Genesis
1–11

VOLUME I A

THE ANCHOR YALE BIBLE is a project of international and interfaith scope in which Protestant, Catholic, and Jewish scholars from many countries contribute individual volumes. The project is not sponsored by any ecclesiastical organization and is not intended to reflect any particular theological doctrine.

THE ANCHOR YALE BIBLE is committed to producing commentaries in the tradition established half a century ago by the founders of the series, William Foxwell Albright and David Noel Freedman. It aims to present the best contemporary scholarship in a way that is accessible not only to scholars but also to the educated nonspecialist. Its approach is grounded in exact translation of the ancient languages and an appreciation of the historical and cultural contexts in which the biblical books were written, supplemented by insights from modern methods, such as sociological and literary criticism.

John J. Collins
General Editor

THE ANCHOR YALE BIBLE

Genesis 1–11

A New Translation with
Introduction and Commentary

RONALD HENDEL

THE ANCHOR YALE BIBLE

Yale UNIVERSITY PRESS

New Haven & London

Yale University Press books may be purchased in quantity for educational, business, or promotional use. For information, please e-mail sales.press@yale.edu (U.S. office) or sales@yaleup.co.uk (U.K. office).

Set in Adobe Garamond type by Newgen North America.

Printed in the United States of America.

Library of Congress Control Number: 2023944448

ISBN 978-0-300-14973-9

A catalogue record for this book is available from the British Library.

This paper meets the requirements of ANSI/NISO Z39.48–1992 (Permanence of Paper).

10 9 8 7 6 5 4 3 2 1

For Ed and Nat

The most beautiful yet most difficult task of the exegete,
to read between the lines of the text.
—*Hermann Gunkel*

Contents

Preface

E. A. Speiser's Genesis commentary of 1964 was the first volume of the Anchor Bible series, founded by William F. Albright and David Noel Freedman to be an accessible, scholarly, and "fresh approach to the world's greatest classic." Speiser's volume served its purpose well, but it has become dated because of flaws in his approach—particularly regarding the family customs in Genesis, which are not as early as he thought (see Winitzer 2010)—and new discoveries and innovations in biblical scholarship. When Freedman invited me in 1988 to write a new commentary to replace Speiser's, I was thrilled but also daunted by the size of the task. This was a time when many of the "assured results" of biblical scholarship were under reconsideration, and new approaches—including a sophisticated literary criticism—were emerging. One of the many results of this ferment in biblical scholarship is that it has taken me far longer to write this book than I imagined. In the meantime, I have explored the many issues concerning Genesis, including its textual history, language, literature, religion, historical context, and history of reception. I am long past my due date for this volume, but I am glad that Noel stuck with me, and since Noel's passing, John Collins. Without their advice and patience, the task would have been overwhelming. The second volume (on chapters 12–50) will go more quickly.

I describe my approach as a literary philology, which combines detailed historical-critical scholarship with attention to the nuances of literary conventions, style, and resonance. Hermann Gunkel was the first biblical scholar to bring these domains into conversation in his great Genesis commentary of 1901. My aim is to renew this linkage of literary and philological forms of attention. As Friedrich Nietzsche—a classics scholar—emphasizes in the preface to *Daybreak,* philology is the art of slow reading: "it teaches to read *well,* that is to say, to read slowly, deeply, looking cautiously before and behind, with reservations, with doors left open, with delicate eyes and fingers." And it requires every other art—and science—to inform it.

I owe many intellectual debts during my long work on Genesis, beginning with my teachers Frank Moore Cross, William Moran, Thomas Lambdin, and Albert Lord.

I have learned much over the years from my friends, colleagues, and students. Those whom I have plied with questions about Genesis and other texts are too many to enumerate, but I am grateful to them all. I owe particular thanks to Bill Propp for his elegant drawings for this volume; to Bob Alter, John Day, and Jeff Stackert for their astute remarks on the manuscript; to Jessie Dolch for untangling my thicket of words; and to John Collins for being an ideal editor. This book is dedicated to my two sons, Ed and Nat, who grew up while I was (intermittently) writing it. It has been a joy.

This book is not intended to be read continuously, with the possible exception of the Introduction. Each section includes a translation with text-critical notes (Textual Notes), followed by Notes elucidating the text and its nuances, and synthesizing Comments. The latter address literary design, major themes, and contexts in the Bible and the ancient Near East and, where applicable, doublets and multiple editions. The whole is encyclopedic in the sense of the original encyclopedias of Bayle and Diderot, that is, a mix of philology, history, literary criticism, and opinion (mostly my own). It is, naturally, an unfinished task, which leaves much for future commentary.

All biblical translations are my own.

Abbreviations

Abbreviations not listed here (e.g., biblical books) are from *The SBL Handbook of Style,* 2nd ed. (Atlanta: SBL Press, 2014).

Biblical Sources

D	Deuteronomist
E	Elohist
J	Yahwist source (roman text in the Translation)
P	Priestly source (**boldface** text in the Translation)
R	"the redactor"—one or more redactors (*italics* text in the Translation)

Texts and Versions

LXX	Septuagint (Old Greek translation)
MT	Masoretic Text
Q	Qumran text (e.g., 4QGen[d])
SP	Samaritan Pentateuch

Reference Works

ABD	*The Anchor Bible Dictionary.* Edited by D. N. Freedman. New York: Doubleday, 1992.
AHw	*Akkadisches Handwörterbuch.* W. von Soden. Wiesbaden: Harrassowitz, 1981.

ANET	*Ancient Near Eastern Texts Relating to the Old Testament.* Edited by J. B. Pritchard. 3rd ed. Princeton: Princeton University Press, 1969.
BDB	Brown, F., S. R. Driver, and C. A. Briggs. *A Hebrew and English Lexicon of the Old Testament.* Oxford: Clarendon, 1907.
CAD	*The Chicago Assyrian Dictionary.* Edited by M. T. Roth. Chicago: Oriental Institute, 2010.
CANE	*Civilizations of the Ancient Near East.* Edited by J. M. Sasson. New York: Scribner's, 1995.
CAT	*The Cuneiform Alphabetic Texts from Ugarit, Ras Ihn Hani, and Other Places.* Edited by M. Dietrich, O. Loretz, and J. Sanmartín. Münster: Ugarit, 1995.
COS	*The Context of Scripture.* Edited by W. H. Hallo. Leiden: Brill, 2002.
DDD	*Dictionary of Deities and Demons in the Bible.* Edited by K. van der Toorn, B. Becking, and P. W. van der Horst. Leiden: Brill, 1995.
GKC	*Gesenius' Hebrew Grammar.* Edited by E. Kautzsch. Translated by A. E. Cowley. 2nd ed. Oxford: Clarendon, 1910.
HALOT	*The Hebrew and Aramaic Lexicon of the Old Testament.* L. Koehler, W. Baumgartner, and J. J. Stamm. 4 vols. Leiden: Brill, 1994–1999.
IBHS	*Introduction to Biblical Hebrew Syntax.* B. K. Waltke and M. O'Connor. Winona Lake: Eisenbrauns, 1990.
KAI	*Kanaanäische und aramäische Inschriften.* H. Donner and W. Röllig. 2nd ed. Wiesbaden: Harrassowitz, 1966–1969.
TDOT	*Theological Dictionary of the Old Testament.* Edited by G. J. Botterweck, H. Ringgren, and H.-J. Fabry. Translated by J. T. Willis, G. W. Bromiley, and D. E. Green. Grand Rapids: Eerdmans, 1974–2018.
TLOT	*Theological Lexicon of the Old Testament.* Edited by E. Jenni and C. Westermann. Translated by M. E. Biddle. Peabody: Hendrickson, 1997.

Journals and Series

ATANT	Abhandlungen zur Theologie des Alten und Neuen Testaments

AYB	Anchor Yale Bible
AYBRL	Anchor Yale Bible Reference Library
BAR	*Biblical Archaeology Review*
BASOR	*Bulletin of the American Schools of Oriental Research*
BZAW	Beihefte zur Zeitschrift für alttestamentliche Wissenschaft
CBQ	*Catholic Biblical Quarterly*
DSD	*Dead Sea Discoveries*
FAT	Forschungen zum Alten Testament
FRLANT	Forschungen zur Religion und Literatur des Alten und Neuen Testaments
HeBAI	*Hebrew Bible and Ancient Israel*
HSM	Harvard Semitic Monographs
HTR	*Harvard Theological Review*
JANER	*Journal of Ancient Near Eastern Religions*
JANES	*Journal of Ancient Near Eastern Studies*
JAOS	*Journal of the American Oriental Society*
JBL	*Journal of Biblical Literature*
JCS	*Journal of Cuneiform Studies*
JNES	*Journal of Near Eastern Studies*
JSJSup	Supplements to the Journal for the Study of Judaism
JSOT	*Journal for the Study of the Old Testament*
JSOTSup	Journal for the Study of the Old Testament Supplement Series
LCL	Loeb Classical Library
VT	*Vetus Testamentum*
VTSup	Supplements to Vetus Testamentum
WAW	Writings of the Ancient World
WMANT	Wissenschaftliche Monographien zum Alten und Neuen Testament
ZA	*Zeitschrift für Assyriologie*
ZAH	*Zeitschrift für Althebraistik*
ZAW	*Zeitschrift für die alttestamentliche Wissenschaft*

INTRODUCTION

I.

Text, Sources, and Style

Text

The oldest manuscripts of Genesis are from the Dead Sea Scrolls. Some twenty-five fragmentary manuscripts of Genesis date from the second century BCE to the second century CE, with the oldest (4QpaleoGen^m) perhaps from the third century BCE (Lange 2009: 43–56; Perrot and Richelle 2022: 44–45). They are written on parchment scrolls, usually in square (Aramaic) script, with three in paleo-Hebrew script. Three are written in small format (4QGen^{d,g,f}) and may not have contained the whole book, and another three are written in large "deluxe" format (4QpaleoGen-Exod^l, 4QGen^b, and MurGen) and may have had special prestige (Tov 2004: 98, 126). Most of these manuscripts agree with the readings of the Masoretic Text (MT), although they occasionally agree with details in the Samaritan Pentateuch (SP) or the Greek Septuagint (LXX).

We can be more precise about some of their textual affiliations (Hendel 2016: 209–24). Two manuscripts belong to the "outer circle" of the proto-MT textual family (4QGen-Exod^a and 4QpaleoGen-Exod^l), meaning they diverge only slightly from the medieval manuscripts of the MT and lack the distinctive features of the other ancient textual families. Three manuscripts belong to the "inner circle" of the proto-MT family (4QGen^b, SdeirGen, and MurGen-Exod-Num^a), meaning they diverge no more than the medieval MT manuscripts do among themselves, primarily in orthography. The oldest of these "inner-circle" texts dates to the late or post-Herodian period (ca. 50–100 CE). The preponderance of this textual type at sites outside Qumran indicates that the proto-MT texts were growing in authority during the first century CE.

For Genesis and other books of the Pentateuch, the three identifiable textual families—proto-MT, proto-SP, and proto-LXX—are distinguished mostly by a series of large and small harmonizations. In Genesis 1–11, about a dozen small harmonizations are shared in proto-SP and proto-LXX texts. One large harmonization is found only in the SP (Gen 10:19, harmonized with Gen 15:18 and Deut 11:24; Hendel 1998: 81–92), and a highly harmonized version of Genesis 1 is found only in the LXX (Hendel 1998: 16–35).

3

Another distinguishing feature of the three textual families is the three different editions of the chronologies in Genesis 5 and 11 (Hendel 1998: 61–80). It is possible that there were more than three editions of Genesis in antiquity, but these are the only ones discernible in the textual evidence. Manuscripts from these three families became authoritative in different communities: a proto-SP text in paleo-Hebrew script for the Samaritans, a proto-MT text in square script in Palestinian Jewish communities, and a proto-LXX text translated into Greek in the Greek-speaking Jewish diaspora, and later in Christianity.

The name "Genesis" derives in part from a harmonization in the proto-LXX family. A Hebrew scribe harmonized Gen 2:4 with 5:1, yielding in both cases *zeh sēper tôlədōt*, "This is the book of the genealogy (of heaven and earth/of Adam)." This was translated into Greek as *autē hē biblos geneseōs*, "This is the book of origin/genesis." Hence the book is called Genesis in Greek and other languages. Notice that this self-reference ("*this* is the book") in 2:4 (LXX) is itself a secondary reading. The name Genesis applies to the book as such, irrespective of variant readings. The earliest Greek evidence for this name is from Philo of Alexandria (first century CE): "the first [book] is called and inscribed Genesis, from the creation of the world, which it contains at the beginning. It received this title despite dealing with a myriad of other matters" (*Abraham* 1).

The Hebrew name of the book, *Bereshit*, comes from the first word of Genesis, *bərē'šît*, "In the beginning." The practice of referring to a book by its opening words (or *incipit*) is common in antiquity. Our oldest attestation of this book name is on a fragmentary dust jacket (*page de gard*) from Qumran, reading *bršt*, a colloquial form of *bərē'šît* (4QGen[h-title], Hendel 1998: vii). Since there were many manuscripts of Genesis at Qumran, we may assume that this name of the book pertained to all of them. The name of the book applied to all its material instantiations, without regard for text-type or variants. The book of Genesis—or the book of *Bereshit*—is a concept that includes all its manuscripts and editions, as long as the community of readers holds them to be valid copies (Hendel 2016: 101–25). The concept of the book of Genesis holds together the idea of the work and all its material instantiations.

But Genesis was not composed as an independent book. It has a complicated compositional history that yielded a composite text whose contents extended from creation to the death of Moses. This composite text came to be written on five scrolls, the Pentateuch (lit. "five scrolls") or Torah. As Haran (1984: 343) observes, the book divisions of the Pentateuch were determined by the length of scrolls (made from sewn-together parchment sheets) and by the editorial discernment of distinct narrative cycles, with the result that "each book encompasses a particular subject matter." The book of Genesis encompasses the primeval and ancestral narrative cycles and closes at a "passage from one thematic cycle to another" (344). This point of passage, after the death of Jacob, Joseph, "and all that generation" (Exod 1:6), marks the genealogical transformation of the "children of Jacob/Israel" from a family to a people, which begins the story of Egyptian bondage and exodus. The book of Genesis has a multilayered coherence in its thematic independence and as the first volume of a larger work.

Sources and Style

Genesis has a complex compositional history, for which we lack direct manuscript evidence. Here I sketch a revised standard model of Genesis's composition, which draws on the classical model constructed by Wellhausen, Kuenen, Driver, and others in the late nineteenth and early twentieth centuries. By blending philological and literary analyses, I hope to resolve some of the problems that divide contemporary scholars on these issues (see Hendel 2011, 2019a). But let us begin with the bigger picture.

Building on the insights of other early modern scholars—especially Masius, Pererius, and Hobbes—Spinoza (2007: 122, original 1670) examined the contradictions and repetitions in the Pentateuch and concluded that it "was not written by Moses but by someone else who lived many generations after Moses." He proposed that the writer or editor, perhaps Ezra the scribe, "made no final version . . . but merely collected narratives from different writers" (130). In the centuries since Spinoza, scholars have further developed these analyses into detailed models of the Pentateuchal sources.

The standard model of the composition of the Pentateuch, formulated in the nineteenth century, posits four main sources, called J (the Yahwist; roman in the TRANSLATION), E (the Elohist), P (the Priestly source; boldface in the TRANSLATION), and D (the Deuteronomist); plus R (one or more redactors; italics in the TRANSLATION), who edited the sources together; and a variety of later supplements and glosses. Of the main sources, J, E, and P begin in Genesis, and D begins in Deuteronomy. Genesis 1–11 is a combination of J and P. There are many variations and developments of this model, including multiple strata of the main sources (see Römer 2013a; Rofé 2009; Baden 2012; cf. Schmid 2021).

A major variation on the standard model is the block-and-supplement model, which posits a continuous P source but replaces J and E with a series of discrete textual blocks and supplements (see Blum 1984, 1990; Carr 1996; Ska 2006; Schmid 2010; cf. C. Levin 2022). I have argued that this model is flawed because it undervalues the stylistic and literary continuities in the non-P sources, focusing instead on the lack of "explicit" interconnections (Hendel 2019a).

Only two of the main sources are relevant to Genesis 1–11, P and J. The E source makes its first appearance in Genesis 20 and continues intermittently until the death of Moses. As we will see, the implicit interconnections are sufficiently extensive to support the concept of a continuous J source.

Some evangelical Protestant and orthodox Jewish scholars deny the validity of both models, arguing for the composition of the Pentateuch in the era of Moses, that is, the Late Bronze Age (see Baker et al. 2020; Berman 2017). Like some medieval and early modern commentators, they admit occasional post-Mosaic supplements. This position is marred by its avoidance of the details that modern scholarship addresses and a close reading of the text reveals (see Barton 2007; B. J. Schwartz 2012a).

Let us turn to the results of such a close reading. I focus on the literary styles and strategies of the sources of Genesis 1–11, combining a revised standard model with literary criticism in a modern sense. I first turn to the issues of double representation, redaction, and narrative continuity, and then to the relationship between the sources' styles—particularly their versions of the *Leitwort* style—and their larger literary designs.

DOUBLE REPRESENTATION AND REDACTION

The J and P sources share the same general sequence in Genesis 1–11, although the particulars differ. The connective structure in both is mostly supplied by genealogies,

Table 1. Double representation and redaction

	P	J	R
Creation	1:1–2:3	2:4b–3:24	2:4a; *'ĕlōhîm* in 2:4b–3:24
Adam to Noah	5:1–28, 30–32	4:1–26, 5:29, 6:1–4	5:1–3*
Flood	6:9–22; 7:6, 11, 13–16, 18–21, 24; 8:1–5, 7, 13a, 14–19; 9:1–19, 28–29	6:5–8; 7:1–5, 7, 10, 12, 16–17, 22–23; 8:2–3, 6, 8–12, 13b, 20–22	6:7*; 7:3*, 8–9, 23*
Noah to Abraham	10:1a, 2–7, 20, 22–23, 31–32; 11:10–27, 31–32	9:20–27; 10:1b, 8–19, 21, 25–30; 11:1–9, 28–30	10:21*, 24; 11:28*

Note: P, Priestly source; J, the Yahwist; R, the redactor. Supplements within a verse are marked with an asterisk.

presented separately or embedded in the narrative. A smaller layer of connective tissue was supplied by R, who inserted occasional supplements at the editorial seams between the two sources. The shared general sequence and the redactional supplements are shown in Table 1.

As a consequence of this double representation of events and genealogies and R's combinatory strategy, it is unlikely that we can restore the original sources in their entirety. As Table 1 shows, however, we can untangle the work to a considerable degree and restore much of the original sources. The gain in doing so is to grasp the compositional history of Genesis and to read more richly the composite text. Many of the interpretive problems that arise when reading the composite text are understandable when the double representation and redaction are taken into account.

Let us first consider R's technique (see, e.g., Halpern 1995; B. J. Schwartz 2012b). In general, R used two complementary procedures. Where the sources presented double representations of the same event or genealogy—as in the flood, the Table of Nations, and the migration of Abraham—R combined the two sources into a composite text with the sources alternating by paragraphs, sentences, or smaller grammatical units, fitted into the progression of narrative time. Where parallel accounts in J and P were sufficiently different—as in the two creation stories or the two genealogies of the descendants of Adam (in Genesis 4 and 5)—R placed them in sequence as consecutive or perhaps simultaneous situations. The difference between these two procedures—combined in a composite unit or linked in a sequence—shows how R perceived and negotiated the harmonies and disharmonies of the two sources. R seems to have omitted some disharmonious text when combining double representations into a single unit (e.g., the absence of the descendants of Japheth in the J Table of Nations, and the absence of Yahweh's command to build the ark in the J flood story). It seems that some source text, primarily from J, was omitted from the composite text. R was a resourceful editor, adroitly managing the similarity of general structure and the differences of particulars in the two sources.

To reduce the dissonances that the combination of sources produced, R added a series of harmonizing glosses. It is possible that some of the glosses were produced by later scribes, but since the technique and motivation are consistent, it is economical to postulate a single R (or a family-like series: R_1, R_2, R_3). To the double representation of creation in Genesis 1–3, R added a transitional gloss at 2:4a, the seam between P and J, "This is the genealogy of heaven and earth, when they were created" (see NOTES at 2:4). This draws on the P formula "This is the genealogy of *X*," now semantically extended to "heaven and earth." This transition echoes the diction of 1:1, serving as a transition and resumptive repetition. To soften the clash of divine names in the transition to the J creation story, R expanded the divine name in 2:4b–3:24 from Yahweh (*yhwh*) to Yahweh God (*yhwh ʾĕlōhîm*), harmonizing with the divine name God (*ʾĕlōhîm*) in 1:1–2:3 (P). (There is variation from this pattern when the characters speak: note that the snake and the woman refer to God [*ʾĕlōhîm*] in 3:1–4; similarly, 4:25.) The harmonization of divine names smooths the transition between the two sources in the double representation of creation.

In the double representation of the flood, R added several glosses to harmonize local discrepancies, mostly concerning the number and kinds of animals on the ark. In 6:7 and 7:23, R added to the J text a P-like list of creatures, "from humans to land animals to crawling creatures to the birds of heaven," clarifying that all the animals from Genesis 1 are included. In 7:3, R added a gloss to the J text to clarify that birds—as mentioned in the previous addition—are included: "also of every bird of heaven take them seven by seven, male and female." In 7:8–9, R added two verses to specify the animals that entered the ark, in this case importing into the J context the number "two of each" from 6:19–20 (P). In all of these cases we can discern R's concern for harmonizing perceived gaps and disharmonies between J and P. Notably, all these pluses were added to the J text, which seems to have been fitted into the framework of the P text. Additionally, R seems to have reordered the J text at the onset of the flood to fit into the P sequence (the original J sequence is arguably 7:10, 7, 16, 12; see Skinner 1930: 153). As noted above, R may have omitted portions of J that too clearly duplicated P (e.g., God's command to build the ark). In these details, we may discern the strategies of R's editorial hermeneutics (see Levinson 2015).

R also added transitional and harmonizing supplements in the genealogies. To the "book of Adam's genealogy" in Gen 5:1, R added a bridge from the preceding P text (1:1–2:3), recapitulating the creation of the first humans and adding the phrase "in his likeness, according to his image" to Adam's procreation of a son. This is a striking extension of creation language, which compensates for the separation of creation and genealogy.

In the double representation of the genealogy of Shem in the Table of Nations (Genesis 10), R added two glosses to harmonize the genealogies of J and P. In 10:21, R adds "all the sons of" before "Eber" to obscure the direct descent of Eber from Shem in J. Similarly, R added to 10:24, "Arpachshad fathered Shelah, and Shelah fathered Eber," taken from the P genealogy in 11:10–15. Both harmonizations make the J genealogy conform to the P genealogy. These additions show R's attention to genealogical details.

R omitted other details from J's genealogy, such as the descendants of Japheth, in favor of the P genealogy. This may have been a less significant lineage in R's eyes and therefore not needing harmonization of details.

The double representation of the migration of Abraham also has a harmonization of detail. In 11:28, R added "in Ur of the Chaldeans" to "the land of his kin" (J) in order to harmonize the J text with the P locale, "Ur of the Chaldeans" (11:31). The harmonization of such details—names, numbers, places, species—seems to be R's main tendency in Genesis 1–11. Beyond these supplements, there is no indication of systematic harmonization or rewriting.

These transitional and harmonizing glosses reveal R's editorial sensibility, which aimed to reduce local disharmonies between the sources by adding strategic glosses. This task required editorial acuity and tact. In all, R seems to have been motivated primarily to combine the sources in a minimally harmonized composite text. Wellhausen (1899: 2–3) aptly describes R's technique in Genesis 1–11:

> The work of the editor consists primarily in the skillful intermingling of the sources, whereby he leaves the content as unabridged as possible, the wording and the order of the narrative as unchanged as possible. But he cannot always do this without his own intervention. Sometimes he makes additions, for example to eliminate a contradiction or to cover a gap, e.g., Gen 7:6–9. Another time he adjusts one source to adapt it to the context of the other, e.g., 7:16c. . . . R has made all sorts of abbreviations and omissions. Just as his interventions in Gen. 1–11 are done at JE's expense—[P] is taken as the basis, JE is adapted to it—so the omissions mostly also concern this source.

R created Genesis 1–11 as a work of bricolage, reassembling and supplementing preexisting material. He (or less likely, she or they) wove the originally independent sources into an intelligible composite work. The careful transitions and harmonizations show that, as Levinson (2015: 123) observes, R "read synthetically . . . [and] engaged and recognized the inconsistencies among the sources without, however, erasing them." R's editorial procedures contrast with those of some other biblical books, such as Deuteronomy, where D consistently rewrites source texts, including J and E (Levinson 1997; Baden 2009a: 99–195). In ancient Israelite scribal and literary circles, there was more than one way to edit texts and manage disharmonies.

DIVERSITY AND CONTINUITY IN J AND P

When we turn to the main sources of Genesis 1–11, J and P, we find that within their shared overall structure from creation to flood to Abraham, there are considerable differences and disharmonies. As Wellhausen (1899: 7) observes, the P text is "a work of unitary conception." P's sequence—creation, genealogy, flood, genealogy—is tightly connected. While P's literary style favors variation within repeating structures (see McEvenue 1971), there is only one juncture where inconsistency occurs, and that at the level of chronology. In the genealogy of Genesis 5, P uses a source text, the "book of Adam's genealogy" (5:1). The ages of Lamech, Methuselah, and Jared seem originally to have lasted beyond the onset of the flood, as told in the following narrative. This discrepancy caused scribes in different textual families (proto-MT, proto-LXX, and proto-SP) to adjust the numbers accordingly (Hendel 1998: 61–71). Aside from this disharmony between the flood narrative and this prior genealogical source, the P text is unified and consistent.

The J text differs in its degrees of consistency and disharmony. As Wellhausen (1899: 7) comments, the J narrative draws on "heterogenous components" from Israel's narrative traditions. Each story or episode coheres internally, but the sequence of stories and episodes generates disharmonies. The "internal disharmonies," Wellhausen (1899: 8) observes, "are largely concerned with connections, not individual stories." These disharmonies can be described as "continuity errors" between the stories.

The following are some of the discontinuities in the J primeval narrative (see Gunkel 1997: 1–2). These disharmonies, generated by the sequence of stories and episodes, have puzzled interpreters over the centuries:

- Cain complains to God, "I will be a restless wanderer on the earth, and whoever meets me will kill me" (4:14). But according to the previous narrative, Adam and Eve are the only other people on earth. Who else could kill Cain? Some later interpreters speculated that Cain was murdered by his descendant Lamech, who in 4:23 boasts that he killed a man (e.g., *Tanḥ. Ber.* 11; Rashi on Gen 4:15).
- After his exile to the land of Wandering, "Cain knew his wife" (4:17). But according to the previous narrative, the only woman is Eve. The genealogy in Genesis 5 states that Adam "fathered sons and daughters" (5:4, P), leading many interpreters to gather that Cain's wife was his sister (e.g., Jub. 4:9; Josephus, *Ant.* 1.53).
- "[Jabal] was the father of herdsmen who dwell in tents. . . . [Jubal] was the father of all who play lyres and pipes . . . Tubal-Cain, [the father of all who] work metal, forging bronze and iron" (4:20–22). The persistence of these professions in the postflood world is an interpretive puzzle, since no descendants of Jabal, Jubal, or Tubal-Cain were on the ark. Some later interpreters attributed all antediluvian knowledge to Noah, perhaps by means of heavenly tablets that Enoch wrote (1 Enoch 81).
- "The Nephilim were on the earth in those days, and also later" (6:4). This also seems to conflict with the flood story, since no Nephilim were on the ark. The comment "and also later" may acknowledge this discrepancy. Later interpreters speculated that the giant Nephilim survived the flood either by being taller than the flood or by holding onto the ark (e.g., *b. Zebaḥ.* 113b).
- "When Noah awoke from his wine, and he knew what his youngest son had done to him, he said, 'Cursed be Canaan'" (9:24–25). Noah's response is in tension with the previous verse, "Ham, Canaan's father, saw his father's nakedness" (9:23), and the transition to this story, "Noah's sons who left the ark were Shem, Ham, and Japheth" (9:18). Noah's response indicates that Ham (his middle son) or Canaan (his grandson) is Noah's "youngest son." Later interpreters addressed this discrepancy by taking "youngest son" as meaning "worthless son," referring to Ham or Canaan (e.g., *Gen. Rab.* 36.7).
- "The chief cities of his [Nimrod's] kingdom were Babel and Erech and Akkad and Calneh, in the land of Sumer" (10:10). This verse is in tension with the following Tower of Babel story, in which Babel is destroyed before it is completed, with no mention of King Nimrod. Later interpreters assumed that Nimrod ruled in Babel during the period of its construction (e.g., Josephus, *Ant.* 1.113–14).

- "The name of the first [son] was Peleg, for in his time the earth was divided" (10:25). This verse is also in tension with the following Tower of Babel story, during which "Yahweh spread them out from there over all the earth" (11:8). Later interpreters assumed that Peleg, like Nimrod, was a member of the generation of Babel (e.g., Jub. 10:18–19).

These disharmonies between the stories and episodes indicate that the J writer was a bricoleur of sorts, compiling traditional stories that circulated independently and were not necessarily consistent with each other. As Wellhausen (1899: 8) suggests, the J composition "brought into connection all kinds of things that had no internal relationship." Yet because of these disharmonies, he supposes only the Garden of Eden story (2:4b–3:24), the story of the Cainites (4:17–24), and the Tower of Babel story (11:1–9) belonged to the original J source (his J¹). Gunkel (1997: 2) comments similarly, "the old legends did not originally exist in the current combination, but each existed independently in oral tradition." Yet he too divides J into different strata because of these disharmonies. In my view this is overly atomistic.

The continuity of the J primeval narrative was created largely by stylistic means. This is a feature that has yet to be fully explored. As Wellhausen (1899: 14) writes, "all the parts [of J] . . . of such different origins are related to each other by expressions and style," and Gunkel (1997: lxxiii) emphasizes "the unified diction of the collections." The J and P writers drew upon prior traditions—including oral traditions and written texts (e.g., the "book of Adam's genealogy," Gen 5:1)—and recomposed them as continuous prose narratives. The writers created continuity by setting the stories into a temporal sequence, connected by genealogy and by their literary art. The most salient literary technique in this respect is the *Leitwort* style, which J and P use in distinctive ways.

LEITWORT STYLE AND LITERARY DESIGN IN J

Buber coined the term *Leitwort* style, by analogy with a leitmotif in music, to designate the artful repetition in biblical narrative of verbal sequences—words, word-roots, homonyms, and phrases. Through the *Leitwort* style, he writes, "a connection is established between one passage and another . . . that articulates the deep motive of the narrated event" (Buber and Rosenzweig 1994: 115). This style generates implicit resonances, contributing to the sense that biblical narrative has subtle and undisclosed meanings, a quality that Auerbach (1953: 12) calls *hintergründig,* "fraught with background." The *Leitwort* style is, as Alter (2011: 118) observes, "at once a unifying device and a focus of development in the narrative." It creates a connective tissue in and across narratives and generates interanimations among the repetitions. This style creates arcs of foreshadowing and development.

As Amit (1989: 105) notes, Buber viewed this stylistic feature as highlighting "the basic underlying unity of Scripture," irrespective of individual authors. In a general sense this view is justifiable, since the *Leitwort* style is a shared feature of biblical narrative. But I suggest that, at a more granular level, it is illuminating to trace the distinctive *Leitwort* style of individual sources. This exposes some of the inner workings and continuities of the narrative sources. The *Leitwort* style adds layers of meaning to the sources' plots, providing resonances that complement and complicate the represented events.

In the J primeval narrative, the dense play of the *Leitwort* style imposes a literary and thematic connectivity that cuts across and blurs its disharmonies. Like a leitmotif in a symphony, it creates cohesion and development within disparate and sometimes clashing movements. Since the *Leitwort* style is intrinsic to the compositions, it is apparent that this style is a mark of the author, the J writer, and is not a secondary or tertiary editorial layer. As a component of what Alter (2011: 143) calls the biblical writers' "art of reticence," it has the effect of transforming the heterogeneous stories into a literary unity.

Instances of the *Leitwort* style in the J primeval narrative include variations on the name Noah (*nōaḥ*) in the J flood story; the *Leitwort* pair "the human" (*hāʾādām*) and "the soil/earth" (*hāʾădāmâ*), which connects many of the stories from the Garden of Eden to the transition to the Abraham narrative; and the phrase "to call on the name of Yahweh" (*liqrōʾ bəšēm yhwh*), which connects the J primeval narrative, the ancestral narrative, and the Moses narrative, culminating with Yahweh's final theophany at Sinai. These cases show how J's *Leitwort* style works as a connective tissue on multiple levels: (1) in a single narrative, (2) across the primeval narrative, and (3) across the larger J work (see Hendel 2008 and 2017).

1. Variations of Noah
   5:29 *nōaḥ* (Noah) . . . *yənaḥămēnû* ("will give us relief")
   6:6–7 *wayyinnāḥem* ("regretted") . . . *niḥamtî* ("I regret")
   6:8 *nōaḥ* (Noah) . . . *ḥēn* ("favor")
   8:9 *mānôaḥ* ("resting place")
   8:21 *nîḥōaḥ* ("soothing")
2. Humans and the Soil/Earth
   2:5 *ʾādām* ("human") . . . *hāʾădāmâ* ("the soil"—"work")
   2:7 *hāʾādām* ("human"—"formed") . . . *hāʾădāmâ* ("the soil")
   3:17 *hāʾădāmâ* ("the soil"—"cursed")
   3:19 *hāʾădāmâ* ("the soil"—"return")
   3:23 *hāʾădāmâ* ("the soil"—"work")
   4:2 *ʾădāmâ* ("the soil"—"work")
   4:11 *hāʾădāmâ* ("the soil"—"cursed")
   5:29 *hāʾădāmâ* ("the soil"—"cursed")
   6:1 *hāʾādām* ("humans"—"multiply") . . . *hāʾădāmâ* ("the earth")
   6:7 *hāʾādām* ("humans"—"destroy") . . . *hāʾădāmâ* ("the earth")
   8:21 *hāʾădāmâ* ("the earth"—"curse") . . . *hāʾādām* ("humans")
   9:20 *hāʾădāmâ* ("the soil"—"man of")
   12:3 *hāʾădāmâ* ("the earth"—"families of")
3. Calling on the Name of Yahweh
   4:26 *liqrōʾ bəšēm yhwh* ("to call on the name of Yahweh")
   12:8 *wayyiqrāʾ bəšēm yhwh* ("he called on the name of Yahweh")
   13:4 *wayyiqrā . . . bəšēm yhwh* ("he called on . . . the name of Yahweh")
   21:33 *wayyiqrā . . . bəšēm yhwh* ("he called on . . . the name of Yahweh")

26:25 *wayyiqrā' bəšēm yhwh* ("he called on the name of Yahweh")

Exod 33:19 *wəqārā'tî bəšēm yhwh* ("I will call on the name of Yahweh")

Exod 34:5–6 *wayyiqrā' bəšēm yhwh* ("he called on the name of Yahweh") . . . *wayyiqrā' yhwh yhwh* ("he called, 'Yahweh, Yahweh'")

I emphasize that these are selected examples; there are many more instances in the J narrative (see NOTES).

The consistent style of the J narratives presumes a writer who is at once a literary artist and a curator of traditional stories and cultural memories. J's *Leitwort* style is, among other things, a way to manage disparate narratives, crafting an interconnected design of verbal resonance and thematic development.

LEITWORT STYLE AND LITERARY DESIGN IN P

The literary style of P is, as Polak (2017) observes, intricate and elaborate, characterized by a density of subordinate clauses, long lists, and quasi-poetic features, including rare words and parallel structures. This high style presupposes a cultural setting in learned circles, such as, in this case, the priesthood. P's intricate style contrasts with the "lean, brisk style" of J and other texts, which is characterized by a high frequency of short independent clauses, short lists, and a prosaic register (Polak 2017: 351–53). These features indicate an affinity with oral narrative style. Yet despite its closeness to tradition, J's style is distinctively literate in its terse but suggestive narration of contexts and character, producing an "art of reticence" in Alter's (2011: 143) terms. The differences between the P and J styles are patent, and both styles show artistic technique.

Some examples illustrate how P's intricate and elaborate *Leitwort* style creates a connective tissue of theme and diction. The first consists of variations on corruption and destruction (*šḥt* in different forms) in the P flood story. The second is the refrain "God saw that it was good," occurring in the P creation story, inverted in the P flood story, and repeated at the completion of the tabernacle in Exodus. The third is the divine command "be fruitful and multiply," which recurs across the P primeval narrative, the ancestral narrative, and the transition to the Moses narrative. These examples show how P's *Leitwort* style operates on multiple levels: (1) in a single narrative, (2) across the primeval narrative (with a distant reprise in Exodus), and (3) across the larger P work (see Lohfink 1994: 166–67).

1. Corruption and Destruction
   6:11 *wattiššāḥēt* ("was corrupt"—"the earth")
   6:12 *nišḥātâ* ("was corrupt"—"the earth") . . . *hišḥît* ("had corrupted"—"all flesh")
   6:13 *mašḥîtām* ("destroy them")
   6:17 *ləšaḥēt* ("to destroy"—"all flesh")
   9:11 *ləšaḥēt* ("to destroy"—"the earth")
   9:15 *ləšaḥēt* ("to destroy"—"all flesh")
2. God Saw That It Was Good
   1:4, 10, 12, 18, 21, 25 *wayyar' 'ĕlōhîm . . . kî-ṭôb* ("God saw . . . that it was good")
   1:31 *wayyar' 'ĕlōhîm . . . wəhinnēh-ṭôb məʾōd* ("God saw [all that he had made], and behold, it was very good")

6:12 *wayyar' 'ĕlōhîm . . . wəhinnēh* ("God saw [the earth], and behold [it was corrupt]")

Exod 39:43 *wayyar' mōšeh . . . wəhinnēh* ("Moses saw [all the work], and behold [they had made]")

3. Be Fruitful and Multiply

    1:22 *pərû urbû* ("be fruitful and multiply"—"seas")

    1:28 *pərû urbû* ("be fruitful and multiply"—"earth")

    8:17 *pərû urbû* ("be fruitful and multiply"—"earth")

    9:1 *pərû urbû* ("be fruitful and multiply"—"earth")

    9:7 *pərû urbû* ("be fruitful and multiply"—"earth")

    17:6 *wəhiprētî* ("I will make you fruitful")

    17:20 *wəhiprētî 'ōtô wəhirbêtî 'ōtô* ("I will make him fruitful and will multiply him")

    28:3 *yaprəkā wəyarbekā* ("May he make you fruitful and multiply you")

    35:11 *pərēh urbēh* ("be fruitful and multiply" [singular])

    47:27 *wayyiprû wayyirbû* ("they were fruitful and multiplied")

    48:4 *maprəkā wəhirbîtīkā* ("I am going to make you fruitful and multiply")

    Exod 1:7 *pārû . . . wayyirbû* ("they were fruitful . . . and multiplied")

    Exod 1:9 *rāb* ("many"—"the people of the children of Israel")

The *Leitwort* style in P also has a special elaboration, which Paran (1989) calls the "circular *inclusio*" and McEvenue (1971: 43–44, 51–53) the "short-circuit inclusion." These are sentences or short sequences that repeat the same word, usually in different forms, in initial and final or near-final positions. This type of chiastic repetition derives from poetic convention, but while poetry prefers synonymous or complementary words, this device repeats different forms of the same word. The circular *inclusio* in P has a semipoetic register, sometimes formally indistinguishable from poetry, producing a momentary heightening from the neighboring prose. These passages mark key moments in P's narratives.

This form occurs twice in Genesis 1, in the first and last works of creation (1:5, 27). These key moments are highlighted through this stylistic device. In the creation of humans, the circular *inclusio* turns into a quasi-poetic triad with the third parallel line, "male and female he created them" (1:27). This conclusion complicates the previous circle, creating a progression in the number of humans—from one to two—and their gender—from (grammatically) male to male and female. It also adds complexity to the phrase "image of God," which seems to resolve from a visual image (cf. 5:3) to something more abstract. This form recurs several times in the flood story (6:9, 14; 8:16–19 [twice]; 9:6) and in the transition to the ancestral story (11:27). This stylistic device, an intricate *Leitwort* repetition of sound and sense, occurs at key moment in P's primeval narrative, producing literary focalization and, at times, subtle thematic development.

Supplements

In a letter to a colleague, Wellhausen (2013: 78) emphasizes "the principle that apart from the main sources there have been all kinds of growths, that the supplementary hypothesis is justified." Beyond the characteristics and designs of the main sources in Genesis, we can discern an abundance of supplements, including the transitions and harmonizations of R, some supplementary "promise" texts (including 22:15–18, 26:2–5, and perhaps 28:13–14), and supplementary narratives (including Genesis 14, 15, 24, 34, and 39; see Römer 2018; Joosten 2019). There is also, as Wellhausen noted, a continuity of literary activity in the scribal revisions and new editions of Genesis (e.g., in Genesis 5 and 11), which creates a floating boundary between the book's compositional and textual history. The process by which Genesis came about is marked by literary artistry and complex editorial growth.

II.

The Age of Genesis

How do we ascertain the age of a biblical book? The inquiry into the book's textual history and composition is a first step. Then we see whether there are dateable features, such as references to historical realia—kings, cities, wars, catastrophes, technologies, institutions, etc.—that can serve as external pegs. Finally, the evidence of language is crucial. Patterns of linguistic features can clarify the age in which a book was written and can confirm or falsify arguments based on other evidence. The ideal is a consilience of different patterns of data that converge on a particular time.

In recent years many scholars have argued that Genesis, and particularly Genesis 1–11, is a combination of exilic and postexilic sources, with the J (or non-P) texts originating as supplements to the P text (Blenkinsopp 1992: 64–67, and 2002; Otto 1996; Witte 1998: 28–31; Wenham 1999; Schüle 2006: 24–40; Arneth 2007: 12–18; Ska 2009: 1–22; Gertz 2012; Schmid 2016; cf. Bührer 2015; Carr 2020a: 224–49). These studies mostly rely on arguments from the history of ideas, occasionally accompanied by linguistic details. But the arguments are flawed. I focus on the age of Genesis 1–11, but the implications encompass the book as a whole.

Blenkinsopp (2002: 50), who initiated this trend, argued that the conceptual and moral orientation of the J text of Genesis 1–11 can be dated to the Persian period on the basis of its "somber diagnosis of the human condition and pessimistic assessment of moral potential." This pessimism, he argues, has "its origins . . . in the lay, intellectual milieu of the province of Judah some time during the two centuries of Iranian rule" (60). This model of the history of ideas in ancient Israel is impressionistic and reductive.

The practice of correlating a mood or disposition with a particular period is what Collingwood (1994: 263) criticizes as the "pigeon-holing" method of history, which construes history as "not a chronological scheme merely, but a qualitative scheme, in which 'periods' each with its own pervasive character follow one another in time." As Sommer (2011: 85) aptly observes, "this method of dating holds no validity whatsoever." If the J narratives of Genesis 1–11 are, as I argue below, decisively shaped by the moral emotions of shame and guilt, and laced with "interior moral struggle," this says nothing about the date of the composition—unless one wishes to say that the representation of moral emotions in literature was available only during the Persian era in Israelite history.

Those who date Genesis 1–11 mostly or wholly to the Persian or Hellenistic period also treat the linguistic details poorly. For instance, Blenkinsopp (1992: 65) argues that some words in the J (or non-P) source—including *tāpar* ("sew"), *ʿārûm* ("crafty"), and *neḥmād* ("desirable")—are "elsewhere attested exclusively or primarily in exilic or postexilic texts." But he does not identify an earlier word that these replaced, which makes this a nonargument linguistically. The principle of contrast is necessary for a valid argument about linguistic history. Moreover, several of these words—including *tāpar, ʿārûm,* and passive forms of *ḥmd*—are attested in Classical Biblical Hebrew and neighboring dialects, indicating that they were indeed part of the preexilic lexicon (see Hendel 2021b).

Let us consider more closely the linguistic profile of Genesis 1–11, drawing on the larger picture of the history of Biblical Hebrew (Hendel and Joosten 2018). There are four phases (or chronolects) of Biblical Hebrew: Archaic Biblical Hebrew (ABH), found in old poems such as the Blessing of Jacob (Genesis 49); Classical Biblical Hebrew (CBH), which characterizes the J and E sources; Transitional Biblical Hebrew (TBH), which characterizes the P source and a few other texts in Genesis such as the betrothal to Rebecca (Genesis 24); and Late Biblical Hebrew (LBH), which does not appear in the text of Genesis (although it often occurs in the linguistic updating of forms in the SP and in some Masoretic vocalizations). Because of continuities with the language of Hebrew inscriptions, CBH can be dated to the monarchic period, primarily the Neo-Assyrian era (ninth to late seventh centuries BCE) and TBH to the "long" sixth century, from the Neo-Babylonian era to the second return to Jerusalem in the Persian era (ca. 612–460 BCE).

The J texts are written in CBH and are peppered with an abundance of distinctive features of this chronolect, including syntax, morphology, lexicon, and phonology. One important category of features is what linguists call function words—conjunctions, prepositions, adverbs, etc.—that order the grammatical relationships among the other words in a sentence. Function words are difficult to emulate in later linguistic eras, since they belong to a tacit level of language, embedded as they are in the grammar of speech.

Numerous function words are distinctive to CBH (Hendel and Joosten 2018: 44–45, 68–69), including the following in J of Genesis 1–11:

ṭerem ("before, not yet")
> Gen 2:5 (twice), followed by imperfect. Occurs often in CBH, also Arad 5.12. Persists in TBH, but LBH uses other constructions, for example, *lipnê* + infinitive (2 Chr 33:19); *ʿad ʾăšer (lōʾ)* + imperfect (Eccl 12:1, 2, 6). This particle reemerges in Ben Sira and Qumran Hebrew as an archaism.

pen ("lest")
> Gen 3:3, 11:4. Occurs often in CBH, also Arad 24.16, 20. Persists in TBH, but used in LBH only once in a passage copied from the Chronicler's source (1 Chr 10:4 // 2 Sam 31:4). LBH uses other constructions for negative purpose, for example, *ʾăšer lōʾ* (Eccl 7:21), *ʾăšer lammâ* (Dan 1:10). This particle reemerges in Ben Sira and Qumran Hebrew.

ʿimmādî ("with me")

> Gen 3:12. Occurs often in CBH, where it varies with *ʿimmî;* compare *ʿmd* in an early sixth-century Edomite inscription (Ḥorvat ʿUzza 4). Persists in TBH, but not found in LBH (only *ʿimmî*).

hēn ("given that")

> Gen 3:22. Occurs often in CBH; also Arad 21.3, 40.9. Persists in TBH but not found with this meaning in LBH. Reanalyzed as conditional ("if") in TBH (Hag 2:12) and LBH (2 Chr 7:13 [twice]) by influence of Aramaic *hēn.*

kî ("when")

> Gen 4:12; 6:1, 4. Occurs often in CBH, where temporal *kî* varies with *ka'ăšer.* Persists in TBH, but used in LBH in only two passages copied from the Chronicler's source (1 Chr 17:11 // 2 Sam 7:12; and 2 Chr 6:28, 34 // 1 Kgs 8:37, 44). Note the linguistic updating in 1 Chr 17:1 (*ka'ăšer*) // 2 Sam 7:1 (*kî*).

lākēn ("therefore")

> Gen 4:15. Occurs often in CBH, where it varies with *ʿal-kēn.* Persists in TBH, but used in LBH only once in a passage copied from the Chronicler's source (1 Chr 18:18 // 1 Kgs 22:19).

bō'ăkâ ("in the direction of")

> Gen 10:19 (twice), 30. Occurs six times in CBH, only in J Genesis and 1 Kgs 18:46. Not used in TBH or LBH.

baʿăbûr ("for")

> Gen 3:17, 8:21. Occurs often in CBH, where it varies with *ləmaʿan.* Persists in TBH; used in LBH four times in Chronicles, three in parallel passages (1 Chr 14:2 // 2 Sam 5:12; 1 Chr 17:19 // 2 Sam 7:21; 1 Chr 19:3 // 2 Sam 10:3), productively only in 2 Chr 28:19.

Most of these function words are also found in P, but several linguistic features distinguish the chronolects of J and P. A pattern of verbal contrasts indicates that the J source belongs to an earlier linguistic state than P. Because of the prominence of procreation in Genesis 1–11, various forms of the verb *yld* ("to give birth") are frequent, in both the active voice (*qal* or *hiphil*) and the passive voice (*qal* passive or *niphal*). The source distinctions make sense of these variations in the verbal stems (Hendel and Joosten 2018: 16–19).

	Active (third-person masculine singular)	Passive
J	*qal* (nine times)	*qal* passive (five times)
P	*hiphil* (fifty-five times)	*niphal* (once)

Two diachronic changes are evident here: (1) the disambiguation of gender in the active voice, with the *hiphil* replacing the *qal* for masculine subjects; and (2) the reduction of the number of passive stems, with the *niphal* replacing the *qal* passive. The J texts consistently have the earlier pattern, including the *qal* passive form, which became obsolete in later Hebrew. In the P texts, both of these changes have already occurred. These changes in the verbal system are clearly diachronic—note the expected relationship in the earlier phase of *qal* and *qal* passive, compared with the odd later pairing of *hiphil* and *niphal*. These and other ordered changes show that the J text of Genesis 1–11 has an earlier linguistic profile than the P text.

Another indicator is the distribution of the first-person singular pronouns *ʾănî* and *ʾānōkî* (Driver 1897: 155–56; Hendel and Joosten 2018: 17–18). J varies freely between *ʾănî* and *ʾānōkî,* with a propensity for the latter, while P exclusively uses *ʾănî* (the exception, Gen 23:4, is arguably a post-P text). This pattern of data is consistent with the other features, showing that J has an earlier linguistic state than P. Placed in a broader context, J's usage agrees with the books of Samuel, while P's agrees with the book of Ezekiel.

There are also several indications that J was written in preexilic orthography, in which a final *he* was used to indicate both a final *ā* and *ō,* the latter replaced by *waw* in postexilic orthography. The evidence comes from the following forms:

> *ʾohŏlōh* ("his tent," Gen 9:21). The consonantal *ketiv* (*ʾhlh*) preserves preexilic orthography for *-ō* (third-person masculine singular pronominal suffix), while the *qere* (*ʾhlw*) has the postexilic orthography. The preexilic form (*ʾhlh*) is also found in 12:8, 13:3, and 35:21, all J.
>
> *ləʿobdāh ulšomrāh* ("to work it and to guard it," Gen 2:15). The two final *he*'s preserve preexilic orthography for *-ō* (third-person masculine singular pronominal suffix), misanalyzed in the reading tradition as *-ā* (third-person feminine singular).
>
> *təšûqātô . . . bô* ("its desire . . . over it," Gen 4:7). The two final *waw*'s (for *ô,* third-person masculine singular pronominal suffix) are probably mistaken postexilic revisions of two final *he*'s (for *ā,* third-person feminine singular).

These forms show both sides of the change in orthography of final long vowels from preexilic *he* (for *ā* and *ō*) to its differentiation into postexilic *he* (*ā*) and *waw* (*ō*) (see Hendel 1998: 44, 46, 57–58).

The linguistic data cohere with the details of cultural history in Genesis 1–11. For instance, the classical linguistic features of the Nimrod pericope (J)—including the *qal* stem of *yld* with a male subject, and *mamlākâ* for "kingdom"—are consistent with the schematic history of Mesopotamian kingship in this passage, which ends with the Neo-Assyrian period (10:8–12; Hendel and Joosten 2018: 108–9). Similarly, the chronological implications of the place names in the Table of Nations (Genesis 10) are consistent with the linguistic evidence, indicating the era of J in the Neo-Assyrian period and the era of P in or around the Neo-Babylonian period (see COMMENTS on Genesis 10).

In sum, the evidence indicates that the J text belongs to the era of CBH (ninth to seventh centuries BCE), and P belongs to the era of TBH (late seventh to early fifth centuries BCE). The linking and harmonizing additions of R probably also belong to the era of TBH, although the evidence is sparse.

As mentioned previously, there are also later compositions in Genesis, including variant editions of the chronologies in Genesis 5 and 11, the harmonized edition of Genesis 1 in the LXX, and other supplementary passages and chapters. But the main sources and the first edition of Genesis 1–11 can be dated to this centuries-long span from the monarchic to the early postexilic periods, according to the evidence of language and history. These eras provide the relevant context for our interpretation of Genesis 1–11, including its religious, political, and literary horizons.

The Settings of the Sources

In the light of the consilience of the linguistic and historical evidence, we may draw some implications for the sources of Genesis 1–11. It is difficult to be precise about the life settings (*Sitz im Leben,* Gunkel's term) of J and P, but we can infer some things with a reasonable degree of confidence.

The J texts were composed by a writer of uncanny skill sometime in the Neo-Assyrian period. As scholars have observed, the prominence of Judean locales and the prominence of Judah as a character in Genesis 37–50 indicate that the writer was probably a Judean (Dillmann 1897: 10–11; Skinner 1930: lvi–lvii; Friedman 1997: 61–69). Regarding J's social location, from the sparse details about authors in other books we can speculate that J may have been a landowner (cf. Amos), a member of a priestly family (cf. Jeremiah and Ezekiel), a scribe (cf. Baruch, Jeremiah's scribe), a sage (cf. Proverbs), or a member of the administrative class (cf. Nehemiah and possibly Isaiah). Members of the military were also known to be literate (Lachish Letter 2). This circle of writers indicates the kinds of people with the learning and opportunity to write works of religious literature.

This circle also points to the literary tradition to which J belonged. The floruit of CBH and Classical Hebrew literature, including narrative and poetry, belongs to the monarchic period. The distinctive conventions of biblical narrative prose crystallized during this era, involving transformations of older written and oral conventions. One such new convention is the *Leitwort* style of Classical Hebrew prose, examined above. As Kawashima (2004a: 73–76) has emphasized, the techniques of verbal repetition in biblical narrative differ markedly from comparable techniques in older and other Northwest Semitic literatures. The finely wrought narrative prose that we find in the J texts and other sources of the Pentateuch and Former Prophets represents a new literary tradition.

Another striking feature of this new tradition is the technique of what Kawashima (2004a: 77–123) calls represented consciousness, in which the presentative particle *hinnēh,* used in situations of perception, effects a deictic shift to the character's perspective. As Driver (1892: 202) describes this narrative syntax, "the stress lies not so much on the mere circumstance as such, but on *the impression it produces* upon the principal subject" (emphasis in original). In the following example from the J flood story, this technique provides a glimpse into Noah's perceptions, allowing the reader access to his unspoken interiority: "The dove returned to him toward evening, and behold (*wəhinnēh*), in its beak was a plucked olive leaf, and Noah knew that the water had subsided on the face of the earth" (8:11). The grammatical shift to Noah's perspective allows us to see through Noah's eyes, while the consequence of his perception shifts back to the narrative voice: "and Noah knew." As Kawashima (2004a: 114) observes, this technique provides the "means to represent consciousness in order to suggest the unspoken inner thoughts of their characters . . . [creating a] perspectival play of foreground and background, surface and depth."

The conventions of Classical Hebrew narrative, shared across various texts, allow us to perceive something of the socio-literary setting of the J source. The J writer was, in a manner obscure to us, a member of the community of writers in which these new techniques coalesced into a distinctive literary practice. Whether the formation of this literary community involved education in scribal schools or a less formal curriculum, perhaps in the family or village, we cannot say.

The display of literary texts on plastered walls at Kuntillet ʿAjrud (a Divine Warrior hymn, ca. 800 BCE) and Deir ʿAlla (a prophetic narrative of Balaam in a Transjordanian dialect, ca. 800 BCE) may be samples of the advanced curriculum of scribal schools in this era (Schniedewind 2019: 147–64), but these are short texts. The reading and destruction of Jeremiah's scroll in the royal chamber (Jeremiah 36) provides a glimpse of the production and circulation of longer scrolls, as does the discovery of a "scroll of the law" (*sēper hattôrâ*) in the temple archive (2 Kings 22). Somewhere in or around these settings the J writer composed a book of genealogically linked narratives drawing on older lore and composed in a distinctively literary style. The communicative network of Classical Hebrew literature, with links in Jerusalem, created the conditions and context for J's work.

The setting of J in the Neo-Assyrian era also allows us to discern some political nuances in Genesis 1–11. For instance, the history of Nimrod in Gen 10:8–12, as van der Kooij (2006: 16) observes, "reflect[s] in one way or another Assyrian imperialism." I do not think Nimrod represents a particular Neo-Assyrian king or regime, but subtle criticisms of Neo-Assyrian kingship seem to be embedded in the story. This political subtext is what Scott (1990) calls a "hidden transcript," a literary mimicry and critique of the imperial power (Hendel 2005b). This is a common strategy of weak or dominated groups, which employ verbal ambiguity, humor, distortion, and other types of disguised criticism to assert their identity in relation to the dominant power.

In the Nimrod story there are two signs of this hidden transcript. The first is the description of Nimrod as "the first to be . . . a mighty hunter before Yahweh. Therefore it is said, 'Like Nimrod, a mighty hunter before Yahweh'" (10:8–9). The repetition of "mighty hunter" (*gibbōr-ṣayid*) seems like emphatic praise. But the repetition of "before Yahweh" (*lipnê yhwh*) adds a note of dissonance. This is an odd phrase in context. The Neo-Assyrian royal topos of the king as a great hunter, appended to "before Yahweh," indicates a relationship in which Yahweh is the superior party, perhaps even Nimrod's patron god. To those who understand that Nimrod is the exemplar of Neo-Assyrian kingship, the superiority of Yahweh over the Assyrian king has a distinctive political message, a hidden transcript that subordinates the Assyrian king to the God of Israel (cf. the similar positioning in Isaiah 10).

The second detail is Nimrod's name, which seems to be a distortion of the name of Ninurta, the patron god of Neo-Assyrian kings. In Hebrew the name *nimrōd* transparently means "we will rebel" or "let us rebel," from the root *mrd* ("to rebel"). Nimrod is implicitly tied to rebellion, perhaps against the proper order of things ordained by Yahweh (van der Kooij 2006: 16). But it is also possible that the plain sense of the name, "we will rebel" or "let us rebel," reflects a desire on the part of Israelites—or the J writer—to rebel against Neo-Assyrian domination (Hendel 2005b 30–31; cf. Day 2022: 197). On any construal, the name of Nimrod, with its distortion of Ninurta and resonance of rebellion, is a veiled criticism of the ideology of Neo-Assyrian kings.

The Tower of Babel story provides a complementary critique of the ideology of Mesopotamian imperial power through its depiction of the hubris and destruction of Babylon—the most famous Mesopotamian city throughout the first millennium BCE—projected into the primeval era. This story's hidden transcript seems to mock the Mesopotamian city's claim to universal hegemony. Other J stories in the ancestral narratives have submerged political nuances reflecting the conditions of this era, particularly regarding relations with neighboring peoples—Ammon, Moab, Arab tribes, Aram, and Edom (Hendel 2018).

The social setting of the P source is the institution of priesthood, probably connected with the Jerusalem temple. The language of P indicates a context in the late monarchic, exilic, or early postexilic era. While there are multiple strata in the P source, I see no sign of stratification in the P texts of Genesis 1–11 (cf. Arnold 2012). The production of the P work in priestly circles may indicate that its circulation was limited to the priesthood. For this reason, Haran (1978: 143) plausibly characterizes P as an esoteric teaching: "What is written in its scrolls is in the nature of a *tôrāh* in the priestly sense of this term. . . . If that *tôrāh* deals with matters which are solely the concern of priesthood, it would remain an esoteric in-group teaching." This inference may illuminate the place and orientation of the P work.

If P was initially an esoteric or even utopian work, it is an historical irony that R combined P with the other literary sources, with the aim of creating a composite work that could serve as a religious and political charter in the postexilic era. The scene of Ezra reading the Torah to the assembled public in Jerusalem (Nehemiah 8) is a literary representation of this project. If P was written as an esoteric priestly instruction, it became the framework of the public Torah. This literary process ultimately created a religious culture based on the Torah's authority, which reconfigured the prerogatives of the priestly class.

It is difficult to discern details in the P work that reflect on the Neo-Babylonian or early Persian era. Some argue that P's creation account is a countertext to the Babylonian creation myth *Enuma Elish,* but the implicit arguments in the text engage primarily with native Israelite traditions. But there is one feature that may reflect P's perspective on Neo-Babylonian matters: the locale of Abram's family in Ur of the Chaldeans (Gen 11:31). In the J text, Abram's family dwells in Haran in Upper Mesopotamia. The locale in P seems to be an updating of this older tradition, plausibly reflecting the locale of the Judean exiles in Lower Mesopotamia. As Wellhausen (1885: 342) observes, since "Abraham is said to have migrated into Palestine from Ur, in Chaldea, it is hardly possible to reject the idea that the circumstances of the exile had some influence." Abram's homeland in Ur, south of the Nippur countryside where most of the exiles lived, may express a hidden transcript, a hope that the descendants of Abraham would journey once again from southern Mesopotamia to the promised land. A repetition of Abram's journey would erase the forced exile imposed by the Neo-Babylonian regime. But this transcript, if legible, is well-hidden.

The Scene of History

The evidence of language and the references to historical details outside the text indicate that the J text of Genesis 1–11 was composed during the monarchic era, more particularly in the Neo-Assyrian period, and the P text was composed during the late monarchic, exilic, or early postexilic period, during the Neo-Babylonian or early Persian era.

This is a return to the view of Wellhausen and other scholars in the late nineteenth and early twentieth centuries, but it is counter to the positions of many recent scholars. Those who date the texts later or reverse the chronology of the P and non-P texts are liable to the criticism that they ignore or undervalue the linguistic history of Biblical Hebrew (Hendel 2021b). Since our texts are linguistic discourses, this avoidance is problematic.

To paraphrase Bloch (1953: 122) on Pascal, the style of J and P belongs to their authors, but their language belongs to their time. Grammatical patterns that change over time are difficult to emulate in a later period and therefore provide our most reliable basis for ascertaining the age of biblical texts. The coherence of the linguistic data with other traces of history in the text, as in the references to foreign affairs, is the best test for the adequacy of our historical models.

Why does the age of Genesis 1–11 matter? In my view, it is not important as an end in itself but as a means to a more informed reading of the text. It is one step in a larger process. This step involves, as Bloch (1953: 41) writes, "return[ing] [texts] to their milieu, where they are immersed in the mental climate of their time." Then we bridge the gap from our milieu and mental climate, yielding to some degree recognition across time and space. In sum, we read the text as a letter from a distant land, whose ideas, perceptions, and thought styles we wish to understand, with a desire not to superimpose our own. This is a peculiarly modern method of reading Genesis, which has its own limitations and rewards. In this approach, as Lévi-Strauss (1966: 262) writes, "the search for intelligibility . . . [does not come] to an end in history. Rather it is history that serves as the point of departure." The historical setting of Genesis 1–11 is not the end, but the beginning.

III.

Genesis 1–11 as Genealogy and Mythology

When we ask what kind of text Genesis 1–11 is, we are posing a question about genre. To do this well, as Ben-Amos (2020: 40–63) advises, it is important to take account of the difference between ethnic and analytical genres. Ethnic genres are those found in the text's own literary culture, for instance Hebrew *šîr* ("song, poem"), *qînâ* ("dirge, lament"), *māšāl* ("proverb, fable"), and *dibrê hayyāmîm* ("chronicle"). Analytical genres, in contrast, are categories devised by scholars to describe literary forms that are inferable from the texts (Newsom 2019: 55–66). Terms such as "myth," "legend," "epic," and "folktale" are analytical categories, which must be tailored to suit the material. Although analytical genres are scholarly constructions, they are often illuminating, like the analytical categories of noun, verb, and grammar in the study of language. Analytical categories are, to varying degrees, cross-culturally relevant, while ethnic categories reflect locally relevant features. We should be able to use native and analytical categories as supplements to each other, juxtaposing them to expand our interpretive sensibilities.

In Genesis, the salient ethnic genre category is *tôlədôt* ("offspring, descendants, genealogy"), used in a semantically extended sense in the P source for genealogically linked narrative sequences. The relevant analytical category for Genesis 1–11, as we will see, is myth or mythology. Many features of the text are illuminated by these categories, yielding a rich understanding of the text's implicit and explicit meanings. I explain the relevance of these ethnic and analytical genres and then explore their expressive dimensions in Genesis 1–11, including explanation, legitimation and orientation, narrative, repetition, and memory.

Ethnic Genre: Genealogy

Tôlədôt is a plural noun derived from the causative stem of *yld* ("beget"). It generally means "offspring, descendants, genealogy." A special formula, found in the P source, is *'ellê tôlədōt* PN, "this is the genealogy of PN," where PN is the name of a male ancestor. This formula introduces new sections throughout Genesis and once in Numbers. In this formula, *tôlədōt* has a semantically extended sense, meaning something like "account of a man and his descendants" (BDB, 410), "family history" (Gunkel 1997: 103), "story of the descendants" (Blum 2022: 41), or simply "story" (Speiser 1964: 8). This extended sense designates a genealogical discourse, a combination of narratives and genealogies. In Genesis, the chain of these *tôlədôt* extends from the era of creation to the descent into Egypt by Jacob/Israel and his children, the ancestors of the twelve tribes. This designation defines Genesis as a connective genealogy of Israel's ancestral past, linking together cosmic and ethnic origins. The stories of the distant past are a genealogy of the present.

The extended sense of *tôlədōt* to designate genealogical narrative is an innovation of the P writer, with further semantic development by R, who combined the sources (see Carr 1998; Hendel 2012a: 76–78; Bauks 2019). The occurrences of the *tôlədōt* formula indicate a deliberate distribution: five times in Genesis 1–11 and five times in Genesis 12–50 (with *'ellê tôlədōt ēśāw*, "this is the genealogy of Esau," in 36:9 as a resumptive repetition of 36:1). Each rubric serves as a transition to a new literary section.

The instances of this formula in Genesis 1–11 and their transitional features are as follows:

—"These are the *tôlədôt* of heaven and earth, when they were created" (2:4a; transition to J creation story)
—"These are the *tôlədôt* of Noah" (6:9; transition to P flood story)
—"These are the *tôlədōt* of the sons of Noah" (10:1; transition to P Table of Nations)
—"These are the *tôlədōt* of Shem" (11:10; transition to P postdiluvian genealogy)
—"These are the *tôlədôt* of Terah" (11:27; transition to P story of Abraham)

With the exception of the first instance, each formula introduces P material. The exception, Gen 2:4a, introduces J material. As commentators have observed, the formula in

2:4a is a redactional passage, providing a narrative bridge between the P and J texts. R was compensating for the separation of the P text from its continuation in 5:1, "This is book of the *tôlədôt* of Adam," by adapting the P formula and applying the subject "heaven and earth" (Skinner 1930: 41; Carr 1998: 169). This yields a semantic extension of *tôlədôt* to a nonbiological genealogy, meaning something like the temporal or causal succession after the creation of heaven and earth, that is, what happens next.

With this semantic extension of the formula, the origin of the cosmos is the beginning of Israel's genealogy. The last link in this genealogical chain—from P or a supplemental stratum—occurs in Num 3:1, "These are the *tôlədôt* of Moses and Aaron," which introduces the lineage of Israel's high priests (Eissfeldt 1966: 458–59; Hieke 2003: 226–32). This notice reflects the social matrix of the P source. The institutional authority of the priests is here built into the genealogy as the final link in its chain.

The semantics of *tôlədôt* as an ethnic category for the genre of Genesis is grounded in the language of kinship descent, which was an organizing principle of Israelite society (Chapman 2016; Hieke 2003: 347–49). In everyday life, genealogical relationships provide a basis for rules of marriage, inheritance, political alliance, and the administration of justice, as well as for institutions such as kingship and priesthood. Genealogies provide connective links with other peoples and polities, who are represented as near or distant kin. Genealogical language blends synchrony with diachrony, grounding the present order of things in the collective past. It orders the succession of time, the divisions of space, and the rules of household and tribe (Hendel 2018).

To describe the stories of the past as a chain of *tôlədôt* is consistent with the authority-bestowing strategies of genealogies. And like other ancestral lore, it is transmitted by those with genealogical authority, including parents, elders, and priests. Accordingly, the priest and prophet par excellence, Moses, instructs the Israelites in the Song of Moses:

> Remember the days of old,
>> Consider the years of ages past,
> Ask your father, and he will inform to you,
>> Your elders, and they will tell you. (Deut 32:7)

Moses's words express the importance that stories of "the days of old" possess, as well as the kinds of people who have the authority to tell them. Moses then relates how God divided the nations in the distant past. Interestingly, this is a different version of the division of nations from what we find in the Table of Nations (Genesis 10) or the Tower of Babel story.

While the J source does not use the term *tôlədôt*, this category also suits the J text, which like P is a genealogical narrative. Particularly in Genesis 1–11, J is structured as a complex genealogy that is filled out with narrative, from the creation of the first couple to the family of Abraham, including genealogical branching for the three sons of Adam and Eve and the three sons of Noah. The verb *yld*, "to bear children, to beget" (and in the passive, "to be born"), occurs more than twenty times in J of Genesis 1–11, highlighting the progression of generations. While the P term *tôlədôt* names this category, the J text implicitly participates in it.

The term *tôlədôt* illuminates the structure and the contents of Genesis, which revolve around genealogical issues. As Westermann (1985: 36) emphasizes, Genesis consists mostly of family stories. In Genesis 1–11 the domestic family is created and its internal tensions explored, including conflicts between husband and wife (Genesis 3), brother and brother (Genesis 4), and father and sons (9:18–27). The families of the world proliferate and separate in the Table of Nations (Genesis 10) and the Tower of Babel story (Genesis 11). This proliferation of peoples is a precondition of the transition from the primeval narrative (Genesis 1–11) to the ancestral narrative (Genesis 12–50), when the universal genealogy narrows to the family of Abraham.

As Gunkel (1997: xi–xii) observes, this narrowing of the genealogy at the juncture of Genesis 11 and 12 introduces a shift of focus, yielding a distinction within the larger genealogical narrative:

> Two groups of material are clearly evident. (1) Stories concerning the origin of the world and the ancestors of humanity, the narratives to the Tower of Babel. The arena of these accounts is the remote past, their sphere of interest the whole world. (2) Stories concerning Israel's fathers, Abraham, Isaac, and Jacob, and his sons. The arena here is Canaan and its environs and the interest concentrates on a family with the more-or-less background implication that the people of God descended from them.

The two types of genealogical narrative—which Gunkel calls "primal stories" (*Ursagen*) and "patriarchal stories" (*Vätersagen*)—have different horizons of time and space. The temporal scope of Genesis 1–11 is the remote past, and its geographical scope is the whole world. The temporal scope of Genesis 12–50 is the era of Israel's direct ancestors, and the geographical scope is the land of Canaan, with excursions from and to its neighboring regions. Genesis 1–11 covers a vast scope of time—in P it covers twenty generations with long lifespans (Methuselah tops out at age 969)—while Genesis 12–50 slows down to cover only four generations of lesser lifespans (Abraham dies at age 175).

This bipartite narrative is also marked by a change in moral economy. As von Rad (1972: 154) comments: "Previously the narrative concerned humanity as a whole, man's creation and essential character, woman, sin, suffering, humanity, nations, all of them universal themes. In [Gen 12:1], as though after a break, the particularism of election begins." Wolff (1982: 49–55) adds a stylistic note to this shift: in J, the verb *'rr* ("to curse") occurs five times in the primeval era and then takes a new direction with the fivefold repetition of *brk* ("to bless") in the call of Abraham. This new economy of blessing includes the universal with the blessing channeled to "all the families of the earth" (*kōl mišpəḥōt hāʾādāmâ*, Gen 12:3), resuming the *Leitwort* relationship of humans and the earth. The particular and the universal are interrelated in this genealogical turn. The different moral coloring of the primeval era versus the ancestral era gives the whole genealogy a trajectory, a sense of moral development, even as the Israelite ancestors have their own complications.

In light of these features, the native genre of Genesis as *tôlədōt* positions its first part, Genesis 1–11, as a special phase in the genealogical chain. The concept of genealogical narrative defines the text as a connective discourse linking the past with the present. It serves to explain and organize the present world, to make it intelligible and livable. The many expressive meanings of the text as *tôlədōt*, we will see, complement the analytical genre of Genesis 1–11 as mythology.

Analytical Genre: Myth

Biblical scholars are often uncomfortable with the term "myth" as a descriptive category for Genesis 1–11. As Rogerson (1984) observes, "myth" is a slippery term, often used imprecisely or colored by religious biases (see Von Hendy 2002). M. S. Smith (2010: 142) similarly cautions, "we should be skeptical about discovering some relatively neutral definition of myth beyond the basic (and arguably banal) definition of myth as a type of religious story." I submit that the past use, and misuse, of a category is not sufficient reason to reject it. Analytical categories are scholarly constructs, and as such can be improved. The value of any category lies in its elucidation of relevant features. We can fashion a multilayered concept of myth that suits Genesis 1–11.

Gunkel's (1997: xi) definition of myth as "stories about gods" (*Göttergeschichte*) was drawn from the Grimm brothers, who drew a distinction between myth and legend as pivoting on the agency of gods versus humans. Since, as Gunkel writes, "a divine story requires at least two gods . . . [t]he characteristic feature of Yahwism does not favor myths" (xiii). At most one finds "mythical accounts . . . in faded colors" (xii), such as Gen 6:1–4. The monotheistic religion of ancient Israel resists the genre of myth.

This definition of myth holds that the genre draws a boundary between polytheists and monotheists. Theologically, this rests on the distinction between pagan and revealed religion. But differences in concepts of divine personhood are not relevant to matters of literary genre. As M. S. Smith (2010: 141) observes, "The logic behind this distinction does not seem particularly strong: why should the form of divinity serve as the criterion for the genre of myth?" Fishbane (2003: 5–6) makes a similar criticism: "the exclusive identification of a literary phenomenon (myth) with a specific religious or cultural form (natural polytheism) is both tendentious and tautological." It is arguably a category error to draw a binary distinction between myth (a genre) and monotheism (a theological system).

There is a restricted sense in which the Genesis primeval narrative has an aversion to myth. The P creation account rejects or reinterprets several mythic motifs, such as the sea monster as a divine adversary. In 1:21 "the great sea monsters" (*hattannīnim haggədōlīm*) are mere creatures. But the J stories include many mythic motifs, such as the garden of God and the food of immortality, and feature a variety of divine beings, including cherubim (3:24) and the Sons of God (6:1–4), who have sex with human women and beget a race of mighty warriors. The close relationship between the flood stories in Genesis 6–9 and the Mesopotamian flood stories also falsifies a genre distinction between polytheistic myth and monotheistic primal stories.

Folklore scholarship since the Grimm brothers provides more sophisticated models of myth. Bascom (1984: 9) gives a useful working definition: "Myths are prose narratives which, in the society in which they are told, are considered to be truthful accounts of what happened in the remote past. . . . Myths account for the origin of the world, of mankind, of death, or for characteristics of birds, animals, geographical features, and the phenomena of nature." I would strike the qualifier "prose," since many myths in antiquity are poetry. Dundes (1988: 1) offers a revised definition: "A myth may be defined as a sacred narrative explaining how the world or humans came to be in their present form." These formulations posit that the analytical genre of myth is widespread, perhaps a cultural universal. People seem to have a deep-seated desire for narratives about origins that illuminate present realities. As these definitions suggest, myths have multiple meanings and functions. As Doniger (2011: 8) observes, "Myth is the most interdisciplinary narrative." Myths have many expressive facets: they are descriptive and prescriptive, practical and abstract, political and religious, and by turns edifying and terrifying.

Within biblical studies, H.-P. Müller (1991a: 34) has proposed a nuanced philosophically inclined definition of myth, emphasizing several of its dimensions: "myth . . . calls humans and their 'world' back, as it were, to their origins, in order to ground and legitimize their past and present existence." Myths not only explain the world, as Dundes's definition states, but also orient and legitimize a people's existence in the world. Müller places a Heideggerian accent on the task of orienting humans in the lived world. In this sense, myths transform features that might seem strange or arbitrary into the legitimate features of the world. As Blumenberg (1985: 113) similarly observes, myths enable humans to be "at home in the world" by making "what is uncanny familiar and addressable."

I would extend Müller's formulation to include other kinds of legitimation and orientation beyond the existential. As Malinowski (1948: 84–85) established, myths provide a charter for social institutions and laws: "myth comes into play when rite, ceremony, or a social or moral rule demands justification, warrant of antiquity, reality, and sanctity." These everyday legitimations are essential functions of myth. Myths also have psychological effects that orient the individual's perception of self and others. As the psychoanalyst Jacob Arlow (in Segal 2004: 99) observes, myth "constitutes a form of adaptation to reality and to the group in which the individual lives . . . it influences the crystallization of the individual identity." Cognitive classification is addressed by Durkheim and Mauss (1963: 77): "Every mythology is fundamentally a classification." The ways we relate to reality are mediated by the categories and schemes embedded in the myths.

Pulling these threads together, one can see that myth explains the present world, it legitimates its features and orients people to them. It has distinctive representational features as a literary genre, including its ways of deriving the present world from the era of origins. The relationship of the past and the present in myth is dialectical, creating a potential for the repetition of mythic events in rituals and other literary genres. Finally, myth is a form of cultural memory, a way that groups represent the past as relevant for the present, shaping their shared identity. The features of Genesis 1–11 are illuminated by a robust and multilayered theory of myth, which in turn enriches the native category of Genesis as *tôlǝdōt*. Let us explore these dimensions of Genesis 1–11 as mythology.

EXPLANATION

Genesis 1–11 explains how the world and humans came to be in their present form. The stories may be more than explanations, but they surely do this. The explanatory function is often called etiology ("knowledge of causes"), which explains a phenomenon by explaining what caused it. The prestige of origins is basic to etiology, relying on the idea that the origin of a thing reveals its essence. By showing how the universe, life, and civilization came into being, Genesis 1–11 explains their essential meanings. As Gunkel (1997: xiii) observes, Genesis 1–11 explains the origin of many features of the world:

> The creation narrative asks, "What are the origins of heaven and earth?" and, "Why is the Sabbath holy?" The Paradise account asks, "What is the origin of human reason and mortality?" as well as "What is the origin of the human

body and spirit? The origin of human language? The origin of sexual love (2:4)? How is it that the woman has so much pain in childbirth, that the man must cultivate the resistant field, that the serpent crawls on its belly? etc."

Along with these questions about the origins of the world and humans, the stories also answer questions about the origins of civilization:

A certain class of etiological accounts . . . asks about the origins of human civilization: "How old and what are the origins of the consumption of fruits and flesh, clothing with leaves and skins, animal husbandry, farming, the arts of the smith and the musician, construction of cities and civic life?" The narratives of Paradise, of the Cainites, and of the construction of the Tower record answers to such questions. (Gunkel 1997: xiv)

We can expand this list of etiologies. Genesis 1–11 explains the causes and origins of other features of nature and culture, including:

- The daily cycle of light and darkness (i.e., the divisions of time)
- The spatial domains of sky, land, and sea (i.e., the divisions of space)
- The heavenly bodies (sun, moon, and stars)
- The kinds of living things (plants and animals)
- Food (vegetarian and carnivore) and food laws
- Religious practices and rites (altars, prayer, sacrifice)
- Human lifespan
- The rainbow
- Wine
- The multiplicity of languages and peoples

Genesis 1–11 explains many phenomena by describing their origins. The causal agent for these phenomena is in most cases God, but innovations of civilization are often caused by people, the culture heroes of old, for example Noah, who invented wine, and Tubal-Cain, who invented metallurgy. The burdensome features of human existence—including subsistence labor, painful childbirth, consciousness of mortality, and unintelligible languages—are the consequence of human transgression and divine punishment, which fix new limits on humankind. Other etiologies are beneficial, such as music or God's creation of woman to solve the human's loneliness. The phenomena of the present world were caused by the interactions of divine and human agency, with assists by a few others, including a crafty snake.

The etiologies of the world and humankind in Genesis 1–11 have a complicated history in modern thought, due to the troubled relationship between religion and science. The first modern formulation of myth as explanation, Fontenelle's *De l'origine des fables* (1724), makes an exception for Genesis 1–11. He defines myths and fables as "stories [that] supply reasons for natural events" (Fontenelle 1972: 16). But since they derive from "the ignorance of the first men" (15), they inevitably supply false reasons. He concludes that, despite the pleasure they bring, they should be rejected as human folly: "Let us not look for anything in the fables except the history of the errors of the human mind" (18).

Fontenelle (1972: 16) makes one exception to this rule: "There are no peoples whose history does not begin in fables, except the chosen people, among whom a particular care on the part of providence has preserved the truth." Genesis 1–11 is not a fable since it is not fabulous—its explanations are true. There may be some self-censorship in Fontenelle's exception, since he was not an orthodox believer. Starobinski (1991: 729) suggests that Fontenelle "makes an exception for the 'true religion' only as a precaution." But his exception shows the problem of his theory, which itself is an etiology. Fontenelle's exclusion of Genesis is disingenuous. Its etiologies cannot be excluded from the human desire for explanations.

From the standpoint of modern science, most or all of the etiologies in Genesis 1–11 belong to what Fontenelle calls the history of error. None of the explanations listed above is plausible in the modern age. In our time, we rely on science and historical inquiry to explain the origins of things. For most moderns, the idea that Genesis 1–11 is an accurate explanation of origins of the world and humans has lost its footing. Some still zealously affirm the explanations of Genesis 1–11 and reject the explanations of science; others reject Genesis 1–11 as a farrago of falsehood. Both sides of this contemporary dispute view Genesis 1–11 as primarily or exclusively an etiology.

But myths do more than explain. The view that Genesis 1–11 is an explanation of causes is a partial response to its multilayered meanings. The model of myth as explanation is necessary but insufficient. Myths, whether true or false, are more than explanations. What this model leaves out—myth's more subtle concerns—shows why we still have a stake in Genesis 1–11.

LEGITIMATION AND ORIENTATION

Herder (1993b: 80), a late eighteenth-century pioneer of modern biblical scholarship, responded sharply to the theory of myth as explanation. In contrast to the view of myths as "lapses of human reason, or lamentable cases of blind superstition," he argued for a view of myth as a combination of reason and subjectivity. Myths embody, in Herder's view, the "tactics of the heart and mind" (80). They are not just explanations, but are a way that people orient themselves in the world. Myths participate in the construction of a shared reality, for "we live in a world we ourselves create" (Herder 1892: 252). As Weber (1978: 499), one of Herder's heirs, emphasizes, myths respond not only to empirical questions but also to "an inner compulsion to understand the world as a meaningful cosmos and to take up a position towards it." Myths provide an orientation and behavioral guide to the world as a meaningful cosmos. Herder (1833: 2.31) aptly describes the stories of Genesis as life-enhancing fictions: "How beautiful, considered even as fictions, are these traditional tales."

Genesis 1–11 offers a mental map for understanding the world as a meaningful cosmos and taking up a position toward it. The P creation myth (1:1–2:3) is a rich instance of this kind of world-making. It tells how God created the universe as an intricately organized system. Humans are made "in the image of God," and their role is to rule the world and all living creatures. As God's representatives on earth, humans have power and mastery—and responsibility to rule wisely. This "position toward the world" includes an ethical relation within it.

The mythic task of legitimation and orientation includes grounding social and religious institutions in the order of creation. In the P creation myth, God rests after his work of creation and sanctifies the seventh day. This act anticipates and justifies the

Sabbath law (Exod 20:11, 31:17). The Sabbath is, in a sense, implicit in the structure of creation. Similarly, when God gives the first food law (Gen 1:29), this event anticipates later food laws (Gen 9:3–4; Leviticus 11). The priests have the duty to regulate the distinctions between clean and unclean and between holy and profane (Lev 10:10, 11:47), just as God creates these and other distinctions in the cosmos. In this respect, priestly authority is embedded in the structure of creation.

The J myths use their powers of legitimation and orientation in a less systematic way, with greater moral ambiguity in the passage from creation to the present world. The J myths, as H.-P. Müller (1991a: 99) emphasizes, depict a growth of limits on the human condition, a "reduction of being" (*Daseinsminderung*). When humans are expelled from Eden, their lives are burdened by hard labor, suffering, and mortality. Women are subordinated to men, and people are burdened by shame and guilt. Civilization is itself tinged with danger, division, and hubris, represented by the ruins of the Tower of Babel and the unintelligible languages of the world's peoples. The problems of human life are made "familiar and addressable," in Blumenberg's (1985: 113) phrase, even as they are also messy or tragic.

Alongside these limits and burdens, there are benefits. In the J myths, humans gain the "knowledge of good and evil," a quality that makes people "like gods," even as its acquisition requires exile from paradise. Men and women are partners, and in their marriage and sexual pleasure they recover a primal unity, rejoined as one. Music and wine provide other kinds of pleasure. *Dasein* ("being there") is not wholly bleak. The world to which the J myths orient is a blend of good and evil, pain and pleasure, knowledge and ignorance. The human condition, nested in the relationship between Yahweh and humans, is complicated and perplexing, but there are various kinds of favor and right living.

The J myths, like P, justify social and religious institutions. Abel, Cain, and Noah offer the first sacrifices, which, if Yahweh accepts them, bring blessing and uplift. In Enosh's generation people begin to call on the name of Yahweh, establishing new religious practices (vows, prayers, etc.). The institution of marriage is justified in 2:24: "Therefore a man leaves his father and mother and cleaves to his wife." In the J myth, these social practices find, in Malinowski's (1948: 84–85) terms, "justification, warrant of antiquity, reality, and sanctity."

The J myths also provide moral and psychological education, another kind of orientation. This function is expressed in Yahweh's exhortation to Cain to master his violent impulses: "sin crouches at the door—it desires you, but you can rule over it" (4:6). This conflict, pictured as a struggle with a predator, is of course an internal struggle. The psychological and moral conflict takes place within one's heart, or—to use a modern translation—one's psyche. In this scene, Yahweh educates the reader's moral self. The myth describes this inner turmoil and gives moral and psychological instruction.

Classification also belongs to the sphere of orientation and legitimation. In some respects, Genesis 1–11 is, in Durkheim and Mauss's (1963: 77) phrase, "fundamentally a classification." The P myths have many classificatory features. The creation myth features the divisions of space—above and below the vault of heaven (1:6–8), and the earth and sea (1:9–10)—and divisions of time, including the daily cycle of day and night (1:4–5) and the weekly cycle capped by the seventh day. Creatures are classified into three spatial domains—sky, water, and land—and distinct species. The hierarchy of creatures is capped by the creation of humans, who are to rule them. A taxonomy of peoples is established by the Table of Nations (Genesis 10), with genealogy as its formal classification scheme.

The J myths also articulate classificatory systems. In the Eden myth, the categories of human, animal, and god are drawn through a series of oppositions and mediations. Yahweh creates the first human as a "living being" (*nepeŝ ḥayyâ*), a term whose scope includes animals. Yahweh then creates the animals. Finally, Yahweh creates the woman: she is the man's true companion, and he names her *'iŝŝâ* (female) as a taxonomic counterpart to his *'iŝ* (male) (3:23). In contrast to the complementarity of woman and man, a contrast is drawn between humans and animals, which includes the distinctive feature of language.

A complication occurs in the myth with the appearance of the snake, an animal who speaks like humans and who has knowledge of things divine. The snake is a mediator who crosses the domains of animal, human, and the divine. His clever speech spurs a dangerous passage between the domains of humans and gods, enticing the woman to eat the forbidden fruit of the Tree of the Knowledge of Good and Evil. In his speech, the snake mingles truth with deception, a mark of a trickster. Yahweh admits that the humans have "become like one of us, knowing good and evil" (3:22), and as a consequence expels them, lest they become immortal. Yahweh casts them into the all-too-human world of hard labor, suffering, and death. The awareness of these categorical distinctions—human/animal, male/female, human/divine, life/death, etc.—is articulated through these mediations, yielding the classificatory scheme of the present world.

The J myths yield a complicated and ambiguous picture of reality, which in many respects still rings true. We strive to overcome the limits of this classification, to become more godlike, to reduce pain and mortality, to return to a lost paradise. In some respects we have reduced these limits, but many of them stubbornly persist—mortality, evil inclinations, subsistence labor, painful childbirth, shame, and guilt. The orientations in the myths, in these respects, are truthful, despite their lack of scientific facticity. They are, in Herder's sense, "tactics of the heart and mind."

The myths of Genesis 1–11 disclose, in Malinowski's (1948: 107) words, a "relevant reality, by which the present life, fates, and activities of [hu]mankind are determined." They do not merely explain, but also illuminate, justify, classify, and mediate. They are a commentary on a meaningful cosmos and a guide to living in it. We can critique and modify their prescriptions about the world, but we must still, in Weber's term, take up a position to the world. The myths redescribe a world that in many respects we still inhabit, despite the advances of modernity.

SACRED NARRATIVE

As a sacred narrative, in Dundes's formulation, myth communicates through features shared with all narrative, along with features specific to it. Among these features, as Gunkel (1997: xii) comments, is a distinctive scope of time and space: "The arena of these accounts is the remote past, their sphere of interest the whole world." Bakhtin (1981: 84–258) describes a genre's relationship of time and space as a "chronotope" (lit. "time-space"). In myth, he observes, this relationship is a "historical inversion" of the present world, projected back into the time of origins as a primeval utopia, which then yields the present world as a damaged version of the utopia. The present world is "somehow empty and fragmented," while bringing to consciousness a fuller reality (147). This chronotope is a deep feature of myth as sacred narrative.

The genre of myth has other distinctive literary features, including its plot structure, in which crises and resolutions yield permanent changes. Aristotle's analysis of plot in his *Poetics*, I suggest, helps to elucidate these plot structures in Genesis (Hendel 1995a, 1997b). Aristotle describes the plot (which he calls *muthos*, "myth") as "the organization of events" and the "first principle" (*archē*) (*Poetics* 1450a). The plot imposes a connective tissue over the individual events, yielding an intelligible consonance of beginnings, middles, and ends. As Kermode (1967: 17) comments, this narrative model of "grand temporal consonance" reflects our desire for consonance in our own lives. The plots of myths organize their meaningful connectivity.

Aristotle draws a useful distinction between simple and complex plots (*Poetics* 1452a). Complex plots consist of a movement from an initial situation to its opposite. This movement is caused initially by the protagonist's violent act or error (*hamartia*), which produces suffering for family or neighbors. The complex plot includes many complications, such as sudden reversals (*peripeteia*) and recognitions (*anagnorisis*). In contrast to complex plots, simple plots lack most of these features—no crises caused by violence or error, and no sudden reversals or recognitions.

The P creation myth in Genesis 1 is an exemplary case of a simple plot. The plot is a consistent movement from a primeval state of chaos to a divinely caused cosmic order. It lacks dissonance, crisis, or conflict. As Levenson (1988: 53) observes, the P creation account is a "creation without opposition," predicated on the absolute authority of God. In his uninterrupted work of creation, "God functions like an Israelite priest, making distinctions, assigning things to their proper category and assessing their fitness, and hallowing the Sabbath" (127). There are no complications or reversals in God's work of creation.

A complication does occur between the creation and the flood. In the P flood story, God perceives that the violence of the creatures has corrupted the earth—this is a decisive moment of recognition. God then returns the ordered world to chaos—a sudden reversal. Finally, he re-creates the ordered world with a new set of laws, which resolves the initial crisis. While the P creation myth has a simple plot, the flood story has a complex one.

The J myths consistently have complex plots, filled with violence or error, deceptions, reversals, recognitions, and suffering. The plot of the Garden of Eden story is characterized by many such complications, including the following:

Error
- Yahweh prohibits eating from the Tree of the Knowledge of Good and Evil (2:16), creating potential for error.
- The humans eat the forbidden fruit (3:6).

Deception
- The snake deceives the woman (3:1–5).
- The humans attempt to deceive Yahweh by hiding and deflecting blame (3:8–13).

Sudden reversal
- The humans become "like gods, knowing good and evil" (3:5, 22).
- The snake crawls on his belly and eats dust (3:14).

- The husband rules the wife (3:16, cf. 3:6).
- The soil is cursed to be unfruitful (3:17–18, cf. 2:9,15).
- Yahweh expels the humans (3:23).

Recognition
- Yahweh sees "It is not good for the human to be alone" (2:18).
- The human discovers that the animals are not suitable companions (2:20).
- The man recognizes the woman as his "bone and flesh" and true companion (2:23).
- The woman sees that the forbidden fruit is desirable to eat and to become wise (3:6).
- The humans' eyes are opened and "they knew that they were naked" (3:7).
- Yahweh sees that the humans have violated his command ("Who told you that you are naked?") (3:11).

Suffering
- Enmity exists between the snake and humans (3:15).
- The woman experiences pain during childbirth (3:16).
- The man works and eats from the soil in pain (3:17–19).
- Humans return to the dust (3:19).

This complex plot involves a chain of complications. It creates a connective tissue of beginning, middle, and end that yields permanent change in the human condition. But within its organizing consonance, the narrative has considerable ambiguity. There is abundant suffering and "diminution of being," but, as Yahweh acknowledges, the humans have "become like one of us, knowing good and evil." This represents an ascent in "being." The complicated reversal of the initial situation has a doubled aspect: humans are now more godlike, but they must bear the burdens of a mortal life.

The distinctive shape of complex plots continues in the other J myths of Genesis 1–11, animated by many transgressions. As Aristotle observes, "it is possible to go wrong in many ways" (*Ethics* 1106b). In the J stories, some transgressions are inadvertent, like Ham seeing his father's nakedness, while others are deliberate violent acts, like Cain's murder of his brother. In each myth, the transgression breaks moral boundaries and causes suffering to family, neighbors, and even Yahweh ("his heart was pained," Gen 6:6). The breaches of boundaries occur primarily in two directions: between humans and the divine, and within the family (Table 2).

A few points of clarification to this table: Cain's exile from God's presence ("I will be hidden from your face," 4:14) is a result of his fratricide being a moral breach of the human/divine relationship. The Sons of God violate the boundaries of human/divine from the other side, since they are divine beings who have sex with human women. Noah's curse of Canaan is solely a family affair, with no divine agency or intervention. Each of these complex plots results in permanent changes of the conditions of human life, yielding a mixture of limits (e.g., lifespan, differentiation of languages and people) and benefits (e.g., music, wine, sex).

The myths of Genesis 1–11 create, in a sense, a master plot, a global consonance, linking then and now in an intelligible nexus, binding the accidental with the essential. This is one of the deep functions of myth—making the world a familiar home rather than a series of random events.

Table 2. Transgressions of boundaries

	Human/divine	*Brother/brother*	*Husband/wife*	*Father/son*
Eden	X			
Cain and Abel	X	X		
Sons of God	X		X	
Flood	X			
Curse of Canaan				X
Tower of Babel	X			

As sacred or authoritative narratives, the myths of Genesis 1–11 are, in a sense, revelatory. They disclose the reality that animates the present world. Unlike other literary genres, they describe the shape of reality and prescribe the right position toward it. This mythic narrative does not depict a possible world; rather, as Auerbach (1953:15) comments, "it insists that it is the only real world." This insistence exemplifies what Benjamin (1968: 109) calls the "aura" of the storyteller, whose voice exerts an irresistible claim. The power of this mythic aura creates a dilemma for modern readers, for, as Auerbach (1953: 15) writes, Genesis "seeks to overcome our reality: we are to fit our own life into its world, feel ourselves to be elements in its structure of universal history." In a sense, the modern reader is both a participant and an observer of the myths of Genesis 1–11: we are its product, even as we stand partially outside its complex plot.

REPETITION

In Bakhtin's (1981: 147) terms, the genre of myth projects the world backward into the era of origins, which it then reconstitutes, in fragmented form, in the present. As Kierkegaard (1983: 229) observes, this doubled temporality makes possible an experience of repetition, which allows for a deeper awareness of oneself and the world: "Repetition is the raising of . . . consciousness to the second power." The repetition of the events of myth takes place in memory, ritual, poetry, and prophecy. The myths of Genesis 1–11 have this propensity for repetition, instantiated in various forms of life and literature.

Eliade (1959: 21) emphasizes the experience of repetition in rituals that actualize myth: "Any ritual . . . [takes place] in a 'sacred time' . . . when the ritual was performed for the first time by a god, an ancestor, or a hero." Rituals repeat the "first time" of myth, bringing the mythic past into the present. The rites reconnect contemporary worshipers with sacred time and space, offering a raised consciousness. Repetition in rituals also has a social dimension; as Durkheim (2001: 282) observes, they serve "to awaken certain ideas and feelings, to link the present to the past, the individual to the collectivity." The repetition of myth affects the individual and the community.

A classic example is the P creation myth, whose ritual counterpart is the Sabbath, a repetition of sacred time—"God blessed the seventh day and made it holy, for on it he ceased from all his work" (Gen 1:3). The ritual of the Sabbath—cessation from work—commemorates and emulates God's rest from his work of creation. Through this ritual repetition, as Levenson (1988: 111) comments, "the Priestly account of creation accentuates the possibility of human access to the inner rhythm of creation itself."

In the Sabbath command, the repetition of God's rest is mandated for every Israelite household, including servants and slaves, resident aliens, and even domestic animals: "You shall not do any work, you and your sons and daughters, your servants and your maidservants, your domestic animals, and your resident aliens within your gates" (Exod 20:10). The Sabbath, a repetition of the "first time," suspends the burdens of ordinary time, and its participants—like God on the seventh day—are refreshed (see Exod 31:17).

Repetitions of the Garden of Eden myth occur in rituals and other literary genres (Stordalen 2000). The repetition of life in Eden may seem paradoxical, since in the myth humans are permanently exiled from it. But in other domains—in hymns, temple rites, and apocalyptic prophecies—the paradisiacal existence in Eden is restored in the present or future, even if partially or with different nuances. As commentators have observed, the Jerusalem temple resonates with images of paradise, from the reliefs of cherubs and sacred trees to the worshiper's experience of perfection and immortality within its precincts (Levenson 1985: 127–42; Wenham 1994; Stager 1999). The paradisiacal quality of the temple's sacred space is also evoked in hymns, as in Ps 36:8–10:

> Humankind shelters in the shadow of your wings;
>> They are sated from the rich food of your house;
> You let them drink from the river of your delights;
>> For with you is the fountain of life.

The phrase "river of your delights" (*naḥal ʿădāneykā*) is, as Gunkel (1997: 36) observes, "an ingenious allusion to the river of ʿēden." The "fountain of life" is a variation on the Tree of Life, providing immortality to those who drink from it. The worshiper's experience in the temple is a kind of repetition of life in the primordial paradise. As Levenson (1985: 129) writes, "The same language describes life in Eden, the Garden of Delight, and Zion, the Temple mount, in which the primal perfection of Eden is wonderfully preserved."

The repetition of myth, in which the primeval past breaks into the present, takes a new form in proto-apocalyptic prophecy, where the primeval past is projected into the future, when the chaos of the present era will be overcome. As Gunkel (2006: 233) writes, "In the end time what had happened in primal time will be repeated." The repetition of the mythic past in the perfect future is the final repetition, permanently transforming the world. In Isa 65:17, the prophet proclaims God's promise: "For behold, I am about to create a new heaven and a new earth." A new creation will transform the world into a utopia.

Isaiah 51:3 describes the coming new age as a return to the Garden of Eden: "He will make her wilderness like Eden, / and her desert like the Garden of Yahweh." According to the later apocalypticism of the book of Enoch, on the day of judgment the righteous will eat from the Tree of Life and live forever in God's presence. The angel Michael says to Enoch, "As for this fragrant tree, no flesh has the right to touch it until the great judgment. . . . Then it will be given to the righteous and the pious, and its fruit will be food for the chosen" (1 En. 25:3–6; Nickelsburg 2001: 312).

The eschatological paradise of the righteous will be a future return to Eden, which is available in the present in a different modality, the sacred space of the Jerusalem temple. Similarly, the Sabbath is a repetition of sacred time, breaking into the weekly cycle of mundane time. The way of paradise may have been closed to humans in the mythic past, but in other forms of life and literature it remains open.

Myth, Genealogy, and Memory

Myths and genealogies are forms of cultural memory, which may be defined as a group's representation of the past with present relevance (Hendel 2010). Genesis 1–11 serves as cultural memory in several ways. As Assmann (2003: 10) writes: "Myths are the fundamental figures of memory. Their constant repetition and actualization is one of the ways in which a society or culture affirms its identity." Cultural memory draws on myth's expressive qualities as sacred narrative and repetition, which bind together past and present in an intelligible web of meaning. Legitimation and orientation are also core aspects of cultural memory. As Durkheim (2001: 279) comments, "the traditions whose memory this mythology perpetuates are expressed in the way the society imagines man and the world." A people's worldview, self-consciousness, and practices are grounded in the soil of collective memory.

Cultural memory, like myth, is often plural. In different groups—whether organized by community, class, religion, etc.—there are inevitably contesting claims expressed through rival memories of the past. This is evident today in the memories of what Halbwachs (1992: 224) calls the "legendary topography" of the Holy Land, where "visible facts are the symbols of invisible truths." For instance, Jewish, Christian, and Muslim traditions have rival memories about the location of Adam and Eve's tomb. According to Christian tradition, it is in the Church of the Holy Sepulcher in Jerusalem, at the center of the world, where drops of Christ's blood cleansed Adam and Eve of sin. According to Jewish and Muslim traditions, Adam and Eve's tomb is in the Cave of the Patriarchs in Hebron, where Abraham purchased the family tomb (Genesis 23). These memories actualize the death of Adam and Eve according to different constellations, one organized by the typology of the First and Last Adam (1 Cor 15:45) and the other by a midrashic interpretation of the name Kiryat ʿArba, "The City of Four," which adds Adam and Eve to the other three pairs (e.g., *Pirqe R. El.* 20). These countermemories offer a repetition of the myth at their respective sacred sites and draw boundaries around the religious communities that assert them.

The J and P myths in Genesis 1–11 are, in many respects, countermemories. They may not have been composed in direct response to the other—for instance, there is no allusion in P to J, or vice versa—but they represent the shared mythic past differently. This is evident in their accounts of creation and flood, which are different in details, motives, and orientation. These differences extend to the character of God. In P, God is the prime agent, the transcendent master of creation. When God speaks, it is always a command, never a dialogue. In J, Yahweh has anthropomorphic traits while still a creator. He walks in the Garden of Eden and engages in dialogue with the man and the woman. He feels regret and heartbreak when he perceives the evil imaginings of the human heart. These are clashing memories of God.

These differences show the variability of cultural memory. Yet despite these differences, Genesis presents itself as the authoritative account of origins, linking the present to the constitutive past by the connective web of memory. As Benjamin (1968: 98) comments: "*Memory* creates the chain of tradition which passes a happening on from generation to generation. . . . It starts the web which all stories together form in the end." The biblical writers participate in this chain of cultural memory, both transforming and perpetuating it.

A final aspect of cultural memory bears on the continuing relevance of Genesis 1–11. The myths belong to ancient Israel's cultural memory, as crystallized in the book of Genesis. But there is a double life for any biblical book, one in its era of creation and another in the *longue durée* of its interpretive life. Genesis 1–11 undergoes creative transformations in its interpretive life from antiquity to today (Hendel 2013). Through memories and countermemories of Genesis, communities past and present constitute themselves and their world.

The life of Genesis 1–11 plays a significant role in modern cultural memory. The ways that we explain natural phenomena, justify laws and institutions, and orient ourselves to the world are still intricately tied to the ways that we understand Genesis 1–11. Our political discourse—particularly on issues of religion, sexuality, and science—still hinges on the authority of Genesis, as we see in the clash of interpretations in the public square. Even those for whom Genesis is not authoritative take a position in relation to it. In sum, the myths of Genesis 1–11 are a part of our contemporary memory work. The text continues to exert its claims on us, who are its genealogical heirs.

IV.

Sex, Honor, and Civilization: The Moral World of Genesis 1–11

———————

"The mythology of a group," Durkheim (2001: 279) writes, "is a morality and a cosmology, even as it is a history." The stories of Genesis 1–11 embody a moral code, or perhaps better, a double version of a moral code, with different emphases in J and P. These representations of morality are richly connected to the domains of sex, honor, and civilization. Myths of origin are well suited to articulate the practices and sensibilities of a moral community, since they embed them in an era when the world's distinctive features were crystallizing into their present form. Like all narrative, myths focus the audience's attention onto the protagonists' moral emotions and conflicts.

The moral world of Genesis 1–11 is expressed primarily through action and dialogue rather than rules, with the exception of God's moral prescriptions. The stories exemplify "thick" moral concepts, which are embedded in a particular social world and are not analyzable, without oversimplification, into universal or context-free precepts (Williams 2008: 143–45). The myths, with their rich particulars, provide a two-tiered moral education—for their characters and their audience. They embody what Barton (2014: 170) calls "narrative ethics."

The moral world of this text is laced with gaps, tensions, and ambiguities. Moral behaviors are enacted beliefs, entrenched in everyday habits that are acquired in the process of acculturation. The myths are part of a moral education. They are part of a practical process, laced with implicit concepts that may sometimes collide. They do not constitute a rational systematic ethics, but a practical one.

A challenge in this type of inquiry is the temptation of paraphrase or simple translation into modern categories. The moral world of Genesis is ancestral to our moral world, but it would be a mistake to minimize or harmonize their differences. Even when concepts and practices seem to be equivalent, they exist in different configurations with different accents. Ancient forms of life are different from ours, and we do damage to the texts—and at times to each other—when we conflate the Bible's moral world with our own.

Sex, Shame, and Guilt

The interrelations of shame and guilt—two distinct moral emotions—are central to the narrative dynamics of the J primeval narrative. The dawning of shame and guilt in the Garden of Eden and the Cain story are turning points, exposing the consequences of the humans' transgressions and their awakening to moral consciousness (see Bauks 2010). Shame (bwš) is a reflexive emotion that links the individual's self-image to a wider moral community, rooted in an implicit code of honor. Guilt (ʿwn) subjects the individual to the judgment of moral obligation, whether imposed externally or internally. Notably, these two moral emotions are associated across cultures with the senses of sight and sound. As Williams (2008: 78, 89) observes, "the basic experience of shame is that of being seen, inappropriately," whereas "guilt is rooted in hearing . . . the voice of judgement." In the J myths sight and sound are the primary sensory channels of shame and guilt. Sexuality is subject to shame or guilt when it is inappropriate or out of place. Sexuality, seen in the wrong place or by the wrong person, is shameful, and when it is a violation of law and subject to the voice of judgment, it triggers guilt.

When Adam and Eve eat the forbidden fruit, their newly acquired "knowledge of good and evil" causes an awareness of shame: "The eyes of the two of them were opened, and they knew that they were naked, and they sewed together fig leaves and made loincloths for themselves" (3:7). In the prior situation, "The two of them were naked, the man and his wife, and they felt no shame before each other" (2:25). This was the state of innocence, before the dawn of self-consciousness and shame. Now the couple see their nakedness through their "opened" eyes and feel shame before each other. The verb for "shame" (bwš) is not used, but the wording activates the situation of the earlier verse. The couple now feel exposed and vulnerable. Their new knowledge involves an awareness of their differently sexed bodies. Their sensation of shame is triggered by their sense of sight, which is deepened by insight.

This primal scene of shame does not mean that sexuality itself is bad or sinful. Sex in the right place and with the right person is a moral good, as when two become "one flesh" (2:24) or when "the man knew Eve, his wife" (4:1). This is appropriate sexual knowledge. Becoming "one flesh" is an unalloyed good, a restoration of the oneness and delight of paradise. Sexuality has a complicated resonance as a moral good that is a source of shame or guilt when it is "out of place" (Douglas 1966: 35).

The couple's emotion of shame leads to the moral emotion of guilt when they hear the sound of Yahweh in the garden, and they hide. But they are not simply hiding their nakedness, for they are now wearing loincloths. They hide because they are afraid. The man says, "I heard your sound in the garden and I was afraid, for I am naked, so I hid" (3:10). The couple hide because they fear exposure of their disobedience, not just of their bodies. Their sense of sound—hearing the *qōl* ("sound," with a latent sense of "voice") of Yahweh—elicits a guilty conscience.

Yahweh exposes their guilt by interrogation, "Who told you that you are naked? Have you eaten from the tree from which I commanded you not to eat?" (3:11). This is a leading question, for the couple's guilt is not due to nakedness as such, but to their consciousness of disobedience. This is shown by their attempts to deflect guilt. Adam blames the woman—and Yahweh for creating her—and the woman blames the snake (3:12–13). Their attempts at passing blame expose their guilty consciences.

After Yahweh punishes the couple for disobeying his command, he performs a compassionate act: he "made leather garments for the man and his wife, and he dressed them" (3:21). This is a gift, replacing the humans' fig-leaf loincloths with sturdier garments. In sum, Yahweh punishes their guilt but covers their shame. His compassionate gift adds a positive note to their moral education.

The dynamics of shame and guilt in Eden are echoed and amplified in the story of Cain and Abel. The trigger for Cain's moral descent is Yahweh's acceptance of Abel's sacrifice and disregard for his own: "Yahweh regarded with favor Abel and his sacrifice, but Cain and his sacrifice he did not regard" (*šāʿâ*, lit. "regard, look at," 4:4–5). Yahweh's distributed gaze triggers Cain's emotion of shame; hence "Cain became very angry, and his face was fallen" (4:5). The clause "his face was fallen" (*wayyippəlu pānâw*) is a picture of shame, which in biblical diction is visually associated with the face (Jer 7:19, Ps 44:16). Cain sees himself as others see him, with Yahweh's gaze parceling out honor and shame.

Echoing the judgment scene in Eden, Cain's moral emotion shifts from shame to guilt under Yahweh's interrogation (4:9–12). This is accompanied by a shift from sight to hearing. As in Eden, Yahweh asks a leading question, "Where is Abel, your brother?," to which Cain responds, "I do not know." Then Yahweh exposes the crime, "The voice (*qōl*) of your brother's blood cries out to me from the soil." Abel's postmortem voice motivates Yahweh's judgment: he curses Cain from the soil and condemns him to be a ceaseless wanderer. Cain then ambiguously admits his guilt: "My punishment (*ʿăwōnî*, with a resonance of both "sin" and "guilt") is more than I can bear (*minnnəśoʾ*)" (4:13). While Yahweh's mark will ward off those who may murder him, Cain continues to bear the weight of his guilt.

The strange case of Lamech, Cain's descendant, further amplifies the dynamics of shame and guilt. Lamech lacks the capacity for shame. As such, he stands outside the moral community. He boasts to his wives:

A man I have killed for wounding me,
    a boy for bruising me.
If Cain is avenged sevenfold,
    Lamech will be seventy-seven-fold. (4:23–24)

Lamech confesses to murder and takes delight in it. Although the details are obscure, he seems to say that he has avenged himself for the slightest of wounds and is proud of being more violent than Cain. This is a bizarre boast, which flouts the code of honor. Lamech is insensible to his shame and guilt—he is blind to his shame and cannot hear the voice of conscience.

Lamech represents the extremity of moral evil. His case is a prelude to the cataclysm of the flood, when Yahweh perceives the extent of human evil: "Yahweh saw how great was the evil of humans on the earth, for every design of their hearts was only evil all day long" (6:5). This is a harsh picture of human morality. Lamech's boast—seconded by Yahweh's perception of humankind's evil imaginings—addresses a world that lacks an internal compass of honor, shame, and guilt. At this juncture, Noah is the exception.

Civilization and Its Discontents

The development of moral consciousness in J is linked to the development of civilization. As Wellhausen (1885: 302) writes, "the first step in civilization is clothing," which the first couple devise when "the eyes of the two of them were opened" (3:7). The experience of shame and the invention of civilization are here linked. The next item of culture derives from Yahweh's judgment of their guilt. Yahweh punishes the man with painful agricultural labor, including the cultivation of a new kind of food: "By the sweat of your brow you will eat bread" (3:19). As Kawashima (2004b: 488) observes, this is the first mention of cooked food, a distinctive feature of civilization. The humans previously ate the fruits of the garden, a cuisine natural and raw. Bread is cooked and cultured. But in contrast to the previous cuisine, eating bread "by the sweat of your brow" is a punishment.

The passage from nature to culture is accompanied by the couple's transition from innocence to self-awareness, including knowledge of sexuality. As scholars have long noted, a similar passage is experienced by the wild man Enkidu in the *Epic of Gilgamesh:* after having sex with a prostitute for seven days, he is rejected by the animals and has a changed self-awareness, becoming "wide of understanding" (*Gilg.* I.202; George 2003: 550–51). A prostitute then teaches him to wear clothes, eat bread, and drink beer. A barber cuts his hair and anoints him with oil, and "he became a human" (*awīliš īwe;* Old Babylonian II iii.108; George 2003: 176–77). His development as a fully cultured person is completed when the prostitute takes him to the city of Uruk to encounter his counterpart, Gilgamesh the king (Moran 2002: 13–14). The awakening of sexuality plays a central role in Enkidu's transformation and sets him on the path to human culture. These themes echo in the transformation of Adam and Eve from their innocence in the garden to their experience of self-consciousness, sexuality, and culture.

The passage to civilization in the J myths features many of the same cultural items as Enkidu's ascent—clothes, bread, liquor (beer for Enkidu, wine for Noah), and cities (Gilgamesh's Uruk, Cain's city, and the city of Babylon). These details indicate a common tradition of the rise of human culture. But there is a key difference in moral tone. For Enkidu, the ascent to civilization is an unalloyed good, as he confesses later to Gilgamesh on his deathbed. In these stories in Genesis, civilization has its discontents.

People eat bread by the sweat of their brow. The murderer Cain and the children of the evil Lamech are the inventors of cities, herding, tents, music, and metalwork (4:17–22). Noah's invention of wine leads to the shame of being seen naked by his son. The Tower of Babel casts urban life in a negative light; it is a building project driven by the human desire to ascend to heaven, and which Yahweh is compelled to halt. These stories suggest something troubling about civilization.

Wellhausen (1885: 303) aptly describes the ambivalence of civilization in these stories: "In all this we have the steps of man's emancipation; with his growing civilization grows also his alienation from the highest good; and—this is evidently the idea, though it is not stated—the restless advance never reaches its goal after all; it is a Sisyphus-labor; the tower of Babel, which is incomplete to all eternity, is the proper symbol for it." The ruined Tower of Babel is an emblem of shame. It recalls the hubris endemic to civilization, which perpetually strains at its limits.

The ambivalence of civilization is a striking feature of the J myths. As Albertz (2003: 30) observes, in these stories, humankind "not only increases life with the work of culture, but also continually endangers it." Civilization is an ascent and a descent. Some of this ambivalence may stem from ancient Israel's identity as a people on the periphery of the great civilizations of the Near East. The city of Babel is, after all, Babylon, the most famous of ancient cities. Cain's city is "east of Eden" (4:16), in the distant east. From Israel's standpoint, these cities are foreign as well as ancient. The village-based society of ancient Israel may have looked with suspicion on great cities, where warrior kings like Gilgamesh and Nimrod (10:8–12) hold sway. In this sense, civilization is dangerous because its great exemplars are foreign, including imperial cities where power is concentrated. The city of Babylon evokes the violence of ancient empires, to which Israel was subjugated. From the view beyond the metropolis, civilization can be an ambiguous gift.

The Image of God

The P myths have a different orientation on the interrelationships of sex, honor, and civilization. The P work is theocentric and architectonic, in contrast to J's focus on the messy complexity of the lived world. In P, sex, honor, sin, and civilization are related in varying ways to the larger order of the cosmos. God creates the human world as a harmonious part of the larger cosmic order, but because of creaturely imperfections it devolves into disharmony. To solve this problem, God issues new commands, setting into motion a sequence of covenants, which provides a structure of moral and ritual laws that protects this fragile harmony.

Human sexuality in P is oriented by the dual position of humans in the created order: they are living creatures created by God, and they are representatives of God on earth. When humans are created on the sixth day, God gives them the blessing to "be fruitful and multiply" (1:28), entailing sexuality, as it does for the animals created on the fifth day (1:22). Since it is a blessing, sexuality is consonant with the goodness of creation. Procreation, in a sense, continues God's work of creation through all time, following his command to "fill the earth" with life.

The increase of civilization in P seems to be a natural consequence of God's command to "be fruitful and multiply" (1:28; similarly 9:1, 7). The refrain of the P Table of Nations lists the descendants of Noah's sons "according to their families, languages, lands, and nations" (10:20, 31). Here the diversity of human languages and peoples is a positive good, serving to fill the earth. Sexual fruitfulness entails the growth of civilization.

Moral evil surfaces in the flood story. God says to Noah, "The end of all flesh has come before me, for the earth is filled with violence because of them" (6:13). Unlike the J flood story, the moral corruption in the P story comes from all the kinds of living creatures, for "all flesh had corrupted its way on earth" (6:12). The content of the creatures' violent ways becomes visible only in the covenant after the flood, when God gives laws to regulate killing and murder. Humans and other animals are allowed to kill for food, but humans must not eat the blood, since, as later explained, "the life of flesh is in the blood" (Lev 17:11). The violent bloodshed of humans is prohibited, in terms that invoke their creation in the image of God:

> Whoever sheds the blood of a human,
>   for a human will his blood be shed,
> for in God's image he made humans. (Gen 9:6)

The final poetic line, which comes after a circular *inclusio,* serves as the motive for the prohibition. The law against bloodshed is rooted in the principle of humankind as God's image. This law, a central part of the Noachian covenant, limits the problem of violence that caused the flood. Human bloodshed and murder are departures from the moral code implicit in the order of creation.

The P primeval narrative links together the domains of sexuality, honor, sin, and civilization but in a configuration different from that in the J stories. The organizing concept is the original harmonious order of creation, whose capstone is the creation of humans in the image of God. The code of morality stems from this central core.

A Genealogy of Morals

The myths of Genesis 1–11 present a complicated picture of the emergent moral world. They depict the moral education of their characters and draw the audience into this moral formation. The stories encode the shared norms of ancient Israel, including the dynamics of honor, shame, and guilt. It is a thick morality, which cannot be easily abstracted or translated from its local practices and habits.

In the modern world, where the forms of family, economy, and nation differ markedly from those of the ancient world, many of these norms no longer seem natural, and the invitation to inhabit these horizons can be problematic. For instance, the subordination of women (3:16) is nowadays seen as a violation of moral norms. It is virtually unthinkable to condone slavery, which is presented as a normal institution (9:26). Yet many other features of morality in Genesis 1–11 still seem vital, such as the challenge of self-mastery over sin's desire, or the capacity for shame and the experience of guilt. It seems to be that an implicit code of honor and shame and a rule of law that entails guilt are necessary for any family or society. In other words, humans seem to share a basic range of moral commitments, even as they are configured and entangled differently from place to place.

In Genesis 1–11, these commitments are configured differently in the J and P sources. To echo Nietzsche, these writers present different genealogies of morals. They explore the origins of the categories and norms that shape our moral orientation, which they situate in the era that shapes the human world. Morality is not a supplement to the lived world but is intrinsic to its deep structure. In this sense, the myths do for morality what they do for other aspects of existence: they explain, justify, orient, and commemorate, through the verbal form of sacred narrative.

As with their stylistic tendencies, the moral worlds of J and E differ. That of J is ambiguous and fraught with background, dependent on the imperfect choices and imaginings of the human heart and the compassion of an anthropomorphic God. In P, the moral world is explicitly theocentric and hierarchical, organized to restore and maintain the original harmony of creation and its capstone, humans created in God's image. The conditions of sexuality, honor, and civilization have their genealogies in these different approaches to the order of things. But in the book of Genesis, these two genealogies are woven together into a single text, yielding a messy and sometimes contradictory genealogy of morals.

The modern world owes many of its moral commitments to these genealogical narratives, sometimes radically transformed. In the early modern period, political philosophers translated the P moral principle of "image of God" into the modern concept of universal human rights. From this comes Thomas Jefferson's formulation "endowed by their Creator with certain inalienable rights." This is a modern rationalization of P's moral system. Freud's discovery of the unconscious and its moral—and immoral— drives is similarly a rationalization of J's model of interior moral struggle (see 4:7). These are legacies of the moral world of Genesis 1–11.

Some aspects of modern morality contest the genealogy of morals in Genesis 1–11, not only the treatment of women, slaves, and sexuality, but also our valorization of civilization and technology, including skyscrapers with their tops in heaven and technologies that corrupt the earth. Some of the modern changes are morally good, while others diminish our well-being and stewardship of the earth. It is plain to see that there is gain and loss, not a unilinear tale of moral progress, in the history of morality since the world of Genesis.

V.

The Interpretive Life of Genesis

Tracing the interpretive life of Genesis involves a distinction between the book's era of composition and its later eras of interpretation. Benjamin (1968: 73) describes this temporal duality through the metaphor of a text's life and afterlife: "In its afterlife—which could not be called that if it were not a transformation and a renewal of something living—the original undergoes a change." Through its transformations and renewals, the text takes on new dimensions of meaning, some of which may have been unthinkable previously. The book becomes a historical agent, entering novel cultural and religious configurations. Its afterlife renews and extends its life.

But the life and afterlife of Genesis are not two wholly different things. The plain senses of Genesis are never lost as long as readers pay attention to the verbal details and resonances of the text. Even if one believes that the true meaning has to do with abstract spiritual truths or coded prophecies, its narrative power and style are apparent to any careful reader. Its plain meanings are always available, even if they are partially obscured under spiritual castles.

The book of Genesis, as we will see, has always demanded interpretation; but its interpretations change over time. Over the generations, the ways that people have understood Genesis tend to correlate with the ways that they have understood reality, which is to say that the kinds of meaning people expect to find in Genesis are the same kinds that they expect to find in the world outside the text. Over the millennia, the ways that people perceive Genesis both shape and reflect their perceptions of the world. What is perhaps surprising is how radically these ways of perceiving Genesis and reality have changed.

I begin this tour with the earliest scene of the interpretation of Genesis, and end with the interpretive thought-style pursued in this commentary. There are many possible paths and plots in the interpretive life of Genesis, and mine has no claim to completeness. It emphasizes some bits and overlooks others, tracing some connected features in a vast panorama (see further Hendel 2013).

The first scene in this interpretive life occurs in the book of Nehemiah, when the priest Ezra reads from the "Book of the Law of Moses" (*sēper tôrat mōšeh*) before a public assembly in Jerusalem sometime in the mid-fifth century BCE. This is our first glimpse of the Torah or Pentateuch, which may have recently been brought to Jerusalem from the Babylonian exile. According to this originary scene of biblical interpretation:

> [Ezra] read it aloud in the public square before the Water Gate from dawn to midday, to the men, women, and those who could understand. The ears of all the people were attentive. . . . Then [the Levites] read from the Book of the Law of God, translating and giving the meaning, so that they would understand the reading. . . . All the people were weeping as they heard the words. . . . Then all the people went to eat and drink and send portions, and to make a great joyous celebration, for they understood the words that had been made known to them. (Neh 8:3, 8, 9, 12)

In this dramatic scene, the people "understood the words," but not without help. After the priest publicly reads the text, the Levites interpret it, perhaps involving a mixture of explanation, exegesis, and Aramaic translation (Pakkala 2011). As this scene illustrates—even if it is embellished or fictive—from its earliest readings, Genesis has been accompanied by interpretation.

There are many reasons for this need for interpretation. The book's terse style, fraught with background (in Auerbach's [1953: 12] term), with many obscure details of character and context, calls out for interpretation. Its compositional complexity, including disharmonies, contradictions, and doublets, also calls for interpretation. Its linguistic "chronolect," Classical Biblical Hebrew, has features that were forgotten in later dialects. These obscurities, which often triggered scribal errors, also call for interpretation.

Beyond these internal features, the public status of Genesis as the first part of the "Book of the Law of God" also generates a need for interpretation. Law (*tôrâ*, Torah) always requires interpretaion. Henceforth each community requires its own masters of interpretation—like the Levites in Nehemiah 8—to whom the community grants the authority to interpret the sacred texts. For Genesis, these masters of interpretation, differing according to the community, are priests, Levites, rabbis, preachers, bishops, popes, visionaries, theologians, and (sometimes) scholars.

The inevitable conflicts of interpretation among interpreters tend to reflect different claims to authority, either within a community or across different communities. These conflicts often reflect differences, sometimes subtle and sometimes large, in the interpretation of reality. That is, the interpretation of the Word and the world go hand in hand. Let us turn to some of the changes and conflicts in the interpretive life of Genesis, beginning with the discovery—or construction—of its hidden, figural senses.

The Rise of the Figural Sense

When people began to read Genesis closely during the Second Temple period, its complex features gave rise to the idea that it was a cryptic text, holding secret meanings. As Kugel (1998: 15) observes, "The first assumption that all ancient interpreters seem to share is that the Bible is a fundamentally cryptic document." This first assumption is linked with several others, as Kugel delineates (14–19). It was seen as a book of teaching, which, as Paul writes, was "written for our instruction" (Rom 15:4). As such, the book is directly relevant for the present. It was also assumed to be a perfect text, containing no contradictions or mistakes. Finally, it was understood to be God's word, as suggested by the term "Book of the Law of God" (Neh 8:8). The first assumption, that Genesis is cryptic, is linked to these others. The task of the interpreter is to discover its secret meanings, aided by divine revelation, in order to clarify its perfect teaching.

These assumptions gave rise to a twofold model of Genesis, which granted the existence of a publicly available sense and a hidden, figural sense. In the Essene manuals from Qumran, these two levels of the text are called the *niglôt* ("revealed or announced things") and the *nistārôt* ("hidden things"; see Heger 2007). Only the masters of interpretation, such as the Essene's Teacher of Righteousness, had access to the hidden sense, which was revealed to them by divine inspiration (1QpHab ii.8–9, vii.4–5). For the Teacher of Righteousness, as for many other master interpreters in the Second Temple period, the cryptic meaning consists primarily of secrets of the end-time, the era of the coming apocalypse, when the wicked will be destroyed and the righteous redeemed. This is apocalyptic interpretation.

The first master of the apocalyptic interpretation of Genesis is a fictional (or pseudepigraphic) sage, the biblical figure Enoch, who reveals the secrets of Genesis in his memoirs, the book of Enoch (ca. third to first centuries BCE). In Genesis, Enoch is mentioned in an admittedly cryptic passage, where, in the seventh generation from Adam, "Enoch walked with God for 300 years . . . and then was no more, for God took him" (5:22, 24). In his book, Enoch reveals the secrets of this cryptic passage, describing how he ascended to heaven and walked with the angels, who showed him the secret places of heaven and earth, including the places of future judgment and reward.

In his book, Enoch also reveals the full history of the divine Watchers (from Gen 6:1–4) and their wicked deeds before the flood. As a sage and prophet, he describes the coming flood as a punishment for their sins. These prophecies blend into visions of the end-time, as in his opening vision:

> Not for this generation do I expound,
> > but concerning one that is distant I speak. . . .
> Behold, he comes with the myriads of his holy ones,
> > to execute judgment on all,
> > and to destroy all the wicked,
> > and to convict all flesh,
> > for all the wicked deeds that they have done,
> > and the proud and hard words that wicked sinners spoke against him.

> (1 En. 1:2, 9; Nickelsburg 2001: 137, 142)

The imminent destruction by the flood doubles as a prophecy for a distant generation, for whom the destruction of the final judgment will occur.

This prophecy of the end-time is quoted in the New Testament, where it is credited to "Enoch, in the seventh generation from Adam" (Jude 1:14–15). As this reference illustrates, the apocalyptic interpretation in the book of Enoch had considerable influence on Jewish and Christian thought in the late Second Temple period. The hidden meaning of Genesis had an apocalyptic orientation, which the master interpreter reveals for future readers. After the profound impact of Enoch's memoirs, the apocalyptic interpretation of Genesis became a dominant feature in its interpretive life.

Another kind of figural interpretation emerged in the late Second Temple period, primarily in Greek-speaking communities, which perceived its hidden meanings as oriented to spiritual transformation and the ascent of the soul. This is Platonic or allegorical interpretation. While apocalyptic interpretation operates on the axis of time, Platonic interpretation operates on the axis of metaphysical space. In this mode of reading, inspired by Plato's philosophy, the secrets of Genesis point to a greater reality that exists beyond the material world, revealing an invisible and timeless realm of pure being.

For Philo of Alexandria (first century CE), in the Greek-speaking Jewish diaspora, Genesis is a twofold text, whose public or sensible meanings are mere shadows of its hidden, perfect meanings: "The contents of the Law [are] visible symbols of things invisible, expressing the inexpressible" (in Winston 1981: 79). This is the language of Platonic philosophy, transposed into the interpretation of the Torah. To give an example, Philo gives a brilliant interpretation of the doublet of God's creation of Adam in Gen 1:27 and 2:7 (from P and J, respectively). To solve the problem of this twofold creation, Philo explains the deeper philosophical sense, guided by hints in the text. In his comment on Gen 2:7, he writes: "[Moses] shows very clearly that there is an immense difference between the man now fashioned [from the soil] and the one created earlier after the image of God. For the molded man is sense-perceptible, partaking already of specific quality, framed of body and soul, man or woman, by nature mortal; whereas he that was after the image was an idea or genus or seal, intelligible, incorporeal, neither male nor female, imperishable by nature" (in Winston 1981: 103).

In Philo's metaphysical dualism, the first creation of Adam occurs in the intelligible world of pure forms, where God creates Adam "in God's image" (Gen 1:27). This, for Philo, is the heavenly or ideal form of Adam, incorporeal and unchanging. The second creation occurs in the material world, where Adam is fashioned "from the soil's dust," and Adam becomes "a living creature" (2:7). This earthly, living Adam later returns to the dust from which he was taken. The material Adam is mortal, but the ideal Adam exists in the realm of being, beyond this shadow world. For Philo and many others since, this figural mode of reading Genesis revealed the philosophical truth of its cryptic sense.

Ancient interpreters often alternated between apocalyptic interpretation and Platonic allegory, varying according to the text or occasion. The New Testament provides examples of both, sometimes fused together. For instance, Noah and the flood are evoked as symbols of the end-time, continuing from Enoch's memoirs. In the Gospels, Jesus draws an analogy between Noah's flood and the coming end-time: "For as the days of Noah were, so will be the coming of the Son of Man" (Matt 24:37; cf. Luke 17:26). This is Jesus's prophecy concerning the apocalyptic secrets of Genesis 6–9.

First Peter similarly sees a hidden link between Noah's ark and the Christian sacrament of baptism, both of which produce salvation through water: "God waited patiently in the days of Noah, during the building of the ark, in which a few, that is, eight persons, were saved through water. And baptism, which this prefigured, now saves you" (1 Pet 3:20–21). The word for "prefigured" here is *antitupon,* which involves a special link between the "type" (or prefiguration) in Genesis and the "anti-type" (or fulfillment) in the life of Jesus or the church. This is a refinement of apocalyptic interpretation, in which Noah's ark is a figural anticipation of baptism.

Paul uses this model of apocalyptic typology to develop his theology of Christ as the "anti-type" of Adam, "who was a prefiguration (*tupos*) of the one who was to come" (Rom 5:14). The first Adam and the last Adam (1 Cor 15:45) form a temporal arc in which sin is resolved by salvation. By his typological interpretation, Paul uncovers the deep consonance from creation to the end-time.

The prologue of the Gospel of John takes a Platonic turn in its interpretation of Genesis. It begins, "In the beginning was the Word" (John 1:1). This transforms the meaning of Gen 1:1, "In the beginning, when God created heaven and earth," using Platonic language for the preexistent Word (*logos*), which it identifies with the preexistent Jesus. The Word is then identified with God's first creation, light, which descends from the higher world: "The true light, which enlightens everyone, was coming into the world" (John 1:9). When "the Word became flesh" (John 1:14), the ideal Jesus took on material form, and Jesus's earthly ministry began. This remarkable passage is an interpretive fusion of Genesis, Christianity, and Platonism (Attridge 2005).

In these New Testament passages, the cryptic meanings of Genesis are revealed by its master interpreters—Jesus, Peter, Paul, and John—who elucidate its apocalyptic and Platonic secrets to the variety of early Christian communities.

In rabbinic Judaism, the mingled strands of apocalyptic and Platonic interpretation take on a new configuration in midrashic interpretation, a novel mode of figural interpretation. Where apocalyptic interpretation operates on an axis of time, pointing to the redemptive events of the end-time, and Platonic allegory operates on the axis of metaphysical space, midrashic interpretation operates on an axis of intertextuality, making connections within the verbal matrix of scripture (Boyarin 1990). The central assumption of midrash is that the Bible, as the holy word of God, is not bound by the parameters of human language, like context, grammar, or even lexicon. Any detail in Genesis can have a hidden relation to any other detail in the Hebrew Bible. As Sommer

(2012: 67) writes, "Stemming from the mind of God and not merely from the mind of human authors, the Bible is an infinitely complex unity, in which all parts are related to each other." The cryptic sense of Genesis, in midrashic interpretation, yields infinite possible meanings, all of which are intended by God's mysterious words.

For instance, in the classic collections of midrashic interpretation, such as *Genesis Rabbah,* the first word of Genesis is a clue to innumerable hidden meanings. It is the task of the rabbinic masters of interpretation to seek out the cryptic senses of the word *bərē'šît* ("in the beginning") in its interconnections with other words and verses in scripture. An obvious intertext is the speech of Wisdom in Proverbs, "Yahweh created (or acquired) me at the beginning (*rē'šît*) of his way, the first of his works of old" (Prov 8:22). The links of word and theme are obvious to the midrashic interpreter, who on this basis elucidates the hidden meanings of Gen 1:1. In one such midrash, the cryptic sense of the word *rē'šît* ("beginning") is the Torah itself: "The Holy One, blessed be He, looked at the Torah and created the world. The Torah says, 'In the beginning [i.e., with *rē'šît*] God created.' There is no *rē'šît* except for Torah, as Scripture says, 'Yhwh created me as the *rē'šît* of his way [Prov 8:22]'" (*Gen. Rab.* 1.1). This interpretation rests on a chain of intertextual inferences. Even the grammar of Gen 1:1 has hidden senses, accommodating the verse's cryptic meanings.

The logic of this midrash works backwards from the intertext (Prov 8:22) to Gen 1:1. First, Wisdom ("me" in Prov 8:22) is equated with the Torah. This is a long-standing equivalence, already found in Sir 24:23 (second century BCE). Second, the Torah is equated with the word *rē'šît*, yielding a new reading of Prov 8:22, "Yhwh created me as the *rē'šît* of his way." The interpreter then draws a generalization, "There is no *rē'šît* except for Torah." In the light of the new meaning of the intertext, the hidden meaning of Gen 1:1 becomes legible: "With *rešît* (= Torah) God created heaven and earth." Notice that grammar is flexible—as is all of God's language—accommodating this hidden sense by the instrumental use of the preposition *bə* ("with") rather than the temporal ("when").

The logic of this midrash of Gen 1:1 is breathtaking, but it is consistent with its interpretive principles. As the rabbinic sage Ben Bag-Bag says of scripture, "Turn it, and turn it, for everything is in it" (*m. Avot* 5.22). Since it is God's discourse, its grammar and lexicon are nonlinear, with every possible intertextual connection and implication intended by its divine author, including those yet to be discovered.

Like the prologue to John, this midrash on Gen 1:1 has a Platonic dimension. The Torah is conceived as the blueprint for God's creation of the world. This concept descends from Plato's *Timaeus,* where the demiurge or creator uses the ideal forms of the intelligible world as a model for the creation of the material world: "He fixed his gaze on the unseen . . . it was created after the Word (*logos*)" (*Timaeus* 29a). When in our midrash "The Holy One . . . looked at the Torah and created the world," he was consulting the Torah as an ideal form of the cosmos. The Torah is itself a Platonic form, preexistent and incorporeal, by which God created the material world. The deep sense of Gen 1:1 is a transformation of Platonic philosophy.

Midrash also incorporates apocalyptic interpretation. In a midrash on Gen 1:3, God's creation of light is a preparatory anticipation of the messianic era. In the present era, the original glorious light is "hidden and prepared for the righteous in the future to come, as it is said, 'The light of the moon will be like the light of the sun, and the light of the sun will be sevenfold, like the light of seven days' [Isa 30:26]" (*Gen. Rab.* 3.6). The intertext (Isa 30:26) is related to Gen 1:3 by the word "light" (*'ôr*) and by the mention of "seven days," which hints at the seven days of creation. These verbal links indicate, to the midrashic interpreter, that the original glorious light, sevenfold greater than the light of the sun on the fourth day of creation, will be restored "for the righteous in the future to come." This interpretation solves the problem of the relationship of the light created on the first day with the creation of the sun and the moon on the fourth day. In the midrash, these are two different kinds of light—one the light that we see now, and the other the light of the end-time.

Midrashic interpretation has a coherent logic in which the words and verses of Genesis are threads in the infinite web of scripture. Midrash includes and goes beyond apocalyptic and Platonic interpretations. Its context is the biblical archive, which is written in the cryptic language of God.

Between the Figural and the Real

The many forms of figural interpretation agree on the duality between public or announced meanings (the *niglôt*) and the hidden meanings (the *nistārôt*) of scripture. The former is available to any reader and the latter only to the masters of interpretation. But the relationship between these two kinds of meaning can be problematic. For Platonists like Philo, the surface meaning of the text is an illusion, devoid of historical truth: "The words of the [biblical] oracles are, as it were, shadows cast by bodies, whereas the significations therein revealed are the things that have true existence" (in Winston 1981: 272). The exception for Philo is biblical law, whose public sense is binding, even if it diverges from the hidden sense. For apocalyptic and midrashic interpreters, the plain sense had a certain reality, and they did not pay much heed to it. As Sommer (2012: 69) remarks for midrash, "The surface context would suggest various meanings which might be legitimate ones intended by the divine author; but those were unlikely to be the deepest or most interesting meanings, and for the classical rabbis scripture was above all interesting and deep." The same neglect pertains to apocalyptic interpreters, for whom the hidden secrets are the keys to the kingdom.

The church father Augustine (late fourth to early fifth centuries CE) drew the figural and the plain senses of scripture into a fixed relationship. He criticized the pure allegorists, like his predecessor Origen, who deny the historical existence of the Garden of Eden: "[They] give a symbolic meaning to the whole of that paradise. . . . It is, however, arbitrary to suppose that there could not have been a material paradise, just because it can be understood also in a spiritual significance" (Augustine 1972: 534). Augustine maintains that the plain and the hidden senses (primarily allegory and typology) are equally true. Figural interpretation is valid, as long as it conforms to Christian doctrine, but it is not sufficient: "There is no prohibition against such exegesis, provided that we also believe in the truth of the story as a faithful record of historical fact" (535).

For Augustine, the plain meaning is the historical sense (*sensus historicus*), a "record of historical fact." So, for example, the Garden of Eden story is the faithful historical record of the fall and original sin, and at the same time an allegory about spiritual truths: "No one can stop us interpreting paradise symbolically as the life of the blessed; its four rivers as the four virtues, prudence, courage, temperance, and justice; its trees as all the beneficial disciplines; the fruit of the trees as the character of the righteous; the tree of life as wisdom, the mother of all good things" (Augustine 1972: 535). The story is also a typological foreshadowing of Christ and the church: "We can also interpret the details of paradise with reference to the Church, which gives them a better significance as prophetic indications of things to come in the future. Thus paradise stands for the Church itself . . . ; the four rivers represent the four Gospels; the fruit trees, the saints; and the fruit, their achievements; the tree of life . . . must be Christ himself" (535).

For the masters of interpretation, including Augustine, there are endless figural meanings. But according to Augustine, this does not diminish the veracity of the historical sense. The Word—like the world—is both real and symbolic.

But there are problems with this rule of interpretation. Augustine carves out an important exception in cases where the historical sense conflicts with the evidence of reason and science. In his comment on God's creation of light in Gen 1:3, he states that this light could refer to material and spiritual light. But if reason and science should disprove "the existence of material light . . . existing before the heavens," then the figural reference to spiritual light is the only true sense (Augustine 1982: 42). Here Augustine takes refuge in pure allegory. This exception allows him to defend scripture from its critics: "When they are able, from reliable evidence, to prove some fact of physical science, we shall show that it is not contrary to our Scripture" (45). Where science conflicts with the plain sense of Genesis, Augustine holds only to the figural sense. By this pragmatic exception, he accommodates scripture and science. But as we will see, this strategy later became problematic.

In medieval Judaism, the commentator Rashi (1040–1105 CE) formulated a delicate balance between midrash and the plain sense, which limits the scope of midrash. In his comment on Gen 3:8—"They heard the sound of Yahweh God walking about in the garden in the evening breeze"—he writes: "There are many midrashic interpretations, and our rabbis have already collected them in their appropriate order in *Genesis Rabbah* and other midrashic books. As for me, I am only concerned with the plain sense (*pašat*) of Scripture and the midrashic interpretations that explain the words of Scripture in a fitting manner" (in Cohen 1997: 1.50). Rashi is quoting Prov 25:11, "a word spoken in a fitting manner," to characterize the plain sense (*pašat*) of scripture. He is formulating the novel idea that the words of scripture should be interpreted according to their narrative and grammatical contexts, not according to the intertextual linguistic matrix of scripture. He says that his preference for the plain sense means he will include only those midrashic interpretations that fit the context. However, in practice his rules for inclusion are often very flexible.

In his Genesis commentary, Rashi marginalizes the hidden sense and sometimes denies it altogether. In his comment on Gen 10:25—"in his time the earth was divided"—he states: "Scripture is not concerned to hide, but to clearly explain" (in Cohen 1997: 1.112). Rashi here asserts that there are no hidden meanings. The midrashic interpretations that seek out the hidden senses are simply misguided. This is a revolutionary claim.

Rashi's commentary is much beloved because he mingles his comments on the plain sense with a rich collection of midrashic interpretation. But his insistence on the primacy of the plain or contextual sense, and his grammatically focused way of reading, challenged the legitimacy of figural interpretation. The duality between the figural and the real was replaced by a preference for the plain sense of the text. It is no coincidence that Rashi lived during the Renaissance of the twelfth century, the era of the first universities (including one in Paris, not far from Rashi's home in Troyes), the rise of mercantile capitalism (which funded the great Gothic cathedrals), and the transmission of arts and knowledge from Muslim Spain's golden age, including Jewish scholarship on the Hebrew language (Grossman 2012: 7–10). Rashi's insistence on the plain sense accompanies the rise of reason and scholarship during this early Renaissance.

The traditional balance between the plain and the figural senses of scripture was permanently upended by Martin Luther (1483–1546), an Augustinian monk who lived during the early modern Renaissance. After embracing Platonic allegory as a monk, he rejected its validity during his path to Reformation. He later reminisced: "When I was a monk, I was a master in the use of allegories. I allegorized everything . . . even a chamber pot" (Luther 1967: 46). Luther the reformer insisted on the clarity of scripture and the ability of every person to read its plain words: "The literal sense does it—in it there's life, comfort, power, instruction, and skill. The other is foolishness, however brilliant the impression it makes" (406). The duality of scripture's public and secret meanings was collapsing.

Luther's elevation of the plain sense has a political dimension. It gave him a tool to undermine the authority of the church and its masters of interpretation, including the pope, who promulgated figural interpretations. For instance, he denounced the authoritative interpretation by Pope Innocent III that the "two great lights" in Gen 1:16 are allegorical symbols of pontifical and royal authority. Luther points out with relish that this is a crude justification of power (1960: 152): "The pope deserves praise for piety and learning in the matter of allegories . . . [proclaiming] 'The sun is the papal office, from which the imperial majesty derives its light, just as the moon does from the sun.' Oh, such audacious insolence and such villainous desire for power!" For Luther, religious authority rests in scripture alone (*sola scriptura*), whose plain sense is available to any faithful reader. This vacates the religious authority of the "villainous" Catholic Church.

Luther rejects the Platonic duality at the heart of allegory: "What need is there of setting up a two-fold knowledge? . . . [Moses's] purpose is to teach us, not about allegorical creatures and an allegorical world but about real creatures and a visible world apprehended by the senses" (1958: 5). For Luther, the plain sense of scripture and the plain sense of the "visible world" are undeniable. The Word and the world are filled with real things and are not the shadows of invisible ideas. The new learning and realism of the Renaissance are evident in his critique.

Since for the most part the words of scripture are tolerably clear, Luther (1958: 10) writes, "I prefer what is simplest and can be understood by those with little education." Accordingly, he maintains that the Garden of Eden was a real historical place, and its four rivers were real rivers: "These, then, are all historical facts. This is something to which I carefully call attention, lest the unwary reader be led astray by the authority of the fathers, who give up the idea that this is history and look for allegories" (93). Luther delights in ridiculing allegorical interpretation. He did, however, allow for apocalyptic and typological interpretation since they are used in the New Testament. But he consistently prefers the plain sense.

Luther grants, however, that there is a problem with taking the "clear accounts of creation" as consisting solely of "historical facts." He admits that some details of the

Garden of Eden story seem dubious, which is why the allegorists had sought out the hidden sense. Since he denies the validity of allegory, Luther must sacrifice his rational judgment and submit to the historical truth of the plain sense. When commenting on the creation of Eve from Adam's rib (Gen 2:22), he wonders:

> What, I ask you, could sound more like a fairy tale if you were to follow your reason? Would anyone believe this account about the creation of Eve if it were not so clearly told? . . . This is extravagant fiction and the silliest kind of nonsense if you set aside the authority of Scripture and follow the judgment of reason. . . . Although it sounds like a fairy tale to reason, it is the most certain truth. (1958: 123)

This is a hard lesson. He concludes, "The more it seems to conflict with experience and reason, the more carefully it must be noted and the more surely believed" (125). The authority of the plain sense of scripture is now in conflict with the authority of reason, a clash that Augustine's exception allowed the medieval church to avoid. But with the figural sense no longer an option, the plain sense of scripture forces Luther to set aside his "judgment of reason." This narrowing of interpretive options is a consequence of the decline of the figural sense.

Luther undermined the authority of the Catholic Church and invited all people to read and understand, with faith alone, the "certain, accessible, and clear" words of scripture. But for Genesis, this reopened the problem of how to reconcile its plain sense with science and reason. Luther's younger colleague, John Calvin (1509–1564), saw this problem clearly and adopted another interpretive tool to circumvent it. This is the principle of accommodation, which was used already by the classical rabbis and the church fathers.

In his *Commentaries on Genesis,* Calvin consistently appeals to the principle that the Bible "speaks after the manner of men" (at Gen 9:15). This means that the passage is accommodated to the knowledge and worldview of an ancient people. When commenting on the talking snake in Gen 3:1, Calvin (1847: 141) writes:

> Moses, by a homely and uncultivated style, accommodates what he delivers to the capacity of the people; and for the best reason; for not only had he to instruct an untaught race of men, but the existing age of the Church was so puerile, that it was unable to receive any higher instruction. There is, therefore, nothing absurd in the supposition, that they, whom, for the time, we know and confess to have been but as infants, were fed with milk. Or (if another comparison be more acceptable), Moses is by no means to be blamed, if he, considering the office of schoolmaster as imposed upon him, insists on the rudiments suitable to children.

By appealing to the principle of accommodation, Calvin is able to explain the passages in Genesis that appear to be "rudiments suitable to children." This means, as Helm (2004: 394) explains, "Calvin believes that such a statement is not strictly true." With this strategy, Calvin dissolves the contradictions between Genesis and science.

In his comment on Gen 1:7—"God made the vault and separated the water below the vault from the water above the vault"—Calvin (1847: 79–80) acknowledges that the passage poses "a great difficulty":

For it appears opposed to common sense, and quite incredible, that there should be waters above heaven. Hence some resort to allegory, and philosophize concerning angels, but quite beside the purpose. For, to my mind, this is a certain principle, that nothing is here treated of but the visible form of the world. He who would learn astronomy, and other recondite arts, let him go elsewhere. . . . I conclude that the waters here meant are such as the rude and unlearned may perceive.

Calvin holds that the plain sense is accommodated to the way that simple people perceive the world. Rain comes from the sky, so "the rude and unlearned" assume there is water above heaven. And Moses, like a schoolmaster, accommodates his lesson to their capacities. Calvin concludes, "The history of the creation . . . is the book of the unlearned" (80).

By his appeal to accommodation, Calvin solves the problem of the clash between the plain sense of Genesis and the claims of modern science and reason. This provides an exception to the historical veracity of the plain sense. But the consequence is that scripture's "clear accounts of creation" (Luther's term) are not entirely clear and reliable. Its "historical facts" are sometimes unhistorical, accommodated as they are to the mistaken assumptions of simple folk. Calvin's exception requires the aid of masters of interpretation to discern the boundaries between the real and the accommodated fictions. Hence his solution has its own difficulties.

A century later, Baruch Spinoza (1632–1677) gave a new twist to the nature of the plain sense of scripture and in so doing created a new conceptual space for the interpretation of Genesis. Like Luther and Calvin, he criticized sharply those who seek the hidden mysteries of scripture and find the Greek philosophers: "While I admit that they could not express greater veneration for the deepest mysteries of Scripture, what I see in their actual teaching is nothing more than the speculation of the Aristotelians or Platonists. Since they did not wish to appear to be following pagans, they adapted the Scriptures to them. It was insufficient for them to be mouthing nonsense themselves, they also desired . . . to render the prophets equally nonsensical" (Spinoza 2007: 8).

Like other early modern commentators, Spinoza read for the plain sense. But he found in it many contradictions and confusions. He observes that the Joseph narrative in Genesis 37–50 is "obviously riddled . . . with inconsistencies," leading to his inference that "the whole history of Joseph and Jacob has been taken and transcribed from different histories" (2007: 132). His analysis exposes inconsistencies across the Pentateuch: "We have only to notice that everything in these five books . . . is narrated in a confused manner, without order and without respect for chronology, and that stories are repeated, sometimes in different versions" (132). A close reading of the plain sense yields the perception that the Pentateuch is a composite text, compiled from different source documents. This begins the modern scholarly inquiry into the literary history of Genesis and the Pentateuch.

Spinoza gives a twist to Calvin's principle of accommodation, which further opens the conceptual space for a new kind of biblical interpretation. It is a small step from the idea that Genesis is accommodated to the capacities of an ancient people to the simpler—but revolutionary—concept that the reason for these outdated features is that Genesis was written by ancient authors. This explains why "their narratives of things are very much adapted to the presuppositions of their respective times" (Spinoza 2007: 104). As Funkenstein (1986: 221) comments, "This is Spinoza's use of the exegetical principle of accommodation. The theological language . . . was turned on its head." This revision of accommodation clarifies why the plain sense does not agree with modern science—it reflects the worldview of ancient Israel. The book of Genesis speaks in human language because it was written by and for ancient Israelites. Genesis is a human book.

Spinoza's method for the interpretation of Genesis in the light of reason and history took root slowly. Most of his readers viewed Spinoza as a scandalous heretic, but scholars gradually adopted his method, even if they disagreed with its implications. A Catholic priest, Richard Simon, wrote the erudite *Critical History of the Old Testament* (1685), in which he adopted Spinoza's historical-critical method. He wrote to a colleague, "the axioms he lays down . . . are not always false in themselves" (in Hazard 1963: 184). The method of reading Genesis in its own historical context had come to stay, despite its challenge to traditional methods of interpretation.

Treasures of Darkness: The Ancient Near East

A core principle of Spinoza's method of interpretation was, as J. Israel writes, "there can be no understanding of any text which is not in the first place a 'historical' interpretation, setting writings in their intellectual context" (Spinoza 2007: xiii). In modern biblical scholarship, the primary context of Genesis is not the higher Platonic reality, the paradisiacal end-time, the life of the church, or the omnisignificant matrix of the Hebrew Bible. It is the textual, cultural, and material world of ancient Israel and its environs. But this task of understanding, as Spinoza details, is difficult to accomplish, since we know so little about the history of the book and its ancient context. How does one begin, in Spinoza's words, "to assemble a genuine history of it" given "the limitations and difficulties in this method's capacity to guide us toward a full and certain knowledge" (98, 106)?

An important step to recovering the historical and intellectual context of Genesis was taken in the eighteenth and nineteenth centuries with scholarly expeditions to the Middle East in search of the realia of biblical antiquity. The historical method now entailed arduous journeys to pursue what Sheehan (2005: 186–89) calls "a philology of things." The German scholar Johann David Michaelis proposed the first major project in 1761, funded by the king of Denmark. That expedition began the modern recovery of the cultures and texts of the ancient Near East.

A member of this German-Danish expedition, Carsten Niebuhr, made the first accurate copies of cuneiform inscriptions from Persepolis, which led to Georg Friedrich Grotefend's breakthrough in deciphering Old Persian in 1802 (see Daniels 1995). The scholarly expedition accompanying Napoleon's campaign to Egypt in 1798 unearthed the Rosetta Stone, which enabled Jean-François Champollion to decipher Egyptian in 1822–1824. French and British excavations in ancient Dur-Sharrukin (1843), Kalḫu (1845), and Nineveh (1849) uncovered masses of cuneiform texts, including the great library of Ashurbanipal in Nineveh, which enabled Edward Hincks to make his breakthroughs in the decipherment of Akkadian in 1846–1849. These long-buried archives, which Jacobsen (1976) aptly calls "the treasures of darkness" (quoting Isa 45:3), could now be read and studied. The wider literary and religious contexts of Genesis were becoming legible.

The most public moment in this conceptual shift occurred on December 3, 1872, when George Smith reported his discovery of "The Chaldean Account of the Deluge" to the British Society of Biblical Archeology. In the dimly lit rooms of the British Museum, he had painstakingly joined together the flood episode in the eleventh tablet of the *Gilgamesh* epic. At the meeting in London, after reading his translation and summarizing the shared features of the Babylonian text and Genesis 6–9, he concluded, "It is apparent that the events of the Flood narrated in the Bible and the inscription are the same and occur in the same order; but the minor differences in the details show that the inscription embodies a distinct and independent tradition" (G. Smith 1873: 232).

Smith's discovery had enormous implications, but no one was quite sure what they were. According to next day's London *Times,* Prime Minister Gladstone, who was in attendance at the meeting, responded, "I do not know whether it is supposed that inquiries into archaeological and other sciences are to have the effect of unsettling many minds in this our generation, but I must say that for me, as to the very few points on which I am able to examine them, they have a totally different effect." His speech acknowledges a degree of anxiety. His epistemic uncertainty ("I do not know whether it is supposed") serves to distance the dangerous possibility that this discovery will "have the effect of unsettling many minds." His invocation of scientific progress further soothes potential worries, but the discovery posed a problem.

In his erudite but theologically conservative commentary on Genesis that appeared shortly afterwards, Delitzsch (1888: 242) came to a more definite conclusion about the relationship of the deluge accounts: "Tradition gives to this ancient event a testimony of many voices, though these do not always agree in all particulars. And this is confirmed by the Scripture narrative, in which we have, in spite of all discrepancies, the legend of the Flood in its original form." Despite the antiquity of the Babylonian text, the Genesis flood was certainly the original account and describes a historical flood, even if some details are accommodated to ancient minds.

Gunkel thought otherwise in his Genesis commentary of 1901 (revised in 1910). He dismisses the orthodox position of Delitzsch and others: "The 'apologetic' perspective is wont to consider . . . only the question of whether the narrative is a 'true story.' This cannot be seriously discussed" (1997: 77). He gives positive arguments for the derivation of the biblical flood stories from the earlier Mesopotamian tradition, including the story's locale in the east (the mountains of Ararat in Gen 8:4 = ancient Urartu, later Armenia). More important, he observes that "certain elements of the Hebrew legend . . . only receive their proper light from the Babylonian" (71–72). These details include the behavior of Yahweh in the J source: "The god's sudden change of attitude—he thinks quite differently in the beginning of the story than at the end—will also have been given a better foundation [in the Babylonian tradition]" (67). The striking shifts of attitude "can be explained in the Babylonian as the result of [Enlil]'s impetuous character and of Ea's wise, appeasing presentation" (72).

Yahweh's changes of attitude in the J flood story are explicable as a monotheistic revision of a polytheistic plot. In the Mesopotamian tradition, Enlil is the angry god who sends the flood, and Ea is the wise and compassionate god who saves humans, his own creation (George 2003). The roles of creator, destroyer, and savior are distributed among two rival gods in the Mesopotamian story, but in the Israel these roles are combined in a single god. Where in the older polytheistic story, the conflict is chiefly between two gods, the monotheistic transformation yields a divine protagonist with a conflicted and changeable interior life. This insight into the literary dynamics of the flood stories opens a new perspective on their historical relationship. In his commentary, Gunkel shows that the biblical flood has a history, although it is a quite different history from the historical sense (*sensus historicus*) of Delitzsch and other orthodox interpreters.

For modern scholars, the wider context of Genesis 1–11 is the cultural matrix of Israel in its ancient world. When Gunkel (1904: 58) writes, "The idea of 'creation' has its history," he is saying that the text's historicity—its embeddedness in history—is the larger context. In this conceptual shift to modern scholarly interpretation, as Frei (1974: 5) observes, "There is now a logical distinction and a reflective distance between the stories and the 'reality' they depict"; hence, their interpretation relies on the "significance of the literal, narrative shape of the stories for their meaning" (12), without the assumption that they are historical facts. Genesis and the other Pentateuchal books are, as Frei writes, "documents of their culture and community, with analogues in the structure of the religious and mythological literature of the Near East." (12) Many of these ancient Near Eastern and Mediterranean analogues will be addressed in this commentary.

This procedure, in a philosophical sense, provides a way of linking biblical discourse with the real, in an era when, as Certeau (1988: 45) writes, "history has become our myth." In practice, the recovery of the historical context allows innumerable insights into the nuances and resonances of Genesis.

Conclusion: Life and Afterlife

There are many ways to tell the story of Genesis's interpretive life. My tale emphasizes some features, particularly the rise and fall of the figural sense and shifting connotations of the plain sense. It is a complicated story, which here serves as a backdrop to the method of this commentary. Others would tell the tale differently and with different accents, emphasizing, for instance, the shifting boundaries of orthodoxy and heresy, the uses and abuses of biblical interpretation in issues of social justice, or the impacts of economic and institutional structures. Other important parts of the story are the interpretations of Genesis in literature, art, and politics (for some of these threads, see Hendel 2013). The interpretive life of Genesis has endured the past two-and-a-half millennia of Western Civilization—and into the East via Islam and Christianity—and its traces are everywhere.

As we have seen, the interpretation of Genesis has undergone major transformations, due to historical shifts in the relationship between the represented world and the real world and shifts in the critical sensibilities of its readers. As Benjamin (1999) argues, the study of a work should include its afterlife along with its life in the era of composition. He writes, "Their entire life and their effects should have the right to stand alongside the history of their composition. In other words, their fate, their reception by their contemporaries, their translations, their fame" (464). This is a difficult task, but it is correct in theory and reorients our understanding of the book's meanings, all of which in some sense coexist in the present moment, in what Benjamin calls its "now-time"

(*Jetztzeit;* see Hendel 2019b: 81–83). This unrealized idea of condensing a work's whole interpretive life would produce a complex fusion of reading and remembrance.

In a practical sense, the afterlife of Genesis 1–11 inevitably affects our reading of it, even if we try to attend to its plain or native literary senses. How difficult it is to read the Garden of Eden story without importing later interpretations, such as the Fall and Original Sin, or Eve as erotic temptress, or the snake as Satan. These are products of Genesis's afterlife, which are hard to see around. The life and afterlife of Genesis have a tangled relationship with each other, which is to say that Genesis still calls for interpretation.

VI.
Synopsis of *Atraḥasis, Gilgamesh,* and *Enuma Elish*

To provide some guidance for the three major Babylonian texts that form a rich backdrop for Genesis 1–11, here is a synopsis of their contents. Good translations are readily available; see especially Dalley 2000 and Foster 2005. Critical editions with translations are Lambert and Millard 1969, George 2003, Lambert 2013, and Wasserman 2020.

Atraḥasis (Old Babylonian, ca. Seventeenth Century BCE)

Part I. Rebellion of the Lesser Gods (Tablet I.1–339)

Prologue: When the gods did the work (digging rivers and canals). Division of cosmos between Anu (heaven), Enlil (earth), and Enki (waters). Rebellion of the worker gods against Enlil. Enki's solution: He instructs Nintu the birth goddess to create humans to do the work.

Part II. Three Destructions and the Flood (remainder of Tablets I–III, with restorations)

Twelve hundred years pass; multiplication of humans and their noise. Enlil cannot sleep. He commands a plague to destroy humans. Enki's solution: Atraḥasis instructs people to offer gifts to Namtar, god of plague, who ends the plague.

Twelve hundred years pass; multiplication of humans and their noise. Enlil cannot sleep. He commands a drought to destroy humans. Enki's solution: Atraḥasis instructs people to offer gifts to Adad, god of rain, who ends the drought.

Twelve hundred years pass; multiplication of humans and their noise. Enlil cannot sleep. He commands a famine to destroy humans. Enki's solution: He opens the bolt of the waters, lets loose abundance.

Twelve hundred years pass; multiplication of humans and their noise. Enlil cannot sleep. He commands a flood to destroy humans. Enki's solution: He instructs Atraḥasis to build a boat and save life. After the flood Atraḥasis offers a sacrifice, which feeds the starving gods.

Conclusion: Nintu and Enki criticize Enlil for sending the flood. Enlil promises not to destroy humans and grants Atraḥasis and his wife immortality. Enki instructs Nintu to establish a limited lifespan for humans. They create other categories of creatures to limit population, including women who do not bear children and demons who snatch babies.

Gilgamesh (Standard Babylonian, Late Second Millennium BCE)

Part I. Gilgamesh and Enkidu (Tablets I.1–II.192)

Prologue: Praise of Gilgamesh, the mighty king who gained wisdom and recorded his deeds on a tablet at the walls of Uruk.

The goddess Aruru creates Enkidu, a wild man of the steppe, as an equal to Gilgamesh, to tame his excesses. Enkidu has sex with the prostitute Shamḫat (sent by a hunter) for seven days. He becomes knowledgeable, but the animals flee from him. The prostitute teaches Enkidu to wear clothing, eat bread, drink beer, and other aspects of civilized life. She then brings Enkidu to Uruk, where he wrestles with Gilgamesh. Gilgamesh and Enkidu become companions, then Enkidu grows morose.

Part II. Quest for Fame (Tablets II.193–VIII.230)

Gilgamesh makes a plan to slay Humbaba, guardian monster of the Cedar Forest, to revive Enkidu and gain fame. The goddess Ninsun, Gilgamesh's mother, blesses the undertaking despite her misgivings. Gilgamesh has three ominous dreams, which Enkidu explains away. Gilgamesh and Enkidu encounter Humbaba, who pleads for mercy. Gilgamesh slays Humbaba.

When Gilgamesh returns to Uruk, the goddess Ishtar proposes marriage to him. He rejects her advances. Ishtar then sends the Bull of Heaven to kill Gilgamesh, but Enkidu and Gilgamesh slay it. Enkidu mocks Ishtar.

Enkidu has an ominous dream, in which the gods decree his death. Enkidu curses Shamḫat for taking him from the steppe, then, after Gilgamesh's rebuke, he blesses her for initiating him into civilized life. Enkidu dies. Gilgamesh sits by him for seven days, then performs mourning rites.

Part III. Quest for Immortality (Tablets IX.1–XI.328)

Gilgamesh wears animal skins and journeys to the far end of the world to learn the secret of immortality from the flood hero Utnapishtim (a biname of Atraḥasis). He passes under the mountains where the sun rises with the help of the guardian scorpion people. He emerges at a divine garden. He is advised by the divine alewife Siduri, and the boatman Urshanabi takes him across the waters of death.

Gilgamesh reaches Utnapishtim, who tells him the story of the flood (summarizing *Atraḥasis* Tablet III), with the caveat that the circumstances of his immortality are not repeatable. Utnapishtim tests Gilgamesh to see whether he can stay awake for seven days. Gilgamesh falls asleep for seven days. When he awakes, he dreads death. At the urging of his wife, Utnapishtim gives Gilgamesh a parting gift—a plant of rejuvenation. On his return journey, a snake takes the plant while Gilgamesh is bathing, to Gilgamesh's despair.

Conclusion: Gilgamesh returns to the city of Uruk with Urshanabi, to whom he praises its well-built walls and foundations, resuming the praises of the prologue.

Appendix. Enkidu in the Underworld (Tablet XII)

An alternative story of how Enkidu descended to the underworld. Gilgamesh speaks to Enkidu's shade. It is a dark, dusty place: "If I tell you the rules of the Underworld that I saw, sit down (and) weep."

Enuma Elish (Standard Babylonian, ca. Twelfth Century BCE)

Part I. Creation, Conflict, and Birth of Marduk (Tablet I.1–108)

Primeval situation: Mingled waters of Apsu and Tiamat, father and mother of the gods.

Birth of the first generations of gods, who form the structure of the cosmos. The clamor of the younger gods disturbs Apsu and Tiamat; Apsu cannot sleep (cf. *Atrahasis*). Apsu plots to destroy the younger gods, but Ea kills Apsu and takes his crown.

Birth of Marduk, awesome and strong. Anu gives him the four winds as a gift.

Part II. Tiamat's War and Marduk's Victory (Tablets I.109–IV.134)

Marduk's winds disturb Tiamat. She and her allies plot war. She gives birth to fierce monsters. Marduk is chosen as champion of the gods. Marduk defeats Tiamat with his winds, net, and arrows. He kills Tiamat and her allies and recovers the Tablets of Destinies.

Part III. Marduk Creates the World and Humans (Tablets IV.135–VI.46)

Marduk divides Tiamat's corpse to create heaven and earth. He creates the constellations and the pathways of heaven. He creates the geography of the earth, including rivers and mountains. The gods proclaim Marduk as king of the gods. Marduk creates humans to do the work of the gods (cf. *Atrahasis*) and establishes the organization of the gods.

Part IV. Marduk's Enthronement in Babylon (Tablets VI.47–VII.164)

The gods build the temple and ziggurat of Babylon as Marduk's shrine and the gods' place of assembly. The gods commemorate Marduk's enthronement. They pronounce his fifty names, which include the names and attributes of the chief gods, culminating with Ea and Enlil.

Conclusion: The exaltation of Marduk: "Here now is the song of Marduk, (who) defeated Tiamat and took kingship."

BIBLIOGRAPHY

Aharoni, Y. 1979. *The Land of the Bible: A Historical Geography.* 2nd ed. Philadelphia: Westminster.

Aḥituv, S. 2008. *Echoes from the Past: Hebrew and Cognate Inscriptions from the Biblical Period.* Jerusalem: Carta.

Albertz, R. 2003. *Geschichte und Theologie: Studien zur Exegese des Alten Testaments und zur Religionsgeschichte Israels.* Edited by I. Kottsieper and J. Wöhrle. BZAW 326. Berlin: de Gruyter.

Albright, W. F. 1944. "The End of 'Calneh in Shinar.'" *JNES* 3: 254–55.

———. 1957. *From the Stone Age to Christianity: Monotheism and the Historical Process.* 2nd ed. Garden City: Doubleday.

Allen, J. P. 1988. *Genesis in Egypt: The Philosophy of Ancient Egyptian Creation Accounts.* New Haven: Yale Egyptological Seminar.

Al-Rawi, F. N. H. 2008. "Inscriptions from the Tombs of the Queens of Assyria." In *New Light on Nimrud,* edited by J. E. Curtis, H. McCall, D. Collon, and L. Al-Gailani Werr, 119–38. London: British Museum.

Alster, B. 1973. "An Aspect of 'Enmerkar and the Lord of Aratta.'" *Revue d'Assyriologie* 67: 101–10.

———. 1999. "Tiamat." *DDD,* 867–69.

Alter, R. 1996. *Genesis: Translation and Commentary.* New York: Norton.

———. 2011. *The Art of Biblical Narrative.* 2nd ed. New York: Basic Books.

Amit, Y. 1989. "The Multi-Purpose 'Leading Word' and the Problems of Its Usage." *Prooftexts* 9: 99–114.

Anderson, G. A. 1990. "The Interpretation of Genesis 1:1 in the Targums." *CBQ* 52: 21–29.

———. 1992. "Sacrifice and Sacrificial Offerings (OT)." *ABD* 5, 870–86.

———. 2001. *The Genesis of Perfection: Adam and Eve in Jewish and Christian Imagination.* Louisville: Westminster John Knox.

Annus, A. 2002. *The God Ninurta in the Mythology and Royal Ideology of Ancient Mesopotamia.* Helsinki: Neo-Assyrian Text Corpus Project.

Anonymous. 2014. "Where Noah Landed?" *BAR* 40.6 (2014): 12–13.

Arie, E., B. Rosen, and D. Namdar. 2020. "Cannabis and Frankincense at the Judahite Shrine of Arad." *Tel Aviv* 47: 5–28.

Armstrong, J. F. 1960. "A Critical Note on Genesis VI 16aα." *VT* 10: 328–33.

Arneth, M. 2007. *Durch Adams Fall ist ganz verderbt . . . Studien zur Entstehung der alttestamentlichen Urgeschichte.* FRLANT 217. Göttingen: Vandenhoeck & Ruprecht.

Arnold, B. T. 2009. *Genesis.* Cambridge: Cambridge University Press.

―――. 2012. "Genesis 1 as Holiness Preamble. In *Let Us Go up to Zion: Essays in Honour of H. G. M. Williamson,* edited by I. Provan and M. J. Boda, 332–43. VTSup 153. Leiden: Brill.

Assmann, J. 2003. *The Mind of Egypt: History and Meaning in the Time of the Pharaohs.* Cambridge, MA: Harvard University Press.

Astour, M. C. 1981. "Ugarit and the Great Powers." In *Ugarit in Retrospect,* edited by G. D. Young, 3–29. Winona Lake, IN: Eisenbrauns.

―――. 1995. "Overland Trade Routes in Ancient Western Asia." *CANE,* 1401–20.

Attridge, H. W. 2005. "Philo and John: Two Riffs on One Logos." *Studia Philonica Annual* 17: 103–17.Attridge, H. W., and R. A. Oden. 1981. *Philo of Byblos, The Phoenician History: Introduction, Critical Text, Translation, Notes.* Washington, DC: Catholic Biblical Association.

Atwood, P. 2018. "ḪQ/GR-Based Toponyms on the Shoshenq-Inscription of Karnak's Bubastite Portal: Some Phonological, Semantic, and Anthropological Reflections." *Jaarbericht van het Vooraziatisch-Egyptisch Gezelschap "Ex oriente lux"* 47: 3–18.

Auerbach, E. 1953. *Mimesis: The Representation of Reality in Western Literature.* Princeton: Princeton University Press.

Augustine. 1972. *City of God.* Translated by H. Bettenson. New York: Penguin.

―――. 1982. *The Literal Meaning of Genesis,* Vol. 1. Translated by J. H. Taylor. New York: Newman.

Baden, J. S. 2009a. *J, E, and the Redaction of the Pentateuch.* FAT 68. Tübingen: Mohr Siebeck.

―――. 2009b. "The Tower of Babel: A Case Study in the Competing Methods of Historical and Modern Literary Criticism." *JBL* 128: 209–24.

―――. 2012. *The Composition of the Pentateuch: Renewing the Documentary Hypothesis.* AYBRL. New Haven: Yale University Press.

―――. 2022. "'His Tent': Pitched at the Intersection of Orthography and Source Criticism." In *"Like 'Ilu Are You Wise": Studies in Northwest Semitic Languages and Literatures in Honor of Dennis G. Pardee,* edited by H. H. Hardy II, Joseph Lam, and Eric D. Reymond, 283–90. Chicago: Oriental Institute.

Bailey, L. R. 1989. *Noah: The Person and the Story in History and Tradition:* Columbia: University of South Carolina Press.

Baker, L. S., K. Bergland, F. A. Masotti, and A. R. Wells, eds. 2020. *Exploring the Composition of the Pentateuch.* Winona Lake, IN: Eisenbrauns.

Bakhtin, M. M. 1981. *The Dialogic Imagination: Four Essays.* Translated by C. Emerson and M. Holquist. Austin: University of Texas Press.

Bal, M. 1987. *Lethal Love: Feminist Literary Readings of Biblical Love Stories.* Bloomington: Indiana University Press.

Barr, J. 1992. *The Garden of Eden and the Hope of Immortality.* Minneapolis: Fortress.

―――. 2013. *Bible and Interpretation: The Collected Essays of James Barr. Vol. II: Biblical Studies.* Edited by J. Barton. Oxford: Oxford University Press.

———. 2014. *Bible and Interpretation: The Collected Essays of James Barr. Vol. III: Linguistics and Translation.* Edited by J. Barton. Oxford: Oxford University Press.

Barré, M. L. 1999. "Rabiṣu." *DDD,* 682–83.

Barth, F. 1961. *Nomads of South Persia: The Basseri Tribe of the Khamseh Confederacy.* Boston: Little, Brown.

Barton, J. 2007. *The Nature of Biblical Criticism.* Louisville: Westminster John Knox.

———. 2014. *Ethics in Ancient Israel.* Oxford: Oxford University Press.

Bascom, W. 1984. "The Forms of Folklore: Prose Narratives." In *Sacred Narrative: Readings in the Theory of Myth,* edited by A. Dundes, 5–28. Berkeley: University of California Press.

Bassett, F. W. 1971. "Noah's Nakedness and the Curse of Canaan: A Case of Incest?" *VT* 21: 232–37.

Batto, B. F. 1987. "The Sleeping God: An Ancient Near Eastern Motif of Divine Sovereignty." *Biblica* 68: 153–77.

Bauks, M. 1997. *Die Welt am Anfang: Zum Verhältnis von Vorwelt und Weltentstehung in Gen 1 und in der altorientalischen Literatur.* Neukirchen-Vluyn: Neukirchener.

———. 2010. "Nacktheit und Scham in Genesis 2–3." In *Zur Kulturgeschichte der Scham,* edited by M. Bauks and M. Meyer, 17–34. Hamburg: Meiner.

———. 2012. "Sacred Trees in the Garden of Eden and Their Ancient Near Eastern Precursors." *Journal of Ancient Judaism* 3: 267–301.

———. 2016. "'Soul-Concepts' in Ancient Near Eastern Mythical Texts and Their Implications for the Primeval History." *VT* 66: 181–93.

———. 2019. "Intratextual Exegesis in the Primeval History: The Literary Function of the Genealogies in View of the Formation of Gen 1–11." *ZAW* 131: 177–93.

Becking, B. 1995. "Japheth." *DDD,* 462–63.

———. 1999. "Sasam." *DDD,* 725–26.

Beckman, G. 1999. *Hittite Diplomatic Texts.* 2nd ed. WAW 7. Atlanta: Scholars Press.

Beitzel, B. J. 1992. "The Old Assyrian Caravan Road in the Mari Royal Archives." In *Mari in Retrospect: Fifty Years of Mari Studies,* edited by G. Young, 35–57. Winona Lake, IN: Eisenbrauns.

Ben-Amos, D. 2020. *Folklore Concepts: Histories and Critiques.* Bloomington: Indiana University Press.

Ben-Dov, J. 2008. *Head of All Years: Astronomy and Calendars at Qumran in Their Ancient Context.* Leiden: Brill.

———. 2021. "A 360-Day Administrative Year in Ancient Israel: Judahite Portable Calendars and the Flood Account." *HTR* 114: 431–50.

Benjamin, W. 1968. *Illuminations: Essays and Reflections.* Edited by H. Arendt. New York: Schocken.

———. 1999. *Selected Writings,* Vol. 2, Part 2, 1931–34. Edited by M. W. Jennings, H. Eiland, and G. Smith. Cambridge, MA: Harvard University Press.

Berman, J. A. 2017. *Inconsistency in the Torah: Ancient Literary Convention and the Limits of Source Criticism.* New York: Oxford University Press.

Bernstein, M. J. 1994. "4Q252 i. 2 *lōʾ yādûr rûḥî bāʾādām ləʿōlām:* Biblical Text or Biblical Interpretation?" *Revue de Qumran* 16: 421–27.

Berry, G. R. 1899. "The Interpretation of Gen. 6:3." *American Journal of Semitic Languages and Literature* 16: 47–49.

Bird, P. 1997. *Missing Persons and Mistaken Identities: Women and Gender in Ancient Israel.* Minneapolis: Fortress.

Blenkinsopp, J. 1976. "The Structure of P." *CBQ* 38: 275–92.

———. 1992. *The Pentateuch: An Introduction to the First Five Books of the Bible.* AYBRL. New York: Doubleday. Reprint, New Haven: Yale University Press.

———. 2002. "A Post-Exilic Lay Source in Genesis 1–11." In *Abschied vom Jahwisten: Die Komposition des Hexateuch in der jüngsten Diskussion,* edited by J. C. Gertz, K. Schmid, and M. Witte, 49–61. BZAW 315. Berlin: de Gruyter.

Bloch, M. 1953. *The Historian's Craft.* New York: Vintage.

Blum, E. 1984. *Die Komposition der Vätergeschichte.* WMANT 57. Neukirchen-Vluyn: Neukirchener.

———. 1990. *Studien zur Komposition des Pentateuch.* BZAW 189. Berlin: de Gruyter.

———. 2009. "Hosea 12 und die Pentateuchüberlieferungen." In *Die Erzväter in der biblischen Tradition: Festschrift für Matthias Köckert,* edited by A. C. Hagedorn and H. Pfeiffer, 291–321. BZAW 400. Berlin: de Gruyter.

———. 2010. *Textgestalt und Komposition: Exegetische Beiträge zu Tora und Vordere Propheten.* Edited by W. Oswald. FAT 69. Tübingen: Mohr Siebeck.

———. 2022. "Once Again: The Literary-Historical Profile of the P Tradition." In *Farewell to the Priestly Writing? The Current State of the Debate,* edited by F. Hartenstein and K. Schmid, 27–62. Atlanta: SBL Press.

Blumenberg, H. 1985. *Work on Myth.* Translated by R. M. Wallace. Cambridge, MA: MIT Press.

Borger, R. 1994. "The Incantation Series *Bīt Mēseri* and Enoch's Ascension to Heaven." In *"I Studied Inscriptions from Before the Flood": Ancient Near Eastern, Literary, and Linguistic Approaches to Genesis 1–11,* edited by R. S. Hess and D. T. Tsumura, 224–33. Winona Lake, IN: Eisenbrauns.

Botterweck, G. J. 1990. "*yônâ.*" *TDOT* 6, 32–40.

Bourdieu, P. 1962. *The Algerians.* Boston: Beacon.

Boyarin, D. 1990. *Intertextuality and the Reading of Midrash.* Bloomington: Indiana University Press.

———. 1993. *Carnal Israel: Reading Sex in Talmudic Culture.* Berkeley: University of California Press.

Braudel, F. 1980. *On History.* Chicago: University of Chicago Press.

Brentjes, G. 1995. "The History of Elam and Achaemenid Persia: An Overview." *CANE,* 1001–21.

Breton, J.-F. 1999. *Arabia Felix from the Time of the Queen of Sheba: Eighth Century B.C. to First Century A.D.* Notre Dame: University of Notre Dame Press.

Brockelmann, C. 1956. *Hebräische Syntax.* Neukirchen: Moers.

Bryce, T. 1998. *The Kingdom of the Hittites.* Oxford: Clarendon.

Buber, M., and F. Rosenzweig. 1994. *Scripture and Translation.* Translated by L. Rosenwald. Bloomington: Indiana University Press.

Budde, K. 1883. *Die biblische Urgeschichte (Gen. 1–12,5).* Giessen: Ricker.

Bührer, W. 2014. *Am Anfang . . . : Untersuchungen zur Textgenese und zur relativchronologischen Einordnung von Gen 1–3.* Göttingen: Vandenhoeck & Ruprecht.

———. 2015. "The Relative Dating of the Eden Narrative Gen *2–3." *VT* 65: 365–76.

Burke, A. A. 2021. *The Amorites and the Bronze Age Near East: The Making of a Regional Identity.* Cambridge: Cambridge University Press.

Burstein, S. M. 1978. *The Babyloniaca of Berossus.* Malibu, CA: Undena.

Calvin, J. 1847. *Commentaries on the First Book of Moses Called Genesis.* Translated by J. King. Edinburgh: Calvin Translation Society.

Carr, D. M. 1996. *Reading the Fractures of Genesis: Historical and Literary Approaches.* Louisville: Westminster John Knox.

———. 1998. "*Biblos Geneseōs* Revisited: A Synchronic Analysis of Patterns of Genesis as Part of the Torah." *ZAW* 110: 159–72, 327–47.

———. 2020a. *The Formation of Genesis 1–11: Biblical and Other Precursors.* New York: Oxford University Press.

———. 2020b. "Standing at the Edge of Reconstructable Transmission-History: Signs of a Secondary Sabbath-Oriented Stratum in Genesis 1:1–2:3." *VT* 70: 17–41.

———. 2021. *Genesis 1–11.* Stuttgart: Kohlhammer.

Cassuto, U. 1961. *A Commentary on the Book of Genesis. Part 1: From Adam to Noah.* Translation by I. Abrahams. Jerusalem: Magnes.

———. 1964. *A Commentary on the Book of Genesis. Part 2: From Noah to Abraham.* Translation by I. Abrahams. Jerusalem: Magnes.

Celestino, S., and C. López-Ruiz. 2016. *Tartessos and the Phoenicians in Iberia.* Oxford: Oxford University Press.

Certeau, M. de. 1988. *The Writing of History.* New York: Columbia University Press.

Chapman, C. R. 2016. *The House of the Mother: The Social Roles of Maternal Kin in Biblical Hebrew Narrative and Poetry.* AYBRL. New Haven: Yale University Press.

Chen, Y. S. 2013. *The Primeval Flood Catastrophe: Origins and Early Development in Mesopotamian Tradition.* Oxford: Oxford University Press.

Childs, B. S. 1962. *Memory and Tradition in Israel.* London: SCM Press.

———. 1979. *Introduction to the Old Testament as Scripture.* Philadelphia: Fortress.

Clay, J. S. 2003. *Hesiod's Cosmos.* Cambridge: Cambridge University Press.

Clements, R. E. 1980. *Isaiah 1–39.* Grand Rapids: Eerdmans.

Clifford, R. J. 1994. *Creation Accounts in the Ancient Near East and in the Bible.* Washington, DC: Catholic Biblical Association.

Clines, D. J. A. 1990. *What Does Eve Do to Help? and Other Readerly Questions to the Old Testament.* JSOTSup 94. Sheffield: JSOT Press.

Cogan, M., and H. Tadmor 1977. "Gyges and Ashurbanipal: A Study in Literary Transmission." *Orientalia* 46: 65–85.

Cohen, M., ed. 1997. *Mikra'ot Gedolot 'Haketer': Genesis.* 2 vols. Ramat-Gan: Bar-Ilan University Press.

Collingwood, R. G. 1994. *The Idea of History.* Rev. ed. Oxford: Oxford University Press.

Collins, A. Y. 1996. "The Seven Heavens in Jewish and Christian Apocalypses." In *Cosmology and Eschatology in Jewish and Christian Apocalypticism,* 21–54. Leiden: Brill.

Collins, A. Y., and J. J. Collins. 2008. *King and Messiah as Son of God: Divine, Human, and Angelic Messianic Figures in Biblical and Related Literature.* Grand Rapids: Eerdmans.

Collins, J. J. 1983. "Sibylline Oracles." In *The Old Testament Pseudepigrapha: Vol. 1: Apocalyptic Literature and Testaments,* edited by J. H. Charlesworth, 317–472. Garden City, NY: Doubleday.

———. 2005. *The Bible After Babel: Historical Criticism in a Postmodern Age.* Grand Rapids: Eerdmans.

———. 2017. "The Pre-Christian Adam." In *La Vie d'Adam et Ève et les traditions adamiques,* edited by F. Amsler, A. Frey, J.-D. Kaestli, and A.-L. Rey, 273–88. Lausanne: Zèbre.

Crawfoot, J. W., and G. M. Crawfoot. 1938. *Early Ivories from Samaria.* London: Palestine Exploration Fund.

Cross, F. M. 1973. *Canaanite Myth and Hebrew Epic: Essays in the History of the Religion of Israel.* Cambridge, MA: Harvard University Press.

———. 1998. *From Epic to Canon: History and Literature in Ancient Israel.* Baltimore: Johns Hopkins University Press.

———. 2003. *Leaves from an Epigrapher's Notebook: Collected Papers in Hebrew and West Semitic Palaeography and Epigraphy.* HSM 51. Winona Lake, IN: Eisenbrauns.

Dalley, S. 2000. *Myths from Mesopotamia: Creation, the Flood, Gilgamesh, and Others.* 2nd ed. Oxford: Oxford University Press.

Dandamayev, M. A. 1992. "Slavery: Ancient Near East." *ABD* 6, 58–62.

Daniels, P. T. 1995. "The Decipherment of Ancient Near Eastern Scripts." *CANE,* 81–93.

Darshan, G. 2016. "The Calendrical Framework of the Priestly Flood Story in Light of a New Akkadian Text from Ugarit (RS 94.2953)." *JAOS* 136: 507–14.

———. 2018. *After the Flood: Stories of Origins in the Hebrew Bible and Eastern Mediterranean Literature* [Hebrew]. Jerusalem: Bialik.

———. 2019. "*Ruaḥ 'Elohim* in Genesis 1:2 in Light of Phoenician Cosmogonies: A Tradition's History." *Journal of Northwest Semitic Languages* 45: 51–78.

Day, J. 1985. *God's Conflict with the Dragon and Sea: Echoes of a Canaanite Myth in the Old Testament.* Cambridge: Cambridge University Press.

———. 2000. *Yahweh and the Gods and Goddesses of Canaan.* JSOTSup 265. Sheffield: Sheffield Academic Press.

———. 2013. *From Creation to Babel: Studies in Genesis 1–11.* London: Clark.

———. 2022. *From Creation to Abraham: Further Studies in Genesis 1–11.* London: Clark.

Delitzsch, F. 1888. *A New Commentary on Genesis, Vol. I.* Translated by S. Taylor. Edinburgh: Clark.

del Olmo Lete, G. 2004. *Canaanite Religion According to the Liturgical Texts of Ugarit.* Winona Lake, IN: Eisenbrauns.

del Olmo Lete, G., J. Sanmartín. 2004. *A Dictionary of the Ugaritic Language in the Alphabetic Tradition.* 2 vols. Leiden: Brill.

Dijkstra, M. 1999. "Mother." *DDD,* 603–4.

Dillmann, A. 1897. *Genesis: Critically and Exegetically Expounded, Vol. I.* Translated by W. B. Stevenson. Edinburgh: Clark.

Doniger, W. 2011. *The Implied Spider: Politics and Theology in Myth.* 2nd ed. New York: Columbia University Press.

Douglas, M. 1966. *Purity and Danger: An Analysis of the Concepts of Pollution and Taboo.* London: Routledge & Kegan Paul.

Drews, R. 1992. "Herodotus 1.94, the Drought ca. 1200 BC, and the Origin of the Etruscans." *Historia* 41: 14–39.

Driver, S. R. 1892. *A Treatise on the Use of the Tenses in Hebrew.* 3rd ed. London: Oxford University Press.

———. 1897. *An Introduction to the Literature of the Old Testament.* 6th ed. New York: Scribner's.

———. 1904. *The Book of Genesis.* London: Methuen.

Dundes, A., ed. 1988. *The Flood Myth.* Berkeley: University of California Press.

Durand, J.-M. 2004. "Peuplement et sociétés à l'époque amorrite: (1) Les clans bensim'alites." In *Nomades et sédentaires dans le proche-orient ancient,* edited by C. Nicolle, 111–97. Paris: Éditions recherche sur les civilisations.

Durkheim, E. 2001. *The Elementary Forms of Religious Life.* Translated by C. Cosman. Oxford: Oxford University Press.

Durkheim, E., and M. Mauss. 1963. *Primitive Classification.* Chicago: University of Chicago Press.

Eco, U. 1995. *The Search for the Perfect Language.* Oxford: Blackwell.

Edzard, D. O. 1987. "Deep-Rooted Skyscrapers and Bricks: Ancient Mesopotamian Architecture and Its Imagery." In *Figurative Language in the Ancient Near East,* edited by M. Mindlin, M. J. Geller, and J. E. Wansbrough, 13–24. London: University of London.

———. 2002. "Eas doppelzüngiger Rat an Adapa: Ein Lösungsvorschlag." *Orientalia* 71: 415–16.

Eichler, R. 2021. *The Ark and the Cherubim.* FAT 146. Tübingen: Mohr-Siebeck.

Eissfeldt, O. 1927. "The Smallest Literary Unit in the Narrative Books of the Old Testament." In *Old Testament Essays,* edited by the Society for Old Testament Study, 85–93. London: Griffin.

———. 1966. "*Biblos Geneseōs.*" In *Kleine Schriften,* vol. 3, edited by R. Sellheim and F. Maass, 458–70. Tübingen: Mohr.

Elat, M. 1982. "Tarshish and the Problem of Phoenician Colonisation in the Western Mediterranean." *Orientalia Lovaniensia Periodica* 13: 55–69.

Eliade, M. 1959. *Cosmos and History: The Myth of the Eternal Return.* New York: Harper.

Emerton, J. A. 1987–1988. "An Examination of Some Attempts to Defend the Unity of the Flood Narrative in Genesis." *VT* 37: 401–20, and 38: 1–21.

———. 1992. "The Source Analysis of Genesis XI 27–32." *VT* 42: 37–46.

Eph'al, I. 1982. *The Ancient Arabs: Nomads on the Borders of the Fertile Crescent, 9th–5th Centuries B.C.* Jerusalem: Magnes.

Ernst, A. 1990. "'Wer Menschenblut vergiesst . . .' Zur Übersetzung von *b'dm* in Gen 9,6." *ZAW* 102: 252–53.

Esse, D. 1984. "Harran: City of Abraham and the Moon God." *Bulletin of the Canadian Society for Mesopotamian Studies* 8: 5–13.

Evans-Pritchard, E. E. 1940. *The Nuer: A Description of the Modes of Livelihood and Political Institutions of a Nilotic People.* Oxford: Oxford University Press.

Ewald, H. 1879. *Syntax of the Hebrew Language of the Old Testament.* Translated by J. Kennedy. Edinburgh: Clark.

Fales, M. 2014. "Hamlets and Farmsteads in the Balīḫ River Valley: The Middle Assyrian and the Neo-Assyrian Evidence." In *Settlement Dynamics and Human-Landscape Interaction in the Dry Steppes of Syria,* edited by D. M. Bonacossim 227–41. Wiesbaden: Harrassowitz.

————. 2017. "Ethnicity in the Assyrian Empire: A View from the Nisbe, (III) 'Arameans' and Related Tribalists." In *At the Dawn of History: Ancient Near Eastern Studies in Honour of J. N. Postgate,* edited by Y. Heffron, A. Stone, and M. Worthington, 133–77. Winona Lake, IN: Eisenbrauns.

Feldman, L. H. 2004. *Flavius Josephus, Judean Antiquities 1–4: Translation and Commentary.* Leiden: Brill.

Finkel, I. 2014. *The Ark Before Noah: Decoding the Story of the Flood.* New York: Doubleday.

Finkelstein, J. J. 1963. "The Antediluvian Kings: A University of California Tablet." *JCS* 17: 39–51.

————. 1966. "The Genealogy of the Hammurapi Dynasty." *JCS* 20: 95–118.

Fischer, G. 2018. *Genesis 1–11 übersetzt und ausgelegt.* Freiburg: Herder.

Fishbane, M. 1985. *Biblical Interpretation in Ancient Israel.* Oxford: Clarendon.

————. 2003. *Biblical Myth and Rabbinic Mythmaking.* Oxford: Oxford University Press.

Fitzmyer, J. A. 1995. *The Aramaic Inscriptions of Sefire.* 2nd ed. Rome: Pontifical Biblical Institute.

Fleming, D. E. 1998. "Mari and the Possibilities of Biblical Memory." *Revue d'assyriologie et d'archéologie orientale* 92: 41–78.

Fokkelman, J. 1991. *Narrative Art in Genesis: Specimens of Stylistic and Structural Analysis.* 2nd ed. Sheffield: Sheffield Academic Press.

Fontenelle, B. 1972. "Of the Origin of Fables." In *The Rise of Modern Mythology: 1680–1860,* edited by B. Feldman and R. D. Richardson, 10–18. Bloomington: Indiana University Press.

Foster, B. R. 2005. *Before the Muses: An Anthology of Akkadian Literature.* 3rd ed. Bethesda, MD: CDL Press.

Fox, J. 2003. *Semitic Noun Patterns.* Winona Lake, IN: Eisenbrauns.

Fox, M. V. 1974. "The Sign of the Covenant: Circumcision in the Light of the Priestly 'ôt Etiologies." *Revue biblique* 81: 557–96.

————. 2000. *Proverbs 1–9.* AYB 18A. New York: Doubleday. Reprint, New Haven: Yale University Press.

Frahm, E. 2010. "Counter-texts, Commentaries, and Adaptations: Politically Motivated Responses to the Babylonian Epic of Creation in Mesopotamia, the Biblical World, and Elsewhere." *Orient: Reports of the Society for Near Eastern Studies in Japan* 45: 3–33.

————. 2013. "Creation and the Divine Spirit in Babel and Bible: Reflections on *mummu* in Enūma eliš I 4 and *rûaḥ* in Genesis 1:2." In *Literature as Politics, Politics as Literature: Essays on the Ancient Near East in Honor of Peter Machinist,* edited by D. S. Vanderhooft and A. Winitzer, 97–116. Winona Lake, IN: Eisenbrauns.

Frame, G. 1997. "Chaldeans." In *The Oxford Encyclopedia of Archaeology in the Near East,* vol. 8, edited by E. M. Meyers, 482–84. New York: Oxford University Press.

Frayne, D. 2001. "In Abraham's Footsteps." In *The World of the Aramaeans I: Biblical Studies in Honour of Paul-Eugène Dion,* edited by P. M. Michèle Daviau, J. W. Wevers, and M. Weigl, 216–36. Sheffield: Sheffield Academic Press.

Freedman, D. N., and M. O'Connor. 1986. "*YHWH.*" *TDOT* 5, 500–521.

Frei, H. 1974. *The Eclipse of Biblical Narrative: A Study in Eighteenth and Nineteenth Century Hermeneutics.* New Haven: Yale University Press.

Friberg, J. 1992. "Numbers and Counting." *ABD* 4, 1139–46.

———. 2007. "The Beginning and the End of the Sumerian King List." In *A Remarkable Collection of Babylonian Mathematical Texts: Manuscripts in the Schøyen Collection, Cuneiform Texts I,* 231–43. New York: Springer.

Friedman, R. E. 1997. *Who Wrote the Bible?* 2nd ed. New York: Simon & Schuster.

Fritz, V. 1982. "'Solange die Erde steht'—Vom Sinn der jahwistischen Fluterzählung in Gen 6–8." *ZAW* 94: 599–614.

Frymer-Kensky, T. 1977. "The Atrahasis Epic and Its Significance for Our Understanding of Genesis 1–9." *Biblical Archaeologist* 40: 147–55.

Funkenstein, A. 1986. *Theology and the Scientific Imagination: From the Middle Ages to the Seventeenth Century.* Princeton: Princeton University Press.

Galambush, J. 1993. "*ʾādām* from *ʾădāmâ, ʾiššâ* from *ʾîš:* Derivation and Subordination in Genesis 2.4b–3.24." In *History and Interpretation: Essays in Honour of John H. Hayes,* edited by M. P. Graham, W. P. Brown, and J. K. Kuan, 33–46. Sheffield: Sheffield Academic Press.

Garr, W. R. 1985. *Dialect Geography of Syria-Palestine, 1000–586 B.C.E.* Philadelphia: University of Pennsylvania Press.

———. 1992. "The Grammar and Interpretation of Exodus 6:3." *JBL* 111: 385–408.

———. 2003. *In His Own Image and Likeness: Humanity, Divinity, and Monotheism.* Leiden: Brill.

———. 2004. "God's Creation: *brʾ* in the Priestly Source." *HTR* 97: 83–90.

———. 2021. "Reflexivity: The Cases of the *Niphal* and *Hithpael.*" *JNES* 80: 341–56.

Gaster, T. H. 1969. *Myth, Legend, and Custom in the Old Testament.* New York: Harper & Row.

Gelb, I. J. 1994. "The Name of Babylon." In *"I Studied Inscriptions from Before the Flood": Ancient Near Eastern, Literary, and Linguistic Approaches to Genesis 1–11,* edited by R. S. Hess and D. T. Tsumura, 266–69. Winona Lake, IN: Eisenbrauns.

George, A. R. 1993. *House Most High: The Temples of Ancient Mesopotamia.* Winona Lake, IN: Eisenbrauns.

———. 1997. "'Bond of the Lands': Babylon, the Cosmic Capital." In *Die orientalische Stadt: Kontinuität, Wandel, Bruch,* edited by G. Wilhelm, 125–46. Berlin: Deutsche Orient-Gesellschaft.

———. 2003. *The Babylonian Gilgamesh Epic: Introduction, Critical Edition and Cuneiform Texts.* 2 vols. Oxford: Oxford University Press.

———. 2005. "The Tower of Babel: Archaeology, History and Cuneiform Texts." *Archiv für Orientforschung* 51: 75–95.

———. 2007. "The Gilgameš Epic at Ugarit." *Aula Orientalis* 25: 237–54.

———. 2011. "A Stele of Nebuchadnezzar II." In *Cuneiform Royal Inscriptions and Related Texts in the Schøyen Collection,* edited by A. R. George, 153–69. Bethesda, MD: CDL Press.

———. 2016. "Die Kosmogonie des alten Mesopotamien." In *Anfang & Ende: Vormoderne Szenarien von Weltenstehung and Weltuntergang,* edited by M. Gindhart and T. Pommerening, 7–25. Darmstadt: von Zabern.

Gertz, J. C. 2009. "Antibabylonische Polemik im priesterlichen Schöpfungsbericht." *Zeitschrift für Theologie und Kirche* 106: 137–55.

———. 2012. "The Formation of the Primeval History." In *The Book of Genesis: Composition, Reception, and Interpretation,* edited by C. A. Evans, J. N. Lohr, and D. L. Petersen, 107–35. VTSup 152. Leiden: Brill.

———. 2015. "Genesis 5: Priesterliche Redaktion, Komposition oder Quellenschrift?" In *Abschied von der Priesterschrift? Zum Stand der Pentateuchdebatte,* edited by F. Hartenstein and K. Schmid, 65–93. Leipzig: Evangelische Verlagsanstalt.

———. 2018. *Das erste Buch Mose (Genesis): Die Urgeschichte Gen 1–11.* Alte Testament Deutsch. Göttingen: Vandenhoeck & Ruprecht.

Glassner, J.-J. 2004. *Mesopotamian Chronicles.* WAW 19. Atlanta: Society of Biblical Literature.

Glessmer, U. 1999. "Calendars in the Qumran Scrolls." In *The Dead Sea Scrolls After Fifty Years: A Comprehensive Assessment,* edited by P. W. Flint and J. C. VanderKam, 213–78. Leiden: Brill.

Goff, M., L. T. Stuckenbruck, and E. Morano. 2016. *Ancient Tales of Giants from Qumran and Turfan: Contexts, Traditions, and Influences.* Tübingen: Mohr Siebeck.

Goldenberg, D. M. 2003. *The Curse of Ham: Race and Slavery in Early Judaism, Christianity, and Islam.* Princeton: Princeton University Press.

Goldenberg, G. 2013. *Semitic Languages: Features, Structures, Relations, Processes.* Oxford: Oxford University Press.

Golka, F. W. 1980. "Keine Gnade für Kain." In *Werden und Wirken des Alten Testaments: Festschrift für Claus Westermann,* edited by R. Albertz, H.-P. Müller, W. Ch. Zimmerli, and H. W. Wolff, 58–73. Göttingen: Vandenhoeck & Ruprecht.

González, J. M. 2010. "The *Catalogue of Women* and the End of the Heroic Age (Hesiod fr. 204.94-103 M-W)." *Transactions of the American Philological Association* 140: 375–422.

Gordon, R. P. 2011. "'Couch' or 'Crouch'? Genesis 4:7 and the Temptation of Cain. In *On Stone and Scroll: Essays in Honour of Graham Ivor Davies,* edited by J. K. Aitken, K. J. Dell, and B. A. Mastin, 195–209. BZAW 420. Berlin: de Gruyter.

———. 2012. "Who 'Began to Call on the Name of the Lord' in Genesis 4:26b?: The MT and the Versions." In *Let Us Go up to Zion: Essays in Honour of H. G. M. Williamson,* edited by I. Provan and M. J. Boda, 57–68. VTSup 153. Leiden: Brill.

Grayson, A. K. 1976. *Assyrian Royal Inscriptions: From Tiglath-Pilesar I to Ashur-nasir-apli II.* Wiesbaden: Harrassowitz.

———. 1987. *Assyrian Rulers of the Third and Second Millennia BC (to 1115 BC).* Toronto: University of Toronto Press.

———. 1991. *Assyrian Rulers of the Early First Millennium BC. Vol. I (1114–859 BC).* Toronto: University of Toronto Press.

———. 1996. *Assyrian Rulers of the Early First Millennium BC. Vol. II (858–745 BC).* Toronto: University of Toronto Press.

Greenberg, M. 1983. *Ezekiel 1–20.* AYB 22. New York: Doubleday. Reprint, New Haven: Yale University Press.

———. 1997. *Ezekiel 21–37.* AYB 22A. New York: Doubleday. Reprint, New Haven: Yale University Press.

Greenfield, J. C. 1984. "A Touch of Eden." In *Orientalia J. Duchesne-Guillemin Emeriot Oblata,* edited by P. Lexoq, 219–24. Leiden: Brill.

Greenspahn, F. E. 1994. *When Brothers Dwell Together: The Preeminence of Younger Siblings in the Hebrew Bible.* New York: Oxford University Press.

Greenstein, E. L. 1997. "Kirta." In *Ugaritic Narrative Poetry,* edited by S. B. Parker, 9–48. WAW 9. Atlanta: Scholars Press.

Grossman, A. 2012. *Rashi.* New York: Oxford University Press.

Guichard, M. 2013. "Bédouins et sédentaires au pays de l'Ida-Maraṣ." *Semitica* 55: 61–74.

Gunkel, H. 1904. *Israel and Babylon: The Babylonian Influence on Israelite Religion.* Philadelphia: McVey.

———. 1997. *Genesis: Translated and Interpreted.* Translated by M. E. Biddle. Macon, GA: Mercer University Press.

———. 2006. *Creation and Chaos in the Primeval Era and the Eschaton: A Religio-Historical Study of Genesis 1 and Revelation 12.* Translated by W. Whitney Jr. Grand Rapids: Eerdmans.

Haag, E. 2004. "*šabbāt.*" *TDOT* 14, 387–97.

Haag, H. 1980. "*ḥāmās.*" *TDOT* 4, 478–87.

Halbwachs, M. 1992. *On Collective Memory,* edited by L. A. Coser. Chicago: University of Chicago Press.

Hallo, W. W. 1970. "Antediluvian Cities." *JCS* 23: 57–67.

Halpern, B. 1992. "Kenites." *ABD* 4, 17–22.

———. 1995. "What They Don't Know Won't Hurt Them: Genesis 6–9." In *Fortunate the Eyes That See: Essays in Honor of David Noel Freedman,* edited by A. B. Beck, A. H. Bartelt, P. R. Raabe, and C. A. Franke, 16–34. Grand Rapids: Eerdmans.

———. 2009. *From Gods to God: The Dynamics of Iron Age Cosmologies.* FAT 63. Tübingen: Mohr-Siebeck.

Hamilton, V. P. 1990. *The Book of Genesis: Chapters 1–17.* Grand Rapids: Eerdmans.

Haran, M. 1978. *Temples and Temple-Service in Ancient Israel.* Oxford: Clarendon.

———. 1984. "The Size of Books in the Bible and the Division of the Pentateuch and the Deuteronomistic Work" [Hebrew]. *Tarbiz* 53: 329–52.

Hasel, G. F. 1980. "*zāʿaq.*" *TDOT* 4, 112–22.

Hasselbach, R. 2004. "The Markers of Person, Gender, and Number in the Prefixes of G-Preformative Conjugations in Semitic." *JAOS* 124: 23–35.

Hawkins, J. D. 1995. "Karkamish and Karatepe: Neo-Hittite City-States in North Syria. *CANE,* 1295–1307.

Hayden, R. M. 1979. "The Cultural Ecology of Service Nomads." *Eastern Anthropologist* 32: 297–309.

Hayes, K. M. 1997. "Jeremiah IV 23: *Tōhû* Without *Bōhû.*" *VT* 47: 247–48.

Hazard, P. 1963. *The European Mind, 1680–1715.* Cleveland: Meridian.

Healey, J. 1999. "Tirash." *DDD,* 871–72.

Heger, P. 2007. "The Development of Qumran Law: *Nistarot, Niglot* and the Issue of 'Contemporization.'" *Revue de Qumran* 23: 167–206.

Heimpel, W. 2003. *Letters to the King of Mari.* Winona Lake, IN: Eisenbrauns.

Helm, P. 2004. *John Calvin's Ideas.* Oxford: Oxford University Press.

Heltzer, M. 1981. *The Suteans.* Naples: Istituto universitario orientale.

Hendel, R. 1985. "The Flame of the Whirling Sword: A Note on Genesis 3:24." *JBL* 104: 671–74.

———. 1987. "Of Demigods and the Deluge: Toward an Interpretation of Genesis 6:1–4." *JBL* 106: 13–26.

———. 1995a. "Tangled Plots in Genesis." In *Fortunate the Eyes That See: Essays in Honor of David Noel Freedman,* edited by A. B. Beck, H. Bartelt, P. R. Raabe, and C. A. Franke, 35–51. Grand Rapids: Eerdmans.

———. 1995b. "4Q252 and the Flood Chronology of Genesis 7–8: A Text-Critical Solution." *DSD* 2: 72–79.

———. 1996. "In the Margins of the Hebrew Verbal System: Situation, Tense, Aspect, Mood." *ZAH* 9: 152–81.

———. 1997a. "Aniconism and Anthropomorphism in Ancient Israel." In *The Image and the Book: Iconic Cults, Aniconism, and the Veneration of the Holy Book in Israel and the Ancient Near East,* edited by K. van der Toorn, 205–28. Leuven: Peeters.

———. 1997b. "The Poetics of Myth in Genesis." In *The Seductiveness of Jewish Myth,* edited by S. D. Breslauer, 157–70. Albany: SUNY Press.

———. 1998. *The Text of Genesis 1–11: Textual Studies and Critical Edition.* New York: Oxford University Press.

———. 1999. "Serpent." *DDD,* 744–47.

———. 2000. "'Begetting' and 'Being Born' in the Pentateuch: Notes on Historical Linguistics and Source Criticism." *VT* 50: 38–46.

———. 2004. "The Nephilim Were on the Earth: Genesis 6:1–4 and Its Ancient Near Eastern Context." In *The Fall of the Angels,* edited by C. Auffarth and L. T. Stuckenbruck, 11–34. Leiden: Brill.

———. 2005a. *Remembering Abraham: Culture, Memory, and History in the Hebrew Bible.* New York: Oxford University Press.

———. 2005b. "Genesis 1–11 and Its Mesopotamian Problem." In *Cultural Borrowings and Ethnic Appropriations in Antiquity,* edited by E. S. Gruen, 23–36. Stuttgart: Franz Steiner.

———. 2007. "Table and Altar: The Anthropology of Food in the Priestly Torah." In *To Break Every Yoke: Essays in Honor of Marvin L. Chaney,* edited by R. B. Coote and N. Gottwald, 131–48. Sheffield: Sheffield-Phoenix Press.

———. 2008. "Leitwort Style and Literary Structure in the J Primeval Narrative." In *Sacred History, Sacred Literature: Essays on Ancient Israel, the Bible and Religion in Honor of Richard E. Friedman,* edited by S. Dolansky, 93–109. Winona Lake, IN: Eisenbrauns.

———. 2010. "Cultural Memory." In *Reading Genesis: Ten Methods,* edited by R. Hendel, 28–46. Cambridge: Cambridge University Press.

———. 2011. "Is the 'J' Primeval Narrative an Independent Composition? A Critique of Crüsemann's 'Die Eigenständigkeit der Urgeschichte.'" In *The Pentateuch: International Perspectives on Current Research,* edited by T. B. Dozeman, K. Schmid, and B. J. Schwartz, 181–205. FAT 78. Tübingen: Mohr Siebeck.

———. 2012a. "Historical Context." In *The Book of Genesis: Composition, Reception, and Interpretation,* edited by C. A. Evans, J. N. Lohr, and D. L. Petersen, 51–81. Leiden: Brill.

————. 2012b. "A Hasmonean Edition of MT Genesis?: The Implications of the Editions of the Chronology in Genesis 5." *HeBAI* 1: 448–64.

————. 2013. *The Book of Genesis: A Biography.* Princeton: Princeton University Press.

————. 2015. "Ritual." In *The Oxford Encyclopedia of the Bible and Law,* edited by B. A. Strawn, 238–45. New York: Oxford University Press.

————. 2016. *Steps to a New Edition of the Hebrew Bible.* Text-Critical Studies 10. Atlanta: SBL Press.

————. 2017. "God and the Gods in the Tetrateuch." In *The Origins of Yahwism,* edited by J. van Oorschot and M. Witte, 239–66. BZAW 484. Berlin: de Gruyter.

————. 2018. "Politics and Poetics in the Ancestral Narratives." In *The Politics of the Ancestors: Exegetical and Historical Perspectives on Genesis 12–36,* edited by M. Brett and J. Wöhrle, 11–34. FAT 124. Tübingen: Mohr Siebeck.

————. 2019a. "Abram's Journey as Nexus: *Literarkritik* and Literary Criticism." *VT* 69: 567–93.

————. 2019b. "The Life of Metaphor in Song of Songs: Poetics, Canon, and the Cultural Bible." *Biblica* 100: 60–83.

————. 2021a. "The Landscape of Memory: Giants and the Conquest of Canaan." In *Collective Identity and Collective Memory: Deuteronomy and the Deuteronomistic History in Their Context,* edited by J. U. Ro and D. Edelman, 263–88. BZAW 534. Berlin: de Gruyter.

————. 2021b. "How Old Is the Hebrew Bible? A Response to Konrad Schmid." *ZAW* 173: 61–70.

Hendel, R., and J. Joosten. 2018. *How Old Is the Hebrew Bible? A Linguistic, Textual, and Historical Study.* AYBRL. New Haven: Yale University Press.

Hendel, R., C. Kronfeld, and I. Pardes. 2010. "Gender and Sexuality." In *Reading Genesis: Ten Methods,* edited by R. Hendel, 71–91. Cambridge: Cambridge University Press.

Hensel, B. 2011. *Die Vertauschung des Erstgeburtssegens in der Genesis: Eine Analyse der narrative-theologischen Grundstruktur der ersten Buches der Tora.* BZAW 423. Berlin: de Gruyter.

Herder, J. G. 1833. *The Spirit of Hebrew Poetry.* Translated by J. Marsh. 2 vols. Burlington, VT: Edward Smith.

————. 1892. *Übers Erkennen und Empfinden in der menschlichen Seele.* In *Sämmtiliche Werke,* vol. 8, edited by B. Suphan, 236–62. Berlin: Weidmann.

————. 1993a. *Älteste Urkunde des Menschengeschlechts.* In *Schriften zum Alten Testament,* edited by R. Smend, 179–660. Frankfurt am Main: Deutscher Klassiker.

————. 1993b. *Against Pure Reason: Writings on Religion, Language, and History,* edited and translated by M. Bunge. Minneapolis: Fortress.

Hess, R. S. 1990. "Splitting the Adam: The Usage of ʾādām in Genesis i–v." In *Studies in the Pentateuch,* edited by J. A. Emerton, 1–15. VTSup 41. Leiden: Brill.

————. 1992a. "Nahor." *ABD* 4, 997.

————. 1992b. "Serug." *ABD* 5, 1117–18.

————. 1993. *Studies in the Personal Names of Genesis 1–11.* Neukirchen-Vluyn: Neukirchener.

Hiebert, T. 1996. *The Yahwist's Landscape: Nature and Religion in Early Israel.* New York: Oxford University Press.

———. 2007. "The Tower of Babel and the Origin of the World's Cultures." *JBL* 126: 29–58.

Hieke, T. 2003. *Die Genealogien der Genesis.* Freiburg: Herder.

———. 2014. "Die Völkertafel von Genesis 10 als genealogische Raumordnung: Form, Funktion, Geographie." In *Genealogie und Migrationsmythen im antiken Mittelmeerraum und auf der Arabischen Halbinsel,* edited by A.-B. Renger and I. Toral-Niehoff, 23–40. Berlin: Topoi.

Hillers, D. R. 1987. "Dust: Some Aspects of Old Testament Imagery." In *Love and Death in the Ancient Near East: Essays in Honor of Marvin H. Pope,* edited by J. H. Marks and R. M. Good, 105–9. Guilford: Four Quarters.

Hoch, J. E. 1994. *Semitic Words in Egyptian Texts of the New Kingdom and Third Intermediate Period.* Princeton: Princeton University Press.

Hoftijzer, J. 1958. "Some Remarks to the Tale of Noah's Drunkenness." *Oudtestamentische Studiën* 12: 22–27.

Holloway, S. W. 1991. "What Ship Goes There: The Flood Narratives in the Gilgamesh Epic and Genesis Considered in Light of Ancient Near Eastern Temple Ideology." *ZAW* 103: 328–55.

Holmstedt, R. D. 2008. "The Restrictive Syntax of Genesis i 1." *VT* 58: 56–67.

Holzinger, H. 1898. *Genesis.* Freiburg: Mohr Siebeck.

Hornung, E. 1982. *Conceptions of God in Ancient Egypt: The One and the Many.* Ithaca, NY: Cornell University Press.

Horowitz, W. 1996. "The 360 and 364 Day Year in Ancient Mesopotamia." *JANES* 24: 20–44.

———. 1998. *Mesopotamian Cosmic Geography.* Winona Lake, IN: Eisenbrauns.

———. 2016. "All About Rainbows." In *Laws of Heaven—Laws of Nature: Legal Interpretations of Cosmic Phenomena in the Ancient World,* edited by K. Schmid and C. Uehlinger, 40–51. Fribourg: Academic Press.

Hoyland, R. G. 2001. *Arabia and the Arabs: From the Bronze Age to the Coming of Islam.* London: Routledge.

Huehnergard, J. 1987. *Ugaritic Vocabulary in Syllabic Transcriptions.* Atlanta: Scholars Press.

———. 2006. "On the Etymology of the Hebrew Relative *šɛ.*" In *Biblical Hebrew in Its Northwest Semitic Setting: Typological and Historical Perspectives,* edited by S. E. Fassberg and A. Hurvitz, 103–25. Winona Lake, IN: Eisenbrauns.

Hunger, H., and J. Steele. 2019. *The Babylonian Astronomical Compendium MUL. APIN.* London: Routledge.

Hurowitz, V. A. 2008. "In Search of Resen (Genesis 10:12): Dūr Šarrukīn?" In *Birkat Shalom: Studies in the Bible, Ancient Near Eastern Literature, and Postbiblical Judaism Presented to Shalom M. Paul,* edited by C. Cohen, V. A. Hurowitz, A. M. Hurvitz, Y. Muffs, B. J. Schwartz, and J. H. Tigay, 511–24. Winona Lake, IN: Eisenbrauns.

Hutter, M. 1999. "Heaven-and-Earth." *DDD,* 390–91.

Hutzli, J. 2010. "Tradition and Interpretation in Gen 1:1–2:4a." *Journal of Hebrew Scriptures* 10. https://doi.org/10.5508/jhs.2010.v10.a12.

Izre'el, S. 2001. *Adapa and the South Wind: Language Has the Power of Life and Death.* Winona Lake, IN: Eisenbrauns.

Jacob, B. 1934. *Das erste Buch der Tora: Genesis.* Berlin: Schocken.

Jacobsen, T. 1976. *The Treasures of Darkness: A History of Mesopotamian Religion.* New Haven: Yale University Press.

Janowski, B. 1993. "Herrschaft über die Tiere: Gen 1,26–28 und die Semantik von *rdh*." In *Biblische Theologie und gesellschaftlicher Wandel: Für Norbert Lohfink SJ,* edited by G. Braulik, W. Gross, and S. McEvenue, 183–98. Freiburg: Herder.

Japhet, S. 1993. *I and II Chronicles: A Commentary.* Old Testament Library. Louisville: Westminster John Knox.

Jenni, E. 1989. "Erwägungen zu Gen 1,1 'am Anfang.'" *ZAH* 2: 121–27.

———. 1997. "Yahweh." *TLOT,* 522–26.

Joannès, F., and A. Lemaire. 1996. "Contrats babyloniens d'époque achéménide du Bît-Abî Râm avec une épigraphe araméene." *Revue d'assyriologie et d'archéologie orientale* 90: 41–60.

Joosten, J. 2019. "The Linguistic Dating of the Joseph Story." *HeBAI* 8: 24–43.

Joüon, P., and T. Muraoka. 1993. *A Grammar of Biblical Hebrew.* 2 vols. Rome: Pontifical Biblical Institute.

Kamrin, J. 2009. "The Aamu of Shu in the Tomb of Khnumhotep II at Beni Hassan." *Journal of Ancient Egyptian Interconnections* 1: 22–36.

Kawashima, R. S. 2004a. *Biblical Narrative and the Death of the Rhapsode.* Bloomington: Indiana University Press.

———. 2004b. "*Homo Faber* in J's Primeval History." *ZAW* 116: 483–501.

———. 2010. "Sources and Redaction." In *Reading Genesis: Ten Methods,* edited by R. Hendel, 47–70. Cambridge: Cambridge University Press.

Keel, O. 1985. *The Symbolism of the Biblical World: Ancient Near Eastern Iconography and the Book of Psalms.* New York: Crossroad.

Kellermann, D. 1997. "*migdāl.*" *TDOT* 8, 69–73.

Kermode, F. 1967. *The Sense of an Ending: Studies in the Theory of Fiction.* New York: Oxford University Press.

Kierkegaard, S. 1983. *Fear and Trembling / Repetition.* Translated by H. V. Hong and E. H. Hong. Princeton: Princeton University Press.

Kilmer, A. D. 1987. "The Symbolism of the Flies in the Mesopotamian Flood Myth and Some Further Implications." In *Language, Literature and History: Philological and Historical Studies Presented to Erica Reiner,* edited by F. Rochberg-Halton, 175–80. New Haven: American Oriental Society.

King, P. J., and L. E. Stager. 2001. *Life in Biblical Israel.* Louisville: Westminster John Knox.

Kitchen, K. A. 1996. *Ramesside Inscriptions Translated and Annotated, Vol. II: Ramesses II, Royal Inscriptions.* Oxford: Blackwell.

Kitz, A. M. 2019. "The Verb **yahway.*" *JBL* 138: 39–62.

Klein, J. 2011. "A New Look at the Theological Background of the Mesopotamian and Biblical Flood Stories." In *A Common Cultural Heritage: Studies on Mesopotamia and the Biblical World in Honor of Barry L. Eichler,* edited by G. Frame, E. Leichty, K. Sonik, J. H. Tigay, and S. Tinney, 151–76. Bethesda, MD: CDL.

Klein, R. W. 1974. "Archaic Chronologies and the Textual History of the Old Testament." *HTR* 67: 255–63.

Knapp, A. B. 1995. "Island Cultures: Crete, Thera, Cyprus, Rhodes, and Sardinia." *CANE,* 1433–49.

Knauf, E. A. 1988. *Midian: Untersuchungen zur Geschichte Palästinas und Nordarabiens am Ende des 2. Jahrtausends v. Chr.* Wiesbaden: Harrassowitz.

———. 1992a. "Lotan." *ABD* 4, 374–75.

———. 1992b. "Uz." *ABD* 6, 770–71.

Koch, K. 1983. "Is There a Doctrine of Retribution in the Old Testament?" In *Theodicy in the Old Testament,* edited by J. L. Crenshaw, 57–87. Philadelphia: Fortress.

Kraeling, E. G. H. 1922. "Terah." *ZAW* 40: 153–54.

Krašovec, J. 1977. *Der Merismus im Biblisch-Hebräischen und Nordwestsemitischen.* Rome: Biblical Institute Press.

Kraus, H.-J. 1993. *Psalms.* 2 vols. Minneapolis: Fortress.

Kselman, J. S. 1978. "The Recovery of Poetic Fragments from the Pentateuchal Priestly Source." *JBL* 97: 161–73.

Kugel, J. L. 1981. *The Idea of Biblical Poetry: Parallelism and Its History.* New Haven: Yale University Press.

———. 1998. *Traditions of the Bible: A Guide to the Bible As It Was at the Start of the Common Era.* Cambridge, MA: Harvard University Press.

Kvanvig, H. S. 2011. *Primeval History: Babylonian, Biblical, and Enochic: An Intertextual Reading.* Leiden: Brill.

Lambert, W. G. 1960. *Babylonian Wisdom Literature.* Oxford: Clarendon.

———. 1967. "Enmeduranki and Related Matters." *JCS* 21: 126–38.

———. 1998. "The Qualifications of Babylonian Diviners." In *tikip santakki mala bašmu: Festschrift für Rykle Borger,* edited by R. Borger and S. Maul, 141–58. Cuneiform Monographs 10. Groningen: Styx.

———. 2013. *Babylonian Creation Myths.* Winona Lake, IN: Eisenbrauns.

Lambert, W. G., and A. R. Millard. 1969. *Atra-Ḫasīs: The Babylonian Story of the Flood, with the Sumerian Flood Story by M. Civil.* Oxford: Clarendon.

Lange, A. 2009. *Handbuch der Textfunde vom Toten Meer. Vol. 1: Die Handschriften biblischer Bücher von Qumran und den anderen Fundorten.* Tübingen: Mohr Siebeck.

Lanser, S. 1988. "(Feminist) Criticism in the Garden: Inferring Genesis 2–3." *Semeia* 41: 67–84.

Layton, S. C. 1990. *Archaic Features of Canaanite Personal Names in the Hebrew Bible.* Atlanta: Scholars Press.

———. 1997. "Remarks on the Canaanite Origin of Eve." *CBQ* 59: 22–32.

Leichty, E. 2011. *The Royal Inscriptions of Esarhaddon, King of Assyria (680–669 BC).* Winona Lake, IN: Eisenbrauns.

Leith, M. J. 2021. "The Garden of Eden: Don't Sweat It!" *BAR* 47/1: 66–68.

Levenson, J. D. 1985. *Sinai and Zion: An Entry into the Jewish Bible.* Minneapolis: Winston.

———. 1988. *Creation and the Persistence of Evil: The Jewish Drama of Divine Omnipotence.* San Francisco: Harper & Row.

Levin, C. 2003. "Tatbericht und Wortbericht in der priesterschriftlichen Schöpfungserzählung." In *Fortschreibungen: Gesammelte Studien zum Alten Testament,* 23–39. BZAW 316. Berlin: de Gruyter.

———. 2022. "The Priestly Writing as a Source: A Recollection." In *Farewell to the Priestly Writing? The Current State of the Debate,* edited by F. Hartenstein and K. Schmid, 1–26. Atlanta: SBL Press.

Levin, Y. 2002. "Nimrod the Mighty, King of Kish, King of Sumer and Akkad." *VT* 52: 350–66.

———. 2010. "Sheshonq I and the Negev *Ḥăṣērīm*." *Maarav* 17: 189–215.

Levinson, B. M. 1997. *Deuteronomy and the Hermeneutics of Legal Innovation*. New York: Oxford University Press.

———. 2008. *"The Right Chorale": Studies in Biblical Law and Interpretation*. FAT 54. Tübingen: Mohr Siebeck.

———. 2015. "A Post-Priestly Harmonization in the Flood Narrative." In *The Post-Priestly Pentateuch: New Perspectives on Its Redactional Development and Theological Profiles,* edited by F. Giuntoli and K. Schmid, 113–23. FAT 101. Tübingen: Mohr Siebeck.

Lévi-Strauss, C. 1966. *The Savage Mind*. Chicago: University of Chicago Press.

Levy, T. E., and M. Najjar. 2006. "Edom and Copper: The Emergence of Ancient Israel's Rival." *BAR* 32/4: 24–35, 70.

Lewis, J. P. 1978. *A Study of the Interpretation of Noah and the Flood in Jewish and Christian Literature*. Leiden: Brill.

Lewis, T. J. 1997. "El's Divine Feast." In *Ugaritic Narrative Poetry,* edited by S. B. Parker, 193–96. WAW 9. Atlanta: Scholars Press.

Lichtheim, M., ed. 1976. *Ancient Egyptian Literature. Vol. II: The New Kingdom*. Berkeley: University of California Press.

———, ed. 1980. *Ancient Egyptian Literature. Vol. III: The Late Period*. Berkeley: University of California Press.

Lipiński, E. 1966. "Nimrod et Assur." *Revue biblique* 73: 77–93.

———. 1990. "Les Japhétites selon Gen 10,2–4 et 1 Chr 1,5–7." *ZAH* 3: 40–53.

———. 1992. "Les Chamites selon Gen 10,6–20 et 1 Chr 1,8–16." *ZAH* 5: 135–62.

———. 1993. "Les Sémites selon Gen 10,21–30 et 1 Chr 1,17–23." *ZAH* 6: 193–215.

Liverani, M. 2014. *The Ancient Near East: History, Society and Economy*. London: Routledge.

———. 2017. *Assyria: The Imperial Mission*. Winona Lake, IN: Eisenbrauns.

Lohfink, N. 1994. *Theology of the Pentateuch: Themes of the Priestly Narrative and Deuteronomy*. Minneapolis: Fortress.

Lovejoy, A. O., and G. Boas. 1935. *Primitivism and Related Ideas in Antiquity*. Baltimore: Johns Hopkins University Press.

Luther, M. 1958. *Luther's Works, Vol. 1: Lectures on Genesis, Chapters 1–5*. Edited by J. Pelikan. St. Louis: Concordia.

———. 1960. *Luther's Works, Vol. 2: Lectures on Genesis, Chapters 6–14*. Edited by J. Pelikan. St. Louis: Concordia.

———. 1967. *Table Talk*. Edited by T. G. Tappert. Philadelphia: Fortress.

Machinist, P. 1992. "Nimrod." *ABD* 4, 1116–18.

———. 2006. "Kingship and Divinity in Imperial Assyria." In *Text, Artifact, and Image: Revealing Ancient Israelite Religion,* edited by G. Beckman and T. J. Lewis, 152–88. Providence, RI: Brown Judaic Studies.

Malinowski, B. 1948. *Magic, Science and Religion and Other Essays*. Edited by R. Redfield. Boston: Beacon.

Marchesi, G. 2001. "On the Divine Name ᵈBA-Ú." *Orientalia* 71: 161–72.

Marcus, D. 1997. "The Betrothal of Yarikh and Nikkal-Ib." In *Ugaritic Narrative Poetry,* edited by S. B. Parker, 215–18. WAW 9. Atlanta: Scholars Press.

Mauss, M. 1990. *The Gift: The Form and Reason for Exchange in Archaic Societies*. New York: Norton.

McCarter, P. K., Jr. 1984. *II Samuel*. AYB 8. New York: Doubleday. Reprint, New Haven: Yale University Press.

———. 1999. "Id." *DDD*, 446.

McEvenue, S. E. 1971. *The Narrative Style of the Priestly Writer*. Rome: Biblical Institute.

McKane, W. 1986. *Jeremiah 1–25: A Critical and Exegetical Commentary*. International Critical Commentary. Edinburgh: Clark.

McNutt, P. M. 1990. *The Forging of Israel: Iron Technology, Symbolism, and Tradition in Ancient Society*. Sheffield: Almond Press.

Mettinger, T. N. D. 1999. "Cherubim." *DDD*, 189–92.

———. 2007. *The Eden Narrative: A Literary and Religio-historical Study of Genesis 2–3*. Winona Lake, IN: Eisenbrauns.

Meyers, C. 1988. *Discovering Eve: Ancient Israelite Women in Context*. New York: Oxford University Press.

———. 2014. "Was Ancient Israel a Patriarchal Society?" *JBL* 133: 8–27.

Michel, A. 1997. *Theologie aus der Périphérie: Die gespaltene Koordination im Biblischen Hebräisch*. BZAW 257. Berlin: de Gruyter.

Miles, J. 1995. *God: A Biography*. New York: Knopf.

Milgrom, J. 1991. *Leviticus 1–16*. AYB 3. New York: Doubleday. Reprint, New Haven: Yale University Press.

———. 2001. *Leviticus 23–27*. AYB 3B. New York: Doubleday. Reprint, New Haven: Yale University Press.

Millard, A. R. 1984. "The Etymology of Eden." *VT* 34: 103–6.

———. 2001. "Where Was Abraham's Ur?" *BAR* 27/3: 52–53, 57.

Miller, P. D. 1965. "Fire in the Mythology of Canaan and Israel." *CBQ* 27: 256–61.

———. 1966. "*Yeled* in the Story of Lamech." *JBL* 85: 477–78.

———. 1973. *The Divine Warrior in Early Israel*. Cambridge, MA: Harvard University Press.

———. 1978. *Genesis 1–11: Studies in Structure and Theme*. Sheffield: JSOT Press.

Moberly, R. W. L. 2000. "Why Did Noah Send Out a Raven?" *VT* 50: 345–56.

Moorey, P. R. S. 1994. *Ancient Mesopotamian Materials and Industries: The Archaeological Evidence*. Oxford: Clarendon.

Moran, W. L. 1988. "*Enūma eliš* I 1–8." *Nouvelles assyriologiques brèves et utilitaires*: 15–16.

———. 2002. *The Most Magic Word: Essays on Babylonian and Biblical Literature*. Edited by R. Hendel. Washington, DC: Catholic Biblical Association.

Most, G. W. 2006. *Hesiod: Theogony, Works and Days, Testimonia*. LCL 57. Cambridge, MA: Harvard University Press.

Mullen, E. T. 1980. *The Assembly of the Gods*. HSM 24. Chico, CA: Scholars Press.

Müller, H.-P. 1991a. *Mythos—Kerygma—Wahrheit: Gesammelte Aufsätze zum Alten Testament in seiner Umwelt und zur Biblischen Theologie*. BZAW 200. Berlin: de Gruyter.

———. 1991b. "Drei Deutungen des Todes: Genesis 3, der Mythos von Adapa und die Sage von Gilgamesh." In *Altes Testament und christlicher Glaube*, edited by I. Baldermann et al., 117–34. Neukirchen-Vluyn: Neukirchener.

Müller, W. W. 1992a. "Abimael." *ABD* 1, 20.

———. 1992b. "Diklah." *ABD* 2, 198–99.

———. 1992c. "Hadoram." *ABD* 3, 16.

———. 1992d. "Havilah." *ABD* 3, 81–83.

———. 1992e. "Hazarmaveth." *ABD* 3, 85–86.

———. 1992f. "Jobab." *ABD* 3, 871.

———. 1992g. "Obal." *ABD* 5, 4–5.

———. 1992h. "Pishon." *ABD* 5, 374.

———. 1992i. "Raamah." *ABD* 5, 597.

———. 1992j. "Sabtah." *ABD* 5, 861–62.

———. 1992k. "Seba." *ABD* 5, 1064.

———. 1992l. "Uzal." *ABD* 6, 775–76.

Naʼaman, N. 1986. "Ḫabiru and Hebrews: The Transfer of a Social Term to the Literary Sphere." *JNES* 45: 278–85.

Nachmanides (Ramban). 1971. *Commentary on the Torah: Genesis.* Translated by C. B. Chavel. New York: Shilo.

Nagy, G. 1979. *The Best of the Achaeans: Concepts of the Hero in Archaic Greek Poetry.* Baltimore: Johns Hopkins University Press.

Newsom, C. A. 1988. "4Q370: An Admonition Based on the Flood." *Revue de Qumran* 13: 23–43.

———. 2019. *Rhetoric and Hermeneutics: Approaches to Text, Tradition and Social Construction in Biblical and Second Temple Literature.* FAT 130. Tübingen: Mohr Siebeck.

Nickelsburg, G. W. E. 2001. *1 Enoch 1: Chapters 1–36, 81–108.* Hermeneia. Minneapolis: Fortress.

Niditch, S. 1985. *Chaos to Cosmos: Studies in Biblical Patterns of Creation.* Chico, CA: Scholars Press.

Niehr, H. 1999: "Host of Heaven." *DDD,* 428–30.

Nihan, C. 2007. *From Priestly Torah to Pentateuch: A Study in the Composition of the Book of Leviticus.* FAT 25. Tübingen: Mohr Siebeck.

Noort, E. 1998. "The Stories of the Great Flood: Notes on Gen 6:5–9:17 in Its Context of the Ancient Near East." In *Interpretations of the Flood,* edited by F. García Martinez and G. P. Luttikhuizen, 1–38. Leiden: Brill.

Olender, M. 1992. *The Languages of Paradise: Race, Religion, and Philology in the Nineteenth Century.* Cambridge, MA: Harvard University Press.

Olyan, S. M. 2004. *Biblical Mourning: Ritual and Social Dimensions.* New York: Oxford University Press.

———. 2005. "Exodus 31:12–17: The Sabbath According to H, or the Sabbath According to P and H?" *JBL* 124: 201–9.

Otto, E. 1996. "Die Paradieserzählung Genesis 2–3: Eine nachpriesterschriftliche Lehrerzählung in ihrem religionshistorischen Kontext." In *"Jedes Ding hat seine Zeit . . ." Studien zur israelitischen und altorientalischen Weisheit,* edited by A. A. Diesel, R. G. Lehmann, E. Otto, and A. Wagner, 167–92. BZAW 241. Berlin: de Gruyter.

Ottosson, M. 1974. "ʾereṣ." *TDOT* 1, 388–405.

Pakkala, J. 2011. "The Quotations and References of the Pentateuchal Laws in Ezra-Nehemiah." In *Changes in Scripture: Rewriting and Interpreting the Authoritative*

Traditions in the Second Temple Period, edited by H. Weissenberg, J. Pakkala, and M. Martilla, 193–221. BZAW 419. Berlin: de Gruyter.

Paran, M. 1989. *Forms of the Priestly Style in the Pentateuch: Patterns, Linguistic Usages, Syntactic Structures* [Hebrew]. Jerusalem: Magnes.

Pardee, D. 2002. *Ritual and Cult at Ugarit.* WAW 10. Atlanta: Society of Biblical Literature.

Parker, S. B. 1997. "Aqhat." In *Ugaritic Narrative Poetry,* edited by S. B. Parker, 49–80. WAW 9. Atlanta: Scholars Press.

———. 1999. "Sons of (the) God(s)." *DDD,* 794–800.

Parpola, S. 1970. *Neo-Assyrian Toponyms.* Neukirchen-Vluyn: Neukirchener.

Pat-El, N. 2014. "The Morphosyntax of Nominal Antecedents in Semitic, and an Innovation in Arabic." In *Proceedings of the Oslo-Austin Workshop in Semitic Linguistics,* edited by L. Edzard and J. Huehnergard, 28–47. Wiesbaden: Harrassowitz.

Paul, S. M. 2012. *Isaiah 40–66: Translation and Commentary.* Grand Rapids: Eerdmans.

Pearce, L. E., and C. Wunsch. 2014. *Documents of Judean Exiles and West Semites in Babylonia in the Collection of David Sofer.* Bethesda, MD: CDL.

Peckham, B. 1987. "Phoenicia and the Religion of Israel: The Epigraphic Evidence." In *Ancient Israelite Religion: Essays in Honor of Frank Moore Cross,* edited by P. D. Miller Jr., P. D. Hanson, and S. D. McBride, 79–99. Philadelphia: Fortress.

Pedersen, J. 1926. *Israel: Its Life and Culture.* 2 vols. London: Oxford University Press.

Perdue, L. G., J. Blenkinsopp, J. J. Collins, and C. Meyers. 1997. *Families in Ancient Israel.* Louisville: Westminster John Knox.

Perrot, A., and M. Richelle. 2022. "The Dead Sea Scrolls' Paleo-Hebrew Script: Its Roots in Hebrew Scribal Tradition." In *The Hebrew Bible Manuscripts: A Millennium,* edited by E. Attia and A. Perrot, 1–72. Leiden: Brill.

Petersen, D. L. 1976. "The Yahwist on the Flood." *VT* 26: 438–46.

Pitard, W. T. 1994. "Arameans." In *Peoples of the Old Testament World,* edited by A. J. Hoerth, G. L. Mattingly, and E. M. Yamauchi, 207–30. Grand Rapids, MI: Baker.

Polak, F. H. 1999. *Biblical Narrative: Aspects of Art and Design* [Hebrew]. 2nd ed. Jerusalem: Bialik.

———. 2002. "Poetic Style and Parallelism in the Creation Account (Genesis 1.1–2.3)." *Creation in Jewish and Christian Tradition,* edited by H. G. Reventlow and Y. Hoffmann, 2–31. London: Sheffield.

———. 2017. "Syntactic-Stylistic Aspects of the So-Called 'Priestly' Work in the Torah." In *Le-maʿan Ziony: Essays in Honor of Ziony Zevit,* edited by F. E. Greenspahn and G. A. Rendsburg, 345–82. Eugene, OR: Wipf & Stock.

Pongratz-Leisten, B. 2015. *Religion and Ideology in Assyria.* Berlin: de Gruyter.

Postgate, N. 2007. *The Land of Assur and the Yoke of Assur: Studies on Assyria.* Oxford: Oxbow.

Potts, D. T. 1997. *Mesopotamian Civilization: The Material Foundations.* Ithaca, NY: Cornell University Press.

Propp, W. H. 1990. "Eden Sketches." In *The Hebrew Bible and Its Interpreters,* edited by W. H. Propp, B. Halpern, and D. N. Freedman, 189–203. Winona Lake, IN: Eisenbrauns.

———. 1999. *Exodus 1–18.* AYB 2. New York: Doubleday. Reprint, New Haven: Yale University Press.

————. 2006. *Exodus 19–40.* AYB 2A. New York: Doubleday. Reprint, New Haven: Yale University Press.

Rainey, A. F. 1996. "Who Is a Canaanite? A Review of the Textual Evidence." *BASOR* 304: 1–15.

Reeves, J. C. 1993. "Utnapishtim in the Book of Giants?" *JBL* 112: 110–15.

Reis, P. T. 2002. "What Cain Said: A Note on Genesis 4:8." *JSOT* 27: 107–13.

Rendsburg, G. A. 1990. *Diglossia in Ancient Hebrew.* New Haven: American Oriental Society.

————. 2016. "Alliteration in the Book of Genesis." In *Doubling and Duplicating in the Book of Genesis: Literary and Stylistic Approaches to the Text,* edited by E. R. Hayes and K. Vermeulen, 79–95. Winona Lake, IN: Eisenbrauns.

Rendtorff, R. 1961. "Genesis 8,21 und die Urgeschichte des Jahwisten." *Kerygma und Dogma* 7: 69–78.

Ritner, J. K. 2009. *The Libyan Anarchy: Inscriptions from Egypt's Third Intermediate Period.* WAW 21. Atlanta: Society of Biblical Literature.

Robson, E. 2008. *Mathematics in Ancient Iraq: A Social History.* Princeton: Princeton University Press.

Rochberg, F. 2004. *The Heavenly Writing: Divination, Horoscopy, and Astronomy in Mesopotamian Culture.* Cambridge: Cambridge University Press.

————. 2010. *In the Path of the Moon: Babylonian Celestial Divination and Its Legacy.* Leiden: Brill.

————. 2016. *Before Nature: Cuneiform Knowledge and the History of Science.* Chicago: University of Chicago Press.

Rofé, A. 2009. *Introduction to the Literature of the Hebrew Bible.* Jerusalem: Simor.

Rogerson, J. W. 1984. "A Slippery Term: Myth." In *Sacred Narrative: Readings in the Theory of Myth,* edited by A. Dundes, 62–71. Berkeley: University of California Press.

Rollinger, R. 2013. "Mita of Mushki." In *The Encyclopedia of Ancient History,* edited by R. S. Bagnall, K. Brodersen, C. B. Champion, A. Erskine, and and S. R. Huebner, 4543–44. Hoboken, NJ: Wiley.

————. 2017. "Assyria and the Far West: The Aegean World." In *A Companion to Assyria,* edited by E. Frahm, 275–85. Malden: Wiley Blackwell.

Römer, T. 2013a. "'Higher Criticism': The Historical and Literary-Critical Approach—with Special Reference to the Pentateuch." In *Hebrew Bible/Old Testament: The History of Its Interpretation. Vol. III/1: The Nineteenth Century,* edited by M. Sæbø, 393–423. Göttingen: Vandenhoeck & Ruprecht.

————. 2013b. "La création des hommes et leur multiplication. Lecture comparée d'Atra-Hasis, de Gilgamesh XI et de Genèse 1; 6–9." *Semitica* 55: 147–56.

————. 2018. "Joseph and the Egyptian Wife (Genesis 39): A Case of Double Supplementation." *Supplementation and the Study of the Hebrew Bible,* edited by Saul M. Olyan and Jacob L. Wright, 69–83. Providence: Brown Judaic Studies.

Rösel, M. 1994. *Übersetzung als Vollendung der Auslegung: Studien zur Genesis-Septuaginta.* BZAW 223. Berlin: de Gruyter.

————. 1998. "Die Chronologie der Flut in Gen 7–8: Keine neuen textkritischen Lösungen." *ZAW* 110: 590–93.

————. 2018. *Tradition and Innovation: English and German Studies on the Septuagint.* Atlanta: Society of Biblical Literature.

Rosenthal, F. 1989. *The History of al-Ṭabarī. Vol. I: General Introduction and From the Creation to the Flood.* Albany: State University of New York Press.

Rüterswörden, U. 1988. "Der Bogen in Genesis 9: Militärhistorische und traditionsgeschichtliche Erwägungen zu einem biblischen Symbol." *Ugarit-Forschungen* 20: 247–63.

Rüterswörden, U., and Warmuth, G. 1993. "Ist *br'šyt* mit Artikel zu vokalisieren?" In *Biblische Welten,* edited by W. Zwickel, 84–90. Neukirchen-Vluyn: Neukirchener.

Sanders, S. L. 2017. *From Adapa to Enoch: Scribal Culture and Religious Vision in Judea and Babylon.* Tübingen: Mohr Siebeck.

Sasson, J. 1975. "Word-Play in Gen. 6:8–9." *CBQ* 37: 165–66.

———. 1978. "A Genealogical 'Convention' in Biblical Chronography?" *ZAW* 90: 171–85.

———. 1980. "The 'Tower of Babel' as a Clue to the Redactional Structuring of the Primeval History [Gen. 1–11:9]." In *The Bible World: Essays in Honor of Cyrus H. Gordon,* edited by G. Rendsburg, R. Adler, M. Arfa, and N. H. Winter, 211–19. New York: Ktav.

———. 1983. *"Reḥōvōt 'ir."* *Revue biblique* 90: 94–96.

———. 1985. *"welō' yitbōšāšû* (Gen 2,25) and Its Implications." *Biblica* 66: 418–21.

———. 1992. "Time . . . to Begin." In *"Shaʿarei Talmon": Studies in the Bible, Qumran, and the Ancient Near East Presented to Shemaryahu Talmon,* edited by M. Fishbane and E. Tov, 183–94. Winona Lake, IN: Eisenbrauns.

———. 2000. "'The Mother of All . . . ' Etiologies." In *A Wise and Discerning Mind: Essays in Honor of Burke O. Long,* edited by S. M. Olyan and R. C. Culley, 205–20. Providence, RI: Brown Judaic Studies.

———. 2014. *Judges 1–12.* AYB 6D. New Haven: Yale University Press.

———. 2015. *From the Mari Archives: An Anthology of Old Babylonian Letters.* Winona Lake, IN: Eisenbrauns.

Sawyer, J. F. A. 1986. "Cain and Hephaestus: Possible Relics of Metalworking Traditions in Genesis 4." *Abr-Nahrain* 24: 155–66.

Scharbert, J. 1977. "*'rr.*" *TDOT* 1, 405–18.

Schellenberg, A. 2011. *Der Mensch, das Bild Gottes? Zum Gedanken einer Sonderstellung des Menschen im Alten Testament und in weiteren altorientalischen Quellen.* ATANT 101. Zurich: Theologischer.

Schloen, J. D. 2001. *The House of the Father as Fact and Symbol: Patrimonialism in Ugarit and the Ancient Near East.* Winona Lake, IN: Eisenbrauns.

Schmid, K. 2008. "Loss of Immortality? Hermeneutical Aspects of Genesis 2–3 and Its Early Receptions." In *Beyond Eden: The Biblical Story of Paradise and Its Reception History,* edited by K. Schmid and C. Riedweg, 58–78. Tübingen: Mohr Siebeck.

———. 2010. *Genesis and the Moses Story: Israel's Dual Origins in the Hebrew Bible.* Winona Lake, IN: Eisenbrauns.

———. 2015. "Von der Gegenwelt zur Lebenswelt: Evolutionäre Kosmologie und Theologie im Buch Genesis." In *Cosmologies et cosmogonies dans la littérature antique,* edited by T. Fuhrer and M. Erler, 51–95. Geneva: Droz.

———. 2016. "Post-Priestly Additions in the Pentateuch: A Survey of Scholarship." In *The Formation of the Pentateuch: Bridging the Academic Cultures of Europe, Israel, and North America,* edited by J. C. Gertz, B. M. Levinson, D. Rom-Shiloni, and K. Schmid, 589–604. FAT 111. Tübingen: Mohr Siebeck.

———. 2021. "The Neo-Documentarian Manifesto: A Critical Reading." *JBL* 140: 461–79.

Schmidt, B. 1995. "Flood Narratives of Ancient Western Asia." *CANE,* 2337–51.

Schmidt, W. H. 1973. *Die Schöpfungsgeschichte der Priesterschrift: Zur Überlieferungsge-schichte von Genesis 1,1–2,4a und 2,4b–3,24.* Neukirchen-Vluyn: Neukirchener.

Schniedewind, W. M. 2019. *The Finger of the Scribe: How Scribes Learned to Write the Bible.* New York: Oxford University Press.

Schorch, S. 2021. *The Samaritan Pentateuch. Vol. 1: Genesis.* Berlin: de Gruyter.

Schüle, A. 2006. *Der Prolog der hebräischen Bibel: Der literar- und theologiegeschichtliche Diskurs der Urgeschichte (Genesis 1–11).* ATANT 86. Zurich: Theologischer.

———. 2009. *Die Urgeschichte (Gen 1–11).* Zurich: Theologischer.

Schwartz, B. J. 2000. "Israel's Holiness: The Torah Traditions." In *Purity and Holiness: The Heritage of Leviticus,* edited by M. Poorthuis and J. Schwartz, 47–59. Leiden: Brill.

———. 2007. "The Flood Narratives in the Torah and the Question of Where History Begins" [Hebrew]. In *Shai le-Sara Japhet: Studies in the Bible, Its Exegesis and Its Language,* edited by M. Bar Asher, 139–54. Jerusalem: Bialik.

———. 2012a. "The Pentateuch as Scripture and the Challenge of Biblical Criticism: Responses Among Modern Jewish Thinkers and Scholars." In *Jewish Concepts of Scripture: A Comparative Introduction,* edited by B. D. Sommer, 203–29. New York: New York University Press.

———. 2012b. "How the Compiler of the Pentateuch Worked: The Composition of Genesis 37." In *The Book of Genesis: Composition, Reception, and Interpretation,* edited by C. A. Evans, J. N. Lohr, and D. L. Petersen, 263–78. Leiden: Brill.

———. 2016. "The Pentateuchal Sources and the Former Prophets: A Neo-Documentarian's Perspective." In *The Formation of the Pentateuch: Bridging the Academic Cultures of Europe, Israel, and North America,* edited by J. C. Gertz, B. M. Levinson, D. Rom-Shiloni, and K. Schmid, 783–94. FAT 111. Tübingen: Mohr Siebeck.

Schwartz, G. M. 1989. "The Origins of the Arameans in Syria and Northern Mesopotamia: Research Problems and Potential Strategies." In *To the Euphrates and Beyond: Archaeological Studies in Honour of Maurits N. van Loon,* edited by O. Haex, H. Curvers, and P. Akkermans, 275–91. Rotterdam: Balkema.

Schwartz, M. 2002. "Qumran, Turfan, Arabic Magic, and Noah's Name." In *Charmes et sortilèges: Magie et magiciens,* edited by R. Gyselen, 231–38. Leuven: Peeters.

Scott, J. C. 1990. *Domination and the Arts of Resistance: Hidden Transcripts.* New Haven: Yale University Press.

Scurlock, J., and R. H. Beal, eds. 2013. *Creation and Chaos: A Reconsideration of Hermann Gunkel's* Chaoskampf *Hypothesis.* Winona Lake, IN: Eisenbrauns.

Seebass, H. 1996. *Genesis I: Urgeschichte (1,1–11,26).* Neukirchen-Vluyn: Neukirchener.

Segal, R. A. 2004. *Myth: A Very Short Introduction.* New York: Oxford University Press.

Seybold, K. 1976. "Der Turmbau zu Babel: Zur Entstehung von Genesis XI 1–9." *VT* 26: 453–79.

Sheehan, J. 2005. *The Enlightenment Bible: Translation, Scholarship, Culture.* Princeton: Princeton University Press.

Shryock, A. 1997. *Nationalism and the Genealogical Imagination: Oral History and Textual Authority in Tribal Jordan.* Berkeley: University of California Press.

Singer-Avitz, L. 1999. "Beersheba: A Gateway Community in Southern Arabian Long-Distance Trade in the Eighth Century B.C.E." *Tel Aviv* 26: 3–75.

Sjöberg, Å. W., and E. Bergmann. 1969. *The Collection of the Sumerian Temple Hymns.* Locust Valley, NY: Augustin.

Ska, J.-L. 1981. "Séparation des eaux et de la terre ferme dan le récit sacerdotal." *La nouvelle revue théologique* 113: 512–32.

———. 2006. *Introduction to Reading the Pentateuch.* Winona Lake, IN: Eisenbrauns.

———. 2009. *The Exegesis of the Pentateuch.* FAT 66. Tübingen: Mohr Siebeck.

Skinner, J. 1930. *A Critical and Exegetical Commentary on Genesis.* 2nd ed. Edinburgh: Clark.

Smith, G. 1873. "The Chaldean Account of the Deluge." *Transactions of the Society of Biblical Archaeology* 2: 213–34.

Smith, M. S. 2001. *The Origins of Biblical Monotheism: Israel's Polytheistic Background and the Ugaritic Texts.* New York: Oxford University Press.

———. 2010. *The Priestly Vision of Genesis 1.* Minneapolis: Fortress.

———. 2014. *Poetic Heroes: Literary Commemorations of Warriors and Warrior Culture in the Early Biblical World.* Grand Rapids: Eerdmans.

———. 2016. *Where the Gods Are: Spatial Dimensions of Anthropomorphism in the Biblical World.* AYBRL. New Haven: Yale University Press.

———. 2019. *The Genesis of Good and Evil: The Fall(out) and Original Sin in the Bible.* Louisville: Westminster John Knox.

Smith, M. S., and W. T. Pitard. 2009. *The Ugaritic Baal Cycle, Vol. II: Introduction with Text, Translation and Commentary of KTU/CAT 1.3–1.4.* VTSup 114. Leiden: Brill.

Soggin, J. A. 1997. *Das Buch Genesis.* Darmstadt: Wissenschaftliche Buchgesellschaft.

Sommer, B. D. 2011. "Dating Pentateuchal Texts and the Perils of Pseudo-Historicism." In *The Pentateuch: International Perspectives on Current Research,* edited by T. B. Dozeman, K. Schmid, and B. J. Schwartz, 85–108. FAT 78. Tübingen: Mohr Siebeck.

———. 2012. "Concepts of Scriptural Language in Midrash." In *Jewish Concepts of Scripture: A Comparative Introduction,* edited by B. D. Sommer, 64–79. New York: New York University Press.

Sonnet, J.-P. 2010. "God's Repentance and 'False Starts' in Biblical History (Genesis 6–9; Exodus 32–34; 1 Samuel 15 and 2 Samuel 7)." In *Congress Volume: Ljubljana 2007,* edited by A. Lemaire, 469–94. VTSup 133. Leiden: Brill.

———. 2020. "Between Poetic Justice and Poetic Mercy: God in the Flood Narrative." *Nova et Vetera* 18: 1247–65.

Sparks, K. L. 2007. "*Enūma Elish* and Priestly Mimesis: Elite Emulation in Nascent Judaism." *JBL* 126: 625–48.

Speiser, E. A. 1964. *Genesis.* AYB 1. Garden City: Doubleday. Reprint, New Haven: Yale University Press.

———. 1967. *Oriental and Biblical Studies: Collected Writings of E. A. Speiser.* Edited by J. J. Finkelstein and M. Greenberg. Philadelphia: University of Pennsylvania Press.

Sperling, S. D. 1999. "Pants, Persians, and the Priestly Source." In *Ki Baruch Hu: Ancient Near Eastern, Biblical, and Judaic Studies in Honor of Baruch A. Levine,* edited by R. Chazan, W. W. Hallo, and L. H. Schiffman, 373–85. Winona Lake, IN: Eisenbrauns.

Spina, F. A. 1992. "The 'Ground' for Cain's Rejection (Gen 4): *'adāmāh* in the Context of Gen 1–11." *ZAW* 104: 319–32.

Spinoza, B. 2007. *Theological-Political Treatise.* Translated by M. Silverthorne and J. Israel. Cambridge: Cambridge University Press.

Stackert, J. 2011. "Compositional Strata in the Priestly Sabbath Law: Exodus 31:12–17 and 35:1–3." *Journal of Hebrew Scriptures* 11. https://doi.org/10.5508/jhs.2011.v11.a15.

———. 2016. "How the Priestly Sabbaths Work: Innovation in Pentateuchal Priestly Ritual." In *Ritual Innovation in the Hebrew Bible and Ancient Judaism,* edited by N. MacDonald. 79–111. BZAW 468. Berlin: de Gruyter.

Stadelmann, L. I. J. 1970. *The Hebrew Conception of the World: A Philological and Literary Study.* Rome: Pontifical Biblical Institute.

Stager, L. E. 1985a. "The Archaeology of the Family in Ancient Israel." *BASOR* 260: 1–35.

———. 1985b. "The Firstfruits of Civilization." In *Palestine in the Bronze and Iron Ages: Papers in Honour of Olga Tufnell,* edited by J. N. Tubb, 172–88. London: Institute of Archaeology.

———. 1995. "The Impact of the Sea Peoples." In *The Archaeology of Society in the Holy Land,* edited by T. E. Levy, 332–48. London: Leicester University Press.

———. 1999. "Jerusalem and the Garden of Eden." *Eretz-Israel* 26: 183*–94*.

Starobinski, J. 1991. "Fable and Mythology in Seventeenth- and Eighteenth-Century Literature and Theoretical Reflection." In *Mythologies,* edited by Y. Bonnefoy, 2.722–32. Chicago: University of Chicago Press.

Steck, O. H. 1971. "Genesis 12:1–3 und die Urgeschichte des Jahwisten." In *Probleme biblischer Theologie: Gerhard von Rad zum 70. Geburtstag,* edited by H. W. Wolff, 525–54. Munich: Kaiser.

———. 1981. *Der Schöpfungsbericht der Priesterschrift: Studien zur literarkritischen und überlieferungsgeschichtlichen Problematik von Genesis 1,1–2,4a.* 2nd ed. Göttingen: Vandenhoeck & Ruprecht.

Steiner, R. C. 1977. *The Case for Fricative-Laterals in Proto-Semitic.* New Haven: American Oriental Society.

———. 2005. "On the Dating of Hebrew Sound Changes (*Ḥ > Ḥ and *Ġ > ʿ) and Greek Translations (2 Esdras and Judith)." *JBL* 124: 229–67.

Stenmans, P. 1997. "*mabbûl.*" *TDOT* 8, 60–65.

Stern, S. 2012. *Calendars in Antiquity: Empires, States, and Societies.* Oxford: Oxford University Press.

Sternberg, M. 1985. *The Poetics of Biblical Narrative: Ideological Literature and the Drama of Reading.* Bloomington: Indiana University Press.

———. 1990. "Time and Space in Biblical (Hi)story Telling: The Grand Chronology." In *The Book and the Text: The Bible and Literary Theory,* edited by R. Schwartz, 81–145. Oxford: Blackwell.

Stewart, F. H. 1994. *Honor.* Chicago: University of Chicago Press.

Stordalen, T. 2000. *Echoes of Eden: Genesis 2–3 and Symbolism of the Eden Garden in Biblical Hebrew Literature.* Leuven: Peeters.

Stuckenbruck, L. T. 2004. "The Origins of Evil in Jewish Apocalyptic Tradition: The Interpretation of Genesis 6:1–4 in the Second and Third Centuries B.C.E." In *The Fall of the Angels,* edited by C. Auffarth and L. T. Stuckenbruck, 87–118. Leiden: Brill.

Tal, A. 1980. *The Samaritan Targum of the Pentateuch: A Critical Edition.* 3 vols. Tel Aviv: Tel Aviv University Press.

———. 2015. *Genesis.* Biblia Hebraica Quinta 1. Stuttgart: Deutsche Bibelgesellschaft.

Talmon, S. 1994. "The Reckoning of the Day in the Biblical and Early Post-Biblical Periods: From Morning or from Evening?" In *The Bible in the Light of Its Interpreters,* edited by S. Japhet, 109–20. Jerusalem: Magnes.

Teissier, B. 1996. *Egyptian Iconography on Syro-Palestinian Cylinder Seals of the Middle Bronze Age.* Fribourg: University Press.

Thompson, C. M., and S. Skaggs. 2013. "King Solomon's Silver? Southern Phoenician Hacksilber Hoards and the Location of Tarshish." *Internet Archaeology* 35. doi: 10.6078/M78913SW.

Thompson, T. L. 1974. *The Historicity of the Patriarchal Narratives: The Quest for the Historical Abraham.* BZAW 133. Berlin: de Gruyter.

Tigay, J. H. 1982. *The Evolution of the Gilgamesh Epic.* Philadelphia: University of Pennsylvania Press.

Tov, E. 1985. "The Nature and Background of Harmonizations in Biblical Manuscripts." *JSOT* 31: 3–29.

———. 2004. *Scribal Practices and Approaches Reflected in the Texts Found in the Judean Desert.* Leiden: Brill.

———. 2012. *Textual Criticism of the Hebrew Bible.* 3rd ed. Minneapolis: Fortress.

———. 2015. "The Genealogical Lists in Genesis 5 and 11 in Three Different Versions." In *Textual Criticism of the Hebrew Bible, Qumran, Septuagint: Collected Essays,* 221–38. VTSup 167. Leiden: Brill.

Trebilco, P. R. 1991. *Jewish Communities in Asia Minor.* Cambridge: Cambridge University Press.

Trible, P. 1978. *God and the Rhetoric of Sexuality.* Philadelphia: Fortress.

Turner, L. A. 1993. "The Rainbow as the Sign of the Covenant in Genesis IX 11–13." *VT* 43: 119–24.

Uehlinger, C. 1990. *Weltreich und "eine Rede": Eine neue Deutung der sogenannten Turmbauerzählung (Gen 11,1–9).* Freiburg: Universitätsverlag.

———. 1999. "Nimrod." *DDD,* 627–30.

Uehlinger, C., and S. Müller-Trufaut. 2001. "Ezekiel 1, Babylonian Cosmological Scholarship and Iconography: Attempts at Further Refinement." *Theologische Zeitschrift* 57: 140–71.

Ullendorff, E. 1954. "The Construction of Noah's Ark." *VT* 4: 95–96.

Ur, J. 2017. "Physical and Cultural Landscapes of Assyria." In *A Companion to Assyria,* edited by E. Frahm, 13–35. Malden, MA: Wiley-Blackwell.

VanderKam, J. C. 1984. *Enoch and the Growth of an Apocalyptic Tradition.* Washington, DC: Catholic Biblical Association.

———. 2002. *From Revelation to Canon: Studies in the Hebrew Bible and Second Temple Literature.* JSJSup 62. Leiden: Brill.

van der Kooij, A. 2006. "The City of Babel and Assyrian Imperialism: Genesis 11:1–9 Interpreted in the Light of Mesopotamian Sources." In *Congress Volume: Leiden 2004,* edited by A. Lemaire, 1–17. VTSup 109. Leiden: Brill.

van der Toorn, K. 1994. *From Her Cradle to Her Grave: The Role of Religion in the Life of the Israelite and the Babylonian Woman.* Sheffield: JSOT Press.

———. 1996. *Family Religion in Babylonia, Syria and Israel: Continuity and Change in the Forms of Religious Life.* Leiden: Brill.

van der Toorn, K., and P. W. van der Horst. 1990. "Nimrod Before and After the Bible." *HTR* 83: 1–29.

van Ruiten, J. T. 2005. "Back to Chaos: The Relationship Between Jeremiah 4:23–26 and Genesis 1." In *Creation of Heaven and Earth: Re-interpretations of Genesis I in the Context of Judaism, Ancient Philosophy, Christianity, and Modern Physics,* edited by G. H. van Kooten, 21–30. Leiden: Brill.

Vansina, J. 1985. *Oral Tradition as History.* Madison: University of Wisconsin Press.

Vanstiphout, H. 2003. *Epics of Sumerian Kings: The Matter of Aratta.* WAW 20. Atlanta: Society of Biblical Literature.

Vervenne, M. 1993. "'The Blood Is the Life and the Life Is the Blood': Blood as Symbol of Life and Death in Biblical Tradition (Gen. 9,4)." In *Ritual and Sacrifice in the Ancient Near East,* edited by J. Quaebegeur, 451–70. Leuven: Peeters.

———. 1995a. "All They Need Is Love: Once More Genesis 6.1–4." In *Words Remembered, Texts Renewed: Essays in Honour of John F. A. Sawyer,* edited by J. Davies, G. Harvey, and W. G. E. Watson, 19–40. Sheffield: Sheffield Academic Press.

———. 1995b. "What Shall We Do with the Drunken Sailor? A Critical Reexamination of Genesis 9.20–27." *JSOT* 68: 33–55.

Vogels, W. 1987. "Cham découvre les limites de son père Noé (*Gn* 9,20–27)." *Nouvelle Revue Théologique* 109: 554–73.

Vollers, K. 1899. "Zur Erklärung von *ydwn* Gen. 6,3." *ZA* 14: 349–56.

Von Hendy, A. 2002. *The Modern Construction of Myth.* Bloomington: Indiana University Press.

von Rad, G. 1972. *Genesis: A Commentary.* Old Testament Library. Philadelphia: Westminster.

von Soden, W. 1985. *Bibel und Alter Orient: Altorientalische Beiträge zum Alten Testament.* Berlin: de Gruyter.

Wachsmann, S. 1998. *Seagoing Ships and Seamanship in the Bronze Age Levant.* College Station: Texas A&M University Press.

Wagner, M. 1966. *Die lexicalischen und grammatikalischen Aramaismen im alttestamentlichen Hebräisch.* Berlin: Töpelmann.

Wallace, H. N. 1985. *The Eden Narrative.* HSM 32. Atlanta: Scholars Press.

———. 1990. "The Toledot of Adam." In *Studies in the Pentateuch,* edited by J. A. Emerton, 17–33. VTSup 41. Leiden: Brill.

Wasserman, N. 2020. *The Flood: The Akkadian Sources. A New Edition, Commentary, and a Literary Discussion.* Leuven: Peeters.

Weber, M. 1978. *Economy and Society: An Outline of Interpretive Sociology.* Edited by G. Roth and C. Wittich. Berkeley: University of California Press.

—————. 2009. *From Max Weber: Essays in Sociology.* Edited and translated by H. H. Gerth and C. Wright Mills. London: Routledge.

Weinfeld, M. 1978. "Gen. 7:11, 8:1–2 Against the Background of Ancient Near Eastern Tradition." *Die Welt des Orients* 9: 242–48.

—————, ed. 1982. *The Book of Genesis* [Hebrew]. Tel-Aviv: Revivim.

—————. 2004. "God the Creator in the Priestly Source and Deutero-Isaiah." In *The Place of the Law in the Religion of Ancient Israel,* 95–117. VTSup 100. Leiden: Brill.

Weippert, M. 1971. *The Settlement of the Israelite Tribes in Palestine.* London: SCM Press.

—————. 1998. "Tier und Mensch in einer menschenarmen Welt: Zum sog. *dominium terrae* in Genesis 1." In *Ebenbild Gottes—Herrscher über die Welt: Studien zu Würde und Auftrag des Mesnchen,* edited by H.-P. Mathys, 35–55. Neukirchen-Vluyn: Neukirchener.

Wellhausen, J. 1885. *Prolegomena to the History of Israel.* Translated by J. S. Black and A. Menzies. Edinburgh: Black.

—————. 1899. *Die Composition des Hexateuchs und der historischen Bücher des Alten Testaments.* 3rd ed. Berlin: Reimer.

—————. 2013. *Briefe.* Edited by R. Smend. Tübingen: Mohr Siebeck.

Wells, B. 2017. "Adam as Temple Oblate: The Yahwist's Garden and the Eanna and Ebabbar Temples." Paper presented at the Annual Meeting of the Society of Biblical Literature. Boston, 20 November 2017.

Wenham, G. J. 1987. *Genesis 1–15.* Word Biblical Commentary. Waco, TX: Word.

—————. 1994. "Sanctuary Symbolism in the Garden of Eden Story." In *"I Studied Inscriptions from Before the Flood": Ancient Near Eastern, Literary, and Linguistic Approaches to Genesis 1–11,* edited by R. S. Hess and D. T. Tsumura, 399–404. Winona Lake, IN: Eisenbrauns.

—————. 1999. "The Priority of P." *VT* 49: 240–58.

Wente, E. F. 2003. "The Book of the Heavenly Cow." In *The Literature of Ancient Egypt,* edited by W. K. Simpson, 289–98. 3rd ed. New Haven: Yale University Press.

West, M. L. 1966. *Hesiod: Theogony.* Oxford: Clarendon.

—————. 1971. *Early Greek Philosophy and the Orient.* Oxford: Clarendon.

Westbrook, R. 1992. "Punishment and Crimes." *ABD* 5, 546–56.

Westenholz, A., and U. Koch-Westenholz. 2000. "Enkidu—the Noble Savage?" In *Wisdom, Gods, and Literature: Studies in Assyriology in Honour of W. G. Lambert,* edited by A. R. George and I. L. Finkel, 437–51. Winona Lake, IN: Eisenbrauns.

Westermann, C. 1984. *Genesis 1–11: A Commentary.* Translated by J. J. Scullion. Minneapolis: Augsburg.

—————. 1985. *Genesis 12–36: A Commentary.* Translated by J. J. Scullion. Minneapolis: Augsburg.

Wevers, J. W. 1993. *Notes on the Greek Text of Genesis.* Atlanta: Scholars Press.

White, L. 1967. "The Historical Roots of Our Ecologic Crisis." *Science* 156: 1203–7.

Whiting, R. M. 1995. "Amorite Tribes and Nations of Second-Millennium Western Asia." *CANE,* 1231–42.

Wiggermann, F. A. M. 1994. "Mischwesen. A. Philologisch." *Reallexikon der Assyriologie* 8: 222–45.

———. 2010. "Wein, Weib und Gesang in een Midden-Assyrische nederzetting aan de Balikh." *Phoenix* 15: 17–58.

Williams, B. 2008. *Shame and Necessity.* 2nd ed. Berkeley: University of California Press.

Wilson, K. A. 2005. *The Campaign of Pharaoh Shoshenq I into Palestine.* FAT 2.9. Tübingen: Mohr Siebeck.

Wilson, R. R. 1977. *Genealogy and History in the Biblical World.* New Haven: Yale University Press.

Winitzer, A. 2010. "Toward Assessing Twentieth-Century Ancient Near Eastern Scholarship: The Case of E. A. Speiser." In *Gazing on the Deep: Ancient Near Eastern and Other Studies in Honor of Tzvi Abusch,* edited by J. Stackert, B. N. Porter, and D. P. Wright, 379–410. Bethesda, MD: CDL.

———. 2013. "Etana in Eden: New Light on the Mesopotamian and Biblical Tales in Their Semitic Context." *JAOS* 133: 441–65.

Winnett, F. V. 1970. "The Arabian Genealogies in the Book of Genesis." In *Translating and Understanding the Old Testament: Essays in Honor of Herbert Gordon May.* Edited by H. T. Frank and W. L. Reed, 171–96. Nashville: Abingdon.

Winston, D. 1981. *Philo:* The Contemplative Life, The Giants, *and* Selections. New York: Paulist.

———. 2001. *The Ancestral Philosophy: Hellenistic Philosophy in Second Temple Judaism.* Edited by G. E. Sterling. Providence, RI: Brown Judaic Studies.

Winter, I. J. 2010. *On Art in the Ancient Near East.* 2 vols. Leiden: Brill.

Witte, M. 1998. *Die biblische Urgeschichte: Redaktions- und theologiegeschichtliche Beobachtungen zu Genesis 1,1–11,26.* BZAW 265. Berlin: de Gruyter.

Wolff, H. W. 1982. "The Kerygma of the Yahwist." In *The Vitality of Old Testament Traditions,* edited by W. Brueggemann, 41–66. 2nd ed. Atlanta: Knox.

Wood, A. 2008. *Of Wings and Wheels: A Synthetic Study of the Biblical Cherubim.* BZAW 385. Berlin: de Gruyter.

Woods, C. 2004. "The Sun-God Tablet of Nabu-apla-iddina Revisited." *JCS* 56: 23–103.

———. 2005. "On the Euphrates." *ZA* 95: 7–45.

———. 2009. "At the Edge of the World: Cosmological Conceptions of the Eastern Horizon in Mesopotamia." *JANER* 9: 183–239.

Wright, D. P. 1992. "Unclean and Clean" *ABD* 6, 729–41.

———. 1996. "Holiness, Sex, and Death in the Garden of Eden." *Biblica* 77: 305–29.

Wyatt, N. 1986. "Cain's Wife." *Folklore* 97: 88–95.

Younger, K. L., Jr. 2016. *A Political History of the Arameans: From Their Origins to the End of Their Polities.* Atlanta: SBL Press.

Zadok, R. 1980. "Notes on the Biblical and Extra-Biblical Onomasticon." *Jewish Quarterly Review* 71: 107–17.

———. 1984. "The Origin of the Name Shinar." *ZA* 74: 240–44.

Zakovitch, Y. 1980. "Explicit and Implicit Name-Derivations." *Hebrew Annual Review* 4: 167–81.

———. 1995. *Through the Looking Glass: Reflection Stories in the Bible* [Hebrew]. Tel Aviv: Kibbutz Meuchad.

————. 1999. "The Exodus from Ur of the Chaldeans: A Chapter in Literary Archaeology." In *Ki Baruch Hu: Ancient Near Eastern, Biblical, and Judaic Studies in Honor of Baruch A. Levine,* edited by R. Chazan, W. W. Hallo, and L. H. Schiffman, 429–39. Winona Lake, IN: Eisenbrauns.

Zatelli, I. 1991. "Astrology and the Worship of the Stars in the Bible." *ZAW* 103: 86–99.

Zenger, E. 1983. "Beobachtungen zu Komposition und Theologie der jahwistischen Urgeschichte." In *Dynamik im Wort: Lehre von der Bibel, Leben aus der Bibel,* edited by Katholisches Bibelwerk, 35–54. Stuttgart: Katholisches Bibelwerk.

Zevit, Z. 2013. *What Really Happened in the Garden of Eden?* New Haven: Yale University Press.

Zimansky, P. E. 1995. "The Kingdom of Urartu in Eastern Anatolia." *CANE,* 1135–46.

Zumthor, P. 1990. *Oral Poetry: An Introduction.* Minneapolis: University of Minnesota Press.

TRANSLATION

Creation

1 ¹In the beginning, when God created heaven and earth—²the earth was desolate chaos, and darkness was over the face of the ocean, and a wind of God was soaring over the face of the water—³God said, "Let there be light," and there was light. ⁴And God saw that the light was good, and God separated the light from the darkness. ⁵And God called the light "day," and the darkness he called "night." There was evening and there was morning, one day.

⁶God said, "Let there be a vault within the water, and let it separate water from water." ⁷And God made the vault and separated the water below the vault from the water above the vault. And it was so. ⁸And God called the vault "heaven." There was evening and there was morning, a second day.

⁹God said, "Let the water below heaven be gathered into one place, so that dry land may appear." And it was so. ¹⁰And God called the dry land "earth," and the pool of water he called "seas." And God saw that it was good.

¹¹God said, "Let the earth grow seed-bearing plants and fruit trees with seed-bearing fruit on the earth." And it was so. ¹²And the earth yielded seed-bearing plants of every kind and trees with seed-bearing fruit of every kind. And God saw that it was good. ¹³There was evening and there was morning, a third day.

¹⁴God said, "Let there be lights in the vault of heaven to separate the day from the night. And let them be signs for festivals, days, and years, ¹⁵and let them be lights in the vault of heaven to light up the earth." And it was so. ¹⁶And God made the two great lights—the greater light to rule the day and the lesser light to rule the night—and the stars. ¹⁷And God set them in the vault of heaven to light up the earth, ¹⁸to rule the day and the night, and to separate the light from the darkness. And God saw that it was good. ¹⁹There was evening and there was morning, a fourth day.

²⁰God said, "Let the waters teem with teeming living creatures, and let birds fly over the earth across the vault of heaven. ²¹And God created the great sea monsters and every kind of moving life with which the waters teem, and every kind of winged bird. And God saw that it was good. ²²And God blessed them and said, "Be

---

In the translations, boldface = P, roman type = J, italics = R.

fruitful and multiply, fill the water of the seas, and let the birds be fruitful on the earth." ²³There was evening and there was morning, a fifth day.

²⁴God said, "Let the earth yield every kind of living creature—domestic animals, and crawling creatures and wild animals of the earth of every kind." And it was so. ²⁵And God made wild animals of the earth of every kind and domestic animals of every kind and land-crawling creatures of every kind. And God saw that it was good.

²⁶God said, "Let us make a human in our image, according to our likeness, so that they may rule the fish of the sea and the birds of heaven and the animals and every crawling creature on earth."

²⁷God created the human in his image;
in God's image he created him;
male and female he created them.

²⁸And God blessed them, and God said to them, "Be fruitful and multiply, fill the earth, and subdue it. Rule the fish of the sea and the birds of heaven and every creature that moves on earth." ²⁹And God said, "I hereby give to you all seed-bearing plants on the whole face of the earth and all trees with seed-bearing fruit. They will be food for you. ³⁰And for every creature on earth, for every bird in heaven, for everything that moves on earth, that has life's breath within it, all green plants will be food." And it was so. ³¹And God saw all that he had made, and behold, it was very good. There was evening and there was morning, the sixth day.

2   ¹Now heaven and earth and all their array were complete. ²On the sixth day God completed his work that he had made, and on the seventh day he ceased from all his work that he had made. ³And God blessed the seventh day and made it holy, for on it he ceased from all his work that God had made in creation.

The Garden of Eden

2   ⁴*This is the genealogy of heaven and earth, when they were created.*

On the day Yahweh *God* made earth and heaven—⁵when wild plants of the field were not yet on the earth, when grasses of the field had not yet grown, for Yahweh *God* had not sent rain on the earth, and there was no human to work the soil, ⁶but a river would flow from the earth and water the whole surface of the soil—⁷Yahweh *God* formed a human from the soil's dust. He blew life's breath into his nostrils, and the human became a living being. ⁸Yahweh *God* planted a garden in Eden, in the east, and placed there the human he had formed. ⁹Yahweh *God* caused to sprout from the soil every tree that is desirable to see and good for food, and the Tree of Life in the middle of the garden, and the Tree of the Knowledge of Good and Evil.

¹⁰A river flows from Eden to water the garden, and from there it splits into four branches. ¹¹The name of the first is Pishon—it circles the whole land of Havilah, where there is gold. ¹²The gold of that land is excellent, and bdellium and carnelian are there. ¹³The name of the second river is Gihon—it circles the whole land of Cush. ¹⁴The name of the third river is Tigris—it flows east of Assyria. The fourth river is Euphrates.

¹⁵Yahweh *God* took the human and placed him in the Garden of Eden to work it and guard it. ¹⁶And Yahweh *God* commanded the human, "From all the trees of the

garden you may surely eat, ¹⁷but as for the Tree of the Knowledge of Good and Evil, you shall not eat from it, for on the day you eat from it you shall die."

¹⁸Yahweh *God* said, "It is not good for the human to be alone. I will make a companion to help him." ¹⁹Yahweh *God* formed from the soil every animal of the field and every bird of heaven, and he brought them to the human to see what he would call them. Whatever the human would call each living being, that was its name. ²⁰The human named every domestic animal, every bird of heaven, and every animal of the field, but the human did not find a companion to help him. ²¹Yahweh *God* cast a trance over the human, and he slept, and he took out one of his ribs and closed the flesh behind it. ²²Yahweh *God* built up the rib that he had taken from the man into a woman, and he brought her to the man. ²³The man said, "This time at last!

> Bone from my bones,
>   and flesh from my flesh.
> This one shall be called 'woman,'
>   for from man she was taken."

²⁴Therefore a man leaves his father and mother and cleaves to his wife, and they become one flesh. ²⁵The two of them were naked, the man and his wife, and they felt no shame before each other.

3 ¹Now the snake was more cunning than all the animals of the field that Yahweh *God* had made. He said to the woman, "Did God really say, 'Do not eat from all the trees of the garden?'" ²The woman said to the snake, "We may eat fruit from the trees of the garden, ³but about the fruit of the tree in the midst of the garden, God said, 'Do not eat from it, and do not touch it, lest you die.'" ⁴The snake said to the woman, "You shall not die. ⁵Indeed, God knows that on the day you eat from it your eyes will be opened, and you will become like gods, knowing good and evil." ⁶The woman saw that the tree was good for food, that it was a delight to the eyes, and desirable to make one wise. She took from its fruit and ate, and she also gave it to her husband beside her, and he ate. ⁷The eyes of the two of them were opened, and they knew that they were naked, and they sewed together fig leaves and made loincloths for themselves.

⁸They heard the sound of Yahweh *God* walking about in the garden in the evening breeze. And the man and his wife hid themselves from Yahweh *God* in the midst of the trees of the garden. ⁹Yahweh *God* called out to the man and said to him, "Where are you?" ¹⁰He said, "I heard your sound in the garden and I was afraid, for I am naked, so I hid." ¹¹He said, "Who told you that you are naked? Have you eaten from the tree from which I commanded you not to eat?" ¹²The man said, "The woman, whom you gave to be with me, she gave to me from the tree, and I ate." ¹³Yahweh *God* said to the woman, "What have you done?" The woman said, "The snake deceived me, and I ate."

¹⁴Yahweh *God* said to the snake, "Because you have done this, cursed are you, out of all the domestic animals and all the wild animals of the field. You shall crawl on your belly and eat dust all the days of your life. ¹⁵I will set hatred between you and the woman, and between your offspring and hers. They will strike at your head, and you will strike at their heels." ¹⁶To the woman he said, "I will greatly multiply your labor pains from pregnancy—in pain you shall bear children. You shall desire your husband, and he shall rule over you." ¹⁷To the man he said, "Since you listened to your wife's voice and ate from the tree about which I commanded you 'Do not eat from it,' cursed

is the soil because of you. In painful labor you shall eat from it all the days of your life. [18]Thorns and thistles it will sprout for you, and you shall eat the grasses of the field. [19]By the sweat of your brow you shall eat bread, until you return to the soil, for from it you were taken. For you are dust, and to dust you shall return."

[20]The man named his wife Eve, for she was the mother of all life. [21]Yahweh *God* made leather garments for the man and his wife, and he dressed them. [22]Yahweh *God* said, "Behold, the human has become like one of us, knowing good and evil. Now, lest he reach out his hand and take from the Tree of Life and eat and live forever . . ." [23]Yahweh *God* expelled him from the Garden of Eden to work the soil from which he was taken. [24]He banished the humans, and he stationed east of the Garden of Eden the cherubim and the flame of the whirling sword to guard the path to the Tree of Life.

Cain and Abel

4   [1]The man knew Eve, his wife, and she conceived and gave birth to Cain. She said, "I have gotten a man with Yahweh." [2]She gave birth again to his brother, Abel. Abel was a herder of flocks, and Cain worked the soil. [3]After some time, Cain offered a sacrifice to Yahweh from the fruit of the soil. [4]Abel too offered a sacrifice from the fat firstborns of his flock. Yahweh regarded with favor Abel and his sacrifice, [5]but Cain and his sacrifice he did not regard. Cain became very angry, and his face was fallen. [6]Yahweh said to Cain, "Why are you angry? Why has your face fallen? [7]Is it not so that if you are good, it will be lifted? But if you are not good, sin crouches at the door—it desires you, but you can rule over it." [8]Cain said to Abel, his brother, "Let us go out to the field," and when they were in the field Cain rose up against Abel, his brother, and killed him.

[9]Yahweh said to Cain, "Where is Abel, your brother?" He said, "I do not know. Am I my brother's keeper?" [10]He said, "What have you done? The voice of your brother's blood cries out to me from the soil. [11]Now, cursed are you from the soil, which opened its mouth to take your brother's blood from your hand. [12]When you work the soil it will no longer yield its strength to you. You shall be a restless wanderer on the earth." [13]Cain said to Yahweh, "My punishment is more than I can bear. [14]You have banished me today from the face of the soil, and I will be hidden from your face. I will be a restless wanderer on the earth, and whoever meets me will kill me." [15]Yahweh said to him, "Therefore whoever kills Cain will suffer vengeance sevenfold." Yahweh placed a sign on Cain so that whoever met him would not kill him. [16]Cain departed from Yahweh's presence and dwelled in the land of Wandering, east of Eden.

[17]Cain knew his wife, and she conceived and gave birth to Enoch. He built a city and named the city after Enoch, his son. [18]To Enoch was born Irad, and Irad fathered Mehiyael, and Mehiyael fathered Methushael, and Methushael fathered Lamech. [19]Lamech took two wives for himself, the first named Ada and the second Zillah. [20]Ada gave birth to Jabal—he was the father of herdsmen who dwell in tents. [21]His brother's name was Jubal—he was the father of all who play lyres and pipes. [22]As for Zillah, she too gave birth to Tubal-Cain, [the father of all who] work metal, forging bronze and iron. Tubal-Cain's sister was Naamah. [23]Lamech said to his wives:

"Ada and Zillah, hear my voice,
     Lamech's wives, listen to my speech.
A man I have killed for wounding me,

a boy for bruising me.
²⁴If Cain is avenged sevenfold,
    Lamech will be seventy-seven-fold."

²⁵Adam knew his wife, and she gave birth to a son. She named him Seth, "For God has set me another seed to take the place of Abel, for Cain killed him." ²⁶As for Seth, a son was born to him, and he named him Enosh. Then was it begun to call on the name of Yahweh.

Generations from Adam to Noah

5   ¹**This is the book of Adam's genealogy.** *On the day when God created Adam, in God's image he made him;* ²*male and female he created them. And he blessed them, and he called them "human," on the day that they were created.*

³**Adam lived 130 years and fathered** *a son in his likeness, according to his image, and he named him* **Seth. ⁴After he fathered Seth, Adam's days were 800 years. He fathered sons and daughters. ⁵All the days of Adam's life were 930 years, and he died. ⁶Seth lived 105 years and fathered Enosh. ⁷After he fathered Enosh, Seth lived 807 years. He fathered sons and daughters. ⁸All the days of Seth were 912 years, and he died. ⁹Enosh lived 90 years and fathered Kenan. ¹⁰After he fathered Kenan, Enosh lived 815 years. He fathered sons and daughters. ¹¹All the days of Enosh were 905 years, and he died. ¹²Kenan lived 70 years and fathered Mahalalel. ¹³After he fathered Mahalalel, Kenan lived 840 years. He fathered sons and daughters. ¹⁴All the days of Kenan were 910 years, and he died. ¹⁵Mahalalel lived 65 years and fathered Jared. ¹⁶After he fathered Jared, Mahalalel lived 830 years. He fathered sons and daughters. ¹⁷All the days of Mahalalel were 895 years, and he died. ¹⁸Jared lived 62 years and fathered Enoch. ¹⁹After he fathered Enoch, Jared lived 900 years. He fathered sons and daughters. ²⁰All the days of Jared were 962 years, and he died. ²¹Enoch lived 65 years and fathered Methuselah. ²²After he fathered Methuselah, Enoch walked with God for 300 years. He fathered sons and daughters. ²³All the days of Enoch were 365 years. ²⁴Enoch walked with God and then was no more, for God took him. ²⁵Methuselah lived 67 years and fathered Lamech. ²⁶After he fathered Lamech, Methuselah lived 902 years. He fathered sons and daughters. ²⁷All the days of Methuselah were 969 years, and he died. ²⁸Lamech lived 88 years and fathered** a son. ²⁹He named him Noah and said, "He will give us relief from our work, from our painful manual labor on the soil that Yahweh has cursed." ³⁰**After he fathered Noah, Lamech lived 665 years. He fathered sons and daughters. ³¹All the days of Lamech were 753 years, and he died. ³²Noah was 500 years old, and Noah fathered Shem, Ham, and Japheth.**

The Sons of God and the Daughters of Humans

6   ¹When humans began to multiply on the face of the earth, and daughters were born to them, ²the Sons of God saw that the daughters of humans were beautiful, and they took for themselves wives from whomever they chose. ³Yahweh said, "My breath will not be strong in humans forever, inasmuch as they are also flesh. Let their days be 120 years." ⁴The Nephilim were on the earth in those days, and also later, when the

Sons of God used to couple with the daughters of humans, who would bear children for them—they were the warriors of old, the men of renown.

The Flood

[5]Yahweh saw how great was the evil of humans on the earth, for every design of their hearts was only evil all day long. [6]Yahweh regretted that he had made humans on the earth, and his heart was pained. [7]Yahweh said, "I will wipe out humans *whom I created* from the face of the soil, *from humans to land animals to crawling creatures to the birds of heaven,* for I regret that I made them." [8]But Noah found favor in the eyes of Yahweh.

[9]**This is the genealogy of Noah. Noah was a righteous man, blameless in his generations; Noah walked with God. [10]Noah fathered three sons, Shem, Ham, and Japheth. [11]The earth was corrupt before God, for the earth was filled with violence. [12]And God saw the earth, and behold, it was corrupt, for all flesh had corrupted its way on earth.**

[13]**God said to Noah, "The end of all flesh has come before me, for the earth is filled with violence because of them. I am now going to destroy them and the earth. [14]Make yourself an ark with gopher wood, with reeds build the ark, and seal it inside and out with pitch. [15]This is how you shall make it: 300 cubits the ark's length, 50 cubits its width, and 30 cubits its height. [16]Make a roof over the ark and finish it 1 cubit from the top. Make a door in its side. Make a lower, a second, and a third deck. [17]As for me, I am going to bring the flood—water on the earth—to destroy all flesh under heaven that has within it life's breath. Everything on earth will die. [18]But I will make my covenant with you, and you shall enter the ark, you and your sons, your wife, and your sons' wives with you. [19]Of all living things, of all flesh, two of each you shall bring into the ark to save their lives with yours—they shall be male and female. You shall bring two of all living things, male and female of all flesh, into the ark to save their lives with yours. [20]Every kind of bird, every kind of land animal, every kind of creature that crawls on the earth—two of each will come to you to save their lives with you. [21]As for you, take every kind of edible food and gather it, for it will be your food and theirs." [22]Noah did everything as God commanded him, thus he did.**

7 [1]Yahweh said to Noah, "Enter the ark, you and all your household, for I see that you are a righteous man before me in this generation. [2]Of every clean animal, take them seven by seven, a male and its mate, and of every unclean animal take two, a male and its mate, [3]*also of every bird of heaven take them seven by seven, male and female,* to keep their seed alive on the whole earth. [4]For in seven days, I am going to bring rain on the earth for forty days and forty nights, and I will wipe off the face of the soil all living things that I have made." [5]Noah did everything as Yahweh commanded him.

[6]**Noah was 600 years old when the flood was on the earth.** [7]Noah, *his sons, his wife, and his sons' wives with him* entered the ark because of the flood waters. [8]*Of the clean land animals, the unclean animals, the birds, and all creatures that crawl on the earth,* [9]*two of each came to Noah in the ark, male and female, as God commanded Noah.* [10]The seventh day came, and the flood waters were on the earth. [11]**In the 600th year of Noah's life, in the second month, on the seventeenth day of the month, on that day,**

> all the wellsprings of the great ocean burst,
>> and the windows of heaven were opened.

[12]It rained on the earth for forty days and forty nights. **[13]On that very day Noah and Noah's sons—Shem, Ham, and Japheth—and Noah's wife, and his sons' three wives with them entered the ark. [14]Every kind of wild animal, every kind of domestic animal, every kind of creature that crawls on the earth, and every kind of bird [15]came to Noah in the ark, two by two of all flesh that has within it life's breath. [16]Those that came, male and female of all flesh, came as God had commanded him.** Then Yahweh shut him in.

[17]The flood was on the earth for forty days. The water rose and lifted the ark, and it was high above the earth. **[18]The water grew strong and multiplied mightily on the earth, and the ark floated on the face of the water. [19]The water grew so very strong on the earth that it covered every high mountain beneath all of heaven. [20]Fifteen cubits higher the water rose, and the mountains were covered. [21]All flesh that moved on the earth died—birds, domestic animals, wild animals, every creature that crawls on the earth, and all humans.** [22]Everything with life's breath in its nostrils, everything that lived on dry land, died. [23]He wiped off the face of the soil all living things—*from humans to land animals to crawling creatures to the birds of heaven. They were wiped off the earth.* Only Noah and those with him on the ark survived. **[24]The water grew strong on the earth for 150 days.**

8   **[1]Then God remembered Noah and all the wild and domestic animals that were with him on the ark. God sent a wind over the earth, and the water subsided. [2]The wellsprings of the ocean and the windows of heaven were shut fast.** Then the rain was withheld from heaven. [3]The water receded gradually on the earth. **The water began to diminish after 150 days. [4]In the seventh month, on the seventeenth day of the month, the ark came to rest in the mountains of Ararat. [5]The water continued to subside until the tenth month. In the tenth month, on the first day of the month, the mountain peaks appeared.**

[6]At the end of forty days, Noah opened the window of the ark that he had made. **[7]He sent out a raven, and it went back and forth until the water was dry on the earth.** [8]He sent out a dove that was with him to see if the water had subsided on the face of the soil. [9]But the dove did not find a place to rest its feet, so it returned to him on the ark, for the water still covered the whole face of the earth. He reached out his hand and caught it and brought it back into the ark. [10]He waited another seven days and again sent the dove from the ark. [11]The dove returned to him toward evening, and behold, in its beak was a plucked olive leaf, and Noah knew that the water had subsided on the face of the earth. [12]He waited another seven days and sent out the dove, but it did not return to him again. **[13]In his 601st year, in the first month, on the first day of the month, the water dried off the earth.** Noah removed the ark's cover, and he looked, and behold, the face of the soil was dry. **[14]In the second month, on the twenty-seventh day of the month, the earth was dry.**

[15]God said to Noah, **[16]"Go out of the ark, you and your wife, your sons, and your sons' wives with you. [17]Every living creature with you, all flesh—birds, land animals, and every creature that crawls on the earth—bring them out with you. Let them be fruitful and multiply on the earth." [18]Noah went out with his sons,**

his wife, and his sons' wives with him. ¹⁹Every living creature, every bird, and every creature that crawls on the earth came out of the ark, according to their families.

²⁰Noah built an altar for Yahweh. He took one of every clean animal and every clean bird and offered burnt offerings on the altar. ²¹Yahweh smelled the soothing aroma, and Yahweh said in his heart, "I will never again curse the soil because of humans, for the designs of the human heart are evil from their youth. Never again will I destroy all life as I have done. ²²For all the earth's days these shall never cease:

> seedtime and harvest, cold and heat,
>> summer and winter, and day and night."

9 ¹God blessed Noah and his sons and said to them, "Be fruitful and multiply and fill the earth. ²Dread and fear of you will come upon every creature on earth, every bird of the sky, everything that moves on the earth, and every fish of the sea. They are in your hands. ³Every living, moving creature will be your food. I hereby give them all to you, as I did the green plants. ⁴But flesh with its life's blood in it you shall not eat. ⁵Indeed, for your lives I will demand your blood. I will demand it from every creature and from humans. From a man regarding his brother, I will demand the man's life.

> ⁶Whoever sheds the blood of a human,
>> for a human will his blood be shed,
> for in God's image he made humans.

⁷As for you, be fruitful and multiply, teem over the earth, and rule it."

⁸God said to Noah and his sons with him, ⁹"As for me, I am going to make my covenant with you, with your descendants after you, ¹⁰and with every living creature that is with you—birds, land animals, and all the earth's creatures, everyone that left the ark. ¹¹I will make my covenant with you: Never again will all flesh be cut off by the flood waters; never again will there be another flood to destroy the earth." ¹²God said, "This is the sign of the covenant that I am making with you and all living creatures with you, for everlasting generations. ¹³I have set my bow in the clouds, and it will be a sign of the covenant between me and the earth. ¹⁴Whenever I bring rain clouds over the earth, the bow will appear in the clouds. ¹⁵And I will remember my covenant between me, you, and all living creatures, all flesh, and never again will the water become a flood to destroy all flesh. ¹⁶The bow will appear in the clouds, and I will see it and remember the eternal covenant between God and all living creatures, all flesh that is on earth." ¹⁷God said to Noah, "This is the sign of the covenant that I have made between me and all flesh that is on earth."

The Curse of Canaan

9 ¹⁸Noah's sons who left the ark were Shem, Ham, and Japheth. Ham was Canaan's father. ¹⁹These three were Noah's sons, and from them all the earth spread out.

²⁰Noah, a man of the soil, was the first to plant a vineyard. ²¹He drank some wine and became drunk and exposed himself within his tent. ²²Ham, Canaan's father, saw his father's nakedness, and he told his two brothers outside. ²³Shem and Japheth took a robe and draped it over both of their shoulders, and they went in backwards and covered their father's nakedness. Since they faced backwards, they did not see their

father's nakedness. ²⁴When Noah awoke from his wine, and he knew what his youngest son had done to him, ²⁵he said, "Cursed be Canaan—he shall be the lowest slave to his brothers!" ²⁶He said, "Blessed be Yahweh, the God of Shem—may Canaan be his slave. ²⁷May God enlarge Japheth—may he dwell in Shem's tents, and may Canaan be his slave."

²⁸**After the flood Noah lived 350 years. ²⁹All the days of Noah's life were 950 years, and he died.**

The Table of Nations

10 ¹**This is the genealogy of Noah's sons, Shem, Ham, and Japheth.** Sons were born to them after the flood.

²**Japheth's sons were Gomer and Magog and Maday and Yavan and Tubal and Meshech and Tiras. ³Gomer's sons were Ashkenaz and Diphat and Togarmah. ⁴Yavan's sons were Elisha and Tarshish, the Kittites and the Rodanites. ⁵From these the maritime nations branched off. These are Japheth's sons by their lands, each according to his language, families, and nations.**

⁶**Ham's sons were Cush and Egypt and Put and Canaan. ⁷Cush's sons were Seba and Havilah and Sabtah and Raamah and Sabteka. Raamah's sons were Sheba and Dedan.** ⁸Cush fathered Nimrod. He was the first to be a warrior on earth. ⁹He became a mighty hunter before Yahweh. Therefore it is said, "Like Nimrod, a mighty hunter before Yahweh." ¹⁰The chief cities of his kingdom were Babel and Erech and Akkad and Calneh, in the land of Sumer. ¹¹From that land he went up to Asshur and built Nineveh and Rehovot-Ir and Calah ¹²and Resen, between Nineveh and Calah, the great city. ¹³Egypt fathered the Ludites and the Anamites and the Lehabites and the Naphtuhites ¹⁴and the Patrusites and the Casluhites, from which came the Philistines, and the Caphtorites. ¹⁵Canaan fathered his firstborn, Sidon, and Heth ¹⁶and the Jebusites and the Amorites and the Girgashites ¹⁷and the Hivites and the Arkites and the Sinites ¹⁸and the Arvadites and the Zemarites and the Hamatites. Afterwards the families of Canaan spread out. ¹⁹Canaan's boundaries extended from Sidon in the direction of Gerar as far as Gaza, and in the direction of Sodom, Gomorrah, Admah, and Zeboiim as far as Lasha. ²⁰**These are Ham's sons according to their families, languages, lands, and nations.**

²¹As for Shem, sons were also born to him. He was the father of *all the sons of* Eber, and he was Japheth's older brother. ²²**Shem's sons were Elam and Asshur and Arpachshad and Lud and Aram. ²³Aram's sons were Uz and Hul and Gether and Mash.** ²⁴*Arpachshad fathered Shelah, and Shelah fathered Eber.* ²⁵As for Eber, two sons were born. The name of the first was Peleg, for in his time the earth was divided, and the name of his brother was Joktan. ²⁶Joktan fathered Almodad and Shaleph and Hazarmaveth and Yarah ²⁷and Hadoram and Uzal and Diklah ²⁸and Obal and Abimael and Sheba ²⁹and Ophir and Havilah and Jobab—all of these were Joktan's sons. ³⁰Their territory extended from Mesha in the direction of Sepharah, the eastern mountain. ³¹**These are Shem's sons according to their families, languages, lands, and nations.**

³²**These are the families of Noah's sons according to their genealogy and nations. From these the peoples branched out over the earth after the flood.**

The Tower of Babel

11 ¹All the earth had one language and one set of words. ²As they journeyed in the east they came upon a valley in the land of Sumer, and they settled there. ³Each one said to his neighbor, "Come, let us mold bricks and bake them in fire"—for bricks served as stone for them, and pitch served as mortar for them. ⁴They said, "Come, let us build for ourselves a city and a tower with its top in heaven, and let us make a name for ourselves, lest we be spread out over all the earth."

⁵Yahweh came down to see the city and the tower that the children of humans had built. ⁶Yahweh said, "Behold, they are one people with one language for all of them, and this is what they begin to do. Now there will be no restraining them from whatever they plan to do. ⁷Come, let us go down and confuse their language there, so that no one will understand his neighbor's language." ⁸Yahweh spread them out from there over all the earth, and they ceased building the city. ⁹Therefore they call its name Babel, for there Yahweh confused all the earth's language, and from there Yahweh spread them out over all the earth.

Generations from Shem to Abram

11 ¹⁰This is the genealogy of Shem. Shem was 100 years old and fathered Arpachshad, two years after the flood. ¹¹After he fathered Arpachshad, Shem lived 500 years. He fathered sons and daughters. ¹²Arpachshad lived 35 years and fathered Shelah. ¹³After he fathered Shelah, Arpachshad lived 403 years. He fathered sons and daughters. ¹⁴Shelah lived 30 years and fathered Eber. ¹⁵After he fathered Eber, Shelah lived 403 years. He fathered sons and daughters. ¹⁶Eber lived 34 years and fathered Peleg. ¹⁷After he fathered Peleg, Eber lived 370 years. He fathered sons and daughters. ¹⁸Peleg lived 30 years and fathered Reu. ¹⁹After he fathered Reu, Peleg lived 209 years. He fathered sons and daughters. ²⁰Reu lived 32 years and fathered Serug. ²¹After he fathered Serug, Reu lived 207 years. He fathered sons and daughters. ²²Serug lived 30 years and fathered Nahor. ²³After he fathered Nahor, Serug lived 200 years. He fathered sons and daughters. ²⁴Nahor lived 29 years and fathered Terah. ²⁵After he fathered Terah, Nahor lived 119 years. He fathered sons and daughters. ²⁶Terah lived 70 years and fathered Abram, Nahor, and Haran.

²⁷This is the genealogy of Terah. Terah fathered Abram, Nahor, and Haran, and Haran fathered Lot. ²⁸Haran died before his father Terah in the land of his kin, *in Ur of the Chaldeans.* ²⁹Abram and Nahor took for themselves wives. Abram's wife's name was Sarai, and Nahor's wife's name was Milcah, the daughter of Haran, who was the father of Milcah and Iscah. ³⁰Sarai was barren; she had no son. ³¹Terah took his son Abram, and Haran's son Lot, his grandson, and his daughter-in-law Sarai, his son Abram's wife, and he sent them from Ur of the Chaldeans to go to the land of Canaan. They came to Haran and settled there. ³²The days of Terah's life were 205 years, and Terah died in Haran.

NOTES AND COMMENTS

Creation (1:1–2:3; **P**)

1   ¹In the beginning, when God created heaven and earth—²the earth was desolate chaos, and darkness was over the face of the ocean, and a wind of God was soaring over the face of the water—³God said, "Let there be light," and there was light. ⁴And God saw that the light was good, and God separated the light from the darkness. ⁵And God called the light "day," and the darkness he called "night." There was evening and there was morning, one day.

⁶God said, "Let there be a vault within the water, and let it separate water from water." ⁷And God made the vault and separatedᵃ the water below the vault from the water above the vault. And it was so.ᵇ ⁸And God called the vault "heaven."ᶜ There was evening and there was morning, a second day.

⁹God said, "Let the water below heaven be gathered into one place,ᵈ so that dry land may appear." And it was so.ᵉ ¹⁰And God called the dry land "earth," and the pool of water he called "seas." And God saw that it was good.

¹¹God said, "Let the earth grow seed-bearing plants and fruit trees with seed-bearing fruitᶠ on the earth." And it was so. ¹²And the earth yielded seed-bearing plants of every kind and trees with seed-bearing fruit of every kind. And God saw that it was good. ¹³There was evening and there was morning, a third day.

¹⁴God said, "Let there be lights in the vault of heavenᵍ to separate the day from the night. And let them be signs for festivals, days, andʰ years, ¹⁵and let them be lights in the vault of heaven to light up the earth." And it was so. ¹⁶And God made the two great lights—the greater light to rule the day and the lesser light to rule the night—and the stars. ¹⁷And God set them in the vault of heaven to light up the earth, ¹⁸to rule the day and the night, and to separate the light from the darkness. And God saw that it was good. ¹⁹There was evening and there was morning, a fourth day.

²⁰God said, "Let the waters teem with teeming living creatures, and let birds fly over the earth across the vault of heaven.ⁱ ²¹And God created the great sea

monsters and every kind of moving life with which the waters teem, and every kind of winged bird. And God saw that it was good. ²²And God blessed them and said, "Be fruitful and multiply, fill the water of the seas, and let the birds be fruitful on the earth." ²³There was evening and there was morning, a fifth day.

²⁴God said, "Let the earth yield every kind of living creature—domestic animals, and crawling creatures and wild animals of the earth of every kind." And it was so. ²⁵And God made wild animals of the earth of every kind and domestic animals of every kind and land-crawling creatures of every kind. And God saw that it was good.

²⁶God said, "Let us make a human in our image, according to our likeness, so that they may rule the fish of the sea and the birds of heaven and the animalsʲ and every crawling creature on earth."

²⁷God created the human in his image;ᵏ
in God's image he created him;
male and female he created them.

²⁸And God blessed them, and God said to them, "Be fruitful and multiply, fill the earth, and subdue it. Rule the fish of the sea and the birds of heaven and every creature that moves on earth." ²⁹And God said, "I hereby give to you all seed-bearing plants on the whole face of the earth and all trees with seed-bearing fruit.ˡ They will be food for you. ³⁰And for every creature on earth, for every bird in heaven, for everything that moves on earth, that has life's breath within it, all green plants will be food." And it was so. ³¹And God saw all that he had made, and behold, it was very good. There was evening and there was morning, the sixth day.
2   ¹Now heaven and earth and all their array were complete. ²On the sixthᵐ day God completed his work that he had made, and on the seventh day he ceased from all his work that he had made. ³And God blessed the seventh day and made it holy, for on it he ceased from all his work that God had made in creation.

Textual Notes

a. The LXX adds *ho theos* = ʾlhym ("God") as the agent of *wybdl* ("separated"), an explication of an ambiguity (Hendel 1998: 23).

b. The LXX has this refrain "and it was so" at the end of 1:6, before the *Tatbericht* ("deed report"), a harmonization to the refrain's position in later verses (Hendel 1998: 20–23).

c. The LXX has the refrain "and God saw that it was good" after the *Tatbericht*, a harmonization to the refrain's position in later verses. The refrain is lacking here in the MT and SP, yielding a sevenfold repetition in all (including variations) in 1:4, 10, 12, 18, 21, 25, 31 (Hendel 1998: 23–24).

d. Reading *mqwm* ("place") with the MT and SP. The LXX and 4QGenʰ have *mqwh* ("pool"), probably a harmonization with this word later in the verse (Rösel 1994: 38–39; Tal 2015: 78*; cf. Hendel 1998: 24–25).

e. The LXX and (partially) 4QGenᵏ have a longer reading, providing the *Tatbericht* to this work of creation, which is lacking in the MT and SP. The longer version is probably a harmonizing plus, following the structure of the other works of creation (Tov 1985: 21–22; cf. Hendel 1998: 25–27).

f. Reading with the LXX. The MT, SP, and 4QGen[b] add *lmynw* ("of every kind"), which breaks up the phrase *pry 'šr zr'w bw* ("seed-bearing fruit," lit. "fruit that has its seed in it"). The plus is probably a harmonization with the corresponding phrase *pry 'šr zr'w bw lmynhw* in 1:12 (Hendel 1998: 28).

g. The SP and LXX add *lh'yr 'l h'rṣ* ("to light up the earth") after *hšmym* ("heaven"), a harmonization with the same sequence in 1:15, 17 (Hendel 1998: 28–29).

h. Reading *wl* with 4QGen[k] and the LXX. The MT lacks *l*, which disrupts the pattern of coordinated nouns (Hendel 1998: 41–42).

i. The LXX has the refrain "and it was so" between the *Wortbericht* ("word report") and *Tatbericht*, as elsewhere in the text. The refrain is lacking here in the MT and SP, yielding a sevenfold repetition (including variations) in 1:3, 7, 9, 11, 15, 24, 30 (Hendel 1998: 20–23).

j. The MT, SP, and LXX add *wbkl h'rṣ* ("and all the earth"), an anomalous phrase that is probably a corruption of the sequence that follows, *wbkl . . . h'rṣ* (Hendel 1998: 42–43). The LXX also has this phrase in 1:28, harmonized from 1:26.

k. The LXX omits *bṣlmw* ("in his image"), a homoiarkton (omission by similar beginnings) in the sequence *bṣlmw bṣlm* ("in his image, in the image") (Hendel 1998: 29–30).

l. Reading with the LXX. The MT and SP add *'ṣ* ("tree") to *pry* ("fruit"), which makes no sense here and was probably an accidental anticipation of the phrase *pry 'ṣ* in 3:2 and 3:3 (Hendel 1998: 32).

m. Reading *hššy* ("sixth") with the SP and LXX, a reading also attested in the Syriac Peshitta and Jub. 2:16. The MT reads *hšby'y* ("seventh"), probably by a scribal anticipation of *hšby'y* in a nearly identical word sequence in the second half of the verse: *bywm hšby'y mkl ml'ktw 'šr 'śh* ("on the seventh day from all his work that he had done") (Hendel 1998: 32–34).

Notes

1:1. *In the beginning, when God created.* Genesis begins with a wordplay and a rare grammatical construction: *bərē'šît bārā' 'ĕlōhîm.* The wordplay is the sonic echo in the first two words, *bərē'šît bārā'*—note the common letters *br'* (Sasson 1992: 186 n. 13). A striking sequence of sounds and sense (*bərē' . . . bārā' 'ĕlōhîm*) begins this chapter, creating a rhythmic opening to God's work of creation. The verb *bārā'* ("create") is used only with God as a subject; it is a technical term for God's unique power of creation (Garr 2004). This verb recurs in God's creations of the great sea dragons (1:21) and humans (1:27), in the last verse of the account (2:3), and in the transition to the following story (2:4a, R). The latter two verses consciously echo the phraseology of the opening verse, repeating the phrases *bārā' 'ĕlōhîm* ("God created") and *haššāmayim wəhā'āreṣ* ("heaven and earth"), forming a literary frame (*inclusio*) around the whole creation account. The wordplay at the beginning announces key thematic and literary structures of the text. It also subtly anticipates the role of words and sounds in God's acts of creation.

The rare grammar has a construct noun, *bərē'šît*, as the head of a verbal clause, *bārā' 'ĕlōhîm.* Grammarians have argued about whether *bərē'šît* should be construed in the absolute state, "In the beginning, (God created . . .)," or in the construct state, "In the beginning of (God created . . .)." The temporal sense of the latter can be highlighted by translating with a temporal adverb, "In the beginning, when (God created . . .)." Rashi and Ibn Ezra solved this problem already in favor of the construct reading. An updated version of their solution is as follows.

This type of grammatical construction, with a noun in construct with a verbal clause (called an unmarked or asyndetic relative clause), is attested elsewhere in the Bible and is common in Semitic languages (see *IBHS* §9.6d–e; G. Goldenberg 2013: 231–41; Pat-El 2014). In Hebrew this construction usually occurs with situations of time or place, for example, *təḥillat dibber-yhwh bəhôšēaʿ* ("In the beginning when Yahweh spoke to Hosea" or "When God began to speak to Hosea," Hos 1:2) and *qiryat ḥānâ dāwīd* ("the city where David camped," Isa 29:1). It also occurs before negated verbs, for example, *śəpat lō-yādaʿtî* ("a language I do not know," Ps 81:6). The temporal/spatial situation also occurs in a seventh-century BCE Philistine inscription from Ekron: *bt bn ʾkyš* ("the house that Akayus built," Aḥituv 2008: 336–38). Many instances of this construction are in poetry, indicating that it has a high stylistic register. It is an authentic grammatical construction in Classical Hebrew, which became obsolete in Late Biblical Hebrew. (Cf. the more common construction of a temporal noun in construct with an infinitive, e.g., *bəyôm bərōʾ ʾĕlōhîm*, "on the day of God's creating" or "on the day that God created," Gen 5:1.)

The word in construct with the verbal clause lacks a definite article. Hence the LXX translates the first word as *en archē* ("in beginning")—it would have translated the definite form *bārēʾšît* with an article, *en tē archē* ("in the beginning," Wevers 1993: 1). Evidence from some Greek Hexaplaric transliterations suggests that the vocalization with a definite article existed in some reading traditions (but see the cautions of Rüterswörden and Warmuth 1993). The Samaritan reading tradition vocalizes the word as indefinite, *bārāšət*, but the Samaritan targum and the Samaritan Arabic translation imply a definite form (Schorch 2021: xlvii). The latter would be explicable as a linguistic modernization of an archaic grammatical construction.

However, as Barr (2013: 180–81) has observed, words for remote time commonly lack the definite article even when they are semantically definite (e.g., *mērēʾšît*, "from *the* beginning," Isa 46:10). Hence *bərēʾšît* could be grammatically definite without the definite article. But the absolute reading "In the beginning, God created heaven and earth," taken as a punctual event, is contradicted by the subsequent references to heaven and earth. The earth exists in 1:2, but it is a desolate chaos. Heaven is created on the second day (1:6–7), rendering the punctual reading of 1:1 unlikely. But the view of 1:1 as a punctual event has its defenders, taking the creation to be an inchoate heaven and earth (Wenham 1987: 12–13; Day 2013: 7–8). It is also possible to regard the absolute reading as a rubric or superscription for the whole account rather than as a punctual event (so Jenni 1989; Barr 2013: 178–82; Gertz 2018: 36–37; similarly, Westermann 1984: 97), but this sits awkwardly with the description of the earth in 1:2 as *tōhû wābōhû* ("desolate chaos") and lacks analogies in biblical prose narrative. Early translators and interpreters adopted various exegetical strategies to resolve the difficulties of the meaning of the absolute reading, which was usually taken to be the natural reading in postbiblical Hebrew (see Anderson 1990; Kugel 1998: 44–47).

The construct reading, in which *bərēʾšît* is the head of a temporal clause, makes good sense in context, followed by the background clause in 1:2 and the first punctual clause in 1:3. The introduction with a temporal clause is common in other biblical and ancient Near Eastern creation myths, including Gen 2:4b, "On the day that Yahweh God made earth and heaven," and *Enuma Elish,* "When the heavens above did not exist, / And earth beneath had not come into being" (Lambert 2013: 50–51). This construction in Hebrew suits the solemnity of the occasion. For these and similar reasons, most modern treatments prefer this reading (e.g., Ewald 1879: §332d; Joüon and Muraoka 1993: §129p3; Speiser 1964: 12–13; Bauks 1997: 81–86; Holmstedt 2008).

The postbiblical "forgetting" of the Classical Hebrew construction eventually gave rise to the idea of creation out of nothing (*creatio ex nihilo*) (Kugel 1998: 60–63). This idea seems to be first expressed in 2 Macc 7:28: "God did not make them [heaven and earth] out of existing things." But the phrase "existing things" (*ontōn*) may refer to formed matter in contrast to unformed primordial matter (Winston 2001: 60). Other biblical passages, such as Isa 44:24, "It is I, Yahweh, who created everything," contributed to the later concept of *creatio ex nihilo.* (It is possible that this verse in Second Isaiah is actually contesting the plural subject of Gen 1:26, "Let us make . . . ," by insisting that Yahweh was the sole creator; Weinfeld 2004: 115–16).

The Classical Hebrew construction, which is attested but rare, has a literary effect here, beginning the account in an unusual and quasi-poetic register of speech. This colors the account as other than normal speech—more formal, ancient, and authoritative.

heaven and earth. This phrase is a merism, that is, a pair of polar opposites that denotes the totality encompassed by them (Krašovec 1977: 16–25). In this sense, "heaven and earth" is a concrete expression for "the cosmos," a usage found elsewhere in the ancient Near East (Ottosson 1974: 389–93; cf. the divine title "Creator of heaven and earth" in Gen 14:19–22). In the context of 1:1, which anticipates what is to come, the phrase clearly means more than just two things—"heaven" and "earth"—since God creates many more things. Moreover, God doesn't seem to create the earth; it is presented as part of the preexisting chaos in 1:2. The sense of the phrase "heaven and earth" as "cosmos" changes somewhat in the retrospective statement in 2:1, "Now heaven and earth and all their array were complete." In this resumption of the phrase, the merism breaks down into its individual components: heaven, earth, and everything that fills them. This is part of the literary style of the piece, distinguished by repetition with subtle variations. In other words, the merism in 1:1 unravels into its components. The words "heaven" and "earth" anticipate the subsequent focus on earth (1:2, 10) and heaven (1:6–8).

Probably unrelated to the usage of this phrase is the Canaanite double deity "Earth-and-Heaven" (*'arṣ wšmm*), listed in Ugaritic ritual texts as a recipient of sacrificial offerings (Pardee 2002, texts 1–3 and 12). This reflects the common practice of divinizing cosmic features in ancient Near Eastern religions (del Olmo Lete 2004: 75–78). A similar tendency is the invocation of divine or semidivine pairs such as "heaven and earth" as witnesses in treaties, as found in Hittite, Mesopotamian, Canaanite, and Aramean texts (Hutter 1999). This custom is shared in biblical texts, in which heaven and earth are summoned as witnesses in prophetic judgment oracles and other covenantal texts (e.g., Deut 4:26, 32:1; Isa 1:2; Mic 6:2; Ps 50:4; see Cross 1998: 80–81).

1:2. *the earth was desolate chaos, and darkness was over the face of the ocean, and a wind of God was soaring over the face of the water.* Grammatically, 1:2 is a series of three disjunctive clauses, providing background information. This is marked by conjunctive *waw* + noun at the head of each clause. The types of verbs in these clauses—statives or participles ("was," "was soaring")—further indicate the background quality of these situations.

These three clauses describe the chaotic state of the universe before the beginning of God's work of creation, at the time "when God began to create." Each of the physical features of this primeval chaos—earth, air, darkness, and water—is reconfigured by God during the first three days to become functional aspects of the ordered cosmos (Zenger 1983: 83–84; see COMMENTS). By this process, God transforms the features of the primordial world into functioning parts of the ordered cosmos.

The three disjunctive background clauses give a complicated and obscure picture of the primordial chaos. Stylistically, these background clauses add a meandering complexity to the text's opening sequence. They also have a quasi-poetic effect—note the parallelisms of sound and sense among the final noun phrases in the three clauses: *tōhû wābōhû* ("desolate chaos"), *'al-pənê təhôm* ("over the face of the ocean"), and *'al-pənê hammāyim* ("over the face of the water"). *Tōhû* has an alliterative echo in *təhôm*, and *'al-pənê təhôm* has a parallelism of sound and meaning in *'al-pənê hammāyim*. This rhythmic and complicated sequence shifts dramatically in 1:3 into the first foregrounded sequence—the terse statement of God's creation of light. The initial obscurity is resolved with respect to style, syntax, and content.

the earth. The repetition of "the earth" at the end of 1:1 and the beginning of 1:2—*hā 'āreṣ wəhā 'āreṣ* ("the earth . . . the earth")—presents an artful transition and contrast. The two "earths" have different meanings, the first as part of the merism "heaven and earth," and the second as a picture of the chaotic, primordial earth. In the disjunctive background clause of 1:2, the earth is shown to be submerged in watery darkness and hence unsuitable for life. Creation is a process whereby God transforms this primordial chaos into a well-ordered world, filled with life and governed by humans under God's authority. It is in this sense that the earth becomes "complete" (2:1).

desolate chaos. Hebrew *tōhû wābōhû* is a rhyming phrase connoting chaos, desolation, and emptiness. Formally it is a hendiadys, a sequence of two nouns connected by conjunctive *wā-* in which one noun modifies the other. The word *tōhû* usually means "wasteland," as in a desert landscape, and by extension, "emptiness, nothingness" (cf. Ugaritic *thw,* probably /*tuhwu*/, "wilderness"; Huehnergard 1987: 287; del Olmo Lete and Sanmartín 2004: 864–65). *Tōhû* also presents a wordplay with *təhôm* ("ocean") later in the verse. *Bōhû* is not an independent word; it occurs only in conjunction with or parallel to *tōhû* (Isa 34:11 and Jer 4:23 [see COMMENTS]) and probably originated as its rhyming partner, like English "helter skelter."

A connection with the Mesopotamian goddess Bau is doubtful, since the first-millennium pronunciation was most likely Babu (Marchesi 2001). The Hellenistic *Phoenician History* of Philo of Byblos has a primordial goddess Baau, but she may be a reflection of biblical *bōhû* (Attridge and Oden 1981: 80). The name of the Gnostic demiurge Yaldabaoth, from Aramaic *yaldā' bōhû,* "child (of) chaos," is exegetically derived from Gen 1:2; compare the Gnostic spirit called Thauthabaoth, a clear reflection of *tōhû wābōhû* (Winston 2001: 63).

darkness. Ḥōšek ("darkness") is the antithesis of *'ôr* ("light"), which is the first work of creation (1:3). Since God sees that the light is "good," darkness is by implication not good. The negative connotation of darkness is reinforced by other passages in the Bible in which darkness is often associated with danger, destruction, evil, or death.

The wicked "walk in the ways of darkness" (Prov 2:13) and "put darkness in place of light" (Isa 5:20); Job curses the day he was born by saying, "May that day be darkness" (Job 3:4); the realm of the dead is "darkness" (Ps 88:13, Eccl 11:8); darkness is a divine plague (Exod 10:21). The darkness of primordial chaos is not overtly evil or threatening; it suggests more an absence of goodness and order, a latent chaos. As such, it provides a backdrop for and foil to God's first act of creation—light, the first clearly good thing.

ocean. The word *təhôm* ("ocean, sea") is generally found in poetry in the Bible, often referring to the deepest part of the sea. It is cognate with Ugaritic *thm(t)* and Akkadian *tiāmtu*, both meaning "ocean, sea." The Akkadian word is personified in the Babylonian creation myth *Enuma Elish* as a primordial watery goddess, Tiamat, and at Ugarit this word is part of the double deity "Mountain-and-Oceans" (*ġrm wthmt*). Babylonian Tiamat is a transformation of the older Sumerian goddess Namma, who is associated with the subterranean waters (*apsû*) and who is "the primeval mother who had given birth to the great gods" (Lambert 2013: 427; *Enki and Ninmah,* line 16).

It is unlikely that *təhôm* in Gen 1:2 has any direct connection with Babylonian Tiamat (Alster 1999), beyond the general idea of the primordial waters preexisting the creation of an ordered cosmos (see COMMENTS). However, an allusion (or counter-text) to *Enuma Elish* cannot be excluded. The primeval ocean is a conceptual feature also shared with Egyptian religion, in the primeval divine waters (Nun), and with archaic Greek religion (Okeanos). The ocean, like the darkness, is a latent force of chaos, both in the primordial world and in the world of human existence (Levenson 1988: 14–25).

In biblical traditions, the primeval ocean can be a static, inchoate force or an active primeval monster. According to Ps 104:6, God covered the earth with the *təhôm* (a tradition different from that of Genesis 1, where the *təhôm* covers the earth before God's work of creation), which then fled in alarm at God's thundering voice. The image of the calm, passive, and purely material ocean in Gen 1:2 may be a revision of the older Israelite tradition of theomachy, God's battle with the primeval sea monster(s) (cf. the reference to "the great sea dragons" in 1:21, below). The word *təhôm* never takes a definite article, which may derive from its background as a personified cosmic figure, but there is no hint of personification in 1:2.

a wind of God. The word *rûaḥ* means "breath, wind," and by extension, "spirit, self, mind." In the Bible, God's breath can be a wind, as when God blows his *rûaḥ* against the waters of the Re(e)d Sea (Exod 15:8, 10). A more abstract sense of God's "spirit" soaring above the waters is possible in the present context, but the more concrete sense of God's breath as wind is suggested by the use of the similar image in the P flood story: "God sent a wind (*rûaḥ*) over the earth, and the water subsided" (Gen 8:1). The end of the flood in P ushers in a new creation, using many of the same images and themes as in Genesis 1. By seeing that the soaring or hovering *rûaḥ* in 1:2 anticipates its return in 8:1, we perceive its role as a *Leitwort* in both verses. In each case the presence of God's wind is a sign that creation (or re-creation) is about to begin (Ska 1981: 528–29).

In the created cosmos, this wind is probably to be understood as the precursor of air, which circulates beneath the vault of heaven. The divine wind may thus be akin to the life-giving breath that Yahweh God blows into the human's nostrils in the J creation story (2:7). That the atmosphere is a later form of the "wind of God" is not explicit in the text, but it may be implicit in its terrestrial location ("over the face of the water").

As with the passive image of the primeval ocean, this image of the divine wind may also be related to the old stories of a cosmic battle in which God's wind is a weapon against the waters (cf. Exod 15:8–10, Job 26:13, the Ugaritic myth of Baal, and the Babylonian myth *Enuma Elish* [Day 1985: 53]). God's wind, in the present context, is not a weapon but a sign of nascent divine activity and perhaps of life-giving air. It is also a prelude to his first speech, which is a form of articulate breath. The creative potential of God's breath/wind has been compared to the primordial principle *mummû* in *Enuma Elish,* which, according to Frahm (2013: 110), "designates creative energy, or spirit, closely associated with the world of the gods and occasionally hypostasized." In the late Phoenician cosmogony in Philo of Byblos's *Phoenician History,* air or wind is the primordial element and "the source of everything" (*tēn tōn holōn archēn*) (Attridge and Oden 1981: 36–37, 75–76; Darshan 2019: 54), which may derive from a mixture of Phoenician and Greek cosmology. Note that air or wind is the "first principle of beings" (*archē tōn ontōn*) in Anaximenes's Presocratic cosmology.

soaring over the face of the water. The phrase *'al-pənê hammāyim* ("over the face of the water") is parallel to the phrase *'al-pənê təhôm* ("over the face of the ocean") in the previous clause. In the rhythmic prose of this description of primordial chaos, this semantic and grammatical parallelism indicates that the "ocean" and the "water" refer to the same watery body, although with slightly different connotations. The word *mayim* (the long *ā* is pausal) lacks the cosmic connotations of *təhôm* and suggests that the primordial body of water is not a personified deity. The equivalence of "ocean" and "water" is counterbalanced by the contrast between the primordial "darkness" over the ocean and the "wind of God" hovering over the water. This latter contrast points toward the movement from chaos ("darkness") to God's incipient activity of creation. The participle *mərahepet* ("hovering, soaring") echoes the sounds of *rûah,* its subject, as if it were its verbal extension. It has a durative and unbounded sense, with a hint of expectation, something about to begin.

1:3. *God said.* This is the first punctual event of the narrative. Grammatically, the verb (a converted imperfect) resumes the foregrounded narrative sequence begun by the temporal clause of 1:1, after the background sequence of disjunctive clauses of 1:2. (On converted imperfects after circumstantial clauses, see *IBHS* §33.2.4a.) Verses 1–3 have the following syntactic structure: "¹when *X* . . . ²at which time . . . ³then *Y.*" This is the same structure as the beginning of the J creation account in 2:4b–7, and it is found in other ancient Near Eastern creation accounts, such as *Enuma Elish* (Speiser 1964: 12). It is plausible that P modeled this sequence after the beginning of the J story or after the wider generic convention (see COMMENTS).

The initial act of creation is a speech-act. The creative word of God is a powerful concept. This method of creation defines God as an unmoving mover, transcendent and omnipotent, establishing the classical conception of God in later Judaism and Christianity. It is worth noting that the priests (including the writer[s] of the P source) often discharged their duties by effective speech-acts, declaring a thing holy or profane, clean or unclean (Lev 10:10). The concept of God in this passage is, in some respects, a cosmic model for the priests' own practice of religious power.

The parallel images of God's breath, speech, and command in this context are presented strikingly in Ps 33:6, 9:

By the word of Yahweh, heaven was created,
And by the breath of his mouth, all its host. . . .
For he spoke, and it was,
He commanded, and it was established.

The concept of God's creative word is also found in ancient Near Eastern religions, as in *Enuma Elish,* where the assembled gods test Marduk (Bēl) to see whether he has the power to create and destroy:

"Your destiny, Bēl, is superior to that of all the gods,
    Command and bring about annihilation and re-creation.
Let the constellation disappear at your utterance,
    With a second command let the constellation reappear."
He gave the command and the constellation disappeared,
    With a second command the constellation came into being again.

(IV.22–26; Lambert 2013: 86–87)

In Egypt the concept of divine creative speech is *ḥw,* "Annunciation" (Allen 1988: 36–38). When the creator-god conceives of his plan and speaks, the effective power of his speech creates the cosmos:

I am the one who made what is and caused what was not to develop:
when I spoke, Annunciation (*ḥw*) developed.

(Coffin Text 4.145; Allen 1988: 38)

In the Memphite Theology, the god Ptah creates the cosmos through his thought and speech:

So were all the gods born,
Atum and his Ennead as well,
For it is through what the heart plans and the tongue commands that every
divine speech has developed.

(lines 20–22; Allen 1988: 44)

"Let there be light," and there was light. The terse and airy quality of God's command, *yəhî 'ôr* ("let there be light"), and its immediate fulfillment, *wayhî-'ôr* ("and there was light"), is a dramatic stylistic counterpoint to the complex and meandering sequence that precedes it. In the only reference to the Hebrew Bible in classical literature, Pseudo-Longinus praises this verse (in its Greek translation) as an example of the sublime in literature (*On the Sublime* 9.9). The brief expressiveness of God's first words and their immediate, precise instantiation show God's mastery over the primeval chaos and his authoritative knowledge. Creation by speech-act also shows that God knows the names of things and summons them into being by invoking their names.

Elsewhere light is often portrayed as a divine attribute. In Ps 104:2 God is "wrapped in light as with a garment," an image of the brilliant glow of God's presence. This lucid substance awakens and illuminates the nascent cosmos. The light of the first day is the binary opposite of the primeval darkness and will alternate with the darkness in the divinely instituted rhythm of time (Gen 1:4–5). On the fourth day it will be coordinated with the movements of the sun (see NOTES at 1:14). This first act of creation sets the chain of subsequent creations into motion and shatters the stasis of primeval chaos.

The grammar highlights this shift, moving from the stative and durative situation of 1:2 to the punctual event of 1:3. God's first speech abruptly starts the transformation of a timeless chaos into a dynamic cosmos.

Because of God's effective speech-act, his command (the *Wortbericht*, "word report") lacks a corresponding statement of the "making" of that creation (the *Tatbericht*, "deed report"; see NOTES at 1:7). Instead, the fulfillment, *wayhî-'ôr* ("and there was light"), is a variation of the refrain *wayhî-kēn* ("and it was so"; see NOTES at 1:7). This refrain occurs seven times in Genesis 1, including the variation in this verse. The narration of the first act of creation is minimalistic yet points toward the elaboration of its stylistic form in the subsequent acts of creation.

This sevenfold repetition, beginning with *wayhî-'ôr*, is one of several uses of seven as a structuring principle in the text. Seven is the number of days in this account, and God sanctifies the seventh day. Seven signifies wholeness or completeness. In Akkadian, the number seven is sometimes translated as "totality" (*kiššatu*), and in the Bible it has the same nuance. God promises that Cain will be avenged "sevenfold" (Gen 4:15); there are seven years of plenty and seven years of famine in the Joseph story (Gen 41:26–27), and festivals generally last seven days (Exod 23:15, etc.). Other sequences of seven can be found in this account; for instance, Cassuto (1961: 12–15) observes that the first verse has seven words. There is also variation from the number seven, as there are eight acts of creation, which occur over six days. Variation of structured repetition is a key feature of P's narrative style.

1:4. *God saw that the light was good.* This is an expansion of the refrain "God saw that it was good," which occurs seven times (1:4, 10, 12, 18, 21, 25, 31; with variations in the first and last instances). As with the refrain "and it was so" (with variation in the first instance in 1:3), sevenfold repetitions circulate in the structure of creation.

God's perception here begins as a purely sensory act—"God saw the light"—as the light comes into being. But it turns into a more nuanced perception with the following subordinate clause, *kî-ṭôb* ("that it was good"). The shift of God's perception from physical luminosity to a moral, aesthetic, and functional judgment shapes our perception of God's power to perceive the outer and inner nature of things.

The word *kî* in the phrase *kî-ṭôb* marks the subordinate clause, "that (it was good)," but can also have an emphatic nuance, yielding the sense "how (good it was)" (Hamilton 1990: 118; *IBHS* §38.8d). The word *ṭôb* ("good") has a wide range of connotations. When the objects of creation are seen to be "good," it seems to mean well-formed, entailing moral and/or functional goodness. It generally signifies God's satisfaction with his works of creation.

God's perception of the goodness of things in Genesis 1 is reversed at the beginning of the P flood story, when God sees that the earth and all flesh have become corrupt (6:12). In this intertextual relationship, the initial goodness of things turns out to be a somewhat fragile quality, capable of being altered by violent deeds. The goodness of things seems to be God's intention, but it is an ideal condition that living things can spoil.

God separated the light from the darkness. The verb *wayyabdēl* ("[he] separated, divided") and its related forms create a *Leitwort* effect during the first four days of creation, occurring five times in 1:4–18. On the first day, God separates light from darkness. On the second day, he creates heaven to separate the waters. On the third day, he separates dry land from sea (but without the verb *bdl,* "to separate"). On the fourth day, he creates the great lights to separate day from night. During the first four days, creation involves separation, demarcating the boundaries and contrasts in the categories of creation. The process of creating order out of a primeval chaos involves not only creating new things but also defining the differences between binary opposites: light/ darkness, day/night, water above/water below, land/water. On subsequent days God continues to make distinctions, but without the verb "to separate": animals of water and sky, humans and other land animals, male and female, ordinary time and sacred time (the seventh day). Creation involves separation, an ordered institution of differences, in contrast to the diffuse unity of primeval chaos.

The authority to determine differences was also part of the religious activity of the priests, who were charged "to separate (*lăhabdîl*) between the holy and the profane, and between the unclean and the clean" (Lev 10:10). The valid separation of categories is a task instituted by God in creation and carried on in religious life by the priests.

1:5. *God called the light "day."* Naming is part of the process of creation, serving to mark the proper categories of the cosmos. According to the ancient conception, the essence of a thing inheres in its name; hence to know the name of a thing is to have some measure of authority over it. God's power to name things signifies his authority over them. Similarly, in 2:19–20, God gives Adam the authority to name the animals. Since the knowledge of names gives power, the divine being refuses to divulge his name to Jacob (Gen 32:20); the angel refuses to reveal his name to Manoah (Judg 13:18); and God is reticent to reveal his true name to Moses (Exod 3:13–14).

By naming the light as "day" and setting it in alteration with night, God institutes the temporal rhythm of the cosmos. In so doing, God creates the category of time (Sasson 1992: 191).

The word *yôm* ("day") has two meanings (as in English): the "day" that is daytime and the "day" that is a full twenty-four-hour day, consisting of daytime and nighttime. Here the former sense is activated, since the light is named "day." In the following clause the latter sense is activated, since "one day" consists of the alternation of light and darkness. The P source has a predilection for varying the meanings of the same term in successive clauses (cf. "earth" in vv. 1–2). An early textual variant in this verse, *ywmm,* "daytime" (4QGen^g, targums, and Peshitta), eliminates this ambiguity (Hendel 1998: 120) but at the price of the varying style of P.

the darkness he called "night." The grammar of this sequence, with the noun *ḥōšek* ("darkness") fronted or clause-initial, signals a disjunction between the two clauses of naming. This disjunction adds focus to the word "the darkness," which may be rendered as a *casus pendens:* "and as for the darkness, he named it night." The disjunctive grammar may also give a sense of simultaneity, as if he named "day" and "night" in the same utterance. The grammar creates a stylistic rhythm and balance, with parallel style, A B C // B′ A′ C′ (see Kselman 1978: 164), raising the rhetorical register of the verse. By naming the darkness, a primordial feature (1:2), God signals that it is now integrated into the order of the universe.

There was evening and there was morning. The twofold repetition of *wayhî* ("and there was") follows closely on *wayhî-'ôr,* "and there was light" (1:3). In the wake of this verbal repetition, the categories of *'ereb* ("dusk, evening") and *bōqer* ("dawn, morning"), that is, the transition from light to darkness and from darkness to light, follow directly from the creation of light. The passage of time is illustrated by this first diurnal variation of light and darkness.

The days in Genesis 1 begin and end at dawn, at the first light. The daily sequence is, God creates X on day Y, and then comes evening and then morning, completing day Y. The creation of light on the first day is the dawn of the first day, which ends at the following dawn. This reckoning of the day as dawn to dawn seems to be the standard in preexilic biblical texts (Cassuto 1961: 28–30; Talmon 1994). The normal way of describing the length of a day is "day and night," and "tomorrow" refers to the time beginning with dawn (e.g., Lev 7:15 [P], Judg 19:4–9, 1 Sam 19:11, 1 Sam 28:19). However, some rites during Israelite festivals begin at evening (e.g., Exod 12:8, 18; see Propp 1999: 391–92), and the fast on the Day of Atonement begins the previous evening and lasts from "evening to evening" (Lev 23:32; Milgrom 2001: 2025–26). Perhaps because of this exegetical basis, by the fifth century BCE the day begins and ends at dusk (Neh 13:19), and this standard of reckoning continued as the norm in Judaism.

This temporal refrain marks a break with the primeval era, when there were no days and nights and no change. The seventh day lacks this refrain, bringing the seven-day rhythm to a close with the creation of sacred time.

one day. This noun phrase has a dual sense. The alternation of light and darkness constitutes "one day" as a complete unit of time, a twenty-four-hour day. However, the cardinal number *ʾeḥād* ("one") can also be used as an ordinal number ("first"), as in 2:11, "The name of the first (*hā ʾeḥād*) river" (Dillmann 1897: 62–63; *IBHS* §15.2.1b). Hence the phrase *yôm ʾeḥād* ("one/first day") has a fruitful ambiguity, both as the culmination of the first work of creation and as the first in a series of seven days. At this point in the narrative, this ambiguity creates a note of hesitation about the possibility of more days to come.

Each "day" in the sequence of days—one/first day, second day, etc.—is a day of the week, a twenty-four-hour day, culminating with the seventh day, anticipating the Sabbath. But postbiblical tradition, beginning with the second-century BCE Jubilees, sometimes redefined the duration of a day by appeal to the poetic metaphor in Ps 90:4, "For a thousand years in your sight / are like yesterday (*kəyôm ʾetmôl*) when it has passed," a reflection on God's vast temporal perspective in contrast to the human experience of fleeting time. Jubilees 4:30 draws the inference that one of God's days is a thousand human years, thus providing an explanation of why God says, "On the day you eat from it you shall die" (Gen 2:17), and yet Adam lived for 930 years (Gen 5:5; see Kugel 1998: 94–95). Jubilees, by linking these biblical verses, infers that 930 years is less than one day in God's reckoning—literalizing the poetic metaphor in order to resolve an exegetical problem in Genesis 2. This exegetical move was applied to the "days" of Genesis 1 by other early interpreters and was revived by biblical literalists in the nineteenth century to expand the days of Genesis 1 to accommodate the vast age of the earth and the universe (the "day-age" theory; Hendel 2013: 179–80).

1:6. *God said, "Let there be a vault within the water.* The noun *rāqîaʿ* ("vault") from the root *rqʿ*, "to spread out, to beat out," signifies the solid expanse of the sky, as if it were beaten out of some hard substance. Elsewhere in P, this verb and a derived noun refer to hammering gold or bronze into sheets for plating (Exod 39:3, Num 17:3–4). An Akkadian cognate, *ruqqu*, means a metal cauldron; in Ugaritic *rq* is a silver "sheet"; and in Phoenician, *mrqʿ* is an object of beaten gold, perhaps a bowl (*HALOT*, 1292).

The LXX translated *rāqîaʿ* as *stereōma*, "solid body"; the Vulgate, as *firmamentum*, "firm thing," whence the King James translation, "firmament." Ezekiel describes the *rāqîaʿ* as having an appearance "like awesome ice" (Ezek 1:22), above which Yahweh is enthroned.

The shape of the *rāqîaʿ* is nowhere specified, but since the sun, moon, and stars are set in it (1:17), and since they describe a semicircle in their daily paths, it is plausible to imagine it as a hemispherical vault (the Akkadian *ruqqu*, "cauldron," may support this). In Job, the perimeter of heaven is described as a *ḥûg* ("circle," Job 22:14), which is supported by the "pillars of heaven" (Job 26:11) (see further Stadelmann 1970: 37–60; Halpern 2009: 428–38). In Mesopotamia, heaven is described as a circle (*kippat šamê* = "circle of heaven") and may have been visualized as a hemispherical vault (Horowitz 1998: 264–65). The word *rāqîaʿ* would be suitable for an inverted bowl or a flat plate. A domelike *rāqîaʿ* may better suit the perception of the curved path of the heavenly bodies and the curve of the rainbow in the sky (Gen 9:13).

The *mayim* ("water") is the primeval water of 1:2, which is now separated into two bodies, above and below. This separation will render the chaotic water useful—the water above as the celestial water that descends as rain, and the water below as the seas (1:10). This separation of water will be reversed in the P flood story, when God reunites the water above the vault with the water below (now called menacingly *təhôm rabbâ*, "the great ocean"), returning the world to watery chaos (7:11).

let it separate water from water. The sequence *wiyhî mabdîl* ("let it separate," *hyh* + predicate participle; *wiy-* is from the Rule of Shewa: **wəyə > wiy*) has the nuance of progressive action, so the vault will "continually separate" the waters (*IBHS* §37.7.1b). The task of separation, initiated by God, is now delegated to the vault of heaven. (Cf. God's separation of light and darkness in 1:4, and his delegation of this process to the heavenly bodies in 1:14.) Just as the separation of light and darkness is the beginning of differentiated time (see NOTES at 1:4), so here the separation of the waters above from the waters below, with the insertion of the sky in between, is the beginning of differentiated space.

1:7. *God made the vault.* On days two through six, the account of God's *word* of creation (the *Wortbericht*, "word report") is followed by a description of the *deed* of creation (the *Tatbericht*, "deed report"). Scholars have conjectured that this dual picture of creation—with the *Tatbericht* recapitulating the *Wortbericht*—may stem from two originally different creation accounts that have been secondarily combined, a supplementation in which one layer is an editorial expansion of the other (see W. H. Schmidt 1973: 160–73; C. Levin 2003; Hutzli 2010). Given the variations and complexities in this scheme, it seems that the word and deed reports are not easily separable, and neither is sufficient for the narrative by itself (Westermann 1984: 82–88; Steck 1981; Carr 2020b: 18–20). Among the complexities are the following: the first day has only a *Wortbericht*, and its fulfillment is fused with the refrain *wayhî-kēn* ("and it was so") (1:3); on the third day the *Wortbericht* commands the water and the earth do the deed, and for the first of these the *Tatbericht* is lacking (1:9, 12); and on the sixth day God instructs a divine plurality ("us") in the *Wortbericht* and acts on his own in the *Tatbericht* (1:26–27).

Moreover, there is a consistent variation of style between each paired *Wortbericht* and *Tatbericht*. In 1:6–7 the stylistic variations are as follows: *wiyhî mabdîl* (1:6) // *wayyabdēl* (1:7) (a participial construction vs. a finite verb); *bətôk hammāyim* and *bên mayim lāmāyim* (1:6) // *bên hammayim ʾăšer mittaḥat lārāqîaʿ ûbên hammayim ʾăšer mēʾal lārāqîaʿ* (1:7) (varying descriptions of the two waters). This style of variation within repetition is characteristic of P's literary technique (see McEvenue 1971).

The duality of word and deed in the picture of creation is probably a juxtaposition of traditional images of creation, yielding a layered and intricate effect. The seeming inconsistency between God saying "let there be a vault" and the statement "God made the vault" may entail some logical friction, but this juxtaposition of command and fulfillment is most plausibly understood as a feature of P's style. The asymmetries and variations in the scheme of *Wortbericht* and *Tatbericht* are like those in the other patterns of Genesis 1 (e.g., the refrains begun in 1:3–5; the sequences of plants and animals in 1:11–12, 24–30; and the variations in command and fulfillment in the P flood story in Genesis 6–9). In these respects, P's style is consistent in its preference for variation within repetition.

and separated the water below the vault from the water above the vault. It is not clear whether the subject of *wayyabdēl* ("separated") is "he" (God) or "it" (the vault of heaven). In 1:6 God says of the vault: "Let it separate water from water." The punctual sense of the converted imperfect *wayyabdēl* in 1:7 is the actualization of the continuous function of separation in 1:6 (*hyh* + participle). Both "God" and "the vault" are mentioned in the preceding clause, so either could be the subject of the verb. The ambiguity of the subject may be intentional, a laconic obscurity. In any case, both God and the vault are involved in the act of separating the water.

An oft-noted parallel is the scene in *Enuma Elish* where Marduk divides the body of Tiamat in two and sets the upper half in the sky to hold back the celestial water:

> One half of her he set up and stretched out as the heavens (*šamāmū*).
> He stretched the skin and appointed a watch
> With the instruction not to let her waters escape.

(IV.137–40; Lambert 2013: 94–95)

As Foster (2005: 462) explicates, "he made the sky to hold back the waters." The similarity with Gen 1:7 is the creator god's act of making the vault of heaven, which holds back the celestial waters from the earth. The difference is that in *Enuma Elish* heaven comes from the body of a vanquished god, whereas in Genesis 1 it is a purely material object, fabricated by God for the occasion. Similarly, in *Enuma Elish* the waters below are remains of the defeated god Apsu. As Horowitz (1998: 113 n. 7) remarks, "the universe [at this point in *Enuma Elish*], consisting of the waters of heaven above, the waters of Apsu below, and perhaps a level of winds, may be compared to the early universe in Genesis 1." The structure of the cosmos is similar, but in Genesis 1 no combat is involved.

In Mesopotamian texts there is also a purely material concept of the "base of heaven" (*šupuk šamê;* Horowitz 1998: 239–41). This is the lowest layer of heaven where the sun, moon, and stars shine. In a Late Babylonian text, the lower heaven is made of jasper stone, on which Marduk set the stars: "The Lower Heavens are jasper. They belong to the stars. He drew the constellations of the gods on them" (Horowitz 1998: 3–4). In this concept the lower heavens are not a divine substance but are a parallel image to the divided body of Tiamat. As Rochberg (2010: 331–32) observes, the double depiction of cosmic phenomena in Mesopotamian texts as manifestations of gods or as physical objects indicates the permeability of "god-talk" and "star-talk." Both pictures

Figure 1. The Egyptian cosmos, with the earth (the god Geb, filled with leaves), the sky (the goddess Nut, filled with stars), and the air (the god Shu, with the sun above), which holds apart heaven and earth. Shu, who is also life-breath, is adorned with symbols of life (*ankh*). The sun god Re rides his celestial boat across the sky. On the left he navigates the celestial waters, and on the right he prepares to reenter the horizon, welcomed by Osiris. Papyrus Tanytamon (detail), twenty-first dynasty (ca. 1070–945 BCE), Bibliothèque Nationale de France. (Drawing by William H. C. Propp)

share the firmament's "function as a barrier between the heavenly waters above and earth below" (344). The rain that falls from above is therefore the "water of heaven" (written A.AN).

Similarly, in Egypt, the goddess Nut is the mythic image of the sky, through which the stars process and above which are the celestial waters (Allen 1988: 1–7).

And it was so. The formulaic assertion of coming into existence, *wayhî-kēn,* occurs seven times (1:7, 9, 11, 15, 24, 30, and with variation in 1:3). This is the same number of repetitions as the refrain "God saw that it was good," which also occurs with variation, beginning with the creation of light (1:4). These two refrains, along with the sequences of evenings and mornings, lend a rhythmic sense of structure and order to the account of creation.

There are several variations in the placement and nuance of this refrain. On day one (1:3), it announces the accomplishment of God's command. On the second day (1:7), it occurs after the "deed report" (the *Tatbericht*) announcing the accomplishment of this act of creation. On the third day, it replaces the *Tatbericht* in the first of the two creations on this day (1:9). Then, on the third, fourth, and sixth days (1:11, 15, 24), the refrain occurs between the *Wortbericht* and the *Tatbericht,* that is, after God's command but before the "making" of that work of creation. The refrain is lacking on the fifth day. Finally, on the second creation of the sixth day (1:30), the refrain occurs at the end of the day's activities, including two acts of creation and blessing, and seems to function as a summary of the preceding actions.

These variations of placement are characteristic of P's style. In general, this refrain serves as an "epexegetical" comment, which Steck (1981: 35–36) argues brings out "the inner connection between word and event." It varies between indicating the accomplishment of God's command or anticipating its forthcoming accomplishment. The variations are most easily regarded as an artistic and conceptual trait of this text, rather than as a sign of complex redaction.

1:8. *God called the vault "heaven."* The name of the vault, *šāmayim* ("heaven, sky"), echoes the word *mayim* ("water"), which occurs five times in the previous two verses. The name of the vault is connected to its function as a divider of water. This word-play may suggest a popular etymology of *šāmayim* from *ša* ("of") plus *mayim* ("water") or *šām* ("there") plus *mayim* (as Rashi and others). The ancestral form is the plural **šamayīm(a),* which was simplified in Hebrew as **šamaym* > *šāmayim* (Huehnergard 1987: 290 n. 108). The Hebrew has the same form as a dual, as if there were two heavens, which may give rise to the expression *haššāmayim ûšmê haššāmayim* ("heaven and the highest heaven," 1 Kgs 8:27). In later Jewish traditions, there are multiple heavens, usually three or seven (three heavens in 2 Cor 12:2, seven heavens in Testament of Levi, 2 Enoch, etc.), a multiplicity that may derive from Mesopotamia, where three heavens is the dominant tradition and some incantations refer to "seven heavens, seven earths" (A. Y. Collins 1996; Horowitz 1998: 217–20).

Although here the vault is named "heaven," in each subsequent mention it is called "the vault of heaven." The reason for this shift of wording is that the word "heaven" usually refers not to the vault, but to the atmospheric space below the vault, that is, the sky. Hence *šāmayim* means "heaven, sky" as a cosmic domain, with its vaulted roof as a more specific image.

The creation of "heaven" is *not* followed by the formula "God saw that it was good," which occurs seven times, including one variation, in Genesis 1 (see NOTES at 1:4). The absence of this formula on the second day preserves the sevenfold repetition but creates a structural gap for this day. It is possible, as commentators have suggested, that the absence of this formula is due to incompletion of this work of creation. On this understanding, the act of separating the waters is not finished until the third day, when the waters below are gathered together and named "seas" (1:10), at which point the goodness formula recurs (*Gen. Rab.* 4.6; Rashi; Dillmann 1897: 67–68; Gunkel 1997: 109; and others). The LXX includes the formula in 1:8, probably reproducing a harmonizing Hebrew text (Hendel 1998: 23–24). The absence of this formula shows again the degree of variation and structure in P's style.

1:9. *be gathered into one place.* The verb *yiqqāwû* ("pool together, gather together") and its related noun, *miqweh* ("pool, gathering place," 1:10), are a *Leitwort* pair in this act of creation. The harmonistic pluses in the LXX (partially preserved in two Qumran fragments, 4QGen^b and 4QGen^k) add two more repetitions (see TEXTUAL NOTES d and e).

so that dry land may appear. The appearance of "dry land" (*yabbāšâ*) recurs at the end of the flood in 8:14 (P), when "the earth was dry" (*yābəšâ hā ʾāreṣ*), signaling the beginning of a new era of creation. This image recurs in the exodus story in P, when the Israelites cross the sea on "dry land" (*yabbāšâ;* Exod 14:16, 22, 29). Ska (1981: 523–31) aptly observes that this motif in the P story of the exodus signals the beginning of new era of creation, modeled after the creation of dry land in our verse.

The *Tatbericht* ("deed report") for this act of creation is absent in the MT, probably reflecting a deliberate stylistic variation by the P writer. The longer harmonized version preserved in the LXX (and partially in 4QGen^k) supplies the *Tatbericht,* in which the waters gather together (see Textual Note e).

1:10. *God called the dry land "earth."* The name *ʾereṣ* ("earth") is the same word as the primeval earth in 1:2, where it has the definite article, *hā ʾāreṣ* ("the earth"). The newly given name seems to indicate a change or transformation in the status of the earth. Whereas before the earth was a "desolate chaos," God now makes it suitable for life by separating it from the water. As a newly constituted part of an orderly cosmos, God grants it a name, even though the name is identical to its primeval designation. This tension between two identical names fits P's style of subtle variation in the semantic scope of repeated words (cf. the two senses of "the earth" in the transition from 1:1 to 1:2).

the pool of water he called "seas." The plural form of the noun *yammîm* ("seas") creates a wordplay with *mayim* ("water") two words previously, which is the primeval substance of the seas—note the reversal of letters, *mym > ymm.* By this stylistic move the water is given a new name that derives from its essence and gives it a new status.

Both the earth and the seas are new creations by virtue of their separation and naming. The transformation of the previously primeval categories makes them suitable for the different forms of life—plants, sea creatures, and land creatures—that God creates subsequently.

Breaking the pattern of the previous days, there are two works of creation on the third day. The doubling of creation on the third day is mirrored by the doubling of creation on the sixth day. Commentators have suggested that this asymmetry stems from a secondary combination of a six-day creation account with eight works of creation (plus the day of rest). This cannot be excluded, but the internal symmetries in this pattern, in which days one through three correspond in various ways with days four through six (see Comments), indicate a deliberate and cohesive design for the narrative. The admixture of structure and variation is more likely a sign of the compositional sophistication of the P writer than evidence for the text's complicated redaction.

1:11. *Let the earth grow seed-bearing plants and fruit trees with seed-bearing fruit.* The word *zeraʿ* ("seed") and its congeners are a *Leitwort* chain in the creation of plants and trees, occurring six times in two verses. The importance of "seed" emphasizes that the plants and trees will continue to propagate their kind. God is the prime creator, but each category of life is granted the ability to create more of its kind. The emphasis on "seed" and "fruit" in 1:11–12 is seconded by the command "be fruitful and multiply" in the creation of animals (1:22) and humans (1:28). The production of progeny, life that re-creates life, is a key part of God's plan of creation.

The phrase *dešeʾ ʿēśeb* ("plants") is an apposition of two words for plants, similar to the later apposition *yereq ʿēśeb* ("green plants") in 1:30. The plants are designated simply *'ēśeb* in 1:29. It is unnecessary to posit different meanings or nuances to these different collocations, although contextually *yereq* *'ēśeb* in 1:30 should include all vegetation, including fruit trees. These variations in terms and in the categories they designate are characteristic of P's style (cf. the designations of animals; see NOTES at 1:24). The phrase *'ēṣ pərî* ("fruit trees") refers to all kinds of trees, including trees whose seed is contained in nuts or cones. Note that in Ezek 17:23, the word *pərî* ("fruit") refers to the "fruit" (i.e., cone) of a cedar tree.

1:12. *the earth yielded seed-bearing plants of every kind and trees of every kind with seed-bearing fruit.* The earth is the agent of creation in 1:12, "yielding" or "bringing forth" plants and trees, following God's command in 1:11. In some respect this is a personification of the earth, but also corresponds to ordinary observation—the earth brings forth produce. The feminine grammatical gender of "earth" gives a sense of the earth as mother, but this is not "Mother Earth" as a deity. The divine command in 1:11 makes it clear who is the ultimate agent of creation.

The *Tatbericht* of 1:12 contains the following stylistic variations on the *Wortbericht* of 1:11: *tadšē'* (1:11) // *wattôṣē'* (1:12); *mazrîa' zera'* (1:11) // *mazrîa' zera' ləmînēhû* (1:12); *'ēṣ pərî 'ōśeh pərî* (1:11) // *'ēṣ 'ōśeh pərî* (1:12); *'al-hā'āreṣ* (1:11) // *ləmînēhû* (1:12). Many of these variations were harmonized away in the proto-LXX tradition, and another harmonization occurred in the proto-MT tradition (see TEXTUAL NOTE f).

1:14. *Let there be lights in the vault of heaven.* The opening sequence, *wayyō'mer 'ĕlōhîm yəhî mə'ōrōt* ("God said, 'Let there be lights'"), pointedly echoes the diction of 1:3, *wayyō'mer 'ĕlōhîm yəhî 'ôr* ("God said, 'Let there be light'"). Various forms and derivations of the root *'wr* ("light") are a *Leitwort* cluster in this act of creation, occurring eight times in five verses: *mə'ōrōt* ("lights," three times), *mā'ôr* ("light," two times), *ləhā'îr* ("to light," two times), and *'ôr* ("light," one time).

to separate the day from the night. This function of the *mə'ōrōt* ("lights") is similar to that of the *raqia'* ("vault") on the second day, that is, to continually separate (*ləhabdîl*) opposite categories in the cosmos: light/darkness, upper water/lower water.

The placement of this command is intriguing since the lights are created three days after God "separated the light from the darkness" and gave names to "day" and "night" (1:4). The lag between the events of the first and fourth days has long puzzled commentators. The solution (first perceived by Herder 1993a: 271–72, original 1774) pertains to the literary structure of the six days of creation, in which God's creations on days four through six are complements to the creations on days one through three (see COMMENTS). Hence, God's creative work on day one—the creation of light, the separation of light and darkness, and the beginning of the temporal rhythm of day and night—is complemented and completed by his creation of the heavenly lights, which now assume the task of separating and governing the light and darkness.

The separate creation of the *mə'ōrōt* ("lights"), on the fourth day, also serves to desacralize or "disenchant" the heavenly bodies, which seems to be a concern of this act of creation. In Israelite religion of the preexilic period, there are numerous indications that the sun, moon, and stars received worship as members of Yahweh's "heavenly host" (e.g., Deut 17:3, 2 Kgs 23:5, Jer 8:2, Ezek 8:16, Job 31:26; and Zatelli 1991). The status of the heavenly lights as lesser deities in Yahweh's divine entourage was probably a normal part of early Israelite religion but came under criticism by the classical prophets and the writers of the Deuteronomistic History (Halpern 2009: 57–97). The desacralization of the sun, moon, and stars in the P text is part of this broader critique. By the creation of light on the first day and the heavenly lights on the fourth day, the text makes it clear that God is the sole authority in the celestial domain, for whom the sun, moon, and stars are merely regulative objects, like the vault of heaven itself (see similarly "their host" in 2:1).

The idea that the sun, moon, and stars in some sense "regulate" or "keep in order" the workings of heaven is also found in Mesopotamian texts: "They installed Sin, Šamaš, and Ištar to regulate (*ana šutēšuri*) the firmament" (Horowitz 1998: 239).

let them be signs for festivals, days, and years. The grammar of this clause is difficult. The first part, *wəhāyû lə'ōtōt*, means "let them become (in a functional sense) signs" (cf. Gen 9:13; Num 10:2, 10; [all P]; Gen 11:3; BDB, 226 §II.2e), and there follows what looks like a conjunctive sequence, *ûləmô'ădîm* (etc.), which should mean "and festivals, etc." But in order to make sense of this sequence, the *waw* before *mô'ădîm* must be taken in a different sense from conjunctive, probably as an "explicating *waw*" (e.g., Skinner 1930: 26; Cassuto 1961: 44; W. H. Schmidt 1973: 114; see BDB, 252 §1b), meaning "let them serve as signs, in particular for festivals, days, and years." In other words, the heavenly lights are signs for marking the major divisions of time. The word *mô'ădîm* can mean "festivals" or "seasons," and it may mean both in this instance; but "festivals" may be the more prominent meaning, given the P source's interest in the cultic calendar.

The statement that the heavenly lights serve as *'ōtōt* ("signs") recalls the traditional conception of the stars as divine signs in the sky. Jeremiah warns the Israelites against heeding the *'ōtot haššamayim* ("the signs of heaven," Jer 10:2). This is part of the prophetic critique of astrology and the worship of celestial gods. In Mesopotamia the starry sky is called "the writing of heaven" (*šiṭir šamê*), indicating the divinatory significance of the heavenly lights (Rochberg 2004: 1). In this conception, the stars are gods or physical objects that are symbols of gods, and they are also coded messages "written" by gods. The following statement from a Babylonian "Diviner's Manual" is indicative: "The signs on earth as well as of the sky bear signals for us; heaven and earth bring us omens; they are not separate from one another; heaven and earth are interconnected" (Rochberg 2004: 166).

When Genesis 1 calls the heavenly lights *'ōtōt* ("signs") but limits their communicative significance to calendrical matters—"festivals, days, and years"—the traditional divinatory role of the heavenly lights is effaced. As Arnold (2012: 342) observes, "the signs of heaven have been transformed from divinatory guidelines to be read by the well-informed into a sacred calendar in the sky on display for all Israelites to follow." The "writing of heaven" becomes solely a way of indicating time.

1:15. *let them be lights in the vault of heaven to light up the earth.* The way that the heavenly bodies serve as lights in the vault of heaven is obscure. Since light was created on the first day, they do not produce light; rather, they regulate the already existing light (cf. Job 38:19, where light and darkness have their own "places," with no mention of the heavenly lights). Halpern (2009: 432–33) has proposed, on the basis of astronomical concepts in the ancient Near East and Greece, that the heavenly lights in Genesis 1 are conceived as membranes in the celestial vault, through which the light above the vault is visible. This concept desacralizes the cosmos, like the naturalistic theories of the Presocratic philosophers in Ionia, who share "the denial of significance to the stars" (441).

Figure 2. Temple of the Babylonian sun god Šamaš in Sippar, with cosmic imagery (Woods 2004): (a) subterranean waters (*apsû*) with stars on their daily procession; (e) sun disk; (f) two-headed snake god with body emerging from the *apsû*; (g) moon disk; (h) sun disk; (i) seven-pointed star disk (Ishtar); (j) enthroned Šamaš statue; (k) bison-headed gods opening the gates of heaven above the eastern mountains, where the sun rises. The king (c) is led by a priest (d) and followed by a goddess (b). Relief from the Sun God Tablet of Nabû-apla-idanna (ca. 860 BCE), British Museum. (Drawing by William H. C. Propp)

1:16. *God made the two great lights—the greater light to rule the day and the lesser light to rule the night.* The text avoids the ordinary words for the sun, *šemeš*, and the moon, *yārēaḥ*. The terms *hammā'ôr haggādōl* ("the greater light") and *hammā'ôr haqqāṭōn* ("the lesser light") are not used elsewhere in the Bible. Interestingly, a similar term, *nyr rbt* ("great light"), is a title of Šapšu, the sun goddess at Ugarit (*CAT* 1.16.i.37; del Olmo Lete and Sanmartín 2004: 655). It seems likely that these terms are substituted for the normal names to emphasize that the heavenly bodies are not independent deities, but physical objects created by God. The sun and the moon were sometimes conceived in Israelite tradition as independent gods and worshiped as such, usually in conjunction with "the host of heaven" (2 Kgs 23:5, Jer 8:2, Ezek 8:16, Job 31:26). Elsewhere in the ancient Near East the sun and the moon were prominent deities; in Canaanite religion the sun goddess (Šapšu) was goddess of justice and ruler of the dead, while the moon (Yarihu) was a male god of fertility. A text from Ugarit recounts the marriage of Yariḫu to the Mesopotamian moon goddess Nikkal-Ib (Marcus 1997).

The word for the task of the greater and lesser lights in this verse, *ləmemšelet*, means "to have rulership/authority over." This word, and its infinitive in 1:18 (*limšōl*), is less forceful than the verb for human rule in 1:26–28, *rādâ*. The authority of the heavenly bodies is part of the larger mechanism of cosmic order.

1:16–18. The *Tatbericht* of this act of creation has several variations from the *Wortbericht* in 1:14–15. The *Wortbericht* has an envelope structure, in which the last clause echoes and extends the first:

A   ¹⁴Let there be lights in the vault of heaven
B   to separate the day from the night.
C   And let them be signs for the festivals, days, and years,
AA ¹⁵and let them be lights in the vault of heaven to light up the earth.

The correspondences in the *Tatbericht* are as follows:

> A and B are fulfilled and explicated in 1:16, with the objects ("lights") and their function ("to separate the day from the night") expanded to "the greater light to rule the day," "the lesser light to rule the night," and "the stars."
> AA is fulfilled more directly in 1:17, "God set them in the vault of heaven to light up the earth."
> C has no explicit fulfillment, but is merely implied.
> B is further fulfilled and explicated in 1:18, "to rule the day and the night, and to separate the light from the darkness," emphasizing the function of the rule from 1:16. The latter phrase, with "light" and "darkness," echoes God's initial separation on the first day: "God separated the light from the darkness" (1:4).

The correspondences and divergences between the *Wortbericht* and *Tatbericht* in this act of creation are artful and deliberate. They indicate the degree of sophistication in P's narrative style.

1:20. *Let the waters teem with teeming living creatures, and let birds fly over the earth across the vault of heaven.* The work of creation on the fifth day consists of two categories of living beings—creatures of the water and creatures of the sky. Both categories have a relation to the work of creation on the second day—the vault of heaven, which separates the water above from the water below. The water below (named "seas" in 1:10) is now inhabited by its appropriate creatures, and the region above the water and below the vault of heaven is inhabited by its creatures. (Note that there are no living creatures for the region above the vault of heaven.) The collocation of the terms *mayim* ("water") and *rəqîaʿ haššāmayim* ("the vault of heaven") echoes the work of creation on the second day.

God's command, "Let the waters teem . . . ," suggests that the waters are now accomplices to creation, similar to the earth on the third day (1:11–12). By implication, the waters and the earth are far from their primeval, chaotic state, since they are now participating in the creation of order and life. Yet there is a grammatical ambiguity, since the jussive sequence *yišrəṣû hammayim* ("Let the waters teem") can be construed either as a command to the waters to do something (similar to "Let the earth grow . . ."), or as a command that this situation come into being, with God as the creative agent (similar to "Let there be light"). This ambiguity is resolved in the *Tatbericht,* in which God is the agent, and the waters are merely the place where the creatures live.

This command emphasizes the abundance and movement of life in the seas by following *yišrəṣû* ("Let [them] teem") with its cognate accusative *šereṣ* ("teeming thing"). The birds are commanded to come into being by a similar alliterative construction, but in reverse order (noun + verb, signaling a change of subject): *ʿôp yəʿôpēp* (lit. "as for flying things, let them fly"). The direction of attention in this verse moves upward—from "the waters" to "the vault of heaven"—taking in the sweep of the livable cosmos.

1:21. *God created the great sea monsters and every kind of moving life with which the waters teem, and every kind of winged bird.* The *Tatbericht* varies from the *Wortbericht* of 1:20 in several respects. The subject is God instead of "the waters," and the verb is the uniquely divine verb of creation, *bārāʾ*, as in 1:1, 27, and 2:3. This emphatic work of creation by God singles out one particular category of sea creature, *hattannînim haggədōlîm* ("the great sea monsters"). Of all the creatures of sky, water, and land, this is the only individual species that is singled out by name (humans are a special case, constituting a separate category). This brief but striking mention seems to have a similar motive to other passages in Genesis 1, such as the creation of sun and moon (1:16)—it clearly subordinates this being to God and clarifies that it is not an independent deity or cosmic force.

Elsewhere in biblical traditions the great sea monsters (or dragons) are depicted as primeval adversaries of God, whom God subdues in cosmic battle (see Cross 1973: 112–63; Day 1985). At that primordial time, "You broke the heads of the dragons (*tannînim*) in the water" (Ps 74:13); "You pierced the dragon (*tannîn*)" (Isa 51:9). In these and other passages (Isa 27:1; Job 7:12; Ezek 29:3, 32:2; Jer 51:34), *tannîn* ("sea monster, dragon") is one of several parallel terms for the primeval monsters of the sea, including Leviathan, Rahab, and Sea. In Genesis 1, the great sea monsters are pointedly domesticated as Yahweh's creatures, not his rivals. This is a revision of Israelite traditions.

In Ugaritic texts, the monster *tnn* (pronounced /*tunnanu*/; Huehnergard 1987: 185) is said to have been defeated by both Baal ("Baal smote . . . the dragon [*tnn*]" [*CAT* 1.82.1]) and Anat ("Surely I lifted the dragon [*tnn*] and destroyed him" [*CAT* 1.3.iii.40]; see Smith and Pitard 2009: 248–58), indicating a multiformity of local traditions. In these texts, *tnn* and other terms (including *ltn,* cognate with Leviathan) are variant designations or instantiations of the primeval sea monster(s), as with Hebrew *tannîn.*

In addition to singling out this species, the *Tatbericht* varies the *Wortbericht* by altering the designation of the sea creatures and sky creatures. The sea creatures are now *nepeš haḥayyâ hārōmeśet ʾašer šārəṣû hammayim* ("moving life with which the waters teem"). This varies from the *Wortbericht* by two moves: the noun *šereṣ* ("teeming thing") is replaced by the synonymous attributive adjective *hārōmeśet* ("moving"), and the initial command, *yišrəṣû hammayim* ("let the waters teem"), is fulfilled in a subordinate clause, *šārəṣû hammayim* ("with which the waters teem"). This latter move clarifies that the waters are a mere place, and not a matrix of creation. The sky creatures are now *ʿôp kānāp* ("winged birds"), a variation of *ʿôp yəʿôpēp* ("let birds fly"), and preserving some alliteration of the *pe*'s. To the sea creatures and sky creatures, the qualifier *kol . . . ləmînêhem/hû* ("every kind of," lit. "every. . . . according to their/its kind") is added, recalling the attention to the different "kinds" in the creation of plants and trees on the third day (1:11–12).

1:22. *God blessed them and said, "Be fruitful and multiply, fill the water of the seas, and let the birds be fruitful on the earth."* The blessing of the sea creatures and birds re-

Figure 3. Mesopotamian warrior god (Ningirsu or Ninurta) slaying a seven-headed dragon. (Cf. the multiheaded Leviathan in Ps 74:14.) Early Dynastic shell plaque (ca. 2800–2600 BCE), Bible Lands Museum, Jerusalem. (Drawing by William H. C. Propp)

sumes the theme of the proliferation of life that began with the emphasis on "seed" in the creation of plants and trees. Living things will continue what God began, that is, the creation of life. There are several artful aspects of this blessing: the assonance and rhythm of *pərû ûrəbu ûmil'û* ("be fruitful and multiply, fill"), the wordplay of *hammayim bayyammîm* ("water of the seas"), the variation of *yireb* ("let [them] be fruitful") with *rəbû* ("be fruitful"), and the semantic balance of *bayyammîm* ("of the seas") and *bāʾāreṣ* ("on the earth"). This blessing also anticipates the fuller blessing of humans in 1:28, where fertility is combined with rule over other living creatures.

1:24. *Let the earth yield every kind of living creature—domestic animals, and crawling creatures and wild animals of every kind.* The creation of land creatures on the sixth day—first animals and then humans—complements the creation of dry land on the third day by filling it with living things. God's grant of plants and fruit trees as food for the land animals also complements his creation of vegetation on the third day. In a blending of these correspondences, the *Wortbericht* here, *tôṣēʾ hāʾāreṣ* ("Let the earth yield . . .") echoes the *Tatbericht* on the third day, *wattōṣēʾ hāʾāreṣ* ("And the earth yielded . . . ," 1:12). However, in the *Tatbericht* here, it is God who "makes" the animals, and the earth is a place for God's creation.

The threefold division of the kinds of *nepeš ḥayyâ* ("living creature") on earth provides a brief animal taxonomy. Yet characteristically for P, the terms for these categories and their semantic content vary in their repetition in subsequent verses (1:25–26). Here the three terms are *bəhēmâ, remeś,* and *ḥaytô-ʾereṣ.* The divisions are relatively clear: *bəhēmâ,* often "cattle," must here include all domestic land animals. The contrast is with the *ḥaytô ʾereṣ,* literally "creatures of the earth," which can mean "animals" or, in contrast with *bəhēmâ,* "wild animals" (on the form, see below). A middle term, *remeś*, "crawling things," refers to insects, reptiles, and the like that inhabit both domestic and wild spaces. The relationships among the terms of this threefold division are complementary.

Each term can have different shades of meaning depending on the contrasting term(s), and in subsequent mentions of land animals these other shades are exploited. In 1:26 land animals are denoted by a twofold division, *bəhēmâ* and *kol-hāremeś hārōmeś ʿal-hāʾāreṣ*, meaning "animals" (domestic and wild) and "every crawling creature on earth." In 1:28 all the land animals are denoted as *kol-ḥayyâ hārōmeśet ʿal-hāʾāreṣ* ("every creature that moves on earth"), with the participle *rōmeśet* referring to movement in general rather than crawling in particular. In 1:30 living creatures as a whole are called *kol-ḥayyat hāʾāreṣ* ("every creature on earth"), and the land animals are now called *kol rômeś ʿal-hāʾāreṣ* ("every living creature that moves on earth"). The semantic scope of the terms *bəhēmâ*, *remeś*, and *ḥayyâ* is varied in each of these passages. This variation of terminology to refer to land animals shows that it is not a strict terminological taxonomy. The variation is motivated by P's style of variation within repetition, thereby allowing shifting terms within a stable overall structure. The taxonomic impulse is overridden by a poetics of variation.

The form *ḥaytô-ʾereṣ* ("wild creatures of the earth") in 1:24 has an unusual form. The noun *ḥaytô* has the archaic nominative case ending *-u* (which lengthens to long *ō* in Hebrew phonology), which has been preserved as a "frozen" archaism in the close juncture of this construct chain. Ordinarily, final short vowels were lost in Hebrew, but in a phonetic environment of close juncture an old case vowel could be preserved, as in some personal and place names: *bənô bə ʿōr* ("son of Beor," Num 24:3), *mətûšāʾēl* (Methushael, lit. "man of God," Gen 4:18), *pənûʾēl* (Penuel, lit. "face of God," Gen 32:32). Two similar terms, *ḥaytô śādāy* ("creatures of the field") and *ḥaytô-yāʿar* ("creatures of the forest"), occur in Ps 104:11, 20, a poetic text that the P writer may have known in some form (so Day 1985: 51–53). These constructions for creatures, which are implicitly definite, lack the definite article.

The use of this archaic term has a notable stylistic resonance in this verse—it is used in God's speech, marking his discourse as a high or quasi-poetic register with an archaic tone. By contrast, in the following verse—the report of the creation in the narrator's voice—the normal form is used, *ḥayyat hāʾāreṣ*. This form has the expected construct form, *ḥayyat*, with the definite article on *ʾereṣ*. God's command has a higher register—as is appropriate for the deity—than the ordinary narration.

1:25. God made wild animals of the earth of every kind and domestic animals of every kind and land-crawling creatures of every kind. The *Tatbericht* varies the agent of creation in the *Wortbericht* from "the earth" to "God" (as noted above), like the variation between "the waters" and "God" on the fourth day (1:20–21). The threefold division of land animals differs slightly in order and form: *ḥayyat hāʾāreṣ* ("wild animals") is moved to first position, rather than *ḥaytô-ʾereṣ* in last; *bəhēmâ* ("domestic animals") correspondingly shifts to the middle from first position; and *remeś hāʾădāmâ* ("land-crawling creatures") is now last, rather than in the middle. These shifts of sequence and variation of form create a sense of structure in motion.

1:26. God said, "Let us make." To whom is God speaking? In the *Tatbericht* (1:27), God alone creates humans. But in the *Wortbericht*, God uses the plural cohortative, *naʿăśeh* ("Let us make"). It is possible that this is a use of the "plural of majesty" (which is better described by the broader class of "intensive plurals," *IBHS* §7.4.3; Garr 2003: 214–15), but this usage is attested only for nouns, never for verbs. (The noun *'ĕlōhîm*, "God," may belong to this category of nouns; Joüon and Muraoka 1993: §136d). The only clear case of a plural self-reference in the Bible is in the Aramaic letter in Ezra 4:18, which purports to be from the Persian king, who writes, "the letter which you sent to us (*'ăleynāʾ*)." But there are no similar examples in Hebrew. There are also no examples of a plural of exhortation or self-deliberation in Hebrew (see Miller 1978: 10–11). The only other texts where God uses a first-person plural address are two J texts in the primeval narrative, "the human has become like one of us" (Gen 3:22) and "let us go down and confuse" (11:7), plus Isa 6:8: "Whom shall I send, and who will go for us?"

The easiest solution to these forms of address is to place them in the context of the biblical picture of God's rule in heaven, where he is accompanied by his divine entourage, the lesser divine beings (see the "Sons of God" in Gen 6:1–4). According to Job 38:7, this divine entourage was present at creation, "when the morning stars sang together, and the Sons of God shouted for joy." The divine assembly is familiar from prophetic visions, such as that of Micaiah: "I saw Yahweh seated on his throne and all the hosts of heaven standing before him on his right and his left" (1 Kgs 22:19). Similarly, Daniel sees God enthroned and served by a myriad of angels, and then "the court sat and the books opened" (Dan 7:9–10). As noted above, Isaiah sees Yahweh enthroned and accompanied by seraphim, after which he overhears Yahweh's deliberations, "Whom shall I send, and who will go for us?" (Isa 6:1–8). In this context, Yahweh is referring both to himself ("I") and to the divine assembly ("us").

Against this backdrop, the "us" in God's speeches in Genesis 1–11 is best understood as referring to the divine assembly (so most commentators; see Gunkel 1997: 112–13; Miller 1978: 9–27; Wenham 1987: 27–28; Garr 2003: 17–21, 85–92). This explains why God announces his decree in a plural address but performs the action by himself—the others are there as the backdrop for his deliberations, but God alone has the authority and power to create.

Another factor that indirectly supports this interpretation is the ancient Near Eastern topos that the gods created humans as a result of decisions in the divine assembly. The following Mesopotamian example, from the "Unilingual/Bilingual Account of Creation," situates this decision after the gods "established the plans for heaven and earth":

[Enlil said to them:]
"What should we do next?
What should we make now?"
The great gods who were present,
And the Anunna-gods, ordainers of destinies,
Both replied to Enlil,
"In Uzumua, the linking-place of heaven with earth,
Let us slaughter Alla-gods,
Let us create humankind from their blood."

(lines 19–26, Foster 2005: 492; Lambert 2013: 354–55)

Similar scenes in Mesopotamian mythology are found in *Atraḫasis* (I.172–220), *Enuma Elish* (VI.1–38), and other texts (Clifford 1994: 54–73). In Canaanite mythology, El, "the Father of Humans" (*'ab 'adm*), creates a healing goddess after deliberations in the divine assembly (*CAT* 1.16.iii), but his creation of humans is lacking in the Ugaritic texts. It is possible that Job 15:7–8 may recall the tradition of the creation of humans in the context of the divine assembly: "Were you the first human born? / Were you made before the hills? / Did you listen in on the assembly of God?"

It is curious that P includes this plural reference in 1:26, since nowhere else in P are angels or other divine beings mentioned. Perhaps this old topos was too well-known to suppress completely. A plausible solution for this anomaly has been advanced by Garr (2003: 202–12). In light of the shift from the plural address in 1:26 to the singular in 1:27—from "let us make" and "our image" to "he created" and "his image"—the P source seems deliberately to acknowledge and then relegate to insignificance the divine assembly. This strategy is comparable to the treatment of other former cosmic powers in Genesis 1—"the great dragons" in 1:21, the sun and the moon (called by other names) in 1:14–18, and the "host/array" of heaven in 2:1. The existence of these other entities is acknowledged (if only nominally), but they are diminished in power and autonomy and thereafter play no active or independent role in the ordered cosmos.

In postbiblical Jewish interpretive traditions, "let us make" was often taken to be an address to the angels or Wisdom, and in classical Christian interpretation it was generally taken to refer to Jesus or the Trinity (Kugel 1998: 51–52). The address to Wisdom depends on Prov 8:22, where Lady Wisdom proclaims, "Yahweh created me at the beginning of his way." The exegetical idea that God speaks to Lady Wisdom in Gen 1:26 has the merit of including a divine duality of male and female in the creation of humans in the image of God(s).

human. The word *ʾādām* ("human, man") is grammatically singular but can also be used in a collective sense. The potential ambiguity—is the first *ʾādām* one person or many?—is partially resolved in the following clause, "so that they may rule," referring to *ʾādām* as a collective plural. Yet a residual ambiguity remains, since the purpose clause could refer to the future (Barr 2014: 568). The ambiguity of *ʾādām* recurs in the *Tatbericht* in 1:27, where it is treated first as grammatically singular ("him") and then as a collective plural ("male and female // them"). The relationship between singular and plural in *ʾādām* is not merely a grammatical issue but is part of the deliberate ambiguity of the word *ʾādām* in Genesis 1. This ambiguity recurs in 5:1–5, where *ʾādām* is first singular ("him"), then a collective plural ("male and female // them"), and then the name of a single male human, Adam. The multivalence of the word *ʾādām* is part of the meaning of the text, and the oscillations between singular and plural, and male and female, are distinctive features. In other words, the text plays on the different meanings of *ʾādām* as it describes *ʾādām*'s origins and destiny.

These grammatical and conceptual shadings of *ʾādām* are exploited by both the P and J creation narratives. The use of *ʾādām* also betrays the conceptuality of a patrilineal and patriarchal culture, that is, a culture where "male" is the gender with greater prestige and where the noun for "people, humankind" is by default male. The wordplay with *ʾādām* is linked to a gender hierarchy (or heterarchy; see Meyers 2014). This presents an ethical problem for many modern interpreters, but it is difficult to "depatriarchalize" it without effacing distinctive features of the text (cf. Trible 1978: 15–21; and the critique by Bird 1997: 140–49).

The semantic multivalence of *ʾādām*—as an individual, as implicitly male, and as the plural humankind—also has significance for the narrative coherence of Genesis, allowing both creation stories to be read together as complementary works of creation (see Barr 2014: 564–68). The usage of this word facilitates the linkage of the two stories and contributes to the narrative continuity of the final text, in which the creation of 'adam and the woman in the Garden of Eden can be interpreted as an elucidation of 1:26–27, as is done in early and classical interpretations (see Anderson 2001; Kugel 1998: 85–86).

in our image, according to our likeness. The terms *bəṣalmēnû* ("in our image") and *kidmûtēnû* ("according to our likeness") may be used synonymously here (e.g., Gunkel 1997: 113; Westermann 1984: 145–46), or they may have an overlapping core but differing contextual nuances (see Garr 2003: 117–76), perhaps with *ṣelem* emphasizing god-likeness with respect to authority, and *demût* emphasizing god-likeness with respect to (pro)creation. The P source unsettles a clear elucidation of the differences by using only *ṣelem* in subsequent references to this situation—in the *Tatbericht* (1:27) and the Noachian covenant (9:6). The redactional expansion in 5:1–3 also unsettles a distinction by using *bidmût* ("in God's image") in 5:1, and using both terms, but with reversed order and prepositions (*bidmûtô kəṣalmô*), when Adam fathers a son in his image. This variation of terms belongs to the *Leitwort* style, in which each reference is qualified or expanded by the others.

Elsewhere in the Bible both terms usually have a concrete physical referent, for example, "images (*ṣalmê*) of Chaldeans" and "a likeness (*dəmût*) of Babylonians" carved on the wall in Ezek 23:14–15. However, both can be used more abstractly, for example, "only as an (evanescent) image (*ṣelem*) does a human go about" (Ps 39:7). Only the context can determine the nuance of the terms.

The meaning of this doubled phrase in God's speech is obscure and suggestive (see most thoroughly Garr 2003), and doubtless deliberately so. Complicating the ambiguity is the implication of the plural possessive pronoun "our," which most easily points to God and his heavenly entourage (see above). Note that according to some biblical texts, including the prophetic visions of Isaiah 6 and Ezekiel 1–2, God and his divine entourage don't look very much alike. The members of the divine entourage have multiple wings and other distinctive features, and in Ezekiel even multiple faces. In these texts God has a generally human form, even though much larger and more awesome. Ezekiel's vision describes God's form as a transcendent anthropomorphism (Hendel 1997a: 207–12), though it is difficult to describe: "on top of the likeness (*dəmût*) of the throne there was the likeness (*dəmût*) of an appearance of a man upon it" (Ezek 1:26). P's use of ambiguous but evocative language to describe humans as made in the image of the divine is comparable to this transcendent anthropomorphism. The plural reference in the phrase "in *our* image, according to *our* likeness" arguably serves to complicate or deflect the idea that it refers to a physical image of God (so Gunkel 1997: 113; Bird 1997: 142 n. 49).

The idea that humans were created in the physical image of God as an "image in the round" seems to be partially implied (as in Gen 5:3, "[Adam] fathered a son in his likeness, according to his image"), but it is also problematic—since women and men obviously have different bodily features, as do God and his divine entourage, and God's image is not easily conceivable. The non-synonymity of the two prepositions—*bə* ("in, as," emphasizing proximity or contiguity) and *kə* ("like, similar to," emphasizing a metaphorical similarity; see Garr 2003: 95–117)—also complicates an easy equivalence of the human and divine bodies. The varying emphases seem to present humans as in some way representations of God(s), but not as copies.

The incompleteness of the bodily sense may suggest that a mental or spiritual sense is primary since "in our image, according to our likeness" need not be restricted to the visual. Humans may be made in God's image with respect to goodness, knowledge, compassion, and the like. The idea in the Garden of Eden story that man "has become like one of us, knowing good and evil" (3:22) correlates generally to this implication in 1:26–27. But there is a crucial difference: in Genesis 1 this likeness is willed by God, whereas in Genesis 3 it is willed by humans, violating God's command. The "knowledge of good and evil" is a mental or spiritual/moral quality, providing an analogy for a mental or spiritual dimension of "image of God."

Another sense of these words is implied in the following purpose/result clause, "so that they may rule the fish of the sea and the birds of heaven and the animals and every crawling creature on earth" (1:26). The idea that humans collectively have governing authority over all life on earth is warranted by their being made in God's image. The phrase "image of God" in this sense has a functional or political effect; it signifies the authority to rule (so many commentators; see von Rad 1972: 59–60; W. H. Schmidt 1973: 142–49; Bird 1997: 132–38; Schellenberg 2011: 68–127). On this meaning, being made in God's image means having been chosen by God to rule in his stead, like a king's regent or governor. These different meanings—functional, cognitive, and bodily—probably complement each other. Because humans look like God and have other godlike capacities, they are entitled to rule in his name. As Dillmann (1897: 80) comments, "By reason of their likeness to God, humans are to rule."

The physical, spiritual, and political senses often coalesce in the ancient Near Eastern usage of the term "image of god," which usually refers to the king. This term is a royal epithet in Mesopotamian texts, describing the king as the image (*ṣalmu*) of a god: for example, *ṣalmu ša Šamaš* ("the image of Shamash"), *ṣalam Enlil* ("the image of Enlil"), *ṣalam Marduk* ("the image of Marduk"), and *ṣalam Bēl* ("the image of the Lord") (see Bird 1997: 135–38; Garr 2003: 145–49; Machinist 2006; Schellenberg 2011: 106–13). This epithet describes the king as the chosen instrument of the god to rule the earth, the earthy representation of the god's greatness and perfection. In all respects, according to an Old Babylonian letter, "the king is the mirror (*muššuli*) of the god" (Lambert 1960: 282). Mesopotamian statues of the king often depict him as the physical mirror image of the high god, and these royal statues were sometimes treated as objects of worship (Winter 2010: 2.167–87). In his person, as Machinist (2006: 162) writes, "[the king's] body serves as the statue of the god." The king's perfect body expresses the political sense of the "image of god." As Pongratz-Leisten (2015: 222) comments, "This virtual image of royal perfection . . . served to advance the notion of homogeneity in action between the gods and the king."

In Egypt the pharaoh is sometimes described as the "image" of a high god (Hornung 1982: 135–42; Schellenberg 2011: 98–106). This suits the royal ideology in which the king was a god, an earthly incarnation of Horus. The wisdom text "Instruction to Merikare" (ca. 2100 BCE) expands this royal connotation, describing humans collectively as made in the creator god's image: "They are his images, who came from his body" (Lichtheim 1976: 106).

Figure 4. Assyrian king Ashurnasirpal II in battle as an earthly double of the god Aššur. Relief (detail restored) from Northwest Palace, Calah (ca. 860 BCE), British Museum. (Drawing by William H. C. Propp)

The idea in Gen 1:26–27 that humans are created "in our image, according to our likeness" draws on this older Near Eastern concept but, perhaps like the "Instruction to Merikare," democratizes and spiritualizes it. Loosened from its mooring in the royal ideology, the idea that humans are made "in the image of God"—implying physical, spiritual, and functional attributes—emphasizes an appreciation of the value of human life (see NOTES at 9:6). The Enlightenment principle that "all men are created equal," adopted in the U.S. Constitution, flows directly from these verses (and is taken up in other emancipatory movements; see Hendel 2013: 204–7).

so that they may rule the fish of the sea and the birds of heaven and the animals and every crawling creature on earth. The verb *wəyirdû* is a jussive, "let them rule." In this type of clause sequence, with a volitional (jussive, imperative, or cohortative) followed by another volitional (jussive or cohortative), the second verb often has a meaning of purpose or result (*IBHS* §34.6). By virtue of their qualities as God's earthly "image," humans are entitled to rule the other creatures of the earth. The geographical scope of their rule is emphasized by naming the locales of the three divisions of living creatures: "sea," "heaven," and "earth."

The precise kind of "rule" (from *rdh*) is not specified. In the blessing of 1:28, the idea that humans will "subdue" (from *kbš*) the earth is linked to their rule (*rdh*) over the animals (*wəkibšuhā ûrədû*, "subdue it, and rule . . ."). These verbs can have various nuances, but in general they belong to the semantics of kingship and military conquest (Garr 2003: 156–63). The type of rule or dominance that humans should exercise is analogous to that of the king, who ideally exercises force, authority, justice, and mercy. These qualities of ideal rule are implied in the conceptual scope of "image of God." As

Janowski (1993: 194) comments, "Their caring *and* commanding rule over the animals is a concretizing of their having been made in the image of God." The ideal king is just and wise (e.g., the portraits of David and Solomon in 2 Sam 14:20 and 1 Kgs 3:9) but is also a strong authority. As Weippert (1998) observes, this is the outlook of a people for whom the world of nature was often dangerous and unpredictable, and often symbolically aligned with chaos. It is a hierarchical view of the cosmos, in which humans are near the top of the chain of being (cf. Psalm 8). It is not necessarily an ecological ideal (see White 1967).

At this point the human "rule" over the animals does not include the authority to kill them for food. This becomes clear in 9:3, when God grants this authority as part of the Noachian covenant. In Genesis 1, humans and land animals are created to be vegetarians (1:29–30). The permission to kill and eat animals after the flood (with the provision that their blood not be consumed) addresses the problem of the "violence" that corrupted the earth before the flood (6:11). The ideal relationship between humans and animals entails nonviolent rule, but humans breach this ideal in the era after creation (Schellenberg 2011: 49–68).

1:27. *God created the human in his image; / in God's image he created him; / male and female he created them.* The *Tatbericht* varies the *Wortbericht* in several ways. First, as noted above, the work of creation is done solely by God (using the divine verb of creation *bara'*) and omits any hint of the presence of the divine assembly. Second, as mentioned above, the double descriptors *ṣelem* ("image") and *dəmût* ("likeness") are replaced by repetitions of *ṣelem*. The semantic play on *'ādām* ("human, man") as both singular and plural is intensified by first referring to *hā'ādām* as "him" and then by unpacking the meaning of *'ādām* as "male and female." The function of ruling the animals is covered by the subsequent blessing, in which the list of animals is slightly varied but preserves a tripartite division.

The most striking stylistic variation is the transition into poetry. While there are no explicit criteria to mark a shift from prose to poetry, the density of poetic features—and particularly the syntactic parallelism of the first two lines—argues for a shift of register to poetry (so, e.g., Cassuto 1961: 57; Speiser 1964: 4; Trible 1978: 16–18; Seebass 1996: 82). It is a characteristic of biblical narrative that at climactic moments the prose may shift into poetry (Alter 1996: 32). It is not necessary to posit a different or earlier source for this poetic upspringing, and it seems unlikely in this case (*pace* Kselman 1978), since the *Tatbericht* is expected. The three parallel poetic lines form a triplet:

> God created the human in his image;
>> in God's image he created him;
> male and female he created them.

Each line is a clause containing four words or accentual units (4:4:4), and each line echoes, expands, or intensifies the meanings of the previous line. Each line repeats the governing verb of divine creation, *br'* ("create"), focalizing this special work of creation. The poetic structure of the parallelism, that is, repetition with variation, can be indicated as follows:

> *wayyibrā'* (A) *'ĕlōhîm* (B) *'et-hā'ādām* (C) *bəṣalmô* (D)
> *bəṣelem* (D') *'ĕlōhîm* (B) *bārā'* (A') *'ōtô* (C')
> *zākār ûnəqēbâ* (E) *bārā'* (A') *'ōtām* (C')

The variations in the first two lines are deceptively simple. Each of the four words in line 1 has a counterpart in line 2, each varied in form, word order, or grammatical function. The divine verb of creation, *br'* (A // A'), occurs in first and near-last position in the two lines and pivots around *'ĕlōhîm*, creating a chiastic rhythm and balance. This chiastic rhythm is heightened by the last and first positions of *bəṣalmô* // *bəṣelem* (D // D'), which blends prosodic chiasm and sequential repetition. The fronted *bəṣelem* in the second line emphasizes and focalizes this concept, which the third line explicates. The *bəṣalmô* at the end of the first line also creates an end rhyme with *'ōtô* ("him") in the second line, which is semantically unpacked at the end of the third line as *'ōtām* ("them"). The subtle variations in these lines create a heightening of sound and sense.

The only word that does not differ in form and word order in the first two lines is *'ĕlōhîm* ("God"), but it differs in grammatical function. In the first line it is the subject of the verb, *wayyibrā' 'ĕlōhîm* ("God created"), and in the second line it is the genitive of the indirect object, *bəṣelem 'ĕlōhîm* ("in the image of God"). So this divine term varies even if unchanged.

Line 3 is the climax of the triplet. It adds a new fronted focus, *zākār ûnəqēbâ* ("male and female"), in the syntactic position occupied by *bəṣelem 'ĕlōhîm* ("in the image of God") in the second line. By this parallel position one might expect the line to heighten or explicate the idea of "image of God." But it more directly explicates the thing that was created, which in lines 1 and 2 looked like a single man—*hā'ādām* // *'ōtô* ("human // him")—but now is shown to be a plural of humans (perhaps a single pair, see below)—*zākār ûnəqēbâ* ("male and female") and *'ōtām* ("them")—with their different sexual identities emphasized.

The new elements of line 3 point backward and forward. They deepen and complicate the nature of *'ādām* ("human") in 1:26–27, mobilizing the ambiguity of singular male versus collective male and female, with *'ādām* now clearly a collective consisting of man and woman. It also complicates the idea of "image of God," which has an implicit physical dimension, since men and women have different bodies. Sexual difference becomes focalized, a topic that is further developed in the blessing of procreation that follows. In this crescendo of the poem, God's creation of *'ādām* in his image is now shown to include the human duality of sex and gender, which yet still corresponds to "the image of God." The meanings of these parallel phrases and concepts are not explicitly articulated, leaving a residue of ambiguity regarding how the human duality of male and female articulates "the image of God." God in P does not have sexual features, but these differential qualities—human and divine, male and female, unity and duality—are here interrelated (see Hendel, Kronfeld, and Pardes 2010: 76).

The implication from the blessing is that human procreation is a counterpart—by analogy and extension—to God's creation of humans in his image. "Male and female" specifies and extends the meaning of "image of God" by including human sexuality and procreation as Godlike qualities. (Note that "likeness" is a comparison, not an identity.) This resonance is taken up in the redactional expansion in 5:3 when Adam fathers a son "in his likeness, according to his image." The humans' ability to reproduce—involving their sexual complementary as male and female—is entailed in their creation in God's image.

The senses of this poetic *Tatbericht* are elusive, multiple, and suggestive. The gender issues are particularly difficult (cf. the various positions of Trible 1978: 12–21; Bird

1997: 123–63; Lanser 1988; Galambush 1993; Schellenberg 2011: 131–34). The text may be reticent for good reason, perhaps because of the topics of God's body and sexuality, but the implications of this text go beyond simple obscurity. As noted above, they offer a new concept of human dignity.

1:28. *Be fruitful and multiply, fill the earth.* This blessing to humans echoes the previous blessing for the water and sky animals in 1:22: "Be fruitful and multiply, fill the water of the seas, and let the birds be fruitful on the earth." As a variation, the land animals do not receive their blessing until 8:17, at their exit from the ark: "Let them be fruitful and multiply on the earth." The verb *pərû* ("be fruitful") in all these blessings echoes the *Leitwort pərî* ("fruit") in the creation of trees in 1:11–12. These verses emphasize the importance of the creation of new life as the continuation and extension of God's creation of life. Creation, propagation, and procreation are thus complementary tasks. This blessing is in the form of a command, a divinely mandated good.

In the literary structure of the P narrative, this blessing/command to humans opens a long-range *Leitwort* sequence (see INTRODUCTION I), joining creation with the Noachian and Abrahamic covenants (Gen 9:1, 7; 17:6, 20) and culminating with the multiplication of Israel in Egypt: "The children of Israel were fruitful and teemed and multiplied and increased greatly, and the earth was filled with them" (Exod 1:7). It is one of the connective features in the P narrative (see Lohfink 1994: 165–67).

and subdue it. Rule the fish of the sea and the birds of heaven and every creature that moves on earth. The blessing continues with the charge to rule over the earth and the animals. This fulfills the charge of the *Wortbericht* ("so that they may rule . . ."). By situating this task as the second part of the blessing, it subtly alters its value. The blessing of fertility associates humans with the other animals, who receive similar blessings, but then it moves from "filling the earth" to "subduing it." Humans are both like and unlike the animals, because they not only procreate but rule the other creatures. This connects with the theme of the "image of God," since their authority to rule stems from this unique status of humans as God's earthly representatives. Hence humans "subdue" (*kbš*) the earth—a royal and martial image—and rule the creatures of the habitable domains: sea, heaven, and earth. This obligation to rule is now presented as a blessing, granted by God to his favored creatures of the earth.

1:29. *I hereby give to you all seed-bearing plants on the whole face of the earth and all trees with seed-bearing fruit. They will be food for you.* The opening phrase, *hinnēh nātattî* ("I hereby give"), signals a performative utterance, in which the Hebrew perfect introduced by the deictic particle *hinnēh* expresses an action that is fulfilled in the act of saying it. Usually, such performative utterances are spoken by God, kings, judges, or elders—those with the authority to make such oral grants (*IBHS* §30.5.1d).

According to this verse, humans were originally vegetarians. The following verse assigns vegetarianism to the animals of the earth and sky (the sea creatures are not included). There are variations in wording from the previous lists of land animals (see NOTES at 1:14), and the term for vegetation also varies (see NOTES at 1:11). Where 1:29 refers to 'ēśeb ("plants") and 'ēṣ ("trees"), the corresponding reference in 1:30 is *yereq* 'ēśeb ("green plants"), which must include plants and fruit trees, since animals eat from both. As noted above, this type of variation of terms and reference is characteristic of P's taxonomic and narrative style.

According to this P text, vegetarian cuisine is part of the initial order of creation. This order becomes corrupted by the violence of "all flesh" in the period before the flood (6:12–13). As part of the new dispensation after the flood, God allows humans to eat animal meat as long as they do not consume it "with its life's blood in it" (9:4). In the postdiluvian order, the consumption of meat is allowed as a compromise with the violence of human and animal nature.

The idea that the first humans were vegetarians is found elsewhere in the Bible and the ancient world. In the Garden of Eden story, the first humans are permitted to eat "from all the trees of the garden" (2:16), with the exception of two trees. The implication in this story is that humans did not eat meat, and in the J narrative animal husbandry is introduced after Eden (4:2, 20). The picture of vegetarianism as the ideal state recurs in Isa 11:6–8, where the carnivorous animals return to vegetarianism ("the lion, like the ox, will eat hay") in the future golden age, when violence disappears from the earth.

The vegetarianism of the first humans is found in other ancient cultures. In the Sumerian "Debate Between Ewe and Grain," the first humans ate grass like the animals:

The humans of those far-off days
did not know the eating of bread,
did not know the wearing of clothes.
The people went naked-limbed,
eating grass with their mouths like sheep,
drinking water from ditches.

(George 2003: 450)

The portrait of Enkidu in the *Gilgamesh* epic reflects this tradition: "He ate grass with the gazelles" (I.110). Similarly, in Greek tradition the earliest humans were vegetarians: "they had all good things; for the fruitful earth unforced bare them fruit abundantly and without stint" (Hesiod, *Works and Days* 116–19; similarly, Plato, *Laws* 6.782c; Ovid, *Metamorphoses* 1.101–12; see Dillmann 1897: 87).

The vegetarianism of primeval times seems to have two different colorings: it can be an ideal or paradisical state that has since been lost, or it can be a savage or animal-like past that human culture has risen above (Moran 2002: 24–26). In Greek culture, both tendencies are present. There also seems to be some ambivalence in the Mesopotamian portrayal of Enkidu (Westenholz and Koch-Westenholz 2000). In Genesis 1, the vegetarianism of early days—and the absence of killing among humans and animals—seems to portray a picture of paradise lost. Violence erupts later (see 6:11–12).

1:31. *God saw all that he had made, and behold, it was very good.* This crescendo of the sevenfold refrain (see Notes at 1:4) expresses God's perception and approval of the goodness of creation, now that it is complete. God's carefully articulated plan has transformed primordial chaos into a good world, filled with life and crowned by humans, who represent God's image on earth.

However, this approval of creation also anticipates the next P story, when God will perceive that the world has changed for the worse. Using the same grammatical construction, 6:12 relates this second look: "God saw the earth, and behold, it was corrupt." This sequence, *wayyar' 'ĕlōhîm* X *wəhinnēh* Y, occurs only in these two places, and they clearly mirror each other (Delitzsch 1888: 255; Eissfeldt 1927: 87). God's perception of a good and orderly cosmos is reversed when he perceives its corruption by the violence of the earth's inhabitants. In retrospect, the "goodness" of the cosmos is a fragile quality. God institutes new laws and covenants, beginning with the Noachian covenant, to protect this fragile goodness.

2:1. *Now heaven and earth and all their array were complete.* This concluding or summarizing statement announces the completion of the process of creating "heaven and earth" announced in 1:1. The successive statements that heaven, earth, and their array "were complete" and that God "completed" his work (2:2) create a *Leitwort* effect, which is heightened by the word *kol-* ("all")—*waykullû . . . wəkol . . . waykal.* This sequence emphasizes the sound and sense of the "completion" of the cosmos. The clause sequence with a noun phrase plus *pual* (a medio-passive form) followed by a *piel* (an active form) plus its subject ("God") emphasizes first the object and then the agent of "completion." The resumption of the active verbal sequence with "God completed" provides a transition to the next active clause, God's rest.

The echo of 1:1, "heaven and earth," is varied here with the two-part merism expanded into a three-part description, "heaven and earth and all their array." In this repetition, "heaven and earth" seem to refer to two different domains, above and below, with "their array" as that which fills them (i.e., the lights in the vault of heaven and the living things of land, sea, and sky). The phrase "heaven and earth" in 1:1 is now filled out with the works of creation.

The word *ṣəbā'ām* ("their array") is unusual and suggestive. Usually *ṣābā'* means "army, organized host," referring to soldiers or workers. A special phrase is *ṣəbā' haššāmayim* ("the host of heaven"), which refers to God's divine entourage as a heavenly army (Niehr 1999). A figure called the *śar-ṣəbā'-yhwh* ("commander of Yahweh's army") appears with sword in hand in Josh 5:13–14, and the heavenly army is shown in military action in Judg 5:20, 2 Kgs 6:17, Isa 13:4–5, and other texts (Miller 1973: 74–144). The phrase "host of heaven" is also used of Yahweh's heavenly entourage in nonmartial contexts (1 Kgs 22:19, Zeph 1:5). The divine title *yhwh ṣəbā'ôt* ("Yahweh of hosts/armies"), associated with the Ark of the Covenant (1 Sam 4:4), refers to Yahweh as master of his heavenly army or entourage. Often the "host of heaven" is identified as stars (so Judg 5:20; Job 38:7; Deut 4:19, 17:3; 2 Kgs 23:5), in line with the common ancient Near Eastern equivalence of gods and stars (see NOTES at 1:16).

In Gen 2:1, the meaning "heavenly host" or "stars" does not fit, although an astral association is part of the picture. The P writer is consciously revising the term to make it clear that the "stuff" of the cosmos is not a host of gods, but mere matter (Halpern 2009: 91). Like the use of "greater light" and "lesser light" to refer to the sun and moon (1:16), the use of "host, array" in this verse seems purposefully to exclude the notion that other gods inhabit the cosmos. This revision of the customary notion of the "heavenly host" into a material "array" exemplifies the rationalizing cosmology of Genesis 1 (see COMMENTS).

2:2. *On the sixth day God completed his work that he had made, and on the seventh day he ceased from all his work that he had made.* The MT reading in the first clause, *bayyôm haššəbî'î* ("on the seventh day"), is probably a scribal anticipation of *bayyôm haššəbî'î* in the second clause (both are followed by the same word cluster, *məla'ktô 'ăšer 'āśâ*, "his work that he had made") (see TEXTUAL NOTE m and Hendel 1998:

32–34). This reading in the MT has stimulated much ingenuity by commentators. The clause-initial form *waykal* ("[God] completed") cannot plausibly be read as a pluperfect ("[God] had completed") (so correctly Dillmann 1897: 90; Skinner 1930: 37; *contra* Cassuto 1961: 61–62; Westermann 1984: 169–70; Hamilton 1990: 142), since this normally requires a disjunctive construction (noun-initial + perfect). Some commentators posit a special meaning of the *piel klh* ("to complete, finish") (e.g., Speiser 1964: 7–8, "brought to a close"), but this is also unwarranted, particularly in light of its echo of the same verb (in the *pual*) in the previous clause.

This verse has a rhythmic and quasi-parallel construction, moving from the completion of the cosmos to God's rest. The rhetorical pivot and emphasis is God's work, which is intensified in the second repetition: "his work that he had made" // "all his work that he had made." The qualifier *kol-* ("all") in the repetition echoes *waykal* ("[he] completed") in the first clause. The parallel phrases "on the sixth day" and "on the seventh day" use a numerical parallelism that is common in biblical and Northwest Semitic poetry, following the formula of $X // X + 1$ (e.g., Job 5:19: "From six troubles he will rescue you // From seven no evil will touch you"). Genesis 2:2 is not poetry but is prose of a high register, using the resources and variations of parallel forms. In this sense, "sixth" and "seventh" are parallel, just as "completed" and "ceased" are parallel. Note that parallelism does not imply identity of the two members; they can also be complementary or supplementary. The ascent to the number seven is significant in the literary structure of the creation account—not only are there seven days, but there are seven repetitions of key refrains (with variations, see Notes at 1:4, 7).

The verb *wayyišbōt* ("he ceased") echoes in the following verse with *šābat* ("he ceased"). Its basic meaning is "to cease, stop." The noun *šabbāt* (Sabbath) is not explicitly named in this text, but it is anticipated by this verb in P's *Leitwort* style. In P texts in Exodus, the Sabbath is explicitly derived from God's cessation from his work on the seventh day (Exod 20:11, 31:16–17; see Olyan 2005; Stackert 2011). The repetition of the verb "to cease" creates a sound-play on the Sabbath, whose sense clearly circulates in this text. God's cessation from labor on the seventh day foreshadows the divine command, given at Mount Sinai, for Israel to cease from labor on the Sabbath. As Levenson (1988: 111) observes, in the sacred time of the Sabbath, "Israel can rest the rest of God." Sabbath rest is an *imitatio dei,* which celebrates, recalls, and re-creates the sacred time of the seventh day in Gen 2:2–3.

There is a further nuance in God's cessation of labor as a foreshadowing of the Sabbath. This literary anticipation is visible to the reader, but not yet to God. As Stackert (2016: 97) observes: "The narrator and the reader (if only by virtue of his cultural knowledge) stand in an elevated position vis-à-vis the character Yahweh. That is, they know of the Sabbath that Yahweh has not yet imagined and thus also recognize its foreshadowing in Gen 2:1–3." The Sabbath of the people Israel is not a property of the "very good" cosmos of Genesis 1. It is only after the transgressions that lead to the flood, when God decides to give covenants and laws, that this ritual practice becomes possible. There are no rites—or religion—at the time of creation.

The word and institution of the Sabbath may be obscurely related to the Akkadian *šapattu/šabattu,* the day of the full moon. Some have argued that the Israelite Sabbath was originally also a festival of the full moon, although there is no clear evidence for this meaning in the Bible (E. Haag 2004: 391–92). The seven-day week is an Israelite innovation, justified in this verse, and capped by the Sabbath, which is not only a celebration of sacred time, but also an economic holiday, a respite from labor. Note that in the Covenant Code (Exod 23:12) and the Ten Commandments (Exod 20:10), even slaves and domestic animals rest from their labors on the Sabbath. In Deuteronomy, the Sabbath derives not from God's rest after creation, but from God's deliverance of Israel from slavery (Deut 5:15). The Sabbath is thus an institution with many meanings, blending a suspension of the ordinary burden of labor, an imitation of God's cessation from his work of creation, and an infusion of sacred time.

The idea of God's rest after his work of creation has analogues in other Near Eastern texts (Batto 1987). In *Enuma Elish,* the god Ea rests in his newly acquired temple after his defeat of Apsu and Mummu:

> After Ea had bound and slain his enemies,
> > Had achieved victory over his foes,
> He rested (*inūḫ*) quietly in his chamber.

(I.73–75; Lambert 2013: 54–55)

Later the god Marduk rests (*inūḫ*, IV.135) after his defeat of Tiamat. The resting of the deity after the conquest of chaos seems to be in the distant background of God's rest after his work of creation in Genesis 1. The distinctive differences are the lack of conflict here—it is a creation without opposition—and the later ritual participation in God's rest. According to Exod 31:17 (P), "on the seventh day, he ceased (*šābat*) and was refreshed," and so Israel is commanded to do.

2:3. *God blessed the seventh day and made it holy, for on it he ceased from all his work.* God's last act in the creation account is to bless the seventh day, which he will later call the *šabbāt* ("Sabbath"; Exod 20:11, 31:16–17). This anticipation rings out in the motive clause, "for on it he ceased," using the form *šābat,* which looks and sounds likes the noun *šabbāt.* God's last act in the creation account thus foreshadows the creation of the institution of the Sabbath at Sinai.

The "work" of creation from which God ceased is emphasized by its threefold repetition, with characteristic variations and intensifications, in 2:2–3: "his work that he had made" // "all his work that he had made" // "all his work that God had made in creation." The additions and variations create a heightening effect, with *kol-* ("all") added to the second and third clauses and the name "God" and divine verb of creation, *bārā',* added to the third. The third clause also echoes Gen 1:1 (see below).

God's blessing of the seventh day is to make it holy. The sequence *waybarek . . . wayqaddēš* ("[God] blessed . . . and he sanctified") is a logical or epexegetical sequence, using quasi-parallel diction in the high rhetoric of this verse. Holiness is a key concept in P, as it is in Israelite religion generally (see B. J. Schwartz 2000). God is holy, sacred places and objects are holy, but most things are profane (*ḥōl*). For humans to have a relationship with God, they must come into contact with holy things. Hence, God makes this day holy, which creates the possibility of human contact with holiness in the Israelite celebration of the Sabbath.

that God had made in creation. The last clause of the creation account includes the two main verbs of creation, the uniquely divine verb *bārā'* ("to create") and the more general verb *'āśâ* ("to make"). In the P creation account, *bārā'* occurs in the first and last verses (1:1 and 2:3), in the creation of sea creatures (1:21), and three times in the creation of humans (1:27). Clearly the creation of humans is marked as special by the repetition of this verb (as by other means). The verb *ʿāśâ* is used for God's work of creation seven times (1:7, 16, 25, 26; 2:2 [twice], 3), a number that is significant. The combination of these two verbs in 2:3, with the infinitive *la ʿăśôt* modifying the finite verb *bārāʾ,* is syntactically awkward but rhetorically resonant. It can be rendered precisely, "that God had created actively/makingly."

The first part of this clause, *ʾăšer-bārāʾ ʾĕlōhîm* ("that God had created"), echoes Gen 1:1, *bārāʾ ʾĕlōhîm* ("God created") and functions as a stylistic inclusion. The last words of the creation account connect with the first. This summarizes the text's meaning *in nuce:* "God created." This verbal frame emphasizes by its literary architecture the harmony of creation.

Comments

Genesis 1:1–2:3 is an elegant and intricate account of God's creation of the cosmos. It begins the Bible with a cosmic horizon, an origin for all things and people. It is the opening text of the Pentateuch and the P source, which, after the primeval narrative, tells the story of Israel up to the death of Moses on the threshold of the promised land (for other possibilities of P's ending, see Nihan 2007: 20–68; B. J. Schwartz 2016). The narrative span beginning with Genesis 1 embeds the particular within the universal, establishing a particular ethnic-religious identity within the broader scope of the cosmos. This mixture of the universal and the particular is already signaled in Genesis 1, in which the structure of seven days ends with an implicit anticipation of the Sabbath, a specifically Israelite institution later revealed at Sinai. Genesis 1 creates a backdrop in space and time for the genealogical narrative of Genesis.

LITERARY DESIGN

Genesis 1 is at the same time a myth of origins and a philosophical-theological system. As we have seen, it is a myth in the sense of "a sacred narrative explaining how the world or humans came to be in their present form" (Dundes 1988: 1), which shows "how existence, including human existence, is meaningfully legitimated" (Müller 1991a: 201). Genesis 1 establishes the structure and meaning of the world and human existence as products of God's creation. It has a simple plot, from the first act ("God said, 'Let there be light'") to the last ("God blessed the seventh day and made it holy"). Unlike complex plots (cf. the Garden of Eden story), it lacks antagonists, reversals, or narrative tension. It is a "creation without opposition" (Levenson 1988: 67), which makes it something other than a typical mythic narrative.

As a philosophical-theological system, it often uses abstract or specialized terms— including *bārāʾ* ("create"), *tōhû wābōhû* ("desolate chaos"), and *ṣelem ʾĕlōhîm* ("image of God")—to describe the processes and purposes of creation. Yet, unlike most philosophical productions, there is literary artistry in the telling—Wellhausen (1885: 298) notes "the exalted ease and the uniform greatness that give the narrative its character." Polak (2002: 11) emphasizes the density of poetic terms and parallel style, which "evokes the poetic code, entailing a rhythmic, balanced reading." Genesis 1 combines the features of a literary myth and a philosophical-theological reflection on myth, yielding something novel.

The formal qualities of the text balance a regular structure with subtle but consistent variation. As McEvenue (1971: 81) comments, "structure is present, but it is so overwoven and interlaced with different systems of echo and repetition that the final effect is of a universe of thought which is completely mastered and unified, but whose pattern remains elusive." For instance, the first six days have a consistent but varying design, consisting of the following elements:

> God said, "Let . . ." (*Wortbericht*—"word report")
> And it was so.
> God made . . ." (*Tatbericht*—"deed report")
> God called . . .
> God saw that it was good.
> God blessed . . .
> There was evening, and there was morning, *X* day.

However, this sequence never occurs in full, and never the same way twice. Each work of creation has a *Wortbericht* and, with one exception, a *Tatbericht*, but the correspondences between the two are never exact, and the meaning of words for particular creatures is often fluid. The statements "and it was so" and "God saw that it was good" occur seven times each, with variations, but are distributed unevenly across the seven days (the former is lacking on the fifth day, and the latter on the second day). The naming formula occurs only on the first three days, and the blessing formula only on days five and six. The third and sixth days each have two separate works of creation, but the other days have only one each. The interplay of system and variation—at the levels of literary structure and individual words—is a constant feature.

One of the most striking examples of internal design and "secret" symmetry are the correspondences between the first three days and the second three days. This diptych design was observed in its essentials by Herder (1993a: 271–72, original 1774) and is clearly described by Delitzsch (1888: 69):

> The account of creation as now extant falls into two groups of three days, so arranged that the days' works of the second group accord with the corresponding ones of the first. On the first day light was created, on the fourth the heavenly light-giving bodies; on the second day the vault of heaven dividing the waters from the waters, on the fifth the birds of heaven and the animals of the waters; on the third day, after the appearance of the dry land, the vegetable world; on the sixth land animals, to fill the dry land now provided with herbage for their nourishment, and man, in whom the whole animal creation reaches its climax.

This diptych design can be presented as two triads:

Day 1: Light	Day 4: Heavenly lights
Day 2: Vault of heaven	Day 5: Sky and water animals
Day 3: Dry land	Day 6: Land animals
Vegetation	Humans

The works of creation on the first three days establish, through God's act of separation and naming, the cosmic domains that will be inhabited or regulated by the creations of the second three days. The second series of works of creation complements and, in a sense, completes the first series.

In the correspondence of days one and four, God creates light and "separated the light from the darkness" (1:4), a task that he assigns later to the celestial lights, which are created "to rule the day and the night, and to separate the light from the darkness" (1:18). In the correspondences of days two and five, God first creates the vault of heaven and "separated the water below the vault from the water above the vault" (1:7), while he later fills the new domains below the vault—the sky and terrestrial waters: "Let the waters teem with teeming living creatures, and let birds fly over the earth across the vault of heaven" (1:20). The correspondences of days three and six are more layered, since each has two works of creation. On day three, God creates the earth by separating the land from the waters, and he also creates vegetation on the earth. He later fills the dry land—first with animals and then with humans—and assigns them vegetation for food.

Creation is now, in a sense, a self-regulating system. On the fourth day God assigns the celestial lights to "rule" the progression of time, and on the sixth day he assigns humans to "rule" the other living creatures: "Rule the fish of the sea and the birds of heaven and every creature that moves on earth" (1:28). In all these ways, the second triad of the days of creation form a parallel panel, completing the works of creation of the first triad.

During the first three days, creation involves separation and naming. By these creative acts, the primeval materials—darkness, water, and the unformed earth—are transformed into the distinct temporal and spatial domains of the ordered cosmos. These domains are, as we have seen, populated by the creations of the second three days. The transformations from primeval chaos to the world of time and space on the first three days are indicated as follows:

Primeval state: Chaotic "earth" (*'ereṣ*), "darkness" (*ḥōšek*), "wind" (*rûaḥ*), and "water" (*mayim*)
Day 1: "He separated" (*wayyabdēl*): light from darkness (*ḥōšek*)
Day 2: "He/it separated" (*wayyabdēl*): water (*mayim*) above from water (*mayim*) below
Day 3: "Let it be gathered" (*yiqqāwû*): water (*mayim*) from earth (*'ereṣ*)

In the second three days these domains are filled, and the vocabulary of separation is limited to the celestial lights, which are assigned "to separate the day from the night" and "to separate the light from the darkness" (1:14, 18). Naming (*wayyiqrā'*, "he named") occurs only on the first three days. On the last three days, the vocabulary of blessing (*waybārek,* "he blessed") comes into play. God gives three blessings on days five, six, and seven: to the water and sky animals, to humans, and to the seventh day. These blessings create a pattern across these days.

As we have seen, there are many variations within this structure. Across the two triads, eight acts of creation are distributed over six days, with creation doubled on the last day of each triad. The act of creation on the fifth day includes two different classes of creature—water and sky animals. These variations are features of the text's literary design, and hence need not be seen as irregularities due to multiple layers of composition or redaction (cf. Levin 2003; Carr 2020a: 26–28).

In all of these layered features, we see a subtle play of structure and variation, creating a sense of an overarching plan and an orderly rhythm, which is at the same time colored by shifting meanings and sometimes obscurity. The sophistication of this style of composition has a notable conceptual and didactic implication—the structure of creation may seem understandable, but its details are complex, shifting, and often baffling or obscure. On a cursory reading, Genesis 1 seems simple and repetitive, as many commentators have lamented, but a close reading yields subtle meanings and resonances.

COSMOLOGY

The often elusive intricacy of Genesis 1 makes it difficult to specify in detail the picture of the cosmos that it verbally constructs. Some commentators infer that the cosmos implicit in Genesis 1 is not a physical picture at all, but a symbolic expression of cosmic and theological principles. For example, as Keel (1985: 57) argues, "Modern representations . . . overlook the fact that the ancient Near East never regarded the world as a closed, profane system. Rather, the world was an entity open at every side. The powers which determine the world are of more interest to the ancient Near East than the structure of the cosmic system." These reservations may be valid if one tries to synthesize or harmonize descriptions of the cosmos from a variety of sources or eras, or when dealing with symbolic religious iconography in seals or reliefs. But Genesis 1 describes a cosmos that seems in every respect a physical, material structure.

Unlike other ancient Near Eastern creation accounts, the world in Genesis 1 is no longer filled with gods—the text deliberately excludes the idea that any piece of the cosmos is divine, including sea, earth, sky, and heavenly bodies (cf. Psalm 104, where wind, fire, and sea are quasi-divine; see Day 2013: 21–23). A major premise of Genesis 1 is that God and his creation are wholly distinct—God creates a well-ordered material world. This premise entails a new concept of "nature," which does not seem to exist elsewhere in the ancient Near East (Rochberg 2016). The contours and categories of this natural realm are a central concern of the text. It is worth recalling that the Israelite priests paid close attention to the detail of bodies and objects in their ritual duties, hence it is reasonable to expect that the details of the world were also taken seriously. As Wellhausen (1885: 298) observes, the writer of Genesis 1 "seeks to deduce things as they are."

As we have seen, on the first three days of creation God creates the domains of the cosmos by a process of repeated separations and namings, thereby transforming the pre-existing materials of primeval chaos—chaotic earth, darkness, wind, and water—into the ordered cosmos (Zenger 1983: 83–84). The "wind of God" (1:2) may also play a role as a catalyst or substance that becomes part of the ordered world, probably a precursor of the atmosphere. From these primordial elements, God creates time (on the first day) and space (on the second and third days). God's creative word and actions are the main strategies in this differentiated system.

But there is no clear sense that God dwells in this cosmic structure, indicating again a distinction between the natural world and God. The traditional Israelite view would have God dwelling in a celestial temple above the vault of heaven, as suggested in Ezekiel's elaborate vision of God enthroned on top of a shining, awesome "vault" (*rāqîaʿ*, Ezek 1:26–28). But in Genesis 1, there is no indication of a place in the natural world for God to dwell. This paradox is later foregrounded when God chooses to dwell in the tabernacle, which, when God's "glory" descends into it, is suffused with holiness and danger (Exod 40:34, Lev 9:23–24).

As Halpern (2009: 427–78) emphasizes, Genesis 1 purposefully transforms traditional Israelite concepts of cosmology. Like the Presocratic philosophers of the Greek world, the P writer was engaged in a critique and reformulation of Israelite religion, organized by a new perspective. A line is drawn between the divine world and the natural world, which are henceforth categorically distinct. This conceptual move results in the disenchantment of nature, in which heaven and earth are objects, unmingled with gods. In its context, it is a radically monotheizing cosmology.

The lights of heaven offer a clear instance of this transformation. In traditional Israelite cosmology, the stars were divine beings, equated with the "Sons of God," that is, the members of God's divine entourage (see Gen 1:26, 2:1, and 6:1–4). These were the "host of heaven" who functioned as God's heavenly court and army. According to God's speech in Job, this divine entourage was present at creation:

Where were you when I founded the earth? . . .
When the morning stars sang together,
     and the Sons of God shouted for joy? (Job 38:4, 7)

Yet in Genesis 1, the stars—and every other aspect of heaven and earth—are depersonalized, rendered as purely material phenomena. The "array" (ṣəbāʾām) of heaven and earth in Gen 2:1, a term that clearly echoes the old "host of heaven" (ṣəbāʾ haššāmayim), no longer includes gods or stars but natural objects—celestial and earthly bodies—that fill the natural world. The heavenly bodies serve not as oracular signs, but as "signs" (ʾōtōt) for the calendar (1:14). The sun, moon, and stars are mechanisms for the regulation and observance of the regular cycles of time.

P's cosmology is a theological innovation, in which God is ontologically distinct from the world of nature that he creates and organizes. As in earlier cosmologies, divine commands create the structure of the universe, but the universe is now a wholly material world. This cosmology is a "natural philosophy" in that it is a product of rational inquiry, observation, and speculation. Like most premodern philosophers, P infers that the universe was created from a limited set of preexisting substances, including earth, water, darkness, and wind. These substances were integrated according to a deliberate plan, with hierarchies of time, space, subsistence, and governance. The resulting cosmos runs in a harmonious and predictable fashion, with heavenly bodies regulating light and time, living creatures propagating their kind, and humans ruling over the other living creatures. This is a coherent religious and philosophical system, a cosmology whose novelty is hard for us to perceive, because it forms the cosmological background of much of Western thought.

CONTEXTS

There are many intricate links between Genesis 1 and other P texts, in both the primeval narrative and the larger P work. Many of these links are effected by P's *Leitwort* style, in which repeated words and phrases create a back-and-forth arc of sound and sense across the narratives. Within the P primeval narrative, several *Leitwort* sequences link the creation with the flood, as in the following:

Creation: "A wind of God (*rûaḥ ʾĕlōhîm*) was soaring over the face of the water (*hammāyim*)." (1:2)

Flood: "God sent a wind (*ʾĕlōhîm rûaḥ*) over the earth, and the water (*hammāyim*) subsided." (8:1)

Creation: "God blessed them (*waybārek ʾōtām ʾĕlōhîm*), and God said to them, 'Be fruitful and multiply, fill the earth (*pərû ûrbû ûmilʾû ʾet hāʾāreṣ*), and subdue it.'" (1:28)

Flood: "God blessed (*waybārek ʾĕlōhîm*) Noah and his sons and said to them, 'Be fruitful and multiply and fill the earth (*pərû ûrbû ûmilʾû ʾet hāʾāreṣ*).'" (9:1)

Creation: "God saw (*wayyarʾ ʾĕlōhîm*) all that he had made, and behold (*wəhinnēh*), it was very good." (1:31)

Flood: "God saw (*wayyarʾ ʾĕlōhîm*) the earth, and behold (*wəhinnēh*), it was corrupt, for all flesh had corrupted its way on earth." (6:12)

These are key moments in each narrative. In the P flood they are the complications and turning points, occurring at the plot's beginning, middle, and end. The *Leitwort* repetitions establish a nexus of foreshadowing and backshadowing linking the creation and flood narratives. They signal a reversal from the "very good" cosmos to a situation of chaos and indicate a new beginning with the "wind of God" over the waters and a new era of humankind with God's reiterated blessing to "be fruitful and multiply and fill the earth." As we have seen, the second and third *Leitwort* sequences extend beyond the P primeval narrative, creating a narrative arc between the completion of creation and the completion of the tabernacle (Exod 39:43; cf. 40:33), and a subplot of blessing to "be fruitful and multiply" through the ancestral narratives, culminating in the crisis of Egyptian bondage (Exod 1:7–9).

Other texts in the P source also refer back to Genesis 1, including the Sabbath command in Exod 31:12–17, a P text that was supplemented by the Holiness source (Olyan 2005; Stackert 2011). According to the Holiness supplement, God gave the Sabbath as a sign to Israel "so that you may know that I, Yahweh, am sanctifying you (*məqaddiškem*)" (Exod 31:13). This understanding of the meaning of the Sabbath seems to be an exegesis of Gen 2:3. God's sanctification of the Sabbath now entails his sanctification of Israel. Once again, the meanings of creation reverberate and expand in the covenant at Sinai. God's first act of making something holy—the seventh day—anticipates the complex interweaving of holy things, actions, and people in the covenantal laws.

As many commentators have observed, the last part of the creation account is taken up, through P's *Leitwort* style, in the completion of the tabernacle, in Exodus 39–40 (Jacob 1934: 67; Buber and Rosenzweig 1994: 14–21; Levenson 1988: 78–95; Propp 2006: 691–94). The echoing words and phrases are italicized:

Moses *saw all the work,* and *behold* they *had made* it. . . . And Moses *blessed* them. (Exod 39:43) . . . Moses *completed* the *work.* (Exod 40:33)	God *saw all* that he *had made,* and *behold* it was very good. (Gen 1:31) . . . God *completed* his *work* that he *had made* . . . And God *blessed* the seventh day. (Gen 2:2–3)

The language of God's completion of creation and his blessing of the seventh day rings out again in the completion of the tabernacle and Moses's blessing of the Israelites at

Mount Sinai. The tabernacle will be the place where God will "dwell" with the Israelites and where the atoning and purifying rites of sacrifice will take place. As such it is a cosmic center, a channel of communication and action linking heaven and earth. Its construction echoes, complements, and in some sense completes God's work of creation in Genesis 1.

In the Hebrew Bible outside the P work, there are some allusions, quotations, or reformulations of Genesis 1. The clearest example is in Nehemiah, when the Levites pray after reading from the "book of the law of Yahweh" (*sēper tôrat yhwh*): "You made heaven, the heavens of heaven, and all their array, the earth and all that is on it, the seas, and all that is in it" (Neh 9:6). This is a pious summary of Genesis 1, with the collocation of "heaven" and "all their array" (*kol-ṣəbā'ām*) and "earth" a near quotation of Gen 2:1. The Levites are pictured here as reading from the Pentateuch, beginning with Genesis 1. In this scene, Genesis has already assumed its role as a sacred text, read aloud by priests before an assembled congregation.

Several psalms quote or reformulate portions of Genesis 1, as in this thanksgiving hymn:

> [Praise] to him who made heaven through understanding,
>> for his lovingkindness is forever,
> To him who spread (*rōqa'*) the earth on the waters,
>> for his lovingkindness is forever,
> To him who made the great lights,
>> for his lovingkindness is forever,
> The sun to rule the day,
>> for his lovingkindness is forever,
> The moon and the stars to rule the night. (Ps 136:5–9)

This hymn comments on the works of creation on days two, three, and four: the *rāqîa'* of heaven, the separation of earth from water, and the "great lights" to "rule the day and the night." The hymn is a mixture of quotation and reformulation—notice that it unpacks the "great lights" as the sun, moon, and stars, differently from Genesis 1, and uses *rq'* as a verb in connection with earth, not as a term for heaven. The hymn freely adapts creation in Genesis 1 to its purposes.

In other cases of possible allusion or reuse, it is less clear whether the text of Genesis 1 is being activated or its background concepts. The most interesting cases are in Jeremiah and Second Isaiah, as in the following prophetic vision of destruction:

> I looked at the earth, and behold, it was a waste (*tōhü*),
>> and heaven, and its light was gone.
> I looked at the mountains, and behold, they were quaking,
>> and all the hills were trembling.
> I looked, and behold, the humans were gone,
>> and all the birds of heaven had fled.
> I looked, and behold, the vineyards were desert,
>> and all its cities were ruined,
>> before Yahweh, before his blazing anger. (Jer 4:23–26)

This poem clearly draws on the language of creation, depicting a world returned to chaos. In the first edition of Jeremiah (represented in the LXX), the first line ends with "nothing" (*outhen*), which elsewhere represents Hebrew *tōhü* (1 Sam 12:21; cf. Job 26:7).

In the second edition (represented in the MT), this is expanded to *tōhû wābōhû*, "desolate chaos," a harmonization with Gen 1:2 (Hayes 1997; McKane 1986: 106–7; cf. van Ruiten 2005: 22). In the second edition at least, this text quotes Gen 1:2. (The second edition, written in Transitional Biblical Hebrew, is roughly contemporary with the P source; see Hendel and Joosten 2018: 77–81.)

This prophetic poem blends disaster from different domains: warfare (ruined cities and desiccated vineyards), divine wrath (quaking mountains and hills), and primordial chaos (the earth as waste, darkness in heaven). The absence of humans and birds cuts across these registers. The quotation of Gen 1:2 in the expanded version intensifies the aura of chaos by creating an explicit link with Genesis 1. In so doing, the expansion creates an intertextual arc from Genesis to Jeremiah.

Several passages in Second Isaiah also seem to hover between widespread concepts of creation and the text of Genesis 1:

> I am Yahweh, there is no other,
>> maker (*yôṣēr*) of light and creator (*bôrē'*) of darkness,
>> maker of peace and creator of evil,
> I am Yahweh, who made all these. (Isa 45:6–7)

> For thus says Yahweh, creator (*bôrē'*) of heaven—he is God,
>> maker (*yôṣēr*) of the earth and fashioner of it—he founded it,
> he did not create it as a chaos (*tōhû*),
>> he made it to be inhabited.
> I am Yahweh, there is no other. (Isa 45:18)

Some commentators see these passages as engaged in argument with Genesis 1, contesting its statements that darkness (*ḥōšek*) and chaos (*tōhû*) existed independently of God's work of creation (Weinfeld 2004; Paul 2012: 20–21; cf. Clifford 1994: 167–76). But it is more plausible to see the prophet here asserting a strong form of monotheism against the backdrop of Mesopotamian polytheism, hence the refrain, "I am Yahweh, there is no other." The next chapter explicitly refers to Marduk (Bēl) and Nabu (Nebo), chief gods of the Neo-Babylonian pantheon (Isa 46:1). These prophetic poems have a shared vocabulary with Genesis 1 (and Genesis 2–3: *yṣr*, "make"), but they do not seem to allude to, quote, or reformulate Genesis 1. Second Isaiah in these passages asserts an expansive concept of biblical monotheism and as such is engaged in a task similar to that of the P writer: creating a new religious world picture that transforms older cosmogonies. But his adversary seems to be Babylonian polytheism, not the P source, in his diasporic situation.

Genesis 1 is a unique crystallization and interpretation of older biblical and Near Eastern traditions about creation. It is a particular cultural memory, which draws on concepts and themes that circulated widely in ancient mythology. To discern its nuances, it helps to set it within its wider cultural context. I briefly survey some of these concepts and categories from ancient Near Eastern texts, primarily Mesopotamian and Egyptian.

As George (2016: 18) observes, there is a limited repertoire of "mythemes" in Mesopotamian creation myths, which are recombined and developed in the various texts and genres:

- Watery chaos
- Heaven and earth

- Generations of gods inside them
- Separation of heaven and earth
- Release of sunlight
- Conflicts among the gods
- Slaying of monsters
- Creation of humans
- Civilization through the mediation of sages
- Flood
- Postdiluvian age

Five of the first eight mythemes are found in Genesis 1, with the exception of "generations of gods inside them," "conflicts among the gods," and "slaying of monsters." Genesis 1 is an expression of P's high monotheism, and as such there is no conflict with gods or monsters. The "great sea dragons" are creations rather than adversaries, and God's seeming allusion to other gods (1:26) is resolved into a statement of God's sole creation of humans (1:27). In P's conception, as Levenson (1988: 17) emphasizes, "the confinement of chaos rather than its elimination is the essence of creation, and the survival of ordered reality hangs only upon God's vigilance." One can say the same, with different accents, about Mesopotamian creation myths, with the substitution of Marduk, Enlil, or other divine protagonists.

Most of these mythemes are also found in Egyptian creation myths, with the difference that the great destruction is not a flood, but Hathor's massacre of humans at the behest of the high god Re due to human rebellion ("The Book of the Heavenly Cow," Wente 2003). Let us turn to some of the ancient mythemes shared with Genesis 1.

As Bauks (1997: 2) observes, ancient peoples "did not think about the world order without having the concept of a preexisting not-order." The not-order is often depicted as a watery chaos, as in "The Founding of Eridu":

A pure temple, a temple of the gods, had not been made in a pure place,
A reed had not sprouted, a tree had not been created,
A brick had not been molded, a brick-mold had not been created,
A temple had not been made, a city had not been created. . . .
But all the lands were sea.

(Lambert 2013: 370–71)

In this primordial scene, the not-order is marked by an absence of nature and culture and a presence of endless sea (*tâmtum*). *Enuma Elish* gives this mytheme a more elaborate scope, with the primeval waters as a divine duality:

When the heavens above did not exist,
    And earth beneath had not come into being—
There was Apsû, the first in order, their begetter,
    And demiurge Tiāmat, who gave birth to them all;
They had mingled their waters together
    Before meadow-land had coalesced and reed-bed was to be found—
When not one of the gods had been formed
    Or had come into being, when no destines had been decreed.

(I.1–8; Lambert 2013: 50–51)

In this primeval state, Apsu, the male god of the subterranean ocean, and Tiamat ("Sea") mingle together, a watery chaos that foreshadows procreation. As Moran (1988: 15) observes, these lines are "an apt description of event-less flux," with all the clauses either stative or durative. The punctual sequence begins with the procreation of the gods in the following line (the syntax of Gen 1:1–3 has a similar pattern).

In Egypt the primeval water was the god Nun, the "father of the gods." The creator god Atum emerged out of the static waters of Nun:

> On the day that Atum developed
> Out of the Flood, out of the Waters,
> Out of the Darkness, out of Chaos.

> (Coffin Text 76; Allen 1988: 18)

This precreation state persists in the waters that surround heaven and earth, where the sun's light does not shine. The static world of dark watery chaos will return when the teeming multiplicity of the cosmos comes to an end, as the creator god describes the world's end, "I am going to destroy all that I have made, and this world is going to return to the Waters and the Flood, like its first state" (Book of the Dead 75; Allen 1988: 14).

Shu, the god of air and life-breath, begets heaven (Nut) and earth (Geb) and then separates them. He describes his act of separation:

> I lifted my daughter Nut atop me
> that I might give her to my father Atum in his utmost extent.
> I have put Geb under my feet:
> this god is tying together the land for my father Atum,
> and drawing together the Great Flood [the celestial waters] for him.
> I have put myself between them.

> (Coffin Text 76; Allen 1988: 18)

This is a familiar picture of the Egyptian cosmos, often represented in Egyptian temples and texts (see fig. 1, above).

Shu's separation of heaven and earth enables the sun (Re) to rise, an event that begins the first day. Shu proclaims, "I am the one who made it possible for it [the sun] to give brilliance to the Darkness" (Coffin Text 76; Allen 1998: 19). With the first light, the dynamic movement of time and existence begins.

The sun rises over land that emerged from the primeval waters. In one text, Atum is identified with the emerging land:

> Hail Atum!—
> who made the sky, who created what exists;
> who emerged as land, who created seed.

> (Book of the Dead 79; Allen 1988: 10)

With the sunrise over the primeval hill, the movement of time, space, and life ("seed") begins.

In Mesopotamia the mytheme of the separation of heaven and earth has multiple forms. In some versions the high god Enlil separates them, as in the Sumerian "Myth of the Pickaxe":

The lord brought into being the established order,
The lord, whose decrees cannot be altered,
Enlil, to produce the seed of the land from the earth,
Made great haste to separate heaven from earth,
Made great haste to separate earth from heaven.

(Lambert 2013: 170)

In *Enuma Elish,* Marduk displaces Enlil as the executive god, and this mytheme is linked with the monster-slaying. Marduk (Bēl) divides the body of the defeated monster, who is (or was) Tiamat, into heaven and earth:

Bēl rested, surveying the corpse,
> In order to divide the lump by a clever scheme.
He split her into two like a dried fish:
> One half of her he set up and stretched out as the heavens.
He stretched the skin and appointed a watch
> With the instruction not to let her waters escape. . . .
He heaped up the distant [mountains] on her breasts,
> He bored wells to channel the springs. . . .
[He set up] her crotch—it wedged up the heavens—
> [The half of her] he stretched out and made it firm as the earth.

(IV.135–40, V.57–62; Lambert 2013: 95, 101)

Marduk's creation of the cosmos completed, "He surveyed the heavens and the earth" (V.65). The gods then celebrate his kingship, and Marduk conceives his plan to create humans.

We do not have any Canaanite or West Semitic creation myths outside the Bible, but a Phoenician cosmogony from Hellenistic times is preserved in excerpts from the *Phoenician History* by Philo of Byblos. Philo cites a legendary Phoenician sage, Sakkunyaton: "He posits as the source of the universe a dark and windy gas, or a stream of dark gas, and turbid, gloomy chaos. These things were unbounded, and for ages were without limit. He says, 'When the wind lusted after its own sources, and a mixture came into being, that combination was called Desire.' This was the beginning of the creation of all things" (Attridge and Oden 1981: 37). This Phoenician cosmogony mingles old Canaanite concepts with Greek ones, as one would expect in the Hellenistic era. The birth of Desire (*pothos*) corresponds to the Greek god Eros, the firstborn god in Hesiod's *Theogony.* Philo's description of creation seems to be a learned reflection on old Phoenician traditions, akin to the Egyptian, Mesopotamian, and biblical cosmogonies. In this reflective nature, his creation myth is not unlike the P account in Genesis 1.

A final issue is the P writer's stance toward the older Near Eastern myths and mythemes. Does Genesis 1 know any of these other texts, or does it directly descend from one of them, in particular *Enuma Elish?* Commentators are divided (see Day 2013: 19–20; Scurlock and Beal 2013). For instance, Speiser (1964: 10) maintains that "P's opening account goes back to Babylonian prototypes," because of the correspondence in its details and order with *Enuma Elish.* But some of these correspondences are unwarranted, such as God's creation of light in Genesis 1 compared with "light emanating from the gods" in *Enuma Elish.* The latter refers to the gods' shining aura (see Marduk "clothed with the shining aura of ten gods," I.103; cf. Yahweh "wrapped in light," Ps 104:2). Light is not explicitly created in *Enuma Elish,* nor are vegetation and animals. Most of the analogous details are widespread mythemes. As Bauks (1997: 268) emphasizes, "associations with individual motifs from Gen 1 arise again and again, which makes a one-sided relationship of dependence on Mesopotamian tradition not credible" (similarly, Gertz 2009). Genesis 1 and *Enuma Elish* are part of a general discourse about creation in the ancient Near Eastern world.

Recently Frahm (2010, 2013) has revived the possibility of "intertextual links" between Genesis 1 and *Enuma Elish,* with Genesis 1 composed as a "counternarrative" to the dominant myth of the Neo-Babylonian Empire. In his view, Genesis 1 is a "demythologized account . . . emphasizing that an almighty male god was in charge from the very beginning" (2013: 116). This is similar to Sparks's (2007: 648) argument that Genesis 1 is an elite emulation of a dominant cultural text, composed "to enhance and preserve Jewish identity in the face of threats raised to it." Other scholars see Genesis 1 as a direct response to *Atraḫasis* or other Mesopotamian myths (Frymer-Kensky 1977: 150–51; Römer 2013b). These possibilities cannot be excluded.

But the clear points of allusion and reformulation of other myths and mythemes points in a different direction. In Gen 1:21, God creates "the great sea monsters" (*hattannînîm haggədōlîm*), the only species singled out for mention among the sea, sky, and land animals. This special mention has the purpose of transforming the sea monsters from their older role as primeval adversaries into a purely natural species. This is a reformulation of older Israelite traditions, as in Ps 74:13, "You shattered the heads of the sea monsters (*tannînîm*) on the waters." The sea monsters are now simply sea animals, perhaps transformed into whales, situated within God's cosmic order. This reformulation in Genesis 1 is an inner-Israelite argument.

Similarly, as noted previously, P's creation myth recasts into natural kinds the divine "host of heaven" (*ṣəbāʾ haššāmayim*), who are celestial bodies in older Israelite tradition. The sun, moon, and stars become natural bodies, assigned with regulating time and light. Their traditional function as oracular signs is naturalized into "signs for festivals, days, and years" (1:14). They are now mere mechanisms, set into the material sky. Celestial phenomena are now a part of nature. The P creation story radically revises traditional Israelite concepts.

In sum, Genesis 1 is engaged in a partial disenchantment (*Entzauberung* in Weber's [2009: 139] terminology; see Schmid 2015: 72) of Israelite cosmogonic concepts, constructing a systematic picture of the cosmos that is no longer shot through with gods and supernatural powers. It is a rationalized creation myth, informed by its practices and thought styles of members of the priestly institution.

In a more general sense, Genesis 1 is in conversation with other ancient Near Eastern cosmogonies. While it may not be clearly aware of them, the text speaks in a conceptual language that has a family resemblance across the region, including the mythemes addressed above. Genesis 1 selects, transforms, and crystallizes these conceptual features in a distinctive configuration.

The Garden of Eden
(2:4–3:24; J, *R*)

——————

2   *⁴This is the genealogy of heaven and earth, when they were created.*
On the day Yahweh *God* made earth and heaven—⁵when wild plants of the field were not yet on the earth, when grasses of the field had not yet grown, for Yahweh *God* had not sent rain on the earth, and there was no human to work the soil, ⁶but a river would flow from the earth and water the whole surface of the soil—⁷Yahweh *God* formed a human from the soil's dust. He blew life's breath into his nostrils, and the human became a living being. ⁸Yahweh *God* planted a garden in Eden, in the east, and placed there the human he had formed. ⁹Yahweh *God* caused to sprout from the soil every tree that is desirable to see and good for food, and the Tree of Life in the middle of the garden, and the Tree of the Knowledge of Good and Evil.

¹⁰A river flows from Eden to water the garden, and from there it splits into four branches. ¹¹The name of the first is Pishon—it circles the whole land of Havilah,ᵃ where there is gold. ¹²The gold of thatᵇ land is excellent, and bdellium and carnelian are there. ¹³The name of the second river is Gihon—it circles the whole land of Cush. ¹⁴The name of the third river is Tigris—it flows east of Assyria. The fourth river is Euphrates.

¹⁵Yahweh *God* took the human and placed him in the Garden of Eden to work it and guard it.ᶜ ¹⁶And Yahweh *God* commanded the human, "From all the trees of the garden you may surely eat, ¹⁷but as for the Tree of the Knowledge of Good and Evil, you shall not eat from it, for on the day you eat from it you shall die."

¹⁸Yahweh *God* said, "It is not good for the human to be alone. I will make a companion to help him." ¹⁹Yahweh *God* formed from the soil ᵈevery animal of the field and every bird of heaven, and he brought them to the human to see what he would call them. Whatever the human would call each living being, that was its name. ²⁰The human named every domestic animal, everyᵉ bird of heaven, and every animal of the field, but the humanᶠ did not find a companion to help him. ²¹Yahweh *God* cast a trance over the human, and he slept, and he took out one of his ribs and closed the flesh behind it. ²²Yahweh *God* built up the rib that he had taken from the man into a woman, and he brought her to the man. ²³The man said, "This time at last!

> Bone from my bones,
> > and flesh from my flesh.
> This one shall be called 'woman,'
> > for from man she was taken."[g]

²⁴Therefore a man leaves his father and mother and cleaves to his wife, and they become one flesh. ²⁵The two of them were naked, the man and his wife, and they felt no shame before each other.

3 ¹Now the snake was more cunning than all the animals of the field that Yahweh *God* had made. He said to the woman, "Did God really say, 'Do not eat from all the trees of the garden?'" ²The woman said to the snake, "We may eat fruit from the trees of the garden, ³but about the fruit of the tree in the midst of the garden, God said, 'Do not eat from it, and do not touch it, lest you die.'" ⁴The snake said to the woman, "You shall not die. ⁵Indeed, God knows that on the day you eat from it your eyes will be opened, and you will become like gods, knowing good and evil." ⁶The woman saw that the tree was good for food, that it was a delight to the eyes, and desirable[h] to make one wise. She took from its fruit and ate, and she also gave it to her husband beside her, and he ate. ⁷The eyes of the two of them were opened, and they knew that they were naked, and they sewed together fig leaves and made loincloths for themselves.

⁸They heard the sound of Yahweh *God* walking about in the garden in the evening breeze. And the man and his wife hid themselves from Yahweh *God* in the midst of the trees of the garden. ⁹Yahweh *God* called out to the man and said to him, "Where are you?" ¹⁰He said, "I heard your sound in the garden and I was afraid, for I am naked, so I hid." ¹¹He said, "Who told you that you are naked? Have you eaten from the tree from which I commanded you not to eat?" ¹²The man said, "The woman, whom you gave to be with me, she gave to me from the tree, and I ate." ¹³Yahweh *God* said to the woman, "What have you done?" The woman said, "The snake deceived me, and I ate."

¹⁴Yahweh *God* said to the snake, "Because you have done this, cursed are you, out of all the domestic animals and all the wild animals of the field. You shall crawl on your belly and eat dust all the days of your life. ¹⁵I will set hatred between you and the woman, and between your offspring and hers. They will strike at your head, and you will strike at their heels." ¹⁶To the woman he said, "I will greatly multiply your labor pains from pregnancy—in pain you shall bear children. You shall desire your husband, and he shall rule over you." ¹⁷To the man[f] he said, "Since you listened to your wife's voice and ate from the tree about which I commanded you 'Do not eat from it,' cursed is the soil because of you. In painful labor you shall eat from it all the days of your life. ¹⁸Thorns and thistles it will sprout for you, and you shall eat the grasses of the field. ¹⁹By the sweat of your brow you shall eat bread, until you return to the soil, for from it you were taken. For you are dust, and to dust you shall return."

²⁰The man named his wife Eve, for she was the mother of all life. ²¹Yahweh *God* made leather garments for the man[f] and his wife, and he dressed them. ²²Yahweh *God* said, "Behold, the human has become like one of us, knowing good and evil. Now, lest he reach out his hand and take[i] from the Tree of Life and eat and live forever . . ." ²³Yahweh *God* expelled him from the Garden of Eden to work the soil from which he was taken. ²⁴He banished the humans, and he stationed east of the Garden of Eden the cherubim and the flame of the whirling sword to guard the path to the Tree of Life.

Textual Notes

a. The MT and SP add the definite article *h-* to *ḥwylh* (Havilah). This is ungrammatical on a proper noun and is probably a case of near-dittography (a dittography with graphic confusion)—a scribe accidentally writing *he-ḥet* instead of a single *ḥet* (Hendel 1998: 43).

b. The demonstrative pronoun "that" is spelled as a masculine form *hhw'* but vocalized (correctly) in the MT as a feminine form, as if it were spelled *hhy'*. This peculiar situation (a *qere perpetuum*) occurs frequently for this word in the Pentateuch (seven times in Gen 1–11; 2:12; 3:12, 20; 4:22; 7:2; 10:11, 12). This textual confusion probably stems from the era when the consonants *waw* and *yod* were virtually indistinguishable, as is the case in some early Herodian manuscripts (ca. 40–20 BCE). A later scribe (or scribes) apparently miscopied the *yod* in this word as if it were a *waw* (Hendel 1998: 43). This scribal error occurs some 120 times in the Pentateuch (Hendel 2016: 211).

c. In the sequence *l'bdh wlšmrh* ("to work it and guard it"), the final *he* is a vowel marker (*mater lectionis*) for the pronominal suffix "it." In the MT this suffix is vocalized as a feminine form, -*â*. Grammatically it ought to be a masculine form, vocalized -*ô*, since the referent "garden" is a masculine noun. In preexilic spelling practices, a final *he* often represents the masculine pronominal suffix (final -*ō*), as in *šlmh* (*šəlomoh*, Solomon) or *'hlh* (*'ohŏlo*, "his tent") (Gen 9:21). In postexilic spelling, the vowel marker *waw* is used for a final -*ō*, and a final *he* is limited to -*ā*, -*ē*, and -*e*. In this verse, we are confronted with preexilic consonantal spelling that has been vocalized by the Masoretes according to postexilic conventions (Hendel 1998: 44).

d. Probably read *'t* (direct object marker) before *kl* ("every") with the SP. The MT lacks this particle, which is grammatically necessary (cf. the *'t* marking the following definite noun).

e. Reading *kl* ("every") with the LXX and several other versions (Targum Pseudo-Jonathan, the Syriac Peshitta, and the Latin Vulgate). The MT and SP lack this word, probably by homoioteleuton, the scribe's eye skipping from one *lamed* to the next *lamed* in *wlkl*, thereby skipping *kl* (Hendel 1998: 44).

f. Vocalizing the prefixed preposition in *l'dm* (2:20; 3:17, 21) as *lā-*, meaning "to the human," rather than the MT's *lə-*, meaning "to Adam." The personal name Adam (*'dm*) is first clearly used in 4:25. Beginning with his/its creation in 2:7, this creature is designated *h'dm* ("the human"), with the definite article *he* (twenty times). But three times it occurs with the prefixed preposition *l-* (2:20; 3:17, 21), which could be vocalized with or without a definite article. In each case the Masoretes vocalized without the definite article, but the context (in which the other instances have a definite article) indicates that it should be vocalized with one (see Barr 2014: 478–81).

g. The MT and SP add *z't* ("this"), which is lacking in the LXX. This is probably an explicating plus, clarifying that the subject of the passive verb "was taken" is the same as the *z't* of the previous clause. In addition to the text-critical reasoning, the word is awkward in the rhythm and grammar of this poetic verse (Hendel 1998: 44).

h. The MT and SP add *h'ṣ* ("the tree"), which is lacking in the LXX. This is probably an explicating or harmonizing plus, specifying the subject of the clause and echoing the *h'ṣ* of the first clause of the verse (Hendel 1998: 44–45).

i. The MT and SP add *gm* ("again"), which is lacking in the LXX. This is probably an explicating plus, clarifying that this would be the second time that humans "took" forbidden fruit (cf. 3:6 with the same verb) (Hendel 1998: 45).

Notes

2:4. *This is the genealogy of heaven and earth, when they were created.* This half-verse is a literary bridge contributed by R, who combined the J and P sources (see Day 2013: 18–19). The problem R faced was how to combine the P creation account of 1:1–2:3 with the J creation account that begins in 2:4b. The solution was to link them by a genea-logical formula derived from 5:1: "This is the book of Adam's genealogy." The formula "This is the genealogy of *X*" serves as a structuring principle in P's work (see INTRODUC-TION I). In this verse, R extends the genealogical idiom to include the "genealogy" (in an abstract sense) of the creation of "heaven and earth" in 1:1–2:3. It looks backward at the totality of creation and forward, with its temporal formula, to what happens next. By this strategy, the differences between the two creation stories are somewhat bridged, and the second story is made subordinate to the first (Childs 1979: 145–50). The listing of "heaven and earth" as if they were cosmic parents may be derived from cosmogonic language, in which heaven and earth did have offspring, but here is adapted to the context. This connective bridge shows how the social idiom of genealogical descent was used to conceptualize the past.

The noun *tôlədōt* ("descendants, genealogy," spelled here *plene, tôlədôt*), found only in the plural, is derived from the verb *hôlîd* ("to beget, father"). By the rule of patrilin-eal descent, all of a man's descendants are his offspring (like "the children of Jacob"), so *tôlədōt* can denote one or many generations of descendants. The usage here is more abstract, as if history descends from the creation of heaven and earth.

The clause "when they were created" is a single word in Hebrew, *bəhibbārə'ām*. It is a *niphal* infinitive construct with a prefixed temporal preposition and a suffixed pos-sessive pronoun. This word, which seems stylistically awkward at the end of the clause, sets up an echo or *inclusio* with the opening verb of 1:1, *bārā'* ("to create"). Now heaven and earth have been created, and after this retrospective glance, the primeval narrative continues.

On the day Yahweh God made earth and heaven. The first sentence of the J story begins with a temporal adverb, *bəyôm* ("on the day that"), meaning "at the time that," or simply "when." The word *yôm* ("day") in this expression allows for a sense of continu-ity with the creation account in 1:1–2:3, with this word echoing the days of creation. Although it formally introduces the J creation account, in the composite text it can be read as a temporal clause parallel to the previous temporal clause: "when they were cre-ated, on the day Yahweh God made earth and heaven." It is a common stylistic trait in ancient Near Eastern creation myths to begin with a temporal clause of this type, "when . . . then," as do both the P and J creation accounts.

Yahweh God. The divine name, *yhwh 'ĕlōhîm*, is a combination of names that are usually used separately—*yhwh* ("Yahweh") and *'ĕlōhîm* ("God"). One of the distin-guishing marks of the J source is the use of the divine name *yhwh* beginning with creation. This portrayal of the antiquity of the name Yahweh contrasts with the P and E sources, where this divine name is first revealed to Moses (Exod 3:15 in E; Exod 6:2

in P). The characters in J sometimes use the generic name *'ĕlōhîm,* as do the woman and the snake in Gen 3:2–5 and the woman in 4:25, but the voice of the narrator uses the name Yahweh consistently in J. Unusually, the Garden of Eden story conflates the two divine names, Yahweh Elohim, or as rendered here, Yahweh God. This double name occurs sporadically elsewhere in the Bible (Exod 9:30; 2 Sam 7:22, 25; Jonah 4:6; Pss 72:18; 84:9, 12; 1 Chr 17:16; 2 Chr 6:41) but nowhere else in J. The expansion of an original Yahweh to Yahweh Elohim is usually attributed to R, who attempted to smooth out the abrupt transition of divine names from Elohim to Yahweh in the combination of the P and J creation narratives. This harmonizing expansion (the double name Yahweh Elohim) continues until the end of the J creation story. Interestingly, the LXX presupposes a Hebrew text that supplemented this strategy by often substituting Yahweh Elohim or simply Elohim for Yahweh through the remainder of Genesis 1–11 (Hendel 1998: 35–39).

The vocalization of the divine name *yhwh*—the Tetragrammaton—as Yahweh is a linguistic reconstruction based on two bodies of evidence: (1) the vowel in the first syllable in the short form of the divine name, *yah* or *yahū,* found in the liturgical formula *hălălû-yāh* ("praise Yah") and in personal names such as *'ēliyāhû* (Elijah, "my God is Yahu"); and (2) the vowel in the final syllable in nouns or prefix verbs from the III-weak roots, *-eh* (a contraction of original **iyu*), such as *yihyeh* ("he will be") or *maḥăneh* ("camp"). Some Greek transcriptions of the divine name support this reconstruction, for example, *Iaoue* (Yahweh), *Iabe* (Yahveh) (see BDB, 218; *HALOT,* 395; Freedman and O'Connor 1986; Jenni 1997). The short form *Yahū* (used in the Elephantine papyri with the biform *Yahō*) reflects an alternative contraction or apocope of the final syllable, like the variation of *yištaḥăweh* and *yištaḥû* ("to bow").

The name Yahweh appears to be a nominalization of the causative (*hiphil*) form of the root **hwh,* which has several basic meanings, including "to be, become" and "to fall, blow." The original verbal meaning would be something like "he creates" (i.e., "causes to be") or "he causes to fall" (e.g., the rain, enemies, etc.). The form originally would have been **yahwiyu,* resolving to *yahweh.* Some scholars derive Yahweh from the *qal* of **hwh,* meaning something like "he is" (see Kitz 2019; and cf. the wordplay in Exod 3:12–14). But according to our understanding of the morphology of such stative verbs, this form originally would have been **yihwayu* (see Hasselbach 2004) resolving into *yihweh* (not *yahweh*).

During the Second Temple times the pronunciation of this divine name came to be considered sacrilege, based on an interpretation of the commandment "You shall not take the name of Yahweh, your God, in vain" (Exod 20:7). (This is originally a prohibition of false oaths.) The LXX of the Pentateuch renders *yhwh* as *kurios* ("Lord"), probably reflecting current custom. The medieval Masoretes placed the vowels for *'ădōnāy* ("my Lord") around the Tetragrammaton in vocalized codices of the Hebrew Bible as a continuous *qere,* noting the reading tradition.

earth and heaven. The conceptual contrast between the P and J creation accounts is subtly indicated by the order of the cosmic pair and merism *haššāmayim wəhā'āreṣ* ("heaven and earth," P) versus *'ereṣ wəšāmāyim* ("earth and heaven," J). J's account is situated from an earthly, human-centered point of view. In contrast, P's account is more lofty, abstract, and cosmic in orientation. The primacy of "heaven" in P coheres with the priority of God's point of view, situated above and transcending the earthly locale.

On the linguistic level, it is notable that this phrase in P (and R in 2:4a, modeled after P) has the definite article *ha-* in each occurrence (1:1; 2:1, 4), whereas J lacks the article. (The archaic divine title "creator of heaven and earth" in 14:19 also lacks the definite article.) The expansion of the use of the definite article is a feature of the history of Biblical Hebrew (Barr 2014: 464). This linguistic detail correlates with the view that the J source is earlier than the P source (see Introduction II).

2:5. This verse consists of four disjunctive clauses arranged in quasi-parallel style. Each clause is introduced by a conjunctive *waw* + noun or by the subordinate clause marker *kî*. These four clauses supply background information on aspects of the world that were absent at the time of creation. Notably, each of these absences is later filled, directly or indirectly, during the course of creation. The "when not" sequence of absence–presence is characteristic of ancient Near Eastern creation myths and serves as part of the literary design of this portion of the creation story. Compare, for instance, the beginning of *Enuma Elish:* "When the heavens above did not exist, / And the earth beneath had not come into being / . . . Before meadow-land had coalesced and reed-bed was to be found" (I.1–2, 6; Lambert 2013: 50–51).

when wild plants of the field were not yet on the earth, when grasses of the field had not yet grown. Elsewhere *śîaḥ* ("wild plants") denotes a plant or shrub that grows in the wild (Job 30:4, 7), but here it indicates wild plants in general, in complement to *'ēśeb* ("grasses"), which refers to plants used for food, including domestic grains. Both are qualified with *haśśādeh* ("of the field"), which highlights their earthy locale. Together these terms signify the totality of vegetation on earth, which is absent in the primeval situation. This lack is rectified in 2:8–9 when Yahweh God plants the garden in Eden. The role of vegetation is further defined in the post-Edenic world when Adam is punished by having to eat the *'ēśeb haśśādeh* ("grasses of the field") by his hard labor (3:18). The movement is from absence (in primeval times) to presence (in Eden) to hard subsistence (in the world after the expulsion from Eden).

The verbal constructions prefixed by *ṭerem* ("when not, not yet, before") have a relative future tense value, that is, future relative to the reference point, which is the time of the previous sentence, "On the day that Yahweh God made earth and heaven" (Hendel 1996: 158–61). The use of the relative future to express the absence of these features points forward to the time when these features will exist. The counterpoint to "had not yet grown" (*ṭerem yiṣmaḥ*) occurs in 2:9 when Yahweh God "caused to sprout (*wayyaṣmaḥ*) from the soil," with the causative stem of the same verb. By planting the Garden of Eden, Yahweh God redresses this lack.

for Yahweh God had not sent rain on the earth, and there was no human to work the soil. The presence of Yahweh God at the beginning of creation is counterposed by the absence of any humans, and similarly the absence of human action necessary for cultivation. Interestingly, the Eden story never mentions the onset of the rains (cf. 2:6 on the primeval "river" that waters the earth). The sequence *lō' himṭîr* ("had not sent rain") provides an apt continuation of the previous *ṭerem* ("not yet') clauses—it has the same sense of lack and anticipation, and poses a wordplay with the consonantal sounds *ṭrm* and *mṭr* rearranged.

The second disjunctive clause fronts *'ādām* ("man, human") with a topicalizing sense, "as for the human, there was none." This absence of *'ādām* to work the soil has the most elaborate fulfillment in the story, since not only is *hā'ādām* ("the human"—on the nuances, see NOTES at 2:7) subsequently created from the soil (2:7), but his role "to work the soil" is fulfilled gradually—he is first assigned by God to "work" the garden (2:15), and later he is punished to toil on the cursed soil in hard labor (3:17–19). This verse first sounds the important theme and *Leitwort* relationship of *'ādām* ("man, human") and *'ădāmâ* ("soil"), which will become increasingly problematic and will be resolved only after the flood and, in part, the call of Abraham (see INTRODUCTION I).

The word *'ădāmâ* ("soil") often has a specific sense of "arable earth," "cultivable land," and this is the primary sense in the Eden story. The usage elsewhere in J oscillates between "arable land" and the more general meaning "earth." In the Eden story's beginning (2:5–7), the words *'ădāmâ* ("soil") and *'ereṣ* ("earth") occur three times each, highlighting the presence of one ("earth") and the potential of the other ("soil, cultivable earth").

2:6. *but a river would flow from the earth and water the whole surface of the soil.* This disjunctive clause continues the sequence of background clauses in 2:5, but now it describes what *does* exist in primeval times—an underground river that continually watered the earth. The imperfect verb has a past durative or habitual sense in this temporal context, literally "would rise, used to rise, well up," and is continued by a sequential clause with a converted perfect expressing the same durative sense, "would (continually) water."

The nature of this *'ēd* ("river") is obscure. The word seems related to or derived from Sumerian Id, the name of the primeval river god (McCarter 1999; Woods 2005; note that the spelling ^d*i-id* indicates that it was pronounced *id*). Id is a divine judge in the river ordeal (cf. Ugaritic *ṯpṭ nhr*, "Judge River"). S/he is dual gendered and praised as "creatrix of everything" (*bānât kalāma*). Woods (2009: 204) plausibly suggests that the *pî nārāti*, "mouth of the rivers," where Utnapishtim dwells in the distant east, is "the place from where the headwaters of the cosmic river rise from the Apsû—this is Íd-mah, 'Great River,' the primeval river." A Sumerian text describes it as "the Great River at the place where the sun rises, no one can look at it" (Woods 2009: 220). The primeval river god, rising from the watery abyss, is the mythic backdrop of the biblical *'ēd*.

In the Eden story, the *'ēd* is a primeval river, but it is not a god. In the only other attestation of this word in the Hebrew Bible (Job 36:27), the *'ēd* is a celestial stream or mist. In the thematics of the story, the ceaseless flow of the primeval river anticipates the great river that branches from Eden to water the earth in 2:10–14. Curiously, however, the *'ēd* does not seem to make the soil fruitful, merely moist. The word *'ēd* plays on the words *'ādām* ("man, human") and *'ădāmâ* ("soil"), so that there was yet no *'ādām*, but an *'ēd* on the *'ădāmâ*.

2:7. *Yahweh God formed a human from the soil's dust.* The first punctual action of the story is God's creation of the first human, signaled by the first converted imperfect verb. The grammatical structure of 2:4b–7 is "when *X* . . . (background information) . . . then *Y*," just as in 1:1–3. The style of older Near Eastern creation myths is also in the background (see NOTES at 2:5).

The action of "forming" man suggests a tactile association—the same verb (*yṣr*) is used for the work of a potter forming pots out of clay and the work of a woodcarver. Yahweh God continues this workmanlike mode of creation when he "plants" the garden (2:8), "forms" (*wayyiṣer*, as here) the animals from the earth (2:19), and "builds" the woman out of the man's rib (2:22). The physical sense of Yahweh God's acts of creation is subdued but apparent in this story.

The description of the object of creation—*hā'ādām 'āpār min-hā'ădāmâ* ("the human from the soil's dust")—has many nuances. Humans are defined in part through their origins, and the words used to describe their origins are richly productive, including the *Leitwort* association of *hā'ādām* and *hā'ădāmâ*.

The first human is *hā'ādām* ("the human, man"). As in 1:26–27, this word can mean humankind in general or a particular human, marked as male. It is a singular noun, which can be used as a collective plural. The relevant sense—singular or plural, gender-neutral or gender-specific—is determined by context. The semantic multivalence of *hā'ādām* is exploited in this story. On one level, *hā'ādām* represents humans in general, since this person is "the human," with the definite article implying that "the human" is a kind of prototype. Like the first human, all humans are made of earthy stuff, are enlivened by breathing, and return to the soil at death. On this level *hā'ādām* is the ancestor and symbol of all humans.

At the same time *hā'ādām* is, as the story unfolds, a single male character. The first mention of *'ādām* in 2:5—in his absence—states his role "to work the soil." This is a predominantly male role in the biblical world (see Meyers 1988: 146–49). The singleness and implicit or incipient maleness of the first man becomes foregrounded when Yahweh sets out to make a partner for him, an *'ēzer kənegdô* ("companion to help him"), since "it is not good for the human to be alone" (2:18). God solves this problem by making a woman from the rib of *hā'ādām*. The sexual dimension of the story is prominent thereafter.

In sum, *hā'ādām* is both "humankind" writ large and the first human, incipiently male. Some scholars have tried to de-patriarchalize the figure of *hā'ādām* by emphasizing the collective, gender-neutral meaning, sometimes arguing that *hā'ādām* has no sex or gender at all until the creation of woman (Trible 1978: 80–81, 97–99; Bal 1987: 112–13; but see the apt criticisms of Lanser 1988; Hess 1990; Clines 1990: 40–41; and Galambush 1993). But to regard *hā'ādām* as a sexually polymorphous or unsexed creature is to miss the multivalence of this character, who is both "the human" and "the man." In other words, the de-patriarchalized interpretation treats the word as if it were simply a floating signifier, independent of the story's implied meanings or "implicature" (see Lanser 1988). In the context of its creation, *hā'ādām* is implicitly a symbolically collective "humankind" *and* a single "man," with the dual meanings circulating in different proportions throughout the story. Other figures in Genesis have a similar duality as individuals and as ancestors and symbols of a collectivity (e.g., Canaan, Ishmael, Esau, and, of course, Israel).

The creation of *hā'ādām* explicitly associates him with *hā'ădāmâ* ("the soil," as with his "absence" in 2:5). The repetitions of these words create a *Leitwort* effect in the story. The words echo each other (and are probably etymologically related by the root *'dm*, which has a basic meaning of "red," although this is not significant in the narrative). From this likeness comes many aspects of human nature. The most tangible sense is that humans are physical creatures, made of soil. This earthy, fleshy quality of humans distinguishes them from Yahweh, who is a nonmaterial being, dwelling in heaven (e.g., 11:5, "Yahweh came down to see the city and the tower"). By Yahweh forming the human from the earth's soil, he defines humans as categorically different from gods. This difference—and the human desire to overcome it—is the focal point for the transgression, transformation, and punishment in the story.

The resolution of this crisis in the finitude of life outside of Eden is foreshadowed in the human's earthly nature, as Yahweh God articulates in his judgment, "you are dust, and to dust you shall return" (3:19). The earth's soil is the human's origins and destiny. The woman is included in this destiny, since she is implied in the concept of *hā'ādām*, both because of the word's collective meaning and because of her origins as "bone from my bones and flesh from my flesh" (2:23). All humans must die. Further, the man must work the soil in pain, by the sweat of his brow (3:17–19). Once again, *hā'ādām* oscillates between its collective and its singular (and gendered) meanings. In the complex relationship between *hā'ādām* and *hā'ădāmâ*, we see a philosophy of life in this ancient agricultural society, a painful realism in its understanding of human origins and destiny.

The use of the word *'āpār* ("dust, dirt") in the phrase *'āpār min hā'ădāmâ* ("dust from the soil") subtly emphasizes the idea of death and mortality (Hillers 1987). In Israelite rituals of mourning, the mourners put dust on their heads (Josh 7:6, Ezek 27:30, Lam 2:10, Job 2:12), thus symbolically participating in the death of the loved one (Olyan 2004: 39–45). The word "dust" is used in many circumlocutions for the realm of the dead—"all who go down to the dust" (Ps 22:30), "those who dwell in the dust" (Isa 26:19), "those who lie down in the dust" (Job 20:11, 21:26). (Cf. the Akkadian expression *bīt epri*, "house of dust" as the underworld.) "Dust" is an objective correlate of "death"—though it can symbolize other things as well, such as vast abundance (e.g., Gen 13:16, 28:14) or debasement (see NOTES at 3:14). In the Eden story, the "dust" that man is made of foreshadows and entails his mortality.

The idea that humans were created from soil or clay is a widespread notion in biblical literature (Pss 103:14–15, 104:29; Job 10:9, 33:6; Eccl 3:20) and other ancient Near Eastern traditions. In the Babylonian *Atraḫasis* myth, two wise gods—Ea and Mami, the goddess of birth—create humans out of clay (*ṭiṭṭu*):

> They entered the house of destiny
> Did prince Ea and the wise Mami
> With the birth-goddesses assembled
> He trod the clay in her presence.
> She kept reciting the incantation,
> Ea, seated before her, was prompting her.
> After she had finished her incantation
> She nipped off fourteen pieces of clay.
> Seven she put on the right,
> Seven on the left.
> Between them she placed the (birthing) brick.

> (I.249–59; Lambert and Millard 1969: 60–61)

These pieces of clay became the first seven couples of humankind. In the flood story in *Gilgamesh*, the flood hero looks around when the flood subsides and sees that "all the people had turned to clay" (XI.135; George 2003: 710–11). The idea that humans are made from the earth—from dust, soil, or clay—and return to it is an old tradition (Tigay 1982: 192–94). In a sense, this reflects "a first attempt at organic chemistry" (Gunkel 1997: 6), in which the human body is made from earthly stuff and decomposes to soil after death. This concept has both philosophical and physical implications.

Similarly, in Egyptian mythology the creator god Khnum molds humans, animals, and even gods on a potter's wheel, presumably—for the mortal creatures—out of clay. The "Great Hymn to Khnum" describes him as the maker of all creatures:

He has fashioned gods and men,
He has formed flocks and herds;
He made birds as well as fishes,
He created bulls, engendered cows . . .
Formed all on his potter's wheel.

(Lichtheim 1980: 112)

He blew life's breath into his nostrils, and the human became a living being. The other component of the first human is the life force, the *nišmat ḥayyîm* ("breath of life"). This enlivening breath comes from Yahweh's breath. This idea is found in other biblical passages, for example, Job 33:4, "God's breath (*rûaḥ*) made me, and the Almighty's breath (*nišmat*) gave me life" (the words *rûaḥ* and *nəšāmâ* are used synonymously for God's enlivening breath). In our verse Yahweh's breath makes the earthly body of the human come to life.

This picture of human origins has many nuances. First, it is a practical theory of life, based on observation. Breathing enlivens us, and when we stop breathing, we die and our body returns to the earth. Second, it is a philosophical and theological theory: that which gives us life is a divine substance, Yahweh's breath. Life is a gift from God. The sanctity of life is rooted in this biblical concept (see Gen 9:6 [P], correlated with "God's image"). The fact of being alive with "life's breath" makes humans in some respect godlike. Being created with this divine component subtly anticipates the human desire to be *more* like gods later in the story.

In this portrait of human origins and essence, a duality is inherent in the human condition. We are made of two parts: the earth's soil and Yahweh's breath. The one part makes us physical and mortal; the second part makes us alive and, in some small way, participants in the divine. This is a "soft" dualism, not of mind versus body, but of life-breath and body (see Boyarin 1993: 31–34; Bauks 2016). In the biblical conception, the intellect is seated in the heart or liver, which is part of the body. The life force is rooted in the breath, which is given and taken away by God:

You take away their breath (*rûaḥ*)
    and they die, they return to dust.
You send forth your breath,
    and they are created. (Ps 104:29–30)

Yahweh's speech in Gen 6:3 hinges on this duality: "My breath (*rûaḥ*) will not be strong in humans forever, inasmuch as they are also flesh." The soft dualism of life-breath and body also conditions the crisis and the resolution of the Eden story—humans desire to be more godlike, which they achieve to some extent ("the knowledge of good and evil"), but they are thrown back on their inescapable earthiness. Humans are conditioned by their originary duality, with its inherent frictions and limitations.

The idea that humans are enlivened by divine breath is a widespread Near Eastern concept, often represented in Egyptian art by the ankh symbol held to a human's nose. In a spell from the Coffin Texts, the air god Shu describes his life-giving power:

I will lead them [animals and humans] and enliven them,
through my mouth, which is Life in their nostrils.
I will lead my breath into their throats.

(80.106–8; Allen 1988: 24)

a living being. Usually the term *nepeš ḥayyâ* ("living being") simply means "animal," as at 2:19. Here it includes humans. The word *nepeš* has a range of meanings, including "life," "breath," "throat" (as the place of breath), "personality," or "self." It can also refer to the nonmaterial seat of emotions, perceptions, and desires. The apposition of *nepeš* ("living") and *ḥayyâ* ("creature, animal") coheres with the soft duality of life and body. The implication that humans belong to the same category as animals anticipates Yahweh's creation of animals to be the human's companions, at which point we see that the human is not *just* an animal, and a more suitable companion is required.

2:8. *Yahweh God planted a garden in Eden, in the east.* Usually this garden is called *gan-ʿēden* ("the Garden of Eden"), a proper noun phrase (Gen 2:15; 3:23, 24; Ezek 36:35; Joel 2:3). When it is first created, however, it is described as an indefinite *gan-bə ʿēden,* "a garden in Eden." Eden is a particular place, somewhere "in the east." Similarly, 2:10 speaks of the river that flows "from Eden" to water "the garden." These expressions emphasize that Eden is a geographical locale. Its location is explicated in the description of the four rivers in 2:10–14.

In references outside of Genesis 2–3, the garden is referred to as God's garden. In Gen 13:10 (J) it is "the garden of Yahweh." In Ezekiel it is "Eden, the garden of God" (Ezek 28:13), and Ezek 31:9 refers to "all the trees of Eden that were in the garden of God." Isaiah 51:3 places "Eden" parallel with "the garden of Yahweh." Most of these references evoke the garden as a paradigm of lush abundance, while others refer to events in the Garden of Eden itself. Evidently the Garden of Eden was a well-known topos, and various stories could be told of its prototypical events (on Ezekiel 28, see Comments). In our story, it is the place where Yahweh walks about in the afternoon breeze (3:8), but the emphasis is on its creation as a place for the human: "Yahweh God planted a garden . . . and placed there the human he had formed."

The idea of Yahweh planting a lush garden where he strolls about at his leisure is probably related to the custom of ancient Near Eastern kings (including Solomon) planting such gardens outside of their palaces (Stager 1999; Liverani 2017: 67–70). The "hanging gardens of Babylon" (possibly originally Nineveh) is the most famous example. This display of abundant fertility is suited to the ideology of kings as its providers, including divine kings.

The word *ʿēden* derives from the root *ʿdn,* which means approximately "to be fruitful, abundantly provisioned" (Millard 1984; Greenfield 1984). An Aramaic inscription (from Tell Fekherye) uses the verb *mʿdn* (in the D-stem) to mean "to make abundant" (equated with Akkadian *mutaḫḫidu*). The idea of abundant food and bounty coheres with the use of this root in Hebrew. The Garden of Eden is therefore "the Garden of Plenty," referring to its lush and abundant vegetation. This is an aspect of its paradisical quality, which corresponds with Yahweh's presence and care. Outside of Eden, humans must work and sweat to make the soil bear fruit (3:17–19). The name of the garden and its mythical locale are therefore the converse of the harsh world of human agricultural subsistence, where one ekes food by sweat and labor. In this sense, the word *gan* ("garden, orchard") is rightly rendered by the LXX as *paradeisos,* "paradise." This garden doesn't necessarily have a wall (as do royal gardens), but it does have an entry (see Notes at 3:24).

The directional location of the garden is *miqqedem,* literally "off to the east" (BDB, 578b). The specifics of this location are obscure. This obscurity will be deepened in the description of the four rivers in 2:10–14. The use of the word *qedem* ("east") involves an interesting play on its two meanings: *qedem* can mean "east" or "ancient times." The overt sense in this sentence is directional, "in the east," but it may also convey a resonance of ancient times—Yahweh planted the garden "in ancient times." Many later translations (including the Aramaic targums, the Syriac Peshitta, and the Latin Vulgate) chose to render the second meaning.

The location "in the east" is consonant with the locale of primeval humanity in 11:2 ("As they journeyed in the east they came upon a valley in the land of Sumer") and the idea that Abraham came from Mesopotamia (11:31). A locale near Mesopotamia is also suggested by the names of two of the rivers that flow from Eden (2:14). The east is the direction of antiquity, both linguistically (in the word *qedem*) and in Israel's cultural memory. The east is the cradle of civilization.

In Mesopotamian mythology, the east is the place where the sun rises, inhabited by liminal creatures, and has associations with death and immortality (Woods 2009). In *Gilgamesh,* the passage to the east is guarded by scorpion people who "guard the sun at sunrise and sunset" (IX.45). Beyond this passage are, as Woods (2009: 194, 204) notes, "the gemstone garden, the cosmic sea (*tâmtu*) and the waters of death (*mê mûti*), and, across these waters, the realm of Ūta-napišti at *pî nārāti,* 'the mouth of the rivers,'" which may be "the place from where the headwaters of the cosmic river rise from the Apsû" (see Notes at 2:6). Many of these features echo in the locale and mythic qualities of the Garden of Eden.

and placed there the human he had formed. This clause echoes the beginning of 2:7, "Yahweh God formed a human," and signals a formal close to this scene of creation. The initial destiny of the human is to dwell in the "Garden of Plenty." But complications are afoot, as anticipated by the description of the trees of the Garden.

2:9. *Yahweh God caused to sprout from the soil every tree that is desirable to see and good for food.* The "Garden of Plenty" is now filled with beautiful, appetizing trees. This creation scene also anticipates the moment when the woman contemplates the forbidden Tree of Knowledge: "The woman saw that the tree was good for food, that it was a delight to the eyes, and desirable to make one wise" (3:6). The clause there, *ṭôb hāʿēṣ ləmaʾăkāl* ("the tree was good for food"), is nearly identical to the words here, *ṭôb ləmaʾăkāl* ("good for food"). However, the charged emotion *neḥmād* ("desirable") is there applied to wisdom ("desirable to make one wise"), whereas here it is visual ("desirable to see"). This is a good example of the verbal and thematic echoes and intensifications in the story.

and the Tree of Life in the middle of the garden, and the Tree of the Knowledge of Good and Evil. These two noun phrases, both definite, lack the direct object marker *ʾet,* so it is possible that they should be read as subjects of a disjunctive (noun-initial) background clause: "Now the Tree of Life was in the middle of the garden, and the Tree of the Knowledge of Good and Evil," with the latter a secondary supplement. However, the sequence *kol-ʿēṣ . . . wəʿēṣ . . . wəʿēṣ* ("every tree . . . and the tree . . . and the tree") makes a conjunctive relationship more likely, joining them in a sequence of objects of the verb "caused to sprout." The locative phrase *bətôk haggān* ("in the midst of the garden") applies to both noun phrases, although it comes between them, in a construction that Michel (1997) calls "split coordination."

The term "the Tree of the Knowledge of Good and Evil" consists of a construct phrase, *'ēṣ hadda'at* ("tree of knowledge/knowing"), followed by *ṭôb wārā'* ("good and evil"), which are objects of the infinitive *da'at* ("knowledge, knowing"). This structure is found elsewhere, for example, Jer 22:16, *hadda'at 'ōtî* ("knowledge of me," "knowing me") (GKC §115d). It is possible to read "good and evil" as a merism for "everything," but since "the knowledge of everything," that is, omniscience, is not gained by the humans, a more subtle or multifarious kind of knowledge is needed.

The nature and relationship of these two trees and the benefits of their fruit are matters of considerable complexity and ambiguity. The fruit of the first tree, *'ēṣ haḥayyîm* ("the Tree of Life"), bestows immortality, as Yahweh later states, "lest he reach out his hand and take from the Tree of Life and eat and live forever" (3:22). The Tree of Life is mentioned only here (2:9) and at the story's end (3:22–24). Between these two sections, the references to "the tree" or "the tree in the midst of the garden" (3:3) refer to the Tree of the Knowledge of Good and Evil. Because of this variation, many scholars have suggested that the story originally had only one tree, and that the Tree of Life is a secondary insertion.

However, the thematics of the story require both trees, since the conjunction of knowledge and mortality defines the dramatic arc of the story (Blum 2010: 12–18; Bauks 2012; Day 2013: 41–44). The human situation is precariously perched between these two qualities. With respect to knowledge, humans become "like gods," but with respect to mortality, they remain earthly beings. Both of these qualities are part of the human condition, linking the humans to gods on the one side and to other animals (*nepeš ḥayyâ*, "living beings," 2:7) on the other. Humans are suspended between the categories of beast and god.

The twin qualities of divine knowledge and immortality (that is, the fruits of the two trees) are the hallmarks of the gods in ancient Near Eastern religions. In the Mesopotamian epics of Gilgamesh and Adapa, the heroes discover that they are doomed to human existence because, though they possess great knowledge, they cannot attain immortality. In both cases, immortality (or perpetual rejuvenation) is imparted by food to which the hero momentarily has access: for Adapa the "food of life" and the "water of life," and for Gilgamesh the "plant of heartbeat." These stories are thematically related to the Garden of Eden story (see COMMENTS).

Similarly, in Israel immortality is a divine quality. In Psalm 82, when God condemns the other gods to death because of their injustice, he states, "Therefore, like humans you will die, / and like the princes you will fall" (Ps 82:7). In this unique instance in the Bible where gods die, they are compared to humans in their mortality. This becoming "like humans" is the inverse of the humans becoming "like gods" in the Garden of Eden.

If the qualities imparted by both trees are necessary in the story, then the absence of the Tree of Life in the bulk of the narration is best understood as a feature of biblical narrative style. As Propp (1990: 193) comments, "the Yahwist did not wish to mystify his audience, but he expected it to focus only on one issue at a time, and this differs slightly from Western modes of narration." This is a matter of narrative focalization (similarly Blum 2010: 12–18). After the creation of both trees, the story focuses first on one tree and its consequences, then on the other. The Tree of Life, once introduced, is in the background during the drama of its companion tree and is foregrounded thereafter.

The second tree, 'ēṣ haddaʿat ṭôb wārāʿ, "the Tree of the Knowledge of Good and Evil," is obscure because of the ambiguous meaning of "knowledge of good and evil." What do the humans gain when they eat the fruit of this tree? The snake says, "you will become like gods, knowing good and evil" (3:5). Yahweh confirms the snake's statement when he says, "the human has become like one of us, knowing good and evil" (3:22). But what kind of knowledge is this that makes them "like gods"? The immediate consequence of this knowledge is that "they knew that they were naked" (3:7). Knowledge of bodily nakedness does not seem like a divine knowledge, but rather a bodily and sexual self-consciousness. This is hardly godlike knowledge. The quality imparted by the fruit of the Tree of the Knowledge of Good and Evil seems odd and contradictory. (The common depiction of the fruit in Western Christianity as an apple is due to the homonymity in Latin of the adjective malus, "evil," and the noun malus, "apple"; see Day 2013: 42.)

The qualities imparted by "the knowledge of good and evil" are multiple and layered. It is a multivalent concept, whose various potentialities can be inferred by looking at other biblical texts. It seems to have at least three kinds of meaning, each of which is circulating in the Garden of Eden story (see Wallace 1985: 115–30; Mettinger 2007: 60–63; Schellenberg 2011: 214–19; Bauks 2015).

The first is a quality of intellectual and moral discernment. This is the type of knowledge that an exceedingly wise person possesses. As a woman addresses King David when she seeks from him a wise judicial decision, "My lord the king is like an angel of God, discerning good and evil (lišmōʿa haṭṭôb wǝhārāʿ)" (2 Sam 14:17). She adds, "My lord is wise like the wisdom of an angel of God, knowing (lādaʿat) everything on earth" (2 Sam 14:20). This type of all-encompassing knowledge—which in its context is moral and judicial wisdom—is something quasi-divine, "like an angel of God." Solomon too is credited with such wisdom, "to understand (or distinguish between) good and evil (lǝhābîn bēn-ṭôb lārāʿ)" (1 Kgs 3:9, cf. 3:12). The ability to judge wisely, to know the difference between good and evil, right and wrong, is knowledge that partakes of divine wisdom. Clearly, understanding good and evil, right and wrong, is part of the thematics of the Garden of Eden story. The humans hide from Yahweh because they are ashamed, that is, they know they have done something wrong (3:9). Their behavior is not Solomonic, but it shows a dawning of moral consciousness and discernment.

The second kind is knowledge of the flesh, sexual awareness and self-consciousness. "They knew that they were naked" (3:7) is the immediate consequence of eating the forbidden fruit—this implies a knowledge of sexual difference that they had not previously possessed. The fig-leaf loincloths are designed to hide these previously unperceived sexual features. Sexual or carnal knowledge is expressed in Hebrew by the verb "to know," as when "The man knew (yādaʿ) Eve, his wife, and she conceived and gave birth" (4:1). This "knowing," so closely following the story at hand, activates this nuance of the sexual knowledge gained in Eden.

Elsewhere "knowing good and evil" occasionally requires the sense of sexual knowledge. When the old man Barzillai refuses to go to Jerusalem with King David, he says: "I am now eighty years old. Can I know good and evil (*haʾēdaʿ bēn-ṭôb ləraʾ*)? Can your servant taste what I eat or drink? Can I still hear the voice of the singers?" (2 Sam 19:36). Since Barzillai is still a wise man, the content of "Can I know good and evil?" must be something other than intellectual or moral wisdom. Its association with his waning senses of taste and hearing makes sexual ability the likely sense. This is a tactful way to say to the king that he cannot partake of the voluptuous life that would be his reward in the royal court.

A related kind of knowledge signified by this vocabulary pertains to the knowledge or awareness gained in the transition from childhood to adulthood. This seems to combine bodily, intellectual, and emotional maturity. The human "rite of passage" from the Garden of Eden to the outside world involves the acquisition of sexual awareness, moral knowledge (including shame and guilt), and other features of adult human life—including childbirth, agricultural labor, and knowledge of mortality. This involves a passage from innocence to experience, from childhood to adulthood. Its attendant gains and losses are recapitulated in each person's passage from adolescence to maturity. The sense of "knowing good and evil" as the passage to maturity is explicit in two biblical passages: when Moses tells the Israelites that their children "who today do not know good and evil" (*lōʾ-yādəʿû hayyôm ṭôb wāraʿ*) will enter the promised land (Deut 1:39), and when Isaiah describes the age of maturity as the time when "the young man knows to reject the evil and choose the good" (Isa 7:15–16). This type of knowledge distinguishes children from adults.

These three levels of meaning of "the knowledge of good and evil"—involving moral and intellectual discernment, sexuality, and maturity—are evoked at various points in the story, sometimes intersecting, sometimes conflicting with one another. The multivocality of this concept makes it a rich and complex theme in the story. It is this complexity, among other qualities, that makes the story such an apt and evocative representation of the human condition. But none of these implications is yet signaled at this point of the story. The reference to the two trees provides anticipatory information, whose significance will emerge gradually.

2:10. A river flows from Eden to water the garden, and from there it splits into four branches. A new section of the story begins with a disjunctive clause (noun-initial), followed by a sequence of disjunctive clauses (vv. 10–14). This section is an aside that provides background information. The participle *yōṣēʾ* ("flows") expresses a durative sense, "continually flows," which also makes it stand outside of the punctual sequence of the main storyline. This continuous sense of the participle probably suggests that the great river still flows out of Eden, long after the events of the story. Some commentators regard this disjunctive sequence as a secondary insertion, since it retards the movement of the narrative (e.g., Bührer 2014: 214–20). It is more likely that the function of retarding the action is deliberate. This background description creates a reality effect for the narrative.

The river's purpose, *ləhašqôt ʾet-haggān* ("to water the garden"), recalls the primordial river (*ʾēd*) that used to water (*wehišqâ*) the earth (2:6). However, the river that flows from Eden is fruitful, nourishing the lush vegetation of Eden, unlike the primordial waters that flowed over the lifeless earth.

The "splitting" of the river into four branches is a durative (imperfective) sequence, with the imperfect verb (*yippārēd*) followed by a converted perfect (*wəhāyâ*), similar to the imperfective sequence of the primeval river in 2:6. The sense is iterative and ongoing, of the river "continually splitting" and "continually becoming" four branches (lit. "heads"). The number of branches—four—signifies the totality of the four directions of the world (cf. the Akkadian expression "the four regions," *kibrat erbetti,* originally "four banks" of the rivers). In some Mesopotamian reliefs, the blessing of fertility is indicated by a god or goddess holding a vessel from which flow four streams (Keel 1985: 118). Also related to this scene is the abode of the Canaanite god El, which is located at "the source of the rivers" (*mbk nhrm, CAT* 1.6.i.33).

2:11–14. These verses name the four branches and their locations. They provide a geographical setting for the Garden of Eden that seems real, as if one could follow these clues and rediscover it. However, the directions are impossible, and the location is eternally elusive (Propp 1990: 193). The ancients may have thought that the Tigris and the Euphrates had a common source, but the Gihon (under any construal of its location) does not, nor does the Pishon (which seems to be purely legendary). In other words, using these geographical clues, the Garden of Eden cannot be located. These geographical details describe the garden as a sacred center, a source of the world's fertility, but at the same time a place that differs from ordinary geography.

The sequence of rivers is presented from the most obscure, the Pishon, to the most famous, the Euphrates, "the great river" (Gen 15:18, Deut 1:7). An abundance of geographical and contextual detail is provided for the Pishon, and the amount of detail diminishes until for the Euphrates none is given, since none is necessary.

2:11. *The name of the first is Pishon—it circles the whole land of Havilah, where there is gold.* The name Pishon is derived from the root *pwš,* "to leap, jump." With the *-ôn* ending, a particularizing particle, the name means "leaping one, jumping one," an apt name for a river. There are, however, no known rivers with this name in the ancient Near East. This river may be wholly fictitious, perhaps formed by analogy with the name of the second river, Gihon, with a similar meaning.

The best proposal for an actual river behind the name Pishon is the Wadi Baiš, which in medieval times formed the northern boundary of the region of Ḥaulan in South Arabia (Müller 1992h). This river was known in antiquity (Ptolemy, *Geography* 6.7.5). The name Baiš does not exactly correspond to Hebrew Pîšon (note that the Hebrew *šin* does not correspond to South Arabian *š*). But the location makes it possible that the Baiš is in the background of this river.

This river is specified as "the one that circles (*hû' hassōbēb*) the whole land of Havilah." The participle *sōbēb* can mean "go around, circle" or "meander, wander about," so the river's path in or around Havilah is not entirely clear. The land of Havilah (*ḥăwîlâ*) refers to a region in South Arabia. It represents the name Ḥaulan, which was held by one or more old Arabian tribal federations (Müller 1992d). In the J Table of Nations, Havilah is the son of Joktan (10:29) along with other names of Arabian tribes and locations. Elsewhere in J, Havilah is one of the limits of Ishmaelite territory (25:18). In the P Table of Nations, Havilah is the son of Cush (10:7), which may suggest a North African location. For the Eden story, the J location is pertinent.

2:12. *The gold of that land is excellent, and bdellium and carnelian are there.* South Arabia was famous for its gold, precious stones, and aromatic spices and resins. The queen of Sheba, another South Arabian polity, brought to Solomon "balsam, great amounts of gold, and precious stones" (1 Kgs 9:2). Bdellium (*bədōlaḥ,* cf. Akkadian *budulḫu*) is an aromatic resin from a variety of tree (*Commiphora mukul*) found in South Arabia, similar to myrrh. Carnelian (*'eben haššōham*, cf. Akkadian *sāmtu*) is a reddish gemstone, a variety of quartz. It is one of the precious stones in the priestly ephod and is one of the precious stones worn by the cherub in Ezekiel's version of the Garden of Eden story (Ezek 28:13). Among the varieties of precious stones found in South Arabia is one called Ḥaulanite onyx, from the tribal region of Ḥaulan (Müller 1992d: 82). The specification of the riches of Havilah may lend a sense of exotic wealth to the fertile rivers of Eden.

2:13. *The name of the second river is Gihon—it circles the whole land of Cush.* The name Gihon (*gîḥôn*) literally means "the bubbling, gushing one." There is no known river with this name in or near Cush, which refers either to Nubia or Mesopotamia (see below). In postbiblical times, this river was identified with the Nile (LXX of Jer 2:18; Ben Sira 24:27; Josephus, *Ant.* 1.39).

The name Cush (*kûš*) seems to designate two different locations. In the J Table of Nations, Cush is the father of Nimrod, the legendary hunter and king of Babylon and Assyria (10:8). This Cush is probably to be equated with Akkadian Kuššu/Kaššu, the Kassites, who ruled Babylonia from ca. 1600 to 1150 BCE. In the P Table of Nations (10:6) and elsewhere in the Bible, Cush refers to the region of Nubia and northern Sudan (Egyptian K'š, Akkadian Kūsu). It is not clear which Cush is referred to in this passage. The J usage in 10:8 and the location of Eden "to the east" may favor the Babylonian locale, but it is possible that the dual meaning of the homonymous Cush makes this locale deliberately ambiguous.

The only known river with the name Gihon (*gîḥôn*) is the stream that bubbles up in the Kidron Valley of Jerusalem. This was the principal source of water for Jerusalem and was where Solomon was anointed king (1 Kgs 1:33–45). It is the "river whose streams make joyful the city of God, the holy dwelling of the Most High" (Ps 46:5). In Ezek 47:1–12, a river that flows from the Jerusalem temple makes the desert bloom, the Dead Sea live, and trees grow fruit continuously. This image of new life in abundance, fructified by a river from Jerusalem, seems to make the Gihon a river of paradise, flowing from the cosmic center (Levenson 1985: 129–31). Yet the Gihon of our verse is not easily equated with the Gihon of Jerusalem, since its location is in Cush. A curious indeterminacy accompanies this river. The name is suggestive, in connection with other hints, of the symbolic association of Eden with the Jerusalem temple and its gardens (Stager 1999).

2:14. *The name of the third river is Tigris—it flows east of Assyria. The fourth river is Euphrates.* The last two rivers are the well-known rivers that define Mesopotamia (lit. "Between the Rivers"). Both rivers have their sources in the Taurus Mountains of eastern Turkey, although their sources are some distance apart. It is possible that the ancients thought that the two great rivers had a single source. In a Hittite version of a Canaanite myth (the Elkuniřša myth), the god El dwells in a tent at "the source of the Euphrates" (*COS* 1.149). This locale seems related to the geography of Eden, from which the Euphrates and other rivers flow. In these scenes of the cosmic center, we probably see an intersection of mythic motifs.

The Hebrew name *ḥiddeqel* ("Tigris") comes from Akkadian Idiqlat/Diqlat. The Greek name Tigris comes from the Old Persian Tigra, a representation of Diqlat. The Tigris flows through the heart of Assyria, east of the city of Asshur. Asshur was the capital of the kingdom of Assyria from the fourteenth to ninth centuries BCE and thereafter remained an important Assyrian city. Elsewhere in the Bible the name 'aššûr refers to the land, people, or king of Assyria, not to the city of Asshur. It is likely that the regional sense is also meant here, parallel to the other regional place names (Havilah and Cush) in the description of the rivers of Eden. But it is possible that the city name is meant here, since the city is on the banks of the Tigris.

The Hebrew name pərāt ("Euphrates") comes from Akkadian Purattu. It is the western of the two great rivers of Mesopotamia. Here it needs no further explanation.

2:15. *Yahweh God took the human and placed him in the Garden of Eden to work it and guard it.* The first part of this verse serves as a repetitive resumption (*Wiederaufnahme*), a restating of events that resumes the narrative after a backgrounded or otherwise separate sequence (Polak 1999: 77–80). This is a literary technique used by biblical authors to link episodes together, and also by editors to join disparate texts. In this case, the verse echoes and resumes 2:8, where Yahweh "placed there the man he had formed." According to this literary convention, the narrative sequence is being resumed after the aside in 2:10–14 about the rivers of Eden. Notably, these two repetitions have different emphases. The statement in 2:8 glances backward to the creation of the man in the words 'ăšer yāṣār ("that he had formed"). The repetitive resumption in 2:15 looks forward in the words used to describe the man's task, "to work it and to guard it."

These words, lə'obdōh ûləšomrōh ("to work it and guard it," see Textual Note c), describe the human's purpose in the garden as its gardener and guardian. A comparable role is held by the Babylonian temple slave who is assigned to be a "guard, watchman" (*maṣṣartu*) and "to do work" (*dulla epēšu*) in the temple garden (Wells 2017). In a sense, the human functions as Yahweh's servant. There is some irony in this job description, however, since the human does not have to work to make the garden fruitful, and there does not seem to be anything to guard it from. It is an easy job, which involves no sweat (see Notes at 3:19). A more serious irony inheres in later echoes of these words. At the end of the story, as a consequence of the humans' transgression, Yahweh casts the man out of the garden "to work (la'ăbōd) the soil" (3:23). Thereafter, Yahweh stations fierce divine beings "to guard (lišmōr) the path to the Tree of Life" (3:24). The two infinitives used to describe the human's job in the garden are transferred to the circumstances of his final destiny. He must work the soil, which is now difficult work, and the humans cannot return to the garden, since it is now guarded by powerful creatures. The use of these words effects a reversal from the ease of the work in Eden to the difficulty and limits of human existence outside of Eden.

This purpose for the first human seems to be an attenuation of the older concept that humans were created to do the work of the gods. As Marduk proclaims, "I will create humankind / On whom the toil of the gods will be laid that they may rest" (*Enuma Elish* VI.7–8; Foster 2005: 469; Lambert 2013: 110–11). This concept derives from *Atrahasis* I, where the lesser gods, who bear the burden of forced labor on the land (e.g., digging rivers and canals), go on strike and threaten the high god Enlil. In response, Enki devises a plan to create humans. He instructs the birth-goddess Mami:

> Create a human being, let him bear the yoke,
> The yoke let him bear, the task of Enlil,
> Let man assume the drudgery of god.
>
> (*Atra.* I.195–97; Foster 2005: 236)

The first human in our verse bears a lighter burden, but the task of working and guarding the garden bears the imprint of the older concept that humans were created to relieve the gods of the toil of working the land.

2:16. *And Yahweh God commanded the human, "From all the trees of the garden you may surely eat."* This is Yahweh's first speech in the story and is the point on which the story turns, although the turn is delayed until after the creation of animals and the woman. The speech provides anticipatory information whose significance will become clear only later. The speech itself refers back to 2:9, when Yahweh planted the trees of the garden, including the two special trees. The command seems clear, although it will later be interrogated, contested, and embellished in the dialogue between the snake and the woman. Yahweh will refer to this command when he interrogates and punishes the man (3:11 and 17).

2:17. *but as for the Tree of the Knowledge of Good and Evil, you shall not eat from it, for on the day you eat from it you shall die.* A prohibition given at the beginning of a story often indicates that it will be broken (cf. Chekhov's gun, the principle that the appearance of a gun in the first scene means it will go off later). This is a narrative hinge and a given of human nature. As Mark Twain commented (in *Pudd'nhead Wilson*), "Adam was but human—this explains it all. He did not want the apple for the apple's sake, he wanted it only because it was forbidden."

The consequence of violating this prohibition—"for on the day you eat from it you shall die"—is relatively clear but does not hold true later in the story. The temporal expression *bəyôm* ("on the day") can refer to a particular day but can also mean simply "when" (see NOTES at 2:4). In other words, the consequence will occur either immediately or on the same day. The verbal phrase *môt tāmût* ("you shall die") is an emphatic sequence (infinitive absolute + finite verb), which is a counterpoint to the earlier emphatic sequence in Yahweh's speech, *'ākōl tō'kēl* ("you may surely eat," 2:16). Both verbal expressions give emphasis to Yahweh's command, which consists of a permission and a prohibition.

The statement "you shall die" does not specify the agent or cause of death. It is quite possible, as Gunkel (1997: 10) notes, to take this as a warning to the man that the fruit of this tree is poisonous, and hence he must avoid eating it. But at the same time, it has the sense of a command, that Yahweh will punish transgression with death. Compare the similar diction of King Solomon's command, "On the day that you go out and cross the Kidron Valley, know well that you shall die (*môt tāmût*), and your blood will be upon your head" (1 Kgs 2:37). This direct command from the king—who has the power to enforce a threat of capital punishment—is analogous to the command from the divine king in Eden. In both cases, as Barr (1992: 10) comments, "such warnings make sense only if the punishment for disobedience is speedy."

The complication, of course, is that the humans do not die immediately or shortly after they eat the forbidden fruit. The most plausible way to understand this outcome is, in Gunkel's (1997: 10) words, "as an extraordinary example of divine mercy that he [Yahweh] did not enforce his word." Yahweh's compassion in the face of human disobedience coheres with some of his other actions in the story—his concern that the human is lonely (2:18), and his fashioning of clothes and dressing of the humans (3:21). The amelioration of punishment operates in Cain's case (4:15) and in the aftermath of the flood (8:21), and it would not be surprising to see it in Eden. And yet the punishment involves the anticipation of death—"to dust you shall return" (3:19)—an announcement of mortality. It is possible to see the judgment in this sense as not immediate death, but the anticipation of mortality. The humans do not die on that day, but they bear the knowledge that they will die. This is both a lessening of punishment and an ironic twist—they gain more knowledge (of their own mortality), which in itself is a heavy burden.

The sentence of death for eating the fruit of the Tree of Knowledge, however ambiguous its consequences, points to the implicit complementarity of the two trees and their fruit, which provide godlike knowledge and eternal life. As Blum (2010: 17) comments, "That is why one aspect of the likeness to God 'must' be prohibited [viz. eternal life] with the taking up of the other."

2:18–25. Just as the first mention of the forbidden trees in 2:9 is followed by a delay in the narrative with the introduction of the rivers of Eden, so the divine prohibition of eating the forbidden fruit is followed by a lengthy excursion that further delays this narrative line. In this case the delay is necessary, since the creation of animals and woman is a precondition for the rest of the narrative.

2:18. *Yahweh God said, "It is not good for the human to be alone. I will make a companion to help him."* This second speech by Yahweh is interior speech, no longer addressed to the human. Now he is speaking *about* the human. This shift in address begins this new section with a glimpse of Yahweh's interior disposition, emphasizing his compassion for the human.

Yahweh perceives the human's solitude as *lō'-ṭôb* ("not good"), a judgment emphasized by the fronted position of these words. In contrast to the many things that are *ṭob* ("good") in Genesis 1, this story focuses on other aspects of the human condition. As 1:27 already adumbrates, to be fully human includes the relationship between male and female. The creation of the woman is, in this sense, a continuation and completion of the creation of *hā'ādām*. She is the fitting complement; she is part of him and completes him.

But the identity of this *'ēzer kənegdô* ("companion to help him," or more literally, "a helper corresponding to him") is not yet clear. Yahweh first creates the animals to see whether an *'ēzer kənegdô* is among them. Only when none is found does he conceive the idea to create the woman. Yahweh is compassionate, but he is not omniscient, and he improvises until he finds the right solution. But the first improvisation yields an important result—the other animals are created.

The word *'ēzer* ("helper") does not specify a social inferior or a superior. For instance, the name Eliezer means "my God is a helper," applying this role to God. More important for the sense of this phrase is the other word, *kənegdô* ("corresponding to him, in front of him"). The helper will be the man's counterpart. The type of help is indicated by the value that the companion brings—it will lift the man out of a condition that is "not good." Yahweh solves the problem by bringing him into relation with another of his kind, one who is a counterpart and a completion.

2:19. *Yahweh God formed from the soil every animal of the field and every bird of heaven.* This verse echoes 2:7, "Yahweh God formed a human from the soil's dust." In trying to create the human's companion, Yahweh repeats the process of the human's creation, which issues in the creation of animals, who are earthly beings. The creation of animals extends the range of living things, but for a purpose that doesn't quite work. A verse in the Talmud expounds the comic potential of this scene, explaining that Adam had sex with each kind of animal but got no satisfaction (*b. Yebam.* 63a).

The twofold division of animals—"every animal of the field and every bird of heaven"—is varied in the following verse by a threefold division—"every domestic animal, every bird of heaven, and every animal of the field" (2:20). The phrase "every animal of the field" in 2:19 refers to all animals, but in 2:20 it designates wild animals as opposed to domestic (with the birds in between). This change in meaning is part of the poetics of variation in biblical prose. The subtly changing categories of animals in the P creation account is another example.

The J account of the creation of animals does not strive for completeness, in contrast with the P account. The absence of water creatures and insects shows how the story hews to details relevant to the main narrative plot (note that the snake is introduced as one of "the animals of the field," 3:1). The story omits the creation of many other aspects of the cosmos—stars, sky, etc.—that the P account, with its striving for comprehensiveness, includes.

and he brought them to the human to see what he would call them. Whatever the human would call each living being, that was its name. The imperfect verb *yiqrāʾ* ("would call, name") has a model sense, relating to the human's will in naming animals. Yahweh seems to be curious about the human's capabilities, perhaps expecting that the choice of names will reveal which of the animals is the "companion to help him." The image of Yahweh shepherding the animals to the human and listening as he names them is striking. Yahweh is nurturing and parental, standing aside as the human begins to think and speak.

By naming the animals, the human is shown not only to possess language but to have the power of naming, a prerogative usually reserved for parents, culture heroes, or God. In the P creation story, naming is part of what God does to create an ordered cosmos. God also renames Abram, Sarai, and Jacob (to Abraham, Sarah, and Israel; Gen 17:5, 15; 32:29; 35:10). The patriarchs name various places where they live or pass through, and parents name their children. In each instance of naming, a relationship of authority is exercised by the one giving the name. The power of naming belongs to the superior party in a relationship.

In naming the animals the human exercises his authority and shows his difference from them. As Alter (2011: 34) comments, the human is a "master of language." The power of speech is shared by the humans and Yahweh, and this ability distinguishes them from animals (with the exception of the snake in Genesis 3). This scene does not reveal the human's companion but shows the differences that color the relationship between humans and animals (Schellenberg 2011: 191–201).

The phrase *nepeš ḥayyâ* ("living being") is stylistically awkward in the second sentence. It may be an explicating gloss, clarifying the object pronoun *lô* ("it," not translated here). Nonetheless, the juxtaposition of *hāʾādām* and *nepeš ḥayyâ* in this sentence is thematically relevant, since the point of this encounter is to explore the similarities and differences between humans and animals. The phrase *nepeš ḥayyâ*, here designating the animals, recalls that the human was created as a *nepeš ḥayyâ*, "and the human became a living being" (2:7). The different frames of reference for the term *nepeš ḥayyâ* in the two verses highlight the ambiguous nature of humans—humans are animals, yet distinct from them.

2:20. *The human named every domestic animal, every bird of heaven, and every animal of the field, but the human did not find a companion to help him.* This is the human's first turn as an active agent in the story. But he does not find a companion. There is an element of surprise in the second repetition of "the human," which begins a disjunctive clause ("but . . .") that emphasizes the word *'ādām.* The clause can be read in slightly different ways: "but for the human he did not find," in which case the subject "he" is ambiguous (either Yahweh or the human); "but for the human was not found," taking the verb as having an indefinite subject (Skinner 1930: 68); or "but as for the human, he did not find," taking *wəlā'ādām* as a fronted topic at the head of the clause (cf. clause-initial *ûləyišmā'ē'l,* "but as for Ishmael," in 17:20). I take the human as the subject, since he is the one who later finds his true companion with a speech of recognition (2:23) and then names her, as if continuing this sequence.

The phrase *'ēzer kənegdô* ("a companion to help him") at the end of this verse echoes its first occurrence at the beginning of this section (2:18), providing a stylistic and thematic envelope around the creation of the animals (Alter 2011: 33). The story then moves forward as Yahweh conceives another plan to create "a companion to help him."

2:21. *Yahweh God cast a trance over the human, and he slept, and he took out one of his ribs and closed the flesh behind it.* Yahweh's solution is to take the companion from the human's own flesh and bone (see NOTES at 2:23). This requires surgery, so Yahweh causes a *tardēmâ* ("trance, deep sleep") to fall upon the human. In 15:12, Yahweh causes a similar deep sleep to fall upon Abraham, which prepares him for a dream revelation.

The creation of woman from *'aḥat miṣṣal'ōtāyw* ("one of his ribs") is motivated by several factors. First, it justifies the man's later exclamation, "bone from my bones, and flesh from my flesh" (2:23). This act is a concrete realization of a metaphor for kinship (see 29:14, "You are my bones and flesh"; similarly Judg 9:2; 2 Sam 5:1, 19:13–14). Notice the implication (or metonymy) that flesh is on this bone. Second, this bone has other resonances. The word *ṣēlā'* ("rib") also means, by semantic extension, "side, side-chamber, supporting beam" (Akkadian *ṣēlu,* "rib, side," has the same semantic range). The word has a concrete sense of "rib" in this context, but the other meanings resonate as well, suggesting the complementary of the woman and the man—they are two "sides" of a whole, as dramatized in the phrase "one flesh" (2:24). As his *ṣēlā'* she is beside him, and she supports and even embraces him like one of his own ribs. In all these features, the image of the woman taken from the man's rib indicates their complementary "fit" and their kinship relationship. (For other speculations, see Propp 1990: 193–94; Zevit 2013: 137–50.)

2:22. *Yahweh God built up the rib that he had taken from the man into a woman, and he brought her to the man.* This verse, for the first time, marks a clear gender distinction for *hā'ādām* ("the human, the man"), who is now faced with the newly created "woman" (*'iššâ*). As noted above, *hā'ādām* is already inchoately male (see NOTES at 2:7). Here Yahweh's act of creating woman makes the sexual distinction of male and female explicit, bringing it into the story's foreground. In the following verse the man articulates this distinction, featuring the wordplay of *'îš* ("man") and *'iššâ* ("woman").

The tactile sense of this creative act—he "built up" (*wayyiben*)—has the physicality of Yahweh "forming" (*wayyîṣer*) the human (2:7) and the animals (2:19) out of the soil. The raw material of this creation is not the soil, but the man's flesh and bone, which was formed from the soil. This situation extends the earthy and bodily bond of woman and man—she too is made of soil (albeit at second remove) and will return to it.

The clause *waybî'ehā 'el-hā'ādām* ("and he brought her to the human") directly echoes 2:19, *wayyābē' 'el-hā'ādām* ("and he brought them to the human"). This time Yahweh brings the woman instead of the animals, yielding the desired result. As before, he waits solicitously for the human to identify and name his true companion.

2:23. *The man said, "This time at last! Bone from my bones, / and flesh from my flesh. / This one shall be named 'woman,' / for from man she was taken."* This is the human's first direct speech in the narrative. Previously he had named the animals, but the words were not disclosed. A character's first speech is, as Alter (2011: 93–94) observes, "revelatory, perhaps more in manner than in matter, constituting an important moment in the exposition of character." The man's first speech expresses his recognition and joy that he has at last discovered the right companion. The word *zō't* ("this," feminine) points to this "time, occasion" but also gestures toward the woman, who is referred to as *zō't* ("this [one]") later in his speech.

After his exclamation of joy, the man breaks out into rhythmic, parallel speech that is identifiable as poetry. In biblical narrative style, a transition into poetry—particularly in speech—signals a crescendo or turning point. Other examples from the J primeval narrative are Lamech's poetic taunt (4:23–24) and Yahweh's promise at the conclusion of the flood (8:22, J), and in P, God's creation of humans (1:27) and the new law after the flood (9:6). Here the poetic speech is the rhetorical crescendo of this section, consisting of two couplets with regular rhythm (2:2 and 3:3) in accentual beats:

'eṣem mē'ăṣāmay	Bone from my bones,
ûbāśār mibbəśārî	and flesh from my flesh.
ləzō't yiqqārē' 'iššâ	This one shall be called "woman,"
kî mē'îš luqŏḥâ	for from man she was taken.

The first couplet is characterized by parallelism within and across the two lines. The internal parallelism of "bone" / "my bones" has differences of singular versus plural and indefinite versus possessive. This structure is repeated with slight variation in the second line with "flesh" / "my flesh." The semantic parallelism of "(my) bone(s)" / "(my) flesh" breaks apart the kinship trope "my bones and flesh" (Gen 29:14, discussed above), and intensifies and literalizes it. The phrase "flesh from my flesh" also anticipates the following verse, where "they become one flesh," blending sex, kinship, and a restoration of primal unity.

The second couplet has a more discursive and forensic parallelism, with the second line as a motive clause for the first line. The first line is a naming speech, with the indefinite focus of "this one" resolved into "woman." The verb *yiqqārē'* ("shall be called") is the passive stem (*niphal*) of the verb used when the human named the animals (*wayyiqra'*, 2:19–20), and in a sense completes this activity. The parallel verb in the second line, *luqŏḥâ* ("was taken"), is also a passive stem (*qal* passive). The second line explains that the name *'iššâ* ("woman") is derived from *'îš* ("man"); that is, the name is motivated by the woman's origin. The two parallel words, *'iššâ* and *'îš*, correspond in sound and sense and are, of course, complementary. *'Iššâ* at the end of line 1 also rhymes with *luqŏḥâ* ("was taken") at the end of line 2, completing the poetic speech with an end rhyme.

The parallelism and conceptual relationship of *'iššâ* and *'îš* has many implications. First, it is a literary (or midrashic) etymology, not a linguistic one. *'Iššâ* derives from the root **'nt* (Hebrew *'nš*), while *'îš* derives from a biradical root, *'š*. Second, the word *'iššâ* has already been mentioned in the narration, when Yahweh built up the rib into a "woman" and brought her to the man (2:22). This detail seems to confirm the correctness of the man's naming speech. More important, the wordplay highlights that the woman derives from the man and completes the creation of *hā'ādām* ("the human"). The man will continue to be called *hā'ādām*, since his personhood persists, but now he is also referred to by the gender-specific term *'îš* ("man") in contrast and complementarity to *'iššâ* ("woman"). This speech explicates the gender of *hā'ādām*, yielding the creation of the categories of "man" and "woman." In this sense, the nature of *hā'ādām*— both as an individual figure and as a collective symbol—has been transformed. This is the construction of gender, of the relationship between one (*hā'ādām* alone) and two (*'iššâ* and *'îš* complementing each other). By Yahweh building the woman out of the body of *hā'ādām*, and the man's articulation of it in his naming speech, the category of "human" is completed.

2:24. *Therefore a man leaves his father and mother and cleaves to his wife, and they become one flesh.* This disjunctive verse (introduced by "therefore") departs the narrative line to bring in a durative or iterative consequence, using an imperfective sequence *ya'ăzob . . . wədābaq . . . wəhāyû,* "leaves . . . and cleaves to . . . and become" (imperfect + converted perfects). This is a temporally unbounded action, signaling a proverbial truth that exists outside and independent of the story. This verse states that this timeless situation has its origin in the preceding events, although it looks forward to the time when such things as fathers, mothers, sons, and daughters already exist. In this aside, the narration discloses that the story is constitutive of reality in the era after Eden. The story here functions explicitly as a myth, detailing how the world and humans came into their present form.

For a man to "leave" (*ya'ăzōb*) his parents does not have the negative sense of abandoning them, but seems to have a spatial and legal sense of separating from the household and from his social position as "son" to begin a new household in his new social position as "husband." In practice, ancient Israelite couples often set up house next to or in the same household complex as the husband's parents. This extended patriarchal family and its architectural space was called a *bêt-'āb,* "house of the father" (Stager 1985a). Therefore, the act of "leaving" one's parents was more a change of kinship roles and boundaries.

It is also possible that this verse refers to the custom of holding the wedding and its consummation at the bride's parents' house, in which case the prospective groom literally leaves his parents' house in order to marry and "cleave" to his wife (van der Toorn 1994: 61, 71). This custom may be attested in Babylonia (*Atra.* I.299–304) and may be presumed in Deut 22:16–17, where the bride's father produces the wedding sheet if the husband later challenges the bride's virginity.

The sequence "[he] cleaves to his wife, and they become one flesh," has multiple nuances. It is a description of the sexual union of a man and a woman. It is also a description of the establishment of a new kinship unit, with "one flesh" as a trope for kinship (as in "our flesh," Gen 37:27). "Flesh" is a word for kin, and a woman and a man become "one flesh" in this legal sense through marriage. The bodily and the kinship meanings of this passage are interrelated, since the sexual union following the marriage ceremony is a part of the rite of passage into the married state.

The diction of becoming "one flesh" also provides an explanation or etiology of sex. It defines sexual desire as stemming from the original creation of the woman from the man's body, echoing the word "flesh" (*bāśār*) in the previous speech, "flesh from my flesh" (2:23). In sexual intercourse, man and woman become *bāśār ʾeḥād* ("one flesh") again, re-creating the primeval unity whence they originated. The desire and passion of sex seem to be, in this sense, a recovery of the joy and primal unity of paradise. Even though there is no indication that the first couple have sex in the Garden of Eden (the first statement of this act is 4:1, after their expulsion), the explanation of sex as a return to "one flesh" has an unmistakable sense of Edenic paradise.

In its layered meanings, this verse provides an etiology of human sexual desire and, at the same time, a charter for the institution of marriage.

2:25. *The two of them were naked, the man and his wife, and they felt no shame before each other.* The narrative line resumes (with a converted imperfect) with the man and the woman now a couple ("the two of them"), designated as *hā ʾādām wə ʾištô* ("the man and his wife"). The word *ʾištô* can mean "his woman" or "his wife," and both meanings are relevant here, particularly after the reference to marriage in the previous verse. The apposition of the two noun phrases, "the two of them" and "the man and his wife," provides a numerical contrast with the previous phrase, "one flesh," and places the focus on the relationship between the two as they stand before each other naked (Alter 2011: 35). The brief description of their interior emotional state—"they felt no shame before each other"—highlights their innocence and anticipates their loss of innocence in the events that follow (Sasson 1985).

The description of the couple as naked and unashamed brings to a close the story of the creation of the beloved companion and completes the creation of *hā ʾādām*. This verse functions as a transitional point, looking backward to the creation of *hā ʾādām* and anticipating the turns to come. The adjective "naked" (*ʿărûmmîm*) will echo in the next verse in the "cunning" (*ʿārûm*) of the snake, which will in turn lead to the couple's transgression and their change of self-consciousness: "they knew that they were naked" (3:7). The words "the two of them" (*šənêhem*) and "naked" (*ʿerummim*) in 3:7 clearly echo 2:25—*šənêhem ʿărûmmîm* ("the two of them were naked")—creating an intertextual arc in the story.

The negated verb, *wəlōʾ yitbōšāšû* ("and they felt no shame before each other"), with the reflexive sense of the *hithpael,* emphasizes the relational nature of their lack of shame. The shame of being naked comes from being seen naked by others, as when Ham sees Noah naked (9:22), or when the prophet Isaiah goes naked in public to symbolize the shame of Egypt (Isa 20:2–5). But the couple has not yet undergone their transformation in "knowledge" to experience this ethical emotion (see INTRODUCTION IV). Notice the suggestive description of the couple's interiority—we are not told what they feel, only that they do not feel shame.

3:1. *Now the snake was more cunning than all the animals of the field that Yahweh God had made.* A new direction in the story is signaled by the disjunctive clause introducing the snake (beginning with *waw* + noun + verb). This clause provides background information that introduces the new protagonist. The snake is *ʿārûm* ("cunning"), a wordplay on the statement that the humans were "naked" (*ʿărûmmîm*) in the previous verse. The word 'ārûm signifies a kind of subtle knowledge or intellectual disposition that can have different valences (M. V. Fox 2000: 35–36). In the book of Proverbs, it is a kind of intellectual facility that is possessed by the wise man, in contrast to the foolish or naive (e.g., Prov 12:16, 23; 13:16; 14:15), while elsewhere it often has a negative sense of being deceptive (e.g., Job 5:12, 15:5). In other words, to be 'ārûm is to be intelligent or clever, but what one does with this ability depends on the individual. To translate "cunning" is to emphasize the shady side of this wisdom, but this nuance is not clear until the snake's speech.

The definite article before the noun (ha + nāḥāš) does not mean that "the snake" is already known to the reader. The article is often prefixed to animals (e.g., haddōb, "the bear"), although the animal is grammatically indefinite (Barr 2014: 465–69).

The snake's cunning sets him apart—he is "more cunning than all the animals of the field (mikkōl ḥayyat haśśādeh) that Yahweh God had made." This diction recalls the creation of "every animal of the field" (kol-ḥayyat haśśādeh) in 2:19. By this backwards glance, the introduction of the snake is a supplement to that earlier scene. The snake belongs to the category of "animals of the field," but with a difference—it is more cunning than the others. The consequence of this distinctive feature will later further separate the snake from its fellow animals when Yahweh declares, "cursed are you, out of (or 'more than') all the domestic animals and all the wild animals in the field" (mikkol ḥayyat haśśādeh) (3:14).

The differences that characterize the snake are significant in the thematics of the story. This clever animal plays the role of a trickster, skillfully deceiving the woman into disobeying the divine command about the fruit of the Tree of Knowledge (Hendel 1999). Trickster figures are characteristically ambiguous creatures who cross or blur the ordinary categories of reality. The snake in Eden crosses or blurs the boundaries between the categories of animal, human, and divine. Although the snake is defined as an animal, he differs from them with respect to his cunning intelligence. Like a human, the snake has the power of speech (cf. 2:19–20, where the power of naming differentiates human from animal), and he tricks the woman through his deceptive speech. Unlike the humans, but like Yahweh, the snake knows that the humans will not die upon eating the forbidden fruit, but rather will become "like gods, knowing good and evil" (3:5), as Yahweh later acknowledges to be true (3:22).

The snake's identity partakes of and combines, in complex measure, characteristics of these three distinct categories of being. He is an animal with intelligence and speech and who has access to secret divine knowledge. Like tricksters of other traditions (cf. Prometheus in Greek tradition, Coyote and Raven in Native American, Spider [Ananse] in West African), the boon of the trickster is both a benefit and a loss. The effects of the snake's actions are colored by multiple meanings and ambiguity.

The snake's role as trickster is also motivated by the snake's symbolic associations in ancient Near Eastern traditions. Many snakes in the region are venomous, hence they are associated with death and healing (cf. the "bronze snake," nəḥaš nəḥōšet [Num 21:9], that cures deadly snakebites in the wilderness). Snakes also shed their skins, rejuvenating themselves, hence they were also associated with immortality (see Gilg. XI.305–7, and COMMENTS). The themes of death and immortality in Eden come into play through the snake's intervention.

Snakes were also associated with magic—the noun nāḥāš ("snake") can also mean "divination" (cf. the denominative verb niḥēš, "to practice divination"). The magical quality of snakes is most obvious in the story of the exodus, where Moses's rod turns into a snake (*nāḥāš*), displaying the power of Yahweh (Exod 4:1–5; cf. the doublet with Aaron and the Egyptian magicians in 7:8–12). The snake's secret knowledge in Eden may reflect their magical qualities.

Snakes also have an association with West Semitic goddesses (Wallace 1985: 155–61). In one type of iconography, the goddess is depicted naked, standing on a lion and holding snakes in one or both hands, and sometimes also holding flowers. There are numerous examples of this image in Levantine and Egyptian art from the second millennium BCE. Whether the snake in its association with this Canaanite goddess connotes rejuvenation, magical protection, sexuality, or some other nuance or conjunction of meanings is unclear. There is a tantalizing possibility that the scene of the snake and the naked woman in Eden is somehow derived from this old Canaanite iconography of the snake and the nude goddess. The woman's name, *ḥawwâ* (Eve), and her title, "mother of all life," may also point in this direction (see NOTES at 3:20).

A story that depicts a snake, a naked woman and man, forbidden fruit, and a type of knowledge that includes sexual knowledge also brings to mind the Freudian phallic associations of snakes. This is nowhere explicit in the story, but there are examples of this symbolism in the ancient Near East (e.g., figurines of the Mesopotamian demon Pazuzu, whose erect phallus is sometimes a snake). The unconscious phallic symbolism of snakes bears on why the snake chooses the woman for his deceptive speech, and on the sexual awareness that ensues when the woman and the man eat the forbidden fruit. The snake is also feared by humans (the etiology of this instinctive fear is given in 3:15), which creates an interesting subliminal mixture of desire and fear in the snake's presence.

In later interpretive traditions, the snake was often taken to be an agent of the devil or the devil himself (e.g., Wis 2:24; Rev 12:9; Targum Pseudo-Jonathan; see Kugel 1998: 98–100). This became the dominant interpretation among the classical rabbis and church fathers and into the modern period. This identity is not in the associative matrix of the story itself. As this verse states, the snake is a creature of the field, created by Yahweh. He is an intelligent and sly trickster and is punished to bear the shame of

Figure 5. Seated female (?) and seated male god (with horns) with palm tree and snake. Formerly called the "Adam and Eve" seal. Cylinder seal, greenstone, Old Akkadian period (ca. 2100 BCE), British Museum. (Drawing by William H. C. Propp)

a distinctively snakish existence (3:14–15; for a critical survey of other views, see Day 2022: 42–60).

He said to the woman, "Did God really say, 'Do not eat from all the trees of the garden?'" At this point we discover that the snake can talk. The dialogue between the snake and the woman is a marvelous exchange of truths, lies, and half-truths. The snake is a master of this language game.

The emphatic particle *'ap* in the sequence *'ap kî-'āmar 'ĕlōhîm* ("Did God really say . . .") injects a degree of doubt, "is it so, indeed, really?" This is similar to the tone of Abraham's question to Yahweh, "Will you really (*ha'ap*) destroy the righteous with the wicked?" (18:23), or Sarah's doubt, "Will I really (*ha'ap*) bear a child, now that I am old?" (18:13). This particle is usually used in poetry, perhaps lending an air of formality. The use of *'ap* without the interrogative *he* creates ambiguity about whether this is even a question. Skinner (1930: 73) aptly describes it as "a half-interrogative, half-reflective exclamation." The implication of this reflective interrogation is cunning, since the woman cannot simply respond yes or no.

The snake's words rephrase Yahweh's previous instruction, "From all the trees of the garden you may surely eat, but as for the Tree of the Knowledge of Good and Evil, you shall not eat from it" (2:16–17). The phrase "from all the trees of the garden" (*mikkōl 'ēṣ haggān*) is repeated verbatim, and "you shall not eat" (*lō' tō'kal*) differs only in a change from singular to plural. So God did indeed say these words, but in a different order and with different meaning from those imputed by the snake. Although God allowed eating "from all the trees," he went on to prohibit a particular tree. The snake carefully manipulates those words to draw the woman into conversation, raising doubts about what God had really said. The question catches the attention of his innocent prey.

The snake's use of the name "God" (*'ĕlōhîm*) is consistent with the general usage in J—the narrator consistently uses the name Yahweh, but characters can say either Yahweh or God (Friedman 1997: 265 n. 17). By using the word *'ĕlōhîm,* the snake can play on both of its potential meanings, "God" and "gods," in his description of the transformative gift of the forbidden fruit, "you will become like *'ĕlōhîm*" (3:5).

3:2–3. The woman said to the snake, "We may eat fruit from the trees of the garden, but about the fruit of the tree in the midst of the garden, God said, 'Do not eat from it, and do not touch it, lest you die.'" Now the woman slightly alters the words of God's instructions. Yahweh said "you shall not eat from it" (*lō' tō'kal mimmennû,* 2:17), which the woman restates in the plural (*lō' tō'kəlû mimmennû*). She adds "and do not touch it" (*wəlō' tigg'û bô*), which Yahweh did not say. This embroidery of Yahweh's words suggests that the woman is going to some lengths to contradict the snake, making God's prohibition more emphatic by doubling it.

We are not told how the snake or the woman knows of Yahweh's prohibition. We presume that the man told the woman, and the snake may have been listening. Much background is left open. In any case, both sides of this conversation are embellishing or deviating from the truth by subtle additions or subtraction. Each side is presenting distortions, one from the standpoint of cunning and the other from naiveté.

3:4. The snake said to the woman, "You shall not die." The snake betrays that he knows more than he has let on. His first question drew the woman in, and now he contests her reformulation of Yahweh's words, "lest you die" (*pen-təmūtûn,* in the plural). This injection of doubt undermines the woman's innocent understanding. The snake uses the same emphatic syntax as Yahweh (*môt tāmût,* "you shall die," 2:17), but in the negative and plural (*lōʾ-môt təmūtûn,* "you shall not die"). The trap has sprung.

The snake here tells the truth, an effective bait. He mysteriously knows that the couple will not die when they eat the forbidden fruit. It is Yahweh, he insinuates, who has not told the truth. But the snake does not tell the whole truth, for there will be serious consequences, entailing the affirmation of mortality and death, for violating God's command. The ambiguous play between the truth and the whole truth is central to this exchange and its consequences (see Sternberg 1985: 230–63).

3:5. *"Indeed, God knows that on the day you eat from it your eyes will be opened, and you will become like gods, knowing good and evil."* The snake cleverly rephrases Yahweh's warning, "for on the day you eat from it (you shall die)" (*kî bəyôm ʾăkāləkā mimmennû,* 2:17), changing it to plural, and substitutes, "your eyes will be opened, and you will become like gods, knowing good and evil." This is true, but a selection of the truth, not the whole truth. The snake's assertion, "God knows" (*yōdēaʿ ʾĕlōhîm*), also foregrounds and echoes the quality of knowledge that the humans will gain, becoming "like gods, knowing . . ." (*kēʾlōhîm yōdəʿê*).

What the snake omits to say is that this knowledge has consequences—they will become estranged from Yahweh and from their previous innocence when they "become like gods, knowing. . . ." The snake's words impute that Yahweh's threat of death is a smokescreen to keep humans in their place, that Yahweh is insincere and perhaps jealous of human prerogatives. But these instructions may be protecting humans, to keep them in paradise. The truth, in short, is ambiguous.

The plural translation of *kēʾlōhîm,* "like gods," rather than the singular, "like God," is preferable because of both the plural participle that follows, *yōdəʿê,* "knowers of," and Yahweh's later affirmation, "the human has become like one of us, knowing good and evil" (3:22). The plural of "gods" and "one of us" presumably refers to Yahweh and the lesser deities that accompany him, although the other gods play no active role in the story (see NOTES at 3:22).

3:6. *The woman saw that the tree was good for food, that it was a delight to the eyes, and desirable to make one wise.* As a consequence of this exchange, the woman's perceptions and sensibility are changed. This verse shows her interiority, the only time that we see through her eyes. By this narrative strategy, we see the dawning of the woman's new consciousness and autonomy. This change is provoked by the snake's deceptive speech, which creates trouble but also opens up new possibilities for the humans.

The woman perceives the tree as having three qualities: it is "good for food . . . a delight to the eyes, and desirable to make one wise." The first two are continuous with the permitted trees of the garden, "every tree that is desirable to see and good for food" (2:9). The woman's perception reverses this phrasing—now "good for food" comes first and visual delight comes second. Now she perceives that the forbidden Tree of Knowledge is like the other trees in its positive qualities, and it becomes the object of desire. The last quality sets this tree apart from the other trees: it is "desirable to make one wise," which makes it a forbidden desire. In this verse we see the woman's desire moving upward from bodily pleasure ("good for food") to visual pleasure ("delight to the eyes") and finally to philosophical-ethical pleasure ("desirable to make one wise"). The description of the tree as "good (*tôb*)" for food may echo the content of the last quality, the knowledge of "good" (*tôb*) and evil.

The woman's desire for wisdom that will make the humans "like gods," as the snake says, outweighs her fear of immediate death. She has been persuaded by the snake that Yahweh's command was a ruse and that the tree's fruit imparts godlike wisdom. The *hiphil* infinitive *ləhaśkîl*, "to make (one) wise," has additional connotations. The overt sense in the context of the Tree of Knowledge is the causative meaning, "to make one wise, to give insight (*śēkel*)." But this verb can also mean "to consider, ponder, watch closely," as one who "considers the poor" (Ps 41:2) or "watches closely his words" (Prov 16:20). This sense is activated by the previous phrase, "a delight to the eyes." The tree is, in this doubled sense, "desirable to see" because it is "desirable to make one wise." I have translated the latter sense, but both are probably mingled in this usage.

She took from its fruit and ate, and she also gave it to her husband beside her, and he ate. After a glimpse of the woman's interiority, the narrative continues with the exterior description of her actions. Her interiority is subsequently revealed only through her direct speech. Here the actions are portrayed with a sequence of four verbs in quick succession: *wattiqqaḥ . . . wattōʾkal wattittēn* ("she took . . . she ate, and she gave . . . and he ate"). The woman acts without hesitation. The quickness of her acts, after the swerve into her thoughts, shows the suppleness of biblical style, allowing the writer to shape the characters and the narrative arc with brief strokes.

The husband (*ʾîšāh*, lit. "her man") has not been previously mentioned in this scene. He appears suddenly as the object of her action, "she also gave it to her husband beside her, and he ate." The focus remains on the woman, with the man now described as *ʿimmāh* ("her husband beside her"). The couple had previously been described as *hāʾādām wəʾištô* ("the man and his wife/woman," 2:25), but now the possessive relationship is reversed—the man is "her husband." This change in reference highlights the shift in human agency. Previously the man was the chief agent, naming the animals and the woman. Now the woman is the agent—speaking with the snake, seeing things in a new light, making new choices. The man is subordinate—she gives him the fruit and he eats. The previous master of language is silent, passively taking the fruit and eating it. He is *ʿimmāh* ("with her" or "beside her") and so, without any sign of hesitation, "he ate."

3:7. *The eyes of the two of them were opened, and they knew that they were naked.* The peripeteia or turning point in the story occurs at this point, when the couple eats the forbidden fruit. The prediction of the snake comes true, up to a point, but not as he had implied. He had said, "your eyes will be opened" (3:5), and this happens precisely as stated. But the promised divine knowledge ("you will become like gods, knowing good and evil") turns out to be an unexpected sort of knowledge, "they knew that they were naked." This is knowledge, but hardly (or at best, ambiguously) divine knowledge.

This is an ironic reversal. Rather than becoming "like gods," they now become aware of something that makes them specifically human. They are now aware of the sexual distinction between male and female bodies, which they wish to hide with fig-leaf loincloths to avoid the shame of being seen naked by each other. What they now know is a new degree of self-consciousness or self-awareness. This knowledge of one's body is more than intellectual; it is physical, emotional, and, we might say, cultural, since it thrusts them into human culture (signified by clothing) and social behavior (the code of honor and shame).

The language of this verse is dramatic. The first part, "the eyes of the two were opened, and they knew that . . . ," echoes the speech of the snake and makes it appear as if his prediction were coming true. But then the sense shifts abruptly, " . . . they were naked," replacing the snake's prediction with the earlier description of innocence: "The two of them were naked, the man and his wife, and they felt no shame before each other" (2:25). The words "the two of them" (*šənêhem*) and "naked" (*ʿărûmmîm* in 2:25 and *ʿêrummîm* here, vocalic variants) repeat in these verses, so that it becomes clear that heeding the snake's words reverses the earlier idyllic scene. The *ʿārûm* ("cunning") of the snake has led them to know that they are *ʿêrummîm* ("naked"), and now cunningly intelligent in their own way.

they sewed together fig leaves and made loincloths for themselves. The couple respond to their new perceptions by making clothes. We are not shown their interior responses, only their actions. The motive for their actions is supplied by the echo of the earlier scene in 2:25—the description, *lōʾ yitbōšāšû* ("they felt no shame before each other"), is clearly reversed. The story's terse diction does not state their moral emotion of shame, but it is implied in their action and the activation of the earlier verse.

The fig leaves and loincloths provide some local detail, a sense of realism. The choice of fig leaves is practical—they are large and serviceable for sewing into loincloths. The *ḥăgōrōt* ("loincloths") are simple garments wrapped around the hips (from *ḥāgar,* "to gird"; cf. 1 Kgs 2:5, "the loincloth that is on his loins"). These unisex loincloths alleviate their shame of nakedness, masking the sex of their male and female bodies.

The transformation of the woman and the man into self-conscious humans is accompanied by their invention of clothing. Civilized humans uniquely wear clothing. In the ancient Near East, only barbarians or animals were naked in public. Clothing, as Enkidu discovers, is an essential part of civilized existence (see COMMENTS). With their newfound human knowledge, a purely natural life recedes. This passage is recapitulated in the life cycle of humans generally. Self-consciousness and body knowledge mark the transition from innocence to adulthood.

With the first clothing—an objective correlate of their new knowledge—the scene of the humans' transgression and transformation ends. They have responded to their shame but have not yet confronted their guilt.

3:8. *They heard the sound of Yahweh God walking about in the garden in the evening breeze.* The story turns to the scene of discovery and punishment. Sometime later—whether immediately or after a while, we are not told—they hear "the sound (*qôl*) of Yahweh." The word means "sound" or "voice." In connection with "walking about," the "sound of Yahweh" seems like the right sense. But the word resonates with the other sense, the "voice of Yahweh." Later Yahweh notes that the man "listened to your wife's voice (*qôl*)" (3:17). The implication is that he should have listened to and heeded Yahweh's voice instead. They hear his *qôl,* but they have not heeded his voice, so they hide.

The description of Yahweh "walking about in the garden in the evening breeze" is a picturesque detail, lending momentary lightness to the drama. Yahweh is taking his evening stroll at the time when the heat of day recedes with the cooling winds. Here we are shown—and the couple is reminded—that this is Yahweh's garden, and the humans are only tenants. A correlate to this scene is the opulence of royal gardens in the ancient Near East, with Yahweh taking pleasure in his private garden. But the couple have disobeyed the king, and pleasure will turn to fear.

The *rûaḥ hayyôm* ("evening breeze"), literally "wind of the day," is presumably the wind that rises around sundown (Skinner 1930: 77; Speiser 1964: 24). Compare when Isaac goes outside for a stroll "at the turn of the evening" (24:63). The Garden of Eden is a Middle Eastern enclosed garden, hot in the day and pleasant in the evening breeze.

the man and his wife hid themselves from Yahweh God in the midst of the trees of the garden. The clause "the man and his wife hid themselves" effectively reverses the tone of 2:25, where "the man and his wife . . . felt no shame before each other." The "man and his wife" are still together, but where before they did not see anything wrong with being naked in public, now they hide, fearful that Yahweh will see them in their newly clothed state. The outward act of hiding implies an inner state of shame, fear, and guilt (see INTRODUCTION IV). Their moral emotion of guilt is not foregrounded until Yahweh interrogates them, and they betray their guilty consciences by trying to shift the blame (3:12–13).

There is some irony in the place of their hiding—*bətôk ʿēṣ haggān* ("in the midst of the trees of the garden"). This phrase echoes the woman's description of the Tree of the Knowledge of Good and Evil as *hā ʿēṣ ʾăšer bətôk-haggān* ("the tree in the midst of the garden," 3:3), and more distantly Yahweh planting the two forbidden trees *bətôk haggān* ("in the midst of the garden," 2:9). The word *ʿēṣ* ("tree") is used in our verse as a collective noun, "trees," but the verbal echo links their place of hiding with the tree with which they transgressed Yahweh's command. Their act of hiding evokes the tree itself, as if they were somehow hiding in it.

The narrative order of the two humans reverts to that of 2:25, *hā ʾādām wə ʾištô* ("the man and his wife"). He is no longer "her husband," as he is presented in 3:6, but she is once again "his wife." By this slight stylistic shift, the story brings the woman back from a position of primacy into her role as the man's companion. From here, Yahweh will address the man first and last, with the woman subordinated to him, both in literary style—she is interrogated second—and social hierarchy—she will be subject to his authority (see NOTES at 3:16; and the overview of J. J. Collins 2005: 86–94).

3:9–19. There is artful symmetry in this sequence of interrogation and punishment, which consists entirely of dialogue (Gunkel 1997: 20). The order of address is chiastic: (A) man—(B) woman—(C) snake—(B) woman—(A) man. Yahweh's interrogations are brief, but they elicit all he needs to know. The judgments are carefully crafted to suit the crimes. The consequences create the new features of post-Eden existence, anticipating the couple's expulsion. Yahweh's judgments in 3:14–19 occasionally have a parallel quasi-poetic style, but this style is not consistently maintained. These judgments express a high register of speech, with poetic shadings, marking this divine discourse as a narrative climax (cf. 1:27).

3:9. *Yahweh God called out to the man and said to him, "Where are you?"* Yahweh's question seems a straightforward call for the man to announce his location and show himself. The implication is that Yahweh does not know where the man is. This may be so, since elsewhere in the J narratives Yahweh is not omniscient, as for instance in his failed plan to find a companion for the man among the animals, and in the flood story when he regrets having made humankind (6:6). But it is also possible that this question is intended to elicit the man's confession, and that Yahweh already has surmised the answer, as in Yahweh's question to Cain, "Where is Abel, your brother?" (4:9). This ambiguity in Yahweh's question yields a divine portrayal that is fraught with background (Auerbach's [1953: 12] phrase).

3:10. *He said, "I heard your sound in the garden and I was afraid, for I am naked, so I hid."* The clause-initial *qōləkā* ("your sound/voice") highlights the doubled nuance of "sound" and "voice" (see Notes at 3:8), since Yahweh has just spoken. This is the man's first speech since the transgression and reveals his sense of panic and guilt. A simpler answer to the question would be "Here I am" (cf. 22:1), but instead he gives a terse explanation of why he hid. As Gunkel (1997: 19) observes, the man's speech "is an exceptionally realistic portrayal of a guilty conscience." Stylistically, his statement rephrases the previous description in 3:8 but now supplemented with his interior emotion and perception—"I was afraid, for I am naked." In his rephrasing of 3:8 from his subjective viewpoint, the man speaks in the first-person singular, "I," rather than the plural, "we." In his words, the man subtly sunders the unity of "the man and his wife" in 3:8, which will crumble further in 3:13 when the man shifts the blame to the woman. Furthermore, as Garr (2021: 345) observes, the switch from the reflexive *hithpael* in 3:8, "they hid themselves," to the middle-voice *niphal*, "I hid," subtly evades the man's responsibility, contrasting the narrative report with the speaker's viewpoint.

The man's fear is couched as a fear of shame by being seen naked, but a deeper fear is intimated, which Yahweh perceives (as shown in his next question). The missing link between fear and nakedness is the man's transgression of Yahweh's command—which enabled him to perceive his nakedness—and the mandated punishment of death. Fear of death and the guilt of transgression are in the background of the man's speech.

3:11. *He said, "Who told you that you are naked? Have you eaten from the tree from which I commanded you not to eat?"* Yahweh dissects the man's response, inferring the man's transgression. But he leaves open another possibility, that someone told the man he was naked. The question of guilt is not resolved until the man's reply. By his words, Yahweh knows that "the knowledge of good and evil" imparted by the forbidden fruit includes the awareness of nakedness.

3:12. *The man said, "The woman, whom you gave to be with me, she gave to me from the tree, and I ate."* The man seems again to give a truthful reply, but his phrasing shows that he has become cunning. He attempts to absolve himself by blaming the woman, and subtly passes the blame to Yahweh, who created the woman. The woman "gave to me" (*nātənâ-llî*) the fruit, but since she is the one whom "you gave to be with me" (*nātattâ ʿimmādî*), the act of "giving" ultimately goes back to Yahweh. In this blame game, the man shows cunning and desperation. As Gunkel (1997: 19) comments, "the narrator knows the human heart."

3:13. *Yahweh God said to the woman, "What have you done?"* Yahweh's question of interrogation again has a doubled meaning. This question seems to ask for a simple description ("what?") but also seeks the motivation ("why?"). Speiser (1964: 24) aptly compares Pharaoh's question to Abram, *mah-zzōʾt ʿāśîtā llî* ("what is this you have done to me?," 12:18), where Pharaoh knows what has happened and wants Abram's self-justification. Yahweh's virtually identical words to the woman, *mah-zzōʾt ʿāśît* (lit. "what is this you have done?"), have the same accusatory sense.

The woman said, "The snake deceived me, and I ate." Echoing the man's strategy of deflecting the blame to her, the woman blames the snake. "The snake" is clause-initial in her response, foregrounding him as the culprit. Like the man's response, her deflection is true in part. The snake did deceive her, but she then acted of her own desire and will. Her laconic statement *wāʾōkēl* ("and I ate") echoes the passive role of the man—*wayyō'kal* ("and he ate," 3:6)—adding a touch of irony to her attempt to evade responsibility.

3:14. *Yahweh God said to the snake, "Because you have done this, cursed are you, out of all the domestic animals and all the wild animals in the field."* Yahweh does not interrogate the snake, but turns directly to judgment. He seems deliberately to deny the snake an opportunity for further deceptive speech. Yahweh pivots from his interrogation of the woman—*mah-zzō't 'āśît* ("what have you done?")—to similar diction in his judgment of the snake—*kî 'āśîtā zzō't* ("Because you have done this"). The snake seems now reduced to a mere animal, lacking the agency of speech.

Yahweh carefully crafts the punishment to fit the circumstances of the crime. The snake's punishment undoes his earlier status as an animal with easy access to the woman. First, the snake's status among the animals is redefined via a curse: *'ārûr 'attâ mikkol-habbəhēmâ ûmikkōl ḥayyat haśśādeh* ("cursed are you, out of all the domestic animals and all the wild animals of the field"), which echoes and transforms the initial condition of the snake as *'ārûm mikkōl ḥayyat haśśādeh* ("cunning, more than all the animals of the field," 3:1). In his previous special state, the snake was distinguished from his fellow "animals of the field" by his *'ārûm* ("cunning"), but now he is distinguished by being *'ārûr* ("cursed").

This verse has a small stylistic variation from 3:1, where *ḥayyat haśśādeh* ("animals of the field") designated all animals. Now animals are divided into two categories, *habbəhēmâ* ("domestic animals") and *ḥayyat haśśādeh* ("wild animals in the field"). This stylistic and semantic variation is comparable to the flexible categorizations in the P creation myth (1:24–30).

The curse, *'ārûr 'attâ min* ("cursed are you out of, from"), with the partitive sense of the preposition *min,* describes an estrangement from the community of animals (Scharbert 1977: 409). Yahweh's curse of Cain in 4:11 has similar diction: *'ārûr 'attâ min-hā'ădāmâ* ("cursed are you from the soil"). Cain is now estranged from the soil that sustained him as a farmer. As Yahweh details, the snake's existence will be marked by humiliation and fear.

"You shall crawl on your belly and eat dust all the days of your life." These are humiliating conditions that distinguish the snake from other animals. To crawl on one's belly is an act of self-abasement. Hence a subject bows with face to the ground before a king or superior (cf. the biblical expression, "he/they bowed down with their face to the ground," Gen 19:1, 42:6, 48:12, etc.). The snake moving forever on his belly is an act of perpetual humiliation—he is now inferior to all. The punishment reverses the snake's previous status.

One implication of this reversal is that the snake previously moved upright. Whether he was imagined having legs is not clear. This punishment has the effect of an etiology or "just so" story, explaining why snakes crawl on their bellies. The mystery of snake locomotion ("the way of a snake on a rock") is listed as one of the world's puzzles in Prov 30:19.

To "eat dust" (*'āpār*) is also an expression of abasement; compare Ps 72:9, "may his enemies lick dust (*'āpār*)," and especially Mic 7:17, "they will lick dust like a snake." Isaiah 49:23 combines prostration and eating dirt: "they will bow down to you with their faces on the ground, and they will lick the dust from your feet." Akkadian curses also have similar expressions—"Let dirt be their food" (*ANET,* 533). For the snake, this

Figure 6. Babylonian snake-dragon (*mušḫuššu*): a composite snake with legs.
Glazed relief from the Ishtar Gate of Babylon (sixth century BCE),
Pergamon Museum, Berlin. (Drawing by William H. C. Propp)

humiliation is permanent. The punishment of eating dust is an inversion of the snake's enticement to the woman to eat the forbidden fruit. Dust is a signifier of mortality and death (see Notes at 2:7), the opposite of food that makes one "like gods."

3:15. *"I will set hatred between you and the woman, and between your offspring and hers. They will strike at your head, and you will strike at their heels."* This punishment reverses the circumstance of the easy relationship between the snake and the woman. Rather than open discourse, there will be open enmity. This verse explains why, in the present world, humans have such a negative visceral reaction to snakes.

The balanced couplet *hû' yəšûpəkā rō'š we'attâ təšûpennû 'āqēb* ("they [lit. 'he'] shall strike at your head, and you shall strike at their [lit. 'his'] heels") shows the kind of hate that henceforth colors the relationship between humans and snakes. The pronouns for "they" and "you" are in the singular but are meant as collectives. (The singular pronouns gave rise to later messianic interpretations of this verse in Judaism and Christianity—"he" identified with the messiah and "you" with Satan. Cf. the common Catholic iconography with Mary as the woman with the snake under her feet.) The verb *šûp* in both clauses means something like "bruise, crush." This verb has a wordplay with a type of snake, *šəpîpōn,* which is an onomapoetic name, "the hisser," for a type of venomous snake. (*Nāḥāš,* "snake," and *šəpipon* are parallel terms in 49:17.) This makes the mutual striking like the hissing of snakes. The words "head" and "heels" are objects of the verbs, but elsewhere they connote a merism of totality, "from head to heels," total enmity.

3:16. *To the woman he said, "I will greatly multiply your labor pains from pregnancy—in pain you shall bear children."* The woman's and the man's punishments share the quality of *'iṣṣābôn* ("pain"), which reverses the idyllic condition of life in Eden. These are etiologies of human pain.

The woman's pain concerns childbirth. Yahweh's speech has a parallel rhythm: *harbâ 'arbeh 'iṣṣəbônēk wəhērōnēk / bə'eṣeb tēlədî bānîm* ("I will greatly multiply your pain and your pregnancy / in pain you shall bear children"). Most commentators take *'iṣṣəbônēk wəhērōnēk* ("your pain and your pregnancy") as a hendiadys, in which one noun modifies the other, hence "your painful pregnancy" (Skinner 1930: 82; Trible 1978: 127; Bird 1997: 165–66; cf. Meyers 1988: 95–109). But the next line clarifies that it is not pregnancy that is painful, but childbirth: "in pain you shall bear children."

The sense of this punishment is best elucidated by considering the parallel style:

I will greatly multiply (A) your pain (B) and your pregnancy (C),
　　in pain (B′) you shall bear children (C′).

In the first line *harbâ 'arbeh* ("I will greatly multiply") and *'iṣṣəbônēk wəhērōnēk* ("your pain and your pregnancy") are quasi-rhyming pairs. There is a narrative quality in the movement to the second line, as *hērōnēk* ("your pregnancy") moves to *tēlədî bānîm* ("you shall bear children"). These parallel terms—*hērōnēk* ("your pregnancy) and *tēlədî* ("you shall bear")—tell a miniature story from pregnancy to birth. In both lines this biological process is colored by pain—from *'iṣṣəbônēk* ("your pain") to *bə'eṣeb* ("in pain"). The focus on pain is emphasized by its clause-initial position in the second line.

Through this quasi-poetic diction, Yahweh institutes pain in childbirth as the woman's punishment. This is an etiology that explains this reality. It also changes the quality of sexual knowledge gained from the forbidden fruit, since this kind of "knowing" (see NOTES at 4:1) will culminate in the pain of childbirth. Elsewhere the pangs of childbirth are a trope for maximal pain (e.g., Isa 13:8, 21:3; Mic 4:9; Ps 48:6). Moreover, childbirth was often deadly (e.g., Rachel in Gen 35:16–20), a nuance that goes unstated but which resonates with the original punishment of death (2:17).

The words for pain— *'iṣṣābôn* and *'eṣeb*—form a *Leitwort* sequence in the punishments of the woman and the man, occurring three times in two verses (3:16–17). For the woman the pain is in childbirth, and for the man the pain comes from working the soil. These punishments reverse the paradisical circumstances in Eden. As Cassuto (1961: 165) observes, the words for "pain" present a wordplay with *'ēṣ* ("tree"). This suggests another reversal—the humans ate from the *'ēṣ* ("tree"), but they gain *'iṣṣābôn* and *'eṣeb* ("pain").

"You shall desire your husband, and he shall rule over you." Yahweh also alters the relationship between the woman and the man as a response to their transgression. This is an etiology of family power. In the scene of transgression, the woman was the chief agent—it was she who conversed with the snake, she who chose to eat the forbidden fruit, and also she who "gave it to her husband beside her, and he ate" (3:6). Because she momentarily ruled him, her punishment is to be ruled by him. Furthermore, her desire for the forbidden tree is redirected to a desire for her husband (however the words for "desire" are different—it is *təšûqâ* here). This new regime between the sexes also relates to their new sexual knowledge—the desire (*təšûqâ*) here is sexual, in contrast to the types of desire (with different words) conjured by the tree (culinary, aesthetic, cogni-

tive). The rule of the man over his wife is a reversal of life in Eden. The circumscribed roles allowed women in ancient Israelite society are therefore defined as punishments, fixed in the present world, but an inverted mirror of the ideal world.

As recent commentators have observed, the story seems to say that male dominance is not a primordial essence, but rather an accident, something nonessential. The thematics of the story certainly allow this inference. It is not likely that the punishments pronounced by Yahweh are meant to be reversable. But of course, modern readers are not bound by these etiologies.

The diction of this punishment is echoed in Yahweh's warning to Cain, "sin crouches at the door—it desires you, but you can rule over it" (4:7). Later interpreters sometimes elided the woman with this personified "sin," but this misogynist reading is quite foreign to the portrait of the woman in the text. She is sympathetic—even a tragic hero—and entirely human.

3:17. *To the man he said, "Since you listened to your wife's voice and ate from the tree about which I commanded you 'Do not eat from it.'"* Yahweh's speeches to the woman and the man are colored by the *Leitwort* pair ʾîš ("man, husband") and ʾiššâ ("woman, wife," see NOTES at 2:23), as Yahweh refers to ʾîšēk ("your man/husband," 3:16) and ʾištekā ("your woman/wife," 3:17). This pivoting between wife and husband leads to an alteration of another *Leitwort* relationship, that between hāʾadam ("the human, man") and hāʾădāmâ ("the soil").

Yahweh describes the man as culpable because šāmaʿtā ləqôl ʾištekā ("you listened to your wife's voice"), which contrasts with listening to Yahweh's voice (see 3:10, ʾet qōləkā šāmaʿtî, "I heard your sound"). The man showed weak judgment in following his wife's voice when it conflicted with Yahweh's. In other circumstances, listening to the wife's voice is correct, as God later tells Abraham: "Whatever Sarah tells you, listen to her voice" (21:12; similarly, 16:9).

cursed is the soil because of you. In painful labor you shall eat from it all the days of your life. The reversal in the man's punishment involves his relationship with the soil, proleptically turning his Edenic quality of existence into the hard life of the subsistence farmer. This curse reflects the difficult agricultural environment of ancient Israel (Meyers 1988: 93). The man's share of pain (ʿiṣṣābôn) echoes the woman's pain (ʿiṣṣābôn and ʿeṣeb) in childbirth. It also anticipates the expulsion from Eden and the task stated there, "to work the soil from which he was taken" (3:23). The easy labor and abundant food of Eden turns to painful labor and scarce food.

The curse on the soil diminishes the relationship of hāʾādām ("the human, man") and hāʾădāmâ ("the soil") (see NOTES at 2:5, 7). Previously, the soil of Eden effortlessly yielded good fruit. Henceforth it will no longer do so but will require intensive labor to make it fruitful. This is an etiology of the harsh agricultural economy. The *Leitwort* relationship of hāʾādām and hāʾădāmâ will develop further nuances in the stories of Cain, Noah, and Abraham (see INTRODUCTION I).

The duration of the punishment, "all the days of your life," subtly returns to the mortal condition implicit in the creation of the human from the soil (see NOTES at 2:7). The days of human life are limited because humans are earthly creatures, made from soil. Only divine beings live forever. The relationship between the human and the soil that unfolds in this punishment is twofold: one part consists of the punishment of painful labor on the soil, and the other consists of the human destiny to return to the soil, that is, mortality and death. This latter is related to Yahweh's threatened punishment, "on the day you eat from it you shall die" (2:17), but this punishment is now deferred for "all the days of your life."

3:18. *Thorns and thistles it will sprout for you, and you shall eat the grasses of the field.* This verse explicates the soil's curse by describing a reversal of the previous circumstances in the Garden of Eden. In 2:9, "Yahweh God caused to sprout from the soil every tree," but now all that will sprout are "thorns and thistles." The words "the soil" (*hā'ădāmâ*) and "sprout" (*wayyaṣmaḥ* and *taṣmîaḥ*) clearly echo in these two verses, but the plants that sprout are distinct. "Thorns and thistles," which sprout naturally, are inedible for humans, so they must now cultivate "the grasses of the field" (*'ēśeb haśśādeh*). This latter term echoes the primordial situation: "grasses of the field (*'ēśeb haśśādeh*) had not yet grown (*yiṣmāḥ*)" (2:5). Now these grasses are described as existing, reversing their primordial absence, with the new turn that they serve as humans' primary food, replacing the fruit of the trees of Eden. These three verses—2:5, 2:9, and 3:18—describe a progression of available vegetation from nonexistence to the abundant provisions of Eden to the hardscrabble cultivation of the cursed soil.

3:19. *By the sweat of your brow you shall eat bread.* This is a concrete application of the previous clauses, "in painful labor you shall eat from it" (3:17) and "you shall eat the grasses of the field" (3:18). The general term *'iṣṣābôn* ("pain") now has its embodied result as "the sweat of your brow," and the "grasses of the field" have, through hard human labor, turned into bread. This sentence brings to vivid closure the picture of painful agricultural labor, before Yahweh turns to the second aspect of the man's relationship with the soil—mortality. The rhythm and alliteration of *tō'kal leḥem* ("you shall eat bread") at the end of the verse make the punishment emphatic.

This reversal implies that the humans did not sweat in paradise, where the labor was easy (see Notes at 2:15). This concept is illustrated in Egyptian tomb paintings, where the paradisical quality of the afterlife is shown by people wearing fine clothing when working the soil, suggesting that they do not sweat (Leith 2021).

until you return to the soil, for from it you were taken. For you are dust, and to dust you shall return. This line takes up the second aspect of the new relationship with the soil, signaled earlier in the phrase "all the days of your life" (3:17). The fact of human mortality is now made explicit by revealing to the man his origins and destination in the soil. The life of *hā'ādām* is bounded by *hā'ădāmâ* ("soil") and *'āpār* ("dust"): the human was taken from it and will return to it. This destiny of humankind is implicit in the earthly origins of the human (see Notes at 2:7), but now Yahweh's speech makes it explicit. At this point the gendered sense of *hā'ādām* as bearing the painful labor of working the soil (in contrast to the painful labor of childbirth) merges with the collective sense of *hā'ādām* as "the human," irrespective of gender. That is, mortality concerns humans in general.

This destiny is not presented as a new punishment but as a qualification of the previous punishment. The particles *'ad* ("until") and *kî* ("for, because") introduce dependent clauses, which explicate features of the punishment. These clauses also provide a "backshadowing" reference to the creation of *hā'ādām* from *hā'ădāmâ* in 2:7, "for from it you were taken." In other words, the style and sense of Yahweh's speech present this information not as another punishment, but as a frame for the previous clause, "By the sweat of your brow you shall eat bread," by unpacking the implications of "all the days of your life." It is an explanation of the temporal boundary of this punishment. The knowledge of human origins and destiny—that is, human mortality—is now given to the humans as a supplement to their new consciousness ("knowledge of good and evil").

The punishment implicit in this statement is not death as such, for the humans were already implicitly mortal, since created from the soil's dust (see Barr 1992: 8–14; Schmid 2008: 60–64). But, like animals, they were not aware of their mortality. Yahweh's words create a tragic revision of human knowledge. The topic of death and mortality echoes Yahweh's warning that "on the day you eat from it you shall die." Yahweh does not enforce his threat of capital punishment, but his words effect an alteration in the human condition with respect to death. The humans do not die but gain consciousness of mortality. This is another point of separation between humans and animals, and a further passage from innocence to experience.

Yahweh's speech to the man ends with a parallel couplet—*kî-ʿāpār ʾattâ / wə ʾel-ʿāpār tāšûb* ("For you are dust, and to dust you shall return"). This couplet makes emphatic the knowledge conveyed in the previous clause, raising to consciousness the mortality and frailty of human life. It clearly echoes the scene of the man's creation in 2:7, particularly in the repetition of the word *ʿāpār* ("dust"). This word is not only the physical substance from which the man was created, but it also carries a connotation of frailty, humiliation, and death (see NOTES at 2:7). The Akkadian expression "to return to clay" (*târu ana ṭiṭṭi*) similarly means "to die." Human nature is revealed to the man in this evocative phrase. As Job saw, it is a humbling experience to realize that one is "dust and ashes" (Job 42:6). The human relationship with the soil now includes the knowledge that death is their lot.

3:20. *The man named his wife Eve, for she was the mother of all life.* A new section begins after Yahweh's speech of punishment, consisting of two miscellaneous details (3:20–21), followed by the expulsion from Eden. These verses are the denouement of the story. This verse turns from a contemplation of pain and death to an affirmation of life.

The man's act of naming his wife hearkens back to the scene of her creation, when he exclaimed "This one shall be called 'woman,' / for from man she was taken" (2:23). Now the man gives her a proper name, deriving it from her future identity as the "mother of all life." This perception of her identity brings out the positive side of Yahweh's announcement that the woman will become pregnant and bear children (3:16). Although she is punished with painful labor, pregnancy and childbirth result in new life. From the resonance of her new name, the woman takes on a lofty status as a creator of life.

The name *ḥawwâ* (Eve) literally means "life-giver" (Layton 1997). It is a *qattāl* nominal form, which denotes an agent of the underlying verb (e.g., *gannāb,* "thief"; *dayyān,* "judge"; *rakkāb,* "charioteer"). The root is *ḥwy,* "to live," and in this agentive form it means "giver/producer of life." The explanation of the name, "for she was the mother of all life," is linguistically accurate, since her name is formed from the word "life" (for which there are two root alloforms in Hebrew, *ḥwy* and *ḥyy*). Commentators have long noted that the name *ḥawwâ* sounds like the Aramaic word for "snake," *ḥiwwâ,* found already in Old Aramaic of the eighth century BCE (see *ḥwh* in Sefire I.A.31; Fitzmyer 1995: 88). The coincidence of the name Eve and a word for "snake" in a nearby Northwest Semitic language suggests a double entendre in her name, which would have been perceptible among the ancient Israelites (note the sporadic Aramaic phrases in Classical Hebrew prose: Gen 31:46, Jer 10:11).

The description of Eve as *'ēm kol-ḥāy* ("mother of all life") adds considerable allure to her persona, since not only is she a life-giver, but this phrase resonates with older goddess epithets (Wallace 1985: 147–61). A similar Akkadian epithet, "mother of living creatures" (*ummu šiknat napišti*, lit. "mother of things endowed with life"), is applied to several Mesopotamian goddesses (Dijkstra 1999: 603). This type of epithet is more appropriate for a goddess than a human—note that Eve is not really the "mother of *all* life" (*kol-ḥāy*), but only of human life.

The more-than-human quality of Eve's name and description is suggested by the later use of the epithet *ḥwt*, "life-giver," for a Phoenician/Punic goddess (Wallace 1985: 152–54; Layton 1997: 30). A text from Carthage begins with an invocation to the goddess, *rbt ḥwt 'lt mlkt*, "Great lady, life-giver (*ḥwt*), goddess, queen" (*KAI* 89.1, ca. third to second centuries BCE). It is unclear to which goddess these praises refer—perhaps Astarte (Peckham 1987: 86)—but the Punic word *ḥwt* is cognate with Hebrew *ḥawwâ*. Whether they share a common origin is unknown. The implications of Eve's name and her title, "mother of all life," may point to other versions of the story in Israelite or pre-Israelite traditions in which Eve was a goddess (Wallace 1985: 158). In any case, this description subtly exalts her status as more than an ordinary woman and mother.

3:21. *Yahweh God made leather garments for the man and his wife, and he dressed them.* The brief scene of Yahweh making leather garments (*kotnôt 'ôr*, lit. "tunics of skin") for the humans and dressing them shows the deity caring for his human creations even after punishing them. Characteristically, this brief scene is narrated without any description of Yahweh's emotions or intentions. But the parental tenderness seems patent, since more durable clothes (replacing the fig-leaf loincloths) will be necessary in the harsh environment outside of Eden (cf. Propp 1990: 197). The gift of new clothes and the gesture of dressing the humans are signs of divine care but anticipate the hard life coming.

The invention of clothing—first fig leaves and then leather—also creates a movement from nature to culture. The humans are changing from their original innocent and natural life, naked and unself-conscious (2:25), to the complexities of human consciousness and culture. Yahweh is an agent of this progression, just as he has created the conditions of agricultural labor (3:17–19). Interestingly, in making leather clothes, Yahweh creates a wider breach between humans and animals; in contrast to the Edenic state in which humans and animals lived tranquilly together, this new invention suggests that humans can kill animals in order to wear their skins. Humans and animals implicitly become adversaries when humans begin to wear leather garments (cf. Sasson 2000: 214–15).

3:22–24. The final scene of the story turns the focus to the other forbidden tree— the Tree of Life—after dwelling on the Tree of the Knowledge of Good and Evil. Yahweh casts the humans out of the Garden of Eden so that they may not eat the fruit of both trees. Since they have become "like gods, knowing good and evil," this prevents them from becoming immortal, which would make them wholly gods. Mortality remains the lot of humans. Interestingly, Yahweh's deliberations and actions imply that the Tree of Life has been available to humans until now. The tragedy of expulsion from

Eden is, in part, a lost chance at immortality (Barr 1992: 1–20). This possibility is forever sealed off by the fierce creatures guarding the path to the Tree of Life.

3:22. *Yahweh God said, "Behold, the human has become like one of us, knowing good and evil."* Yahweh confirms the truth of the snake's statement to the woman, "God knows that on the day you eat from it your eyes will be opened, and you will become like gods, knowing good and evil" (3:5). Until this point of the story, one might suspect that the snake's words were both deceptive and false, since the nature of the knowledge gained by the humans is ambiguous, involving knowledge of nakedness, shame, guilt, and a degree of cunning (on the relationship of *ʿărûmmîm*, "naked," and *ʿārûm*, "cunning," see NOTES at 2:25). But Yahweh clarifies that these aspects of knowledge are part of the godlike scope of "the knowledge of good and evil." The precise inventory of this knowledge remains unclear (see NOTES at 2:9), but Yahweh confirms the snake's words that it has made the humans "like one of us," that is, like gods.

The "us" of this statement, as well as the particle of attention, *hēn* ("behold, look"), indicates that Yahweh is addressing a plural audience. As commentators have long noted, this utterance is best explained as an address to Yahweh's divine entourage (e.g., Ibn Ezra; Miller 1978: 20–22). These are a group of lesser deities that accompany or wait upon God in various biblical passages, for example, "Seraphs stood in attendance on him" (Isa 6:2), or "all the host of heaven were standing by him" (1 Kgs 22:19; see Mullen 1980). This plural address is also found in Gen 1:26 ("Let us make . . .") and 11:7 ("Let us go down and confuse . . ."). These attendant beings are not mentioned earlier, as when Yahweh walks about the garden (3:8), but the stationing of the cherubim to guard the garden (3:24) belongs to this notion of the divine assembly, which has various strata, including Sons of God (6:1–2) and angels (18–19). In this scene in Eden, Yahweh deliberates in the plural, addressing his divine attendants, and announces the verdict that the humans must be expelled, lest they go from being "like gods" to becoming gods. The plural reference to "us" serves to emphasize the bounded category of divinity as well as the divide between humans and divine beings, which must not be effaced.

The object of Yahweh's deliberation is *hā ʾādām,* "the man, human," with no mention of Eve or "his wife." This does not mean that the woman is excluded but that she is included or subsumed by the singular reference to *hā ʾādām.* This relates to the collective resonance of *hā ʾādām,* "the humans," invoking the general category of humankind, with which the story began. This usage again subtly emphasizes the contrast between gods and humans.

Now, lest he reach out his hand and take from the Tree of Life and eat and live forever . . . This potential action has not taken place (see Barr 1992: 58). The force of the particle *pen* ("lest, so that not") concerns something that has not happened and must be prevented from happening, for example, *pen-təmūtûn* ("lest you die," 3:3) and *pen-nāpûṣ* ("lest we be scattered," 11:4). This usage suggests "that some precaution has been taken to avert the dreaded contingency" (BDB, 814). The precaution is, in this case, expulsion from the Garden of Eden.

The consequence of eating the fruit of the Tree of Life is disclosed in this verse—it bestows immortality (*ḥay lə ʿōlām,* lit. "alive forever"). Like the "food of life" and the "water of life" in the Mesopotamian myth of Adapa (see COMMENTS), this fruit has the power to turn a mortal into an immortal. The essences of both forbidden trees are revealed by Yahweh in this verse and constitute a complementary pair. One tree has the power to make humans "like gods" with respect to knowledge, and the other makes humans like gods with respect to immortality. Humans may partake of one of these divine qualities, but not the other, lest they cease to be human and become gods.

Although there seem to be some inconcinnities in this relationship between the two trees—why didn't the humans eat from the Tree of Life when they had the chance?—it is difficult to imagine a coherent story without both trees. Humans do, in fact, have a kind of knowledge and consciousness that sets them apart from other animals, but humans cannot live forever. Humans are suspended between beasts and gods, oscillating between earthbound and divine qualities.

3:23. *Yahweh God expelled him from the Garden of Eden to work the soil from which he was taken.* In an abrupt grammatical transition, Yahweh's speech of deliberation ceases and is continued by his action. This shift has a dramatic rhetorical effect (called aposiopesis), as if the speaker were unable or unwilling to continue the thought and, as in this case, acts rather than speaks. This grammatical turn, where the conclusion of a sentence is left out, occurs sometimes in conditional sentences ("if . . . then") in Biblical Hebrew (GKC §167a).

The expulsion resumes the language of the man's punishment of hard agricultural labor (3:17–19), particularly its repetition of the sequence "the soil, for from it you were taken" (3:19). It also echoes 2:15, where the man was placed in the garden "to work it" (*lə'obdōh*), with the same verb, "to work" (*la'ăbōd*), here. Now the task of the man "to work the soil" is transformed to the harsh labor on the unyielding soil outside of Eden, signaling once again the new and difficult relationship between *hā'ādām* and *hā'ădāmâ*, the human and the soil.

By these verbal echoes, Yahweh's motivation for the expulsion weaves the Tree of Life into the previous punishment. The explicit motive is to preclude access to the Tree of Life (3:22). The motive clause given here, "to work the soil from which he was taken," fulfills the punishment of hard labor on the soil, which was a consequence of eating from the Tree of the Knowledge of Good and Evil. Some commentators view these two motives as disparate, perhaps indications of two earlier stories that have been combined (e.g., Westermann 1984: 270). But they may also be seen as a way of bringing the implications of the two trees together, after the story has focused first on one tree and then on the other. The two trees, I have argued, are complementary in the thematics of the story, and hence the two motives for expulsion from the garden may also be seen as complementary rather than clashing. Both motives ensure that humans enter securely into the human world, leaving the possibility of divine existence behind. The one motive looks back to the lost possibilities of life in the garden, while the other looks forward to the hard world of human existence after Eden.

3:24. *He banished the humans, and he stationed east of the Garden of Eden the cherubim and the flame of the whirling sword to guard the path to the Tree of Life.* The initial verbal clause, *waygāreš 'et-hā'ādām* ("He banished the humans"), doubles the previous verbal clause, *wayšalləḥēhû yhwh* ("Yahweh expelled him," 3:23). The reason for this doubling is unclear. It may again be a sign of two stories that have been joined, or it may be a stylistic emphasis of the banishment. It may be a kind of repetitive resumption, moving the story forward after the backward glance of the motive clause of 3:23, "to work the earth from which he was taken," with its reference to the creation of the human from the earth (2:7). The verb *waygāreš* ("banish, drive out") has a sense of finality, like Cain's echoing lament, "You have banished (*gēraštā*) me today from the face of the soil" (4:14).

Yahweh 's stationing of supernatural guardians *miqqedem ləgan-ʿēden* ("east of the Garden of Eden") echoes the scene of his planting a *gan-bə ʿēden miqqedem* ("a garden in Eden, in the east," 2:8), where he first placed the human. Now Yahweh places creatures east of Eden, whose task is to keep the humans out of their original home. This direction not only recalls the earlier verse when the garden was created, but also reveals that there is an entrance to the garden in the east. This detail, along with the image of the cherubim, suggests an echo with the Jerusalem temple, whose entrance faced east and whose inner sanctum had two large images of cherubim (Wenham 1994: 401; Wright 1996: 311). In some respects, the temple and the Garden of Eden have an analogical relationship—they are sacred spaces where God dwells and where one has the possibility of returning to paradise (see COMMENTS). But in the story this allusion is dim, since a return to Eden is disallowed according to Yahweh's actions.

The creatures called *hakkərūbîm* ("the cherubim"), mentioned some ninety times in the Hebrew Bible, are probably to be identified with the winged hybrid creatures depicted in the art of Syria-Palestine (Mettinger 1999; Wood 2008; cf. Eichler 2021). Originally an Egyptian motif—as in the monumental sphinx guarding the way to one of the great pyramids at Giza—it was borrowed into Syro-Palestinian art in the early second millennium BCE (Teissier 1996: 80). Many examples are known in Israelite iconography, including ivory reliefs from the royal palace at Samaria (Crawfoot and Crawfoot 1938) and the ornamentation of the Jerusalem temple (1 Kgs 6:23–35, 8:6–7). The name and function of the cherubim (singular *kərûb*, probably derived from **kurub*) are nearly identical to those of the Mesopotamian *kurību*, winged composite creatures that guard entrances. For example, an inscription of the Assyrian king Esarhaddon states, "I placed (at the entrance of the sanctuary of Asshur) *laḥmu*-creatures and *kurību*-creatures made of reddish gold facing each other" (*CAD* K, 559). The Mesopotamian *kurību* are composite guardian creatures (possibly with bird heads; Wiggermann 1994: 224). The noun *kurību* derives from the verb *karābu*, "to bless, pray." The description of the four-faced cherubim in Ezekiel's vision (Ezekiel 1, 10) is influenced by contemporary Mesopotamian models (Uehlinger and Müller-Trufaut 2001).

In Syro-Palestinian art, including Israelite examples, winged hybrid creatures (perhaps cherubim) with human or bird heads are often shown flanking a stylized date palm tree. In this pose, these hybrid creatures are not only guardians, but may also partake of the fertility and abundance represented by the tree (Teissier 1996: 84; Winter 2010: 1.164–69). This pose seems somehow related to our scene in which the cherubim (two or more) are stationed to guard the way to the Tree of Life.

The role of the cherubim to guard the boundaries of divine places—the Garden of Eden, the temple's inner sanctum, and God's chariot throne (Ezekiel 1, 10)—relates to their representation as awesome, liminal creatures. In their very being, they mix the categories of animal, human, and divine, making them appropriate beings to stand at the threshold between earthly and divine space. Their quality as paradoxical creatures makes them apt emblems for the forbidden entrance to the Garden of Eden—awesome, unreal, and dangerous.

The mysterious *lahaṭ haḥereb hammithappeket* ("the flame of the whirling sword") is another paradoxical object or creature, either held by or stationed alongside the

Figure 7. Stylized palm tree flanked by winged hybrid creatures. Ivory furniture inlay (composite drawing, ca. eighth century BCE) from Nimrud. (Drawing by William H. C. Propp)

cherubim. The cherubim and "the flame of the whirling sword" are both objects of the verb "he stationed" (each is marked by the direct marker *ʾēt*) and must be separate entities. If this "flame of the whirling sword" is an independent being (so Gunkel 1997: 24; Hendel 1985), it remains unclear what it is. It may be a magical weapon, perhaps an animate fiery sword slashing back and forth, which may be a mythic objectification of lightning, a weapon of the storm god (cf. Speiser 1964: 25; Westermann 1984: 274–75).

An interesting parallel is the sun god Shamash's "roving weapon" (*kakku murtap-pidu*) that guards the entry to a mountainous region in the Mesopotamian Etana epic (Winitzer 2013). This seems to be an independent, animate weapon whose function (guarding entry by the transgressor of a taboo) and motion (*Gtn,* iteratively "roving") are similar to the "whirling" (*hithpael,* interative "turning") sword at the entry to Eden. Winitzer (2013: 449) suggests that "the Biblical image is to be understood as a borrowing of the counterpart in *Etana*." The resemblance does not require a direct connection but illuminates the range of animate weapons at the gods' disposal.

Another explanation comes from the evidence for fiery minor deities in Canaan and Israel (Miller 1965). In the Canaanite Baal myth, the god Sea sends two fiery messengers, "a flame, two flames they appear" (*CAT* 1.2.32). Psalm 104:4 presents a similar image of fiery minor deities attending Yahweh: "fire (and) flame are his servants" (vocalizing *lhṭ* as a noun, *lahaṭ*, rather than the participle *lōhēṭ*, which is ungrammatical in context; see Kraus 1993: 295–97). Against this background, "the flame of the whirling sword" may refer to a fiery minor deity who serves as a guardian of the entry, wielding a sword that constantly slashes and turns. The "flame" would, in this interpretation, be parallel to the cherubim—both minor deities in Yahweh's divine entourage, and both paradoxical and fearsome. But the interpretation of this entity remains uncertain.

These creatures are assigned "to guard (*lišmōr*) the path to the Tree of Life." This may be a final irony. Earlier, the human had been assigned to guard the garden (*ləšomrōh,* "to guard it," 2:15), but the human's task has been altered. Now fierce creatures are assigned to guard the garden. Their task is permanent and effective, sealing off forever the possibility of human entry. The human condition is permanently transformed.

Comments

DOUBLETS

The Garden of Eden has a distinctive literary style, cosmology, and theology compared with Genesis 1. But both are myths of creation, explaining how the world and humans came into their present form, beginning with the time of origins. There are many differences in these two creation myths, including the order of creation. In Genesis 1 there are eight acts of creation spread over six days, from light on the first day to humans on the sixth, plus God's rest on the seventh day. In Eden the (hu)man is created first, and his counterpart, the woman, is created last. The style, tone, and plot organization are altogether different. The Eden narrative is a dramatic story, with complications, conflicts, reversals, and recognitions and an abiding sense of tragic realism. Genesis 1 has a simple plot, with no conflict or opposition (see INTRODUCTION III). There are some shared themes, including the hierarchy among God, humans, and animals, in which animals are subordinate to humans, and humans are to some degree "like" God. But the latter is a feature of the divinely created cosmos in Genesis 1, while in Eden it is a fraught consequence of human disobedience. On one level the Eden story is a myth of paradise lost, but on another it is a parable of the real, a profound reflection on the complexities and ambiguities of human life in the world.

LITERARY DESIGN

The text is a continuous narrative, punctuated by four disjunctive sequences that provide background information or an etiology of a custom—the initial condition before creation (2:4b–6), the rivers of Eden (2:10–14), the introduction of the snake (3:1), and the custom of marriage (2:24). There is no indication of the time between events—perhaps the narrative occurs on a single day, as traditional commentators infer. The disjunction that introduces the snake also marks a caesura between two major parts of the narrative: creation (2:4b–24) and the drama of transgression, judgment, and expulsion (3:1–24). The two parts each consist of a sequence of episodes, each with its own internal cohesion, which can be indicated as follows:

A. Creation (2:4b–24)
    1. Introduction and creation of the human and the garden (2:4b–17)
    2. Creation of the animals and the woman (2:18–24)
B. Transgression and judgment (3:1–24)
    3. Complication and reversal: The snake, the woman, and the man (3:1–7)
    4. Recognition and judgment: God and the man, the woman, and the snake (3:8–21)
    5. Resolution: God's expulsion of the humans from Eden (3:22–24)

The literary design of each episode, and the coherence of the whole, is shaped by the narrative's *Leitwort* style. The first episode introduces the *Leitwort* relationship of *hā'ādām* ("the man") and *hā'ădāmâ* ("the soil") in the primeval lack: "there was no human to work the soil" (2:5). Episode 1 continues with the creation of the human and the soil, and the role of the human "to work it and to guard it" (2:15). The episode ends with God's speech prohibiting the human from eating the fruit of the Tree of the Knowledge of Good and Evil (2:17), which sets the stage for the later transgression of this command in the second part of the story.

Episode two begins with a shift from God's direct speech to internal speech—his decision to create an *'ēzer kənegdô* ("companion," lit. "helper corresponding to him"). This decision motivates the creation of animals, among whom is not a corresponding companion, and then the creation of the woman from the man's bone and flesh. The episode ends with the picture of the couple as *'ărûmmîm* ("naked") and unashamed. This sets the stage for the reversal—their loss of innocence and paradise—in the narrative's second part.

Episode three begins by introducing the snake as *'ārûm* ("cunning"), activating a *Leitwort* relationship with *'ărûmmîm* ("naked"). The play between the snake's cunning and the couple's nakedness (and absence of shame) leads to the snake's deceptive dialogue with the woman, her awakening of desire for the forbidden fruit, and her sharing the fruit with the man. The episode ends with their reversal of consciousness: they know that they are naked (with the variant form *'ērummîm*), and they make clothes to hide their nakedness and shame.

Episode four begins with the entry of God on the scene and the couple hiding. Recognition and judgment ensue. As noted above, the formal structure of the sequence of speeches is chiastic, circling from man to woman to snake to woman to man:

God's interrogation and the man's responses (3:9–12)
    God's interrogation and the woman's response (3:13)
        God's judgment of the snake (3:14–15)
    God's judgment of the woman (3:16)
God's judgment of the man (3:17–19)

Notably, God doesn't question the snake, who may be too cunning (*'ārûm*) to interrogate, placing the focus on the human couple. The sequence of judgments and curses, as Gunkel (1997: 20) observes, "involves an intensification that concludes disturbingly": "You are dust, and to dust you shall return" (3:19).

This episode concludes with two unconnected details that partially soften the judgments—the man naming the woman Eve ("life"), which highlights the future continuation of humankind, and God clothing the humans in skins, an improvement from fig leaves and a gesture of God's care.

The final episode begins with another speech by God—his decision to expel the humans from Eden. This decision hearkens back to the two trees introduced in episode one, the Tree of the Knowledge of Good and Evil and the Tree of Life (2:9). Since the humans have eaten from the former and have become like gods, "knowing good and evil," they must be expelled lest they eat from the latter and "live forever" (3:22). The Tree of Life is now focalized, becoming the proximate reason for expulsion, and the episode ends with God assigning anomalous creatures "to guard the way to the Tree of Life."

The beginning and end of the story are linked together not only by the two trees, but also by the transformation of the relationship of *hā'ādām* and *hā'ādāmâ,* the human and the soil. In episode one, the lack of a human to work the soil is remedied by the creation of the first human to work the Garden of Eden. In the process of transgression, reversal, and judgment in the second part of the story, this relationship is reconfigured. God curses the soil because of the man, and he must work the soil in painful labor until he "returns to the soil, for from it you were taken" (3:19). The fate of returning to *hā'ādāmâ* applies to both parts of *hā'ādām,* man and woman, the latter having her own share of pain in bearing children. The *Leitwort* relationship of *hā'ādām* and *hā'ādāmâ* provides a scarlet thread through the Eden narrative, unfolding the complexities of human life out of the original soil.

As is characteristic of biblical narrative, the drama and nuances of character are conveyed primarily through dialogue. This is the case particularly in episodes three and four, which are almost entirely dialogue. As Alter (2011: 79–110) has emphasized, subtle variations in reported dialogue are indicative of the characters' interior motives. The opening gambit of the snake to the woman is a clear example: "Did God really say, 'Do not eat from all the trees of the garden?'" (3:1). The cunning of the snake is subtly articulated in this speech. God had said, "From all the trees of the garden you may surely eat" (2:16), at which point the answer to the snake's question would be "no." But God then adds an important exception: "As for the Tree of the Knowledge of Good and Evil, you must not eat from it, for on the day you eat from it you will surely die" (2:17). There is therefore no uncomplicated answer to the snake's question. One would have to say, "No, but yes for one tree." The snake's question is designed to deceive. Through this brief speech, the character of the snake is articulated as devious and manipulative.

The snake's final remark to the woman is equally cunning: "You shall not die. Indeed, God knows that on the day you eat from it your eyes will be opened, and you will become like gods, knowing good and evil" (3:4–5). This statement is a mixture of truth and deception, also designed to deceive. God had said, "for on the day you eat from it you shall die" (2:17), which the snake negates. The snake is telling the truth, but not the whole truth. The humans do not die, but they lose their life in paradise and are burdened with the consciousness of mortality. Their eyes are indeed opened, but what they see with their opened eyes is their nakedness, and they experience shame. Yet they do become "like gods, knowing good and evil," as Yahweh later confirms (3:22). The snake is a master of cunning, mixing half-truths and deceptions. The trickster quality of the snake, who disrupts life in paradise, is expressed through his finely tuned dialogue with the woman.

Yahweh's character is also articulated through his speech, including interior speech. He prohibits eating from the Tree of the Knowledge of Good and Evil by penalty of death, but he seems to relent in the actual judgment, declaring instead that humans will die after a life of painful toil, returning to the soil from which they were taken (3:19). Yahweh seems to show clemency or compassion in reducing the threatened death penalty "on the day you eat from it" (2:17) into a delayed return of *hāʾādām* to *hāʾădāmâ*. Yahweh's compassion toward humans is realized more explicitly in his internal speech after creating the first human: "It is not good for the human to be alone. I will make a companion to help him" (2:18). This is unalloyed compassion. The creation of animals and the woman follows directly from this expression of divine compassion, yielding a world designed for humankind.

The characters and dispositions of the man and the woman are also fashioned through dialogue. The man expresses his joy in the creation of woman—"This time at last!" (2:23)—and expresses his cowardice in blame-shifting—"The woman, whom you gave to be with me, she gave to me from the tree, and I ate" (3:12). The woman also shifts the blame, "The snake deceived me, and I ate" (3:13). Her addition to God's prohibition in her response to the snake—"God said, 'Do not eat from it, and do not touch it, lest you die'" (3:3)—shows her susceptibility to the snake's guile, as she embroiders truth with untruth. In their speeches the humans show the inconstancy of their characters, which articulates the complexity of human character as such.

ANTHROPOLOGY

Whereas Genesis 1 has a cosmic scope, including "heaven and earth and all their array" (2:1), the Eden narrative is primarily focused on the human world, including the myriad links in the relationship between *hāʾādām* and *hāʾădāmâ*. The wider cosmos—the sun, moon, firmament, light, time, etc.—lies outside this narrative focus. The first part of the Eden narrative is an account of creation, but it is selective, attuned to creating the categories and relationships necessary for the complications in the story's second half. For instance, there is no explicit account of the creation of the world outside of Eden, but it is brought into view implicitly through the brief aside about the four rivers that flow from Eden (2:10–14). The outside world is not a focus of creation, but it is implied and hence available as the place to which God banishes humans at the story's end.

Within this anthropocentric focus on the creation and development of humankind, the episodes in the narrative explore the progressive contours of human existence. In a broad sense, they explore the taxonomy of categories and their relationships, including a larger hierarchy in which *ʾādām* is nested, and the internal subcategories of *ʾādām*. This taxonomy, including the semantic flexibility of its taxa, is shown in Table 3.

Table 3. Taxonomy of humans, gods, and animals

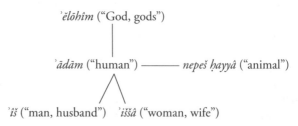

ʾĕlōhîm ("God, gods")

ʾādām ("human") ——— *nepeš ḥayyâ* ("animal")

ʾîš ("man, husband")   ʾiššâ ("woman, wife")

The taxonomy's anthropocentric nature is indicated by the category ʾādām ("human") as the central node, with lines of relationship extending vertically and horizontally. The story explores the origins of this taxonomy and its moral, social, physical, and metaphysical implications. Each relationship illuminates a different dimension of the human condition, and the totality yields a model of the complex embeddedness of humans in the world. Let us consider how each of these relationships is fashioned in the story and how they fit together.

The relationship between ʾādām and ʾĕlōhîm is complicated. In the first act of creation, Yahweh God creates hā ʾādām from the dust of hā ʾādāmâ. The human is clearly subservient to Yahweh, with his assigned role "to work and guard" the garden. In the last action, Yahweh expels hā ʾādām from Eden to the outside world. In the meantime, the relationship between hā ʾādām and ʾĕlōhîm has changed. The human—whom Yahweh differentiates into two beings, ʾîš and ʾiššâ ("male" and "female")—becomes (in the words of the snake) "like ʾĕlōhîm, knowing good and evil" (3:5). Yahweh confirms this change in status: "Behold, hā ʾādām has become like one of us, knowing good and evil" (3:22). Paradoxically, as a result of their disobedience to Yahweh, the humans have become godlike. As a consequence of this nearness, Yahweh institutes a distance. He exiles the humans to the outside world of hard labor, pain, and mortality. Becoming "like gods, knowing good and evil," is a transition upward, into the divine realm but entails an exile outward, into the distinctly human world. Likeness to gods and distance from God go hand in hand in the shaping of the human condition.

The culinary content of the two special trees—the Tree of the Knowledge of Good and Evil and the Tree of Life—are features that first distinguish ʾādām from ʾĕlōhîm and then create a more complicated relationship. The humans gain some aspect of divine knowledge by eating from the forbidden tree, making them "like gods," but they do not become fully gods. Yahweh prevents a full transition by expelling humans from the garden, lest they "take from the Tree of Life and eat and live forever" (3:22). Had they done so, Yahweh implies, they would wholly cross over the boundary between ʾādām and ʾĕlōhîm. They would not be "like gods," but immortal beings, that is, gods. By expelling the humans, Yahweh preserves this boundary, even as it has been blurred with respect to knowledge, which blends moral knowledge ("good and evil"), bodily self-consciousness ("they saw that they were naked"), and divine knowledge. Their godlike knowledge includes an awareness of human sexuality, a self-consciousness that seems to contrast with Yahweh's divine body. By these resonances, which sometimes seem at cross-purposes, the story builds up a complicated picture of the relationship—including similarity and difference—between ʾādām and ʾĕlōhîm.

The category of human is suspended between the taxa of god and animal, while partially overlapping with them. The relationship between ʾādām and nepeš ḥayyâ ("animal, creature") is explored in the second episode, motivated by Yahweh's desire to make an ʿēzer kanegdô ("a companion to help him," lit. "a helper corresponding to him") so that the human will not be alone (2:18). This is an act of care, a recognition of human sociality and need for companionship. Yahweh is compassionate, while not omniscient. His solution—"[He] formed from the soil (hā ʾādāmâ) every animal of the field and every bird of heaven" (2:19)—turns out to be infelicitous, for "hā ʾādām did not find an ʿēzer kanegdô" (2:20). The animals are like hā ʾādām, but they don't sufficiently correspond to him, so Yahweh takes a second try at making a fitting companion.

The human is like the animals in many respects. Yahweh creates both from *hā'ădāmâ* (2:7, 19), and both are called *nepeš ḥayyâ* ("animal, creature," lit. "breath creature," 2:7, 19). Humans and animals are earthly—and hence implicitly mortal—creatures, who, as implied in their name, are enlivened by Yahweh's breath. Both belong to the same general category and are therefore potential companions. The difference between *'ādām* and the other kinds of *nepeš ḥayyâ* becomes apparent only when Yahweh brings the animals to see what *hā'ādām* would name them. This act inscribes a hierarchy between the human and the other animals, establishing *hā'ādām* as a master of language and the animals as subject to his words. The animals are implicitly placed in a subordinate position, with language as a distinguishing feature. By the end of the speech-acts of naming, the animals are found to be wanting. None is an appropriate *'ēzer kənegdô*. The focus on language as establishing a decisive difference between *'ādām* and all the other *nepeš ḥayyâ* will be complicated with the introduction of the talking snake. But this episode defines humans as a distinctive category of living creature. They are like the other animals as a *nepeš ḥayyâ*, made from *hā'ădāmâ*, but they are unlike them with respect to language, bodies, and authority.

The relationship of human and animal is in some respects the inverse of the relationship of human and gods. Humans are mortal creatures like the animals, but they are unlike them in knowledge and power. This reverses the terms of the relationship between humans and God, who are similar with respect to knowledge but different with respect to mortality. The human condition is to be an animal with godlike features or a godlike being with animal features. Humans face both earth and heaven, striving upward but ineluctably bound to earth.

The story explores another taxonomy internal to *hā'ādām*. This is the distinction of male and female, a difference of bodies and sexuality. The woman is the true *'ēzer kənegdô*, made from the flesh and bone of *hā'ādām*. As *hā'ādām* says: "Bone from my bones, and flesh from my flesh. This one shall be called *'iššâ*, for from she was taken" (2:23). In this speech-act the man names the woman, implicitly instituting a hierarchy, as with his previous naming of the animals. Yet the woman is also his equal, made from the same flesh and bones. The relationship of *'îš* and *'iššâ* is complicated, with layers of similarity and difference. They are complementary taxa of *hā'ādām*. When together, they make "one flesh," a term that refers both to sexuality and kinship—as do the terms *'îš* and *'iššâ*, which designate man/woman or husband/wife.

The nature of the relationship between *'iššâ* and *'îš* is developed through the story's narrative arc. The baseline is described at the end of the *'ēzer kənegdô* episode: "The two of them were naked, the *'îš* and his *'iššâ*, and they felt no shame before each other" (2:24). This is their initial state of innocence, when the couple are unself-conscious with respect to their bodies and sexuality. They are like children, living in paradise without a care. In the story's second half, their innocence is lost, they become aware of their bodily difference, and they learn shame and guilt. The "soft" hierarchy at first becomes a strong gender hierarchy in Yahweh's punishment of the woman: "To the *'iššâ* he said . . . 'You will desire your *'îš*, and he will rule over you'" (3:16). The *'iššâ* receives her own kind of painful labor in childbirth, parallel to the painful agricultural labor of the *'îš*. And yet, in spite of the changes in their relationship and their respective burdens, the couple is now more than they were before, since, as we have seen, they have gained forbidden knowledge that makes them like *'ĕlōhîm*. As a consequence of their disobedience, the couple's relationship and consciousness have changed. They are still companions, but their roles have been differentiated in preparation for the harsh life outside of Eden.

Gender hierarchy, male authority, and gender-specific suffering are the outcomes of this transformation, counterbalanced by an ascent to godlikeness, which includes—paradoxically—self-consciousness of sexuality. When the couple clothe themselves to hide their shame at being naked before each other, they become more than children. When their eyes are opened, they become mature human beings, subject to desire and shame. This is their passage to maturity and full humanity, with all the complications that come with being *hā'ādām*.

A question often asked about male and female in Eden is the gender of *hā'ādām* before the differentiation into *'îš* and *'iššâ* (cf. Trible 1978: 79–81; Meyers 1988: 81–82; Bird 1997: 164–66; Day 2013: 32–35). Is the first human a male, as most commentators have assumed, or a creature without gender, as some scholars have argued, or even a hermaphrodite, as a rabbinic midrash infers? The best answer, as with much in this story, is ambiguous and multivalent. Human gender and sexuality are not focalized until Yahweh fashions the rib of *hā'ādām* into the *'iššâ* (2:22). This is the institution of sexual difference. Before this, *hā'ādām* is not explicitly marked for gender and hence is implicitly "the human," a category that includes all humans, irrespective of gender. Yet there is a subtext or foreshadowing of gendered roles, since *hā'ādām* is assigned "to work and guard" the Garden of Eden (2:15). This is a step in the relationship between *hā'ādām* and *hā'ădāmâ*. To work the soil is, as Yahweh's later judgment makes explicit, the destiny of the *'îš*, not the *'iššâ*. Hence, there are multiple resonances of *hā'ādām*—a human made from *hā'ădāmâ*, who will return to *hā'ădāmâ*, as do all humans, and a human who is incipiently male but not explicitly marked as such until the distinction of *'îš* and *'iššâ*. The differentiation of sex and gender is delayed until the *'ēzer kənegdô* episode, which yields the creation of animals and the woman. Thereafter, the doubled semantics of *hā'ādām* continues, sometimes with gender in the foreground—as in the punishment of agricultural labor—and sometimes with the general category of "human" in the foreground—as with the expulsion of *hā'ādām* from Eden.

The condition of being *'ādām* is a unity, a duality, and a multiplicity, in the layered relationships of *hā'ādām* in its internal features and its relationships with *'ĕlōhîm* and *nepeš ḥayyâ*. This is a complicated picture of humanity, a biblical anthropology. The story presents a sequence of formative events in the distant past, but there is also a sense, as many commentators have noted, that the transition from innocence to experience, from paradise to the real world, from unself-conscious ease to a complicated self-awareness is repeated in each of our lives as we transition to adulthood. In a sense, the turning points in Eden are signposts in each of our lives, as we each recapitulate the narrative development of *hā'ādām*. Some aspects have changed over time in some places, most notably the curses of gender hierarchy and subsistence agriculture. But the general conditions of human existence persist: mortality, knowledge, sexuality, labor, our animal lives, our drive to transcend, the ambivalences of desire, shame, and guilt. The story, despite its antique science and cultural biases, remains a brilliant portrait of the human condition.

A lingering question about the anthropology of the story concerns the nature and consequences of the first couple's transgression. As we have seen, this is a multivalent issue. The humans' disobedience of Yahweh's command brings about their expulsion from paradise and their entry into the human world of hard labor and suffering; however, it also brings about their ascent from innocent animals to self-conscious maturity, entailing knowledge "like the gods." This is a layered and complex transformation, characterized by both gain and loss. In the history of interpretation, however, these ambiguities were often simplified into a stark account of loss, yielding the theological doctrine of original sin.

This interpretation first arose under the influence of the apocalyptic and ethical dualism of the late Second Temple period (see J. J. Collins 2017). The fault is either internal, the intrinsic evil of the human heart (cf. the flood story, Gen 6:5), or external, the malign influence of the devil, who comes to be identified with the snake. So the Wisdom of Solomon says that sin entered the world "through the envy of the devil" (Wis 2:24), and the book of Revelation identifies Satan as "the ancient serpent" (Rev 12:9, 20:2). Fourth Ezra laments, "O Adam, what have you done? For though it was you who sinned, the misfortune was not yours alone, but ours also who are your descendants" (4 Ezra 7:118). In all of these texts, the current world of evil will be remedied in the judgment of the apocalypse, which will usher in a new Eden for the righteous.

Paul linked the idea of Adam's sin with the redemption of sin through Jesus's crucifixion and resurrection. In Paul's theology, Christ atoned for "the transgression of Adam, who is a type of the one who was to come" (Rom 5:14). He explains, "just as one man's trespass led to condemnation for all, so one man's act of righteousness leads to justification and life for all" (Rom 5:18). The path from Adam to Christ leads from sin and death to their solution, salvation and eternal life. In these ways we can see how the Eden story became embroidered into Christian theology. The church father Augustine later elaborated Paul's doctrine of original sin, introducing the idea that it is transmitted by sexual intercourse (specifically semen) and that the emotive power of sexuality is the consequence and bodily expression of sin. This melancholy interpretation of the Eden story is motivated by attitudes toward sexuality that are foreign to the anthropology of Genesis.

CONTEXTS

The Eden narrative is woven into the J primeval narrative by style, theme, genealogy, and character (especially that of Yahweh). As we have seen, several *Leitwort* sequences bind the Eden narrative into the larger primeval narrative, most prominently the relationship of *hā'ādām* and *hā'ădāmâ* (humans and the soil/earth). A dense layer of *Leitwort* sequences, some involving the relationship with the soil, joins the Eden narrative with the following story of Cain and Abel, including the following:

Working the soil
Eden: "there was no human to work (*la'ăbōd*) the soil (*hā'ădāmâ*)." (2:5)
"to work (*la'ăbōd*) the soil (*hā'ădāmâ*) from which he was taken." (3:23)
Cain: "Cain worked ('ōbēd) the soil ('ădāmâ)." (4:2)
"When you work (*ta'ăbōd*) the soil (*hā'ădāmâ*) it will no longer yield its strength to you." (4:12)
Desire and rule
Eden: "You shall desire (*təšûqâ*) your husband, and he shall rule (*yimšōl*) over you." (3:16)

Cain: "To you is its desire (*təšûqâ*), but you can rule (*timšōl*) over it." (4:7)

Curses and the soil

Eden: "cursed (*ʾārûr*) are you (*ʾattâ*), out of all the . . . animals." (3:14)

"cursed (*ʾārûrâ*) is the soil (*hāʾădāmâ*) because of you." (3:17)

Cain: "cursed (*ʾārûr*) are you (*ʾāttâ*) from the soil (*hāʾădāmâ*)." (4:11)

Banishment

Eden: "He banished (*waygāreš*) the humans." (3:24)

Cain: "You have banished (*gēraštā*) me today from the face of the soil (*hāʾădāmâ*)." (4:14)

East of Eden

Eden: "[Yahweh] planted a garden in Eden, in the east (*gan-bəʾēden miqqedem*)." (2:8)

"he stationed east of the Garden of Eden (*miqqedem ləgan-ʿēden*)." (3:24)

Cain: "[Cain] dwelled in the land of Wandering, east of Eden (*qidmat-ʿēden*)." (4:16)

Each of these *Leitwort* clusters creates a rhythm of foreshadowing and backshadowing between the two stories, making Cain's destiny a genealogical echo of the events in Eden.

In the J narrative of Abraham, the Garden of Eden is alluded to indirectly when Lot sees the fertile Jordan Valley: "Lot lifted his eyes and said that the whole Jordan valley was well-watered, before Yahweh destroyed Sodom and Gomorrah, like the garden of Yahweh, like the land of Egypt, all the way to Zoar" (13:10). Lot's perception that the lush valley is like "the garden of Yahweh" (*gan-Yhwh*) does not necessarily allude to the Garden of Eden, since the phrase *gan-Yhwh* does not occur there. It might be a figure of speech. However, in its context an allusion to Eden seems likely. The collocation of the "garden of Yahweh" with the "land of Egypt" has a doubled resonance—they are both well-watered lands, desirable to inhabit, but Eden and Egypt are also places of danger and transgression—for the first couple in Eden, for Abraham in Egypt (12:10–20), and for all Israel later in Egypt. This double resonance of beauty and disaster is also suggested by the mention of Zoar, where Lot will take refuge from the destruction of Sodom and Gomorrah (19:30). The imminent danger of this beautiful land is made explicit in the aside, "before Yahweh destroyed Sodom and Gomorrah." In sum, Lot's comparison to the "garden of Yahweh" makes literary sense if the Garden of Eden—the only known garden of Yahweh—is implied.

Beyond the J work, there is an intriguing doublet of the Eden narrative in Ezek 28:11–19, which the prophet has transformed into a poetic dirge (*qînâ*) over the death of the king of Tyre (Greenberg 1997: 579–93; Mettinger 2007: 85–98). The king is cast in the role of the "anointed guardian cherub" (reading with the MT; the LXX and Peshitta read the first word of Ezek 28:14 as *ʾet*, "with [a cherub]," rather than *ʾatt*, "you [were a cherub]," thereby yielding a human protagonist; see Barr 2013: 220–28; cf. Day 2022: 67–70). The cherub guards the Garden of Eden until an unspecified wrongdoing is found in him; then Yahweh destroys him by fire. The description of the king as the guardian cherub activates images of Phoenician luxury goods, such as the ivory carved cherubs and trees that adorned chairs and beds at royal palaces at Nimrud, Samaria (see

Amos 6:4), and presumably Tyre. The parts of the oracle that contain the variant story of Eden are as follows:

> You were the seal of perfection,
>> complete in beauty.
> You were in Eden, the garden of God,
>> every precious stone was your covering,
>
> . . .
>
> Gold work was your filament and settings,
>> prepared on the day you were created.
> You were an anointed guardian cherub,
>> and I set you on the holy mountain of God.
> You walked amid the stones of fire,
>> you were blameless in your ways,
> From the day you were created,
>> until iniquity was found in you.
>
> . . .
>
> I desecrated you from the mountain of God,
>> and I destroyed you, O guardian cherub,
>> from the midst of the stones of fire.
>
> . . .
>
> And I brought out fire from your midst,
>> it consumed you,
> I turned you into ashes on the earth
>> before the eyes of all who saw you. (Ezek 28:12–18)

In this doublet, the Garden of Eden is on "the holy mountain of God," and the protagonist is the cherub, not a human. The cherub is found to be at fault—perhaps, as in the previous judgment against the king of Tyre, because of his pride (Ezek 28:2)—and after his iniquity is discovered, he is destroyed by fire and cast down to earth. These details are not known in this configuration elsewhere, but they are very similar to the story in the Ugaritic myth of Athtar, who is briefly enthroned as king of the gods but is found wanting and descends to earth or the underworld (*CAT* 1.6.i.54–65). The fall of the "Shining One, son of Dawn" in Isa 14:12–15, a parable for the pride and fall of the king of Babylon, is a more direct reflection of the Athtar myth (Day 2000: 166–84).

In Ezekiel's version of the Eden narrative, the most unusual feature is the protagonist as a cherub. In Gen 3:24 and elsewhere (including Ezekiel 1 and 10) the cherub is a fearsome composite creature that guards sacred space—the Garden of Eden, the Jerusalem temple, its inner sanctum and ark, and the divine chariot-throne. It is possible that the cherub as protagonist is Ezekiel's innovation, linked to his evocation of visual imagery of Phoenician luxury goods.

Ezekiel's description of the location of the Garden of Eden on "the holy mountain of God" may also have a Phoenician resonance. According to the *Gilgamesh* epic, the Cedar Mountain, at the heart of the cedar forest of Lebanon, was "the dwelling of the gods, the throne of the goddesses" (*mūšab ilī parak dirnini;* V.6), and was guarded by a fierce composite creature, Ḫumbaba (George 2003: 602–3). In Ugaritic ritual texts, "the gods of Lebanon" (*'l lb[]n*, Akkadian *ilū Labana*) receive sacrifices (Pardee 2002: 18–19, 48–49), suggesting, as M. S. Smith (2016: 89) observes, that "the deities have a known site of meeting in the Lebanon mountains." In Ezekiel 31, the location of the Garden of Eden seems to be in Lebanon, as indicated in the sequence "all the trees of Eden, the best and choicest of Lebanon" (Ezek 31:16). In this text the prophet compares the king of Assyria to a "cedar of Lebanon," which was taller than the "cedars in God's garden" and envied by "all the trees of Eden, which were in the garden of God" (Ezek 31:8–9). The association of the Garden of Eden with "the mountain of God" in Ezekiel 28 seems to be rooted in this general picture, in which the divine garden is in the mountains of Lebanon. This suits a dirge for the king of Tyre, but it is a different locale from the Garden of Eden in Genesis, which is "in the east" (Gen 2:8).

We may infer that there were different versions of the Garden of Eden story in ancient Israel and its environs, with variations in characters, plots, and locales. The flexibility of the story allowed for innovations by tellers and authors, as perhaps for the cherub as protagonist in Ezekiel's version. The stories in Genesis and Ezekiel seem to be independent doublets, with no indication that either is aware of the other. This does not mean that Genesis 2–3 is later than Ezekiel but does suggest that he did not know the book of Genesis (which was promulgated after the return to Zion; see Nehemiah 8). The two texts came to be interpreted together in later tradition, as, for instance, in the LXX translation of Ezekiel 28, which has a human with the cherub in the Garden of Eden (by interpreting *'att,* "you," in 28:14 as the preposition *'et,* "with"), and the cherub expels the human.

Some of the themes and motifs of the Garden of Eden story echo in other biblical texts, with different inflections in different genres, including psalms, wisdom literature, and prophecy. It is difficult to tell whether these are allusions to the Garden of Eden story in Genesis or to other versions of the Eden story, which, as Ezekiel 28 shows, circulated in multiple and changeable forms. Some of these echoes of Eden texts offer alternative pathways back to Eden, through its repetition and actualization in worship, wisdom, and eschatology. An example is this praise of Wisdom in Proverbs:

> Length of days is in her right hand,
> in her left are wealth and honor.
> Her ways are pleasant ways,
> and all her paths are peace.
> She is a Tree of Life for those who grasp her,
> happy are those who hold on to her. (Prov 3:16–18)

Wisdom is often personified in Proverbs as a quasi-goddess, a divine principle who, like Egyptian Ma'at, gives life and knowledge. Here Wisdom holds in her hand "length of days" (i.e., long life), much like personified Ma'at holds the *ankh* ("life") symbol. This portrait is further developed by the metaphorical description of wisdom as a "Tree of Life" (*'ēṣ ḥayyîm*), intensifying the long life of the wise into a kind of immortality. By activating this Eden allusion—whether to the Genesis story or to its multiple forms in Israelite culture—the mythic repetition aligns the path of wisdom with the path back to the Tree of Life. The fruit of immortality, which is blocked forever in the myth, reopens at another level in the cultivation of wisdom, where a kind of immortality is again possible.

The repetition of Eden motifs in proto-apocalyptic prophecy also hovers between the multiform Eden tradition (as in Ezekiel) and the particular text in Genesis. An interesting mingling of the two occurs in a vision of the paradisical end-time in Third Isaiah:

> The wolf and the lamb will graze together,
>> and the lion will eat straw like the ox,
>> but the snake's food will be dust.
> They will not do evil nor destroy,
>> in all my holy mountain. (Isa 65:25)

In this passage, which echoes and abbreviates the vision of future paradise in Isa 11:6–9, the world is a peaceful place, where wild predators become herbivores, grazing alongside their former prey. The concept of God's paradise on his holy mountain, as in the psalms of Zion and (with a different locale) Ezekiel 28, now describes a future paradise on "my holy mountain."

In the midst of this idyllic picture, which evokes the general themes of Eden, a particular Eden motif intrudes: "but the snake's food will be dust" (*wǝnāḥāš 'āpār laḥmô*). This line—probably a scribal gloss—changes the tenor of the previous lines and harmonizes the peaceful culinary habits of wolves and lions with the snake's punishment in the Garden of Eden: "you will eat dust all the days of your life" (Gen 3:14). The snake is an exception to the happy scene, since he must forever bear his punishment in the first Eden. The repetition of the general myth of paradise is interrupted by the fate of the snake in Genesis 3, qualifying the snake as an exception to the perfection of the future paradise.

In the wider ancient Near Eastern context, there are many parallels to Eden motifs, such as cherubim, sacred trees, and divine gardens (Wallace 1985). As for the major themes of the story, two Babylonian texts stand out as important antecedents, *Adapa* and *Gilgamesh* (H.-P. Müller 1991b; Mettinger 2007: 99–122). Both deal with the nature of the human condition in comparison with the gods, including the quest for knowledge and immortality, with some striking similarities in particular motifs, including the food of life and a trickster's role in its loss, and the role of sexuality in the passage of primeval humans from nature to culture.

Adapa is a wise man and a patron of magic, one of the seven *apkallu* who preserved knowledge from before the flood (Izre'el 2001). His benefactor Ea, the god of wisdom and magic,

> made him perfect in wisdom,
> revealing the designs of the land.
> To him he granted wisdom,
> eternal life he did not grant him.

>> (*Adapa* A i 3–4; Foster 2005: 526; Izre'el 2001: 9–10)

In this respect, Adapa is like Adam and Eve. He achieves wisdom (*nemēqu*), but since he is human, he lacks eternal life (*napištu darītu*). In the course of the story, he has the opportunity to achieve eternal life, but he fails because of the deceptive speech of Ea.

When Adapa violates a taboo by breaking the wings of the wind, he is summoned to heaven. Ea instructs his protégé to refuse the offer of the food and water of death, which are presumably deadly: "If they offer you food of death, do not eat! / If they offer you water of death, do not drink" (B 28–31; Foster 2005: 528; Izre'el 2001: 18–19). As

Edzard (2002) points out, these seem to be conditional commands, marked with *ma* ("if"). As it turns out, however, Adapa is offered the "food of life" (*akal balāṭi*) and the "water of life" (*mê balāṭi,* B 61–62). Not perceiving this deviation from Ea's instructions, Adapa turns them down. The god Anu laughs in astonishment:

> Anu looked at him, he laughed at him,
> "Come, Adapa, why did you not eat or drink?
> Hence you will not live. Alas for inferior humankind!"
>
> (B 66–68; Izre'el 2000: 20–21)

Adapa loses his chance for immortality because he followed Ea's deceptive instructions. This loss illuminates the human condition. As Izre'el (2001: 120) comments: "The reason for Ea's deceit is quite clear. Because Adapa is 'a seed of humankind' (Frag. D 12), he simply cannot have both wisdom and immortality. In this regard he is a symbol of humanity and its status on earth." Anu's laughter punctuates this condition: "Alas for inferior humankind!" Adapa's failure reflects on the inevitable mortality of humankind.

Like Adam and Eve, Adapa gains knowledge like the gods—in Adapa's case, magical knowledge. But he does not become a god, since he fails to eat the food of life, also like Adam and Eve, who are banished from proximity to the Tree of Life. In both stories the proximate cause for their loss is the deceptive speech of the trickster—the snake in Eden or Adapa's patron, Ea. The deeper cause is the nature of the human condition, which entails that the border of immortality is impassible. Knowledge like the gods is achievable, but not eternal life.

The *Gilgamesh* epic treats many of the same themes, which seem to be widely shared in antiquity. Gilgamesh the king is an exemplar of knowledge. Like Adapa, he learned "the totality of wisdom," including knowledge of secrets from before the flood (I.6–8; George 2003: 538–39). But his attempts to achieve eternal life fail. In an Old Babylonian tablet, the divine barmaid Siduri warns him that his quest is futile:

> O Gilgamesh, where are you wandering?
> Life, which you seek, you cannot find.
> When the gods created humankind,
> For humankind they established death,
> Life they kept for themselves.
>
> (Old Babylonian Sippar iii 2–5; George 2003: 278–79)

Gilgamesh fails at two attempts at immortality, one a test of overcoming sleep (a facsimile of death), administered by the flood hero Utnapishtim. Gilgamesh falls asleep instantly (*Gilg.* XI.210–11). The second failure, resonant of Eden and Adapa, is his failure to eat the plant of rejuvenation, a parting gift from Utnapishtim and his wife. On his journey home, while taking a break to bathe in a pool of water, Gilgamesh loses the "plant of heartbeat" (*šammu nikitti*) to a snake:

> A snake smelled the fragrance of the plant,
> > [silently] it came up and bore the plant off;
> > as it turned away it sloughed a skin.
> Then Gilgamesh sat down weeping,
> > the tears streaming down the side of his face.
>
> (XI.305–9; George 2003: 722–23)

Gilgamesh loses this form of immortality, rejuvenation, to a snake, who ever after sheds its skin and regains youth. This snake is not an intelligent trickster, like the snake in Eden, but it is a snake nonetheless, which has the gift of shedding its skin and regaining—it seems—perpetual youth. As a consequence of his loss, Gilgamesh gains wisdom. As the introduction says, "He returned from a distant road, weary but at peace" (I.9; George 2003: 538–39; Moran 2002: 7).

The birth of Gilgamesh's counterpart Enkidu and his transition from the state of nature to civilization also has a close relationship to themes in Eden. Enkidu is created from clay by the birth goddess, Aruru:

> Aruru washed her hands,
>> she took a pinch of clay, she threw it down in the wild.
> In the wild she created Enkidu, the hero,
>> an offspring of silence, knit strong by Ninurta.

(I.101–4; George 2003: 544–45)

As George (2003: 450) observes, the creation of Enkidu is a repetition of the creation of primeval humankind: "He lives in an animal state: hairy and unclothed, . . . feeding with the gazelles on grass and water (I.105–12). In these particulars . . . , he is a replica of the first man, dwelling far removed from civilization, both in space and in behavior."

Like Adam and Eve, Enkidu transitions from this primeval state—naked, unself-conscious, and innocent—to a state of sexual maturity, self-consciousness, and civilization. Like in Eden, this transition involves sexuality. A trapper brings a prostitute to distract Enkidu from his animal companions. She accomplishes her task:

> The two of them were making love together,
>> he forgot the wild where he was born.
> For seven days and seven nights
>> Enkidu was erect and coupled with Šamkatum.
> The harlot opened her mouth,
>> saying to Enkidu:
> I look at you, Enkidu, you are like a god,
>> why with the animals do you range through the wild?

(Old Babylonian II ii 46–62; George 2003: 174–75)

The harlot then clothes Enkidu and leads him to the shepherds, where he learns to eat bread and drink beer, has his hair cut, and anoints himself with oil. He "became a human" (awīliš iwê; iii 108).

In all these respects, the transition of Enkidu from nature to civilization echoes the transition of Adam and Eve from their creation in Eden to the world of human existence outside of paradise. There is an ascent of knowledge, a self-consciousness associated with sexuality, and a loss of innocence. Enkidu gains wisdom or understanding (ḫasīsu), but there is also diminishment, a loss of innocence and purity, which the animals recognize and run away from him. The human condition is, it seems, an ascent from the state of nature to civilization and knowledge, but this transition also entails a loss of innocence.

Cain and Abel (4:1–26; J)

4 ¹The man knew Eve, his wife, and she conceived and gave birth to Cain. She said, "I have gotten a man with Yahweh." ²She gave birth again to his brother, Abel. Abel was a herder of flocks, and Cain worked the soil. ³After some time, Cain offered a sacrifice to Yahweh from the fruit of the soil. ⁴Abel too offered a sacrifice from the fat firstborns of his flock. Yahweh regarded with favor Abel and his sacrifice, ⁵but Cain and his sacrifice he did not regard. Cain became very angry, and his face was fallen. ⁶Yahweh said to Cain, "Why are you angry? Why has your face fallen? ⁷Is it not so that if you are good, it will be lifted? But if you are not good, sin crouches[a] at the door—it[b] desires you, but you can rule over it."[c] ⁸Cain said to Abel, his brother, "Let us go out to the field,"[d] and when they were in the field Cain rose up against Abel, his brother, and killed him.

⁹Yahweh said to Cain, "Where is Abel, your brother?" He said, "I do not know. Am I my brother's keeper?" ¹⁰He said, "What have you done? The voice of your brother's blood cries out to me from the soil. ¹¹Now, cursed are you from the soil, which opened its mouth to take your brother's blood from your hand. ¹²When you work the soil it will no longer yield its strength to you. You shall be a restless wanderer on the earth." ¹³Cain said to Yahweh, "My punishment is more than I can bear. ¹⁴You have banished me today from the face of the soil, and I will be hidden from your face. I will be a restless wanderer on the earth, and whoever meets me will kill me." ¹⁵Yahweh said to him, "Therefore whoever kills Cain will suffer vengeance sevenfold." Yahweh placed a sign on Cain so that whoever met him would not kill him. ¹⁶Cain departed from Yahweh's presence and dwelled in the land of Wandering, east of Eden.

¹⁷Cain knew his wife, and she conceived and gave birth to Enoch. He built a city and named the city after Enoch, his son. ¹⁸To Enoch was born[e] Irad, and Irad fathered Mehiyael,[f] and Mehiyael fathered Methushael, and Methushael fathered Lamech. ¹⁹Lamech took two wives for himself, the first named Ada and the second Zillah. ²⁰Ada gave birth to Jabal—he was the father of herdsmen who dwell in tents. ²¹His brother's name

211

was Jubal—he was the father of all who play lyres and pipes. ²²As for Zillah, she too gave birth to Tubal-Cain, [the father of all who]ᵍ work metal, forging bronze and iron. Tubal-Cain's sister was Naamah. ²³Lamech said to his wives:

> "Ada and Zillah, hear my voice,
>> Lamech's wives, listen to my speech.
> A man I have killed for wounding me,
>> a boy for bruising me.
> ²⁴If Cain is avenged sevenfold,
>> Lamech will be seventy-seven-fold."

²⁵Adam knew his wife,ʰ and she gave birth to a son. She named him Seth, "For God has set me another seed to take the place of Abel, for Cain killed him." ²⁶As for Seth,ⁱ a son was born to him, and he named him Enosh. Then was it begunʲ to call on the name of Yahweh.

Textual Notes

a. Reading *trbṣ* ("crouches"), a feminine verb. The major versions (MT, SP, LXX) all read *rbṣ* ("crouches"), a masculine participle. The problem with the transmitted reading is that the noun *ḥṭ't* ("sin") is feminine. The easiest solution to this ungrammatical sequence is to assume a scribal haplography ("single writing") of *taw* in the sequence *ḥṭ't ⟨t⟩rbṣ* ("sin crouches") (Dillmann 1897: 189; Hendel 1998: 45–46; similarly, Gordon 2011: 196).

b. Reading *tšwqt⟨h⟩* ("its desire"), with a feminine pronominal suffix. The MT and SP read *tšwqtw* with a masculine pronominal suffix. As in the previous TEXTUAL NOTE, the problem with the transmitted reading is that the antecedent, *ḥṭ't* ("sin"), is a feminine noun. In preexilic spelling, a final *he* could represent a final *-ā* or final *-ō*. In postexilic practice, a final *waw* was used for a final *-ō*. Scribes generally modernized preexilic biblical texts to reflect postexilic spelling practices, such that a final *he* representing a final *-ō* was usually replaced with a final *waw*. In this case, *tšwqth* was probably wrongly modernized to *tšwqtw* (Dillmann 1897: 189; Hendel 1998: 46). This is an economical solution to the grammatical problem.

c. Reading *b⟨h⟩* ("it"), with a feminine pronominal suffix, rather than the MT's and SP's *bw* with a masculine pronominal suffix. See the previous TEXTUAL NOTE.

d. Reading *nlkh hśdh* ("Let us go out to the field"), with the SP, LXX, and several minor versions (the Palestinian targums, the Latin Vulgate, and, with minor variation, the Syriac Peshitta). The MT lacks this reading, which makes the verse in the MT unintelligible as it stands. Early interpreters of the MT tended to supply Cain's missing speech in imaginative ways (Kugel 1998: 160–62). The agreement among all the non-MT versions makes a strong case for the originality of this reading. The MT probably lost this reading by a scribe's anticipation of the similar sequence in the second half of this verse: *qyn 'l hbl 'hyw . . . qyn 'l hbl 'hyw* (Hendel 1998: 46–47; cf. Tal 2015: 88*). Medieval MT codices often mark this lacuna with a break in the middle of the verse (*pisqa' bə'emṣa' pasuq*) (Hendel 2016: 4–5).

e. It is likely that the consonants should be vocalized as a *qal* passive, **wayyulad > wayyûllad* (cf. 4:26), rather than the *niphal*, *wayyiwwālēd*, of the MT. The *niphal* replaces the *qal* passive for this verb over the course of the Classical Biblical Hebrew period, but the J source preserves the earlier usage (Hendel 2000).

f. Reading *mhyy'l* ("Mehiyael"), with the SP and LXX. The MT reads *mhwy'l* ("Mehuyael") for the first instance of the name and *mhyy'l* ("Mehiyael") for the second. It is not clear which of the two variants preserved in the MT is the original—the difference consists of a simple variation of *yod* and *waw,* letters that are liable to scribal confusion. The easiest solution is to suppose that the original was Mehiyael and that the reading with *waw* (Mehuyael) was influenced by anticipation of the vocalic pattern of Methushael, the next name in the sequence (Hendel 1998: 47–48).

g. The verse as it stands is corrupt. Judging from the parallel descriptions of the other sons of Lamech in 4:20–21, a phrase like *'by kl* ("the father of all who") is expected (Targums Onqelos and Pseudo-Jonathan supply similar phrases) (Hendel 1998: 48).

h. The MT and SP add *'wd* ("again"), which is lacking in the LXX. This is an explicating plus, clarifying that this is Adam and Eve's second reported sexual congress (Hendel 1998: 48).

i. The MT and SP add *gm hw'* ("him too"), which is lacking in the LXX. This is probably a harmonizing plus with *wslh gm hy'* ("Zillah too") in 4:22, and similarly 10:21 (Hendel 1998: 49).

j. The MT reads *'z hwhl.* The LXX reads *zh hwhl,* and the SP reads *'z hhl,* both reading the verb as active. The latter are probably influenced by the active sequences with *hhl* in 6:1, 9:20, and 10:8 (cf. Hendel 1998: 49; Gordon 2012).

Notes

4:1. The man knew Eve, his wife, and she conceived and gave birth to Cain. This verse begins with a disjunctive (noun-initial) clause, signaling the beginning of a new scene or episode (*IBHS* §39.2.3c). The style of this opening verse is highlighted by its repetition, with variation, twice more in this story: "Cain knew his wife, and she conceived and gave birth" (4:17), and "Adam knew his wife, and she gave birth" (4:25). These three acts of "knowing" and birth structure the narrative into three parts: Cain and Abel, Cain's descendants, and Seth and descendants.

The diction of this verse also ties together several themes of the Garden of Eden story. The man (*hā'ādām*) knew (*yāda'*) his wife, that is, they had sex—perhaps for the first time, although this is not highlighted. This fulfills the rule "Therefore a man . . . cleaves to his wife, and they become one flesh." (2:24). The marital reference to the woman as *hawwâ 'ištô* ("Eve, his wife") emphasizes their relationship, which has been evolving since she was created from the man. In their next act of conception, it is Adam who is named (for the first time with a proper name), and Eve is referred to simply as "his wife" (4:25). At the beginning of this story, Eve is in the foreground, conceiving, giving birth, and naming the child. Interestingly, her painful labor is not mentioned (cf. 3:16)—her brief exclamation after the birth of the child expresses only joy.

The child's name, *qayin* ("Cain"), is a wordplay on Eve's exclamation, *qānîtî* ("I have gained, acquired"). This name is also related to its lexical cognates and ethnic affiliation—"metalsmith" and the Kenites (Day 2013: 51–60). The word **qayn* (which becomes *qayin,* "Cain") and its congeners mean "smith, metalworker" in Central Semitic—so Arabic *qayn,* Syriac *qaynāyā,* and Jewish Aramaic *qênā'â* (*HALOT,* 1097).

The Hebrew word *qênô* (2 Sam 21:16), apparently from **qayn,* may be a word for a weapon or armor with metal parts (or it may be a scribal error; see McCarter 1984: 448). Although Cain is a farmer, not a smith or metalworker, this meaning is close to the surface in Cain's descendant Tubal-Cain, who is the ancestor of those who "work metal, forging bronze and iron" (Gen 4:22). The meaning "metalsmith" is part of the resonance of Cain's name.

Metalsmiths in the preindustrial world were (and today still are) often itinerant, wandering from place to place, making a meager living, and often looked down upon by townspeople and villagers. Examples of this phenomenon are the Roma people of Europe, the Sleybs of Arabia, and the Falashas of Ethiopia, itinerant groups or tribes that practice metalwork and other crafts, economically useful but often despised by their hosts (Skinner 1930: 113; other examples in McNutt 1990: 70–82). These instances of wandering, low-status metalworkers seem an apt sociological backdrop to the story of *qayin,* "smith," whom Yahweh curses to be "a restless wanderer on the earth" (see COMMENTS).

The name *qayin* also has an ethnic resonance, designating the *qênî* ("Kenites"). The Kenites are mentioned in a handful of biblical texts (see Day 2013: 51–60). In Judges 4–5, Heber the Kenite and his wife Jael live in the countryside between Megiddo and Taanach as tent-dwelling shepherds, serving milk and curds from their flock to their guests (cf. Cain's descendant Jabal, "the father of herdsmen who dwell in tents," in Gen 4:20). They have political relations with Canaanites and Israelites and live in the boundary region between them. Elsewhere the Kenites live in the Negeb south of Arad (Judg 1:16; similarly, 1 Sam 15:6) and have a connection to "the city of palms," probably Tamar ("palm"), in the Wadi Arabah south of the Dead Sea (Aharoni 1979: 215). According to 1 Chr 2:55, Kenites also lived in the city of Jabez, near Bethlehem in Judah, where they migrated from Hamath of Syria. The Kenites seem to be widely dispersed people who have cordial relations with many peoples—Israelites, Amalekites (1 Sam 15:6), the Canaanites (Judg 4:17), Syrians (1 Chr 2:55), and the Midianites (note that the two are interchanged or confused in the ethnic affiliation of Moses's father-in-law).

Although the Kenites are not directly associated with metalwork, it is possible that their ethnonym, *qênî,* perhaps "smith people," can be explained in connection with the extensive copper industry in the Wadi Arabah region south of the Dead Sea, which flourished through the ninth century BCE (see Levy and Najjar 2006; Sawyer 1986). Major copper mining and smelting sites include Timna, Feinan (biblical Pinon/ Punon), and Khirbet en-Nahas. The tribal polity of Edom was also probably involved in copper production at these sites; note the names Timna and Pinon in the list of the chiefs of Esau/Edom (Gen 36:40–41). The Kenites may have been employed in the metalworking industry in this period, and from this occupation derived their name. In any case, it is a region associated with Kenite origins, and it is a center of the metal industry.

The association of Cain with the Kenites (as their eponymous ancestor?) may stem from this tribal history in the copper trade. By the time of the biblical writings, the Kenites had an economy of tents and herds, in essence shifting from Tubal-Cain's lifestyle to Jabal's (4:20–22). This historical reconstruction accounts for several otherwise disparate details.

The Cain-Kenite connection is also suggested by the geographical associations of some names in Cain's genealogy. The names Adah and Naamah, Lamech's wife and daughter (4:19–22), are elsewhere linked with the region of Edom: Adah is Esau's wife (36:2), and Naamah is the home of Zophar, one of Job's comforters (Job 2:11; Sawyer 1986: 159). A place called *haqqayin,* meaning "the Kenite" or "the smith," is listed in Josh 15:57, perhaps to be read in combination with the previous place name as "Zanoah of the Kenites." This city is presumably located in the Arabah region. These names and places associate Cain's kin with the homeland of the Kenites.

She said, "I have gotten a man with Yahweh." This is a folk etymology or naming midrash, which relates the name to the thematics of the narrative context. The child is named *qayin* ("Cain") because the mother said *qānîtî* ("I have gotten, acquired"). This wordplay is an implicit name-derivation (Zakovitch 1980). Eve's joyful exclamation attributes the production of a child to a divine act, hence she credits Yahweh's participation. She seems to leave her husband out of the picture, substituting the prime creator. Notably, Eve names the child, taking on the task of naming that previously belonged to the man. Elsewhere it is common for the woman to name the child (e.g., Genesis 29–30, 35:18; 1 Sam 1:20), although in some texts (e.g., the P source; Gen 16:15, 17:19, 21:3) it is the father's prerogative.

This exclamation corresponds to the image of Eve as the "mother of all life" (3:20). Here she revels in the child she has "gotten, acquired." The verb *qānâ* can have the sense of "created" in the context of childbirth; compare the personal name Elkanah (*'elqānâ*), "God has created," which also celebrates the birth of a child. The sense in which Eve's work of creation has been done "with Yahweh" is not clear but points to the deep meaning of procreation.

4:2. *She gave birth again to his brother, Abel.* The sequence *wattōsep lāledet* can mean "she continued to give birth" or "she gave birth again." It is unclear whether the second birth occurs immediately after the first, in which case Cain and Abel are twins, or occurs sometime later. This issue is not highlighted in the story. What is emphasized is that Abel is *'āḥîw* ("his brother"). The words *'āḥîw* ("his brother") and *'āḥîkā* ("your brother") occur seven times in the story, six times during the scenes of murder and discovery (4:8–11). The seemingly superfluous mention that Abel is "his brother" anticipates the resonance of this *Leitwort* in the verses that follow.

In contrast to the naming of Cain, Abel's name (*hebel, hābel* in the pausal form) receives no explanation. It is possible that it means "herder"; compare Syriac *habālā',* "swineherd, camel herder" (Day 2022: 81). This would suit his occupation. But the ordinary Hebrew meaning seems to express Abel's fate. *Hebel* means "vapor, breath," and by semantic extension, "evanescent, unsubstantial, worthless, nothingness." This word is used to describe the fleeting insubstantiality of human existence, as in the following poetic verses:

A human (*'ādām*) is like a breath (*hebel*),
> their days like a passing shadow. (Ps 144:4)

I despise it, I would not live forever,
> leave me be, for my days are a breath (*hebel*). (Job 7:16)

In the book of Ecclesiastes *hebel* is a *Leitwort,* as in the proclamation that "everything is *hebel,*" meaning futile, insubstantial, evanescent (Eccl 1:1). This quality of human existence, that it is a passing breath, is expressed in Abel's name. As an exemplar of *hebel*, he is born to have a brief, transitory life.

Abel was a herder of flocks, and Cain worked the soil. The occupations of the two brothers are contrasted as shepherd and farmer. More important to the story, their offerings are also contrasted, and the shepherd's is preferred. Many commentators infer that this expresses a preference for shepherds over farmers, tracing this back to Israel's putative pastoral origins. But there is no reason to think that the Israelites originated as shepherds or mobile pastoralists. The economy of ancient Israel was throughout its history based on a mixed peasant economy of farming and herding (King and Stager 2001: 85–122). Even the patriarchs are pictured as involved in farming and herding (e.g., Gen 26:12–14; 37:7, 12). This mixed economy diversifies food production and reduces the risk of famine; it is reflected in the economy of the first family, in which the older son (like his father) is a farmer, and the younger son is a shepherd. Note that the father's role is taken up by the older son, while the younger tends the sheep (cf. David in 1 Sam 16:11; and the younger daughter Rachel in Gen 29:9). Abel and these other younger siblings are domestic herders, not mobile pastoralists like Cain's descendant Jabal (see NOTES at 4:20).

The contrastive terms for these professions, *rō'ēh ṣō'n* (lit. "herder of sheep") and *'ōbēd 'ădāmâ* (lit. "worker of soil")—both participle + noun in construct—have further resonances in the story. Abel's occupation as *rō'eh* ("shepherd") may resound in Cain's later protest, "Am I my brother's keeper (*šōmēr*)?" (4:9). The verb *šāmar* ("keep, watch, guard") is often used for shepherding (e.g., Gen 30:31, 1 Sam 17:20, Hos 12:13). More decisively, Cain's occupation as *'ōbēd 'ădāmâ* ("worker of the soil") echoes his father's task, *la'ăbōd 'et-hā'ădāmâ* ("to work the soil," 3:23). Cain is following in his father's footsteps, with its legacy of transgression and punishment. The term also recalls the curse on the soil (3:17) and anticipates his own punishment: "cursed are you from the soil. . . . When you work the soil it will no longer yield its strength to you" (4:11–12).

The style of contrasts between the two brothers continues through 4:5, highlighting the potential friction between them. As Cassuto (1961: 204) observes, this is a repeating alternation—Cain-Abel (4:1–2), Abel-Cain (4:2), Cain-Abel (4:3–4), Abel-Cain (4:4–5)—which creates literary symmetry. It also disturbs the expected priority of the firstborn, Cain, and rhetorically highlights the unspoken question of which son—the older or the younger?—will receive favor. The varying order of the two brothers insinuates on the level of style a sense of unresolved relationship between them, building toward the crisis.

The grammar of these verses accentuates the stylistic alternation. Beginning in 4:2 the clause sequences alternate between sequential (concerning one brother) and disjunctive (concerning the other). The disjunctive (noun-initial) clause in each pair may signify that the action is simultaneous rather than successive, as in the contrastive sense of "Abel was a herder of flocks, and Cain worked the soil," or it may simply signify a contrast, "Abel was a herder of flocks, *but* Cain worked the soil." The contrastive sense is palpable in the last alternation, "*but* Cain and his sacrifice he did not regard" (4:5).

4:3. *After some time, Cain offered a sacrifice to Yahweh from the fruit of the soil.* The temporal span is unspecified—*miqqēṣ yāmîm* is literally "at the end of (some) days." Elsewhere *yāmîm* ("days") alone can mean an indefinite amount of time, as in 40:4 ("for some time").

The word for Cain's sacrifice," *minḥâ,* literally means "gift, present." In non-P texts it is a term that includes all types of sacrifice and offerings. In P texts—and also in Iron Age Phoenician texts—the term *minḥâ* takes on a more specialized usage as "grain offering" (Anderson 1992: 873–75). The usage in Genesis 4 reflects the general meaning since it applies to both Cain's and Abel's sacrifices. As a "gift," one expects that it will be accepted. In the ancient code of honor and shame, to refuse a gift, as Yahweh does to Cain, is to shame the donor. A person's public honor is closely tied to the giving and receiving of gifts (Pedersen 1926: 296–304). Sacrifice is a ritualized expression of such reciprocal exchanges (Hendel 2015).

Cain's sacrifice is taken *mippĕrî hāʾădāmâ* ("from the fruit of the soil"). It is a gift of produce or grain (cf. Deut 26:2) and is the fruit of Cain's agricultural labor. There is no reason why a vegetation offering should be unacceptable, in contrast to Abel's animal offering. The fault in Cain's offering presumably lies elsewhere than in its agricultural origin (cf. Spina 1992).

4:4. *Abel too offered a sacrifice from the fat firstborns of his flock.* Abel's offering is from his professional domain, *mibbǝkōrôt ṣōʾnô ûmēḥelbēhen,* literally "from the firstborns of his flock and from their fat." The last phrase, "and from their fat," may be explanatory (with the *waw explicativum*), "namely, from their fat" (GKC §154a, n. 1b), but this is unlikely for a nontechnical description of sacrifice (particularly if this is an ordinary *zebaḥ* sacrifice). This sequence is better read as a hendiadys, in which two nouns joined by *waw* form a single expression, one modifying the other. Hence Speiser (1964: 29–30) reads, "the finest of the firstlings of his flock." The word *ḥēleb* ("fat, suet") has the extended sense of "best, choicest," and this sense is fitting here. With flocks, the best ones are also the ones with the most fat, so the multiple meanings of "fat" coexist. This type of sacrifice probably involves burning the whole animal, including the fat and the meat.

In the contrast between Cain's gift and Abel's, the only verbal difference of ritual value is that Abel's offering is *mibbǝkōrôt* ("from the firstborns"). Cain's gift from the fruit of the soil lacks this qualification. For produce, the term would be *bikkûrîm,* "firstfruits" (e.g., Exod 23:16, 19) or *rēʾšît,* "first," as in "the first of every fruit of the soil" (Deut 26:2). As commentators have observed, the value of Abel's offering is increased by being from the firstborns. But a sacrifice that is not from the firstfruits should still be acceptable.

The absence of a counterpart to *bǝkōrôt* ("firstborns") in Cain's offering may have a slightly different resonance. An issue in the story is the rivalry between brothers over the honor due to the firstborn son (*bǝkôr*). The word *bǝkōrôt* in Abel's offering subtly activates this theme (Greenspahn 1994: 92). The rivalry in the story is not between Cain and Abel as members of different professions, but as older and younger brothers—a common theme in Genesis. The link of "firstborns" with Abel, and not with Cain, accompanies the incipient friction over their status.

4:4–5. *Yahweh regarded with favor Abel and his sacrifice, but Cain and his sacrifice he did not regard.* No obvious reason is given for Yahweh's decision to favor Abel's sacrifice and not Cain's. This is part of the rich obscurity of the story. There may be an ethical reason for Yahweh's decision—Yahweh raises ethical issues in his subsequent speech to Cain (4:6–7); or the quality of Abel's offering—it is from the "fat firstborns," while Cain's is from the everyday "fruit of the soil"—may motivate the preference (see Day

2022: 81–83); or Yahweh's decision may simply be a "given" in the plot, which generates a complication. In the terse narration, Yahweh's choice seems mysterious and is perhaps inscrutable.

The verb *šā'â* ("look at, gaze at, regard") is often used in poetry in parallel with the ordinary term *rā'â* ("see," e.g., Isa 17:7–8). Both verbs have extended senses, including "consider, pay attention to." The more formal or elevated term is used here for Yahweh's acceptance or nonacceptance of sacrifice. The procedure by which Yahweh's favor or disfavor is ascertained is obscure—perhaps we are to assume an oracular or supernatural sign (cf. Judg 13:30). This absence of detail is part of the terse style of the narrative.

The objects of Yahweh's gaze or non-gaze are "Abel and his sacrifice" and "Cain and his sacrifice." These phrases seem to focus on the brothers as much as on the sacrifices. The contrast is between *'el-hebel wə'el-minḥātô* ("Abel and his sacrifice") and *wə'el-qayin wə'el-minḥātô* ("but Cain and his sacrifice"). In this diction, Yahweh seems to focus on the offerer first, then on the sacrifice.

Cain became very angry, and his face was fallen. Cain's response is described with an emotion and its visual expression—*wayyiḥar ləqayin mə'ōd* ("anger kindled greatly for Cain") and *wayyippəlû pānāyw* ("his face fell"). In both a literal and a figurative sense, Cain's body registers anger, dejection, and shame. So the grieving Job declares, "I will not raise my head, full of shame" (Job 10:15), and he recalls better days when "the light of my face never fell" (Job 29:24). In Cain's case, his diminished state registers in his fallen face. Among the modern Bedouin, for whom the code of honor and shame is still strong, the word "face" can also denote "honor" (Stewart 1994: 99). Cain's anger and his fallen face are complementary images.

4:6. Yahweh said to Cain, "Why are you angry? Why has your face fallen?" A deceptively simple pair of questions, like the later question, "Where is Abel, your brother?" (4:9). In each of these instances, the question seems to be a subtle interrogation, as in Yahweh's straightforward questions in the Garden of Eden, "Where are you?," "Who told you?," and "What have you done?" (3:9–13). Here Yahweh's questions do not elicit a response from Cain but set up a moral exhortation. Yahweh seems already to know the reasons for Cain's anger.

Yahweh does not acknowledge his own role in instigating Cain's anger but is rather concerned with Cain's ethical state. Unlike the interrogation scene in Eden, there is no description of how or where Yahweh encounters Cain, now or later (4:9). It is perhaps ironic that Yahweh addresses Cain, revealing that he knows Cain's emotions, just after he has chosen not to "see" (*lō' šā'â*) Cain.

4:7. Is it not so that if you are good, it will be lifted? Yahweh's words are slightly cryptic. The conditional clause *hălô' 'im-têṭîb śə'ēt* means, "is it not so that if you act rightly, (there is) uplift." In the condition (protasis), the verb *têṭîb* has the sense of "doing what is right, good" when contrasted with doing evil, for example, "cease to do evil, learn to do good" (*hêṭēb*, Isa 1:16–17). In the biblical conception, being good involves doing what is good; it is a moral disposition with practical content. The terse consequence (apodosis), "(there is) uplift," expressed by one word, *śə'ēt*, seems to correspond with the idiom of "face" as the repository of shame or honor. If Cain is good and does what is right, he will regain his honor, that is, his face will be lifted up. A raised face is the consequence and the tangible image of a good person. The moral condition conveyed in Yahweh's speech is what Pedersen (1926: 434) calls "the old law of Israel, viz. that goodness bears blessing within itself."

But if you are not good, sin crouches at the door—it desires you, but you can rule over it. Whereas being and doing good yields honor and a raised face, doing evil opens the door to sin. *Ḥaṭṭāʾt* ("sin, transgression") is pictured here as an objective force, poised like a predatory animal crouching (*tirbaṣ*, see TEXTUAL NOTE a) at the doorstep (cf. the animal metaphor in 49:9, "he lies down, he crouches (*rābaṣ*) like a lion"). The image of sin lying in wait at the door may have as its conceptual background the activity of demons who lurk at thresholds and doorways. Amulets were attached to doorways to ward off such demonic creatures; compare a Phoenician amulet from Arslan Tash (seventh century BCE): "Sasam, let (the door) not be opened for him. Let him not come down to the doorposts (*mzzt*)" (*KAI* 27; Cross 2003: 265–69; Becking 1999).

Some commentators have suggested that the form *rōbēṣ* ("crouching, croucher") in the MT may actually be the name of a demon, translating "sin is the *rōbēṣ*-demon at the door" (Speiser 1964: 33; see M. S. Smith 2019: 67–69; Day 2022: 85–86). A category of demon called *rābiṣu* ("croucher, one who lies in wait") is known from Mesopotamia, and this would correspond to the form *rōbēṣ* in Hebrew. But a demon of this name is not known in Hebrew or other West Semitic languages. (In Ugaritic and Amarna Canaanite, *rābiṣu* is an "inspector" or "commissioner.") Moreover, the grammar of this verse makes it difficult to read *rōbēṣ* as a substantive (Barré 1999: 683). The context is most easily accommodated by reading this form as a predicate, "crouches" (Gordon 2011).

Yahweh's further description of Cain's situation—"it desires you, but you can rule over it"—continues the metaphor of sin as a predatory animal or demon. The question is whether sin's desire will overwhelm Cain, or whether he will tame and rule it, like domesticating a wild animal. This dialectic of desire and discipline is projected as an exterior relationship, as if sin were a dangerous creature, but of course the exhortation is aimed at Cain's ability to control his inner self. In the psychoanalytical model of Freud, he similarly describes this dangerous inner drive as a quasi-independent agent, "it" (German *es*), rendered in translation with the Latin word *id*. Within us, therefore, in both the biblical and Freudian pictures, is the allure of destructive/sinful tendencies and drives, warring with our better selves.

Yahweh cautions Cain that unless he engages this struggle forthrightly, he will succumb to sin. Cain has free will in this struggle, such that the outcome is not preordained, but victory over one's evil inclination is difficult and ongoing. To have mastery over sin, one must choose to engage the struggle. The emphasis in this sequence is on *ʾattâ* ("you") preposed to the verb—"but *you* can rule over it." Personal commitment and initiative are necessary.

In the Freudian model—a secularization of this moral discourse—Yahweh's words may be seen as a divine voice of conscience. Yahweh instructs Cain in the complexities of a moral life, which Cain (and the reader) should internalize. Yahweh has the role of the *Über-ich,* the "above-I" (superego), speaking to Cain's "I" (ego), about the seductive evil power of "it" (the id). Freud's tripartite structure of the psyche is a transposition or transformation of the biblical picture in this verse. It is, in a sense, a modern version of biblical moral discourse.

4:8. *Cain said to Abel, his brother, "Let us go out to the field," and when they were in the field, Cain rose up against Abel, his brother, and killed him.* Rather than responding to Yahweh's previous question and exhortation, Cain speaks to Abel. This abrupt transition may suggest that Cain is unwilling to respond or incapable of responding to Yahweh's speech. His lack of response is jarring, in contrast to his responses to Yahweh's questions and punishment after the murder (4:9, 13–14). The abrupt shift—without any indication of time passing—adds to the terseness and tenseness of the story.

Because of the lack of the clause "let us go out to the field" in the MT (see TEXTUAL NOTE d and below), some commentators have tried to read the initial verb, *wayyōʾmer* ("[he] said"), with an unusual meaning here (e.g., Cassuto 1964: 213–15: "appointed a place to meet"; Reis 2002: "spoke against"). But the sixfold use of this verb in the story, all in the sequence *wayyōʾmer PN ʾel-PN* ("PN said to PN"), argues against an unusual meaning here. In Classical Hebrew "*ʾmr* never means to say without indicating what is stated" (*HALOT,* 66), so we expect a speech to follow. The speeches in this story are significant, composing the majority of the story, particularly in this section.

Moreover, Cain's speech to Abel, *nēlǝkâ haśśādeh* ("Let us go out to the field"), is his first utterance, which tends to highlight the character and his motivation. In the context of biblical diction and custom, it has nuances that are activated when Yahweh confronts Cain with his crime. The word *śādeh* ("field") can mean agricultural land or pastureland, or it can refer to wild country. In either case, going to the field means leaving the settled domain, the city or village. The intent to go out to the field can mean, as Skinner (1930: 107) comments, "they were safe from observation." This is the sense when Jonathan says to David, "Come, let us go out to the field" (*lǝkâ nēṣēʾ haśśādeh,* 1 Sam 20:11), where Jonathan confides his plans to David in secret. Similarly, the prophet Ahijah tears Jeroboam's robe into twelve pieces "when the two of them were alone in the field" (1 Kgs 11:29), away from prying eyes. Cain's brief speech indicates that he wishes to speak to Abel in private.

There is also a more covert resonance to this speech. In laws about violent crimes, the locale—city verses field—is significant. This holds in ancient Near Eastern law generally (Westbrook 1992: 552). The distinction between city and field turns on whether the victim can "cry out" (*ṣāʿaq*) and be heard by others. In the city the presumption is that the cry can be heard, since other people are within earshot, but in the field the presumption is that the cry cannot be heard. This distinction of locale is explicit in the laws about murder and rape in Deuteronomy: "As when a man rises against his neighbor and murders him, so it is in this case. For he found her in the field (*śādeh*), and the betrothed woman cried out (*ṣāʿǎqâ*), but there was none to save her" (Deut 22:26–27). There was none to save her because in the field there is no one to hear her cry.

In this juridical context, Cain's statement, "Let us go out to the field," suggests his criminal intent, since the field is a place where Abel's cry cannot be heard, and no one can save him. The dramatic irony is that Cain's plan fails, for Yahweh hears the cry: "The voice of your brother's blood cries out (*ṣōʿǎqîm*) to me from the soil" (4:10). Cain's calculated statement to Abel indicates a plan that is ultimately thwarted. Cain is punished by being exiled beyond the fields, to a place where murder is unnoticed and licit (4:14). He becomes a placeless wanderer, far from civilization and from Yahweh's presence.

The legal implications of murder in the field recur in two other biblical narratives: Joseph and his brothers (Gen 37:15–36) and the story of the woman of Tekoa's two sons

(2 Sam 14:6). Both involve fratricide. These stories support the idea that these juridical concepts circulate in Cain's invitation to Abel.

The image that Cain "rose up" (*wayyāqom*) against his brother has a violent sense—"as when a man rises against his neighbor and murders him" (Deut 22:26)—and it also plays on the image of sin as a crouching beast in Gen 4:7, now rising to attack. The theme of fratricide is also subtly emphasized by the repetition of "Abel" and "his brother" twice in this verse. The term "his/your brother" resounds throughout the scenes of murder and punishment (six times in 4:8–11; see NOTES at 4:2).

4:9–12. The scene of interrogation and judgment has many echoes with the similar scene in the Garden of Eden. Note these correspondences: "Where is Abel, your brother?" and "Where are you?" (4:9 and 3:9); "What have you done?" (4:10 and 3:13); "the voice of your brother's blood" and "your wife's voice" (4:10 and 3:17); "Cursed are you from the soil" and "Cursed is the soil because of you" (4:11 and 3:17); and "work the soil" (4:12 and 3:23). The concluding verses also echo the Eden story: "You have banished me" and "He banished the man" (4:14 and 3:24); and "east of Eden" and "east of the Garden of Eden" (4:16 and 3:24). In this section, the quite different story of Cain and Abel becomes a thematic counterpart of the Garden of Eden story. With Yahweh's discourse of interrogation and judgment, the two stories highlight the images of human transgression, duplicity, and guilt, and their weighty consequences.

4:9. *Yahweh said to Cain, "Where is Abel, your brother?"* Yahweh's question seems simple. The idea that he doesn't know where Abel is, that is, that Yahweh is not omniscient, is unproblematic in this context and was probably a normal concept in classical Israel. Cain assumes that this is the case, since he boldly lies to Yahweh in response. But Yahweh does know, since he has heard the voice of Abel's blood (4:10). In retrospect we realize that Yahweh has been investigating the matter because of the blood's cry (cf. the "cry" about Sodom and Gomorrah in 18:20–21). The reader—and Cain—does not know about Abel's blood crying out until after Cain's duplicitous reply, allowing the implications of the question to resonate until Yahweh reveals what he knows, and Cain is trapped in a lie.

He said, "I do not know. Am I my brother's keeper?" Cain responds by lying—"I do not know"—and poses an evasive question, "Am I my brother's keeper?" Both responses evoke deeper issues. To say *lōʾ yādaʿtî* ("I do not know") echoes the *Leitwort* of the Eden story, *yādaʿ* ("to know"), with its complicated legacy. But Cain does know; his claim of ignorance is mere cunning. Knowledge and duplicity are interwoven in this story. Cain's claim to lack knowledge, his false witness, does not hide his sin but compounds it.

The evasive question "Am I my brother's keeper?" sharpens the concept of Cain's sin. The word *šōmēr* ("keeper, guardian") calls to mind Abel's occupation as a shepherd, whose responsibility it is to protect his flocks (see NOTES at 4:2). It also echoes the first human's task "to guard" the garden (2:15). If humans are to protect gardens and flocks, how much more so one's brother? The absence of a reply to Cain's evasive question makes it hang in the air. That Cain is, in fact, his brother's murderer, not his keeper, complicates this question. Later in Genesis, the older brothers, Reuben and Judah, try to save Joseph from murder at the brothers' hands and pledge to protect Benjamin (37:21–30, 42:37, 43:8–9). In a tribal society such as ancient Israel, it is the responsibility of older brothers to protect the lives and honor of younger siblings (cf. 34:13–31). But Cain rejects his responsibility.

The literary style also affects this question. In the repetition of the *Leitwort* "his/ your brother" (4:2, 8 [twice], 9 [twice], 10, 11), this is the first time that the name Abel is omitted. This omission gives Cain's question a broader reference (Seebass 1996: 155). Are we, and to what extent ought we be, our brother's keeper? The question that begins as a criminal's evasion turns into a question of responsibility toward our brothers and sisters.

4:10. *He said, "What have you done? The voice of your brother's blood cries out to me from the soil."* After Cain's denial, Yahweh confronts him with proof of the murder—the dead victim's cry. Blood, which we are told elsewhere is "life" (9:4), has an eerie life of its own here, crying out its accusation from the soil where it was spilled. The blood, it seems, still has enough life essence to accuse its murderer (Gaster 1969: 65–69). The concept that postmortem blood still has the power to "cry out" is found elsewhere: "Earth, do not cover up my blood (*dāmî*); let there not be a resting place for my outcry (*za'āqātî*)" (Job 16:18).

The idea of blood crying out from the earth is not only uncanny, but also carries a forensic or legal connotation. The root *ṣ'q* and its alloform *z'q* ("cry out") can refer to a legal accusation of crime (Hasel 1980: 116–19). In this case the blood of the murdered victim is crying out its accusation to the divine judge. As with the *ṣə'āqâ*, "cry," that comes to Yahweh regarding the crimes of Sodom and Gomorrah (Gen 18:20–21; similarly Exod 22:22, 26), this term signifies "a cry of distress, a cry for help, often to those legally bound to assist . . . and, in the case of Genesis, the rest of the legal community failing, to the ultimate custodian of the community and its law" (Moran 2002: 58 n. 45). The voice of Abel's blood is not just "crying out" in pain or distress; it is acting as a witness against Cain, accusing him of fratricide. Cain's plan to lure Abel out into the field, where the victim's cry would not be heard, has failed (see NOTES at 4:8).

The diction of this sentence makes the picture of the murder more precise. The word *dāmîm* ("blood," *dəmê* in construct) is in the plural, signifying an abundance of blood, particularly blood spilled in violence (BDB, 196). This plural form is used only for blood from human bodies (*IBHS* 7.4.1b). Hence, *dəmê 'āḥîkā* ("your brother's blood") indicates that it is blood shed in violent murder.

4:11. *Now, cursed are you from the soil, which opened its mouth to take your brother's blood from your hand.* Cain's punishment severs his relationship to the soil. This is an extension and echo of Yahweh's punishment of the man in Eden—compare the curses, *'ārûr 'āttâ min-hā 'ădāmâ* ("cursed are you from the soil") with *'ărûrâ hā 'ădāmâ ba'ăbûrekā* ("cursed is the soil because of you," 3:17). This involves, of course, the Leitwort *hā 'ădāmâ* ("soil"). Cain had been an *'ōbēd 'ădāmâ* ("worker of the soil," 4:2), the role allotted to the man in Eden (3:17–19). He had offered a sacrifice from *pərî hā 'ădāmâ* ("the fruit of the soil," 4:3). Now, because he shed his brother's blood on the soil—a perversion of agriculture and sacrifice—his bond with the soil is severed. He can neither work the soil nor be at home on it.

The statement that Cain is cursed *min-hā 'ădāmâ*, with the preposition *min* ("from") used in a partitive sense, "away from," involves a separation from the arable land, entailing the loss of his livelihood as farmer and an exile from settled communities. It is an occupational change *and* a geographical separation.

The gruesome image of the personified soil "which opened its mouth to take your brother's blood from your hand" is a play on the proper cultivation of the earth. A farmer feeds the soil with water, not his brother's blood. By this grotesque inversion of agriculture, Cain earns his curse from the soil. Note the emphatic repetition of the possessive pronoun, indicating the guilty party: "*your* brother's blood from *your* hand."

As in Eden, the punishment fits the crime. This correspondence is highlighted by an artful chiasm: *dəmê ʾāḥîkā . . . min-hā ʾădāmâ* ("your brother's blood . . . from the soil," 4:10) and *min-hā ʾădāmâ . . . dəmê ʾăḥîkā* ("from the soil . . . your brother's blood," 4:11). The punishment is presented as cause and effect: because your brother's blood (A) cried out from the soil (B), you are cursed from the soil (B), which received your brother's blood (A). Yahweh's verdict is poetic justice.

4:12. *When you work the soil it will no longer yield its strength to you.* This punishment echoes Cain's identity as an *ʿōbēd ʾădāmâ* ("worker of the soil"). The arable soil, still personified, will not give its strength to Cain because it received Abel's strength—his lifeblood—from Cain's hand. There is a logical progression in the soil's actions, from *lāqaḥat* ("to *take* . . . from your hand," 4:11) to *tēt* ("no longer *give* . . . to you," 4:12), again showing that the punishment fits the crime.

You shall be a restless wanderer on the earth. The phrase *nāʿ wānād* ("restless wanderer") is an alliterative hendiadys, like *tōhû wābōhû* ("desolate chaos") in 1:2. The two words are synonyms for "wanderer." This construction conveys an intensive or emphatic sense, as well as having internal rhyme. The verbal form *nāʿ* can also have the sense of "tremble (with fear)," and it is possible that this sense of trembling accompanies the idea of being a restless wanderer.

The *hā ʾāreṣ* ("the earth") which Cain must wander has a different referential scope from *hā ʾădāmâ* ("the soil") from which he is cursed. The contrast is between arable land and the wider world. Because he has shown himself to be uncivilized, Cain is banished from the civilized regions, the land of the sown, to the wild world. He is in exile from the soil of human culture. There may be a thematic intensification in this punishment with Cain's words to Abel, "Let us go out to the field" (4:7). Since the intent of these words is to take Abel out of the domain of human habitation, so that there will be no one to hear his cry, it is apt that Cain's punishment takes him farther away from human settlements to the "land of Wandering" (*ʾereṣ-nôd*, 4:16), where murder goes unpunished (4:14). In this respect Cain's murderous plan turns on him.

The punishments of exile and wandering are found elsewhere in the Bible, for example, "Let his children wander (*nôaʿ yānûʿû*) and beg, and seek (food) out of their desolate places" (Ps 109:10); "God was angry against Israel, and he made them wander (*waynîʿēm*) in the wilderness for forty years" (Num 32:13). For murder, a capital offense, the punishment is death (Gen 9:6, Exod 21:12), but in practice a murderer can also be exiled. So David allows Absalom to go in exile and commutes the bloodguilt of the woman of Tekoa's fictive son—both for crimes of fratricide (2 Sam 13:37–38, 14:11). Yahweh's choice of exile and wandering as punishment may involve a degree of mercy, an alternative way to absolve the bloodguilt of murder in a way that does not eliminate the sole surviving son.

Exile is a form of social death, a severing of one's identity as a member of family and community. This form of punishment occurs in many societies, as in pre-Islamic Arab culture: "If a person had committed a crime within his own kinship group or threatened their peace and stability, then that group might decide to banish him from their presence and protection. This meant that a person's blood was licit, and he was forced to live as an outlaw" (Hoyland 2001: 124). This description precisely fits Cain's punishment. A similar punishment of wandering is found in a curse inscribed in an Assyrian royal tomb at Calah, directed at the spirit of any future grave robber: "let his spirit wander in thirst in the open country" (Al-Rawi 2008: 119–24, lines 13–14). The outside land is a liminal zone filled with danger for those condemned to wander.

4:13. *Cain said to Yahweh, "My punishment is more than I can bear."* With this reply, Cain seems crushed by the consequences of his crime. The word *'āwōn* ("punishment") has several meanings, which deepens his response: (1) a sin or misdeed, (2) the guilt that is a consequence of a sin or misdeed, and (3) the punishment for a sin or misdeed (*HALOT,* 800). Because of the semantic link between sin and punishment in this and some other words, scholars have suggested that in Israelite thought sin entails both guilt and punishment, what Koch (1983) calls the "sin-disaster connection." Something like this concept shapes the correspondence of sin and punishment in the stories of Eden and Cain, although Yahweh's agency and moral authority as judge should not be downplayed (see Barton 2014: 211–26).

Because of this semantic multivalence, early interpreters often understood Cain's outburst as the first act of repentance, reading it as "my sin (or guilt) is more than I can bear" or "my sin (or guilt) is too great to forgive" (already in the LXX; see Kugel 1998: 155). But the ambiguity that allows for these divergent readings is clarified in the next verse—Cain is speaking about his punishment, not out of remorse for his sin or guilt. The openness of his initial statement may raise a brief hope that Cain has begun to change and to master sin (as Yahweh exhorts in 4:7), but this hope diminishes as his speech continues.

4:14. *You have banished me today from the face of the soil, and I will be hidden from your face.* Cain's summary of his punishment echoes the end of the Eden story, "He banished (*waygāreš*) the man . . ." (3:24). The banishment now goes further—whereas the man and woman were banished from the Garden of Eden, Cain is now banished from the whole *pənê hāʾădāmâ* ("face of the soil"). Humans are exiled from paradise, and Cain is exiled from the habitable earth. This cultural and geographical exile, as Cain points out, is also a religious exile from Yahweh's presence.

The diction of Cain's complaint builds from *pənê hāʾădāmâ* ("face of the soil") to *ûmippānêkā ʾessater* ("and from your face I will be hidden"). He equates the exile from the land with an exile from God. The semantics of "face" shifts in this sentence from "surface" to "presence," while the verbal image of God's "face" retains a visual connotation (as when God's face "shines upon you," Num 6:25). Exile now seems to be a spiritual as well as a social death.

To be hidden from Yahweh's face/presence is a terrifying concept in biblical writings. It does not mean that Yahweh is absent in an absolute sense, but that he withdraws from his relationship to a person or people. His blessing and protection are withdrawn. So Yahweh warns Moses: "On that day my anger will burn against them and I will abandon them and hide my face from them; they will be easy prey, and many evils and troubles will find them" (Deut 31:17). In Psalms, the opposite of God's "hiding the face" is his responsive presence: "He did not hide his face from him, and when he cried out to him, he heard" (Ps 22:25). When Cain laments that he will be "hidden from your face," he implies that Yahweh will no longer protect him. He will be on his own, vulnerable and frail, easy prey. Note also the progression from Cain's "fallen face" to his exile from the "soil's face" and banishment from Yahweh's "face"—another correspondence of moral fault and its consequences.

I will be a restless wanderer on the earth, and whoever meets me will kill me. Cain draws out the danger of his exile from the face of the soil and Yahweh's face. Outside of cultivated land and civilization, there is no civil justice and, as Cain assumes, no divine justice or protection. Hence a *nāʿ wānād* ("restless wanderer") is vulnerable to one and all. This is an image of wild nature, the opposite of civilization, in which, as Hobbes famously observed, there are "no arts; no letters; no society; and which is worst of all, continual fear and danger of violent death" (*Leviathan,* ch. 13). This Hobbesian picture corresponds to the general ancient Near Eastern image of the danger and lawlessness of primitive times, which still exists outside the boundaries of civilization.

As many commentators have observed, Cain's complaint presupposes that there are other people in the world who could meet him and kill him. This situation clashes with the narrative context in J in which the only other people alive are Adam and Eve. Who are these other people whom Cain fears? The number of possibilities is limited. The P source states that Adam "fathered sons and daughters" (5:4). The J source may presume the same tradition, in which case Cain may be anticipating other members of his family traveling in the outlands who might execute him for blood vengeance or kill him for no cause (cf. Lamech's violence in 4:23).

But Cain's complaint is not directed at family members; the term *kol-mōṣaʾî* ("anyone who finds me" or "whoever meets me") refers to people generally. As we have noted (INTRODUCTION I), the Cain and Abel story seems to presume a narrative context other than its placement in J directly after the Garden of Eden story. In a different narrative context, the reference to other humans would be unproblematic, as would the later reference to Cain's wife (4:17). The puzzle of Cain's potential encounter with other people is most plausibly a consequence of the literary linkage of two stories that may have previously circulated in other configurations. The numerous verbal echoes show that the two stories have been artfully joined, but the gaps and frictions that remain testify to a legacy of other forms of the stories in prior narrative traditions.

4:15. *Yahweh said to him, "Therefore, whoever kills Cain will suffer vengeance sevenfold."* Yahweh acknowledges that Cain's complaint is justified, since a punishment of wandering and exile should not entail violent death. Yahweh adds provisions to protect Cain from murder. There is some irony in this gesture of divine protection. "Am I my brother's keeper?" was Cain's evasive reply to Yahweh, but now Yahweh becomes Cain's protector. In a sense, Cain's cunning question is undermined by his own plea for protection, and Yahweh grants to Cain what he denied his own brother. This modification of Cain's punishment may be a gesture of mercy. But Yahweh's response to Cain's complaint also ensures that his intention will be carried out—Cain will be a "restless wanderer in the world" and not a victim of murder (Golka 1980: 69).

The meaning of *šibʿātayim* ("sevenfold") vengeance is unclear. The bloodguilt for murder usually requires that the murderer be executed or make restitution. In some cases additional family members may be killed to avenge the bloodguilt of one person. An example is the execution of seven of Saul's sons to atone for Saul's bloodguilt in slaying the Gibeonites (2 Sam 21:1–9). Some commentators suggest that sevenfold vengeance means that seven of his kin (including the murderer) will be executed to atone for the bloodguilt of murdering Cain. In this case, however, it may be a rhetorical emphasis for "complete" vengeance.

Yahweh placed a sign on Cain so that whoever met him would not kill him. Yahweh marks Cain with a protective *'ôt* ("sign"). The type of sign is not specified (see Day 2022: 91–92). A close analogy is the mark placed on enslaved people to identify their status as slave. According to biblical law, a Hebrew debtor slave who wishes to remain a slave after seven years is marked by having his ear pierced with an awl by his master (Exod 21:6, Deut 15:17). Other marks for slaves are attested in Mesopotamia. The name of the slave owner could be branded with a red-hot iron on the slave's hand, or the slave's ears could be pierced, as in Israel. Another type of mark, the *abbuttum,* was "probably a special mark placed on the shaven head" of a slave (Dandamayev 1992: 60). Yahweh's sign on Cain is similar in function to these slave marks, since it displays to others that Cain is under the protection of his master. Another parallel is the "mark" (*tāw,* referring to the *X*-shaped *taw* in paleo-Hebrew) that Yahweh instructs an angel to place on the foreheads of those in Jerusalem who bewail the people's abominations, and only those with the mark are spared from being killed (Ezek 9:3–7).

The motive clause, "so that whoever met him would not kill (*hakkôt*) him," echoes and varies the previous diction, "whoever meets me will kill me (*yəhargēnî*)" (4:14) and "whoever kills (*hōrēg*) Cain" (4:15). These variations create an artful repetition of the image of someone murdering Cain and recalls the severity of Cain's crime—*wayyahargēhû* ("and he killed him," 4:8). Again, the conditions of the punishment respond directly or indirectly to the crime itself.

4:16. *Cain departed from Yahweh's presence and dwelled in the land of Wandering, east of Eden.* The first clause can be rendered simply as "Cain departed from Yahweh (*millipnê yhwh*)." The compound preposition *millipnê* means "from before" or "from the presence of," and in this context it is also an echo of the *pənê yhwh,* "face of Yahweh" (4:14). By this wordplay the feared outcome that "I will be hidden from your face" is accomplished.

Beyond Yahweh's presence is the *'ereṣ-nôd* ("the land of Wandering"). This land is the geographical correlate of Cain's identity as a *nā' wānād* ("restless wanderer"). With this wordplay—the *nād* ("wanderer") who dwells in the land of *nôd* ("Wandering")—Cain begins his exile in a restless and rootless land, beyond civilization. The location of this land, *qidmat-'ēden* ("east of Eden"), echoes the locale of the previous story, where Eden is *miqqedem* ("in the east," 2:8), and its fearsome guards are *miqqedem ləgan-'ēden* ("east of the Garden of Eden," 3:24). The last words of this narrative segment recall the end of the Eden story, tying the two scenes of exile together. The paradise of Eden is gone, and Cain now dwells in a land that is even farther from Eden—homeless, unfruitful, solitary, violent, and apart from Yahweh's presence.

4:17–24. The second part of the story tells of Cain's descendants, culminating in the speech of Lamech, whose lawlessness and violence make him the ultimate descendant of Cain. Curiously, among the Cainites are cultural heroes: Cain builds the first city, and Lamech's three sons are the ancestors of mobile herdsmen, musicians, and metalworkers. These cultural inventions are partially motivated by wordplays with the name of Cain (*qayin*). There is a mixed message in the account of Cain's descendants— on the one hand the account culminates in total lawlessness; on the other, several valuable institutions of human culture are founded by these ancients. This mixture may suggest that civilization itself is tinged with violence (see INTRODUCTION IV).

It is customary in Genesis to list the descendants of the nonlineal ancestors before returning to the main narrative of the ancestors of Israel. So Cain's descendants are listed, and then the narrative returns to the line of Seth. Later Japheth's and Ham's descendants are listed, and then the narrative returns to Shem (Genesis 10). This pattern continues in the patriarchal narratives, as in the listing of Nahor's descendants (22:20–24), then returning to Abraham's family; and listing Esau's descendants (Genesis 36), then returning to Jacob's family.

The descendants of Cain in Genesis 4 (J) and the descendants of Adam (through Seth) in Genesis 5 (P) appear to be biforms of an old genealogical tradition (see COMMENTS).

4:17. *Cain knew his wife, and she conceived and gave birth to Enoch.* This verse echoes, with variations, the beginning of the story: "The man knew Eve, his wife, and she conceived and gave birth to Cain" (4:1). Although the grammar makes it continuous with the previous verse (note the succession of converted imperfect verbs), this verse signals a new beginning, marked by a new birth. The final segment of the story begins similarly (4:25).

In this new beginning, Cain's wife is not named, in contrast to Eve in 4:1. Cain's wife is anonymous and mysterious, since it is unclear how she came to exist (cf. Wyatt 1986). This gap in the story probably points to other tellings of the tale in which this story was not the direct sequel to the Garden of Eden story (see NOTES at 4:15). Early interpreters solved the problem of the origin of Cain's wife by reading this verse in conjunction with Gen 5:4, "(Adam) fathered sons and daughters," inferring that Cain married one of his sisters (e.g., Jub. 4:9; see Kugel 1998: 148–49).

The name of Cain's son Enoch (*ḥănôk*) means "dedicated," perhaps a short form (hypocoristicon) of the name "dedicated to/of God." Compare the pattern of the name Zadok (*ṣādôq*), "righteousness," which is a short form of a longer name, for example, Zedekiah (*ṣidqiyyāhû*), "Yahweh is my righteousness." In its present context, the meaning "dedicated" may be connected to the building of the city, which was "dedicated" by the name of Enoch (Cassuto 1961: 229). According to Deut 20:5, it was the custom to "dedicate" (*ḥānak*) a new house (cf. 1 Kgs 8:63, where Solomon "dedicated" [*wayyaḥnəkû*] the temple).

Enoch is the name of a son of Midian in the J list of the descendants of Abraham and Keturah (Gen 25:4). In the P lists, Enoch is the name of Reuben's first son (Gen 46:9, Exod 6:14, Num 26:5). These texts suggest that Enoch was a tribe or group in southern Transjordan or northern Arabia, which came to be associated with the Transjordanian lineage of Israel. Knauf (1988: 81–84) has noted a south Arabian tribe called the *banū l-Ḥanīk* ("children of the expert"?), which may have north Arabian roots and may be relevant. The geographical and ethnic setting of the Midianite Enoch may relate to the Kenite connection of the Cainites (Day 2022: 99). There is no known city named Enoch, although the next verse posits one. There is possibly a relationship with the "cities of the Kenites" (1 Sam 30:29).

In the P Sethite genealogy in Genesis 5, *ḥănôk* (Enoch) is the son of Jared and the father of Methuselah (5:18–24), and he dies mysteriously: "Enoch walked with God and then was no more, for God took him" (5:24). In the J Cainite genealogy, he is Cain's son and the father of Irad (the parallel of Jared), with no mention of his death. It is possible that the idea of a man "dedicated" to God inspired the idea of Enoch's exalted status in Genesis 5.

He built a city and named the city after Enoch, his son. The sequence *wayhî bōneh ʿîr,* literally "he was the builder of a city," recalls the verbal structure of Abel's and Cain's occupations (a construct phrase consisting of participle + noun: *rōʿēh ṣōʾn* ("herder of sheep") and *ʿōbēd ʾădāmâ* ("worker of soil"), which are narrated immediately after they are born (4:2). This parallel may suggest that the occupation here should be that of the son, not the father (so Cassuto 1961: 229–30). Further, if the builder were Enoch, and he named the city after his son, Irad, there would be a wordplay between *ʿîr* ("city") and *ʿîrād* (Irad) (Sasson 1978: 174). But in the text the subject is clearly Cain, since the city is named *kəšēm bənô ḥănôk* ("after the name of his son, Enoch"), hence the builder must be Enoch's father (R. R. Wilson 1977: 139–40). Part of the connection between father and son is contained in the wordplay between *bōneh* ("builder") and *bənô* ("his son").

Cain's role as builder of the first city is curious since this seem to violate his sentence to be a "restless wanderer on the earth." Perhaps he builds the city for his children who are not condemned to wander, which motivates naming the city after his son (Seebass 1996: 167). Or this action could stem from a multiform of the story of Cain that does not include a sentence of perpetual wandering.

The association of Cain with the first city may also suggest that cities are places of violence or lawlessness, a fear that comes to fruition in the story of the Tower of Babel in 11:1–9. Those builders "journeyed in the east" (11:2)—recalling the direction of Cain's wanderings "east of Eden" (4:16). Yet outside of the primeval narrative there is no indication that cities are inherently bad. For example, God promises to give the Israelites "large and good cities, which you did not build" (Deut 6:10; see Westermann 1984: 328).

4:18. *To Enoch was born Irad, and Irad fathered Mehiyael, and Mehiyael fathered Methushael, and Methushael fathered Lamech.* The sequence of the genealogy, Cain— Enoch—Irad—Mehiyael—Methushael—Lamech, is clearly related to the sequence in the Sethite genealogy in Genesis 5. Each name has a matching variant: Cain/ Kenan (both begin with the letter *qop*), Enoch/Enoch, Irad/Jared, Mehiyael/Mahalalel, Methushael/Methuselah, Lamech/Lamech. The only difference of sequence is that of Enoch—Irad—Mehiyael (Genesis 4), which in Genesis 5 is reversed: Mahalalel— Jared—Enoch. These variations are best explained by positing differing oral versions of this genealogy in Israelite tradition, one preserved in J (Genesis 4) and the other preserved in P (Genesis 5), while each author may have revised details in the inherited traditions (see COMMENTS).

The etymology of the name *ʿîrād* (Irad) is obscure. It may mean "wild ass, onager" (Hebrew *ʿārôd;* Arabic *ʿard*), from the category of animal names used as personal names. This word is used for personal names in Amorite and Neo-Babylonian (Hess 1993: 40). In its narrative context, *ʿîrād* suggests a wordplay with the *ʿîr* ("city") of 4:17. Some have suggested that Irad may be a reminiscence of the Sumerian city Eridu (Hallo 1970: 64), but this seems unlikely, and the guttural *ʿayin* is an obstacle in this equation. The parallel name in Genesis 5 is *yered* (Jared, 5:16–20). Jared is arguably a later form of the same name, reflecting a weakening of the guttural *ʿayin.*

The name Mehiyael (*məḥiyyā'ēl*) appears to be a *piel* or possibly *hiphil* participle of *ḥyy*, meaning "to enliven," plus the word for god, *'ēl* (*HALOT*, 568). Such a name, which would be vocalized *məḥayyī'ēl* (*piel*) or *maḥyī'ēl* (*hiphil*), meaning "God enlivens," would refer to the birth of the child. Names with this root are common in the West Semitic onomasticon (Hess 1993: 41–43). In its MT vocalization, the word has apparently been connected with the root *mḥy*, "to strike, smite," and taken to mean "stricken, smitten of God" (cf. *məḥî* "stroke," in Ezek 26:9). This meaning may have been derived from the context of Cain's punishment. The parallel name in Genesis 5 is Mahalalel (*mahălal'ēl*, 5:12–17), probably reflecting a weakening of the guttural *ḥet*.

The name Methushael (*mətûšā'ēl*) is an archaic form, meaning "man of God" (cf. Layton 1990: 66–72; Hess 1993: 43–45). The first element, *mətû* ("man"), reflects **mutu,* with the old nominative case ending *-u*. The second element, *šā* ("of"), is the relative *ša* known from Akkadian and early Hebrew (cf. Judg 5:7, *šaqqāmtî*, from *ša* + *qāmtî*), which becomes *še* in later Biblical Hebrew. This element occurs elsewhere in the biblical personal name Mishael (*mîšā'ēl*, "who is of God?," Exod 6:22) and in the name of a Middle Babylonian physician, *Raba-ša-Marduk* ("great one of Marduk," Beckman 1999: 143). The third element is *'ēl,* "God." Similar names are common in West Semitic tradition—compare Amorite *mutu-Dagan,* "man of Dagan," and Ugaritic *mtb'l,* "man of Baal"—but there is no exact cognate to Methushael. The parallel name in Genesis 5 is Methuselah (*mətûšelaḥ,* "man of Shelah"?, 5:22–27), which differs in the final sequence: *'aleph—lamed* versus *lamed—ḥet.* It is not clear how to account for this variation of *lamed* and guttural consonant.

The meaning of Lamech's name (*lemek, lāmek* in pause) is obscure. It may mean "powerful man" (cf. Arabic *yalmak* [*HALOT*, 532]). The name *lamki* (the ancestral form of Hebrew *lemek/lāmek*) is found at Mari in the early second millennium BCE (Hess 1993: 46). In Genesis 5, Lamech is the father of Noah (5:25–31). There is an interesting relationship between these two versions of Lamech: one is the epitome of violence and lawlessness, and the other is the father of the righteous man who survives the flood, which was caused by the excess of human violence. One can imagine a version of the story in which Lamech the father of Noah is the same as Lamech the man of violence. The violent Lamech of Genesis 4 is in the seventh generation, often a special place in biblical genealogies (cf. Enoch as the seventh generation in Genesis 5; Sasson 1978: 173).

4:19. *Lamech took two wives for himself, the first named Ada and the second Zillah.* The vertical genealogy descending from Cain now spreads horizontally to include Lamech's wives and four children. Perhaps the wives are named to provide a context for the Song of Lamech, which refers to them.

Lamech is the first man with multiple wives in the Bible, followed by Abraham (Gen 25:1), Jacob (Genesis 29), Esau (Gen 26:34, 28:8), Elkanah (1 Sam 1:2), Boaz (Ruth 1:1), David (2 Sam 3:2–5), and Solomon (1 Kgs 11:3) (Perdue et al., 1997: 64, 121–22). Deuteronomic law regulates inheritance rights in cases of polygamy (Deut 21:15–17). Although polygamy was an option in Israelite society, during the monarchy it may have become rare outside of the royal family. According to the implications of Gen 1:27 (P) and 3:22–23 (J), monogamy was the ideal, as in the marriage of Adam and Eve.

The name of Lamech's first wife, Ada (*'ādâ*), means "ornament," from the root *'dy*, as in the longer personal name *'ădî'ēl,* "ornament of God" (1 Chr 4:36, 9:12). The short

Figure 8. West Semitic traders or service nomads, arriving in Egypt carrying skin bellows (?) for metalwork, a lyre for entertainment, and galena or black eye-paint (Kamrin 2009). The leader, Abi-ša(r), at the right, makes a gesture of submission and offers an ibex and gazelle to the "Administrator of the Eastern Desert," Khnumhotep II (not shown). Wall painting (detail restored), tomb of Khnumhotep II (ca. 1880 BCE), Beni Hassan, Egypt. (Drawing by William H. C. Propp)

form is also found in Ugaritic (*'dy*), and numerous other West Semitic names have this root (Hess 1993: 47–48). This name has an association with the region of Edom, since Esau has a wife named Ada, whose son Eliphaz (whose concubine is Timnah, the great copper mining site) and grandsons are clans and places in Edom (Gen 36:2–16; Sawyer 1986: 159)

The name of Lamech's second wife, Zillah (*ṣillâ*), is from the root *ṣll*, which has several meanings in Hebrew. The sense most used in names is "shade, protection," as in Bezalel (*bəṣal'ēl*), "in the shadow/protection of God" (Exod 31:2, etc.). Numerous other Hebrew and West Semitic names have this root (Hess 1993: 48–49). In the context of the Cainite genealogy, the meaning "little bell" (*məṣillâ,* Zech 14:20) might resonate in the name of Zillah (*ṣillâ*)—note that she is the mother of Naamah, whose name may be associated with music.

4:20–22. Lamech's three sons—Jabal, Jubal, and Tubal-Cain—are the founding fathers of nomadic herders, musicians, and metalworkers, respectively. Their names are all variations of the root *ybl,* "to bring," hence they are the "bringers" of these cultural vocations. These vocations all seem connected to the name and vocations of the Kenites (*qênî*) and their eponymous ancestor Cain (*qayin*) (Cassuto 1961: 235; Halpern 1992: 17–18). The description of the vocations of each of these cultural heroes follows a similar pattern: "father" or "father of all who" + participle(s) + double object. Their names and their vocations have an interconnecting rhythm.

4:20. *Ada gave birth to Jabal—he was the father of herdsmen who dwell in tents.* Jabal is the *'ăbî yōšēb 'ōhel ûmiqneh,* literally "father of those who dwell in tents and (with) herds." Jabal is the ancestor of herders who move seasonally—and hence dwell in tents—following the pasturage. These are mobile pastoralists. This differs from the category of sedentary herders in an agro-pastoral family setting, as is Abel's occupation. But there may be an echo between Jabal and Abel in the similar features of their names and occupations. The word *ûmiqneh* ("and herds") is a bit elliptical in this grammatical sequence, but the sense is clear, and it provides a wordplay with *qênî* (Kenites). This vocation seems to have been led by some Kenites, for example, Jael and Heber in Judges

4–5, who live in a tent and have dairy products at hand, indicating herds. The word *ʾăbî* ("father") has the extended sense of "founder" or "originator" as well as the genealogical sense of ancestor (*HALOT,* 1).

4:21. *His brother's name was Jubal—he was the father of all who play lyres and pipes.* Jubal is the founding father of musicians, who play the lyre (*kinnôr*), a stringed instrument of the harp family, and the *ʿûgāb,* perhaps a flute or other wind instrument. The targums translate as flute, but the LXX translates as harp. There are analogies with other tribal groups that specialize in metalworking, music, and other crafts, as in the West Semitic clan pictured in the Egyptian Beni Hassan relief bearing metalworking tools and musical instruments. There may be an implicit wordplay with Jubal's profession and the root *qyn,* one of whose meanings has to do with making music and singing (cf. Hebrew *qînâ* ["elegy, lament, funeral song"], Ethiopic *qanaya* ["to make music"], and Arabic *qaynat* ["songstress"]) (*HALOT,* 1097).

4:22. *As for Zillah, she too gave birth to Tubal-Cain, [the father of all who] work metal, forging bronze and iron.* After Jabal and Jubal, one expects the third son to be Tubal (*tûbāl*), a t-preformative noun from the root *ybl.* The addition of Cain (*qayin*) to his name may indicate that the meaning *qayin* ("metalsmith") is operating here, since that is Tubal's legacy. Tubal-Cain's name also has an association with the place name Tubal (Gen 10:2, Ezek 27:13), a Neo-Hittite kingdom in Asia Minor that was a center of metallurgy. The region of Tubal traded in "bronze implements" (*kəlê nəḥōšet,* Ezek 27:13). Tubal-Cain is the ancestor of metalworkers, including those in Tubal.

The description of Tubal-Cain's vocation is grammatically difficult. He is the ancestor of *lōṭēš kol-ḥōrēš nəḥōšet ûbarzel,* literally "those who sharpen, all who forge bronze and iron." This difficult sequence requires *ʾăbî* ("father") or *ʾăbî kol-* ("father of all who") for it to make sense (see Textual Note g) (cf. *ʾăbî* and *ʾăbî kol-* in the parallel expressions for Jabal and Jubal). The rest of the sequence is also difficult, particularly the redundancy of *lōṭēš* ("those who sharpen") and *kol-ḥōrēš* ("all who forge"). The original text was probably something like *ʾăbî kol-lōṭēš nəḥōšet ûbarzel* ("father of all who sharpen bronze and iron"), that is, metalworkers, which is stylistically parallel to Jabal's and Jubal's descriptions. The awkward and redundant phrase *kol-ḥōrēš* ("all who forge") can easily be viewed as an explicating plus, inserted by a later scribe to explain the obscure word *lōṭēš.* In this explanation, the awkward grammar of the present text is explicable by ordinary scribal practices (Hendel 1998: 48). Even in its present difficult state, the sense is relatively clear. In many cultures metalworking is associated with violence and war (Sawyer 1986: 156–57), and hence both the name and occupation of Tubal-Cain make him an apt descendant of the violent Cain.

Tubal-Cain's sister was Naamah. Naamah is the first daughter or sister named in Genesis. Like Dinah, Jacob's sole daughter (Gen 30:22), she lacks the distinguishing textual traits—an occupation, a naming speech—granted to her older brothers. The name Naamah (*na'ămâ*) has several resonances. The root *n'm*, meaning "to be pleasant, lovely," is common in personal names (Hess 1993: 54–55); compare Naomi (*no'ŏmî*, "my lovely"), Ruth's mother-in-law. Another meaning of this root, found in several Northwest Semitic languages (but not attested in Biblical Hebrew), is "to sing." In this semantic association, Naamah's name may ring with her mother Zillah's name and her brother Jubal's musical occupation. Her name may also have a connection with the metalworking region of the Arabah, since Naamah is the home of Zophar (Job 2:11) and is presumably located in Edom or Midian (Sawyer 1986: 159). In these associations of her name, she is an apt sibling of Jubal and Tubal-Cain.

4:23–24. The Song of Lamech is a boasting or taunting song, in which he claims that his ferocity is even greater than Cain's. It depicts a situation in which there are no limits on revenge, evoking a sense of total lawlessness. The transition from Cain to Lamech is therefore a progression from bad to worse, culminating in unbridled violence worthy of a flood.

As elsewhere (cf. 1:27, 2:23), the prose narrative transitions into poetry—often the poetry of reported speech—at a decisive moment. Since the Song of Lamech tells how he killed a man, it enters into the semantic domain of a *qînâ*, a lament or funeral song. But since this song is a boast of murder and limitless revenge, it represents an uncivilized inversion of a *qînâ*. Formally the song consists of three couplets, each of which exhibits parallelism on various levels, creating a tightly structured expression of brute violence.

4:23. *Lamech said to his wives: "Ada and Zillah, hear my voice, / Lamech's wives, listen to my speech. / A man I have killed for wounding me, / a boy for bruising me."* The opening clause, "Lamech said to his wives," frames the poetic discourse. This is Lamech's first and only speech, which reveals his immorality. The prosody of the first two couplets is as follows:

'ādâ wəṣillâ šəma'an qôlî	Ada and Zillah, hear my voice,
nəšě lemek ha'zēnnâ 'imrātî	Lamech's wives, listen to my speech.
kî 'iš hāragtî ləpiṣ'î	A man I have killed for wounding me,
wəyeled ləhabbūrātî	a boy for bruising me.

The key formal feature—synonymous parallelism with a variety of intensifications—can be mapped as A B C // A′ B′ C′ and A B C // A′ C′.

The parallelism in the first couplet is "Ada and Zillah" // "Lamech's wives"; "hear" // "listen"; and "my voice" // "my speech." In each, subtle semantic shifts intensify the diction (see Alter 2011: 4–7). In the first line, the women are hailed as separate individuals. In the second Lamech intensifies his claim on their attention—they are "Lamech's wives," which shows his claim on them and their obligation to attend and obey him. Similarly, the verb "hear" (*šəma'an*) is stylistically intensified by "listen" (*ha'zēnâ*, a denominative *hiphil* from *'ōzen*, "ear"), a poetic word with a higher register, which has the sense of "listen closely, heed carefully." Similarly, "my voice" (*qôlî*) is intensified with "my speech" (*'imrātî*), another poetic word with a higher register, which specifies a discourse, referring to the poetic speech-act. The parallel effects of this couplet, when read attentively (as Lamech requests), draw the audience—Ada, Zillah, and the readers/ hearers—into Lamech's poetic performance.

The second couplet reveals Lamech's violent act (or acts), which is the occasion for his taunt poem. He revels in having murdered someone, or perhaps two people, as revenge for a wound. The ambiguities of this couplet are part of its rhetorical effect—it piles up violent images, even if the events are unclear. As in the first couplet, there is an intensifying parallelism between the two lines. The word "man" (*'îš*) is seconded by "boy" (*yeled*), which makes Lamech's murder in the second line more heinous. The parallelism of *piṣ'î* ("my wound," translated as "wounding me") and *ḥabbūrātî* ("my bruise," translated as "bruising me") may have a subtle intensification from general to concrete, since the latter has a visual sense of "slash, stripe."

The governing verb in the second couplet, *hāragtî*, is most easily read as a past punctual event, "I killed." It is also possible to read it as an expression of timeless intent (the "gnomic" perfect), "I kill" or "I would kill" (so Kugel 1981: 32; but cf. Dillmann 1897: 206). In the context of a man informing his wives of his violent deeds, the past punctual sense may be preferable. Further, the parallel with Cain's murder of Abel makes an actual (rather than generalized) murder thematically apt.

What is unclear is whether the parallelism of "man" and "boy" refers to the same person or two people ("a man and a boy") (see Miller 1966). The dynamics of parallelism can go either way. The word *yeled* can mean someone older than a boy (e.g., *haylādîm,* "the young men" in 1 Kgs 12:8), but Lamech's boast of extreme violence and excessive revenge is better served by maximal carnage in this verse—that is, two murders, first a man and then a boy. This would have the effect of making Lamech a double murderer, including a boy—worse than Cain. The ambiguity of the murder(s)—is it one or two?—focuses attention on Lamech's barbarity, rather than on the body count. That he would boast of killing a "boy" puts Lamech outside the pale of civilization.

There is also a rhyming effect in these two couplets. The four lines all end with *-î* ("my," the first-person pronominal suffix). The end-line rhymes are about "my voice," "my speech," "my wound," "my bruise." Lamech's song is all about "me," a violent Song of Myself.

4:24. *"If Cain is avenged sevenfold, / Lamech will be seventy-seven-fold."* In the final couplet Lamech turns the focus to a comparison with Cain. Having shown that his violence exceeds Cain's, he elaborates on Yahweh's previous statement "whoever kills Cain will suffer vengeance sevenfold" (4:15). Lamech boasts by saying that his vengeance also exceeds Cain's.

The prosody is as follows (the translation reflects the word order):

kî šib'ātayim yuqqam-qāyin	If sevenfold is avenged Cain,
wəlemek šib'îm wəšib'â	Lamech will be seventy-seven-fold.

The semantic parallelism is A B C // C' A', varying the form of the previous couplets. This couplet has a chiastic form, in which the first and last elements of the first line (A and C) are reversed in the second line (C' and A'). The parallelism, as before, has an intensifying force. "Sevenfold" (*šib'ātayim*) is increased exponentially to "seventy-seven-fold" (*šib'îm wəšib'â*) in the second line. This exemplifies the incremental numerical parallelism of biblical poetry (e.g., "Saul has slain his thousands; and David his tens of thousands," 1 Sam 18:7). The progression here also involves a verbal doubling, as *šib'ātayim* is intensified to *šib'îm wəšib'â* ("seventy and seven"). The parallel numbers have an internal rhythm, ending in doubled sevens.

The name "Cain" in the first line is intensified in the second by the greater murderer, "Lamech." The latter name is grammatically disjunctive (clause-initial, prefixed by *waw*), making it emphatic and focused ("as for Lamech . . ."). In the first line the accents land on *táyim* and *qáyin,* creating an internal rhyme between the number (*šib'ātayim,* "sevenfold") and the name of Cain (*qayin*).

In Lamech's world, the violent man prevails. But in the ancient civilized world, tribal and state law provided judicial control on personal violence and revenge. As Westbrook (1992: 548) comments, "Uncontrolled revenge was considered the antithesis of legal order, as in the boast of Lamech, which typified the wicked, lawless society before the Flood." The Song of Lamech is the last word of the Cainite genealogy, and it is a vivid poetic expression of sheer barbarity, which provides a concrete backdrop to Yahweh's decision to send a flood.

4:25–26. The final section of the Cain and Abel story returns to Adam and Eve and the birth of a new child, whose lineage will lead in a different direction than the lineage of Cain. The end of the story returns to its beginning and offers a new, more hopeful path. As elsewhere, the glimpse at the future descendants of a nonlineal ancestor (Cain) loops back to the central branch of the genealogy.

4:25. *Adam knew his wife, and she gave birth to a son.* This verse echoes the beginning of the previous two sections: "The man knew Eve, his wife, and she conceived and gave birth" (4:1) and "Cain knew his wife, and she conceived and gave birth" (4:17). The small variations are revealing: "the man" (*hā'ādām*) is now for the first time referred to as Adam ('*ādām*), a personal name (lacking the definite article *ha-*). This places Adam on the same level as Eve (and unlike the anonymous wife of Cain). The shift of '*ādām* ("man/human") to Adam is presumably contextually motivated. As Dillmann (1897: 207) observes, now there are other men about, and so the term '*ādām* "for the first man, must necessarily become a proper name." Adam, now properly named, begins to fade into the background as the generations progress.

She named him Seth, "For God has set me another seed to take the place of Abel, for Cain killed him." Eve again names her child, as she did with Cain, describing him as a replacement for Abel. The name Seth (*šēt*) is a play on her phrase "God has set (*šāt*)." A similar personal name is found in Phoenician, *b'lšt,* "Baal has placed (a son)" (Hess 1993: 66). Seth is also the name of the eponymous ancestor of "the children of Seth" (*bənê-šēt*), a Transjordanian people mentioned in Balaam's oracle (Num 24:17, parallel to Moab). It is possible that these Sethites are related to the Šutû tribes (Suteans) of second-millennium Syria, mentioned in Akkadian and Egyptian texts (Heltzer 1981).

Eve's comment "for Cain killed him" indicates that she knows what has happened between Cain and Abel. We are not shown her grief or anger; rather, she expresses gratitude that God has granted a substitute for her lost son. Her brief comment is terse and unemotional, but seems dramatic, since it is all the mother says.

4:26. *As for Seth, a son was born to him, and he named him Enosh. Then was it begun to call on the name of Yahweh.* The birth of Enosh to Seth continues the new line of humans, presenting a positive face in comparison to the Cainite line. But like the Cainites, Enosh's generation participates in the invention of culture, in this case a religious practice described as *liqrō' bəšēm yhwh* ("to call on the name of Yahweh"). The medio-passive *hûḥal* ("was begun") suggests that the inventor is not just Enosh but his generation. Elsewhere "to call on the name of Yahweh" means to invoke or pray to God. The phrase is particularly associated with Israel's ancestors and Moses, forming a long-range *Leitwort* thread in the J source (Gen 12:8, 13:4; 21:33, 26:25; Exod 33:19, 34:5–6; see INTRODUCTION I).

The theme of people who "began" (*hḥl*) to do new things continues in the J primeval narrative when humans "began to multiply on the face of the earth" (6:1), when Noah "began (or was first) to plant a vineyard" (9:20), and when Nimrod "began (or was first) to be a warrior on earth" (10:8). In our verse the form *hûḥal* ("was begun") perhaps echoes the form *yullād* ("was born"), also a medio-passive, earlier in the verse. It also varies the form of *hḥl* ("to begin") in this J *Leitwort* sequence.

This beginning of "calling on the name of Yahweh" seems slightly odd, since Cain and Abel had previously offered sacrifices to Yahweh (4:3–4), which presumes the existence of religious worship, and Eve had previously spoken Yahweh's name (4:1). Part of the rationale for this has to do with the wordplays in the verse. The diction of Seth naming his child—*wayyiqrā' 'et-šəmô 'ĕnôš* (lit. "he called his name Enosh")—recurs when people begin to call on the divine name—*liqrō' bəšēm yhwh* ("to call on the name of Yahweh"). The sequence repeats: *qr'* + *šem* + name. This invention of sacred invocations makes sense verbally, even if there is friction with previous events.

Enosh's name, which means "human" (*'ĕnôš*, cf. the common plural for "people," *'ănāšîm*), is another contributing factor to this invention. In some sense Enosh is a double of Adam, since they are both named "man/human." (The word *'ĕnôš* appears primarily in poetry as a parallel heightening of *'ādām*.) Hence the worship of Yahweh begins with "human," even if it is a later generation. The chronological problem—that others have already worshiped Yahweh—is ameliorated by this name, which in some sense is a repetition of the first human.

The institution of religious prayer and worship is a salutary endpoint for a story that was otherwise characterized by violence and punishment. The early history of humans turns in a new direction with the new lineage of Seth and Enosh. Seth takes the place of Abel, and Enosh and his generation invent right worship, in contrast to the Cainites' violent killings.

The genealogy of Adam → Seth → Enosh is recapitulated in the P genealogy of Genesis 5, where it continues with a variation of the Cainite genealogy. The branching family tree in Genesis 4, in which Adam's sons are Cain, Abel, and Seth, becomes a single line in Genesis 5, in which only Seth is Adam's son, and Kenan (a biform of Cain) is Seth's grandson.

Comments

The Cain and Abel story continues from the Eden story, recounting the events of the first post-Eden generations. In this era, life outside of paradise seems to be, in Hobbes's terms, "poor, nasty, brutish, and short" (*Leviathan,* ch. 13). Cain murders his brother, and his descendant Lamech boasts about his own acts of murder. In the midst of violence, new forms of civilization are invented—cities, herding, music, and metalworking. In a final sign of hope, swerving back to the lineage of Seth and Enosh, people begin to worship Yahweh, pointing to a better way forward than total violence.

LITERARY DESIGN

The Cain and Abel narrative consists of three sections. Each begins with an act of procreation, repeating with variations the birth formula "*X* knew his wife, and she conceived and gave birth to *Y*":

> *wəhāʾādām yādaʿ ʾet-hawwâ ʾištô wattahar wattēled ʾet-qayin* (4:1)
> "The man knew Eve, his wife, and she conceived and gave birth to Cain."

> *wayyēdaʿ qayin ʾet-ʾištô wattahar wattēled ʾet-ḥănôk* (4:17)
> "Cain knew his wife, and she conceived and gave birth to Enoch."

> *wayyēdaʿ ādām ʿôd ʾet-ʾištô wattēled bēn* (4:25)
> "Adam knew his wife, and she gave birth to a son."

These variations are characteristic of J's literary style and illustrate the *Leitwort* technique. Notice the subtle changes: grammatically from disjunctive (4:1) to conjunctive sequences (4:17 and 25); verbally from the double action "she conceived and gave birth" (4:1, 17) to the simplified "she gave birth" (4:25); and three nominal changes: from "the man" (4:1) to Adam (4:25)—the first time *ʾādām* is used as a personal name; from "Eve, his wife" (4:1) to the simplified "his wife" (4:17, 25), with Cain's wife unnamed and Adam's previously known; and from the named sons Cain and Enoch to "a son" (4:25), whose name is deferred to the following clause. Clearly, this is a story about intertwined generations, which begins and swerves back to the children of Adam and Eve.

The naming sequences that follow these births are also stylistically varied. The first and third feature Eve's direct speech, with the verb motivating the child's name: *qānîtî* ("created, acquired") motivating *qayin* (Cain), and *šāt* ("set, put") motivating *šēt* (Seth). The middle one varies by having Cain name a city after the child (4:17), rather than the mother naming the child. Eve's second naming speech also creates a closure by naming Seth as God's compensation for Abel: "For God has set me another seed to take the place of Abel, for Cain killed him" (4:25). The tragedy of the first section is partially resolved by the birth of a new child in the third and final section.

Within each of the three sections there are other stylistic features that shape the narrative. The first section divides into two parts dramatically, although it is presented as a single temporal sequence:

> Introduction, initial complication, and transgression (4:1–8)
> Recognition, judgment, and resolution (4:9–16)

The first part consists of third-person narration and speeches by Eve, Yahweh, and Cain, but there is no dialogue among the characters. The second part is entirely a dialogue between Yahweh and Cain until the third-person narration in the last verse. In both parts, the drama is mostly carried by direct speech—note the repetition of *wayyōʾmer* ("and he said") six times, plus *wattōʾmer* ("and she said") once at the beginning.

The first part is stylistically shaped by an oscillation between Cain and Abel. Note the consistent variation in the order of names:

Birth: Cain and Abel (4:1–2)
Professions: Abel and Cain (4:2)
Sacrifices: Cain and Abel (4:3–4)
Responses: Abel and Cain (4:3–5)
Yahweh's speech to Cain (4:6–7)
Cain's speech to Abel (4:8)

The back-and-forth of the two brothers subtly dramatizes the instability of their relationship. Cain, as the firstborn, ought to have priority over the younger son, but the stylistic fluidity sets Cain's priority into question. The complication, that Yahweh accepts Abel's offering (from the "firstborns of his flock") and not Cain's (the firstborn son), is orchestrated by this repeated variation of their order. Cain's resentment that his genealogical authority is set aside triggers his shame and anger, which leads to his murder of Abel in cold blood.

The second part of this first section—recognition, judgment, and resolution—is laced with intertextual echoes of the corresponding part of the Eden narrative, creating a parallelism of narrative events across the first two generations. These repetitions show how J's *Leitwort* style creates resonances across the stories:

Questions

Eden: *wayyōʾmer lô ʾayyekkâ* (3:9)
"[Yahweh] . . . said to him, 'Where are you?'"

Cain: *wayyōʾmer yhwh ʾel-qayin ʾê hebel ʾāḥîkā* (4:9)
"Yahweh said to Cain, 'Where is Abel, your brother?'"

Eden: *wayyōʾmer yhwh ʾĕlōhîm lāʾiššâ mah-zzōʾt ʿāśît* (3:13)
"Yahweh God said to the woman, 'What have you done?'"

Cain: *wayyōʾmer meh ʿāśîtā* (4:10)
"[Yahweh] said, 'What have you done?'"

Curse

Eden: *ʾărûrâ hāʾădāmâ baʿăbûrekâ* (3:17)
"cursed is the soil because of you."

Cain: *wəʿattâ ʾārûr ʾattâ min-hāʾădāmâ* (4:11)
"Now, cursed are you from the soil."

Banishment

Eden: *waygāreš ʾet-hāʾādām* (3:24)
"[Yahweh] banished the humans."

Cain: *hēn gēraštā ʾōtî hayyôm* (4:14)
"You have banished me today."

Location

Eden: *miqqedem ləgan-ʿēden* (3:24)
"[Yahweh] stationed east of the Garden of Eden."

Cain: *wayyēšeb bəʾereṣ-nôd qidmat-ʿēden* (4:16)
"[He] dwelled in the land of Wandering, east of Eden."

These sequences in the Cain and Abel story activate a series of associations with the Garden of Eden story, from Yahweh's initial question, which opens the interrogation and grudging confession of Adam and Cain, to Yahweh's judgment and punishment, including curses that affect the relationship between human and soil (*hā'ādām* and *hā'ădāmâ*) and banishment. The closing echo in the phrase "east of Eden," the last words of this section, presents the fate of Cain as a repetition of his parents' exile from Eden, the next movement of humankind away from paradise.

The second major section of the narrative begins after Cain's banishment, with the birth of Cain's son, "Cain knew his wife, and she conceived and gave birth to Enoch" (4:17). The transition to this section is awkward, lacking an introduction of Cain's wife or a connection with Cain's wandering. But the repetition of the birth formula provides a degree of connectivity to the narrative, introducing the theme of Cain's genealogy, which is the topic of this section.

The genealogical history of the Cainites, as Halpern (1992: 17–18) has observed, is punctuated by a series of wordplays and semantic associations with the name *qayin* (Cain). The generation of cultural heroes and their father Lamech have several associative links. Tubal-Cain's name echoes Cain's, and he is the father of metalworkers, which is the meaning of *qayin*. Jabal is the father of pastoralists with herds (*miqneh*—a wordplay on *qyn*). As a murderer in cold blood, Lamech carries the legacy of Cain. At the end of this section, Lamech invokes his ancestor, claiming some kind of precedence: "If Cain is avenged sevenfold, / Lamech will be seventy-seven-fold" (4:24). In this poetic couplet, Lamech is not only Cain's descendant, but his intensified double.

The genealogy of the Cainites, interspersed with their famous and infamous deeds, is a branching in the genealogical narrative of Genesis. This creates an interesting temporal and thematic effect, as the narrative goes forward through seven generations of Cainites and then swerves back in time to the birth of Seth, Cain's younger brother. This is a consistent literary technique in Genesis, where the genealogies of peripheral sons or affines are supplied after their last appearance, and the story then doubles back to the main ancestral lineage of Israel. Cain's lineage is here presented fully, after which the story returns to the birth and lineage of Seth, Cain's brother. Similarly, in the Table of Nations (Genesis 10) the lines of Japheth and Ham are narrated before doubling back to the branch of Shem. In the rest of Genesis, this technique recurs for the lineages of Lot (Genesis 19), Ishmael (Genesis 25), and Esau (Genesis 36). As Sternberg (1990: 119) observes, there is a theological impulse in this temporal movement: "At every fork in the course of humanity toward Israel, from Adam to Isaac, the narrative sooner or later temporarily leaves behind the God-elected son to execute a summative prospection on the line of the rejected." The genealogical plot moves in a zigzag manner toward the children of Israel, punctuated by the genealogical histories of the other branches.

The third section of the narrative returns to the main branch, resuming the genealogy of Adam and Eve through their third son, Seth. This section begins with a repetition of the birth notice, as the narrative pivots to a resumption of the endangered lineage. In Eve's speech, "For God has set me another seed to take the place of Abel, for Cain killed him" (4:25), this birth restores the family after Cain's fratricide. Her use of the name God also leaves open some linguistic space for the generation of Enosh to be the first to "call on the name of Yahweh" (4:25). These are the last words of the narrative, but they point forward to a larger narrative trajectory in J—the repetition of this phrase across the generations until the time of Moses, when both Moses and Yahweh "call on the name of Yahweh" in the divine revelation at Sinai (Exodus 33–34).

FRATRICIDE

The relationship between brothers is fraught in any family, and particularly in traditional societies where the firstborn has priority for inheritance, family honor, and blessing. As Bourdieu (1962: 99) observes for traditional tribal societies such as ancient Israel, "The ambiguity of the whole system may . . . be found in the basic unit on which it is modeled, namely the family. . . . Each brother is the potential breaking point of the family continuum." Cain's hatred of his brother is a manifestation of the rivalry of brothers, which is a potential breaking point in any family. But Cain takes this rivalry to an extreme. Murder of one's brother is a heinous crime, for which Cain is cursed. In Shakespeare's *Hamlet,* Claudius alludes to Cain after murdering his brother (Hamlet's father): "Oh, my offence is rank. It smells to heaven. It hath the primal eldest curse upon't."

There are some mysteries in the backdrop to Cain's murder. The initial complication occurs when Yahweh does not accept Cain's sacrifice (*minḥâ*, lit. "gift," 4:5). No reason is given for this choice, which contrasts with Yahweh's acceptance of Abel's sacrifice. The giving of gifts, like sacrifice, is a central practice in traditional cultures, serving as a way to create, define, and maintain relationships (Mauss 1990). For a figure of authority to reject a gift is to shame the gift-giver, hence "Cain became very angry, and his face was fallen" (4:5). A "fallen face" is an expression of personal shame, as if one's face were a window onto the self, seen both by oneself and by others. In what anthropologists call the "logic" of the gift, Cain is justified in feeling shame and anger. He was placed in this situation by Yahweh's rejection of his gift. So Yahweh is responsible, in the first instance, for shaming Cain.

Yahweh admonishes Cain to resist the temptation to respond with bad intent: "Why are you angry? Why has your face fallen? Is it not so that if you are good, it will be lifted? But if you are not good, sin crouches at the door—it desires you, but you can rule over it" (4:6–7). In some sense, this statement is a test of Cain's moral compass. Yahweh knows why Cain is angry and his face has fallen, but he raises the situation as a challenge. Can Cain rule over his anger and his desire for sin, that is, achieve self-mastery? For Cain, the answer is no. For the readers and audience of the story, Yahweh's admonition lingers as a constant question. Can we humans master our inner Cain?

Yahweh's role as instigator of Cain's shame is one ambiguity in the story. Another is the character of Abel (*hebel*), whose name means "vapor, breath," and by extension, "something evanescent, unsubstantial, worthless, nothingness." This is not the name of a child, but of a passing evanescence, as Job complains, "my days are but a breath (*hebel*)" (Job 7:16). Simply by his name, Abel's character bears the mark of being insubstantial and evanescent. Abel is born to dissipate like a breath, which he fulfills by dying young. This destiny is intimated by his name, adding another layer of ambiguity to the story and the brothers' relationship.

Cain is insensible to Yahweh's warning and does not reply. Instead, he turns his speech to Abel, "Let us go out to the field" (4:8). This is the turning point of the story, where Cain's calculated words lure Abel into a place where no one will hear his cry, and he commits premeditated murder. These words have a double meaning. For Abel, they imply that Cain has something to say in secret, far from prying eyes and ears. In the context of the criminal act of murder or rape (Deut 22:25–27), however, they imply there will be no witnesses to a victim's cry of violence. The irony for this layer of meaning is that there is a nonhuman witness, Yahweh, who hears Abel's posthumous cry: "The voice of your brother's blood cries out to me from the soil" (4:10). The crime is exposed by the victim's unrequited blood persisting in its cry for justice, which is heard by Yahweh.

The connection with the soil, "which opened its mouth to take your brother's blood from your hand" (4:11), activates the relationship between humans and the soil ('ādām and 'ădāmâ), which was central to the Eden story. Now Cain, who was a farmer like his father, is cast away from his livelihood—"Now, cursed are you from the soil" (4:11)—and exiled to be a "restless wanderer on the earth" (4:12). Cain's expulsion from arable land and agriculture makes him a pariah, wandering in a region outside of civilization, where there is no law or authority. Hence, he complains, "whoever meets me will kill me" (4:14). There is irony in his complaint, since he killed Abel in cold blood but fears it for himself. The implication is that Cain has been cast out from civilization to barbarism, where murder is licit and commonplace. It is a place outside of any social or moral norms, a state of social death. But Yahweh shows compassion by placing his mark on Cain, protecting him from murder, comparable to his compassion to Adam and Eve before their expulsion, when he clothes them with durable clothes to protect them.

In a sense, Cain's expulsion from the arable soil is a doubling and extension of Adam and Eve's expulsion from Eden. They were exiled from paradise, where the soil yielded its fruit freely, to the outside world, where the soil is cultivated with pain: "In painful labor you shall eat from it all the days of your life" (3:17). Cain's exile takes him outside the domain of the arable soil, where humans can live, to the land of Wandering, outside of morality and common law, where human life is cheap. This is a place far from Yahweh's presence; as Cain complains, "I will be hidden from your face" (4:14). The expulsion from Eden has taken another leap, to the farthest point from paradise, a place "east of Eden" (4:16). This is the antipode of Eden.

This state of abyss mysteriously transitions to the Cainites' invention of culture—the first city and the activities of herding, music, and metalworking. This is a surprising twist, which is perhaps motivated more by Cain's name (qayin, "metalworker") and his eponymous tribe, the Kenites (qênî), than by the narrative logic. But the mocking elegy (qînâ) by Lamech revives Cain's moral abyss in the fifth generation after Cain (the seventh overall). Lamech has no shame, no capacity for experiencing guilt. He is a cold-blooded killer and proud of it. With Lamech's unrequited bloodguilt, Cain's genealogy ends. Lamech exemplifies the extreme state of barbarism, the farthest point from Eden. It is a niche that lacks both honor and shame, where no one hears the cry of violent bloodshed.

CONTEXTS

The immediate context for the themes of the Cain and Abel narrative is the fragility of family and morality in primeval times. In the J source, the crime and dishonor that stem from the rivalry between brothers is seconded in the story of the curse of Canaan (9:18–27), where the son dishonors the father, and the lineage of his son (Canaan) is cursed to be a slave to the lineages of his brothers (Shem and Japheth). In this narrative relationship, the complicated rivalry of the three sons of Adam (Cain, Abel, and Seth) repeats with variation in that of the three sons of Noah (Shem, Ham, and Japheth). Noah, the first postdiluvian ancestor, formally echoes the position of Adam, the first ancestor. The Adam–Noah relationship is marked more clearly in Noah's birth in J, where his father says of Noah, "He will give us relief from our work, from our painful manual labor on the soil that Yahweh has cursed" (5:29), referring to the legacy of Adam.

The broader context for the main themes in the Cain and Abel story is the fraught relationship between older and younger siblings in Genesis and other biblical books (Greenspahn 1994; Hensel 2011). In the ancestral narratives of Genesis 12–50, the rivalry between brothers is a recurring theme. Abram's firstborn is Ishmael, but Sarah bears Isaac, who will receive the blessing and promise of the firstborn son. In this generation it is Sarah who endangers the life of the firstborn, both in J (Genesis 16) and in E (Gen 21:8–21). In the next generation, Isaac's firstborn is Esau, who is in conflict with the younger son, Jacob, beginning in their mother's womb (25:22–25). When Jacob succeeds, through deception, in gaining Isaac's blessing, Esau decides to kill his brother: "And Esau hated Jacob because of the blessing with which their father blessed him, and he said in his heart, 'When the days of mourning for my father arrive, I will kill Jacob, my brother'" (27:41). When their mother, Rebekah, learns of Esau's murderous intent, she commands Jacob to flee. When Jacob finally returns, he is still afraid that Esau will murder him (Genesis 33). But Esau has become more civilized—and eloquent—and the brothers part in peace.

The next generation features the rivalry between Joseph and his older brothers. Because of their jealousy and hatred, the brothers decide to murder Joseph: "Now come, let us kill him and cast him into one of the cisterns, and we will say, 'A wild animal ate him'" (37:20). But Joseph is rescued by—or sold to—wandering traders, who take him down to Egypt. The treachery of the older sons echoes the murderous plan of Cain. But since all the sons are ancestors of the twelve tribes, the plan must go awry—like Esau's plan to murder Jacob—and becomes a complication rather than a crime.

The sibling rivalries in Genesis include conflict between two sisters, Leah and Rachel. The firstborn, Leah, prevails genealogically, by being Jacob's first wife and bearing his first children, but Rachel prevails thematically by winning Jacob's love and bearing his favored child, Joseph, the ancestor of the most powerful and numerous tribes (Ephraim and Manasseh).

In 2 Samuel, the rivalries between King David's sons also activate these themes. Absalom murders his older brother Amnon because Amnon has shamed his sister Tamar, and Absalom flees. A wise woman tells David a fabricated story about her sons to elicit David's compassion for Absalom: "Your maidservant had two sons, and the two of them struggled in the field, but there was no one to separate them, and one struck the other and killed him" (2 Sam 14:6). As commentators have noted, this story recalls Cain's murder of Abel "in the field," where, as Gunkel (1997: 44) observes, "Abel had no helper and the murder no witness." Solomon's rivalry and his murder of his older brother Adonijah over the succession (1 Kings 1–2) continues the same theme.

Another context concerns the sociological and ethnic associations of Cain. Since Cain's name *qayin* means "smith, metalworker" in other Semitic languages, scholars have inferred that, as Gunkel (1997: 48) writes, "Cain may have been a tribe of desert smiths." Cain is a wanderer on the outskirts of civilization, and his descendants are herders who live in tents, musicians, and metalworkers; these features suit the lifestyle of a nomadic tribe. These details point to the Kenites (*qênî*, from **qaynî*), for whom Cain (*qayin*, from **qayn*) is plausibly the eponymous ancestor (see Day 2013: 51–60).

The Kenites are nowhere depicted as metalworkers, but some are described as living in tents, like Jabal, who was "the father of herdsmen who dwell in tents" (4:20). In the Song of Deborah, Jael the Kenite is "the most blessed of women in tents" (Judg 5:24), and she feeds her guest dairy products (milk // curds, Judg 5:25), indicating access to domestic herds. Other Kenites live in the desert, in the "Negeb of the Kenites" (1 Sam 27:10; probably the Wadi al-Qeini; cf. Judg 1:16), a region where various tribal peoples live (e.g., Jerahmeelites and Amalekites). There are also indications that Kenites lived in the desert regions of Edom and Midian, where there were copper mines in antiquity (see NOTES at 4:1). The Kenites were arguably a tribal people that included mobile pastoralists and "service nomads" (Hayden 1979), who provided goods and services like metalwork and musical entertainment.

A broader perspective on the sociological context of Cain as the ancestor of pastoral and service nomads is provided by ethnographic parallels. Skinner (1930: 113) adduces the Solubba or Sleyb, a pariah tribe in Bedouin regions of Jordan and Saudi Arabia, and the smiths of the Masai of East Africa. McNutt (1990: 70–82) compares other groups of African metalworkers, who were often regarded by their clients, the major tribes, as dangerous or impure. Other Middle Eastern groups are the Ghorbati tribe of Persia, who are low-status tinkers and smiths who accompany the Bedouin on their migrations (Barth 1961: 91–92).

The Solubba may be related to the Šalappāya, known from Middle and Neo-Assyrian records as foreign ironworkers in Assyria (Postgate 2007: 178–79). Such metalworkers, as Aeschylus writes, "are savage and not to be approached by strangers" (*Prometheus Bound* 715–16). These ethnographic parallels indicate the *longue durée* of mobile—and feared—metalworkers in the Middle East.

Generations from Adam to Noah (5:1–32; **P**, J, *R*)

----

5   ¹**This is the book of Adam's genealogy.** *On the day when God created Adam, in God's image he made him;* ²*male and female he created them. And he blessed them, and he called them "human," on the day that they were created.*

³**Adam lived 130 years and fathered** *a son*[a] *in his likeness, according to his image, and he named him* **Seth.** ⁴**After he fathered Seth, Adam's days were 800 years. He fathered sons and daughters.** ⁵**All the days of Adam's life were 930 years, and he died.** ⁶**Seth lived 105 years and fathered Enosh.** ⁷**After he fathered Enosh, Seth lived 807 years. He fathered sons and daughters.** ⁸**All the days of Seth were 912 years, and he died.** ⁹**Enosh lived 90 years and fathered Kenan.** ¹⁰**After he fathered Kenan, Enosh lived 815 years. He fathered sons and daughters.** ¹¹**All the days of Enosh were 905 years, and he died.** ¹²**Kenan lived 70 years and fathered Mahalalel.** ¹³**After he fathered Mahalalel, Kenan lived 840 years. He fathered sons and daughters.** ¹⁴**All the days of Kenan were 910 years, and he died.** ¹⁵**Mahalalel lived 65 years and fathered Jared.** ¹⁶**After he fathered Jared, Mahalalel lived 830 years. He fathered sons and daughters.** ¹⁷**All the days of Mahalalel were 895 years, and he died.** ¹⁸**Jared lived 62**[b] **years and fathered Enoch.** ¹⁹**After he fathered Enoch, Jared lived 900**[c] **years. He fathered sons and daughters.** ²⁰**All the days of Jared were 962 years, and he died.** ²¹**Enoch lived 65 years and fathered Methuselah.** ²²**After he fathered Methuselah, Enoch walked with God for 300 years. He fathered sons and daughters.** ²³**All the days of Enoch were**[d] **365 years.** ²⁴**Enoch walked with God and then was no more, for God took him.** ²⁵**Methuselah lived 67**[e] **years and fathered Lamech.** ²⁶**After he fathered Lamech, Methuselah lived 902**[f] **years. He fathered sons and daughters.** ²⁷**All the days of Methuselah were 969 years, and he died.** ²⁸**Lamech lived 88**[g] **years and fathered** a son. ²⁹He named him Noah and said, "He will give us relief from our work, from our painful manual labor on the soil that Yahweh has cursed." ³⁰**After he fathered Noah, Lamech lived 665**[h] **years. He fathered sons and daughters.** ³¹**All the days of Lamech were**[d] **753**[i] **years, and he died.** ³²**Noah was 500 years old, and Noah fathered Shem, Ham, and Japheth.**

Textual Notes

a. The word *bn* ("son") occurs after all the other instances of *wywld* ("fathered") in Genesis 5 and 11 (thirty-five times) and should be read here. This word was probably lost by eye-skip (homoiarkton), the scribe's eye skipping from the initial letter (*bet*) in *bn* to the same initial letter in the following word (Hendel 1998: 49–50).

b. Reading 62 with the SP. The MT and LXX have 162. See COMMENTS.

c. Restoring 900 (see below). The MT and LXX have 800, and the SP has 785.

d. Reading *wyhyw* ("and [they] were") with the SP and LXX at 5:23 and 31. The MT reads *wyhy* ("and [it] was"), probably because of a near-haplography ("single writing" of two graphically similar letters) of *yod* and *waw*. The plural form is grammatically correct and occurs in this date formula in 5:5, 8, 11, 14, 17, 20, and 27 (Hendel 1998: 50).

e. Reading 67 with the SP (see below). The MT has 187; and the LXX, 167.

f. Restoring 902 (see below). The MT has 782; the SP, 653; and the LXX, 802.

g. Restoring 88 (see below). The MT has 182; the SP, 53; and the LXX, 188.

h. Restoring 665 (see below). The MT has 595; the SP, 600; and the LXX, 565.

i. Reading 753 with the LXX (see below). The MT has 777; and the SP, 653.

Notes

5:1. *This is the book of Adam's genealogy.* As has long been noted, this rubric seems to refer to a separate document, a *sēper* ("written document") of Adam's genealogy, that the P writer has incorporated into his text (e.g., Eissfeldt 1966; Cross 1973: 301–5; Blum 1984: 451–52; Carr 1996: 70–73; cf. Gertz 2015). In later times, this verse was taken as a self-reference to the book of Genesis. The Greek title *Genesis* ("origins") derives from this rubric (and the similar rubric in the LXX of 2:4), which in Greek is *hē biblos tōn geneseōs anthrōpōn,* "the book of the origins of humankind." Hence, via the Greek translation, this originally separate document gave its name to the book into which it was incorporated.

The *sēper tôlədōt 'ādām* ("book of Adam's genealogy") probably originally consisted of a genealogy from Adam to Abram. It included the linear genealogy of 5:3–32, from Adam to the birth of Noah's sons, and then continued with 9:29: "All the days of Noah's life were 950 years, and he died." It probably continued with the linear genealogy from Shem to the birth of Abram (11:10b–26) and ended with the death of Terah (11:32). The postdiluvian section has a slightly abbreviated style, lacking a statement of the ancestors' age at death until Terah.

The genealogy follows the rule of patrilineal descent through the firstborn son, with variation in the horizontal branching at the midpoint (Noah's sons) and end (Terah's sons). In this two-part structure, the tenth generation (Noah) branches into three sons (Shem, Ham, and Japheth), and the twentieth generation (of Terah) consists of three sons (Abram, Nahor, and Haran). The horizontal branching into three sons at the midpoint and end of a linear genealogy is comparable to the J Cainite genealogy in Genesis 4, which branches at the end of a linear genealogy into three sons and a daughter.

We can discern P's technique for making the "book of Adam's genealogy" a connective tissue in the P primeval narrative. In P the "book of Adam's genealogy" follows immediately after Gen 2:3, the close of the creation account. The first part of the genealogy, ending with Noah and his sons, is followed by the flood narrative, with Noah's death (9:29) placed after the flood. The second part of the genealogy, beginning with Shem (11:10b–26 + 32), resumes after the Table of Nations, which ends with the Shemites. The P writer augmented these transitions with three additional notices in the flood story: a resumptive repetition of 5:32 (the birth of Noah's sons) in 6:10, a verse about Noah's age at the onset of the flood (7:6; cf. 7:11), and the formula for his remaining years after the flood (9:28). As part of his editorial technique, P composed a series of connective passages modeled after the rubric of 5:1— 'elleh tôlədōt PN ("this is the genealogy of PN")—to structure the work (see INTRODUCTION I).

R supplemented this genealogy with the J text of the naming of Noah (5:29) after the mention of his birth (5:28). R probably also composed the restatement of God's creation of humans and the birth of Seth (5:1b–3, see below). Finally, in the place where the "book of Adam's genealogy" originally began in the P work, he composed a transitional rubric, "this is the genealogy of heaven and earth" (2:4), followed by J texts (2:4b–4:26). Hence the "book of Adam's genealogy" assumed its present textual situation.

5:1b–2. *On the day when God created Adam, in God's image he made him, male and female he created them. And he blessed them, and he called them "human," on the day they were created.* This sequence is a rhythmic and quasi-poetic recapitulation of God's creation of humans in 1:26–28, framed by a blending of the first words of the P and J creation accounts (1:1 and 2:4b) and the R transition in 2:4a. It is also chiastic, beginning with a temporal clause with the divine verb of creation, *bārā'*, with God as the subject, and ending with a temporal clause with the same verb in a passive construction, *hibbārə'ām* ("they were created"). This sequence echoes and distills the P creation of humans, harmonized with J and R diction.

The multivalence of *'ādām* ("man, human, Adam") is exploited in this sequence. The "book of Adam's genealogy" uses *'ādām* as a proper name both in the rubric in 5:1 and in the genealogy in 5:3–5. The précis of the creation of humans in 5:1b–2 seems initially to use *'ādām* as a proper name but then complicates this usage echoing the diction of 1:27, "he called them *'ādām*," which refers to the genus "human." Through this play on *'ādām*, the creation of humans is funneled into the "book of Adam's genealogy."

The writer of this bridging verse deliberately varies the diction of the source text, 1:1–2:4. Instead of *bərē'šît bārā'* ("in the beginning, when [God] created," 1:1) we have *bəyôm bərō'* ("on the day that God created"), both of which having essentially the same meaning but with different temporal adverbs and forms of *bārā'* ("to create"). The sequence *bəyôm* ("on the day when") plus infinitive absolute echoes the beginning of the J creation story, *bəyôm 'ăśôt* ("on the day when [Yahweh God] made," 2:4). The next clause echoes 1:27, *bəselem 'ĕlōhîm bārā' 'ōtô* ("in God's image he created him"), but rephrases it as *bidmût 'ĕlōhîm 'āśâ 'ōtô*, substituting the noun *dəmût* for *selem* (both mean "image" with slightly different nuances) and substituting the verb *'āśâ* for *bārā'* (both mean "create" here). The next clause varies from the source text only slightly, reducing *bārā' 'ōtām* (1:27) to *bərā'ām*, "(he) created them." The following clause, *wayyiqrā' 'et šəmām 'ādām* ("he called their name 'human'"), is wholly new and is modeled after the naming formula in J texts (e.g., 4:26, *wayyiqrā' 'et šəmô*, "he called his name . . ."), rather than the naming formula in Genesis 1 (*wayyiqrā' lə . . .* , in 1:5, 8, 10). The last clause, "on the day they were created," differs from 2:4 by expanding one word, *bəhibbārə'ām* ("when they were created"), into two, *bəyôm hibbārə'ām*.

Since these clauses allude to and recast diction from P, J, and R, we may infer that the composer of 5:1b–2 is not P but someone who knows P, J, and R. This is plausibly R (Wallace 1990: 19–21; Blum 1990: 280; Holzinger 1898: 58–59; cf. Carr 1996: 71 n. 44). This redactional supplement is, in some sense, a resumptive repetition of the P creation of humans, compensating for the insertion of J material in 2:4b–4:26. The same editorial strategy occurs in the expansion in 5:3b, which may be from the same hand.

5:3–5. Adam lived 130 years and fathered a son in his likeness, according to his image, and he named him Seth. After he fathered Seth, Adam's days were 800 years. He fathered sons and daughters. All the days of Adam's life were 930 years, and he died. The genealogical pattern in this chapter for the most part has the following form: "PN$_1$ lived X years and fathered PN$_2$. After he fathered PN$_2$, PN$_1$ lived Y years. He fathered sons and daughters. All the days of PN$_1$'s life were Z years, and he died." The chief exceptions are Adam, Enoch, and Lamech, which have expanded entries. (Noah has some smaller variations.) It is likely that these large expansions are from the hand of P (for Enoch) and R (for Adam and Lamech). Adam's genealogy has been expanded in 5:3 by the sequence "a son in his likeness, according to his image, and he named him." This expansion, like the supplement in 5:1b–2, uses the diction of the creation of humans in Genesis 1 blended with the J naming formula, *wayyiqrā' 'et šəmô* ("he named him"; see the previous Note).

The sequence "he fathered a son in his likeness, according to his image" strikingly reformulates its source text (1:26) and applies it to human procreation. God had said, "Let us make a human in our image, according to our likeness" (1:26). The last two words are *bəṣalmēnû kidmûtēnû* ("in our image, according to our likeness"). Genesis 5:3 reformulates this sequence (reversing the words and prepositions) to *bidmûtô kəṣalmô* ("in his likeness, according to his image"). The result is an extension of the concept of God's creation of humans in his image to the father' procreation of sons in his image.

The text blends these concepts of divine creation and human procreation. As Garr (2003: 153) comments, "Inherent in the human race from its inception, the early history of the 'image' demonstrates that it is perdurable as well." It might seem that "image" in the relationship between son and father has a predominantly bodily sense. But the allusion to God's creation of humans "in his image" complicates this assumption, invoking the multiple qualities of "image" that the creation text carries (see Notes at 1:26).

The begetting of "sons and daughters," part of the genealogical formula, refers to the younger sons and daughters, who are not named and not genealogically memorialized. This follows from the linear form of the genealogy, which records the central patriline from father to firstborn son. The genealogy branches horizontally at the midpoint and endpoint, with Noah's and Lamech's three sons, who are named and have their own genealogies.

Adam's lifespan is 930 years. The other antediluvians also have huge lifespans. Most are in or near the 900s, topped by Methuselah's 969. Lamech's dips to 753. The exception is Enoch, who lives for 365 years and then "was no more, for God took him" (5:26). There is no obvious pattern to the lifespans, no numerology that we can detect (but see below on Enoch). The lifespans of the antediluvians in the Sumerian king lists, which provide a useful comparison, are tens of thousands of years (see Comments).

In the postdiluvian era, the spans gradually decline to more recognizable proportions, from Abraham at 175 years (Gen 25:7) to Moses at 120 years (Deut 34:7).

The verbal forms *wayyôled* and *hôlîd* ("he fathered, begat") are *hiphil* causatives of the root *yld* ("to give birth"). In the J source the corresponding verbal form is the *qal* verb *yālad*, used for the father (e.g., 4:18) or mother (e.g., 4:1). This difference between *qal* and *hiphil* for a male subject indicates a difference in the historical phases of Hebrew represented in J and P. The linguistic evidence for this verb in its various forms (including the *qal* passive and *niphal*) shows that J's usage represents an earlier phase of Hebrew than P's (Hendel 2000).

5:6–8. *Seth.* Adam's son Seth is the same figure as Seth in the Cainite genealogy (4:25). Whether this genealogy knows of Cain and Abel as Adam's other sons is unclear. (See below on Kenan as a biform of Cain.) As in J, the main branch of the genealogy goes through Seth.

5:9–11. *Enosh.* Seth's son Enosh is the same figure as Enosh in the Cainite genealogy (4:26), although here he lacks any narrative context. As the father of Kenan (a biform of Cain), Enosh functions again as a biform of Adam, both of whose names mean "man, human." In the lacuna of the J Cainite genealogy, it is possible that Enosh was the father of Noah (see NOTES at 5:29).

5:12–14. *Kenan.* The name Kenan (*qênān*) resembles the name Cain (*qayin*) and probably comes from the same root (*qyn*), plus the hypocoristic affix *-ān* (Hess 1993: 67–68). This figure looks like a biform of Cain but lacks the significance of Cain in the J narrative.

5:15–17. *Mahalalel.* The name Mahalalel (*mahălal'ēl*) means "praise of God," which probably relates to the gratitude at the birth of a child (Hess 1993: 68–69). This figure is a biform of Mehiyael (*məḥiyyā'ēl*) in the Cainite genealogy, whose name probably originally meant "God enlivens" (see NOTES at 4:18). The *he* of Mahalalel is arguably a weakened form of the *ḥet* of Mehiyael, which indicates that the Cainite form is earlier. The change from *yod* to *lamed* in Mahalalel is plausibly an assimilation to the other *lamed*'s, or to the common root *hll*.

5:18–20. *Jared.* The name Jared (*yered*) appears to derive from the root meaning "to descend." There are other similar-looking names in the West Semitic world (e.g., Jared in 1 Chr 4:18), but its meaning is unclear (Hess 1993: 69). This figure is a biform of Irad (*'îrād*) in the Cainite genealogy (4:18), whose meaning is also obscure. The initial *yod* in Jared may be a weakening of the initial *'ayin* in Irad, which would suggest that the Cainite form is earlier, as with other correspondences.

5:21–24. *Enoch lived 65 years and fathered Methuselah. After he fathered Methuselah, Enoch walked with God for 300 years. He fathered sons and daughters. All the days of Enoch were 365 years. Enoch walked with God and then was no more, for God took him.* The most mysterious antediluvian is Enoch. In the Cainite genealogy, Enoch is the third generation, after Adam and Cain, and is the father of Irad. In Genesis 5, Enoch is the seventh generation—a propitious number in biblical genealogies (Sasson 1978: 175–76)—and is the son of Yered. The identical names and similar contexts indicate that these two Enochs are biforms, but this Enoch is invested with much more detail and mystery (see COMMENTS).

Enoch's genealogy in 5:21–24 diverges from the standard form at two points. In 5:22 we expect the formula, "After he fathered PN$_2$, PN$_1$ lived *Y* years." Instead, the text reads, "After he fathered Methuselah, Enoch *walked with God* for 300 years." The substitution of *wayyithallēk ḥănôk ʾet-hāʾĕlōhîm* ("Enoch walked with God") for *wayḥî ḥănôk* ("Enoch lived") is striking. Another expansion occurs in 5:24, where we expect the formula, "All the days of PN,'s life were *Z* years, and he died." Our text reads, "All the days of Enoch were 365 years. *Enoch walked with God and then was no more, for God took him.*" The expected final word, *wayyāmōt* ("and he died"), has been replaced by the long sequence *wayyithallēk ḥănôk ʾet-hāʾĕlōhîm wə̄ʾênennû kî-lāqaḥ ʾōtô ʾĕlōhîm* ("Enoch walked with God and then was no more, for God took him"). This expansion supplies a very mysterious ending.

In addition to these departures from the expected form, Enoch's lifespan (365 years) is considerably shorter than that of the other antediluvians, whose lifespans range from 753 to 969 years. Most commentators infer that the number 365 refers to the number of days in a year according to the solar calendar. But this is odd, since ancient Israel operated by a lunar (or more precisely, lunisolar) calendar, in which there are 354 days in a year. There was also a schematic calendar, as in the P flood chronology, with 30 days in a month and 360 days in a year (see Notes at 7:11). In antiquity, a "corrected" calendar—adjusted from the lunisolar or schematic calendar—generally had 364 days, not 365 (Ben-Dov 2008, 2021).

The earliest indication of a 364-day duration may be from a calculation in the early first-millennium BCE astronomical text Mul.Apin (II.ii.11–12): "You proclaim a leap month (every) three years; the amount for (one) year is 10 additional days for 12 months" (Horowitz 1996: 40–41; Ben-Dov 2008: 164–67; Hunger and Steele 2019: 152–53, 214–15). Although Mul.Apin works with a schematic 360-day year, the leap month occurs only in the lunisolar calendar. This notice may indicate that a "corrected" year is 364 days (= 354 + 10), a calculation based on a leap month of thirty days every three years in the lunisolar calendar. But other interpretations of this notice are possible—it may simply derive a ten-day period for intercalation without drawing any implications for the duration of the year (see Stern 2012: 198–200). While a 364-day year is explicitly used only in later literature (see the Astronomical Book of Enoch, ca. third century BCE), this type of calendrical inquiry may have influenced priestly circles earlier (Ben-Dov 2008: 245–50). In any case, Enoch's lifespan of 365 years is probably tinged with astronomical speculation.

These features in Enoch's genealogical account are not entirely explicable, but they can be illuminated by considering their connotations and literary features. The construction *wayyithallēk ḥănôk ʾet-hāʾĕlōhîm* ("Enoch walked with God," 5:22, 24) recurs in the P flood story, with a slight change of word order: *ʾet-hāʾĕlōhîm hithallek-nōaḥ* ("With God, Noah walked," 6:9). The context is "Noah was a righteous man, blameless in his generation." From this parallel usage we may infer that "walking with God" is a metaphor for moral virtue in P. A similar expression, *hithallēk* + *ləpānay/ləpānāyw* ("walk before me/him"), is used in P for Abraham and Isaac (17:1, 48:15; cf. 24:40, a post-P text). These expressions link Enoch, Noah, Abraham, and Isaac in the P narrative. The near-verbatim repetition of the expression for Enoch and Noah links them most closely.

In the P text, this description of Noah follows the genealogy in Genesis 5. The parallel diction in this tight sequence clearly marks Enoch and Noah as righteous men par excellence. There may be a further wordplay in this repeated construction. As Sasson (1975: 166) observes, there is a sound-play between *hithallek-nōaḥ* ("Noah walked," 6:9) and *hănôk* (Enoch). If one reverses the last three consonants in the Noah sequence, one finds Enoch's name: *knh > hnk*. In this possible wordplay, the direct allusion to Enoch In the word sequence has a cryptic allusion in the letter sequence. Whether or not this argument is compelling, Noah and Enoch are clearly alike with respect to walking with God, and even in the sounds in their names. Therefore, on one or more levels, Enoch (*hnk*) is "like Noah" (*knh*).

The repetition of "Enoch walked with God" in 5:24 is expanded by the mysterious description of his end: "Enoch walked with God and then was no more, for God took him." The closest comparison in the Hebrew Bible is to Elijah, who at the end of his life was "taken" (*lqh*) by God (this expression repeats with variations in 2 Kgs 2:3, 5, 9, 10), and "Elijah ascended to heaven in a storm-wind" (2 Kgs 2:11). Elijah's end is narrated more explicitly than Enoch's, but it shows that a nonordinary death can be denoted by the verb *lāqaḥ* ("to take"), and an ascent to heaven—rather than the expected descent to Sheol—is thinkable for legendary biblical figures. The text does not say where God "took" (*lāqaḥ*) Enoch, but his end is not an ordinary death. This is indicated not only by what the text says, but also by what it does not—the omission of the formulaic ending, "and he died."

Many extrabiblical figures have mysterious ends that are unlike an ordinary human death. From Greek tradition there are heroes like Sarpedon and Herakles. But the closest parallels are from Mesopotamia. The lists of antediluvian kings and sages include several figures who ascend to heaven, and whose traditions may have influenced the depiction of Enoch (VanderKam 1984: 23–51). Adapa, the first of the primeval sages (*apkallu*), ascended to heaven and lost a chance for immortality (Izre'el 2001). Enmeduranki, sometimes listed as the seventh of the antediluvian kings, ascended to heaven and became the founder of a divinatory guild (Lambert 1998). Utuabzu is the seventh sage (*apkallu*) in some lists and "ascended to heaven" in unknown circumstances (Borger 1994). Any or all of these Mesopotamian figures may illuminate the fate of Enoch. But it seems that all of these ascended to heaven during their lives—not at their end—after which, according to the preserved traditions, they returned to earth.

As several commentators have observed, the closest analogue to Enoch in Genesis 5 is the Mesopotamian flood hero, variously called Atraḫasis, Ziusudra (in Sumerian), and Ut(a)napishtim (Budde 1883: 180; Dillmann 1897: 226; Sasson 1975: 166). The flood hero is famous in Mesopotamian traditions for his wisdom (Atraḫasis means "exceedingly wise") and for being the only human—along with his wife—to be granted immortality. As Utnapishtim recounts in the *Gilgamesh* epic, after the flood had ended:

[Enlil] touched our foreheads, standing between us to bless us:
"In the past, Utnapishtim was (one of) mankind,
but now Utnapishtim and his wife shall be like us gods!
Utnapishtim shall dwell far away, at the mouth of the rivers!"

(XI.202–5; George 2003: 716–17)

The Mesopotamian flood hero does not ascend to heaven but is granted immortality by the high god and taken to a mysterious place, apart from other humans. Genesis 5:24 does not say that Enoch ascended to heaven but that "Enoch walked with God and then was no more, for God took him." As VanderKam (1984: 50) observes, "Enoch, like the flood hero, was taken; he did not ascend." The P writer is reticent about Enoch's fate, but a transcendence of death is implied (as for Elijah), as is a translation to a special place.

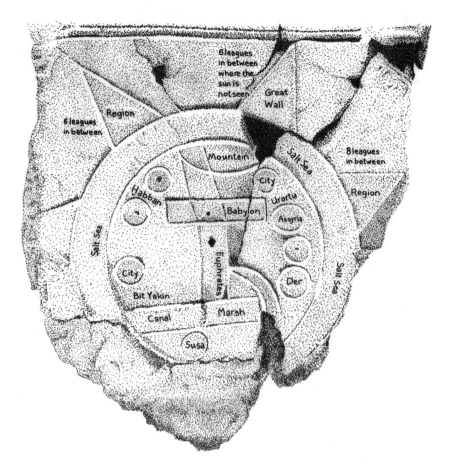

Figure 9. Babylonian world map. The accompanying text indicates that
one of the regions beyond the world ocean (Salt Sea) "where the sun is not seen"
is the home of the flood hero Utnapishtim (Horowitz 1998: 23, 36). In *Gilgamesh* X,
this region is past the eastern mountain where the sun rises and beyond the Waters
of Death. From relief on Late Babylonian tablet (copy of original ca. eighth to
seventh century BCE), British Museum. (Drawing by William H. C. Propp)

Notice that this is not the fate of Noah, the biblical flood hero. Noah has the
expected formulaic ending to his genealogical notice: "All the days of Noah's life were
950 years, and he died" (9:29). It is plausible that an older tradition for the flood hero
has been displaced to Enoch, who is, as we have seen, analogous to Noah in P. As Budde
(1883: 180) writes, "It seems as if what is stated about the hero of the Babylonian flood
has been here divided into two people." Enoch in the Cainite genealogy has no such
fate, nor does Noah. But according to the supplemental material in P, Enoch had a
marvelous life and death, like Noah in some respects ("walking with God") and like the
Mesopotamian flood hero in another. Enoch echoes and supplements Noah in surprising ways.

The mysteries of Enoch in 5:21–24 generated a rich tradition in postbiblical litera-ture, particularly in the pseudepigraphic books of Enoch, whose earliest parts are from the third century BCE. These elaborations are exegetically derived from Genesis and expanded with esoteric speculations about what Enoch saw while he walked with God (Nickelsburg 2001; VanderKam 2002: 276–304).

5:25–27. *Methuselah.* The name Methuselah (*mətûšelaḥ*) consists of the word *mutu* ("man," with the archaic nominative case ending) plus *šelaḥ*, whose significance is un-clear. Some have proposed that Šelaḥ is the name of a god, hence "man of (the god) Šelaḥ," but no such god name is known (Hess 1993: 70–71). It is more likely a garbled version of Methushael (*mətûšāʾēl*), to which it corresponds in the Cainite genealogy (4:18). In later exegetical traditions, Methuselah becomes a figure of interest because he is the longest lived of the ancestors, and his death is mysterious—in the MT he dies in the year of the flood, and in the LXX he dies fourteen years after the flood (see COM-MENTS, "Editions").

5:28–31. *Lamech.* This figure clearly corresponds to Lamech in the Cainite geneal-ogy but lacks the notoriety of his genealogical double. This Lamech is the father of the exemplary Noah, who is rescued from the flood, in contrast to the other Lamech, who is the exemplar of violence and barbarity. The violent Lamech of the Cainite geneal-ogy is the father of three sons and a daughter, ending the genealogy with a branching, while in this genealogy it is the righteous Noah who has three sons, from whom come the three branches of humanity. There is thus a layered relationship of multiformity between the two Lamechs and their offspring.

5:28–29. *a son. He named him Noah and said, "He will give us relief from our work, from our painful manual labor on the soil that Yahweh has cursed."* The naming of Noah has been inserted here (by R) from the J text. The clues of J provenance include the naming formula (*wayyiqrāʾ ʾet-šəmô PN*, cf. 4:17, 25, 26), the use of the divine name Yahweh, and the clear allusions to 3:17 and 8:21, both J texts. According to the formula in the "book of Adam's genealogy," 5:28 would have ended *wayyôled ʾet-nōaḥ* ("and [he] fathered Noah"), which has been changed to *wayyôled bēn* ("and [he] fathered a son"). The sequence from *bēn* ("son") onward was originally from the J text and has been carefully spliced into a P text, which itself is incorporating a prior document (the book of Adam's genealogy).

This J inset does not name Noah's father. It is presumably not Lamech, who was a descendant of Cain. If we follow the genealogical sequence in Genesis 4, the last man born was Enosh, in whose time "was it begun to call on the name of Yahweh" (4:26). This association with religious speech makes Enosh an appropriate father for the flood hero, who "found favor in the eyes of Yahweh" (6:8). The sequence from Enosh to Noah in J makes sense thematically but was presumably omitted by R because of its friction with the P genealogy.

The naming of Noah in 5:29 picks up the words and ideas of Yahweh's curse on the soil in Eden, "cursed is the soil because of you. In painful labor you shall eat from it all the days of your life" (3:17). The sequence *mēʿiṣṣəbôn yādênû min-hāʾădāmâ ʾăšer ʾērərāh yhwh* ("from our painful manual labor on the soil that Yahweh has cursed") reformulates Yahweh's words, *ʾărûrâ hāʾădāmâ baʿăbûrekā bəʿiṣṣābôn* ("cursed is the soil because of you. In painful labor," 3:17). The prediction that Noah will provide relief (*nōaḥ . . . yənaḥămēnû*) relies on a wordplay between *nōaḥ* (Noah, meaning "rest") and *nāḥam* ("to comfort, relieve"). This motivates Noah's name and foretells his great destiny—he will repair the cursed relationship between *hā᾽ādām* ("man, humankind") and *hā᾽ădāmâ* ("the soil"). This prediction lingers in the background of the flood story.

Curiously, Yahweh's final speech in the J flood story seems to confirm this destiny, "I will never again curse the soil because of humans" (8:21), using the same diction. But there, "curse the soil" seems primarily to refer to the destruction brought by the flood. Noah has another opportunity to provide relief after the flood, when "Noah, a man of the soil, was the first to plant a vineyard" (9:20). The gift of wine, Noah's legacy, provides a measure of relief from "our painful manual labor on the soil." Both texts—Yahweh's promise after the flood and Noah's viticulture—seem to recall and affirm the destiny that Noah's father predicts, albeit in different ways.

Wordplays on the name Noah (*nōaḥ*) occur throughout the flood story (Cassuto 1961: 289; Sasson 1975). Noah found "favor" (*ḥēn*, 6:8); the ark "came to rest" (*wattānaḥ*, 8:4); the dove did not find a "place to rest" (*mānôaḥ*, 8:9); and Yahweh smelled the "soothing" aroma (*nîḥôaḥ*, 8:21). The echoes of Noah's name create a connective tissue in the story.

Noah (*nōaḥ*), as mentioned above, means "rest." This root is fairly common in personal names, as in Samson's father Manoah (*mānôaḥ*) (see Hess 1993: 28–29; on other etymologies, see Witte 1998: 208–10). M. Schwartz (2002: 236–37) has proposed that there may be a linguistic connection between the name of Noah and the name Utnapishtim, one of the names of the Mesopotamian flood hero. On the basis of a late form of Utnapishtim found in the Manichaean *Book of Giants*, *᾽tnbyš* (Atnabish), we can infer that a similar form existed in the Aramaic *Book of Giants*, fragments of which were found at Qumran (so also Reeves 1993). In an earlier time than the *Book of Giants*, a short form like *᾽tnpyš* or *᾽tnbyš* could easily have been (mis)analyzed by a West Semitic speaker as a Dt (*hithpael*) verb of the root npš, "to be refreshed, rested" (cf. the alloform nbš in inscriptional Hebrew and Aramaic; *HALOT*, 711). It is possible that a local flood tradition could have substituted for the name *᾽tnpš* a more familiar verbal root, *nwḥ* ("to rest"), yielding the name *nōaḥ* ("rest"). This conjectural derivation of the name is an interesting possibility.

5:32. Noah was 500 years old, and Noah fathered Shem, Ham, and Japheth. The genealogical entry for Noah has two departures from the formulaic pattern (see NOTES at 5:3–5). Noah's entry begins *wayhî-nōaḥ ben-X šānâ* ("Noah was X years [old]"), adding the word *ben*, a variation that recurs with Noah's son Shem (*šēm ben-X šānâ*, "Shem was X years [old]," 11:10). More importantly, three of Noah's sons are listed, which effects a horizontal branching in the genealogy. This feature recurs with the three sons of Terah (11:26), which may have originally closed the "book of Adam's genealogy."

The remaining text of Noah's genealogy has been displaced by the P writer to 9:29, "All the days of Noah's life were 950 years, and he died." By this means, the P writer incorporated the flood narrative into Noah's lifespan. The P writer supplemented Noah's genealogy with three further notices: a resumptive repetition about Noah fathering three sons (6:10, which reformulates 5:32); a notice about his age at the flood, "Noah was 600 years old when the flood was on the earth" (7:6); and his lifespan after the flood, "After the flood Noah lived 350 years" (9:28). By these relocations and supplements, the P writer folded the flood into Noah's genealogy (see Carr 1996: 73–74).

On the names of Shem, Ham, and Japheth, see NOTES at 10:2 (Japheth), 10:6 (Ham), and 10:21 (Shem).

Comments

EDITIONS

There are three variant editions of the chronology in Genesis 5, which seem to be independent revisions in the three extant textual families, proto-MT, proto-SP, and proto-LXX. The proto-SP chronology is attested in Jubilees, while the proto-LXX chronology, revised occasionally to the MT, is attested in Josephus, *Jewish Antiquities,* and Pseudo-Philo, *Biblical Antiquities.* The most plausible text-critical analysis of these developments was formulated by R. W. Klein (1974) and revised in Hendel 1998: 61–80 (see also Hendel 2012b; and cf. Tov 2015; Gertz 2015: 83–90; Rösel 2018: 89–107). This analysis begins with the following three clues: in the MT, Methuselah dies in the year of the flood; in the SP, Jared, Methuselah, and Lamech die in the year of the flood; and in the LXX, Methuselah outlives the flood by fourteen years. The anomaly of ancestors dying after the flood is arguably the exegetical problem that motivated scribes in the Second Temple period to revise the chronology. Scribes in the proto-MT and proto-SP traditions devised systems to have the three problematic ancestors—Jared, Methuselah, and Lamech—die before or in the year of the flood, while the system devised by proto-LXX scribes was more systematic, extending from Adam to Lamech, but only partially successful, leaving Methuselah as a survivor of the flood (as noted with dismay by Josephus, Augustine, and others).

We can infer the following revision strategies in the three extant textual families. In proto-MT and proto-SP, revisions were made only for Jared, Methuselah, and Lamech, who were the three problematic cases. In proto-LXX, the same scheme was imposed on all the ancestors from Adam to Lamech.

Proto-MT

> *Jared:* Add 100 to Jared's age at begetting, and subtract 100 from the remainder of his lifespan, leaving the age at death unchanged.
> *Methuselah:* Add 120 to Methuselah's age at begetting, and subtract 120 from the remainder of his lifespan, leaving the age at death unchanged.
> *Lamech:* Add 94(?) to Lamech's age at begetting, and subtract 70 from the remainder of his lifespan.
> *Result:* Jared and Lamech die before the flood, and Methuselah dies in the year of the flood.

Proto-SP

> *Jared:* Subtract 115 from Jared's remainder of lifespan.
> *Methuselah:* Subtract 149 from Methuselah's remainder of lifespan.
> *Lamech:* Subtract 35(?) from Lamech's age at begetting, and subtract 65 from the remainder of his lifespan.
> *Result:* Jared, Methuselah, and Lamech die in the year of the flood.

Proto-LXX

> *Adam to Lamech:* Subtract 100 from age at begetting, and add 100 to the remainder of their lifespans.
> *Result:* Ages at death unchanged, but the increases of age at begetting expands the timespan before the flood.

These three revision strategies are independent and relatively simple, and from them we can infer the archetype that underlies them, with uncertainties only for the revisions of Lamech's numbers in proto-MT and proto-SP (as indicated by the question marks above). In Table 4, the archetype, derived by triangulation from the three editions, approximates the original P chronology. The year of the ancestor's death after creation (*anno mundi*, AM), which is not in the text but easily added up, is supplied in parentheses. The values given are *b*, age at begetting; *r*, remainder of lifespan; and *d*, age at death (= *b* + *r*). The other signs are ", unchanged from archetype; and *, reconstructed archetype (i.e., not attested in any edition). The latter occur only for Jared, Methuselah,

Table 4. Editions of antediluvian chronology

	Archetype	MT	SP	LXX
Adam *b*	130	"	"	230
r	800	"	"	700
d	930	"	"	"
	(930 AM)	"	"	"
Seth *b*	105	"	"	205
r	807	"	"	707
d	912	"	"	"
	(1042 AM)	"	"	(1142 AM)
Enosh *b*	90	"	"	190
r	815	"	"	715
d	905	"	"	"
	(1140 AM)	"	"	(1340 AM)
Kenan *b*	70	"	"	170
r	840	"	"	740
d	910	"	"	"
	(1235 AM)	"	"	(1535 AM)
Mahalalel *b*	65	"	"	165
r	830	"	"	730
d	895	"	"	"
	(1290 AM)	"	"	(1690 AM)
Jared *b*	62	162	"	162
r	*900	800	785	800
d	962	"	847	"
	(1422 AM)	"	(1307 AM)	(1922 AM)
Enoch *b*	65	"	"	165
r	300	"	"	200
d	365	"	"	"
	(887 AM)	(987 AM)	"	(1487 AM)
Methuselah *b*	67	187	"	167
r	*902	782	653	802
d	969	"	720	"
	(1556 AM)	(1656 AM)	(1307 AM)	(2256 AM)
Lamech *b*	*88	182	53	188
r	*665	595	600	565
d	753	777	653	753
	(1407 AM)	(1651 AM)	(1307 AM)	(2207 AM)
Flood	(1342 AM)	(1656 AM)	(1307 AM)	(2242 AM)

Note: b, age at begetting; *r*, remainder of lifespan; *d*, age at death; AM, *anno mundi*; ", unchanged from archetype; *, reconstructed archetype.

and Lamech, where the archetype is derived from the regular formula in the LXX. The year of the flood is derived from Noah's age of six hundred years at its onset.

From the revision strategies in the three editions, we can derive the archetype and isolate the exegetical problem that stimulated the revisions. In the archetype, Jared dies 80 years after the flood, Methuselah dies 214 years after the flood, and Lamech dies 65 years after the flood. This conflicts with the flood narrative, where "only Noah and those with him on the ark survived" (7:23), listed as "Noah and his sons and his wife and his sons' wives" (8:18). The three revision strategies resolve this exegetical problem for the most part, except for Methuselah in the proto-LXX revision, in which a systematic application of its formula leaves Methuselah alive fourteen years after the flood.

The proximate cause of the initial exegetical problem is the incorporation of the "book of Adam's genealogy" (see Notes at 5:1) into the P narrative. Apparently, the P writer failed to harmonize the chronology with his date for the flood in Noah's six-hundredth year (7:6). Later scribes did the calculations and sought to harmonize the discrepancy using the three separate strategies above.

Compare the treatment of Tov (2015: 236), who agrees with most details of the above analysis: "In chapter 5, the numbers in SP and the LXX, possibly also in MT, were probably meant to postdate the flood, avoiding a situation where the patriarchs would be alive after the flood." He grants that "the three texts display different versions, possibly recensions, of the same list" (234). However, he prefers to equate the archetype or hyparchetype with the MT: "It seems to me that a text like MT formed the basis of the revised form of the two parallel lists [in SP and LXX], but MT itself could also have revised an earlier list" (229). Others prefer the SP as preserving the earlier P chronology (e.g., Gertz 2015: 88–90). As we have seen, given the different strategies in proto-MT, proto-SP, and proto-LXX, it is more plausible to posit three independent revisions of the antediluvian chronology.

LITERARY DESIGN

Genesis 5 is an expanded genealogy, a literary elaboration of the "book of Adam's genealogy" (*sēper tôlədōt 'ādām,* 5:1). The prologue in 5:1–2, reprising the creation of humans in Genesis 1, is a supplement to the original document. An additional supplement occurs in the next verse, where Adam begets "a son in his likeness, according to his image, and he named him" (5:3, see Notes). This expanded beginning, incorporating language from previous texts, functions as a kind of resumptive repetition of Genesis 1 and presumably was composed by R, who was resuming the P text from 2:3. R also inserted the naming of Noah from the J source into 5:29, "He named him Noah and said, 'He will give us relief from our work, from our painful manual labor on the soil that Yahweh has cursed,'" which resumes the *Leitwort* theme of the relationship between humans and the soil (*hā'ādām* and *hā'ădāmâ*). These expansions connect the genealogy with diction and themes of the surrounding P and J texts, richly embedding the genealogy into its context.

Aside from these expansions and the enigmatic description of Enoch in 5:24–26, the literary form of the "book of Adam's genealogy" is formulaic. This creates an internal rhythm of the cycle of generations, with life, procreation, and death following each other in regular order. The formula is "PN$_1$ lived X years and fathered PN$_2$. After he fathered PN$_2$, PN$_1$ lived Y years. He fathered sons and daughters. All the days of PN$_1$'s life were *Z* years, and he died." We may presume that this was the original form of the "book of Adam's genealogy," which the P author incorporated into his work directly after the creation account (see Bauks 2019).

For the tenth generation, that of Noah, the formula is changed to include Noah's three sons, with a corresponding omission of "he fathered sons and daughters." At this point the P writer broke up Noah's genealogy to insert the flood story. The next part of Noah's genealogy is presented undisturbed in 5:32, "Noah was 500 years old, and Noah fathered Shem, Ham, and Japheth," and his death notice concludes the covenant after the flood, "All the days of Noah's life were 950 years, and he died" (9:29). P includes other genealogical details in the flood story, modeled after the style of Genesis 5, in 6:10, 7:6 (cf. 7:11), and 9:28, with a resumptive repetition of the birth of Noah's sons, his age at the flood, and the remainder of his lifespan after the flood. Here we see the P writer at work, weaving together the "book of Adam's genealogy" and the flood narrative. In a tangible sense, the flood story is embedded within the genealogy. It is an event firmly founded in genealogical time.

GENEALOGIES

Genesis 5 articulates the passage of time from the creation of Adam to the generation of Noah. It is a chain that links creation and flood. The idiom of this connective chain is genealogy. Stripped of the chronological details and formulae, the structure of the account is a linear genealogy from Adam to Noah, which branches into a horizontally segmented genealogy of Noah's three sons (Table 5). There are ten generations in the

Table 5. Antediluvian genealogy in P

Adam
|
Seth
|
Enosh
|
Kenan
|
Mahalalel
|
Jared
|
Enoch
|
Methuselah
|
Lamech
|
Noah
┌──────┴──────┐
Shem   Ham   Japheth

linear genealogy from Adam to Noah, with the eleventh generation of Shem, Ham, and Japheth pointing forward to the branching of the human genealogy in the Table of Nations (Genesis 10).

The key figures are the first and last members of the linear genealogy, Adam and Noah, who are famous for their roles in the creation and flood. With the exception of Enoch, whose fame is alluded to and partially foreshadows Noah, there is no narrative about any of the other figures in the linear genealogy. It seems that the passage of ten generations is the primary point, that is, the passage of time in the epoch from creation to flood.

The names and lifespans in this genealogy, other than Adam and Noah, are in a sense flexible placeholders. They are part of what Vansina (1985: 168–69) calls the "floating gap" in the middle of the genealogy. With the exception of Enosh (whose name means "human"), none of the names has any obvious meaning or associations.

When we compare this P genealogy with the antediluvian genealogy in the J source (Genesis 4 + 9:18–19) (Table 6), we find variations of the same genealogical details. The J genealogy, however, is more richly segmented, with seven generations from Adam to Lamech. It is not clear who is Noah's father in J (note that Lamech, Noah's father, is in the P genealogy), but Enosh is a reasonable candidate. With some uncertainty (indicated by the broken line after Enosh), there are approximately four generations from Adam to Noah.

As commentators have long noted, the J and P genealogies are variants in content and form. The names of seven of the antediluvian ancestors are identical (Adam, Seth, Enosh, Enoch, Lamech, Noah, and Shem, Ham, and Japheth). In the intermediate generations, four of the names are similar: Kenan and Cain, Mahalalel and Mehiyael, Jared and Irad, and Methuselah and Methushael. Apart from Adam at the top and Noah and his sons at the bottom, the genealogies have a different order in P and J. In

Table 6. Antediluvian genealogy in J

the middle—the floating gap—the names and order differ. The correspondences of the variant names are clearer in Hebrew:

P	J	
qênān	qayin	Both derive from *qayn, PN[P] adds the ending -ān
mahălal'ēl	məḥîyā'ēl	ḥ in PN[P] is a weakened version of ḫ in PN[J]
yered	'îrād	y in PN[P] is a weakened version of ' in PN[J]
mətûšelaḥ	mətûšā'ēl	šelaḥ in PN[P] is a variant of šā'ēl in PN[J]

In two of these correspondences, the P name has later linguistic features than the J name. This corresponds to the relative chronology established previously. These features indicate that the "book of Adam's genealogy" is later than the J genealogy. A final difference regards gender: the J genealogy includes women in the segmented generations, including the daughter Naamah and the wife/mothers Eve, Cain's wife (not named), Adah, and Zillah. The P genealogy includes only males.

What are we to make of the striking similarities and differences between the two genealogies? It does not appear that one is a literary revision of the other, since the form, content, and linguistic details are so divergent. As most commentators infer, they probably depend on variant genealogies in Israelite oral tradition, or a mixture of oral and written sources (R. R. Wilson 1977: 161–66). The J genealogy seems closer stylistically to traditional genealogies. As Skinner (1930: 120) observes, "The alliterations, Yābāl— Yûbal—Tûbal, are a feature of legendary genealogies, cf. Arab. Habîl and Qabîl, Shiddîd and Shaddâd, Mâlik and Milkân, etc."

The P genealogy races from creation to flood, with no intervening stories of human tragedy or human-divine encounters. The linear form of the genealogy expresses this streamlined strategy. The male-centered progression is arguably rooted in the conceptual world of P, the priesthood, where priestly status was inherited along the patrilineal genealogy. Women are not prominent agents in the priestly world or the P source. In a general sense, the P genealogy, drawn from the "book of Adam's genealogy," is an abstracted or simplified revision of the richer segmented genealogy that is represented in J. There is fluidity between the two genealogies, particularly in the "floating gap" in the middle between the apex (Adam) and the main branching point (Noah). The P genealogy reflects the well-ordered world of the priests, without the meandering and colorful branches of the J source and (presumably) Israelite folklore.

A final point about genealogies is important for Genesis 5. In societies like ancient Israel that are organized by tribal segments and affiliations, genealogies provide a conceptual map or charter for intergroup relationships, obligations, and claims (Shryock 1997; Hendel 2018). In a linear genealogy, the key ancestors are at the branching points that lead to groups in the present. Noah is the father of three branches, Shem, Ham, and Japheth, whose descendants are groups in the present. This branching after the flood indicates geographical or ethnic distance. Israel, a descendant of Shem, viewed itself as more distantly related to the Hamite and Japhethite people. The main exception, the Canaanites, who are Hamites, are defined by the genealogy as distant, which here indicates their social distance, marking an ethnic boundary, despite their geographical proximity.

This is how genealogical distinctions work in traditional societies. They define proximity and distance in the current world by constructing a genealogical past that anchors the present in the past, through the structures of shared and diverging ancestry.

As indicated more decisively in the genealogical relationships in Genesis 12–50, Israel defined itself in relation to its neighbors through genealogies and genealogical narratives. This process begins with Adam, has a branching point with Noah, and resumes with the lineages and dramas of Abraham's family and heirs.

CONTEXTS

In the genealogical narrative of P, the "book of Adam's genealogy (*tôlədōt*)" is a temporal bridge between two eras: creation and flood. At both ends of the genealogy, there are echoes and extensions of its diction and themes. In P this genealogy is positioned between 2:3 (the last verse of the P creation account) and 6:9 (the introduction to the P flood). The genealogical formula "this is the genealogy (*tôlədōt*) of PN" forms a long-range continuation of this genealogy. In 6:9, the P source resumes, "This is the genealogy of Noah." This phrase recurs through the remainder of Genesis, serving as a structuring principle for the book. All the subsequent repetitions arguably belong to the P writer, who used this genealogical idiom as a unifying thread from Adam to Joseph. This makes all of Genesis an extended or amplified genealogy, whose core is Genesis 5 and whose *telos* or goal is Israel.

R added a version of this rubric in 2:4a, using its connective quality to join together the two creation stories. In this move, the genealogy becomes a metaphor, a way of bridging the creation of heaven and earth in 1:1–2:4a with another creation in 2:4b–3:24, now defined as a figurative "offspring" of the prior account. In this notice, the genealogical coloring of Genesis takes on a cosmic scope, beginning not with the creation of humans (as in 5:1), but with the creation of the universe.

Another context for the genealogy concerns the lifespans of the ancestors. In the first ten generations, the lifespans cluster in the range of 800 to 900 years, beginning with Adam's 930 years, and peak with Methuselah's 969. At the shorter end of the curve is Lamech's 753 years. The only outlier is Enoch, who lives 365 years, making him unusually young. The number seems to suggest calendrical speculation (see NOTES at 5:21–24) but also marks Enoch as a special case. Enoch does not die as the others do, but in a departure from the pattern, he "was no more, for God took him" (5:24). P may have revised and supplemented the details about Enoch from the source text to make him a special figure, as befits the seventh generation.

After the flood, lifespans decrease. Although Noah lives to a ripe age of 950, the ages in the genealogy of Genesis 11 decline from Shem's 600 to a low of Nahor's 148, with a slight spike at the end to Terah's 205. In P's genealogical notices through the rest of Genesis, the ancestors' lifespans are merely in the 100s: Abraham dies at 175, Sarah at 127, Ishmael at 137, Isaac at 180, Jacob at 147, and Joseph at 110. From the beginning of Genesis to its end, the lives of the ancestors decrease by almost 90 percent, from the huge lifespans before the flood to the lesser ones in Joseph's generation. The trajectory is from the mythical to the merely extraordinary, marking the passage from the era of origins to the limits of the present world.

In the ancient world several traditions have a comparable trajectory in which people in the first era had extraordinary lifespans. The most striking case is the list of antediluvian kings contained in the Sumerian King List, also known as the Chronicle of the Single Monarchy (Glassner 2004: 55–60, 117–21; Friberg 2007). The antediluvian list also circulated as an independent text. As Finkelstein (1963: 51) observes, "it seems to have remained more or less a loose and fluid tradition with greater or lesser variations occurring in every detail: number of kings, the names, the cities, the sequence of both kings and cities, the length of their reigns, and the choice of formulae and phraseology."

Many scholars have argued for the dependence of Genesis 5 on this list (see Day 2013: 61–76 and references). This is not an obvious inference, since all the names and dates are different, but it does provide a context and analogue for the biblical antediluvian genealogies. Most versions of the list are from the Old Babylonian period, but some were known in the first millennium, including the late version in Berossos's *Babyloniaca* (third century BCE). The closest to the era of P is the version in the Babylonian Royal Chronicle, known from Neo-Assyrian and Neo-Babylonian texts.

Table 7 presents the details of city, king, and reign from the Babylonian Royal Chronicle and Berossos's *Babyloniaca* (Glassner 2004: 128–29; Friberg 2007: 236–37; Burstein 1978: 18–19). These two versions are probably related, since they share the sequence of the dynasty of Sippar (or its king, Enmeduranki) followed by the dynasty of Larak, while all the earlier versions have the reverse. The reigns of the kings are written as units of 3,600 (ŠAR) and 60 (GEŠ) years, with ŠAR borrowed into Greek as *saroi*.

The Sumerian King List is a different kind of text than the "book of Adam's genealogy," cataloguing the reigns of the first kings, whose dynasties are not genealogically

Table 7. Two versions of the Sumerian King List

Babylonian Royal Chronicle ("five cities, nine kings")	Berossos, Babyloniaca ("ten kings and 120 s")
Eridu	*Babylon*
Alulim 10 Š (36,000)	= Aloros 10 *s* (36,000)
Alalgar 12 Š (43,200)	= Alaparos 3 *s* (10,800)
Badtibara	*Badtibara*
Enmeluana 12 Š (43,200)	= Amelōn 13 *s* (46,800)
	Ammenōn 12 *s* (43,200)
Enmegalana 13 Š+ (46,800+)	= Amegalaros 18 *s* (64,800)
Dumuzi [—]	= Daōnos 10 *s* (36,000)
Sippar	
Enmeduranki 15 Š 1 G (54,600)	= Euedōrankhos 18 *s* (64,800)
Larak	*Larak*
Ensipaziana 10 Š 2 G+ (37,200+)	= Amempsinos 10 *s* (36,000)
Šuruppak	
Ubartutu [—]	= Otiartes 8 *s* (28,800)
Ziusudra [—]	= Xisouthros 18 *s* (64,800)

Note: Š, 3,600 (ŠAR) years; G, 60 (GEŠ) years; *s*, ŠAR borrowed into Greek as *saroi*. A dash (—) indicates broken text (the number is missing).

related. But it shares several distinctive features with Genesis 5. The kings have extraordinarily long reigns before the flood, ending with the reign of the flood hero Ziusudra. The antediluvian ancestors in Genesis 5 have extraordinarily long lives, ending with the flood hero Noah. However, the Sumerian kings live much longer, with lifespans in the tens of thousands of years. Their reigns range from a low of 36,000 years for the first king, Alulim (= Aloros), to a high of 54,600 or 64,800 for Enmeduranki (= Euedōrankhos) and another 64,800 for Xisouthros. The list of antediluvian kings, with its fiction of a single kingship moving from one city-state to another, is a different genre from that of Genesis 5, but the broad concepts are comparable.

The only detail that specifically corresponds to Genesis 5 is the final position of the flood hero. Many scholars have argued that Enmeduranki, in sixth position in the Babylonian Royal Chronicle and in seventh position in Berossos, is the inspiration for Enoch, who occupies the seventh position in Genesis 5 (cf. Sanders 2017: 13–18). While the seventh position indicates a special status for Enoch, who is special in other ways, there is no cause to derive his features from Enmeduranki. Enmeduranki was revered as the ancestor of the diviners who practice lecanomancy (mixing oil and water in a bowl) and hepatoscopy (reading the marks in livers). He was a king who was initiated into the arts of the diviner by the gods of divination, Shamash and Adad. He was brought to the divine assembly, where the gods "showed him how to observe oil on water . . . they gave him the tablet of the gods, the liver, a secret of heaven and [the underworld]" (Lambert 1967: 132). Afterward, Enmeduranki initiated specialists from Nippur, Sippar, and Babylon into these divinatory arts.

None of these features characterizes Enoch in Genesis 5 (but some of them may color Enoch in the Hellenistic book of Enoch; see VanderKam 1984: 110–40). As observed previously (see NOTES at 5:21–24), Enoch has closer affinities to the flood heroes. He is linked to Noah, who also "walked with God" (6:9). He seems to have inherited the flood hero's destiny in being "taken" by God instead of dying, like Ziusudra and his Akkadian counterpart Utnapishtim. As Berossos relates: "Xisouthros was no longer visible to them, but a voice from the sky ordered them to be reverent. Because of his piety, he had gone to live with the gods" (Burstein 1978: 20; similarly, *Gilg.* XI.199–204). In sum, Ziusudra is the antediluvian king who has the most affinities with Enoch and Noah, who seem to inherit different traits of the Mesopotamian flood hero. This split legacy coheres with the other broad and detailed correspondences between the Mesopotamian and biblical flood traditions.

The concept that humans had prodigious lifespans in the distant past is shared by other cultures in antiquity. According to Hesiod, the silver generation had a long childhood: "A boy would be nurtured for a hundred years at the side of his cherished mother." But after the boys reached puberty, "they would live for a short time only, suffering pains for their acts of folly" (*Works and Days* 130–34; Most 2006: 96–99). This is reminiscent of a Sumerian parody of the antediluvian king list: "at that time the human race in its carefree infancy had a hundred years" (Lagash Chronicle; Glassner 2004: 146–47). The first mythical dynasties in Egypt also had long reigns. According to the first columns of the Turin king list (from the Ramesside period), in the first era, when gods, demigods, and spirits were kings, Thoth ruled for 7,726 years, Maat ruled for more than 200, and a variety of spirits ruled for more than 13,420 years (Kitchen 1996: 540–41).

In this company, Enoch remains mysterious. His lifespan of 365 years sounds like speculation on the solar year, his "walking with God" is obscure—is it a tour, or a metaphor?—and "God took him" seems like a translation to heaven (cf. Elijah). All of these exegetical options were taken up in the book of Enoch, whose earliest parts were composed in the third century BCE (Nickelsburg 2001: 118–19). In this book Enoch describes his ascent to heaven and his tour of the cosmos, accompanied by angels. This is an exegetical transformation of Enoch "walking with God," with "walking" taken literally and *ĕlōhîm* ("God, gods") understood as angels—Enoch traveled with angels and was "taken up" to God's heavenly throne. This is the starting point of the Enochic apocalyptic traditions (see VanderKam 1984). Enoch disciplines the fallen watchers (the Sons of God from Gen 6:1–4) and dispenses advice to Methuselah and other off-spring about the coming of the great destruction. He also expounds the astronomical details of the 364-day solar year. In his admonitions and prophecies, the flood becomes a foreshadowing of the final judgment of the wicked and the redemption of the righteous. The author and his cohort must have expected the end-time soon. (There is no indication that P knew this Enochic material, contra Kvanvig [2011] and others.) In this book, written in Aramaic and infused with details of Mesopotamian and Greek mythology, the brief verses about Enoch in Genesis 5 are expanded marvelously into the esoteric revelations of this mysterious antediluvian sage.

The Sons of God and the Daughters of Humans (6:1–4; J)

---

6 ¹When humans began to multiply on the face of the earth, and daughters were born to them, ²the Sons of God saw that the daughters of humans were beautiful, and they took for themselves wives from whomever they chose. ³Yahweh said, "My breath will not be strong[a] in humans forever, inasmuch as they are also flesh. Let their days be 120 years." ⁴The Nephilim were on the earth in those days, and also later, when the Sons of God used to couple with the daughters of humans, who would bear children for them—they were the warriors of old, the men of renown.

Textual Notes

a. The MT and SP read *ydwn,* whose meaning is unclear but plausibly "be strong" (see NOTES at 6:3). A Qumran commentary (4QCommGenᵃ) quotes this text with *ydwr* ("dwell"), which agrees with the translation "dwell" in the LXX, Targum Onqelos, the Syriac Peshitta, the Vulgate, and Jub. 5:8. Apparently *ydwn* and *ydwr* were textual variants. The former is obscure, and probably original. The latter is an Aramaic loanword (BDB, 192; Wagner 1966: no. 68) found in late and postbiblical Hebrew (Ps 84:11; Ben Sira 33:11, 50:26; and seven occurrences in the Aramaic of Daniel) and is most likely a linguistic modernization of the obscure and archaic *ydwn* (cf. Bernstein 1994).

Notes

6:1–2. The first two verses introduce the protagonists, "the daughters of humans" and "the Sons of God," and describe their encounter. These verses are one continuous sentence, consisting of a backgrounded temporal clause sequence ("when . . . and . . ."), followed by the foregrounded action sequence ("[they] saw . . . and they took . . ."). The background sequence provides the preliminary information—the multiplication of humans and the birth of daughters—for the foregrounded action. The language of reproduction and sexuality in the human realm, which is normal and expected, provides a thematic backdrop for the sexuality and reproduction among gods and humans in 6:2, which is unexpected.

6:1. *When humans began to multiply on the face of the earth, and daughters were born to them.* The beginning of a new story is marked by the temporal clause *wayhî kî . . .* ("And it was, when . . . ," cf. 27:1). The background situation continues the theme of human reproduction, which began when "the man knew Eve, his wife, and she conceived and gave birth" (4:1) and progressed in the accounts of the Cainite and Sethite generations. But here no specific lineage is invoked; rather, we are told of the multiplication of *hā'ādām* ("humankind"), that is, humanity as a whole.

The word *hā'ādām* is used here as an unambiguously collective term (rather than a specific individual) for the first time. This is explicit in the use of the plural pronominal suffix "them" at the end of the verse. Previously in the J source *hā'ādām* referred to "the human," a male individual who was the ancestor and prototype of the collective (see NOTES at 2:7). After other men are born, the individual is called *'ādām* (Adam), now a proper name (see NOTES at 4:25). The word *hā'ādām,* with the definite article *ha-,* henceforth refers to the collective. But just as the previous usage of *hā'ādām* implied the collective, so now the collective use still carries the resonance of the first man, Adam. The semantics of *hā'ādām* is also affected by the collocation with *bānôt* ("daughters")— these are the daughters of humankind and also, indirectly, the daughters of Adam. This latter resonance suggests an element of incipient danger.

This is the first mention of daughters in the J source (cf. the formula "he fathered sons and daughters" in Genesis 5 [P]). The diction, with the *qal* passive, *yullədû* ("were born"), echoes the previous birth notice in 4:26 (J), "to Seth was born (*yullad*) a son." This notice is given in a disjunctive clause (*waw* + noun + verb), placing focus on this collectivity of young women. In a society like ancient Israel, the emphasis on daughters raises the charged issues of proper marriage, kinship, sexuality, and offspring.

There are several verbal links between this introduction and the surrounding verses (4:26, 5:29, and 6:5) in J. The sequence *hēḥēl* ("began") + *lə* ("to") + infinitive ("multiply") is a variation on 4:26, *hûḥal* + *lə* + infinitive ("begun to worship"). These activities are different, but there is a connective echo between them. The *Leitwort* relationship between *hā'ādām* ("the human, humankind") and *hā'ădāmâ* ("soil, earth") is also signaled in the diction of *hā'ādām* multiplying on the face of *hā'ădāmâ* (with the general nuance of "the earth"). This relationship has just been recalled in the naming of Noah in 5:29, referring to Yahweh's curse on *hā'ădāmâ* ("the soil"). This is a prelude to the flood story, but the multiplication of *hā'ādām* on *hā'ădāmâ* also serves as background to the flood. This *Leitwort* relationship will take a new turn in the flood story.

The beginning of the J flood story also has verbal and thematic links with our verse. Whereas here *hā'ādām lārōb* ("humans [began] to multiply") on the earth, the flood story begins with the multiplication of human evil: *rabbâ ra'at hā'ādām* ("great was the evil of humans," 6:5). The word *hā'ādām* ("man, humankind") and the verbal root *rbb* ("to be great, multiply") occur in both verses; but here it is the multiplication of human population, and in 6:5 it is the multiplication of human evil. In both stories, divine beings (the Sons of God, Yahweh) perceive this multiplication, and the stories turn on their reactions. While 6:1–4 is not directly tied to the flood story by its narrative events, these verbal echoes provide a thematic bridge.

The background information provided in 6:1 is the consequence of normal human marriage, sexuality, and reproduction. The population expansion is presented neutrally and is itself not seen as a problem (cf. the Mesopotamian flood tradition, where the multiplication of humans is a crucial problem, since the resulting noise disturbs Enlil's sleep; see the COMMENTS to the J flood story). This background of human sexual behavior and kinship serves as an implicit counterpoint to the extraordinary marriages and sexual couplings that follow and the extraordinary offspring that are born. The notice of the birth of daughters—*yullədû lāhem* ("[they] were born to them")—also anticipates their subsequent procreation of marvelous offspring: *wəyālədû lāhem* ("they would bear children for them," 6:4). The change from passive to active of *yld* provides an unexpected turn in the human genealogy.

6:2. *the Sons of God saw that the daughters of humans were beautiful, and they took for themselves wives from whomever they chose.* The punctual action of the story begins with the male gaze of "the Sons of God," who see "the daughters of humans." The *bənê-hā'ĕlōhîm* ("the Sons of God") are collectively the antithesis of *bənôt hā'ādām* ("the daughters of humans"). This defining contrast prepares for the activation of the male/female contrast and the divine/human contrast that follows. As "sons" and "daughters" of different fathers, they are ripe for the sexual attraction, marriage, and procreation that follow. But as their lineages are divine and human, respectively, this brings into play the crucial focus on the God/human relationship, which, as the previous J narratives have shown, is fraught with danger. The mingling of these categories—male/female and divine/human—is anticipated in the shape of these identifying phrases.

The word *benê* can mean "children," "sons," or "members (of a group or class)," depending on the context. Here the meaning "sons" is indicated by the contrast with "daughters" (*bənôt*) and by the acts of marriage, sex, and reproduction that follow. The word *hā'ĕlōhîm* can mean "god/God" (lit. "the god") or "the gods," singular or plural, depending on context. The context here allows for either meaning. As we will see, *benê-hā'ĕlōhîm* in origin refers to El (lit. "God") as the father of his divine children. The singular, "God," is the presumptive meaning of *hā'ĕlōhîm*.

The "Sons/Children of God" are mentioned several times in the Hebrew Bible and other West Semitic texts and must have been a well-known group in Israelite religion. They are members of Yahweh's heavenly entourage, divine beings who function in biblical texts as Yahweh's heavenly council, divine courtiers, and (rarely) the gods of the nations (Parker 1999; Mullen 1980). Under a related term, "host of heaven," these gods function as Yahweh's heavenly army. However, nowhere else in the Hebrew Bible do they behave sexually, and rarely are they depicted acting on their own volition, independent of Yahweh.

The Sons/Children of God (*bənê-hā'ĕlōhîm* in prose, and in poetry *bənê 'ĕlōhîm* and *bənê 'ēlîm*, cf. *bənê 'elyôn*, "Sons/Children of the Most High") are depicted elsewhere acting collectively in the heavenly realm. This is their sphere of activity from creation onward. The passages that clearly name this group are as follows:

When the Most High apportioned the inheritances of the nations,
   when he divided the sons/children of humans (*bənê 'ādām*),
He established the borders of the peoples
   according to the number of the Sons/Children of God
      (*bənê 'ĕlōhîm*). (Deut 32:8, reading with 4QDeut^j [*bny 'lwhym*]
         and the LXX)

Ascribe to Yahweh, O Sons/Children of God (bǝnê ʼēlîm),
   ascribe to Yahweh glory and strength. (Ps 29:1)

The heavens praise your wonders, O Yahweh,
   your faithfulness also, in the assembly of the Holy Ones.
For who in the heaven can be likened to Yahweh?
   Who can be compared to Yahweh among the Sons/Children of God
   (bǝnê ʼēlîm)? (Ps 89:6–7)

I have said that you are gods (ʼĕlōhîm),
   all of you are the Sons/Children of the Most High (bǝnê ʽelyôn).
But you shall die like a human,
   and like one of the princes, you shall fall. (Ps 82:6–7)

It was the day when the Sons/Children of God (bǝnê hā ʼĕlōhîm) came to present themselves before Yahweh. (Job 1:6, cf. 2:1)

Where were you when I founded the earth? . . .
When the morning stars sang together,
   and all the Sons/Children of God (bǝnê ʼĕlōhîm) shouted praise?
   (Job 38:4, 7)

These brief glimpses of "the Sons/Children of God" show a variety of actions: they sing praises to Yahweh at creation and later; the Most High (probably understood as a title of Yahweh) assigns one for each nation; they assemble in heaven before Yahweh; they are lesser beings compared with Yahweh; and Yahweh pronounces their death sentence. This latter decree (Ps 82:6–7) comes from a time when the logic of Israelite monotheism precipitated a rejection of the concept of other deities, even those subordinate to Yahweh. A similar tendency can be seen in the MT of Deut 32:8, where a pious scribe of the Second Temple period substituted yśr'l ("Israel") for the original 'l or 'lhm ("God") (Tov 2012: 248–49).

By the late Second Temple period, "the Sons/Children of God" came to be identified with the angels, two classes of divine beings that had previously been separate (M. S. Smith 2001: 45–46). In Dan 3:25 the king sees a figure in the fiery furnace "whose appearance is like a Son of God" (bar-ʼĕlāhîn, in Aramaic), a divine messenger who in earlier times would have been called a malʼāk ("angel"). Because of this reduction of divine classes, "the Sons of God" of Gen 6:2 are called "angels" in works of this period (e.g., Jub. 5:1).

The implication of divine parentage in the phrase "the Sons/Children of God" derives from the older West Semitic phrase bn ʼil ("the sons/children of El") and the idea that the active gods are all (or nearly all) offspring of the high god El ("God"). One of El's epithets at Ugarit is ʼab bn ʼil, "Father of the Children of El" (CAT 1.31.i.25, etc.). In its biblical use, the notion of God's actual parentage is not explicit. In the Hebrew Bible it is an old term whose original nuances have probably diminished through time, while maintaining its general reference to divine beings (so Parker 1999: 794–95).

In this verse, the Sons of God—divine beings subservient to Yahweh—gaze upon "the daughters of humans" and desire them. This desiring gaze motivates their sexual transgression of the metaphysical boundary of divine/human. Unlike Eve's desirous gaze of the fruit of the Tree of the Knowledge of Good and Evil (3:6), it looks at the divine/human boundary from the divine side, and the woman is the object of the gaze, rather than its subject.

This act of perception by the Sons of God also sets up a contrast with Yahweh's later perception in the flood story (6:5). The diction of this sequence, *wayyir'û . . . 'et-banôt hā'ādām kî ṭōbōt* ("[they] saw . . . that the daughters of humans were beautiful)," is echoed and inverted in 6:5: *wayyar' . . . kî . . . rā'at hā'ādām* ("[He] saw . . . that . . . the evil of humans"). Whereas "the Sons of God" saw the *ṭōbōt* ("goodness") of the daughters of humans, meaning their beauty and desirability, Yahweh saw the *rā'â* ("evil") of humans, an ethical and interior condition. One sees the "good" (*ṭōb*); the other sees the "evil" (*ra'*). These related scenes subtly denigrate "the Sons of God" in comparison with Yahweh—the former, driven by sexual desire, see only beautiful bodies, whereas the latter sees the moral condition of the human heart.

The beauty of women is often noted in biblical narrative as a prelude to danger, seduction, or even rape, as in the beauty of Sarah (Gen 12:11), Rebekah (Gen 26:7), Bathsheba (2 Sam 11:2), and Tamar (2 Sam 13:1). The mention of male beauty can have the same nuance of danger, as in the description of Joseph's beauty (Gen 39:6), immediately before Potiphar's wife gazes at him with sexual desire. But the beauty of a woman—as with Rachel (29:17)—can also be noted in the context of love, courtship, and marriage.

The sequence *wayyiqḥû lāhem nāšîm* ("they took for themselves wives") is a normal biblical idiom for marrying (e.g., 4:19, 11:29, 25:1, 28:9) but takes on a harsh tone linked with *mikkōl 'ăšer bāḥārû* ("from whomever they chose"). Normally marriage arrangements are negotiated with a woman's father or another head of the household (as 24:34–60, 28:15–30). The sense here is that the Sons of God did not observe the formal procedures of marriage arrangements, suggesting rashness and unregulated power. In ancient Israel, the preferred marriage was within the patrilineal kinship group (e.g., 24:4, 28:1–2, 29:12). The farther one strayed from this ideal, the more perilous the marriage. Marriages with deities is, according to this kinship logic, maximally perilous. Yet the danger is only hinted at in this verse, which describes the events, not their implications.

The polytheistic implication of this verse—the existence of "many gods," even if subservient to Yahweh—led many postbiblical interpreters to identify the Sons of God with a human group, of which contextually only the Cainites or Sethites are available. However, these identifications fail to account for the semantic contrast with "the daughters of humans." As Cassuto (1961: 291–92) observes, "these words ['daughters' and 'humans'] cannot be understood in this verse in a different sense from that which they have in 6:1, which definitely refers to the human species as a whole; hence 'the sons of God' must be entities existing outside the sphere of humankind." The plain sense became problematic in Jewish and Christian interpretation (in part because angels were thought to be celibate); for instance, "Rabbi Simeon ben Yoḥai cursed any who called them Sons of God" (*Gen. Rab.* 26.5), and Augustine wrote, "these were not really angels but human beings" (*City of God* 15.23; see Kugel 1998: 210).

Note that the singular "son of God" has a different derivation, rooted in concepts of divine or divinely authorized kingship (e.g., Pss 2:7, 45:7, 89:27–28; 2 Sam 7:14) and in the Second Temple period becoming a messianic title (see Collins and Collins 2008).

6:3. Yahweh said, "My breath will not be strong in humans forever, inasmuch as they are also flesh." This verse bristles with difficulties, not least its relation to the narrative context. Yahweh's speech appears to be interior monologue, not addressed to the Sons of God or the daughters of humans. It is a punishment that diminishes the lifespan of humans. Although Yahweh does not refer to the story's protagonists, he does draw out a divine/human antithesis in the implicit contrast between *rûḥî* ("my breath"), the divine breath that animates humans, and *bāśār* ("flesh"), the earthy material of human bodies. The duality of divine breath and human flesh recalls Yahweh's creation of the first human out of the soil, when "He blew life's breath into his nostrils" (2:7). This is a "soft dualism" of body and life-spirit that is characteristic of biblical anthropology (see NOTES at 2:7). The flesh is adduced to signify mortality, to which Yahweh adds a fixed lifespan so that humans will not live "forever" (*lə ʿōlām*). This punishment echoes and extends the expulsion of humans from Eden so that they cannot eat from the Tree of Life "and live forever" (*wāḥay lə ʿōlām,* 3:22).

It is not clear why this punishment of limited lifespan is a consequence of the marriages of the Sons of God with the daughters of humans. It is relevant on a thematic level, since it concerns the junction of divine and human domains; however, the limitation of human lifespan is not directed solely at the offspring of these mixed marriages but applies to all humans. Moreover, this consequence does not seem to affect the instigators of the apparently illicit marriages, the Sons of God. It is, as commentators have noted, a punishment that does not quite fit the crime. It does, however, fit a larger movement of the J primeval narrative, providing a step in the gradual, episodic construction of the conditions and limits of human existence, here focused on the boundaries between the human and the divine.

Notice that humans are already subject to death, as made explicit in 3:19, "until you return to the soil, for from it you were taken." Here the limitation of death is further constrained by a fixed lifespan. A comparable progression occurs in the Mesopotamian myth of Atraḫasis, where humans are subject to death from the time of their creation—particularly by disease or calamity—but receive a decree of natural death, that is, a limited lifespan, only after the flood:

> [Enki] opened his mouth and [addressed] Nintu, the Womb:
> "[You, the W]omb, creatress of destinies, [assign death] to
> the people, [put a man] to sleep [(in the grave)]."
>
> (*Atra.* III.vi.47–49; Wasserman 2020: 29, 36)

As Wasserman (2020: 58) comments, "This line describes the creation of natural death as a biologically unavoidable process (as opposed to death in an unexpected cataclysm)." Mortality and a fixed lifespan, in these traditions, are limits that arise at different moments in the story of early humanity.

Yahweh's brief speech contains two linguistic puzzles: the verb *yādôn* and the compound particle *bəšaggam*. The verb *yādôn* (translated here as "be strong") is obscure and occurs only here. Many etymologies have been proposed, with varying degrees of linguistic plausibility. At first it looks like it should be from the common root *dyn,* "to judge," but there are morphological and semantic problems: the form should be *yādîn,* and the meaning does not fit the context. Yahweh's *rûaḥ* ("breath, spirit") does not "judge" in humans but enlivens them.

The most plausible explanation of *yādôn* was proposed independently by Vollers (1899) and Berry (1899). They adduced the root *dnn*, attested in the Akkadian verb *danānu*, "to be strong," and related words. Formally there is no difficulty with this root; as Speiser (1967: 36) correctly notes, "the received reading can be reconciled only with **dnn*." For the stative imperfect of a geminate root one might expect the form *yēdan* or *yiddôn* (like biforms *yētam* and *yittôm*), but there are other stative geminate forms of this type, for example, *tā'ōz* (Ps 89:14), which also means "be strong." It is unusual to find a geminate imperfect with full (*plene*) spelling, but there are other such examples, particularly with uncommon geminate roots, for example, *yāgôddû* ("band together," Ps 94:21). The *plene* spelling clarifies the form of an uncommon word. Also, as Vollers and Berry note, the Hebrew place name Dannâ ("fortress, stronghold," Josh 15:49) derives from *dnn*, "to be strong" (although place names can be very old). The meaning "be strong" (from *dnn*) for *yādôn* is contextually and linguistically plausible and has been adopted by many scholars (e.g., Jacob 1934: 174; Hendel 1987: 15; Hendel 2004: 15; Vervenne 1995a: 27; Seebass 1996: 193; Day 2013: 88–89; Carr 2021: 205).

The compound particle *bəšaggam* is best read as *bə* (preposition) + *ša* (relative) + *gam* (adverb), meaning "in that [they] also" (so most commentators), or, to capture the archaic flavor of the compound word, "inasmuch as [they] also." The vocalization with a *patach* in the final syllable is found in all of the oldest MT manuscripts (Hendel 1998: 133) and in manuscripts closely affiliated with them (Cohen 1997: 74), clarifying that the reading tradition understood *gam* ("also") as the final part of the compound. The doubling of the *gimel* is due to close juncture after *ša* (cf. Judg 5:7, *'ad šaqqamtî*, "until you arose"; see Sasson 2014: 289–90).

Some later manuscripts and editions of the MT (including the Second Rabbinic Bible, which formed the basis for the *textus receptus*) vocalize this word with a *qamets* in the final syllable, which makes the final -*ām* a pronominal suffix ("their") and presumes an analysis of the word as *bə* + infinitive construct of *šāgag* ("to stray, sin") + the third-person masculine plural suffix -*ām*, yielding "in/because of their sinning." The plural suffix, however, conflicts with the grammatically singular antecedent *bā'ādām* ("in humankind") and the following singular pronoun *hû'* ("he"). This vocalization, therefore, is ungrammatical and is probably a reanalysis of an obscure compound form.

The relative particle *ša* is an old form, found in Akkadian, Ugaritic, and elsewhere. In Classical Hebrew the equivalent form (although etymologically unrelated) is *'ăšer*. In Late Biblical Hebrew the dominant form is *še*, which may be a clipped form of *'ăšer* (Huehnergard 2006). The old relative *ša* occurs in archaic Hebrew poetry (Judg 5:7, and probably Num 24:3, 15) and in frozen form in names (*mətûšā'ēl*, "man of God," Gen 4:18; and *mîšā'ēl*, "who is of God?," Exod 6:22), and probably persisted in the northern dialect of Hebrew (as in Judg 6:17, 7:12, 8:26; see Rendsburg 1990: 113–18). The compound form *ba'ăšer* (Gen 39:9, 23) is equivalent to *bəša*- here. The corresponding Late Biblical Hebrew form is *bəše*- (Eccl 2:16). The effect of this archaic-sounding compound preposition, in conjunction with the unique verb *yādôn*, is to color Yahweh's speech as lofty and archaic. Yahweh speaks in a high register here, befitting his divinity and antiquity, but with an aura of obscurity.

The sense of Yahweh's utterance is that the divine portion in humans will not be strong forever because humans are also flesh, an earthly and mortal substance (see NOTES at 2:7). Humans are a compound of earthly and divine substances, but this compound creature must remain mortal. Yahweh here sets the proper temporal relation between flesh and life-spirit, apparently preventing the mixed marriages of the Sons of God and daughters of humans from tilting the balance too much toward the divine side, toward immortality.

Let their days be 120 years. The finitude of human creatures is sealed by the penalty of a limited lifespan. The use of *yāmāyw* ("their days") to signify lifespan is common in Hebrew, as in Gen 3:14, 17 (J), *kol-yəmê ḥayyêkā* ("all the days of your life") or the lifespan formula in Genesis 5 (P), *kol-yəmê PN* ("all the days of PN"). The temporal duration of the earth is signified in the same manner: *kol-yəmê hā'āreṣ* ("all the days of the earth," 8:22, J). The limit of 120 years is a reasonable number considering actual human longevity, and as a multiple of twelve it is a good formulaic number (cf. the twelve tribes). It is probably significant that Moses, according to both the Deuteronomist and P, lives for 120 years (Deut 31:2, 34:7). According to Ps 90:10, a lifespan (*yəmê-šənôtênû*, "the days of our years") of seventy or eighty years is a good long life.

A maximum lifespan of 120 years is a shared concept in the ancient Near East. As J. Klein (2011: 165–66) observes, the Sumerian folktale *Enlil and Namzitara* (found in a bilingual version at Late Bronze Age Emar) expresses this notion in a passage about the transience of life:

> The days of the human being are approaching,
>> Day to day they verily decrease,
> Month after month they verily decrease,
>> Year after year they verily decrease!
> One hundred twenty years (are) the years of humankind—verily it is their bane;
>> (This is so) from the time that humanity exists until today!

A problem for traditional interpreters in understanding this lifespan is that everyone afterwards in Genesis, except for Joseph, lives for longer than 120 years: Noah lives 950 years; Shem, 600; Shelah, 433; Abraham, 175; Jacob, 147; and Joseph, 110. The reason for this friction is that 6:3 is from J and all the other lifespan numbers in Genesis are from P. Hence early interpreters understood Yahweh's words in 6:3 as not referring to the human lifespan but to some other duration of time. The LXX, the targums, and a Qumran commentary on Genesis (4QCommGen[a]) take this span to be the time remaining until the flood: "their days" is interpreted as "their remaining days" before the flood (see Kugel 1998: 183–85). This interpretation makes sense of the text in its final form—and is perhaps the only way to make it yield consistent sense—but then this decree loses its resonance with the theme of immortality and becomes an odd foreshadowing of Yahweh's later, and differently motivated, decision to send the flood.

6:4. *The Nephilim were on the earth in those days, and also later, when the Sons of God used to couple with the daughters of humans, who would bear children for them—they were the warriors of old, the men of renown.* Verse 4 consists of a sequence of disjunctive clauses, each qualifying the known narrative situation. The new information includes the name and characteristics of the Nephilim, who are (in an awkward sequence) identified as the offspring of the Sons of God and the daughters of humans. These statements bring the story to an obscure conclusion. Gunkel (1997: 58–59) rightly observes that v. 4a reads "like a parenthetical note," and v. 4b elucidates this parenthesis. The verse is, in a sense, a complex antiquarian aside. Cassuto (1961: 299) detects an echo of 6:1–2 in the sequence "Sons of God . . . daughters of man . . . bear them," but now the children born are the mysterious Nephilim.

The grammar is awkward. The initial disjunctive (noun-initial) clause, "The Nephilim were on the earth in those days," is the stable part of this sentence, with each further phrase or clause referring to it. The phrase "and also later" seems an afterthought, conditioned by the mention of the Nephilim in Num 13:33 long after the flood (see below). The temporal clause "when the Sons of God . . ." that recapitulates the reproductive acts of the Sons of God and the daughters of humans seems an awkward clarification that the Nephilim are to be identified as the offspring. The final disjunctive (noun-initial) clause also qualifies the Nephilim as legendary figures. There is a particularly rough transition to the final clause, lāhem hēmâ ("for them—they"), in which the two pronouns have different antecedents. The preposition lāhem ("for them") refers to the Sons of God, but hēmâ refers to their offspring, the Nephilim.

The identity of the Nephilim is obscure. Their epithets, "the warriors of old, the men of renown," indicate that their stories were well-known, but their legendary exploits have been lost. The only other reference to the Nephilim is the report by the Israelite spies who were commissioned by Moses to reconnoiter the hill country of the promised land. They report to Moses: "The land we went through to spy is a land that eats its inhabitants. All the people we saw in it are men of great size. There we saw the Nephilim (the Anakites are from the Nephilim) and we seemed in our own eyes like grasshoppers, and so we seemed to them" (Num 13:32–33, J). According to this fearful report, the Nephilim are giants, "men of great size" (ʾanšê middôt) (cf. Deut 1:28, Amos 2:9; see Hendel 2021a).

The statement that "the Nephilim were on the earth in those days, and also later," links these legendary warriors before the flood to the Nephilim who are mighty giants in Canaan at the time of the Israelite conquest. This dual signification of the Nephilim is odd, but the continuity of the antediluvian and postdiluvian Nephilim is clear enough. Following this equation, the LXX translates the Hebrew "Nephilim" in Gen 6:4 as "giants" (gigantes), and most early interpreters understood the Nephilim similarly.

The etymology of nəpîlîm (Nephilim) may be important in understanding their identity, although this too is unclear. The word is a passive adjectival construction from npl, "to fall," and means "ones who are fallen." In Hebrew, the term "fallen ones" evokes the idea of one who has fallen in battle, for example, "How have the mighty fallen?" (2 Sam 1:19, 25, 27), and "the fallen warriors of old" (Ezek 32:27, reading "of old" with the LXX). This latter phrase may refer to the Nephilim of Gen 6:4, although this is not clear (see Hendel 2004: 22 n. 28). This evocation of death ("fallen ones") fits the fate of the Nephilim, who are destroyed by the flood and/or by the Israelite conquest.

There is, of course, a logical problem with the twofold reference of the Nephilim as the antediluvian warriors and the giant aboriginal inhabitants of Canaan. The flood intervenes, which kills all living creatures on earth, with the exception of those on the ark (7:22, J). The persistence of the Nephilim contradicts the flood story—providing a lively subject for postbiblical interpreters. The likely solution to this problem is that

J combined traditions about the Nephilim that were not internally consistent or that were told independently of the flood story.

The epithets of the Nephilim—*haggibbōrîm 'ăšer mē'ôlām 'anšê haššēm* ("the warriors of old, the men of renown")—presumably triggered well-known associations that are now obscure. The word *mē'ôlām* ("of old, ancient") echoes *lə'ôlām* ("forever") in 6:3, providing a counterpoint between the now dead heroes and the theme of mortality (Cassuto 1961: 299). The word *haššēm* (lit. "the name," meaning "renown, fame") provides a linkage with the mention of *šēm* (Shem), son of Noah, in the flood story that follows. More importantly, it sets up the theme of the desire for a great name that later animates the builders of the Tower of Babel (11:4) and that echoes in the call of Abraham ("I will make your name great," 12:2). However, the Nephilim and the builders of the tower remain anonymous, providing a counterpoint to Abraham's great name. This repetition of *šēm* ("name, fame") yields a *Leitwort* sequence that culminates with the call of Abram. Whereas the Nephilim were "men of renown (*šēm*)," a form of cultural immortality, this status is neutralized or ironized by the absence of their famous deeds in the text. The reason for their fame is omitted, and their collective name Nephilim ("fallen ones") signals their anonymous death.

Comments

This is a strange text, filled with enigmas and gaps. Male gods having sex and offspring with mortal women seems more suited to ancient Greece than Genesis. As Josephus writes, "The deeds that tradition ascribes to them [the Nephilim] resemble the audacious exploits told by the Greeks of the giants" (*Ant.* I.73–74). While Josephus seems to discount the truth of the Greek stories, he grants their resemblance to this biblical tradition. This story, however, seems to be truncated. As Gunkel (1997: 59) comments, "It can hardly be called a story. . . . The original narrative must have been much richer." By its style and diction, it is a J text, but there were things J did not want to tell. The story is only four verses long, and only the first two present a continuous story. Something about lusty gods, beautiful women, and the birth of demigods made the J writer hesitant to tell the whole story. And yet it includes a different angle on some central themes in the primeval narrative, particularly the dangerous boundary between humans and gods. It also supplies a backdrop for later events in the J source, when the Nephilim were on the earth.

LITERARY DESIGN

In this short text, there are several instances of J's *Leitwort* style. The text begins, "When humans began (*hēḥēl*) to multiply" (6:1), which repeats in the active voice the verb of the previous verse in J: "Then was it begun (*hûḥal*) to call on the name of Yahweh" (4:24). The language of beginnings pivots from religious speech to procreation. The *Leitwort* relationship of "humans" (*hā'ādām*) and "soil/earth" (*hā'ădāmâ*) also resounds here, as "the humans" (*hā'ādām*) multiply on the face of "the earth" (*hā'ădāmâ*). This expansion of humans on the earth subtly echoes the problematic relationship of the previous humans to the soil and may signal that more problems are to come. The chief problem is a consequence of the multiplication of humans and the birth of daughters, who attract the attention of the Sons of God.

While the first verse has *Leitwort* echoes of the previous J narrative, the first two verses have *Leitwort* anticipations of the next story, the J flood. After the humans begin "to multiply" (*lārōb*), the sons of God "see" (*wayyir'û*) that the daughters of humans are "beautiful/good" (*ṭōbōt*, 6:2). This diction echoes in the next story in 6:5, "Yahweh saw (*wayyar'*) how great (*rabbâ*) was the evil of humans (*rā'at ha'ādām*)." This time it is Yahweh who sees, not the Sons of God, and he sees the great extent of human evil, not the goodness/beauty of the abundant human daughters. But Yahweh sees differently than the Sons of God: he sees the interior moral disposition of humans, while the Sons of God see the exterior form of the human women. These verbal echoes and inversions set the two stories in relation to each other. The Sons of God see humans with a sexual gaze, while Yahweh sees the human heart.

After setting the initial condition of the story with these developments, the protagonists, the Sons of God, take action: "they took for themselves wives from whomever they chose" (6:2). This is the complication and turning point of the story. Although there is no direct comment on these marriages, the implication is that they are improper. The partners belong to different orders of being, gods and humans, which should not be mixed. This is the clear implication of the Garden of Eden story, where Yahweh says, "the human has become like one of us, knowing good and evil," whereupon he expels the couple, lest they "take from the Tree of Life and eat and live forever" (3:22). Humans have encroached on the divine realm and are prevented from becoming immortal, that is, wholly gods. The marriages and offspring of gods and humans also constitute a breach of these boundaries. Although Yahweh's speech in 6:3 does not directly address this problem, it seems to effect a separation of humans and gods, so that the breach of boundaries may be repaired.

Yahweh's speech in the third verse of the story seems to hover around this complication, while punishing humans with a limited lifespan. This seems an odd punishment, since the Sons of God were the agents of the transgression, not the humans. Yahweh addresses the divine/human relationship only with respect to humans, not with respect to their husbands and in-laws, the Sons of God. He says, using somewhat obscure diction, "My breath will not be strong in humans forever, inasmuch as they also are flesh. Let their days be 120 years" (6:3). The divine "breath" that animates humans recalls Yahweh's creation of the first human: "And he blew life's breath into its nostrils, and the human became a living being" (2:7). The word for "breath" is different (*rûaḥ* in 6:3, *nəšāmâ* in 2:7), but the concept is the same. Humans are made of "flesh" (*bāśār*) taken from the soil's dust, and breath from Yahweh. This is a "soft" duality, which separates at death. The punishment of a fixed lifespan marks a clear separation between humans and gods. Humans are mortal—as shown already in the expulsion from Eden and in the murders committed by Cain and Lamech—and now have a strictly limited lifespan. This adds a new limit to the human condition. It also seems to pertain to the hybrid offspring of the dangerous marriages.

The fourth and last verse addresses these offspring in a sequence of disjunctive clauses, backfilling the story, as it were, with asides rather than resuming a connected narrative. The new details include the offspring of the divine-human marriages, called obscurely the Nephilim, who seem to be described in the last clause—the grammar is unclear, perhaps deliberately so—"they were the warriors of old, the men of renown" (6:4). The cause of their "renown" (*šēm*, lit. "name") is lacking. Although they are "men of renown," their famous deeds seem to be forgotten. This is an obscure end for famous warriors. One of the embedded clauses, however, gives a hint: "The Nephilim were on the earth in those days, *and also later.*" Although this aside may be a secondary gloss, it may well be a subtle hint by the J writer that these hybrid offspring have a role to play in a future era, long after the flood, when the Nephilim will still be on the earth. This is a puzzle, since in the flood story all the people not on the ark will die. But the story tells us, all too briefly, that the Nephilim are an exception, and may be revisited later.

The story is framed by the birth of human daughters and the birth of the Nephilim. These two birth scenes are cast in echoing clauses, first passive and then active: "[they] were born to them" (*yullədû lāhem,* 6:1) and "they would bear for them" (*wəyālədû lāhem,* 6:4). The birth of daughters follows from previous stories where sons were born, for example, "a son was also born to him" (*gam-hû' yullad-ben,* 4:26). The birth of the Nephilim to the daughters of humans, however, shows a world gone awry, for they are hybrids, crossing the boundaries of divine and human.

HYBRIDS

As Douglas (1966: 164–65) emphasizes, creatures that fall between categories are often treated as dangerous anomalies, sometimes holy and sometimes abominable, but always "matter out of place." The Nephilim exemplify this anomalous character. As neither wholly god nor wholly human, their existence suggests a system gone awry, whose categories and boundaries lack coherence. The implicit danger of the crossed boundary that they exemplify, the difference between divine and human, motivates Yahweh's intervention. He must impose restrictions to restore and safeguard the stable categories of the cosmos. To do this, in a surprising move, he imposes stricter limits on human mortality. This intervention prevents humans, and by implication their hybrid offspring, from living "forever" (*lə'ōlām,* 6:3), which is solely a divine prerogative.

The fathers of these hybrid creatures, however, do live forever, for they are gods. They are "the Sons of God" (*bənê hā'ĕlōhîm*), who are mentioned only here in the J source. But as members of Yahweh's divine entourage, they seem to be alluded to twice in J, where Yahweh refers to "us"—"like one of us" (*kə'aḥad mimmennû,* 3:22) and "let us go down and confuse" (*nērədâ wənābəlâ,* 11:7). While grammatically these plurals could be "plurals of majesty" or "plurals of intensification" (attested in royal letters; see NOTES at 1:26), they more likely refer to Yahweh's divine assembly. This group consists of lesser gods, called collectively "the Sons/Children of God" (*bənê hā'ĕlōhîm* and similar terms) or "the host of heaven" (*ṣəbā' haššāmayim* and similar terms, e.g., 1 Kgs 22:19). There are also messenger gods; the angels (*mal'ākîm*), as in the story of Sodom and Gomorrah (Gen 19:1, 15; cf. Gen 18:22, where they are called simply "the men," *hā'ănāšîm*); and assorted other divine creatures, like the guardian cherubim (Gen 3:22). The Sons/Children of God have more autonomy than the lesser classes of divine creatures, although they too are subservient to Yahweh. Elsewhere they report to Yahweh in the divine assembly (Job 1:6, 2:1) and sing praises to Yahweh (Pss 29:1, 87: 6–7). They were already singing praises when Yahweh created the world (Job 38:7).

As gods, the Sons/Children of God are also physically manifested as stars in the sky, as reflected in their designation "the host of heaven" (*ṣəbā' haššāmayim*). This term often has a martial sense, since they fight Yahweh's battles from heaven (Josh 5:14–15,

Judg 5:20). In some texts the Sons/Children of God are also the gods of foreign nations (Deut 4:19 and 32:8, reading for the latter *banê ʾělôhîm* with 4QDeut^j and the LXX). The theological end of the Sons/Children of God occurs in Psalm 82, when God decides to execute them for injustice:

> I had taken you for gods,
>> and the children of the Most High (*bənê ʾelyôn*) all of you.
> But like humans you shall die,
>> and like one of the princes you shall fall. (Ps 82:6–7)

This is a strong assertion of biblical monotheism. An earlier text in which one of the celestial gods dies is Isa 14:12–20, which relates the fall of "Shining One, son of Dawn," a pretender to the heavenly throne who was cast down to Sheol like a falling star. (For the disappearance of the divine assembly in P, see NOTES at 1:26.)

In Gen 6:1–4, the focus is on the male members of the Sons/Children of God. Their sexual desire is awakened by the beauty of the daughters of humans. The story's turning point—"they took for themselves wives from whomever they chose"—suggests the illicit nature of the marriages. Unlike honorable marriages, there is no consultation or negotiation with the women's kin (cf. Genesis 24 and 29). The Sons of Gods wield dangerous agency in the human world. Their sexual and social incursion into the human world, which is a dangerous incursion, produces children who are demigods, part god and part human. These children are hybrids whose very being confuses the boundary between human and divine. This distinction of realms has been marked as dangerous since the first humans crossed this boundary when they ate the forbidden fruit of knowledge, becoming "like gods," and were then expelled from Eden lest they eat from the fruit of life and "live forever" (3:22).

The fate of the hybrid offspring is suggested by their collective name, Nephilim (*nəpîlîm*). This means "fallen ones," which evokes the idea of warriors fallen in battle, as in David's lament, "How have the warriors fallen?" (*ʾêk nāpəlû gibbôrîm,* 2 Sam 1:9, 27). Although they are described as heroes—"the warriors of old, the men of renown" (6:4)—their name indicates their collective death, hinting at a tragic fate, presumably in battle. But the details are omitted. They are a generation of hybrids, half god and half human, but the human half makes them mortal, and so they are doomed to die. This doom is not explicit, but suggested, both concealed and revealed in their name and epithets.

Yahweh does not act explicitly against the hybrids themselves, nor against the Sons of God who were the agents of the transgression. His focus is on the human world, and he sets a limit on lifespan that further separates humans from the divine world. This response to transgression expands Yahweh's previously imposed limits in J (note that the P genealogies in Genesis 5 and 11 are unaware of the 120-year limit on lifespan). Yet the hybrid Nephilim persist and, in a brief aside, are on the earth "also later" (*gam ʾaḥărê-kēn,* 6:4). This comment acknowledges that the hybrids exist after the flood, which poses a curious puzzle in the narrative transition to the flood.

CONTEXTS

The fame—or infamy—of the Nephilim is partially revealed in a later story in the J source. In Numbers 13, we learn that they are fearsome giants dwelling in the hill country of Canaan, whom Yahweh promises to deliver to destruction. In the era of the conquest, the giants are hybrids, dangerous beings who are betwixt and between, but in a different configuration. They stand between Israel and the promised land and pose a deadly threat to those who would cross that boundary.

When Moses sends spies to reconnoiter the hill country of Judah, they discover the Nephilim, who are called "children of Anak" ('ănāq means something like "long-necked"). Upon their return, the spies report to Moses:

> "We came to the land where you sent us, and indeed it is flowing with milk and honey, and this is its fruit. However, the people who live in the land are strong, and the cities are fortified and very great, and also we saw there the children of Anak" . . . Caleb quieted the people before Moses and said, "Let us immediately go up and possess it, for we are able to prevail over it." But the people who went up with him said, "We are not able to go up against the people, for it is stronger than us. . . . And there we saw the Nephilim (the children of Anak are from the Nephilim) and we seemed in our eyes like grasshoppers, and so we seemed in their eyes." (Num 13:27–28, 30–31, 33; J)

A later scribe added the gloss (indicated by the parentheses) that "the children of Anak are from the Nephilim" (Num 13:33; this clause is lacking in the LXX). Here and in Gen 6:4 the LXX translates Nephilim as "giants" (*gigantes*), because this is how they are pictured here. Even the fruit of the Nephilim is giant fruit, since it takes two men to carry a single grape-cluster on a pole (Num 13:23).

The spies express their terror at the giant Nephilim with a striking metaphor: "we seemed in our eyes like grasshoppers, and so we seemed in their eyes" (Num 13:33). This metaphor transposes the relationship between humans and giants to a different scale—in the metaphor, people are like grasshoppers while giants are like people. In metaphor and reality, the giants have overwhelming mastery. Caleb does not dispute the accuracy of the report but argues "we are able to prevail" because of Yahweh's superior power. He is correct, but the crowd's fear of the giants prevails, and they refuse to go up into Canaan. The people's refusal triggers Yahweh's wrath. This is a turning point in the narrative.

At Moses's insistence, Yahweh relents from destroying the people, but they are punished with forty years of wandering in the wilderness: "None of those who saw my glory and my signs that I did in Egypt and in the wilderness and tested me these ten times and have not heeded my voice, will see the land that I promised to their fathers" (Num 14:22–23). The giants are the occasion for the decisive act of backsliding and punishment. The good spy, Caleb, is the only one who will enter the land. In the J source, this is the last we hear of the Nephilim, the giant inhabitants of Canaan.

The fate of the Nephilim (and other ethnonyms for the indigenous giants of Canaan) is taken up in other biblical books—Deuteronomy and Joshua rewrite and extend the earlier J narrative, while Amos gives an independent account (Hendel 2021a: 265–72). In Deut 1:28, Moses rephrases the spies' description from Num 13:28 (above): "It is a people greater and taller than us, and great cities fortified up to heaven." He later informs the Israelites that Yahweh will destroy the giants so that they may dispossess them and dwell in the promised land:

> Hear O Israel, you are going to cross the Jordan today to go in and dispossess nations greater and mightier than you, with great cities fortified up to heaven, a people great and tall, the children of the Anakim, whom you know. And you have heard it said, "Who can stand before the children of Anak?" But know today that Yahweh, your God, He is going to cross before you as a devouring flame. And He will destroy them and subdue them before you, and you will dispossess them and destroy them quickly, as Yahweh has promised you. (Deut 9:1–3)

Deuteronomy here supplements Yahweh's promise that "My presence will go with you" (Exod 34:14) with dual agency, such that both Yahweh and Israel will destroy the native inhabitants, using synonymous verbs—"he will destroy them" (*hûʾ yašmîdēm*) and "you will destroy them" (*haʾabadtām*). Yahweh's metaphorical presence as "a devouring flame" will clear the way to the destruction of the giants.

In the account of the conquest of Canaan by Joshua and his troops, after the eradication of the Canaanites and their kings, Joshua destroys the giants: "At that time Joshua came and cut off the Anakim from the hill country, from Hebron, from Debir, from Anab, and from all the hill country of Judah and from all the hill country of Israel, with their cities. Joshua eradicated them. No Anakim remained in the land of the children of Israel; only in Gaza, Gath, and Ashdod did they remain" (Josh 11:21–22). This seems to be a secondary aside, supplementing the annihilation (*ḥerem*) of the Canaanites with the annihilation of the giant Anakim. Notably, it harmonizes the different locales of the Anakim in Numbers and Deuteronomy. In Numbers 13, the Anakim are located in the Judean hill country around Hebron, whereas in Deuteronomy 1 and 9 their location is generalized to the whole land. The Joshua passage links these different geographies and includes an anticipatory link to the story of David and his men slaying four Philistine giants, including a certain Goliath (see 1 Samuel 17; 2 Sam 21:15–22).

The book of Amos also recalls the destruction of the indigenous giants, but in this account the conqueror is Yahweh alone:

> It was I who destroyed the Amorite before them,
> > whose height is like the height of cedars,
> > and whose strength is like oaks.
> I destroyed his fruit above,
> > and his roots below. (Amos 2:9)

The conquest is recalled as a total destruction of the Amorites, who are presented as giants. (The ethnonyms for the indigenous giants are somewhat varied among the texts; here "Amorite" is the general designation.) Their fearsome stature is expressed through metaphor, likening their height to cedars, the tallest known tree, and their strength to mighty oaks. In the final couplet, the metaphor is developed into a mini-narrative, as Yahweh destroys the giant Amorites totally, from above (fruit) to below (root).

The common denominator in these traditions is that the giants were once the indigenous inhabitants of the land but were destroyed—by Yahweh, Joshua, or David and his men. In the current era after the conquest, the giants are dead. This seems to be a collective resonance of their ethnonyms: Nephilim ("fallen ones"), Rephaim (*rəpāʾîm*, "healthy ones[?]," elsewhere denoting the spirits of the dead), Emim (*ʾēmîm*, "terrors"), and Zamzummim (*zamzummîm*, "whisperers"). They once were giants, but now they sleep in the dust.

Some postbiblical Jewish texts were troubled by the survival of the hybrid Nephilim after the flood and filled this gap by having them destroyed by the flood or by each other. In the book of Enoch, they destroy each other before the flood. God sends an angel to implement a war of destruction:

> Go, Gabriel, to the bastards, to the half-breeds, to the sons of miscegenation;
>   and destroy the sons of the watchers from among the sons of men;
>   and send them against one another in a war of destruction.

(1 En. 10:9; Nickelsburg 2001: 215)

The destruction of the hybrid Nephilim in a great war may draw on Greek traditions about the destruction of the hybrid heroes in the Trojan War (see below). The term "watchers" (*'îrîn* in Aramaic; Dan 4:14) refers generally to angels and here to the Sons of God. In the book of Enoch, the watchers descend to earth to marry human women and reveal to them and their violent offspring forbidden secrets—sorcery and divination, the cutting of roots and plants, metallurgy and weapons, and even makeup. This is the origin of evil on earth, which brings on the great flood (see Stuckenbruck 2004: 99–104).

In other interpretations the Nephilim die in the flood, as the context in Genesis seems to indicate. According to an "Admonition Based on the Flood" from Qumran, "All tha[t was on] dry land was [wiped out], and humans and [beasts and all] birds, every winged thing, d[ie]d. And the g[ian]ts did not escape" (4Q370 i 6; Newsom 1988: 28). This interpretation makes sense of the immediate context of the Nephilim but omits their persistence after the flood so that they could be destroyed (again) in the conquest of Canaan. The "Book of Giants" from Qumran and later Manichaean texts expand on the tales of the demonic giants, albeit fragmentarily (Goff, Stuckenbruck, and Morano 2016).

A broader context for the biblical stories about the birth and death of demigod warriors can be found in ancient Near Eastern and Greek texts (Hendel 1987, 2004; Darshan 2018: 113–34). Genesis 6:1–4 does not seem to be directly influenced by these other texts; rather, they all belong to a family of traditions in which narrative memories of the heroic past take different forms in various communities in an interconnected cultural sphere. The stories have shared themes and categories, which are articulated through local frameworks of memory. As George (2003: 57) surmises from the Greek parallels to the Gilgamesh traditions, "Greek poetry imported from the eastern Mediterranean region motifs, episodes, imagery and modes of expression that were always traditional in the narrative poetry of the area." The biblical story of the Sons of God and the daughters of humans is part of this multiform river of poetic and prose traditions, from which each culture drew in its portraits of the past.

Let us turn to the Mesopotamian and Greek traditions. The most famous Mesopotamian hero, Gilgamesh, was a warrior-king of old and a man of renown. He was also the hybrid offspring of a goddess and a human king. These features make him an analogue of the Nephilim. Because of Gilgamesh's human father he was mortal, and because of his divine mother he was superhuman and huge in stature. As described in the epic's prologue, he was a mighty warrior with an impressive ancestry and size:

Wild bull of Lugalbanda, Gilgamesh, perfect of strength,
> suckling of the exalted cow, Wild-Cow Ninsun.

Gilgamesh so tall, perfect and terrible . . .
> two-thirds of him god but a third of him human.

Bēlet-ili drew the shape of his body,
> Nudimmud brought his form to perfection.

[. . .] was majestic [. . .]
> [a giant(?)] in stature, eleven cubits [was his height,]

[Four cubits was] the width of [his chest,]
> a triple cubit his foot, half a rod his leg,

six cubits was the length of his stride.

(Gilg. I.35–37, 48–58; George 2003: 540–41, and 2007: 247–48)

Gilgamesh is a giant hybrid, two-thirds god and one-third human (perhaps the human chromosome is recessive?), who stood some sixteen-and-a-half feet tall, with a body six feet wide. We may compare these dimensions with the giant King Og in Deut 3:11, whose bed was thirteen-and-a-half feet long and six feet wide. Gilgamesh would have fit the width of Og's bed, but he was a yard too long for it.

In addition to being a famous warrior of old and a giant, Gilgamesh was also a god in the underworld after his death, where he was a judge and ruler of the shades of the dead (George 2003: 119–132). The shades—*utukkū* or *eṭemmū* in Akkadian—are equivalent to the Rephaim in the Bible and Ugaritic texts (see below). In this mixture of traits, we see the heroic status of Gilgamesh, who in life and death is comparable to these biblical figures. He has a richer narrative legacy, but a similar range of heroic concepts.

Josephus first noted the resemblance between the Nephilim and the stories of Greek giants (see above). More recently, classicists have observed that Gen 6:1–4 resembles the story of "the Greek heroes who were born to gods and mortal women and destroyed by the Trojan War" (West 1971: 43 n. 3). The fullest description is in the *Catalogue of Women,* attributed in antiquity to Hesiod. It begins with an invocation to the muse to inform the poet about the sexual unions of male gods and human women and the birth of heroic warrior-kings:

Of these women tell [me the race and the splendid children:]
All those with whom lay [the father of men and of gods,]
Begetting at [first the race of illustrious kings,]
And with which ones Poseidon [. . .]
And [all those whom] Ares [. . .]
[and all those with whom Heph]aestus
[And with which ones] Hermes [. . .]

(1.14–21; Most 2006: 42–43).

The text comes to an end with Zeus devising his plan to destroy the heroic demigods (*hemitheoi*) in the great destruction of the Trojan War:

High-thundering Zeus was devising
wondrous deeds then, to stir up trouble on the boundless earth;
for he was already eager to annihilate the abundant race

of speech-endowed humans, avowedly to destroy
the lives of the demigods, [. . .] to mortals,
children of the gods [. . .] seeing with eyes,
but that the blessed [gods], as before,
should have [beds and] habitations apart from human beings.
[Hence he established] for immortals and for mortal humans
[difficult warfare: for the ones he made] pain upon pain
Zeus [. . .] he destroyed
(10 more fragmentary lines)
[neither] of the blessed gods nor of mortal humans;
[and] the bronze was going to send to Hades many heads
of men, heroes falling in battle-strife.

(155.95–119; Most 2006: 232–35, and González 2010)

The destruction of the demigods restores the separation of humans and gods. In Zeus's words, "but that the blessed [gods], as before, / should have [beds and] habitations apart from human beings." As Clay (2003: 168) comments, "The passing of these half human/half divine hybrids therefore reinstates the status quo ante, *hōs to paros per* ['as before']." While there are other motives for the Trojan War in other texts, the revelation of Zeus's plan makes it a mythic transition from primeval confusion to the distinct domains of "blessed gods" and "mortal humans" in the present world. As Nagy (1979: 220) observes, "besides entailing the death of heroes in the Trojan War . . . the Will of Zeus also entails *the permanent separation of gods and men*" (emphasis in the original).

The separation of the domains of gods and humans is a central theme in the J primeval narrative, but the Nephilim obscurely persist to be annihilated in a later great destruction—the conquest and its aftermath. Although the separation of gods and humans occurs during the primeval era, a remnant of its dangerous hybridity remains until the era of Israel's emergence as a nation, when the present world is fully formed. The hybrid demigods thus animate the boundary between chaos and order in both eras, each marked by a great destruction—the flood and the conquest. In Greek epic, the Trojan War plays this role.

The Nephilim, like the Greek demigods, belong to a past era. As Clay (2003: 169) notes, "In early Greek poetry, the term *hemitheoi* [demigods] always seems to convey not only their hybrid nature, but also a distancing perspective on the heroes that assigns them to a bygone era." The designations of the Nephilim—"the fallen ones," "the warriors of old, the men of renown"—have a similar distancing resonance. They evoke an era of distant memory, of permeable boundaries, of beds shared by gods and humans. In Genesis this memory is half-effaced, but in Greece it animates the great epics of the heroic age.

As a final comparative context, we turn to ancient Canaan. Generally, we would turn to Canaan first, since it is the direct ancestor of ancient Israelite culture. But in this case, we lack a Canaanite story that is directly comparable to Gen 6:1–4. Yet there are several of the ingredients. The Hebrew term "Sons/Children of God" (*bənê hā'ĕlōhîm*) is cognate with Ugaritic *bn 'il* and *bn 'lm* ("Sons/Children of God"), and this term is also found in Phoenician and Ammonite inscriptions (see Notes at 6:2). In Ugaritic, it literally refers to the children of El ("God"), who is the head of the pantheon and the father of the gods. El bears the epithet *'ab bn il* ("Father of the Children of El") and appears in scenes where he begets divine children with various wives and consorts. As far as we can tell, these female partners are gods. We lack any indication that El or the other gods have sex with mortals. In the Aqhat epic, the goddess Anat propositions the mortal hero Aqhat, but he rejects her advance (this has a parallel in the *Gilgamesh* epic, where Gilgamesh rejects Ishtar's advance).

The other ingredient that is cognate in biblical and Canaanite lore is the status of the Rephaim, Ugaritic *rp'um* (probably vocalized *rapa'ūma*). In the Bible, the Rephaim are related to the Nephilim as aboriginal giants in Canaan (e.g., King Og, the last of the Rephaim, Deut 3:11) and as shades of the dead. In Ugaritic texts, as M. S. Smith (2014: 137) observes, "*rp'um* were evidently viewed as heroes of old predating Ugarit's royal line. These *rp'um* enjoyed 'divine' or 'semi-divine status' in their postmortem existence." In the Kirta epic, El blesses Kirta at the birth of his children with the following invocation:

> May Kirta be greatly exalted,
> In the midst of the Rephaim of the underworld,
> In the assembly of Ditanu's company.

> (*CAT* 1.15.iii.13–15, 17–19; Greenstein 1997: 26)

This refers to Kirta's future status as a shade of the underworld, in the company of the *rp'um* and the ancestors of his royal dynasty (headed by Ditanu). Compare the prophet's description of the underworld Rephaim at the death of the king of Babylon:

> Sheol below is stirred up to meet you when you come,
> > it rouses the Rephaim for you, all the chiefs of the earth,
> > it raises from their thrones all the kings of the nations. (Isa 14:10)

Here the Rephaim are the royal dead, greeting the new shade as he arrives in the underworld.

In Ugaritic royal ideology, the king was divinized after death, and while he lived he was regarded as a "son of El" (*bn 'il*), not fully a god, but hedged with divinity. Kirta's son says when his father the king becomes deathly ill:

> Is Kirta not called son of El (*bn 'il*),
> > scion of the Gentle and Holy One?
> Gods, after all—do they die?
> > The Gentle One's son—won't he live?

> (*CAT* 1.16.i.22–23; Greenstein 1997: 30–31)

Since Kirta is mortal, he must die, whereupon he will join the Rephaim and his royal ancestors in the underworld as a divinized shade.

If we gather these threads together, we can see the Canaanite background for the "Sons/Children of God" and the Rephaim. The former are the gods of the pantheon, the consanguineous "Children of El," who have shifting alliances and independent identities. The term "son of El" is semantically extended to the king, who is El's chosen ruler, and who, like medieval kings, has "two bodies," mortal and divine. At his death, the king joins the divine Rephaim in the underworld, uniting with his dynastic ancestors.

If the Nephilim in Gen 6:4 are the partially effaced cultural memory of the heroes and warriors of a past age, then we should expect the Ugaritic texts to provide some of the background for this memory. We may conjecture that in the sexual couplings of the Sons of God and the daughters of humans and the birth of hybrid demigods, we have a confection of old bits of royal ideology combined with tales of heroes, giants, and shades. *Gilgamesh* is a robust version of this tradition, as crystallized in Mesopotamia in the second millennium BCE. The Greek demigods are another version, a transformed memory of Mycenaean kings and warriors of the Late Bronze Age. The Nephilim are probably a similar cultural memory, recalling "the warriors of old, the men of renown" of ancient traditions through Iron Age lenses.

For the Greek demigods and the biblical Nephilim, the memory of this prior age was also preserved in the landscape. The massive ruins of Mycenae, Tiryns, and other sites were visible testimony to the great warrior-kings of old. Similarly, the immense cyclopean walls at Hebron and other hill country sites were visible testimony to the giant Nephilim, and the megaliths and dolmens in Transjordan were testimony to the giant Rephaim, including King Og's giant bed, which still could be seen in Rabbah of Ammon (Deut 3:11; see Hendel 2021).

The Flood According to J
(6:5–8:22, J, *R*)

---

6 ⁵Yahweh saw how great was the evil of humans on the earth, for every design of their hearts was only evil all day long. ⁶Yahweh regretted that he had made humans on the earth, and his heart was pained. ⁷Yahweh said, "I will wipe out humans *whom I created* from the face of the soil, *from humans to land animals to crawling creatures to the birds of heaven,* for I regret that I made them." ⁸But Noah found favor in the eyes of Yahweh.

. . .

7 ¹Yahweh said to Noah, "Enter the ark, you and all your household, for I see that you are a righteous man before me in this generation. ²Of every clean animal, take them seven by seven, a male and its mate, and of every unclean[a] animal take two, a male and its mate, ³*also of every bird of heaven take them seven by seven, male and female,* to keep their seed alive on the[b] whole earth. ⁴For in seven days, I am going to bring rain on the earth for forty days and forty nights, and I will wipe off the face of the soil all living things that I have made." ⁵Noah did everything as Yahweh commanded him.

¹⁰The seventh day came, and the flood waters were on the earth. ⁷Noah, *his sons, his wife, and his sons' wives with him* entered the ark because of the flood waters. ⁸*Of the clean land animals, the unclean animals, the birds, and all creatures that crawl on the earth,* ⁹*two of each came to Noah in the ark, male and female, as God commanded Noah.* . . . . ¹⁶Then Yahweh shut him in. ¹²It rained on the earth for forty days and forty nights.

¹⁷The flood was on the earth for forty days. The water rose and lifted the ark, and it was high above the earth. . . . . ²²Everything with life's breath[c] in its nostrils, everything that lived on dry land, died. ²³He wiped off the face of the soil all living things—*from humans to land animals to crawling creatures to the birds of heaven. They were wiped off the earth.* Only Noah and those with him on the ark survived. . . .

8 . . . ²Then the rain was withheld from heaven. ³The water receded gradually on the earth. . . .

⁶At the end of forty days, Noah opened the window of the ark that he had made. . . . ⁸He sent out a dove that was with him to see if the water had subsided on the face of the soil. ⁹But the dove did not find a place to rest its feet, so it returned to him on the ark, for the water still covered the whole face of the earth. He reached out his hand and caught it and brought it back into the ark. ¹⁰He waited[d] another seven days and again sent the dove from the ark. ¹¹The dove returned to him toward evening, and behold, in its beak was a plucked olive leaf, and Noah knew that the water had subsided on the face of the earth. ¹²He waited another seven days and sent out the dove, but it did not return to him again. . . . ¹³Noah removed the ark's cover, and he looked, and behold, the face of the soil was dry.

. . .

²⁰Noah built an altar for Yahweh. He took one of every clean animal and every clean bird and offered burnt offerings on the altar. ²¹Yahweh smelled the soothing aroma, and Yahweh said in his heart, "I will never again curse the soil because of humans, for the designs of the human heart are evil from their youth. Never again will I destroy all life as I have done. ²²[e]For all the earth's days these shall never cease:

> seedtime and harvest, cold and heat,
>   summer and winter, and day and night."

Textual Notes

a. The MT and SP add a resumptive pronoun *hy'*, which is lacking in the LXX. This is probably an explicating plus (Hendel 1998: 51).

b. The MT and SP add *pny* ("face of"), which is lacking in the LXX. This is a harmonization with the phrase *'l pny kl h 'rṣ* ("on the whole face of the earth," 8:9; 1:29) (Hendel 1998: 51).

c. The MT and SP add *rwḥ* ("breath, spirit"), which is lacking in the LXX. This plus harmonizes the phrase *nšmt ḥyym*, typical of J, with the equivalent P phrase *rwḥ ḥyym* (6:17, 7:15), both meaning "life's breath" (Hendel 1998: 53–54).

d. The MT and SP have suffered a haplography ("single writing") of *yod* in the verb *wyyḥl*, "he waited." The form *wyḥl* in the MT is vocalized as a *hiphil*, but if it were *hiphil* the consonantal spelling would have been *wywḥl* (Hendel 1998: 54).

e. In the MT and SP this verse begins with *'d*, "again," which is lacking in the LXX. This is perhaps a reminiscence of the construction *l' . . . 'wd* ("never again"), twice in the preceding verse. The *'d* in 8:22 would then coordinate with *l' yšbtw* ("never cease") at the end of the verse (Hendel 1998: 56).

Notes

6:5–8. The introduction to the flood story presents an evocative description of Yahweh's motivations for the sending the flood. The text shows Yahweh's own sensibilities: first he sees, then he feels, and finally he speaks (in an internal speech) (Hamilton 1990: 273). In this description, Yahweh's moral agency and inner life contrast with those of humans, who are characterized by their evil designs. In a *Leitwort* sequence, the repeated verb *nḥm* ("regret") contrasts with *nōaḥ* (Noah), whom Yahweh perceives favorably.

This sets up the tension in the story between Yahweh's regret and favor and his subsequent acts of destruction and restoration.

6:5. *Yahweh saw how great was the evil of humans on the earth, for every design of their hearts was only evil all day long.* The opening, *wayyar' yhwh kî* ("Yahweh saw how . . ."), presents a verbal echo and thematic counterpoint to the previous action in 6:2, "the Sons of God saw . . . that . . ." (*wayyir'û banê-hā'ĕlōhîm . . . kî*). But the tenor and gravity of the situation are different. Rather than the erotic gaze of the Sons of God, who see the beauty of human women, now we have the deeper perception of Yahweh, who sees the human heart (cf. 1 Sam 16:7, "for a human looks at the eyes [i.e., appearance], but God looks at the heart").

The object of the verb "saw," *kî rabbâ rā'at hā'ādām bā'āreṣ* ("how great was the evil of humans on the earth"), also echoes the diction of 6:1–2. In 6:1 it was humans who had "multiplied" (root *rbb*) on the face of the earth, whereas now human evil has become great (root *rbb*) on the earth. The progression is from the multiplication of bodies to the multiplication of evil. Similarly, in 6:2 the object of divine sight was the "daughters of humans" (*banôt hā'ādām*), and now it is the "evil of humans" (*ra'at hā'ādām*). The proximity of the two phrases creates an echoing contrast, counterposing illicit sexual desire (by the Sons of God) with human immorality. This is not to say that the sexual mingling of the Sons of God and the daughters of humans is the cause of the flood, but that the verbal echoes allude to the previous story. The other previous transgressions—Adam's and Eve's disobedience, Cain's fratricide, Lamech's violence—are similarly illustrations of the multiplication of human evil.

The nature of human evil is not clearly specified, only that it is widespread and constant: "every design of their hearts was only evil all day long." The phrase *yēṣer maḥšəbōt libbô,* literally "shape/construction of the thoughts of his heart," refers to inner intentions, plans, or imagination. In rabbinic literature, this idea was developed into an internal dualism between the *yēṣer hārā'* ("the evil inclination") and the *yēṣer haṭṭôb* ("the good inclination," e.g., *Gen. Rab.* 27.6). An ethical dualism seems to be implied in Genesis—since some people are good at least some of the time (e.g., Noah, Abraham), and people have the capacity to master this evil impulse (Gen 4:7)—but in this verse evil imaginings are constitutive of humans. This is a dark vision of human nature. Notably, although Noah is saved from the flood, at the end of the story this harsh realism remains unchanged—Yahweh resigns himself to the fact that "the designs of the human heart are evil from their youth" (8:21). The pervasiveness of the human capacity for evil is emphasized by the repetition of *kōl* ("all, every"): *kol-yēṣer* ("every design") and *kol-hayyôm* ("all day long").

6:6. *Yahweh regretted that he had made humans on the earth, and his heart was pained.* Yahweh's regret follows his perception of human evil. In J, Yahweh is susceptible to strong emotions—anger, regret, compassion. He is an anthropomorphic and anthropopathic God, that is, he is described in approximately humanlike shape and with humanlike emotions. The object of his regret is the creation of *hā'ādām* ("humans, the human," implicitly collective and singular) in 2:7. He rejects his decision to create these flawed creatures.

The verb for "regret," *wayyinnāḥem* (in the *niphal*), can also mean its opposite, "to comfort, relieve." Contextually the meaning is clear, but there is a verbal echo of the opposite meaning in the birth of Noah in 5:29 (J), when his father says, "he will give us relief/comfort (yənaḥămēnû)" (in the piel). The root nḥm and the name nōaḥ (Noah) are a *Leitwort* pair in this story (Cassuto 1961: 289; Sasson 1975), and the verbal shape of Yahweh's regret implicitly recalls Noah's destiny and anticipates his entry into the story.

Elsewhere occasionally God regrets or repents (nḥm) of his previous actions or intentions, especially when a prophet or intercessor argues with him, for example, Moses (Exod 32:14) and Amos (Amos 7:3, 6) (cf. Abraham, Gen 18:19–32, without nḥm) (see Sonnet 2010). But in other texts, the idea that God could change his mind is anathema—so Balaam says, "God is not a man that he would lie; nor a son of man, that he would change his mind (wəyitneḥām)" (Num 23:19). Many biblical texts agree with this sentiment. Notice that a God who can regret is not omniscient, which Yahweh is not here. He is heartbroken at how the human experiment has turned out. The concept of God's regret is changeable and disputed among the biblical texts.

The pain that Yahweh feels—wayyit'aṣṣēb 'el-libbô ("he was pained/grieved in his heart")—in some ways echoes the pain of the woman ('iṣṣəbônēk, "your pain," 3:16) and the man (bə'iṣṣābôn, "in pain," 3:17, 5:29). The root ṣb echoes in these scenes as the woman, the man, and Yahweh bear the bitter consequences of human transgression, now redescribed as human evil. Yahweh's pain is caused by his perception of the extent of this evil. The specification of libbô ("his heart") draws us into Yahweh's inward experience of pain and is a counterpart to libbô (lit. "his heart," translated as "their hearts," 6:5), where human evil dwells.

6:7. *Yahweh said, "I will wipe out humans whom I created from the face of the soil, from humans to land animals to crawling creatures to the birds of heaven, for I regret that I made them."* The wordplay of hā'ādām ("humans") and hā'ādāmâ ("the soil, earth") strengthens the allusion to Yahweh's creation of the first human from the soil in 2:7. Now he will "wipe off, out" ('emḥeh) humans from the soil, an obliteration of their creation. Compare Yahweh's statement in 2 Kgs 21:13: "I will wipe out Jerusalem as one wipes off a dish."

R added the phrases 'ăšer-bārā'tî ("whom I created") and mē'ādām 'ad-bəhēmâ 'ad-remeś we'ad-'ôp haššāmāyim ("from humans to land animals to crawling creatures to the birds of heaven") to harmonize with the diction of the P creation account (see Skinner 1930: 151; Carr 1996: 57; Soggin 1997: 130). The phrase 'ăšer-bārā'tî ("whom I created") alludes to the creation of humans in 1:27 (P), in which the verb bārā' ("created") occurs three times. The fuller list of creatures accommodates God's (or Yahweh's) later statements that the flood will destroy "all flesh under heaven that has within it life's breath" (6:17, P) or "all living things that I have made" (7:4, J). This supplement also uses the diction of the P creation account, listing the creatures in reverse order from the sixth day (humans, land animals, and crawling creatures) to the fifth (the birds of heaven) (Levinson 2008: 17). But this sequence is grammatically and stylistically awkward (note the explicating transition "from humans to . . ."). R makes Yahweh's plan more harmonious but adds a degree of grammatical infelicity to his speech.

6:8. *But Noah found favor in the eyes of Yahweh.* The verb nḥm (regret), occurring twice in 6:6–7, provides a verbal backdrop for the introduction of nōaḥ (Noah). For reasons given subsequently (7:1), Noah finds divine favor. There is a clever wordplay in the statement that nōaḥ (Noah) finds ḥēn ("favor"). In the consonantal text, ḥn ("favor") is nḥ ("Noah") spelled backwards, an anagram or palindrome (Cassuto 1961: 307).

This verse is grammatically disjunctive (clause initial *waw* + noun + verb) and is also a narrative turn. Yahweh has determined to wipe out *hā'ādām* ("humans") from *hā'ădāmâ* ("the soil, earth") and regrets that he made them. Saving Noah (and his family) would undermine this plan, since it would preserve humans on the earth. There is a degree of friction here—Yahweh's favor for Noah is at odds with his plan to wipe out humankind. This tension is not resolved until the end of the flood story (8:21), when Yahweh decides never again to destroy all life despite the persistent evil of humans. In our verse, Yahweh's destructive plan seems already to be tempered by compassion. As Sonnet (2020: 1255) comments, "Punishment, we realize, is neither the first nor the last word in God's design; it is *already* accompanied by a movement of grace. . . . [T]he divine character . . . is capable of artfully holding together two answers to the crisis that affects creation."

This friction or duality in Yahweh's plan is, on another level, a consequence of the reduction of characters in the transformation from a divine pantheon to a religion with a single divine lord (albeit with subordinate gods; see NOTES at 6:1–4). In the older Mesopotamian flood tradition (see COMMENTS), an essential part of the story is the conflict between Enlil, who sends the flood to destroy humans, and Enki/Ea, who preserves the flood hero (and humankind) from destruction. As Gunkel (1997: 72) already observes, Yahweh's change of attitude reflects the amalgamation of the roles of Enlil and Enki/Ea: "The deity's strangely sudden change of attitude in J can be explained in the Babylonian [story] as the result of [Enlil's] impetuous character and Ea's wise, appeasing presentation." As H.-P. Müller (1991a: 101) comments, "the conflict of divine parties in the *Atraḫasis* myth . . . is taken up in the biblical flood story as a conflict *in* Yahweh" (see also Westermann 1984: 408). Yahweh takes on the narrative roles of both gods and as a result becomes a god internally complicated, drawn toward destruction and preservation. The classical rabbis perceived this friction and derived the divine change of attitude from an inner clash between his "attribute of justice" (*middat haddîn*) and his "attribute of compassion" (*middat hārăḥămîm*), which they linked to the alternation of the divine names God and Yhwh (*Gen. Rab.* 33.3). By encompassing this clash of Enlil and Ea, or justice and compassion, Yahweh becomes a richly imagined and complex god.

7:1. *Yahweh said to Noah, "Enter the ark, you and all your household, for I see that you are a righteous man before me in this generation."* Yahweh now speaks to Noah and informs him of his plan. Previously Yahweh had been speaking internally to himself.

The term *tēbâ* ("ark") is used only for Noah's boat and Moses's basket (Exod 2:3–5). The word is probably a loanword from Egyptian *tbt*, "container, chest" (*HALOT*, 1678; Propp 1999: 149). The translation "ark" comes from the Latin Vulgate *arca*, "chest, box." The use of this word seems to indicate that the ark is not really a boat, since it is not a means of transport. As Ibn Ezra notes, it does not have the shape of a ship nor does it have oars but is rather a floating container to preserve life.

In J the ark is first mentioned with the command to enter it. Many commentators assume that the J account contained instructions to build the ark, but R included only the P instructions. This is a reasonable inference, but this verse also follows easily from 6:8 in its explication of why Noah merits Yahweh's favor. Moreover, later in this speech Yahweh reveals to Noah his plan to send the flood (7:4), perhaps for the first time. This makes it difficult to imagine an earlier instruction to build the ark. It may be that construction of the ark is simply assumed in J, or perhaps overlooked.

The favor granted Noah encompasses "you and all your household" (*'attâ wəkol-bêtəkā*, lit. "all your house"), which includes his wife, sons, and sons' wives. This is the family unit called the "house of the father" (*bêt 'āb*) in Israelite society. All the members of this "house" fall under the authority of the father and (as here) are covered by his honor or shame. In this way the merits of the fathers accrue to the children (see Exod 20:5–6). This concept of the individual as embedded in the context of family and descent is characteristic of ancient Israel.

The reason that Yahweh is saving Noah is specified in the motive clause, "for I see that you are a righteous man before me in this generation" (*kî-'ōtəkā rā'îtî ṣaddîq ləpānay baddôr hazzeh*). This clause fronts the direct object, *'ōtəkā* ("you"), yielding the sense, "for it is you that I see is a *ṣaddîq* before me in this generation." The agentive noun *ṣaddîq* expresses a range of meanings, someone who is morally innocent, virtuous, wise, just, pious, and truthful. The implication is that Noah alone has these virtues, unlike the others of his generation. There is no implication that he is only *relatively* virtuous, that is, the least bad of an evil generation (as in the later rabbinic interpretation, based partially on his drunken behavior in 9:21). Elsewhere in the Bible, Ezekiel knows of Noah as an exemplar of virtue or righteousness (*ṣədāqâ*), together with Daniel and Job (Ezek 14:14, 20).

Yahweh's "seeing" Noah's virtue contrasts with his "seeing" the evil of human hearts in 6:5. Noah's virtue, however, exists in some tension with the total depravity of humankind in that verse. Noah is the exception to the rule. This tension corresponds to the different perspectives of Enlil and Enki on humankind in the Mesopotamian flood story, which, we have noted, has been transformed into a complexity of perspectives within Yahweh.

7:2. *Of every clean animal, take them seven by seven, a male and its mate, and of every unclean animal take two, a male and its mate.* The word *bəhēmâ* ("animal") can mean "animal," "quadruped animal," "domestic animal," or "cattle," depending on the context. Here it means "animal" as a general category. The distinction between "clean" (*ṭəhôrâ*) and "unclean" (*lō' ṭəhôrâ*) animals is systematized in Leviticus 11 and Deuteronomy 14 but is attested here in an earlier, nonpriestly dietary system. After the flood Noah offers sacrifices "from *every* clean land animal and *every* clean bird" (8:20), though in the priestly system only certain species of clean animals (cattle, sheep, and goats) and clean birds (doves and pigeons) are permitted for sacrifice (Lev 1:10, 14). Another early feature is that the head of the household offers the sacrifice.

The distinction between clean and unclean animals regulates what species are permitted for human consumption and for sacrifice (see Douglas 1966: 41–57; Wright 1992; Hendel 2007). The mention of this distinction anticipates the rite of sacrifice at the end of the flood story (8:20). In J, this distinction exists in antediluvian time, unlike the P source, where it is instituted at the Sinai covenant with Israel (Leviticus 11).

The number of clean animals taken into the ark, *šib'â šib'â* ("seven by seven"), is a formulaic number. For instance, there are seven days in the week, Cain is avenged sevenfold, and there are seven-year cycles of plenty and famine in the Joseph story. In the flood story, Yahweh waits seven days to send the flood (7:4). In the wider ancient Near East, seven has the same connotation—some Mesopotamian lexical texts translate seven (and forty) as "totality" (Friberg 1992: 1144). There is some ambiguity, however, in the sense of "seven by seven." The context suggests that it has a distributive sense of "seven males and seven females" for each kind of clean animal. But it could mean "seven of each (kind), a male and its mate," meaning three pairs and a spare (e.g., Skinner 1930: 152). The parallel expression *šənayim šənayim* ("two by two") means "two of each" in 7:9, 15 (R and P, respectively).

The reason that more than one pair of clean animals must be taken into the ark is that Noah will offer sacrifices "of every clean animal" (8:20). There must be extras of these animals, else they will quickly go extinct. This is another difference from the P story, in which "two of all living things, male and female" enter the ark (6:19–20, 7:14). A pair of each suffices, because sacrifices cannot commence until Sinai, after the sacrificial laws are given and the priests anointed (Lev 9:1–4).

7:3. *also of every bird of heaven take them seven by seven, male and female, to keep their seed alive on the whole earth.* The instruction regarding birds is a redactional expansion, as is their mention in 6:7 (e.g., Skinner 1930: 152). The expressions "birds of heaven" (*ʿôp haššāmayim*) and "male and female" (*zākār ûnəqēbâ*) are P diction (1:26–30, 6:19, 7:16). This instruction also conflicts with the previous verse, where "seven by seven, male and female" applies only for clean animals. Here the distinction between clean and unclean is missing. (The SP and LXX repair this lack by supplying "clean" after "birds of heaven," and the LXX supplies a supplementary instruction about unclean birds; see Hendel 1998: 134.)

R seems to have inserted this supplement to harmonize with 8:20, where Noah sacrifices "one of every clean animal (*bəhēmâ*) and every clean bird (*ʿôp*)." The distinction between animals and birds is not drawn in 7:2, where Noah is instructed to take "of every clean animal (*bəhēmâ*)," with *bəhēmâ* as a general term for animal (inclusive of birds). R, whom Gunkel (1997: 63) describes here as "pedantic," sensed the lexical inconsistency with 8:20 and added the distinction here. In R's harmonization of the two passages, he left traces of his editorial practice, which added consistency but sometimes included new disharmonies (see also NOTES at 7:5–9).

7:4. *For in seven days, I am going to bring rain on the earth for forty days and forty nights, and I will wipe off the face of the soil all living things that I have made.* The numbers seven and forty are both formulaic numbers of wholeness or totality (see NOTES at 7:2; note that Moses spent "forty days and forty nights" on Mount Sinai, Exod 24:18). The seven days before the flood give Noah time to take the animals into the ark. In the Mesopotamian flood story, Enki tells Atraḫasis that the flood will come in seven days, in which time Atraḫasis must build the boat (with the help of workers) and gather the animals into it. The flood then lasts for seven days (*Atra.* III.i.37–III.iv.24; the latter period is in *Gilg.* XI.128–31).

Yahweh's announcement "I am going to bring rain" (*ʾānōkî mamṭîr*) foregrounds his agency ("I") and use the participle to express an imminent future event (*futurum instans;* GKC §116q; *IBHS* §37.6f). The verb for "bring rain" indicates a normal meteorological rain (as in 2:5). This contrasts with the P concept of a cosmic cataclysm (7:11).

The statement "I will wipe off the face of the soil all living things that I have made" repeats Yahweh's internal speech in 6:7 but expands the previous reference to *hāʾādām* ("humans")—in its relationship with *hāʾādāmâ* ("the soil, earth")—to *kol-hayqûm* ("all living things, existing things"). Note that the other animals have done nothing wrong; only humans are culpable (6:5–8). The animals accompany humans to destruction, just as they were created to accompany them (2:19). (Sea creatures, however, seem to be immune to this danger, an issue that piqued medieval interpreters.)

Noah says nothing in response to Yahweh's speech. Rabbinic interpreters compared his silence unfavorably to Abraham's reply to Yahweh's announcement of the destruction of Sodom and Gomorrah (18:22–33). However, since Noah is the only virtuous man in his time (7:1), he has no basis to argue with Yahweh to save the innocent.

7:5. *Noah did everything as Yahweh commanded him.* Noah's obedience is noted in similar words in J and P (6:22), with P adding a circular *inclusio, kēn ʿāśâ* ("thus he did"). In the P story, 6:22 and 7:16 serve as echoing refrains, which now has a third echo in the composite text.

7:7–16. This sequence provides a striking example of the art of R (see Budde 1883: 260–61; Carr 1996: 58–59; Levinson 2008: 17–23). First, to combine the J and P sequences of the onset of the flood and the entry into the ark, R reordered the J text, which was originally 7:10, 7, 16b, 12 (as translated above). Second, in order to harmonize their content, R expanded 7:7 to include the members of Noah's family who came into the ark (using P diction) and added 7:8–9 on the entry of the animals (combining J and P diction). As Levinson (2008: 23) observes, "Consistent with neither [source], the now exegetical text is in fact a new literary creation."

7:7. *Noah, his sons, his wife, and his sons' wives with him entered the ark because of the flood waters.* In this sequence R supplements the subject Noah (*nōaḥ*) with the P sequence from 8:18, "his sons, his wife, and his sons' wives with him" (*ûbānāyw wə ʾištô ûnəšê-bānāyw ʾittô*). This harmonizes the family's entrance into the ark with its exit. The J text either did not mention Noah's family (although they are implied) or perhaps used a different phrase (e.g., *wəkol-bêtô,* "and all his household," cf. *wəkol-bêtəkā,* "and all your household," 7:1).

The phrase "because of (lit. 'from the presence of') the flood waters" (*mipnê mê hammabbûl*) indicates that the inundation has begun, providing a compelling reason to enter the ark. This suggests that the statement "The seventh day came, and the flood waters were on the earth" (7:10) preceded the entry into the ark in the J text (Skinner 1930: 153–54). R arguably shifted 7:10 to its present position in order to harmonize with the onset of the flood in 7:11 (P).

The word "flood" (*mabbûl*) occurs in both versions of the flood story (J and P) and in other references to the flood (10:1, 32; 11:10). Psalm 29:10 states that "Yahweh sits enthroned on the flood (*lammabbûl*)." In this psalm, "the flood" refers to the celestial ocean, the waters above the vault of heaven (see Stenmans 1997). In the J flood, which comes as rain, this nuance has become obscured. In P, the flood comes from the celestial and the subterranean waters. The Akkadian flood stories use the unrelated word *abûbu* ("flood").

7:8–9. *Of the clean land animals, the unclean animals, the birds, and all creatures that crawl on the earth, two of each came to Noah in the ark, male and female, as God commanded Noah.* This redactional supplement harmonizes the commands in J (7:2) and P (6:19–20) and combines them with the animals' entry into the ark in P (7:14–16). Each phrase derives from one of these texts. The resulting picture has all the animals, including the clean and unclean animals, coming into the ark in pairs. This reduces the friction between the two sources (note that the seven pairs of clean animals from 7:2 are not mentioned). As Carr (1996: 58) notes, "this author [R] seems to have intervened at the exact point where the break between the P and non-P systems is strongest: in P and non-P's divergent concepts of the importance and role of animals in the flood destruction and rescue." R's procedure is worth noting: Rather than correcting or deleting the discrepancy between the two sources concerning the numbers and kinds of animals, R added new text to harmonize the differences. This shows a tendency to preserve the source texts along with an exegetical imperative to make their combination intelligible.

7:16. *Then Yahweh shut him in.* This scene apparently refers to "the ark's cover" (*miksēh hattēbâ,* 8:13) that Noah removes when the flood abates. Presumably this is some kind of exterior cover or door to keep out the rain. In the *Atraḫasis* myth, the flood hero seals his own door: "bitumen (*kupru*) was brought, and he sealed his door" (III ii 51). In *Gilgamesh* (XI.95), a boatman named Puzur-Amurru seals the door, for which he receives the flood hero's palace and property as payment. This detail here, with Yahweh as the sealer, changes the older tradition into a picture of Yahweh's care—and foregrounds his anthropomorphic character in J. R has moved this statement to its present position in order to have the entry of Noah's family and the animals (7:13–16, P) precede Yahweh's sealing of the ark.

7:17. *The flood was on the earth for forty days. The water rose and lifted the ark, and it was high above the earth.* The flood itself, following the onset of rain in 7:12, is tersely narrated. The vertical ascent of the waters and the ark—"high above the earth"—is the only measure of the flood's intensity and scope. By this narrow focus, we see the juxtaposition of the fragile ark, the towering waters, and the inundated earth.

7:23. *He wiped off the face of the soil all living things—from humans to land animals to crawling creatures to the birds of heaven. They were wiped off the earth. Only Noah and those with him on the ark survived.* This verse is the fulfillment of Yahweh's intention, stated in 7:4. The first part of the redactional supplement, "from humans to land animals to crawling creatures to the birds of heaven" (*mē'ādām 'ad-bəhēmâ 'ad-remeś wə'ad-'ôp haššāmayim*), harmonizes the J text with the P categories of animals, using precisely the same diction as the parallel supplement in 6:7. The second part of the supplement, "they were wiped off the earth" (*wayyimmāḥû min-hā'āreṣ*), is a resumptive repetition of the beginning of the verse, "He wiped off the face of the soil" (*wayyimaḥ . . . 'al pənê hā'ădāmâ*). The technique of resumptive repetition often serves to frame or fold in supplemental material.

8:6. *At the end of forty days, Noah opened the window of the ark that he had made.* Noah's "opening" window after forty days is the counterpart to Yahweh "shutting" the ark (7:16) at the beginning of the forty days. After two seven-day periods during which he releases birds, "Noah removed the ark's cover" (8:13), bringing the sequence to a close. These seven-day periods echo the seven-day period before the flood (7:4). These actions and dates convey the chronological structure of the J story.

The "window" (*ḥallôn*) has not been mentioned previously, hence the backward-glancing remark, "that he had made." The mention of the window—a rare detail about the ark in J—provides a visual backdrop to the episode of releasing the birds. In a fragment of the Babylonian flood from Ugarit, Ea tells the flood hero to "make a window at the top (of the boat). Release a bird, let it find for you a shore!" (Wasserman 2020: 88–89). The window seems to be a part of the bird type-scene in these traditions (see below and NOTES at 8:7 [P]).

8:8–12. The scene of the sending of the birds shows Noah's resourcefulness and provides a sense of the passage of time. The threefold sending of the dove is an artful mininarrative. The Mesopotamian flood story has a similar episode (in *Gilgamesh* XI and Berossos's *Babyloniaca*), also followed by the flood hero's sacrificial offering. These shared details show the close filiation of the Mesopotamian and biblical flood traditions. In the *Gilgamesh* version, Utnapishtim waits seven days after the end of the flood and sends out three birds in succession: a dove, a swallow, and a raven:

> When the seventh day arrived—
> I brought out a dove, setting it free:
>> off went the dove.
>> No perch was available for it and it came back to [me.]
> I brought out a swallow, setting it free:
>> off went the swallow.
>> No perch was available for it and it came back to me.
> I brought out a raven, setting it free:
>> off went the raven and it saw the waters receding.
>> It was eating, bobbing up and down (?), it did not come back to me.
> I brought out an offering and sacrificed to the four corners of the earth.

(XI.147–57; George 2003: 712–13)

In the biblical versions, each source seems to have selected one bird: the dove in J and the raven in P. The variations within these shared scenes, and the absence of any indication of textual dependence, suggests that the Mesopotamian and Israelite stories are related primarily by oral tradition, mediated by bilingual speakers across cultural boundaries (see COMMENTS).

The cognate relationship of the biblical and Mesopotamian type-scene is further underscored by its nonessential quality in the story. The nautical practice of sending birds as navigational aids is ancient and widespread (George 2003: 517); as Pliny notes of Indian sailors, "they carry birds with them, sending them out quite often, and following the course of their flight as they make for land" (*Natural History* 6.83). However, unlike sailors on the open sea, it is not clear why the flood hero needs them—he can simply look down to see if the water has abated. This scene has folkloric dimensions—the successful third try, the seven-day intervals—and adds a sense of drama and the passage of time.

8:8. *He sent out a dove that was with him to see if the water had subsided on the face of the soil.* The "dove" (*yônâ*) is often a symbol of beauty and love in the ancient world (Botterweck 1990). In Song of Songs, the beloved woman is called "my perfect dove" (5:2, 6:9). Doves are associated with various goddesses (Ishtar, and perhaps Astarte and Greek Aphrodite). However, because of their cooing, doves can also be a symbol of mourning (Isa 38:14, 59:11; Ezek 7:16; Nah 2:8). Perhaps more relevant here, doves are known as strong flyers (Hos 11:11, Ps 55:7). The dove is a clean animal (i.e., permitted for sacrifice and food), so there are extra (seven pairs) on the ark. It is also a domestic bird, which perhaps makes it suitable to be a helper to humankind.

The reason for sending the dove is "to see if the water had subsided on the face of the soil" (*lir'ôt hăqqallû hammayim mē'al pənê hā'ădāmâ*). This motive clause recurs twice more: when the dove returns to the ark, "for the water still covered the whole face of the earth" (8:9), and when the dove later returns with the olive leaf, "and Noah knew that the water had subsided on the face of the earth" (8:11). This threefold repetition—

combined with the repetitions of the verbs for sending and waiting, and the seven-day intervals—gives literary balance to this episode.

In this sequence the words *hā'ădāmâ* ("the soil, earth") and *hā'āreṣ* ("the earth") interchange. The two words are synonymous here but have different intertextual nuances. The phrase *'al pənê hā'ădāmâ* ("on the face of the soil") echoes the plan of destruction and its fulfillment (6:7; 7:4, 23) and activates the *Leitwort* relationship of *hā'ādām* (humankind") and *hā'ădāmâ* ("soil, earth") in the motive for the flood (6:7). In 8:21, Yahweh's promise never again "to curse" (*ləqallēl*) the soil may resonate with the water that "subsided" (*qallû*, from the same root) on the soil here.

8:9. *But the dove did not find a place to rest its feet, so it returned to him on the ark, for the water still covered the whole face of the earth.* The "place to rest" (*mānôaḥ*) is a wordplay on Noah (*nōaḥ*), which means "rest." The dove did not find a *mānôaḥ*, so it returned to *nōaḥ*. This language game with "rest" will culminate in the "soothing" (*nîḥōaḥ*) aroma of Noah's sacrifice (8:21). In this respect, Noah brings rest and comfort (5:29).

He reached out his hand and caught it and brought it back into the ark. This succession of actions slows down the pace of the narrative. Noah extends his hand as a resting place and brings the bird to the safety of the ark. The verb "reached out" (*wayyišlaḥ*) is the same verbal root as when he "sent out" (*wayšallaḥ*) the dove in 8:8, creating a verbal framing of Noah's sending and retrieving the dove.

8:11. *The dove returned to him toward evening, and behold, in its beak was a plucked olive leaf, and Noah knew that the water had subsided on the face of the earth.* The new detail that the dove returned "toward evening" (*lə'ēt 'ereb*) adds a brief "reality effect" to the story. It gives a sense of Noah's long watch until twilight, after which doves do not fly.

The disjunctive clause "and behold, in its beak was a plucked olive leaf" (*wəhinnēh 'ălēh-zayit ṭārāp bəpîhā*),beginning with waw + *hinnēh* (the presentative particle), portrays a vivid moment of perception (*IBHS* §40.2.1b). This effects a perspectival shift to Noah's perception, as if we were seeing through his eyes. Its consequence, "and Noah knew" (*wayyēda' nōaḥ*), resumes the foreground narrative sequence, continuing from the previous converted imperfect clause, "the dove returned to him toward evening." This shows the interweaving of foreground and background in the narrative technique.

The "olive leaf" (*'ălēh-zayit*) is a material sign that the waters have subsided on the earth. Olive trees do not grow at high altitudes, so the bird has flown a distance downward. Olive trees are also a symbol of fruitfulness and plenty. In Jotham's fable, the olive tree refuses to be king because it would have to cease producing olive oil, which honors God and humans (Judg 9:8–9). In Greco-Roman times the olive branch was a symbol of peace (Virgil, *Aeneid* 8.116), although there is no evidence of this specific nuance in Israel or the Near East. The combined image of the dove and the olive leaf is visually evocative.

8:13. *Noah removed the ark's cover, and he looked, and behold, the face of the soil was dry.* This is another construction of vivid perception, marked by the presentative particle *hinnēh* (cf. NOTES at 8:11). Noah sees that the soil is finally dry, and we see through his eyes. This verse fulfills his plan to release birds "to see if the water had subsided on the face of the soil" (8:8). After the dove fails to return—indicating that it has found a place to rest—Noah sees the dry earth for himself.

8:20–22. The final scene in the J flood story reestablishes the bond between Yahweh and humans that was sundered by the flood. Noah's sacrificial offering does so from the human side, and Yahweh responds with a promise never to "destroy all life as I have done." In this conclusion, Yahweh reconciles himself to his flawed creatures.

It is possible that the J story had a scene of disembarkation, which R omitted in favor of the P passage (8:15–19). Given J's preference for brief strokes rather than systematic exposition, the sacrifice may have directly followed the scene of the birds, as it does in *Gilgamesh* (XI.157) (see Note at 8:8–12). In a late fragment of the Babylonian flood story, the god Enlil escorts the flood hero out: "Enlil went up into the b[oat]. He took my hand and escorted me from the boat"; and Enki rebukes Enlil for sending the flood, proclaiming, "From now on, let no Flood be brought about! Verily, let the people last for ever and ever" (Wasserman 2020: 100–102). Here we see a combination of details similar to those of our passage. See Comments.

8:20. *Noah built an altar for Yahweh. He took one of every clean animal and every clean bird and offered burnt offerings on the altar.* An "altar" (*mizbēaḥ*, from *zbḥ*, "to slaughter, sacrifice") is generally a stone structure where one offers sacrifices, a key performative act in Israelite religion. When the worshipers offer sacrifices, God is expected to reciprocate with his blessing (Exod 20:21; see Gen 4:3–5). The altar is sometimes called Yahweh's "table" (*šulḥān*, Ezek 41:22, 44:16; Mal 1:7, 12), showing the underlying concept of sacrifice as a feast offered to and shared with God. In the relationship expressed by this ritual meal, the offerer is the suppliant who honors the divine master (see Hendel 2015).

Noah is the first to build an altar (although Cain and Abel had earlier offered sacrifices). The next person to build an altar is Abraham, in a sentence nearly identical to Noah's: "he built there an altar for Yahweh" (*wayyiben šām mizbēaḥ lyhwh*, Gen 12:7). These two first altars are signs of new beginnings in the relationship between humans and Yahweh.

As observed above (see Notes at 7:2), the distinction between clean and unclean animals is portrayed as a pre-Mosaic custom, part of the worship of Yahweh from primeval times. This is a striking difference from P, for whom the laws of purity and sacrifice stem from the Mosaic era (this is why P lacks a scene of sacrifice in the flood story). The modifier *mikkōl* ("from each/all") has a distributive sense, rendered here as "one of every." This sacrifice is a major event, with many animals offered.

The statement "he offered burnt offerings" (*wayya ʿal ʿōlōt*) is an onomatopoetic phrase. The verb and noun "offered" and "burnt offering" are composed of the same root, *ʿlh* ("to go up"). In this type of offering, the sacrificial animal is wholly burnt in the fire on the altar, and the smoke "goes up" to Yahweh. Unlike the other types of meat offering, the humans do not share in the ritual feast; it is wholly given to Yahweh. This ritual gift establishes a relationship of reciprocity—the worshiper has made a valuable sacrifice, and Yahweh reciprocates with his care and blessing. The form into which the food is transformed—from a physical body to smoke—is appropriate for divine cuisine, which "goes upward" in immaterial form to God

8:21. *Yahweh smelled the soothing aroma, and Yahweh said in his heart, "I will never again curse the soil because of humans, for the designs of the human heart are evil from their youth. Never again will I destroy all life as I have done."* Yahweh responds to Noah's sacrifice with a profound change in his disposition toward humans. Although Yahweh does not consume the sacrifice in the same way as do the gods in *Atrahasis,* by accepting Noah's sacrifice he acknowledges the important value of his relationship with humans. Yahweh's new resolution is presented as interior speech, which forms a counterpoint to his initial interior resolution to destroy humankind (6:7).

The initial clause, "Yahweh smelled the soothing aroma" (*wayyāraḥ yhwh ʾet-rēaḥ hannîḥōaḥ*), is onomapoetic and brings a new turn to the *Leitwort* play on Noah (*nōaḥ*). Now Noah's sacrifices yield a *rēaḥ hannîḥōaḥ* ("soothing aroma"), a fragrance of *nōaḥ* ("rest"). This wordplay provides an artful closure to this *Leitwort* sequence, beginning with Noah's destiny to provide "relief" (see NOTES at 5:29).

The term *rēaḥ nîḥōaḥ* ("soothing aroma") is used in P and Ezekiel as a technical term, preserving in fossilized form the anthropomorphic notion of God smelling the sweet smell of the sacrifice. Here it activates the symbolism of the ritual meal. By partaking of his portion of the sacrifice, Yahweh participates in and restores this broken relationship. Smelling the soothing aroma is the sensible outward correlate of this inner process.

Yahweh's response to this restoration is expressed as interior speech: "Yahweh said in his heart" (*wayyōʾmer yhwh ʾel-libbô*). This corresponds to and resolves the situation at the beginning of the flood story, when "his heart was pained" (*wayyitʿaṣṣēb ʾel-libbô*), followed by an interior speech (*wayyōʾmer,* "he said . . .") expressing his plan to destroy humankind (6:5–7). Now he says in his heart that he will never again do this. Yahweh has experienced, it seems, a change of heart.

The content of his interior speech, "I will never again curse the soil (*hāʾădāmâ*) because of humans (*hāʾādām*), for the designs of the human heart are evil from their youth," reverses his earlier decision to wipe out *hāʾādām* from the face of *hāʾădāmâ* for precisely the same reason (6:5–7). But there are some interesting nuances and ambiguities in this new decision. The sequence "I will never again curse the soil because of humans" (*lōʾ-ʾōsīp ləqallēl ʿôd ʾet-hāʾădāmâ baʿăbûr hāʾādām*) recalls not only 6:5–7, but also Yahweh's pronouncement in the Eden story: "cursed is the soil because of you" (*ʾărûrâ hāʾădāmâ baʿăbûrekā,* 3:17; cf. Noah's naming speech, "the soil that Yahweh has cursed" [*hāʾădāmâ ʾăšer ʾērərāh yhwh*], 5:29). The curse on the soil in our verse clearly alludes to the curse in Eden. The verb differs—here "to curse" is the *piel* of *qll* rather than *qal* of *ʾrr,* but these are synonyms elsewhere in J (see 12:3), so it is unwarranted to propose a different meaning here (*pace* Rendtorff 1961: 70–72; see Steck 1971: 527–31; Petersen 1976: 442–44).

But there is an ambiguity in this double allusion to Yahweh's decision to destroy *hāʾādām* on *hāʾădāmâ* (6:7) and his earlier decree to curse *hāʾădāmâ* because of *hāʾādām* (3:17). How are we to understand this ambiguity? A corresponding grammatical ambiguity inheres in the phrase *lōʾ-ʾōsīp ləqallēl ʿôd,* which can mean "I will never again curse" or "I will not continue to curse." If one takes the referent of "curse" to be the soil's curse in Eden, then "not continue to curse" is apt, and the curse is now removed. Conversely, if one takes "curse" to refer to the flood, then "never again curse" is apt, since the flood is a punctual event, which Yahweh now promises never to send again. Contextually, this statement applies to the flood. This is explicit in the next sentence, "Never again will I destroy all life as I have done." Furthermore, the soil's curse in Eden involves the painful labor of subsistence agriculture, which does not change after the flood. But the *Leitwort* relationship of *hāʾādām* and *hāʾădāmâ,* humans and the soil, clearly resonates with the curse in Eden.

The ambiguity of this verse is by design. The flood and curse on the soil are mingled together suggestively but obscurely. As Zenger (1983: 49) suggests, "the flood judgment qualifies the [curse on the soil] as a destructive curse lying over the earth, which does not become deadly because Yahweh limits it." The curse on the soil is verbally transmuted into the destructive flood, which Yahweh abjures.

The motive clause for Yahweh's decision is nearly identical to his motive for destroying humans in 6:5. Here the motive is, "for the designs of the human heart are evil from their youth" (*kî yēṣer lēb hā'ādām ra' minnə'ūrāyw*). In 6:5 it is, "for every design of their hearts was only evil all day long" (*kî . . . kol-yēṣer maḥšəbōt libbô raq ra' kol-hayyôm*). The slight differences in wording do not change the basic meaning: *kol-yēṣer* ("every design," 6:5) corresponds to *yēṣer* ("[the] designs," 8:21); *raq ra'* ("only evil," 6:5) corresponds to *ra'* ("evil," 8:21); and the temporal modifier *kol-hayyôm* ("all day long/constantly," 6:5) corresponds to *minnə'ūrāyw* ("from their youth," 8:21). It is possible to see a diminution of Yahweh's anger and pain in these slight changes: the constancy of human evil is less emphatic, and there may be an acknowledgment that humans are not born evil but become evil in their youth.

These nuanced differences may reflect a more distanced and reflective state of mind, but they do not change Yahweh's perception of human evil. The evil designs of the human heart have not changed, but Yahweh's disposition to human evil—"in his heart"—has changed. Despite their evil, he will never again destroy them. Yahweh seems to abjure strict justice for human evil and becomes a more compassionate God. He is reconciled to the deep flaws of his human creatures. As Fritz (1982: 612) observes, "humans remain evil, but Yahweh becomes benevolent."

Yahweh follows his deliberations about humans with a parallel clause about all life on earth: "Never again will I destroy all life as I have done." This repeats his pledge of "never again" in the previous clause, extending it to all living creatures. The other animals had been created for the human's company in the Garden of Eden (2:19), and now their survival is correspondingly ensured. The animals are regarded as innocent creatures, lacking the humans' evil intentions.

8:22. *For all the earth's days these shall never cease: seedtime and harvest, cold and heat, summer and winter, day and night.* Yahweh lifts his decision to the temporal horizons of creation. He promises that his response to human evil will never again threaten the existence of the created cosmos, with its concentric rhythms of time (Fritz 1982: 611; cf. Hiebert 1996: 45–47).

The expression "all the earth's days" (*kol-yəmê hā'āreṣ*) means forever. A close parallel is the Ugaritic poetic verse "for the days of the sun and the moon" (*lymt špš wyrḫ, CAT* 1.108.26; Pardee 2002: 192–95), which also means forever. The promise is that "all the earth's days"—that is, the cosmic duration of time—will not be curtailed by another cataclysm and will exist enduringly.

This temporal horizon is characterized by different cycles of time, listed in parallel fashion: "seedtime and harvest, cold and heat, summer and winter, day and night." The climax of the narrative often verges into poetic or quasi-poetic cadence, particularly in divine speech (cf. 1:27, 2:23, 4:23, 9:6). The four temporal rhythms listed here belong to complementary domains: agriculture (seedtime and harvest), weather (cold and heat), seasons (summer and winter; cf. the pairing of *qayiṣ* and *ḥōrep* in Ps 74:17, Amos 3:15, and Zech 14:8), and the daily cycle (day and night). These are a selection of temporal cycles (note that there are other seasons, weather, and agricultural periods), which foreground the ways that humans experience time. Each pair of antonyms brings its own distinctive temporal durations and human sensations. In this evocation of time's rhythms, there is a suggestion that "all the earth's days" will be days of human existence too, time that is experienced and felt.

Comments

The flood story places at risk everything that has come before. Seeing the extent of human evil, Yahweh regrets having created humankind and resolves to destroy it. This will bring to a decisive end the existence of humans and return the world to its primordial state. But Yahweh alters his plan twice. First, he makes an exception for Noah and his household, along with the seed of all animals. Then, after the flood he changes his mind altogether, promising never again to "destroy all life as I have done" (8:21). The flood turns out to be not the end, but an interruption in the movement from creation to the present world. The J flood story is, in a sense, an episode in Yahweh's relationship with humans and the world. It begins with a harsh picture of the pervasiveness of human evil, but it ends with a spirit of generosity in Yahweh's promise that life and the cycles of nature will never cease.

LITERARY DESIGN

The J flood story has a tripartite form: a prologue, the main event, and an epilogue. The main event, the flood, is presented in two sections: Yahweh's instructions and the flood itself. The flood event consists of three subsections, its onset, climax, and recession. These segments are structured by various *Leitwort* sequences:

Prologue (6:5–8)
Flood (7:1–8:13)
      a. Yahweh's instructions to Noah (7:1–5)
      b. Onset, climax, and recession of flood (7:10, 7, 16b, 12, 17, 22–23; 8:2b–3a,
         6, 8–12, 13b)
Epilogue (8:20–22)

Much of the story consists of Yahweh's speech, both internal (in the prologue and epilogue) and spoken to Noah (in the instructions). Noah never speaks, but wordlessly obeys ("Noah did everything as Yahweh commanded him," 7:5). Noah also takes independent actions, including sending out the birds and offering the sacrifice that is the occasion for Yahweh's change of heart. The story as a whole is framed by Yahweh's changing perceptions and decisions about the problem of human evil.

J's *Leitwort* style informs the design of the story and its relationship to other stories. Key moments of the flood story echo the name of Noah (*nōaḥ*): Yahweh's "regret" (*nḥm*, 6:6–7) at creating humans, the dove seeking a "resting place" (*mānōaḥ*, 8:9) when the waters recede, and Yahweh smelling the "soothing" (*nîḥōaḥ*, 8:21) smell of Noah's sacrifice. There is a subtle reversal of Noah's name when *nōaḥ* finds *ḥēn* ("favor," 6:8). Noah is born as a bringer of "comfort, relief" (*nḥm*, 5:29), and he fulfills his destiny, at least in part, by bringing relief to humankind from the flood.

The *Leitwort* pair "the human/humankind" (*hā'ādām*) and "the soil/earth" (*hā'ădāmâ*) activate connections with other J stories. In Yahweh's initial and final speeches, the relationship between humans and the soil is first doomed and finally restored: "I will wipe out humans (*hā'ādām*) from the face of the soil (*hā'ădāmâ*)" (6:7); and "I will never again curse the soil (*hā'ădāmâ*) because of humans (*hā'ādām*)" (8:21). The diction of the latter echoes the curse in Eden, "cursed is the soil because of you" (3:17), although it carries a different nuance, referring to the flood rather than the soil as such. But the resonance between the two verses is mediated by Noah's naming in 5:29: "He will give us relief from our work, from our painful manual labor on the soil (*hā'ădāmâ*) that Yahweh has cursed." Although the implications and resonances are suggested rather than spelled out, the relationship between humans and the soil is now changed. Human life on the soil is still difficult, but it will continue without fear of total destruction.

In the prologue and epilogue, Yahweh's speeches and perceptions focus on the problem of human evil. The words "evil" (*ra'*) and "heart" (*lēb*) circulate in varied ways, sometimes with sound rhymes. In 6:5–6, Yahweh saw that "great was the evil (*rabbâ rā'at*) of humans" and "every design of their hearts (*libbô*) was only evil (*raq ra'*)." As a consequence, "his heart (*libbô*) was pained." The evil of the human heart pains Yahweh's heart. In 8:21, "Yahweh said in his heart (*libbô*)" that "the designs of the human heart (*leb*) are evil (*ra'*)," and yet now this perception is accompanied by Yahweh's change of heart in his relationship to humans. His broken heart at human evil is replaced by his heartfelt accommodation to it.

Nested within these divine perceptions and responses is the central event of the story, the flood. It is presented in four paragraphs, each marked by indications of time. These sections present the flood in its temporal phases, creating an effect of the passage of time. Yahweh's instructions set the stage with its indications of future time. Each phase of the flood actualizes or fills out Yahweh's instructions:

> *Instructions*
> "In *seven days*, I will bring rain on the earth for *forty days and forty nights*" (7:4).
> *Onset of the flood*
> "The *seventh day* came, and the flood waters were on the earth" (7:10).
> "It rained on the earth for *forty days and forty nights*" (7:12).
> *Climax of the flood*
> "The flood was on the earth for *forty days*" (7:17).
> *Recession of the flood*
> "At the end of *forty days*, Noah opened the window of the ark that he had made" (8:6).
> "He waited another *seven days* and (again) sent out the dove" (8:10, 12).

The event of the flood is structured by these repetitions of seven and forty days. The seven-day intervals between sending the birds is a way of emphasizing the passage of time, making the flood's gradual recession sensible, and also frames the flood narrative with seven-day periods.

The postflood epilogue begins with Noah building an altar, which anticipates the future constructions of altars by Abraham and Isaac in J (12:7–8, 26:25) and provides a concrete image of Noah's piety. Noah's ritual gift reestablishes the reciprocity between

Yahweh and Noah, and by extension between Yahweh and all humans. It is the occasion for Yahweh's reevaluation of this relationship, despite the problem of evil. Yahweh's closing speech "to his heart," as noted above, revises his opening internal speech about the evil of the human heart (8:21; cf. 6:5). In the dramatic arc of the story, Yahweh changes his emotional and moral commitment to humankind, in all its complications, as he reconciles himself to the continuance of humans and the earth.

DESTRUCTION AND RESTORATION

The flood story comes after a sequence of other transgressions—by Adam and Eve, Cain, Lamech, the Sons of God, and (by their hybridity) the Nephilim—but it does not refer to any particular transgression. Yahweh's focus is on the general condition of humankind—"every design of their hearts was only evil all day long" (6:5). This is a perception of human interiority, the problem of the human heart.

Yahweh had previously admonished Cain, "if you are not good, sin crouches at the door—it desires you, but you can rule over it" (4:7), but Cain was not able to heed this warning. Now Yahweh perceives that humankind as such is incapable of heeding it. They are daily preoccupied by evil thoughts and deeds. Humans themselves are a moral danger. The multiplication of humans is accompanied by the multiplication of evil.

The problem of human evil causes a dilemma for Yahweh. As Miles (1995: 42) writes, it "exposes the deepest of all fault lines in the divine character. In the story of the flood, the creator . . . becomes an outright destroyer." At the end of the story, Yahweh seems to repudiate this destruction, promising never to do it again. In some sense the flood seems a divine mistake, which provides the occasion for Yahweh's own moral education, learning to leaven justice with compassion.

To gain some traction on Yahweh's response to his moral dilemma, it is helpful to bring in other versions of the flood story, which I explore more fully in the next section. As Gunkel (1997: 72) notes briefly, "the deity's strangely sudden change of attitude in J can be explained in the Babylonian [story] as the result of [Enlil's] impetuous character and of Ea's wise, appeasing presentation." That is, in the Babylonian flood narrative, the different sides of Yahweh's moral dilemma are occupied by different gods: Enlil, who decides to destroy humans, and Enki/Ea, the creator of humans, who saves them from Enlil's wrath by secretly instructing the flood hero to build an ark and save all life. Other gods are allied with one or the other of these major gods. In the J flood story, what was primarily an external moral contest between factions of gods has been transformed into an internal contest in the heart of a single god. Yahweh's moral dilemma is, in some respects, a monotheistic translation of the moral conflicts within a divided pantheon.

The response of the birth goddess Mami in the *Atraḫasis* myth is aligned with Yahweh's. She initially agrees with the decision to destroy humans in a flood, but later changes her mind (see Wasserman 2020: 140–45). At this point she laments:

Let the day grow dark,
     let it turn back to gloom!
In the assembly of the gods,
     how did I agree with them on annihilation? . . .
Of my own accord, from myself alone,
     to my own hurt have I heard (my people's) clamor!

[My] offspring—with no help from me—have become like flies.
>   And as for me, how to dwell in (this) abode of grief, my clamor
>   fallen silent?

>   (*Atra.* III.iii.34–37, 42–46; Foster 2005: 250; Wasserman 2020: 140–41)

Mami juxtaposes her previous hearing of the "clamor" (*rigmu*) of humans, which triggered the decision to send the flood, with her remorseful silence: "my clamor fallen silent." She echoes the silence of destroyed humans. The decision to destroy them was unwise and irrational, a brute decree of annihilation.

Mami's eloquent lament is motivated not only by her relationship with humans as their co-creator, but also by the consequence for the gods during the flood. They are starving because of the lack of sacrificial offerings by humans. While she speaks, "the great gods / were sitting in thirst and hunger" (III.iii.30–31). Her regret is rounded by starvation, which graphically depicts the gods' dependence on humans. The decision in the assembly of the gods had the unintended consequence of the gods' own suffering and imminent demise. The plan was ill-conceived. Only wise Enki's decision to save the flood hero and his family, along with the seed of all animals, rescues the gods from destruction.

Yahweh's situation is akin to that of the gods in the Babylonian flood story—indeed, it derives from theirs (see below)—but it has a different configuration. As Moran (2002: 40) observes, the rebuke of Enlil by Mami and Enki after the flood exposes "Enlil's character as a brutal force." Yahweh's character in this sense contrasts with Enlil's, since Yahweh is motived by morality, while Enlil wants silence simply so that he can sleep. Yet Yahweh, like Enlil, is the destroyer who sends the flood.

Yahweh's moral vision changes, however, and his character becomes more akin to that of Mami and Enki, the co-creators of humans. Like Enki, he tells the flood hero to build an ark to save his family and the seed of all animals. Yahweh saves humankind and life on earth from destruction. At the end, again like Enki, he promises that their destruction will never happen again. Like Mami, he seems to regret his initial decision and has a change of heart. Yahweh realizes that his relationship with humans, activated by Noah's sacrificial offerings, is worth keeping despite the problem of human evil. Yahweh adopts a more forgiving position toward humans, his own imperfect creations. In sum, the conflicts among the gods in the Babylonian myth are transformed into an inner conflict and development within Yahweh. The arena of moral claims is the relationship between Yahweh and humans, which effects changes in Yahweh's heart.

The *Leitwort* emphasis on the interplay of the human heart and Yahweh's heart creates a backdrop for the moral focus of the story. As a consequence of monotheism and the J writer's literary art, the flood story explores the complicated bond between humans and Yahweh. The moral chaos of human evil and Yahweh's decision to destroy resolve into a deeper moral vision in which Yahweh reconciles himself to the human heart, and life on earth can continue.

CONTEXTS

The immediate sequel in J to the flood is the brief story of the Curse of Canaan (9:18–27). This story picks up the theme of the evil imagination of humankind, which is still alive and well as Noah becomes drunk, his son dishonors the father, and Noah curses Canaan, his grandson. Noah, the righteous man, and his descendants seem fully capable of various kinds of moral transgressions, just like humans before the flood. The evil inclinations of the human heart continue unabated, setting a backdrop to the change of moral focus with the call of Abraham.

A larger context for the flood story in J is the *Leitwort* relationship between "humans" (*hāʾādām*) and "the earth/soil" (*hāʾădāmâ*), which forms a connective tissue in the J primeval narrative. This relationship takes on new complications in the flood story's movement from destruction to restoration. The relationship also has a change of focus, turning from curses to blessing, with the call of Abram (see 12:3).

Outside of Genesis 1–11, Noah and the flood are mentioned or alluded to in two prophetic texts, Ezekiel 14 and Isaiah 54. These brief references show that the story had currency in ancient Israel and was not limited to the J and P texts. The ways that Ezekiel and Second Isaiah refer to Noah and the flood indicate that the story was a well-known tradition.

In Ezekiel 14, Yahweh makes the point that when he decides to punish a people—using the examples of famine, wild animals, war, and plague—even the most righteous persons could not turn back God's wrath but would save only themselves. Yahweh repeats this refrain four times, once for each type of punishment. The first and last refrains specify the righteous persons as Noah, Daniel, and Job:

> Even if these three men were in its midst, Noah, Daniel, and Job, by their righteousness they would save only their own lives—declares the Lord Yahweh. (Ezek 14:14)

> Even if Noah, Daniel, and Job were in it, as I live—declares Yahweh—they would save neither sons nor daughters; by their righteousness they would save only their own lives. (Ezek 14:20)

Several points may be gathered. First, Noah, Daniel, and Job are exemplars of righteousness. Second, they are all from non-Israelite lands or epochs. Noah is from the pre-Israelite period, and Job is from Uz in the east (Job 1:1). Since the book of Daniel is later than Ezekiel's time, scholars have inferred that Ezekiel's Daniel is a version of the wise Canaanite patriarch Daniel (or Danel, *dnʾl*), known from the Ugaritic epic of Aqhat (Greenberg 1983: 257). This Daniel, like Noah and Job, is a righteous gentile. Finally, as noted above, Ezekiel's evocation of these three righteous men indicates that these figures were well-known to his audience. The stories of Noah, Dan(i)el, and Job must have been common fare, so that the prophet could appeal to them so briefly. This gives us an insight into the contents of narrative traditions known by Ezekiel's community in exile. Noah and his righteousness were not invented by the writers of Genesis but were part of the widely shared cultural knowledge of ancient Israel.

The same point can be gathered from Second Isaiah's reference to the flood in Isaiah 54. Yahweh compares his recent rejection of and incipient compassion on Israel to the story of Noah:

> In overflowing anger, I hid my face for a moment from you,
>> but with everlasting lovingkindness I will have compassion on you,
>> —says your redeemer Yahweh.

For this is to me like the waters of Noah,

> when I swore that the waters of Noah would no more go over the
> earth,
> thus I swear that I will not be angry with you or rebuke you.
> (Isa 54:8–9)

Here Yahweh appeals to the flood story as a precedent to the current situation, in which the destruction wrought by his past anger will now be rectified by his everlasting compassion. He swears never again to hide his face from Israel as he did during the Babylonian destruction and exile. He cites his oath after the flood as an analogy and precedent for his current oath (reading *kēn nišbaʿtî* as a performative construction, "thus I swear"). We may gather that Second Isaiah's audience know the story of the flood and Yahweh's promise at its conclusion. As we will see, this promise is a feature of other versions of the ancient Near Eastern flood story, not just the versions in Genesis 6–9. The flood story, we can infer, circulated in oral and written traditions in various forms, such that this prophetic analogy could be readily understood independent of the biblical text.

The flood story, as has long been known, has a wider context in the ancient Near East (e.g., B. Schmidt 1995; Noort 1998; Kvanvig 2011: 209–34; Day 2013: 98–112). As Speiser (1964: 54) comments, "That the biblical account as a whole goes back ultimately to Mesopotamian sources is a fact that is freely acknowledged by most modern scholars." While the genealogy of the various flood stories is beyond our ability to map, there is clearly a family relationship between the biblical flood stories—in J and P—and the Mesopotamian flood stories, both in the general plot and in numerous specific details. It would seem that bilingual storytellers, perhaps including a mixture of traders, soldiers, scholars, itinerant workers, and service nomads, mediated the story—perhaps multiple times—from Mesopotamian to Israelite culture. During and after the Neo-Assyrian period, Aramaic may have served as an intermediary since it became the international lingua franca. A clue to its path of transmission may be found at the end of the *Atraḫasis* myth: "I have sung of the flood to all the peoples. Hear it!" (III.viii.18). This reference to sung performance, whose audience is "all the peoples," suggests that the flood was widely known in oral settings. At minimum we can say that, in this instance, the story's self-conception is as a textualized oral performance.

It may be useful to summarize the plot of *Atraḫasis*. The story has two main sections: one the rebellion of the worker gods, which ends with the creation of humans; and the other a series of attempted destructions of humankind that culminate in the flood (Moran 2002: 33–86).

After forty years of hard labor digging watercourses, including rivers (the Tigris and Euphrates), springs, wells, and canals, the worker gods declare a strike and threaten their boss, the leading god Enlil. The wise god Enki, who is sympathetic to the rebellious workers, proposes the creation of humans to take on their burden. He instructs the birth goddess Mami to create humans, which she does from clay mixed with the flesh and blood of the executed rebel leader. She proclaims, "I have imposed your drudgery on humankind" (Foster 2005: 236; Lambert and Millard 1969: 56–57). The creation of humans to assume the hard work of the gods resolves the conflict of the first part.

The second part, culminating in the flood, begins with an unforeseen consequence. Humans have no limit to their lifespan, and so they multiply and make a boisterous clamor (*rigmu*). Enlil complains, "The clamor of humankind [has become burdensome to me], I am losing sleep [to their uproar]" (Foster 2005: 239; Lambert and Millard 1969: 66–67). This is the problem that gives rise to a series of destructions—plague, drought, famine—each of which Enki thwarts through clever instructions to his human protégé Atraḫasis. The fourth and final destruction is the flood.

The flood and its aftermath, which is consistent in all the Mesopotamian versions, is aptly summarized by Wasserman (2020: 130):

> A deity discloses to his devotee a decision to wipe all life off the earth by means of a flood. The god instructs his devotee to build a large boat and orders him to store within sufficient foodstuff. He gives a sign when it is time to embark with his family, thus saving him and through him, all humanity. When the tidal wave washes over the earth, the human protagonists are safe inside the boat. Once the flood is over, the survivors emerge from the boat and offer sacrifices to the gods. A divine promise is given: no flood will occur again.

In *Atraḫasis,* Enlil grants immortality to the flood hero and his wife, while Enki and Mami devise new conditions that will limit the human lifespan, including natural death, demons who kill infants, and classes of holy women who do not bear children.

The Mesopotamian flood story circulated in two forms: as the final episode in a complex story, as in *Atraḫasis;* and as a first-person narrative by the flood hero, who tells only the story of the flood. The second form is found in several second- and first-millennium Akkadian tablets (including three from Ugarit) and Tablet XI of *Gilgamesh* (Wasserman 2020: 60–129). Both forms were transmitted widely in the cuneiform scribal stream of tradition.

The biblical versions of the flood in J and P combine aspects of both forms: they tell only the flood story, but in third-person narration, and they embed the flood into a narrative sequence that begins with creation. We cannot draw a direct line of textual dependence between the biblical flood and a particular form of the Mesopotamian flood. As Lambert writes, "[We must] suppose that an oral tradition existed alongside the copying of texts on clay, but we can only speculate on how the two traditions may have interacted" (Lambert and Millard 1969: 8). In the dissemination of the flood from Akkadian to other languages and cultures, we do not know to what extent written and oral traditions shaped each other. Lambert speculates that flood traditions penetrated West Semitic culture in the Late Bronze Age, when Akkadian was the international language of diplomacy (24). This is plausible, but contacts in the Neo-Assyrian period and later, perhaps mediated by Aramaic, are equally plausible. The version in P may draw on Mesopotamian versions in the Babylonian exile. There may be multiple eras and paths of contact.

Notice that the plot summary of the Mesopotamian flood story above also suits the J and P flood stories. The family resemblance is obvious. The correspondence of certain details brings this resemblance into sharper focus. Let us consider two scenes from Genesis and the Akkadian texts: the birds sequence and the sacrificial offering. The first is in both biblical versions and the second in J only.

The birds sequence, in which the flood hero sends off birds to determine when the waters have abated, is extant in two Akkadian texts, a Middle Bronze tablet from Ugarit and Standard Babylonian *Gilgamesh* XI (see NOTES at 8:8–12). There is a long lacuna at this point in *Atraḫasis,* so we cannot tell whether it had this scene, but it seems likely. The tablet from Ugarit reads:

> At the beginning of the invisibility of the moon, at the beginning of the
> month,
> Ea, the great lord, stood at my side, (saying:)
> "Take a wooden spade and a copper axe, and make a window at the top.
> Release a bird, let it find for you a shore!"
> I heeded the words of Ea, my great lord and advisor.
> I took a wooden spade and a copper axe. I made a window at the top
> above me.
> I released a dove, strong-of-wings.
> She went forth and came back, exhausted her wings.
> I did this again and released a water-bird.
>
> (Wasserman 2020: 88–89)

As Darshan (2016: 511) notes, in this version it is Ea who orchestrates the scene, instructing the flood hero to make a window and release the birds, in contrast to the other versions where the flood hero acts of his own volition. In the other versions, the window (*aptu,* Gilg. XI.137; *ḥallôn,* Gen 8:6, J) or door/entrance (*petaḥ,* Gen 6:16, P) is already built into the ark before the flood.

Other fluid features in this scene are the types of birds and the times of release:

Ugarit: Dove and water bird (crane or pelican?), released on the first of the
month
Gilgamesh XI.148–56: Dove, swallow, and raven, released seven days after the
ark lands (at intervals?)
J (Gen 8:6–12): Dove, released at the end of forty days, then twice more at
seven-day intervals
P (Gen 8:7): Raven, released on the tenth month, the first of the month

These four versions share many features, but those features are embedded in different configurations. First, the birds. The flood hero first releases a dove (Akkadian *summatu,* Hebrew *yônâ*) in both Akkadian versions and the J version. It fails to find a resting place and returns to the ark. The flood hero releases a raven (Akkadian *aribu,* Hebrew *ʿōrēb*) in *Gilgamesh* XI as the last bird of three, and it is the only bird released in P (on the source analysis, see NOTES at 8:7 [P]). The last bird of two in the Ugarit tablet is a water bird (*kumû,* perhaps a crane or pelican), which, as Wasserman (2020: 90) observes, "could more easily find a resting place and stay outside." The water bird is like the raven in this respect.

The release of three different birds in *Gilgamesh* XI (perhaps at intervals, although the text is silent on this point) probably points to different characteristics of the birds. As George (2003: 517) comments, "Though the primary function of the episode of the release of the three birds is to mark the gradual ebbing of the waters, the passage also serves as an aetiology of the different habitats of these birds, the dove and swallow on the one hand, the raven (or crow) on the other." The dove and swallow are habituated to human company, while the raven is more likely to fly away from humans. The three birds (a formulaic number) in *Gilgamesh* XI is comparable to the sequence of one bird sent three times in J. The raven sent once in P echoes a detail of this Mesopotamian sequence but simplifies it into a single bird.

The intervals of time also vary across the versions. Seven-day intervals are found in *Gilgamesh* XI and J but occur in different contexts: before the release of birds in the former and between the releases of birds in the latter. The release occurs on the first of the month in the Ugarit tablet and in P. The literary purpose of the bird scene, as George (2003: 517) remarks, is "to mark the gradual ebbing of the waters." It is a narrative technique to dilate time. It also marks the flood chronology. In the Mesopotamian tradition, this is a threefold sequence of sevens. The god instructs the flood hero that the flood will come in seven days, the flood lasts seven days, and seven days after the flood the bird release begins. The biblical versions expand this timeframe. In J, Yahweh instructs the flood hero that the flood will come in seven days, the flood lasts forty days, and there are two seven-day intervals during the bird episode. The P version expands the time frame considerably, with 150 days for the flood's rise and a longer period for its cessation.

These details and implications in the birds sequence show the degree of flexibility that writers and storytellers had when re-creating this episode. It seems clear that this episode was a well-known feature of the flood in Mesopotamian and Israelite traditions, but there was no expectation of fixity in its literary instantiations. Within the family relationship there was room for innovation, abbreviation and expansion, and new configurations.

The same can be said for the flood hero's sacrificial offering. This is found in multiple versions: *Atraḥasis,* the Sumerian flood myth, *Gilgamesh* XI, Berossos, and J. The prior lines are missing in *Atraḥasis,* but in *Gilgamesh* XI, Berossos, and J the sacrifice occurs directly after the birds sequence. In *Gilgamesh,* the words "I brought out" (*ušēṣi-ma*) recur for the birds and the sacrifice: "I brought out an offering and sacrificed to the four corners of the earth" (XI.157; George 2003: 712–13). Then the gods smell the aroma of the sacrifice:

> The gods smelled the savor,
>> the gods smelled the sweet savor,
>> the gods gathered like flies around the sacrificer.

(XI.161–63; George 2003: 712–13)

According to the older version in *Atraḥasis:*

> [The gods smelled] the savor,
>> They were gathered [like flies] around the sacrifice.
> [. . .] they had eaten the sacrifice,

(III.iv.34–38; Foster 2005: 251; Wasserman 2020: 27, 35)

In the *Gilgamesh* version, the gods gather like flies around the "sacrificer" (*bēl nīqi*) instead of the sacrifice (*nīqi*), and the statement that "they had eaten the sacrifice" is omitted. As Tigay (1982: 227–29) comments, these and other changes serve to eliminate the older version's "implications that the gods starved and thirsted during the flood." These implications, however, provide a powerful motive for Mami's critique of Enlil and the other gods (herself included) for agreeing to send the flood (see above).

The flood hero's sacrifice in the Mesopotamian flood tradition represents a resumption of the regular cult, the ritual "care and feeding of the gods" that took place in local temples. Atraḫasis is a priest (*pašīšu,* Ugarit 1.6; Wasserman 2020: 82–85) and has the authority to make such sacrifices. Notably, in *Gilgamesh* he makes this offering on "the peak of the mountain" (*ziqqurrat šadi*), literally "the ziggurat of the mountain." A ziggurat is a sacred mountainlike structure with a temple on top. Here, as Wasserman (2020: 128) observes, "the mountain *is* the ziggurat." The priest resumes the regular offerings, which reestablish the relationship between humans and gods in which the humans feed the gods. The gods' starvation in the wake of the flood is an ironic echo of the humans' starvation in the previous famine (*Atra.* II.iv.1–18; Chen 2013: 232) and emphasizes that the gods are dependent on their human subordinates. This is why Mami announces, regarding the sacrifice:

> "Let the gods come to the incense,
>> (but) may Enlil not come to the incense,
> Because he lacked counsel and caused the Deluge,
>> and delivered my people into destruction."

(Gilg. XI.168–69; George 2003: 714–15)

The sacrifice repairs the breach between humans and the gods but at the same time highlights the irrationality of Enlil's decision to send the flood to destroy humankind.

Noah's sacrifice in J also occurs directly after the birds sequence, when he "removed the ark's cover" and saw that "the face of the soil was dry" (8:19). Then "Noah built an altar for Yahweh. He took one of every clean animal and every clean bird and offered burnt offerings on the altar. Yahweh smelled the soothing aroma" (8:20–21). The details closely track the Mesopotamian versions; however, Noah is not a priest. Like Abraham and other Israelite ancestors, he builds an altar, a ritual place for sacrifice. His sacrifice consists of "burnt offerings" (*ʿōlōt*) from every ritually clean animal and bird. In a burnt offering, the whole animal is turned into smoke as a ritual gift for God. This is a symbolic transformation of a meal, turned into a "soothing aroma" (*rēaḥ hannîḥōaḥ*), echoing the name of Noah (*nōaḥ*).

When in *Atraḫasis* "the gods smelled the savor," the focus is the gods' hunger and need for nourishment, which only humans can provide. In *Gilgamesh* XI, the focus is on the gods' gratitude to the sacrificer rather than on the sacrifice. Both emphasize the gods' need for humans for their continued well-being. In the J flood, the soothing aroma of Noah's sacrifice has a similar nuance. It provokes an inward reckoning: "Yahweh said in his heart, 'I will never again curse the soil because of humans, for the designs of the human heart are evil from their youth. Never again will I destroy all life as I have done'" (8:21). It is a moral awakening and a letting go, an admission that the reciprocity between humans and God that is activated by the sacrifice is more valuable than the perfect justice of a dead world. Yahweh, like Mami, turns to compassion and a deeper wisdom. For God recognizes that humans are, as Mami says, "my people," despite the ineluctable evil of the human heart. The sacrifice is a turning point in the Mesopotamian and the J flood stories, but it turns in different ways.

The Flood According to **P**
(6:9–9:29)

---

6   9This is the genealogy of Noah. Noah was a righteous man, blameless in his generations; Noah walked with God. 10Noah fathered three sons, Shem, Ham, and Japheth. 11The earth was corrupt before God, for the earth was filled with violence. 12God saw the earth, and behold, it was corrupt, for all flesh had corrupted its way on earth.

13God said to Noah, "The end of all flesh has come before me, for the earth is filled with violence because of them. I am now going to destroy them and the earth. 14Make yourself an ark with gopher wood, with reeds make the ark, and seal it inside and out with pitch. 15This is how you shall make it: 300 cubits the ark's length, 50 cubits its width, and 30 cubits its height. 16Make a roof over the ark and finish it 1 cubit from the top. Make a door^a in its side. Make a lower, a second, and a third deck. 17As for me, I am going to bring the flood—water on the earth—to destroy all flesh under heaven that has within it life's breath. Everything on earth will die. 18But I will make my covenant with you, and you shall enter the ark, you and your sons, your wife, and your sons' wives with you. 19Of all living things, of all flesh, two of each you shall bring into the ark to save their lives with yours—they shall be male and female. You shall bring two of all living things, male and female of all flesh, into the ark to save their lives with yours. 20Every kind of bird, every kind of land animal, every kind of creature that crawls on the earth—two of each will come to you to save their lives with you. 21As for you, take every kind of edible food and gather it, for it will be your food and theirs." 22Noah did everything as God commanded him, thus he did.

. . .

7   6Noah was 600 years old when the flood was^b on the earth. . . . 11In the 600th year of Noah's life, in the second month, on the seventeenth^c day of the month, on that day,

all the wellsprings of the great ocean burst,
and the windows of heaven were opened.

. . . [13]On that very day Noah and Noah's sons—Shem, Ham, and Japheth—and Noah's wife, and his sons' three wives with them entered the ark. [14d]Every kind of wild animal, every kind of domestic animal, every kind of creature that crawls on the earth, and every kind of bird[e] [15]came to Noah in the ark, two by two of all flesh that has within it life's breath. [16]Those that came, male and female of all flesh, came as God had commanded him. . . .

[18]The water grew strong and multiplied mightily on the earth, and the ark floated on the face of the water. [19]The water grew so very strong on the earth that it covered every high mountain beneath all of heaven. [20]Fifteen cubits higher the water rose,[f] and the mountains were covered. [21]All flesh that moved on the earth died—birds, domestic animals, wild animals, every creature that crawls on the earth, and all humans. . . . [24]The water grew strong on the earth for 150 days.

8   [1]Then God remembered Noah and all the wild and domestic animals that were with him on the ark. God sent a wind over the earth, and the water subsided. [2]The wellsprings of the ocean and the windows of heaven were shut fast. . . . [3]The water began to diminish after 150 days. [4]In the seventh month, on the seventeenth[c] day of the month, the ark came to rest in the mountains of Ararat. [5]The water continued to subside until the tenth month. In the tenth month, on the first day of the month, the mountain peaks appeared.

. . . [7]He sent out a raven, and it went back and forth until the water was dry on the earth. . . . [13]In his 601st year, in the first month, on the first day of the month, the water dried off the earth. . . . [14]In the second month, on the twenty-seventh day of the month, the earth was dry.

[15]God said to Noah, [16]"Go out of the ark, you and your wife, your sons, and your sons' wives with you. [17]Every living creature with you, all flesh—birds, land animals, and every creature that crawls on the earth—bring them out with you. Let them[g] be fruitful and multiply on the earth." [18]Noah went out with his sons, his wife, and his sons' wives with him. [19]Every living creature, every bird, and every creature that crawls[h] on the earth, according to their families, came out of the ark.

. . .

9   [1]God blessed Noah and his sons and said to them, "Be fruitful and multiply and fill the earth. [2]Dread and fear of you will come upon every creature on earth, every bird of the sky, everything that moves on the earth, and every fish of the sea. They are in your hands. [3]Every living, moving creature will be your food. I hereby give them all to you, as I did the green plants. [4]But flesh with its life's blood in it you shall not eat. [5]Indeed, for your lives I will demand your blood. I shall demand it from every creature and from humans. From a man regarding his brother, I will demand the man's life.

[6]Whoever sheds the blood of a human,
    for a human will his blood be shed,
    for in God's image he made humans.

[7]As for you, be fruitful and multiply, teem over the earth, and rule[i] it."

⁸God said to Noah and his sons with him, ⁹"As for me, I am going to make my covenant with you, with your descendants after you, ¹⁰and with every living creature that is with you—birds, land animals, and all the earth's creatures,ʲ everyone that left the ark.ᵏ ¹¹I will make my covenant with you: Never again will all flesh be cut off by the flood waters; never again will there be another flood to destroy the earth." ¹²God said, "This is the sign of the covenant that I am making with you and all living creatures with you, for everlasting generations. ¹³I have set my bow in the clouds, and it will be a sign of the covenant between me and the earth. ¹⁴Whenever I bring rain clouds over the earth, the bow will appear in the clouds. ¹⁵And I will remember my covenant between me, you, and all living creatures, all flesh, and never again will the water become a flood to destroy all flesh. ¹⁶The bow will appear in the clouds, and I will see it and remember the eternal covenant between God and all living creatures, all flesh that is on earth." ¹⁷God said to Noah, "This is the sign of the covenant that I have made between me and all flesh that is on earth."

. . .

²⁸After the flood Noah lived 350 years. ²⁹All the days of Noah's life were 950 years, and he died.

Textual Notes

a. The MT and SP add *htbh* ("[of] the ark"), which is lacking in the LXX. This is an explicating plus, qualifying the word "door" (Hendel 1998: 51).

b. The MT, SP, and LXX⁹¹¹ add *mym* ("water"), an awkward harmonization with *hmbwl mym ʿl h'rṣ* in 6:17. LXXᴬ lacks this plus and plausibly represents the original LXX (Hendel 1998: 51–52).

c. In 7:11 and 8:4 the MT and SP read seventeen, while the LXX reads twenty-seven. This variation is most likely a harmonization in proto-LXX (harmonized to 8:14, where all versions read twenty-seven), which serves to "correct" the flood chronology to precisely one year (cf. other views in Hendel 1995b; Rösel 1998; Ben-Dov 2021: 446–49).

d. The MT and SP add *hmh* (SP *hm*), which is lacking in the LXX. This is an explicating plus, including Noah and his family in the procession, but conflicts with the following statement that "they came to Noah on the ark" (7:15). The explication, in other words, misconstrues the picture of who is coming to whom on the ark (Hendel 1998: 52–53).

e. The MT and SP add *kl ṣpwr kl knp* ("every bird, every wing"), probably meaning "every winged bird," which is lacking in the LXX. This phrase, perhaps copied from Ezek 17:23, appears to be an explication of which flying creatures were on the ark, though its sense is not entirely clear. Perhaps this is a scribal comment that other winged creatures (insects?) were not on the ark (Hendel 1998: 53).

f. Reading *gbhw* ("rose") with the LXX, rather than *gbrw* ("was strong") with the MT and SP. The latter is probably a reminiscence of *gbrw* in 7:19 (Hendel 1998: 53).

g. The MT and SP add *wšrṣw b'rṣ* ("let them swarm on the earth"), which is lacking in the LXX. This addition harmonizes the blessing of the animals with the blessing of humans in 9:7, which includes the phrase *šrṣw b'rṣ* ("swarm/teem over the earth") (Hendel 1998: 56).

h. Reading with the SP and LXX *wkl h'wp wkl hrmś* ("and every bird and every creature that crawls"). The MT has suffered a metathesis of *'wp* ("bird") and *rmś* ("crawling creature"), into which an extra *kl* ("every") has been inserted to reduce the chaos, yielding the odd text *kl hrms wkl hwp kl* (*hrms*) ("every crawling creature and every bird, everything [that crawls]") (Hendel 1998: 56).

i. Reading *wrdw* ("and rule"), rather than *wrbw* ("and multiply") (MT, SP, LXX). The latter is a reminiscence of *wrbw* earlier in the verse, whereas the former is probably meant, reviving the blessing of 1:28. The difference between the two readings is a single letter, making the reminiscence an easy scribal error (Hendel 1998: 56–57; cf. Schellenberg 2011: 33).

j. The MT and SP add *'tkm* ("with you"), which is lacking in the LXX. This word is a repetition of *'tkm* earlier in the verse and appears to explicate the phrase "all the earth's creatures," limiting its scope to those that were with Noah on the ark (Hendel 1998: 57).

k. The MT and SP add *lkl ḥyt h'rṣ* ("of all earth's creatures"), which is lacking in the LXX. This is an odd explicating plus. It echoes the phrase *wbkl ḥyt h'rṣ* ("and all the earth's creatures") earlier in the verse and apparently qualifies the phrase *mkl yṣ'y htbh* ("of everyone who left the ark"). If this is an explicating plus, it adds less clarity rather than more (Hendel 1998: 57).

Notes

6:9. *This is the genealogy of Noah.* The formula "this is the genealogy of PN" functions as section headings in Genesis (see INTRODUCTION I). In the P text, these headings occur for Noah (6:9), Noah's sons (10:1), Shem (11:10), and Terah (11:27). In some cases, as Wellhausen (1885: 332) notes, "the contents of the preceding section are first of all briefly recapitulated," as they are in 6:10. Some have suggested that all the headings should be attributed to R, but in 6:9 it prefaces the P flood story, not the composite flood story (one would expect it to preface 6:5 if this were so). Usually these headings introduce sections that feature the descendants of the father named. In this case the father (Noah) has the major role, though he is accompanied by his sons. Although this section begins with a focus on the father, it includes the lineages that descend from him.

Noah was a righteous man, blameless in his generations; Noah walked with God. The grammar of this sentence is unusual. The first part, *nōaḥ 'îš ṣaddîq tāmîm hāyâ,* is often read as a single clause (as it is by the Masoretes), "Noah was a righteous (and) blameless man in his generation." But the verb *hāyâ* ("was") should come after *nōaḥ* in this construal, not at the end of the sequence. It is more plausible, and in keeping with the style of P, to read this as a quasi-poetic introduction, with a pause between *ṣaddîq* and *tāmîm* ("man of virtue, blameless . . .") (see Skinner 1930: 158). Combined with the following clause, this introduction of Noah's qualities has the rhythm of a parallel triplet. This three-part description begins and ends with the name Noah (*nōaḥ*), creating a stylistic *inclusio* (McEvenue 1971: 40). B. J. Schwartz (2007: 147–48) attributes the first two parts to J, but this seems unlikely since the plural *dōrōt* ("generations") with pronominal suffix is typical covenantal language in P (e.g., 17:7–12; cf. the singular *dôr* for Noah in J, 7:1); and the plural *tāmîm* ("blameless") is also characteristic P diction (17:1; cf. the singular *tām* for Jacob in J, 25:27).

As a virtuous man who is *tāmîm* ("blameless, complete, perfect," a **qatīl* adjectival form) and who "walked" (*hitallēk*) with God, Noah is a precursor of Abraham, whom God commands, "walk before me and be blameless" (*hithallēk ləpānay wehyēh tāmîm,* 17:1, P). Through this language, Noah's virtue is linked with Abraham's. This language also links Noah with his virtuous precursor Enoch.

The clause "Noah walked with God" (*'et-hā'ĕlōhîm hithallek-nōaḥ*) elucidates Noah's moral perfection. It echoes and inverts 5:22 (P), "Enoch walked with God" (*wayyithallēk ḥănôk 'et-hā'ĕlōhîm*), using the same grammatical construction. The verb *hithallēk* has an iterative sense, "walk around (with)," or even "walk constantly (with)." The fronting of the clause with the indirect object, "with God" (*'et-hā'ĕlōhîm*), creates an emphatic contrast with the previous object, "in his generation" (*bədōrōtāyw*). Noah's conduct is contrasted with that of his contemporaries—"*with God* Noah walked," not with them.

Sasson (1975: 166) suggests that the text highlights the parallelism between Enoch and Noah not only by using the identical construction *hithallēk* ("walk around") + *'et-hā'ĕlōhîm* ("with God"), but also by ending the verse with a palindrome—the last three letters of *hithallek-nōaḥ*, when read backwards, spell *ḥnk* (*ḥănôk,* Enoch). Noah and Enoch are not only parallel figures but perhaps also palindromes. Their virtues and vocables echo each other.

6:10. *Noah fathered three sons, Shem, Ham, and Japheth.* This verse repeats the diction of 5:32, serving as a resumptive repetition, which picks up the narrative thread from the point of the previous text.

6:11–13. The motive for the flood has a structure like the J sequence in 6:5–7, 7:1–4. In J, Yahweh "saw" (*wayyar'*) the changed situation, "said" (*wayyō'mer*) his decision in an internal speech, then "said" (*wayyō'mer*) his instructions to Noah. P has a comparable sequence of seeing, deciding, and saying. This sequence is rhythmic and quasi-poetic, as is characteristic of P's heightened style (McEvenue 1971: 41–42; Paran 1989: 103–4). The repetition of the terms *šḥt* ("ruin, corrupt, destroy," four times), *ḥms* ("violence, wrongdoing," two times), and *hā'āreṣ* ("the earth," six times) creates a dense and foreboding *Leitwort* texture (see INTRODUCTION I).

6:11. *The earth was corrupt before God, for the earth was filled with violence.* In P, the motive for the flood is not human evil per se, but the consequence of the violent acts of humans and other living creatures, which have corrupted the earth. The focus is on the corrupted earth, consonant with P's cosmic focus, compared with J's anthropocentric focus. The nature of the earth's corruption is not entirely clear. The two parallel clauses in this verse overlay two descriptions of the earth, both with passive verbs: the earth was "ruined, corrupted," with the *Leitwort* verb *šḥt* in the *niphal,* and it was filled with "violence, wrongdoing," with the *Leitwort* *ḥms.* Both are general terms. A land can be "ruined" (in the *niphal*) by insects (Exod 8:20), a pot can be "ruined" by its maker (Jer 18:4), and a loincloth can be "ruined" by being buried in the ground (Jer 13:7). Human behavior can also be "ruinous, corrupt" (Ezek 20:44). The noun *ḥāmās* ("violence, wrongdoing") can refer to a great many misdeeds, including murder, rape, theft, oppression of the poor, and false witness (H. Haag 1980). It is also used as a legal term for "injustice," as when one cries out in public appealing for redress (Jer 20:8, Hab 1:2, Job 19:7; similarly, the "cry" of Abel's blood in Gen 4:10).

The particular violence in this case seems to involve bloodshed (e.g., Westermann 1984: 416), since the solution to this problem in the Noachian covenant is the regulation of bloodshed and prohibition of murder (9:3–6). But this is specified only in retrospect. The text here leaves the range of violence and injustice open. As Wenham (1987: 171) observes, there is an ironic tension between God's blessing to humans, "fill the earth" (*mil'û 'et-hā'āreṣ*, 1:28), and the tragic result, "the earth was filled with violence" (*wattimmālē' hā'āreṣ ḥāmās*).

6:12. *God saw the earth, and behold, it was corrupt, for all flesh had corrupted its way on earth.* After the objective portrayal of the earth's ruin, the text turns to God's perception of it. God's act of "seeing" the earth's corrupt state does not involve divine emotions—regret or grief, as in the J version—but rather registers the profound change from God's vantage point. The wording and syntax of God's perception echo his final perception of creation in 1:31—"God saw" (*wayyar' 'ĕlōhîm*) his work of creation, "and behold, it was very good" (*wəhinnēh-ṭôb mə'ōd*) (Delitzsch 1888: 255; Cassuto 1964: 53). Now God sees (*wayyar' 'ĕlōhîm*) again, but the world he created has turned from "very good" to "corrupt" (*nišḥātâ*). Both verses use the deictic particle *hinnēh* (translated "behold") after a verb of perception to portray the scene from the agent's point of view. The corrupt earth is shown from God's perspective.

The agents of the earth's corruption are specified in the last clause, "for all flesh had corrupted its way on earth." The perpetrators are "all flesh" (*kol-bāśār*), not just humans, in contrast to the J version. Animals are also violent, and humans and animals have both corrupted their "way" (*derek*). What is this way? Presumably the proper mode of being and behaving. The text is reticent on this point, but it fills in the gaps retrospectively with the remedies in the Noachian covenant.

As Skinner (1930: 159) observes, "The fundamental idea of v. 11f. is the disappearance of the Golden Age, or the rupture of the concord of the animal world established by the decree of 1:29f." In this golden age animals and humans were vegetarians, as mandated in 1:29–30. The rupture began with killing: some animals killed others for food, some preyed on humans, and humans killed animals and each other. This is an implicit history of how "all flesh had corrupted its way on earth," with the consequence that the earth itself "was corrupt." The Noachian laws remedy this situation by allowing meat-eating (without the blood) in addition to vegetarianism (9:3). But here only a general impression of violence and corruption is given—the "way" has been ruined.

6:13. *God said to Noah, "The end of all flesh has come before me, for the earth is filled with violence because of them. I am now going to destroy them and the earth."* God's speech to Noah expresses the transcendent position of God as the "unmoved mover," in contrast to the anthropopathic Yahweh in the J version. The "end of all flesh has come before me" (*qēṣ kol-bāśār bā' ləpānay*), just as the earth was "corrupt before God" in 6:11. The divine agent is the objective perceiver, and the problem entails its own response. God's decision merely acknowledges what the situation requires.

The motive clause and its consequence—"for the earth is filled with violence because of them. I am now going to destroy them and the earth"—forms an *inclusio* or envelope structure with 6:11: "The earth was corrupt before God, for the earth was filled with violence" (McEvenue 1971: 29). The beginning and end have *šḥt* ("corrupt, destroy") + *hā'āreṣ* ("the earth"), and the middle has *ml'* ("fill") + *hā'āreṣ* + *ḥāmās* ("violence"). This dramatic structure moves from the objective description to God's response. Because the earth is "corrupt," God will "destroy" (both verbs from the root *ḥt*). The violence of all flesh will be erased by God's destruction, both sides linked stylistically and by the *Leitwort* variation of *šḥt* ("corrupt" in the *niphal* and "destroy" in the *piel*). The construction *wǎhinǎnî mašḥîtām* ("I am now going to destroy them") uses the participle as an imminent future (*futurum instans*). The deictic particle *hinnēh* is often used in this construction to convey the vividness of the situation (*IBHS* §37.6f).

6:14–16. God's speech to Noah shifts topic to the instructions for building the ark. Stylistically, as McEvenue (1971: 44 n. 36) notes, "the text is built as three triplets: gopher—reeds—pitch; length—width—height; roof—door—decks." The decks include another triplet: lower—second—third. These schematic instructions are not comprehensive but give a general sense of technical precision. Several of the terms are rare or unknown—*gōper* ("gopher wood"), *kōper* ("pitch"), *ṣōhar* ("roof?")—giving a sense of reality and obscurity to the ark's construction.

6:14. *Make yourself an ark with gopher wood, with reeds make the ark, and seal it inside and out with pitch.* On the word "ark" (*tēbâ*), used by J and P, see Notes at 7:1 (J). The type of wood, *ʾǎṣê-gōper* ("gopher wood"), is unknown. It is possibly a type of cypress, given its similarity to the Greek *kuparissos* (cypress), which may be a pan-Mediterranean *Kulturwort* (see Delitzsch 1888: 257; Skinner 1930: 161). The targums translate this wood as "cedar," which is probably a guess. In the ancient world, wooden boats were usually made of cypress, cedar, or oak, with some references to pine and palm (Wachsmann 1998: 215–27; cypress, cedar, and oak are listed as the types of wood in Tyrian boats in Ezek 27:5–6). The word *gōper* has an alliterative rhyme with *kōper* ("pitch") later in the verse (Rendsburg 2016: 84).

The word *qnym*, pointed as *qinnîm* ("nests") in the MT, is best read as *qānîm* ("reeds"), since this verse is concerned with materials, and "nests" makes no sense (Jacob 1934: 188; Ullendorff 1954; Wenham 1987: 173; Day 2013: 113–22). If one accepts the traditional reading, *qinnîm* ("nests"), one would have to attribute a more general meaning, "cells, compartments" (e.g., Speiser 1964: 52). However, all twelve instances of *qēn* in the Hebrew Bible (found only in the singular) refer to a bird's nest or, by semantic extension, the bird's family (cf. the denominitive verb *qnn,* "to make a nest"). It is simpler to assume that the reading tradition (already in the LXX) had forgotten the ancient use of reeds in boat construction.

Ancient Mesopotamian boats were often made of wood and reeds (the reeds were used to sew the wood planks together) and caulked and coated with pitch (Potts 1997: 122–37). The boat in the Mesopotamian flood tradition was so constructed in the (broken) scene in *Atraḫasis* III.ii.11–13 (similarly *Gilg.* XI.50–56):

> The carpenter [carried his axe].
> The reed-worker [carried his stone(?)].
> [The rich man carried] the pitch (*kupru*).

(Wasserman 2020: 22, 32)

The instructions, and perhaps even the sequence of materials, for constructing Noah's ark may reflect this Mesopotamian tradition.

The sequence "Make yourself an ark with gopher wood, with reeds make the ark," with the chiasm of *ʿśh* ("make") + *tēbâ* ("ark") + material (wood, reeds), belongs to a favorite style of the P source, the "circular *inclusio*" (Paran 1989: 84–85; Introduction I). The instructions for the ark end in 6:16 with a repetition of *ʿśh* ("make"), creating a larger *inclusio* around this section.

The noun and verb in "seal it . . . with pitch" (*wəkāpartā . . . bakkōper*) occur only here in Biblical Hebrew. The cognate noun *kupru* is the common word for "pitch, bitumen" in Akkadian (see above), whereas the normal Hebrew word for "pitch" is *ḥēmār* (Gen 11:3, 14:10; Exod 2:3). The use of *kōper* here may be another sign of borrowing from Mesopotamian tradition (Noort 1998: 9), or perhaps is a deliberate allusion to Mesopotamian tradition. The repetition of the root in this command creates alliteration, plus an end rhyme with the previous *gōper* wood.

It may be significant that the only other *tēbâ* ("ark") in the Hebrew Bible, that of baby Moses on the Nile (Exod 2:3–5), is made of "reed" (*gōme'*) and caulked and coated with pitch (*ḥēmār*). The words for these materials are different from those used for Noah's ark, but there seems to be a thematic echo in water-going arks that save the lives of ancestors.

6:15. *This is how you shall make it: 300 cubits the ark's length, 50 cubits its width, and 30 cubits its height.* At about 18 inches to the cubit, the ark is approximately 450 feet long, 75 feet wide, and 45 feet high. This is a large vessel, unlike any in use. The detailed dimensions of the ark are complemented by the detailed chronology for the flood (see NOTES at 7:11). These detailed structures in the P flood story complement the well-structured design of creation in Genesis 1.

The dimensions of the tabernacle in P may have some relation to those of the ark. The tabernacle has a surrounding enclosure that is 100 cubits long, 50 cubits wide, and 5 cubits high (Exod 27:18). The Jerusalem temple may have had the same measurements as the tabernacle enclosure (including the side chambers around the temple) but was 30 cubits high (1 Kgs 6:1–6). Noah's ark and the tabernacle/temple share two dimensions, width and height, but the ark is three times longer. On the basis of these measurements, it is possible that the ark has a symbolic link with the temple (Holloway 1991: 348–49).

The dimensions of Noah's ark differ from those of Utnapishtim's boat in the *Gilgamesh* epic. As Utnapishtim relates:

On the fifth day I set in place her surface,
   one *ikû* was her area (?), ten *nindanu* each her sides stood high,
ten *nindanu* each, the edges of her top were equal.
   I set in place her body, I drew up her design:
I gave her six decks,
   I divided her into seven parts.
I divided her interior into nine.

(XI.57–63; George 2003: 706–7)

The ark's height, width, and length are equal at 10 *nindanu* (120 cubits) each, forming a perfect cube (George 2003: 512). This symmetrical shape and its interior division into six decks probably has cosmic significance (the cosmos has six levels in some Mesopotamian texts; Horowitz 1998: xii–xiii, 3–19). As George (2003: 512) comments, "its interior reproduces in miniature the cosmos in its most elaborate structure: six decks stacked vertically." The flood hero's boat is a microcosm of the cosmos.

An Old or Middle Babylonian version of *Atraḥasis* depicts the boat as a circular craft, with the sides only 1 *nindanu* (12 cubits) high and with two decks. Enki instructs the flood hero:

The boat which you will build,
    I will draw it out (for you)—a circular plan:
Her length and breadth should be equal,
    Her base should be one *ikû*; her walls should be one *nindanu* (high).

(Wasserman 2020: 66, 69, Ark 6–9)

As Finkel (2014: 123–44) elucidates, this is a circular boat of traditional kind, a coracle, unlike the cuboid boat in *Gilgamesh* XI.

In the Sumerian flood myth and a Middle Babylonian tablet from Nippur the boat is a large almond-shaped vessel (*maqurqurrum;* Finkel 2014: 121; Wasserman 2020: 78). There is no obvious link between the dimensions of any of these Mesopotamian flood vessels and Noah's ark, but they are all massive and built according to the precise plans given by a deity to the flood hero.

6:16. *Make a roof over the ark and finish it 1 cubit from the top. Make a door in its side. Make a lower, a second, and a third deck.* The word *ṣōhar* ("roof?") is found only here in Biblical Hebrew. On the basis of Akkadian *ṣēru*, Ugaritic *ẓr*, and Arabic *ẓahr*, all meaning "back, upperside, top," it is plausible to read the Hebrew word as "top, roof" (Gunkel 1997: 144; Armstrong 1960; *HALOT*, 1008). The older traditional reading is "skylight, window," related to *ṣohŏrayim* ("noon"). If it means "roof," it is a different type of roof from the Hebrew word *gāg*, which means "flat roof." Perhaps it is a type of pitched or vaulted roof. If so, this would explain the obscure instruction, "finish it 1 cubit from the top," which would refer to the peak of the roof extending 1 cubit higher than the walls, such that the roof slopes down on two sides to meet the top of the walls (so Armstrong 1960: 333; Hamilton 1990: 282–83). A pitched roof would be useful during a deluge. On this understanding, there is a possible gender problem between *ṣōhar* (probably masculine) and the suffix *-ennâ* (feminine) on *təkallennâ* ("finish it"). In any case, as McEvenue (1971: 44–45) observes, the instructions convey a sense of technical language without being entirely clear or comprehensive.

The detail of the *petaḥ bəṣiddāh* ("door in its side") prepares for the entry of the animals and people into the ark. Utnapishtim's boat also has a door or hatch (*Gilg.* XI.89), unlike ordinary ancient boats.

It is possible that the three decks of the ark—"a lower, a second, and a third deck"—may have an analogue in the three stories of the side chambers of Solomon's Temple (Holloway 1991: 349). The three-storied structure of P's inhabited cosmos— sea, earth, and sky—might also have a resonance, with the floating ark as a microcosm of life while the cosmos returns to chaos.

6:17. *As for me, I am going to bring the flood—water on the earth—to destroy all flesh under heaven that has within it life's breath. Everything on earth will die.* Having given his instructions to Noah, God tells him what he will do. The diction echoes God's words to Noah before the instructions about the ark, "I am now going to destroy them and the earth" (6:13), forming an envelope or resumptive repetition around the ark instructions.

The phrase *mayim ʿal hāʾāreṣ* ("water on the earth") seems to be an explanation of the technical term *hammabbûl* ("the flood," see NOTES at 7:7 [J]). It may be a scribal gloss or part of the original composition, explaining the technical term to Noah.

The sequence "to destroy all flesh under heaven that has within it life's breath. Everything on earth will die"—with the *Leitwort* terms *ləšaḥēt* ("to destroy"), *kol-bāśār*

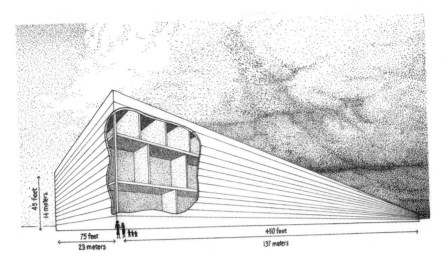

Figure 10. Artist's rendition of details of Noah's ark. (Drawing by William H. C. Propp)

("all flesh"), and *hā'āreṣ* ("the earth")—echoes the ominous beginning in 6:11–13. The dramatic tone of this death sentence is heightened by the spatial diction, echoing the creation account: "under heaven" and "on earth." From this point on, the references to the Genesis 1 creation story mount, creating a sense of reversing creation. In 2:1, "heaven and earth and all their array were complete," but now the ordered cosmos bounded by heaven and earth will return to watery chaos.

The mention of "life's breath" (*rûaḥ ḥayyîm*) reflects the "soft duality" of flesh and life-breath (see NOTES at 2:7). In P and J, creatures consist of a material substance, *bāśār* ("flesh"), which is enlivened by *rûaḥ ḥayyîm* ("life's breath"). In P, the blood is also a carrier of the life force (see NOTES at 9:4).

6:18. *But I will make my covenant with you, and you shall enter the ark, you and your sons, your wife, and your sons' wives with you.* In contrast to "all flesh," Noah and his household have a different fate. God's reference to "my covenant" (*bərîtî*) is not explained here but anticipates the postdiluvian Noachian covenant in 9:8–17. The word "covenant" (*bərît*), cognate with Akkadian *birītu*, "area between or held in common; link, clasp, fetter," begins a major connective theme in the P source. The Noachian covenant, the Abrahamic covenant (Genesis 17), and its renewal in the Mosaic covenant (Exodus 6) are key steps in the reconstitution of cosmic order in P. The anticipation of the covenant theme is appropriate here, mingling the return to chaos with the promise of re-creation.

The command includes Noah's household—"you and your sons, your wife, and your sons' wives with you." This provides a glimpse into the concept of the "father's house" (*bêt 'āb*), which is both a residential unit and a collective identity. This social unit is patrilineal and patriarchal; hence Noah and his sons are listed before their wives. The wives are not named, nor are the sons, all of whom are subordinate to Noah. This list is repeated with variations four times in the P flood story. Each time the list is slightly varied, in accord with the stylistic propensity of P for variation within repetition:

—"you and your sons, your wife, and your sons' wives with you" (6:18)
—"Noah and Noah's sons—Shem, Ham, and Japheth   and Noah's wife, and
     his sons' three wives with them" (7:13)
—"you and your wife, your sons, and your sons' wives with you" (8:16)
—"Noah . . . his sons, his wife, and his sons' wives with him" (8:18)

The order, the naming (of the sons), and the closing prepositions ("with you" and "with them") all vary. As McEvenue (1971: 49) observes, "we seem to have hit again upon a general tendency in the priestly writer to set up a strict system, whose discipline is felt by the reader, and yet to break out of that system by variation."

6:19. *Of all living things, of all flesh, two of each you shall bring into the ark to save their lives with yours—they shall be male and female.* P has one pair of each animal on the ark, in contrast to J's seven pairs of every clean animal and one pair of every unclean animal (7:2 [J]). The reason for this difference derives from the Sinaitic law in P, where the laws of purity and sacrifice are given (Leviticus 1–7, 11). In contrast, J presumes that purity rules and sacrifices are universal custom or natural law, already operating in primeval time. Thus, there is no sacrifice after the flood in P, and one pair of each animal on the ark is sufficient.

This number of animals, "two of each" (*šǝnayim mikkōl*), has a parallel in an Old or Middle Babylonian tablet of *Atraḫasis*:

And so, wild anima[ls from the s]teppe [. . .],
by twos (*šanâ*) [I] did [make enter] into the boat.

(Wasserman 2020: 68, 70, Ark 51–52)

This seems to be an old feature of the flood tradition.

The designation "male and female" (*zākār ûnǝqēbâ*, 6:19; 7:3, 16) differs from the similar designation in J, "a male and its mate" (*'îš wǝ 'ištô*, twice in 7:2). The P diction may be more technical or objective, suiting P's style.

The command to save the lives of "all flesh" (*kol-bāśār*) ameliorates the death sentence for "all flesh" (*kol-bāśār*) in 6:17. There the verb was "to destroy" (*lǝšāḥēt*); now the governing verb is "to save life" (*lǝhaḥăyōt*). As observed above (see Notes at 6:8 [J]), the friction between destroying and saving life in the flood reflects the monotheistic recasting of the old flood tradition, in which a single God must be both the destroyer and the rescuer. In the P story, these are presented as steps in God's plan.

The form *lǝhaḥăyōt* ("to save life") is a *hiphil* infinitive of the root *ḥyh*. The J story uses a *piel* infinitive of this root with the same meaning, *lǝḥayyōt* (7:3). This difference between *piel* and *hiphil* indicates a difference in the dialects or historical phases of Hebrew represented in J and P. The movement of some verbs from *piel* to *hiphil* is a diachronic characteristic of language change in Biblical Hebrew (see Hendel 1998: 134, 142).

6:20. *Every kind of bird, every kind of land animal, every kind of creature that crawls on the earth—two of each will come to you to save their lives with you.* The categories of animals on the ark echo the diction of the creation account in Genesis 1. In both P texts, the diction varies slightly from verse to verse. In God's command here, the animals are categorized as *'ôp* ("birds"), *bǝhēmâ* ("land animals"), and *remeś hā 'ǎdāmâ* (lit. "crawlers of the earth," i.e., rodents, reptiles, insects, etc.). In the subsequent lists of animals, the latter two terms have shifting meanings, depending on the terms they are contrasted with. Another term, *ḥayyâ* ("living creature" or "wild animal"), rounds out the subsequent lists (cf. *ḥay,* "living things," in 6:19):

— "Every kind of wild animal (*ḥayyâ*), every kind of domestic animal (*bəhēmâ*), every kind of creature that crawls on the earth (*ḥāremeś hārōmēś ʿal-hā ʾāreṣ*), and every kind of bird" (7:14)

— "birds, domestic animals (*bəhēmâ*), wild animals (*ḥayyâ*), every creature that crawls on the earth (*haššereṣ haššōrēṣ ʿal-hā ʾāreṣ*)" (7:21)

— "birds, land animals (*bəhēmâ*), and every creature that crawls on the earth (*ḥāremeś hārōmēś ʿal-hā ʾāreṣ*)" (8:17)

— "every bird, and every creature that crawls on the earth (*ḥāremeś harōmēś ʿal-hā ʾāreṣ*)" (8:19)

— "birds, land animals (*bəhēmâ*), and all the earth's creatures (*ḥayyat hā ʾāreṣ*)" (9:10)

The word *bəhēmâ* means "land animal" in 6:20, 8:17, and 9:10, but when contrasted with *ḥayyâ* ("wild animal") in 7:14 and 7:21, it means "domestic animal." The word *remeś* (or its synonym *śereṣ*) refers to crawling creatures in 6:20, 7:21, and 8:17, but when paired only with "birds" in 8:19, it refers to all animals that move on the earth. The word *ḥayyâ,* "wild animal," in 7:14 and 7:21 (when contrasted with *bəhēmâ*) means "living creature" in 9:10 (as does *ḥay* in 6:19). There are other changes in wording that do not alter the terms' meanings. Like the variations in the lists of humans on the ark (see Notes at 6:18), this is a prime example of P's tendency for variety within repetitions. Each list is synonymous, but there is a good deal of artful play in their composition.

6:21. *As for you, take every kind of edible food and gather it, for it will be your food and theirs.* This command refers back to 1:29–30, where God granted all vegetation for humans and animals to consume. The sequence "it will be your food and theirs" (*wəhāyâ ləkā wəlāhem lə ʾoklâ*) echoes 1:29, "they will be food for you" (*lākem yihyeh lə ʾoklâ*). The topic of edible food recalls the peaceful order of creation and anticipates the new dispensation after the flood, when eating meat will be permitted with restrictions (9:3).

6:22. *Noah did everything as God commanded him, thus he did.* This is a formula of execution in P, which often concludes a narrative section (McEvenue 1971: 52–53; Blenkinsopp 1976: 283–84; Paran 1989: 234–35). The diction *wayya ʿaś nōaḥ* ("Noah did") . . . *kēn ʿāśâ* ("so he did") echoes the refrains in creation, *wayya ʿaś ʾĕlōhîm* ("God made/did") and *wayhî-kēn* ("so it was"). Its form here is a circular *inclusio,* beginning and ending with differing forms of *ʿāśâ* ("to do"). It also anticipates later execution statements in P during the Mosaic era:

— "Moses and Aaron did as God had commanded them, thus they did" (Exod 7:6).

— "The Israelites went and did as Yahweh had commanded Moses and Aaron, thus they did" (Exod 12:28).

— "The Israelites did it according to everything Yahweh had commanded Moses, thus they did" (Exod 39:32).

— "According to everything that God had commanded Moses, the Israelites did all the work. Moses saw all the work, and behold, they had done it as Yahweh had commanded, thus they did" (Exod 39:42–43).

—"Moses did it according to everything that Yahweh had commanded him, thus he did" (Exod 40:16).

The latter three instances, at the construction of the tabernacle, are particularly relevant, since this is the final construction work in P. (Note that Exod 40:16 is particularly close to the form of Gen 6:22.) In this respect, Noah's ark and the tabernacle are verbally and thematically linked (see also NOTES at 8:13, on a chronological link). The ark and the tabernacle are, in these respects, corresponding structures in the P narrative, with Noah and Moses as exemplary figures.

7:6. *Noah was 600 years old when the flood was on the earth.* It is likely that this verse (which 7:11 seems to reprise) was originally from the "book of Adam's genealogy" used in Genesis 5, coming immediately after 5:32.

Noah's age at this event, six hundred years, may have some significance in the context of the sexagesimal system of Mesopotamian mathematics. As Skinner (1930: 163) notes, Noah's age equals one Babylonian *nēr,* a mathematical unit. This Akkadian word can signify six hundred or also, by extension, "all, totality." According to one version of the Sumerian King List, the flood hero Ziusudra ruled for thirty-six hundred years when the flood came, a figure that is also a round number in the sexagesimal system (see Cassuto 1964: 17).

7:11. *In the 600th year of Noah's life, in the second month, on the seventeenth day of the month, on that day, all the wellsprings of the great ocean burst, and the windows of heaven were opened.* The onset of the flood is announced in formal language. As Alter (1996: 32) observes, "the precise indications of age and date give the report of the inception of the flood a certain epic solemnity." The concern for chronology is characteristic of P, and the juxtaposition of calendrical data with cosmic events effects a distance between Noah and his terrestrial world. After the deictic emphasis, "on that day" (*bayyôm hazzeh*), the verse turns into quasi-poetry, highlighting this climactic moment.

The chronology of the flood also has a rhetorical effect, creating a "reality effect" in its precise details and duration. It may convey a sense of what Robson (2008: 268) calls "divine quantification," the sense in first-millennium Mesopotamian texts that "the gods' management of time and space was deeply mathematised." The P text has a similar tendency.

The chronological details of the flood are as follows:

2/17 of Noah's 600th year	Flood begins (7:11)
7/17 (150 days later = five months)	Flood waters cease, ark rests on mountain (8:4)
10/1	Mountain peaks appear (8:5)
1/1 of Noah's 601st year	Water dries up (8:13)
2/27	Earth is dry (8:14)

The only date with clear special resonance is 1/1, when the water dries up. This is the first day of the new year and corresponds to the day when the tabernacle is completed (Exod 40:1, 17) and God's glory descends on it (Exod 40:34). It also corresponds to the first day of creation in Genesis 1. (See also NOTES at 8:14 for the possibility that the last date, 2/27, marks the end of a lunar cycle.)

In 7:11 and 8:4, the LXX reads twenty-seven instead of the MT's seventeen. This is probably a harmonization with the date 2/27 in 8:14, yielding a full year for the flood.

The tendency for harmonization in the proto-LXX scribal tradition suggests that the slightly asymmetrical MT chronology is original (see TEXTUAL NOTES 7:11c and 8:4c). The dates of the month—particularly 2/17, 7/17, 10/1, and 2/27—have no explicit significance. "Seven" is a number of wholeness or completion, and the repetitions of this number may carry that sense in the flood chronology.

In the version of the Babylonian flood in Berossos, the flood begins on the fifteenth day of the Babylonian month of Iyyar, the second month of the year (following the spring New Year). Lambert and Millard (1969: 136) comment, "It is not clear if this datum is part of a precise chronology of the flood, like that in Genesis, or if it was a solitary item with some other, perhaps cultic, significance." It is possible that Berossos's date of 2/15 is related to P's date of 2/17 for the beginning of the flood, which would be another sign of the continuity of the flood tradition (see Darshan 2016: 512–14).

One relatively clear implication of this chronology is that P used a calendar with 30 days to a month, such that 150 days (from 2/17 to 7/17) equals five months (see NOTES at 8:4). This is neither a lunar calendar (in which five months = ca. 148 days) nor a solar calendar (in which five months = ca. 152 days). This indicates that P is following the so-called administrative or schematic calendar that was commonly used in Mesopotamian administrative and astronomical/astrological texts (see Glessmer 1999: 215–17, 258; Ben-Dov 2021). This schematic calendar has twelve months of 30 days = 360 days in a year. It was used as an ideal model rather than a practical system, since the actual (solar) year is longer than the schematic year.

The description of the flood's onset is a parallel sequence that is often taken as poetry (Gunkel 1997: 145; Cassuto 1964: 84; Speiser 1964: 48):

> all the wellsprings of the great ocean burst,
> > and the windows of heaven were opened.

The parallel and chiastic structure can be indicated as follows:

> *nibqə'û* (A) *kol-ma'yənōt* (B) *təhôm rabbâ* (C)
> *wa'ărubbōt* (B') *haššāmayim* (C') *niptāḥû* (A')

The accentual rhythm is 4//3. The couplet is framed by a chiasm of the verbs "burst" (A) and "opened" (A'), with a hint of rhyme: *nibqə'û* (A) / *niptāḥû* (A'). The transition between the first and second line is onomapoetic: *rabbâ* / *wa'ărubbōt*. There is antithetical parallelism between "great ocean" (C) and "heaven" (C'), as the spatial extremes of the cosmos. The phrase *təhôm rabbâ* ("great ocean") occurs elsewhere only in poetry (Isa 51:10; Pss 36:7, 78:15; see also Amos 7:4). These poetic features emphasize this key moment, but it is not necessary to see this couplet as an excerpt from a poetic document (Cassuto 1964: 84; Kselman 1978). As Alter (1996: 32) observes, "The grand flourish of this line of poetry is perfectly consonant with the resonant repetitions and measured cadences of the surrounding prose."

The collocation of "ocean" (*təhôm*) and "heaven" (*šamāyim*) recall the beginning of the creation story (1:1–2), to which the cosmos is reverting. The *təhôm* ("ocean") is the primeval water, and God created *šāmayim* ("heaven") to divide the celestial and terrestrial waters (1:6–7). As Gunkel (1997: 146) observes, "The idea is, what God separated at creation, the *waters* and *above* and *below,* rush together again now. A second Chaos fell in on the world." The flood waters represent a reversion to primeval chaos.

The phrase "windows of heaven" (*'ărubbot haššāmayim*) occurs in Mal 3:10, and similar phrases occur in 2 Kgs 7:2, 19 and Isa 24:18. This may be an old formulaic phrase. The idea of a celestial window is also found in Ugaritic texts, when the storm god Baal thunders through the window in his palace, also pictured as a break in the clouds (*CAT* 1.4.vii.25–29; Cassuto 1964: 86–87). The Ugaritic words used for this heavenly window are *ḥln* and *'urbt,* equivalent to Hebrew *ḥallôn* ("window," as in Gen 8:6 [J]) and *'ărubbâ,* the word used in our verse. This word in Hebrew is rare, with a high or poetic register (see Hos 13:3, Isa 60:8, Eccl 12:3).

The paired image of waters pouring down from above and waters surging up from the deeps is also found in *Atraḥasis,* where before the final deluge, the storm god Adad is commanded to bring a drought by withholding his waters (see Weinfeld 1978: 243):

Adad should withhold his rain,
And below, the flood should not come up from the abyss.

(II.i.11–12; Lambert and Millard 1969: 72–73)

In P this unleashing of the celestial and subterranean waters brings cosmic catastrophe.

7:13–16. The detailed entry into the ark is the fulfillment of God's commands to Noah in 6:18–20. The varying lists of Noah's family and the animals change in each repetition, as is characteristic of P's narrative style. Each phrase of the entry into the ark echoes or repeats an earlier phrase, but the combination of phrases is distinctive in each. In addition to the different delineation of animal kinds, the phrase "two of each" (*šənayim mikkōl*) in 6:19 is expanded to "two by two of all flesh that has within it life's breath" (*šənayim šənayim mikkol-habbāśār 'ăšer-bô rûaḥ ḥayyîm*), which incorporates God's prior statement that he will destroy "all flesh under heaven that breathes life's breath" (6:17). This phrase injects a touch of pathos to the description of the animals, implicitly contrasting them with those whose lives are about to be destroyed.

7:13. *On that very day.* This phrase, *bə'eṣem hayyôm hazzeh,* echoes and intensifies the phrase "on that day" (*bayyôm hazzeh,* 7:11). The same phrase "on that very day" (*bə'eṣem hayyôm hazzeh*) occurs at other climactic times in the P narrative (McEvenue 1971: 61–62): Abraham's circumcision (Gen 17:23, 26), the exodus from Egypt (Exod 12:17, 41, 51), and Moses's death (Deut 32:48).

7:18–21, 24. The rise of the flood waters is framed by the phrase "the water grew strong" (*wayyigbərû hammayim*) in 7:18 and 24. Within this frame there are five related wordplays, creating a *Leitwort* effect: *gābərû* ("grew strong," 7:19), *gəbōhîm* ("high," 7:19), *gābəhû* ("grew high, rose," 7:20), and *wayyigwa'* ("died," 7:21). The repetitions of sound and sense are accompanied by three repetitions of "very much" (*mə'ōd,* 7:18–19) and five repetitions of "every, all" (*kōl,* 7:19, 21). These repetitions heighten the vast and destructive quality of the water's rise.

There are also echoes of the creation story with the references to "the earth" (*hā'āreṣ*) and "heaven" (*haššāmayim*) in 7:19, and the categories of animals in 7:21, from birds to land animals to humans, recapitulating their order of creation. The declaration "All flesh that moved on the earth died" (with the relatively rare verb *wayyigwa',* "died," 7:21) fulfills God's plan, "Everything on earth will die (*yigwā'*)" (6:19).

7:20. *Fifteen cubits higher the water rose, and the mountains were covered.* The flood reaches a height at 15 cubits (ca. 22 feet) above the mountains, so that the ark, which is 30 cubits in height, can come to rest on them (8:4). The draft of the ark is approximately half its height. This detail gives a sense of verticality and prepares for the ark's rest on the mountains of Ararat.

7:24. *The water grew strong on the earth for 150 days.* This detail too has a reality effect or technicity. The duration of the flood complements its vast extent—it is a massive catastrophe in space and time. The timespan will be further explicated in 8:4 by the date 7/17, exactly five months since the flood began.

8:1. *Then God remembered Noah and all the wild and domestic animals that were with him on the ark. God sent a wind over the earth, and the water subsided.* This is the turning point of the P flood story. In the Hebrew Bible the act of remembering often involves actions motivated by that memory; it is not simply cognitive (Childs 1962: 31–44). God's remembrance of Noah and the animals motivates his salvific action, sending wind to dry the flood waters. This becomes a leitmotif in P (Kawashima 2010: 56–57). In Gen 19:29, "God remembered Abraham," and he acts on this memory by rescuing Lot and his family from destruction. In Exod 2:24, "God remembered his covenant with Abraham, Isaac, and Jacob" and then turns to rescue Israel from Egypt. Note also God's promise in the Noachian covenant that when the rainbow appears, "I will remember my covenant" (Gen 9:15), and the rains will not become another flood. The act of remembering is a mental focusing, such that now God turns his attention to Noah, implying decision and action.

God's decision to send a "wind" (*rûaḥ*) over the earth evokes the primal scene of chaos, when "a wind of God (*rûaḥ 'ĕlōhîm*) was soaring over the face of the water" (1:2). God's wind over the water here begins a re-creation of an ordered cosmos out of the chaotic waters. This is one of the many interconnections between creation and flood in P. Having returned to watery chaos, creation now begins again.

In the ancient Near East and in some biblical texts, the wind is the warrior god's weapon against the adversary "sea" (e.g., Job 26:12–13; cf. Exod 15:8), but here (and in Gen 1:2) the old image is transposed into God's decision to reassert his mastery over the watery chaos (Day 1985: 53; Levenson 1988: 26–28).

8:2. *The wellsprings of the ocean and the windows of heaven were shut fast.* The verb *wayyissākərû* ("[they] were shut fast") echoes the sounds of the verb in 8:1, *wayyizkōr* ("[God] remembered"). There may be a sense of cause and effect in this wordplay—God's act of remembrance results in shutting of the flood's sources. Note the collocation of God's wind and the primeval "ocean" (*təhôm*) here and in 1:2. This verse ends the resurgence of the celestial and subterranean waters, now narrated in prose (cf. 7:11). The "ocean" (*təhôm*) is no longer called the "great ocean" (*təhôm rabbâ*, 7:11), perhaps because it is no longer a threatening and awesome force, and accordingly, is more prosaic.

8:3–14. The withdrawal of the flood waters is marked by a series of dates, conveying the passage of time. The repetition of verbs for "diminish," "subside," dried," and "dry" forms a counterpart for verbs to "grow strong," "multiply," "cover," and "die" during the waters' rise. A particular focus is the gradual exposure of the mountaintops, which were "covered" by the waters at their height.

8:3. *The water began to diminish after 150 days.* The mention of 150 days resumes the chronology from 7:24, when the water grew strong for 150 days. This is the day when the waters reached their peak and when God sent his wind and closed the sources, and the water began to diminish. R's placement of 8:3a (J), "The water receded gradually on the earth," may suggest that this is a second period of 150 days. The verb "diminish" (*wayyašūbû*) can be read either as inceptive, "began to diminish," or as a complete event, "diminished." The former meaning is evident in the chronology of the P story, but in the composite text the latter meaning is also contextually apt. The date when the ark came to rest, specified in the next verse as the seventeenth day of the seventh month (7/17), five months after the flood began, makes it clear that 150 days refers to the time that elapsed during those five months. There is no room for two sets of 150 days between 2/17 and 7/17. The impression of two such periods is an effect of R's art.

8:4. *In the seventh month, on the seventeenth day of the month, the ark came to rest on the mountains of Ararat.* It may be relevant that 7/17 is one week after the Day of Atonement (Yom Kippur), which occurs on 7/10 (Lev 16:29). But the two dates may have no connection in P's theological system. The repetition of "sevens" may be more resonant—the "seventh month" may echo the "seventh day" of creation, on which God ceases his work.

As noted above (NOTES at 7:11), the equivalence of 150 days with the five months from 2/17 to 7/17 indicates that P is using the schematic calendar, in which each month has 30 days. This is neither a lunar nor a solar calendar (in which five months = ca. 148 or ca. 152 days, respectively). In Mesopotamia the schematic calendar and the lunar calendar were used in different contexts and for different purposes (see Glessmer 1999: 215–17), and it is possible that this was the case in Israel as well. But the evidence is sparse.

The statement that "the ark came to rest" (*wattānaḥ hattēbâ*) echoes the name of Noah (*nōaḥ*). Compare the J story, where Noah's name is part of a *Leitwort* sequence (e.g., the *mānôaḥ*, "resting place," 8:9).

The ark rests on "the mountains of Ararat" (*hārê ʾărārāṭ*), referring to a whole range rather than to a particular mountain. The word "Ararat" is the Hebrew version of the Akkadian word "Urarṭu," which refers to the land and kingdom of the mountainous region around Lake Van in eastern Anatolia (Zimansky 1995). (The kingdom called itself Biainili, from which comes the word "Van.") The name Urarṭu is found in Akkadian records from the thirteenth to the sixth centuries BCE. The mountains of this region are the tallest in the Near East, hence their suitability as the resting place for the ark. The tallest mountain in the region, called Masis by the Armenians and Ağre Dağ by the Turks, is roughly 17,000 feet tall, and in modern times is also called Mount Ararat. The Cilo mountains, south of Lake Van, are also prominent, reaching to 13,500 feet. The landing place of the ark is changeable in postbiblical traditions: for example, the more southerly mountains of Qardu (Kurdistan) in the targums and Peshitta, Mount Lubar (location unknown) in Jubilees, and other sites (J. P. Lewis 1978: 14, 94, 161; and COMMENTS).

In *Gilgamesh* XI.142–43, Utnapishtim's boat lands on Mount Nimush, which has been identified with Pir Omar Gudrun, northeast of Kirkuk in Iraqi Kurdistan (George 2003: 516). This mountain is not as high as the mountains of Urarṭu but is in the Mesopotamian landscape.

8:5. *The water continued to subside until the tenth month. In the tenth month, on the first day of the month, the mountain peaks appeared.* It takes two months and two weeks (74 days) from the water's highest point (on 7/17) until the first signs of earth appear (on 10/1). This is almost half of the 150-day period of the flood waters' rise. The date

10/1 does not have any obvious significance, except that the first of the month (the new moon) is an occasion for sacrifice and feasting (Num 28:11, 1 Sam 20:5–6). The appearance of the mountaintops recalls that the waters rose "15 cubits higher" and covered mountains (Gen 7:20), so presumably the water level has now dropped by this amount. The landmarks on the way up are now being charted on the way down, creating a mental map of the water's withdrawal.

8:7. *He sent out a raven, and it went back and forth until the water was dry on the earth*. It is likely that Noah sending the raven belongs to the P source (Darshan 2016: 512; cf. Westermann 1984: 444–45), since there are some continuities of diction and theme. Its movement—*wayyēṣēʾ yāṣôʾ wāšôb* ("it went back and forth")—echoes the diction and syntax of the gradual movement of the receding flood waters in 8:5, *hāyû hālôk wāḥāsôr* ("[the water] continued to subside"). In each the subject is modified by a finite verb plus two infinitives absolute of verbs of motion. The raven's "back and forth" movement is coordinated with the ongoing recession of the waters. These two continual movements produce a doubled sense of motion and the passage of time (Moberly 2000: 350–51). Both continue "until the water was dry on the earth," a clause that recurs in slightly different formulations here and at 8:13–14:

—"until the water was dry on the earth" (*ʿad-yəbōšet hammayim mēʿal hāʾāreṣ*) (8:7)
—"the water dried off the earth" (*ḥārəbû hammayim mēʿal hāʾāreṣ*) (8:13)
—"the earth was dry" (*yābəšâ hāʾāreṣ*) (8:14)

These repetitions with subtle variation of diction and meaning are characteristic of P's style and emphasize the narrative movement toward the flood's end.

George (2003: 517) has plausibly proposed that the biblical raven is a half-forgotten vestige of the older Babylonian type-scene in which the sequence of birds—dove, swallow, raven—provides an etiology for the birds' current behavior. The dove and the swallow return to the ark, while the raven flies away, thus explaining the current habits of doves and swallows (which nest in human habitations and can be domesticated) versus ravens (which remain wild). In this respect the Babylonian sequence of birds is motivated. In contrast, the biblical scenes have a single bird in each version—a raven in P and a dove (sent three times) in J. The raven plausibly shows a continuity with the Babylonian flood tradition.

Another continuity is the day when the flood hero sends the bird. Noah sends the raven on 10/1 (8:5). In a fragment of the Babylonian flood from Ugarit, the flood hero says:

At the beginning of the invisibility of the moon, at the beginning of the month,
Ea, the great lord, stood at my side, (saying:)
"Take a wooden spade and a copper axe, and make a window at the top.
Release a bird, let it find for you a shore!"

(Wasserman 2020: 88–89)

The Mesopotamian flood hero dutifully builds a window in the ark and releases a dove, parallel to the scene in *Gilgamesh* XI. As Darshan (2016: 512) observes, the date may be a "correspondence between the Akkadian text from Ugarit and the Priestly narrative."

The bird is sent "at the beginning of the month" (*ina rēš arḫi*), although the text does not specify which month (see further at Notes to 8.14).

The definite article (*ha-*) of *hāʿōrēb* ("a raven") does not necessarily mean that the noun is definite ("the"), that is, an individual already identified and known about. Animal names often have the article without being definite (Barr 2014: 465–68; cf. *IBHS* §13.5.1e). Examples are Gen 3:1 (snake), 1 Sam 17:34 (lion and bear), 1 Kgs 20:36 (lion), and Amos 5:19 (lion, bear, and snake).

8:13. *In his 601st year, in the first month, on the first day of the month, the water dried off the earth.* Although "God remembered Noah" (8:1), Noah is not mentioned during the rise of the waters or their withdrawal. His age is here a point of reference at the turn of the year—he is now 601. This recalls the date formula at the beginning of the flood when his age (600 years) is the point of reference (7:11). The symmetry of this date formula is varied by this being only the partial end of the flood; the waters have withdrawn, but Noah and family remain in the ark until the earth is dry, which is roughly two months later (8:14).

The date 1/1, the New Year, is also the date when the priestly tabernacle is erected: "On the first month, in the second year [after the exodus], on the first day of the month, the tabernacle was set up" (Exod 40:17). These two events begin new eras in P's historiography (Blenkinsopp 1976: 283–84). The drying of the waters on the earth also recalls the separation of the waters and the dry land in the P creation account (Gen 1:9). The earth once more emerges from the waters.

8:14. *In the second month, on the twenty-seventh day of the month, the earth was dry.* The end of the flood comes in two steps, with the drying up of the water (on 1/1) and the drying of the earth (on 2/27). The two verbs for drying, *ḥārəbû* ("dried off") and *yābəšâ* ("was dry"), are essentially synonymous, but *yābəšâ* has a special resonance for the earth (see below). The chronological sequence indicates that after the water had dried from the earth on New Year's Day, the earth remained saturated for another eight weeks (fifty-six days).

The statement "the earth was dry" (*yābəšâ hāʾāreṣ*) alludes to 1:9, the separation of the water from the land, where the newly emergent land is called "the dry land" (*hayyabbāšâ*). The earth is once again dry land, habitable for living creatures, as in the process of creation. This allusion signals that the end of the flood is also the beginning of a new era of life on earth.

The significance of the date 2/27 is obscure. It would be more symmetrical for this date to be exactly one year after the onset of the flood on 2/17 (see Notes at 7:11). In the LXX and in some postbiblical texts, the flood does last exactly one year (1 En. 106:15; Jubilees; and 4QCommGenᵃ; see Hendel 1995b; Ben-Dov 2021: 445–49). The P chronology unsettles our expectation of symmetry.

It is possible that there is an esoteric meaning in the ten-day difference between 2/17 (the onset of the flood) and 2/27 (the dry earth). Calendrical speculation in the Astronomical Book of Enoch and later Jewish literature took this difference as an indication of a solar calendar of 364 days. In a lunar (or lunisolar) calendar, a year is 354 days, and if one adds 10 days, the total is 364. There are, however, two problems with this inference: (1) The time difference between 2/17/600 and 2/27/601 is 10 days more than a year according to *any* calendar, so if the text is hinting at the length of the solar year, it is an obscure hint. (2) As we have seen, the enumeration of five months as

150 days (in 8:3–4) indicates that P uses the schematic calendar, in which each month has 30 days, which corresponds to neither the lunar nor the solar calendar. A year in the schematic calendar is 360 days, and 10 days added to 360 yields 370, a number with no calendrical significance.

Ben-Dov (2021: 448 n. 58) suggests that the date 2/27 may indicate that the flood ends on an interlunium day, when the moon disappears. In Mesopotamia this day (*biblu* or *bubbulum*) marks the completion of the lunar cycle, when various rituals are performed. In the fragment of the Babylonian flood myth from Ugarit quoted above (see NOTES at 8:7), this is when Ea gives his command to build a window and release the birds. It is usually the twenty-eighth to thirtieth day of the month but can be the twenty-seventh. This possible connection would link the P flood chronology to the ritual calendar, although P is using a schematic calendar.

8:15–19. The departure from the ark is framed by God's command, "Leave the ark" (*ṣēʾ min-hattēbâ*, 8:16), and its fulfillment, "[they] left the ark" (*yāṣaʾû min-hattēbâ*, 8:19). As McEvenue (1971: 66) observes, the verb *yṣʾ* ("to leave, go out") occurs four times in four verses, each in a different form—*ṣēʾ* (8:16), *hôṣēʾ* (8:17), *wayyēṣēʾ* (8:18), and *yāṣaʾû* (8:19)—and is interleaved in a chiastic sequence: before the humans, after the animals, before the humans, after the animals. At the hinge between the command to exit the ark and its fulfillment is a further command, "be fruitful and multiply." McEvenue describes this as "the most structured and symmetrical unit" in the P flood narrative (66).

8:17. *Let them be fruitful and multiply on the earth.* This blessing and command recapitulate God's blessing to the animals in 1:22, "be fruitful and multiply" (*pərû ûrəbû*). The repetition of this statement marks the emergence from the ark as a passage into a new era of creation. Although the animals participated in the violence that corrupted the earth, they now have a symbolic re-creation, which will be regulated by the Noachian covenant "with every living creature" (9:9). This blessing also anticipates the similar blessing given to Noah and his sons in 9:1 (see INTRODUCTION I).

8:19. The exit of the animals "according to their families" (*ləmišpəhōtêhem*) corresponds to their entry into the ark by couples, "male and female" (7:16). The animals do not leave en masse, but deliberately, species by species. The word "families" also picks up a nuance of the command to "be fruitful and multiply" and anticipates the ordering of Noah's sons "according to their families" (*ləmišpəhōtām*) in the Table of Nations (10:5, 20, 31).

9:1–7. The new order of creation in this section is a reformulation of the cosmic order in Genesis 1. Life on earth essentially begins again under revised rules, which are structured to prevent the corrupting violence of antediluvian times (Frymer-Kensky 1977: 152–54). The new order includes the Noachian covenant, given in the continuation of God's speech (9:8–17), but these two sections are structured as distinct units or topics. This section begins and ends with the blessing to "be fruitful and multiply" (*pərû ûrəbû*, 9:1, 7), with slightly different elaborations.

9:1. *God blessed Noah and his sons and said to them, "Be fruitful and multiply and fill the earth."* This is a close repetition of the blessing to the first humans, "God blessed them, and God said to them, 'Be fruitful and multiply, fill the earth . . .'" (1:28). In this repetition, Noah and his family are the new humanity, charged with repopulating the earth. There are two notable changes in this reformulation: (1) In 1:28 the objects of blessing were *'ōtām* ("them," the humans, male and female), and in 9:1 the objects are *'et-nōaḥ wə 'et-bānāyw* ("Noah and his sons"). The scope of the blessing includes the unnamed wives, who are implied but not named (as is frequent in P). (2) The blessing in 9:1 lacks the continuation in 1:28, *wəkibšūhā ûrədû* ("and subdue it and rule . . ."). But the section ends with the latter verb, *ûrədû* ("and rule," 9:7; see TEXTUAL NOTE i). In the intervening verses the rule of humans over the animals (and over themselves) is regulated to prevent the return of corrupting violence. The blessings of fertility and authority are reformulated to suit the new era of creation.

9:2. *Dread and fear of you will come upon every creature on earth, every bird of the sky, everything that moves on the earth, and every fish of the sea. They are in your hands.* In the new order, animals will fear humans. In the previous era, all creatures were to be vegetarians, implying a peaceful harmony of animals and humans—although this golden age was destroyed through violence.

As Milgrom (2001: 1502) observes, this change of cuisine and the shift in animal relationships are comparable to Enkidu's transformation in the *Gilgamesh* epic. When first created, Enkidu lives in harmony with the animals, eating, drinking, and running with them. But when he is initiated into human culture, the animals flee from him (I.197–98). The change in the relationship between humans and animals is part of the transformation of human existence from a natural to a cultural existence. Similar transformations are found in many other mythologies (Lovejoy and Boas 1935; Lévi-Strauss 1966).

9:3. *Every living, moving creature will be your food. I hereby give them all to you, as I did the green plants.* In the new order, God gives humans the animals to eat, in addition to the "green plants" of the previous order (1:29–30). This revision uses the same performative language as 1:29, "I hereby give them all to you" (*nātattî lākem 'et-kol-*) and "they will be food for you" (*lākem yihyeh lə 'oklâ*). God explicitly refers to the provisions of 1:29 in his statement, "as I did the green plants" (*kəyereq 'ēśeb*). God now sanctions the killing of animals for food, a concession that he grants to the "violence" of humans. He regulates this act by the law in the following verse, so that it no longer generates impurity and corruption. By these means, God ensures that life on earth will not again have to be destroyed—and the earth cleansed—because of unregulated violence and bloodshed.

In Greek tradition the transition from vegetarianism to meat-eating is also part of the decline of the human condition from the golden age to the Bronze Age (Hesiod, *Works and Days* 117–18, 146–47). The P source never makes this sense of decline explicit, but as Lohfink (1994: 169) observes, "it could well be that Pg sees the course of history as an analogous decline from a 'best' world to a new, but only 'second-best' state."

9:4. *But flesh with its life's blood in it you shall not eat.* This is the first prohibition that God gives in the P source. The crisis of the flood now entails that God must regulate human behavior to ensure the survival of life on earth. This command is formulated as a timeless apodictic law, with *lō'* + imperfect to express unbounded duration (imperfectivity). Like other apodictic laws (e.g., the Decalogue), it lacks an explicit penalty.

The logic of this law concerns the life force that is in blood. Like J, P understands living things as composed of a duality of earthly and divine portions. This is the "soft" dualism of flesh and life-breath (see NOTES at 2:7 [J] and 6:17 [P]), but with blood as another form of the divine life-giving essence. When a creature dies, its breath departs; but its blood remains, and its disposition is a crucial issue for P. The culinary rule is that the blood must be drained from the animal before it can be eaten or sacrificed. The classic statement of the priestly view is Lev 17:14 (from the Holiness source), "for the life of all flesh is its blood; anyone who eats it shall be cut off." As Milgrom (2001: 713) observes, "Mankind has a right to nourishment, not to life. Hence the blood, the symbol of life, must be drained, returned to the universe, to God."

The grammar of 9:4 is odd and perhaps deliberately ambiguous (Vervenne 1993: 467–69). The word *dāmô* ("its blood") in the sequence *bənapšô dāmô* ("with its life, its blood") is either in apposition ("with its lifeblood") or is a later explicating gloss. A comparable phrase is in Lev 17:14, *dāmô bənapšô* ("its blood is its life" or "its blood is in its life force," or similarly). Genesis 9:4 may have been secondarily influenced by this phrase in Leviticus, or it may be a parallel construction. In either case it explicates the relationship between blood and life in P's anthropology.

9:5. *Indeed, for your lives I will demand your blood. I shall demand it from every creature and from humans. From a man regarding his brother, I will demand the man's life.* This dense verse moves from the shedding of animal blood (9:4) to the shedding of human blood. This was presumably another type of violence that corrupted the earth before the flood. The verse consists of three clauses, each containing the verb *'edrōš* ("I will seek, require, demand"), meaning God will demand the murderer's lifeblood as recompense (cf. Ps 9:13, *kî-dōrēš dāmîm*, "for He requites bloodshed"). A problem for the interpretation of this verse is that the boundary between the second and third clause is not clearly marked.

The first clause begins with *wə'ak* ("indeed, surely"), which links with the initial *'ak* in the previous clause (9:4). But in 9:4 this particle has a restrictive sense ("but"), and in 9:5 it has an asseverative sense ("surely, indeed"). These two senses of the particle in succession exemplify the style of repetition with variation in P and create a legalistic effect, a high diction that gives the sense of precision, while not clearly explaining its rationale.

The first clause foregrounds the direct object, "your blood" (*dimkem*), which continues the focus on blood and killing. Here, however, blood is what God requires "for your lives" (*lənapšōtêkem*), that is, for the taking of human lives. "Your blood" refers to capital punishment, which is a consequence of taking human lives. Notice the shifting senses of "blood"—in 9:4 it signifies life, and here it signifies judicial death. As Vervenne (1993: 469) observes, "Here, the blood has a bi-polar value as a symbol for life *and* death." By means of this legal reasoning, and in contrast to the prediluvian order, human murder is now regulated by the death penalty.

The second clause specifies that this decree includes animal *and* human perpetrators. An illustrative example of the former is Exod 21:28 (the Covenant Code), where an ox that gores a person to death is stoned to death. The phrase *ûmiyyad hā'ādām* ("and from humans," lit. "and from a human hand") plausibly belongs to this clause (Skinner 1930: 171; Weinfeld 1982: 64), in which case the Masoretic accent (*atnach*) should be moved to the end of this phrase.

The third clause awkwardly reiterates that the death penalty applies to humans. It either begins (as I have taken it) *miyyad 'îš 'āḥîw* ("From a man regarding his brother," lit. "From a man's hand regarding his brother") or continues from the previous clause (as the MT accents and many commentators infer), *ûmiyyad hāʾādām miyyad ʾîš ʾāḥîw* ("and from a man's hand, i.e., from a companion's hand"). In the latter reading the phrase *miyyad ʾîš ʾāḥîw* is coordinated with *ûmiyyad hāʾādām* (so Dillmann 1897: 294) and is perhaps a later gloss. In favor of the former reading is the parallel phrase *rāʾat ʾîš ʾāḥîw* ("the evil of a man against his brother," Zech 7:10; so Skinner 1930: 171). Also in its favor is the semantic and rhythmic balance of *miyyad kol-ḥayyâ* ("from every creature") with *ûmiyyad hāʾādām* ("and from humans"). Either clause division is possible and yields essentially the same meaning.

The use of the word *ʾāḥîw* ("his brother") in the third clause brings to mind Cain's murder of his brother in Genesis 4, prompting Westermann's (1984: 466) observation, "P expounds in principles what J tells in story." A notable difference is that in J, Yahweh protects Cain from the (inadvertent) penalty of capital punishment.

9:6. *Whoever sheds the blood of a human, / for a human will his blood be shed, / for in God's image he made humans.* The first two clauses form a poetic couplet, and the third (the motive clause) may be read as a concluding poetic line. As previously (e.g., 1:27, 7:11), the prose narrative rises to poetry at key moments, particularly in divine speech. The couplet has a parallel and chiastic structure:

šōpēk (A) *dam* (B) *hāʾādām* (C)   Whoever sheds the blood of a human,
      bāʾādām (C′) *dāmô* (B′) *yiššāpēk* (A′)   for a human will his blood be shed

This couplet has symmetry of form, sound, and sense. Each word of the first line is repeated in a different form in the second line, but in reverse order: *šōpēk // yiššāpēk, dam // dāmô,* and *hāʾādām // bāʾādām.* The assonance of *dām* ("blood") and *ʾādām* ("human") in the sequence *dam hāʾādām bāʾādām dāmô* resounds like a drumbeat, surrounding the nexus of crime and punishment. This verse justifies the principle of "blood for blood" (*lex talionis*) by its verbal texture.

The preposition *bə-* on *bāʾādām* may be read in slightly different ways. It can have an instrumental sense, "by a human," that is, by human agency (so GKC §121f; *IBHS* §11.2.5d), or a causal sense, "for a human," or more precisely, "for that human," that is, for the price of the human whose blood was shed (the *bet pretii;* so Brockelmann 1956: §106e; Milgrom 1991: 705; Ernst 1990; cf. 2 Sam 3:27). In this sense *bāʾādām* (C′) refers to *hāʾādām* (C). This meaning may better suit the context, since the previous verse emphasizes God's agency ("I will demand," three times), and the following clause focuses on the value of human life. The principle is comparable to Deut 19:21, "life for life" (*nepeš bənepeš,* with the *bet pretii*), in essence justifying capital punishment. This clause gives a terse rationale, which is unpacked in the following clause.

The motive clause, "for in God's image he made humans" (*kî bəṣelem ʾĕlōhîm ʿāsâ ʾet-hāʾādām*), is a near quotation of Gen 1:27, "in God's image he created him" (*bəṣelem ʾĕlōhîm bārāʾ ʾōtô*). This is a way of saying that human life comes from God and hence is inviolable. It also justifies the new rule by means of the original order of creation. As Fishbane (1985: 320) notes, this is an exegetical move, deriving a law from a biblical text (which continues in postbiblical legal exegesis). In the movement from creation to new creation, it revises the earlier order, drawing out its implications and imperatives for behavior. This reuse of the biblical verse extends its meaning in a new context.

9:7. *As for you, be fruitful and multiply, teem over the earth, and rule it.* This divine speech is closed by a reiteration of the blessing in 9:1, with the variation of *širṣû* ("teem") for *mil'û* ("fill") and the inclusion of *ûrədû* ("and rule"). This blessing and command complete the revision of the rules of creation in 1:28–30. The new regulations ensure that the violence that corrupted the earth will not recur. As Frymer-Kensky (1977: 153–54) observes, the earth is now cleansed of the bloodguilt of murder, and the shedding of blood is strictly regulated. This is the solution to the violence and corruption before the flood.

In the MT the last verb is *ûrəbû* ("multiply"), which is arguably a dittography of the prior *ûrəbû* in the verse (see TEXTUAL NOTE i). The MT reading would seem to lessen or eliminate the rulership of humans over the animals, which has striking implications for the postflood era (Schellenberg 2011: 59–68). However, on either reading the animals now must "dread and fear" humans (9:2), which is a departure from the initial harmony of creation.

9:8–17. The granting of the Noachian covenant consists of two formal sections: the covenant's participants and terms (9:8–11), and the sign of the covenant (9:12–17). The whole and its two sections are framed by layered *inclusios*. Both 9:8 and 9:17 begin with the phrase "God said to Noah" (*wayyō'mer 'ĕlōhîm 'el-nōaḥ*), followed by the "covenant" (*bərît*) that God is "going to make" or "has made" with all living things (9:9, 17). Genesis 9:12 (the second section) and 9:17 each begin with "God said . . . 'This is the sign of the covenant'" (*wayyō'mer 'ĕlōhîm . . . zō't 'ōt-habbərît*), which God "is making" or "has made" with all living things (9:12, 17). In other words, the beginnings of both sections (9:8 and 9:12) are structured by differing *inclusios* with the final verse (9:17). The final verse closes both movements. This connective structure accounts for its remarkable degree of repetition with variation in the covenantal text.

The Noachian covenant has many verbal and thematic echoes with the later P accounts of God's covenant with Abraham (Genesis 17) and his renewal of the Abrahamic covenant to Moses and Israel (Exod 6:2–8) (see Lohfink 1994: 165–72; Garr 1992). This covenantal sequence creates a large-scale temporal structure in P. The first era begins with creation; the second begins with the Noachian covenant; the third begins with the Abrahamic covenant; and the fourth begins when God "remembers" the Abrahamic covenant and renews it with Moses and Israel.

The phases of the covenant each have a sign: the rainbow (Gen 9:12–17), circumcision (Gen 17:9–14), and the Sabbath (Exod 31:12–17). Each form or iteration of the covenant is an "eternal covenant" (*bərît 'ôlām*, Gen 9:16, 17:7; Exod 32:16), a permanent part of the cosmic order that cannot be rescinded. The sequence includes a progressive revelation of God's name: during the first two ages God is known to all as "God" (*'ĕlōhîm*); he reveals his name to Abraham as El Shadday (*'ēl šadday*, perhaps "God of the mountain," Gen 17:1); and he reveals to Moses and Israel the divine name Yahweh (*yhwh*, Exod 6:2). Each of these covenants is conveyed through divine monologue—the human interlocutors do not reply (nor do they need to). The sequence of covenants, and the cosmic ages that they frame, creates a large-scale structure in the P source, a periodization of history that progressively narrows its focus from all of creation to the people of Israel.

9:9. *As for me, I am going to make my covenant with you, with your descendants after you.* The fronting of the pronoun *wa'ănî* ("as for me") changes the focus from *wə'attem* ("as for you") in 9:7. The same change of focus and grammatical construction (*wa'ănî hinənî* + participle) occurred in the transition from God's command to Noah to build the ark to his announcement of his intention in 6:17, "As for me, I am going to bring the flood" (wa'ănî hinənî mēbî' 'et-hammabbûl) These two statements of imminent divine action frame the whole P flood story. The framing is emphasized by God's proleptic statement in 6:18, "But I will make my covenant with you" (wahăqīmōtî 'et-bərîtî 'ittāk). The covenant is part of God's plan from the beginning of the story. Now this plan is fulfilled.

The primacy of "making" the covenant is signaled in the sequence of verbal forms: hinənî mēqîm ("I am going to make," 9:9), wahăqīmōtî ("I will make," 9:11), 'ănî nōtēn ("I am giving, making," 9:12), and hăqīmōtî ("I have made," 9:17). The Noachian covenant is firmly established in this sequence. Notably, the idiom for making the covenant, hēqîm bərît (lit. "setting up a covenant"), differs from the older idiom kārat bərît (lit. "cutting a covenant"). The older idiom probably goes back to rituals of animal sacrifice that accompanied such covenants (cf. Gen 15:7–21; Exod 24:3–8). It is possible, as Day (2013: 123–36) proposes, that P's idiom consciously distances itself from sacrificial connotations, since sacrifice in P does not occur until Sinai.

The concept of the bərît ("covenant") in P is comparable to a royal grant but has an implicit mutuality. Its content is a promise never again to send the flood (cf. the J parallel in 8:21–22). The mutuality is implied in its placement immediately following God's decree of new regulations in 9:1–7. The covenant is, in this respect, both unconditional and conditioned—there is no provision for its ever being annulled, but it is tied to rules that humans (and animals) are commanded to follow. It therefore differs from the concept of covenant in the Deuteronomistic literature. Lohfink (1994: 171) aptly expresses these nuances: "Its validity is no longer dependent, like that of the Deuteronomic bərît, on the fidelity of human beings to the covenant. If a human generation sins, of course, it excludes itself, and punishment falls upon it. But God withdraws nothing, and the next generation can return to the stable, final state of the world."

9:10. and with every living creature that is with you—birds, land animals, and all the earth's creatures, everyone that left the ark. The Noachian covenant includes not only Noah's descendants (i.e., all humans), but also the creatures on the ark and their descendants. The inclusion of the animals is emphasized by the list of creatures, "birds, land animals, and all the earth's creatures" (bā'ôp babbəhēmâ ûbəkol-ḥayyat hā'āreṣ), with the preposition bə- specifying "the parts of which a whole consists" (BDB, 88). This list echoes the categories of creation. The emphasis on all creatures continues with repetitions of "all living creatures" (kol-nepeš ḥayyâ, 9:12, 15, 16) and "all flesh" (kol-bāśār, 9:11, 15, 16, 17) in the following verses. The covenant is with all creatures, just as God's destruction encompassed "all flesh" and "everything on earth" (6:17).

As commentators have long noted, water creatures are not included. This may be paradoxical, since they are living creatures, but they were not on the ark and are not susceptible to destruction by a flood. Hence Genesis Rabbah adds the qualification, "excluding the fish" (pəraṭ laddāgîm, 32.10).

9:11. I will make my covenant with you: Never again will all flesh be cut off by the flood waters; never again will there be another flood to destroy the earth. The covenantal promise is proclaimed in parallel diction, comparable to the couplets in 7:11 and 9:6. As noted above, God's speech often veers into poetry or quasi-poetic diction at key moments. The verb yikkārēt ("be cut off") is seconded by ləšaḥēt ("destroyed"). The former verb is not used previously in the flood story but occurs often in the laws of P as the most severe penalty for extreme transgression. The latter verb is a Leitwort in the P flood narrative, particularly in its prologue (6:10–13). God now pledges that destruction by a flood will not occur again. The phrase "to destroy the earth" (ləšaḥēt hā'āreṣ) closes this *Leitwort* sequence with finality, with "the earth" as a metonym for "all life."

A comparison with Yahweh's promise at the end of the J flood narrative is instructive. There it is a personal pledge, using the first person "I will never again" (lō'-'ōsīp) twice, and concluding with a self-reference, "as I have done" (ka'ăšer 'āśîtî). Yahweh reconciles himself to the evil of the human heart and learns compassion. In contrast, God's promise in P uses third-person passive constructions, "never again will be cut off" (lō'-yikkārēt . . . 'ôd) and "never again will there be a flood to destroy" (lō'-yihyeh 'ôd mabbûl ləšaḥēt). This promise is a divine speech-act that establishes a new feature in the cosmic order, like the speech-acts with which God created the cosmos in Genesis 1. While the promises in J and P are parallel, their nuances proceed in different directions as part of their distinctive theologies and cosmologies.

9:12. *God said, "This is the sign of the covenant that I am making with you and all living creatures with you, for everlasting generations."* Each of the three phases of the covenantal sequence in P has a "sign" (ôt)—the rainbow for the Noachian covenant; circumcision for the Abrahamic (Gen 17:9–14); and the Sabbath for the Mosaic (Exod 31:12–17), which completes the Abrahamic covenant. As M. V. Fox (1974) observes, in each the sign of the covenant is an object of cognition and remembrance. In this case, the rainbow is a mnemonic for God, reminding him to fulfill his promise that there will never be another flood. It is also implicitly mnemonic for humans (and perhaps animals too): when they see the rainbow, they are reminded that God will remember to keep his covenant. There is a mutuality in the perception of the rainbow, although only God is responsible for maintaining his promise to prevent a world-destroying flood. These signs of the covenant are features of the present world—in nature, the body, and time—which function as mnemonics of the relationship between God, the cosmos, and Israel. They are also reminders of the narratives in which they are told. Finally, each sign signifies the covenant's eternal duration—here "for everlasting generations" (lədōrōt 'ôlām; similarly, Gen 17:12; Exod 31:16).

9:13. *I have set my bow in the clouds, and it will be a sign of the covenant between me and the earth.* The "bow" (qešet) is the rainbow, as in Ezek 1:28: "like the appearance of the bow that appears in the clouds on a rainy day." This is an etiology of the rainbow's origin and function as a sign of the Noachian covenant.

Elsewhere the word qešet refers to the bow as a weapon, used with arrows. God as a divine warrior wields his mighty bow, usually in poetic texts: "Laid bare is your bow" (Hab 3:9); "he has bent and prepared his bow" (Ps 7:13; similarly, Lam 2:4, 3:12). In this divine warrior image, God's chariot is storm clouds, his arrows are lightning, and his war shout is thunder (Pss 29:3; 68:5, 34; Hab 3:11; see Day 1985). The concept of the bow as a divine weapon is widespread in the ancient Near East (Rüterswörden 1988). Notably, after Marduk's victory over Tiamat, his bow is set into the sky as a constellation (*Enuma Elish* VI.82–91).

In light of this concept of the divine bow, many commentators have followed Wellhausen (1885: 311) in seeing God's setting his bow in the clouds as a sign of peace after battle: "He lays it out of His hand to signify that He has laid aside His wrath, and it is a token of His reconciliation and favor." Nachmanides (1971: 137) expressed a similar view: "It is indeed the way of warriors to invert the instruments of war which they hold in their hands when calling for peace from their opponents." This sense may be implicit in this scene, but in the P story there is no martial imagery in God's destruction of living creatures. It is possible, as M. V. Fox (1974: 573) suggests, that "P is taking an old—pre-Israelite—motif and removing it from its mythic context by interpreting it as an ʾôt ["sign"], thus fitting it into his own theology and view of history." The bow becomes a pure signifier of the Noachian covenant.

Delitzsch (1888: 290) points to another symbolic aspect of the rainbow: "Stretched between heaven and earth, it is as a bond of peace between both. . . . [T]he idea of the interposition of the two worlds attaches itself to the colored bow resting at both ends firmly on the earth." In other words, the rainbow's shape allows it to function as a cosmic axis, a sign of the mutuality and coexistence of God and his creatures. This meaning may be hinted at by the wording of this verse, in which the rainbow is "a sign of the covenant between me and the earth." The rainbow as a bridge of peace between heaven and earth.

Turner (1993) adds the suggestion that the shape of the rainbow signals the shape and boundary of the dome (rāqîaʿ) of heaven (1:6–8), which will not again be breached by celestial waters to flood the earth. This idea is complementary to the other senses of the rainbow. The rainbow may well have been understood as a divine projection on the curve of the dome of heaven.

9:15. *And I will remember my covenant between me, you, and all living creatures, all flesh, and never again will the water become a flood to destroy all flesh.* As with the point in the flood story when "God remembered" Noah and the animals on the ark (8:1), remembrance plays a key role in the Noachian covenant, linking God's cognition and action. As M. V. Fox (1974: 573) comments, "when [God] sees the rainbow it reminds him of his past promise, and this memory results directly in the maintenance of his vow. For God, no shadow falls between the thought and the reality."

After the flood in *Atraḫasis,* the goddess Mami gathers large flies and proclaims, "Let t[hese] flies be the lapis lazuli around my neck, that I may remember the days" (III.vi.2–4; Wasserman 2020: 28, 35). As Wasserman comments, this necklace is "a *symbolon* serving to remind her of the horrors of the Flood" (56). Kilmer (1987: 179) further suggests that the fly necklace is "a symbolic reference to the rainbow," due to the prismatic reflective quality of flies' wings (see Horowitz 2016). While a link with the rainbow is uncertain, the necklace certainly functions as a visual sign for the deity, causing Mami to remember the flood.

9:16. *The bow will appear in the clouds, and I will see it and remember the eternal covenant between God and all living creatures, all flesh that is on earth.* Although 9:16 seems a restatement of 9:14–15, McEvenue (1971: 77) observes that it turns the conditional structure of the previous sequence, "whenever" (wəhāyâ bə), into an affirmative promise, "The bow will appear" (wəhāytâ haqqešet). This follows P's style of command followed by fulfillment. The major terms of the condition are repeated in the fulfillment: "bow" (qešet), "clouds" (ānān), "see" (rāʾâ), "remember" (zākar), and "covenant" (bərît).

9:17. *God said to Noah, "This is the sign of the covenant that I have made between me and all flesh that is on earth."* The fourth and final divine speech in Genesis 9 echoes and completes the previous instances, each of which begins with a slightly different sequence:

—He said to them (9:1)
—God said to Noah and his sons (9:8)

—God said (9:12)

—God said to Noah (9:17)

The whole of 9:1–17 is one divine discourse, hence 9:17 links up with 9:1. It provides a closing frame for both sections of the text, linking with 9:8 as the conclusion of making the covenant, and linking with 9:12 as the conclusion of creating the sign of the covenant.

The last words of the P flood story—"all flesh that is on earth" (*kol-bāśār ʾăšer ʿal-hā ʾāreṣ*)—repeat the end of the previous verse and provide an apt coda for the whole narrative. It was the relationship between "all flesh" and "the earth" that was the problem at the beginning (where both are *Leitwort* terms), and it is this relationship that has been reordered by the rules and covenant of the postdiluvian order. The world had to be destroyed and begun again in order to reach this point of equilibrium.

9:28–29. *After the flood Noah lived 350 years. All the days of Noah's life were 950 years, and he died.* The notice of Noah's lifespan, probably derived from the "book of Adam's genealogy" (see NOTES at 5:1), is the closing frame of the P flood story. Noah's genealogical sequence is dispersed among three verses:

—"Noah was 500 years old, and Noah fathered Shem, Ham, and Japheth." (5:32)

—"Noah was 600 years old when the flood was on the earth." (7:6)

—"After the flood Noah lived 350 years. All the days of Noah's life were 950 years, and he died." (9:28–29)

This differs slightly from the normal pattern of the antediluvian ancestors, as do the entries for Adam and Enoch. A notable difference is inclusion of the flood, which displaces the birth of Noah's eldest son as the key date of his middle years. Also, Noah fathers three named sons, yielding a three-branched lineage, rather than a single vertical lineage with the firstborn son. This branching anticipates the Table of Nations, which lists the three lineages of Noah's sons.

The P writer restructured this genealogical entry so that it serves as a beginning, middle, and end for the flood narrative. The flood is, in a sense, folded into Noah's genealogy. In the final text, R inserted the J story of the curse of Canaan before 9:28–29, in order to accommodate one more story about Noah and his sons.

Comments
DOUBLETS

The J and P flood stories are a classic example of a doublet in the Pentateuch. Although they have been edited together into one narrative, it is relatively easy to discern the editorial seams and to reconstitute the two stories, with some missing text. Some of the "doubled" features in the composite story are as follows (Gunkel 1997: 139; see also Emerton 1987–1988):

—God sees the evil of humankind (6:5 and 6:11–12)

—God announces to Noah the destruction of humankind by a flood (6:7 and 7:4)

—God commands Noah to enter the ark with his whole household (6:8 and 7:1) and with a specific number of each animal (6:19–20 and 7:2)

—Noah enters the ark with his whole household and the animals (7:7–9 and 7:13–16)
—The flood comes (7:10 and 7:11)
—The waters rise and the ark floats on the waters (7:17 and 7:18)
—All living creatures die (7:21 and 7:22)
—The flood ceases (8:2a and 8:2b)
—Noah learns he can leave the ark (8:6–12, 13b and 8:15–16)
—God promises not to send another flood (8:20–22 and 9:8–17)

Among these doubled actions are several contradictions. The number of animals is "two of each" (*šənayim mikkōl*) in one case (6:19–20), and in the other "seven by seven, a male and its mate" (*šibʿâ šibʿâ ʾîš wəʾištô*) for clean animals and "two, a male and its mate" (*šənayim ʾîš wəʾištô*) for unclean animals (7:2). The distinction between clean and unclean animals corresponds to the postflood sacrifice (8:20), which occurs only once. In this layer, Noah brings more than two of each clean animal so that he can sacrifice from all of them without making that species extinct.

Another contradiction is the timeline in the two layers. In one the flood lasts for 40 days and nights (7:4, 12, 17; 8:6) and in the other it rises for 150 days (7:24) and diminishes for a longer period, yielding a total of about 370 days (in the schematic calendar) until the earth is dry (8:14). The picture of the flood is also different. In the forty-day flood it is a long rain (*gešem*, 7:12, 8:2b). In the ten-month flood it is a resurgence of cosmic waters, caused when "all the wellsprings of the great ocean burst, and the windows of heaven opened" (7:11, 8:2a). This is an undoing of creation in Genesis 1, when God commanded the separation of the waters above from the waters below, and the emergence of dry land from the waters below (1:6–10). There is also a contradiction in how Noah learns he can leave the ark: in one case God commands him (8:15–16), and in the other Noah sends a dove three times to determine when "the face of the soil was dry" (8:6–12, 13b). The language and rationale of God's promise not to send another flood are entirely different in the two layers (cf. 8:21–22 and 9:8–17).

Finally, the name of God is different in the two layers. In one it is Yahweh (*yhwh*), and in the other it is God (*ʾĕlōhîm*). These are the characteristic divine names in the J and P sources (particularly in narration; cf. 3:2–5, 4:25, 9:27 in direct speech). In sum, there are two accounts of the flood from two different sources, J and P, which have been ably combined by R, who alternated the sources paragraph by paragraph at the beginning and end, and in the middle—during the details of the rise and fall of the flood waters—proceeded verse by verse or clause by clause. The composite narrative is well-crafted, preserving most of the two sources and adding some harmonizing words and clauses to smooth over some (but not all) contradictions and inconsistencies (see NOTES at 6:7; 7:3, 8–9, 23).

The P flood is easily recognizable by its literary style and structure and by its intertextual links with Genesis 1 and other P texts.

LITERARY DESIGN

The P flood story, like its J counterpart, has a tripartite structure, consisting of a prologue, main event, and epilogue. The flood, the main event, has three internal sections, with the last echoing the diction of the first, and the middle organized by the flood chronology. The sections and their transitions are indicated by grammar, patterned repetition, and indications of time:

Prologue (6:9–12)
Flood (6:13–8:19)
    a. God's instructions to Noah (6:13–22)
    b. Onset, climax, and recession of the flood (7:6, 11, 13–16a, 18–21, 24; 8:1, 2a, 3b–5, 7, 13a, 14)
    c. Exit from the ark (8:15–19)
Epilogue (9:1–17, 28–29)

Several of these sections are structured by P's "circular *inclusio*" style, which is a type of patterned repetition related to the *Leitwort* style. The prologue begins with the genealogical formula, "This is the genealogy of Noah" (6:9), followed by a circular *inclusio* (translated to show word positions):

> Noah (*nōaḥ*) was a righteous man, blameless in his generation; walked with God, Noah (*nōaḥ*). (6:9)

God's instructions to Noah are framed by two circular *inclusios* (the first one doubled):

> Make (*ʿăśē*) yourself an ark with gopher wood, with reeds make (*taʿăśeh*) the ark, and seal (*wəkāpartā*) it inside and out with pitch (*bakkōper*). (6:14)

> Noah did (*wayyaʿaś*) just as God commanded him, so he did (*ʿāśâ*). (6:22)

The onset of the flood is marked by a *near*-circular *inclusio,* with similar sounding verbs at the beginning and end:

> Burst (*nibqəʿû*) all the wellsprings of the great ocean, and the windows of heaven opened (*niptāḥû*). (7:11)

The exit from the ark consists primarily of two circular *inclusios,* one God's command and the other its fulfillment:

> God said to Noah, "Go out (*ṣēʾ*) of the ark, you and your wife, your sons, and your sons' wives with you. Every living creature with you, all flesh—birds, land animals, and every creature that crawls on the earth—bring them out (*hôṣēʾ*) with you." (8:16–17)

> Noah went out (*wayyēṣēʾ*) with his sons, his wife, and his sons' wives with him. Every living creature, every bird, and every creature that crawls on the earth came out (*yāṣəʾû*) of the ark, according to their families. (8:18–19)

Finally, the Noachian covenant has a circular *inclusio* as its central law:

> Whoever sheds (*šōpēk*) the blood of a human,
> for a human will his blood be shed (*yiššāpēk*). (9:6)

This sentence has a dense circular structure in its middle as well—*dam hāʾādām bāʾādām dāmô* ("blood of the human, for a human his blood")—that intensifies the focusing effect of this style.

Beyond these circular *inclusios,* P's *Leitwort* style provides a connective tissue in and among these sections. The prologue features the *Leitwort* repetition of various forms of *šḥt* ("corrupt, destroy,") and a twofold repetition of *ḥāmās* ("violence"), which binds together the unstable condition of the cosmos with God's perception and decision:

The earth was corrupt (*wattiššāḥēt*) before God, for the earth was filled with violence (*ḥāmās*). And God saw the earth, and behold, it was corrupt (*nišḥātâ*), for all flesh had corrupted (*hišḥît*) its way on earth.

God said to Noah, "The end of all flesh has come before me, for the earth is filled with violence (*ḥāmās*) because of them. I am now going to destroy them (*mašḥîtām*) and the earth." (6:11–13)

This *Leitwort* sequence resumes in the next section, God's instructions, with God's intentions surrounding the detailed instructions for the ark:

the earth is filled with violence (*ḥāmās*) because of them. I am now going to destroy them (*mašḥîtām*) and the earth. (6:13)

I am going to bring the flood—water on the earth—to destroy (*ləšāḥēt*) all flesh under heaven that has within it life's breath. (6:17)

This sequence resumes in the epilogue, repeating God's promise in two subsections of the Noachian covenant:

never again will there be another flood to destroy (*ləšāḥēt*) the earth. (9:11)

never again will the water become a flood to destroy (*ləšāḥēt*) all flesh. (9:15)

This *Leitwort* cluster gives the story a particular thematic resonance, linking together the chaotic state of the world with God's responses. In this verbal structure, God's decision to send a flood of destruction is the right response to the corruption of the earth by its violent creatures, while the laws of the Noachian covenant will contain the problem of future corruption and destruction.

The whole story is framed with genealogical formulae. The prologue begins, "This is the genealogy of Noah" (*'ēlleh tôlədōt nōaḥ,* 6:9), continuing the style of the preceding P text, the "book of Adam's genealogy" (5:1–32). The P flood narrative ends with the formulaic details of Noah's age and death after the flood (9:28–29). The initial rubric marks the flood as a new section in the larger genealogical narrative of P.

The section of God's instructions to Noah consists almost entirely of a single long speech in which God informs Noah of his plan and gives instructions about the construction of the ark, its passengers, and provisions. These instructions will be actualized in the sections that follow, especially in the list of the ark's passengers, which repeat (with variation) in the entry into and exit from the ark (7:13–15, 8:15–19). God's statement to Noah during the instructions, "I will make my covenant with you" (6:18), anticipates the epilogue, which tells the contents and conditions of the covenant. In God's instructions, the flood's end is guaranteed in its beginning.

The main action of the flood, its onset, climax, and recession, is structured literarily by chronology and *Leitwort* repetitions. The latter include *gbr* ("to be strong"), three times as the flood rises (7:18–24), and *ḥsr* ("to diminish, subside"), twice as the flood subsides (8:3–5). Repetitions of the synonyms ḥrb and ybš ("to dry, be dry") also add internal rhythm to the flood's recession.

The indications of time are a framing structure in this section:

> Noah was 600 years old when the flood was on the earth. . . . In the 600th year of Noah's life, in the second month, on the seventeenth day of the month, on that day, all the wellsprings . . . (7:6, 11)

> The water grew strong (gbr) on the earth for 150 days. (7:24)

> The water began to diminish (ḥsr) after 150 days. (8:3)

> In the seventh month, on the seventeenth day of the month, the ark came to rest in the mountains of Ararat. The water continued to subside (ḥsr) until the tenth month. In the tenth month, on the first day of the month, the mountain peaks appeared. (8:4–5)

> In his 601st year, in the first month, on the first day of the month, the water dried (ḥrb) off the earth. . . . In the second month, on the twenty-seventh day of the month, the earth was dry (ybš). (8:13, 14)

The first indication of time begins the section of the flood (7:6, 11), and the last one ends it (8:13, 14). In between, these temporal indicators mark the turning points of the flood, giving a sense of its scope over its long timespan. The chronological markers provide a sense of the passage of time and the flood's durative force.

Two dates seem particularly significant: the turning point after 150 days when "God sent a wind over the earth, and the water subsided" (8:1), and New Year's Day as the time when the waters dried (8:13). Both activate themes of chaos and creation in P, which begin in Genesis 1 and extend through Exodus 40 (see below).

The epilogue to the flood, in which God establishes the Noachian covenant, also participates in the long-range literary structure of P, anticipating the covenant to Abraham (Genesis 17) and its realization in the covenant laws of the Mosaic era (see below). The epilogue is also structured by verbal repetitions. This section consists of three subsections, the blessing and laws (9:1–7), the covenant (9:8–11), and the sign of the covenant (9:12–16), followed by a short summarizing conclusion (9:17).

The three subsections and the summarizing conclusion of the epilogue each begin with a notice of direct speech by God. This is striking since the whole section consists of God's direct speech. The repetition of these notices serves as a literary structuring device, with each indicating the content of that section:

> God blessed Noah and his sons and said to them, "Be fruitful and multiply and fill the earth." (9:1)

> God said to Noah and his sons with him, "As for me, I am going to make my covenant with you, with your descendants after you, and with every living creature that is with you." (9:8–10)

> God said, "This is the sign of the covenant that I am making with you and all living creatures with you." (9:12)

God said to Noah, "This is the sign of the covenant that I have made between me and all flesh that is on earth." (9:17)

The first section (9:1–7), which begins the postflood era, repeats the blessings given to the first humans and ends with an expanded repetition of the same: "As for you, be fruitful and multiply, teem over the earth, and rule it" (9:7). This section repeats the diction in Genesis 1, adding new laws to regulate the violence of earthly creatures in this new era.

The second section (9:8–11) establishes the Noachian covenant with all humans and living creatures. It contains God's promise, "Never again will all flesh be cut off by the flood waters; never again will there be another flood to destroy (ləšaḥēt) the earth" (9:11). This promise activates the *Leitwort* repetition of *šḥt* ("ruin, corrupt, destroy") from the flood prologue and resolves it, stating that God will never again send a flood to destroy. This section also fulfills God's promise to Noah during the instructions, "I will make my covenant with you" (6:18).

In the third section (9:12–16) God creates the sign of the covenant, the rainbow, which will be a perpetual reminder that God will keep his covenant promise. The appearance of the rainbow will be a reminder to God ("I will remember my covenant," 9:15) and also a visible sign to humans and other creatures that God will keep his covenant in perpetuity. It also repeats the covenantal promise, "never again will the water become a flood to destroy (ləšāḥēt) all flesh" (9:15).

The summarizing conclusion (9:17) echoes the diction of the previous notices of divine speech and constructs a closing frame for the covenant section. Notice the temporal progression from incipient action ("I am going to make," 9:9) to ongoing action ("I am making," 9:12) to past action ("I have made," 9:17). God's last speech is a summarizing synopsis of the Noachian covenant, emphasizing that, unlike future covenants, it is with all living creatures on earth.

CHAOS AND RE-CREATION

Genesis 1 ends with God's perception of the goodness of all his works of creation: "And God saw all that he had made, and behold, it was very good" (1:31). The P flood story begins with God's perception that the world has gone very wrong: "And God saw the earth, and behold, it was corrupt" (6:12). The repetition of this image of divine perception expresses a dramatic reversal. The world that was once "very good" is now "corrupt" (nišḥātâ). The P flood story is, in many ways, a reversal and repetition of the P creation story, showing how the good order of the cosmos has gone bad, necessitating God's decision to send a flood and start over. The flood is depicted as the return of the primeval waters, which inundate the dry land, reversing their initial separation (1:9–10). When the flood waters abate and dry land emerges, a new era of creation begins. At the conceptual core of the story is the reversion of the cosmos to chaos—first morally, then materially—followed by God's re-creation of the cosmos, regulated by new laws limiting violence.

The parallel mythic movement from chaos to (re-)creation in the P creation and flood stories is signaled by a network of repetitions of key words and clauses. The first of these is the statement of God's new perception of the cosmos in 6:12 (above), which reverses his perception in 1:31, using the same grammar: "And God saw X, and behold, it was Y." This moment of recognition shows—through God's eyes—the reversal of the world from a state of goodness to corruption. This perception impels God to turn the world back to a primeval chaos.

The repetitions of diction from Genesis 1 in the section of the onset, climax, and recession of the flood further emphasize the parallel movement from chaos to new creation. The flood begins when "all the wellsprings of the great ocean (təhôm) burst, and the windows of heaven (šāmayim) opened" (7:11). This "ocean" activates the description of primeval chaos, when "darkness was over the face of the ocean (təhôm)" (1:2). These are the primeval waters, which God first divided on the second day of creation and separated from dry land on the third. The beginning of the flood reverses these acts of separation. The wellsprings of the ocean burst, releasing the waters below to inundate the dry land, and the windows of heaven open, releasing the waters above to rejoin the waters below into a single watery mass, returning the world to chaos.

God's creative acts of dividing the primeval waters to make the spaces where creatures can live are reversed in the flood. But the underlying structure of the cosmos still exists. The vault of heaven is not destroyed, although its windows are opened. A bubble of air remains between heaven and the surging waters so that the ark can float and its creatures breathe. The flood is a reversion to chaos, but with the basic structures intact so a new era can begin again.

The end of the flood and the beginning of the new era echo the transition from chaos to creation in Genesis 1 on many levels. After the flood's climax, when all creatures on earth have died, God begins the cosmos anew: "God sent a wind (rûaḥ) over the earth, and the water subsided. The wellsprings of the ocean (təhôm) and the windows of heaven (šāmayim) were shut fast" (8:1–2). The "wind" sent from God echoes 1:2, when "a wind (rûaḥ) of God was soaring over the face of the water." Then as now, God's wind signals the onset of a transformation from chaos to cosmos. The collocation of "wind," "ocean," "earth," and "heaven" repeats the cluster of primeval substances from 1:1–2, also signaling a recapitulation of creation. The closing of the ocean's wellsprings and heaven's windows reinstates the separation of the waters and the eventual emergence of dry land. The statement that "the earth was dry" (yābəšâ hā'āreṣ, 8:14) pointedly echoes the third day of creation when God called "the dry land 'earth'" (yabbāšâ 'ereṣ, 1:10).

The kinds of creatures on the ark echo the diction of their creation in Genesis 1, as in God's instructions to Noah: "Every kind of bird, every kind of land animal, every kind of creature that crawls on the earth" (6:20). When the animals exit the ark after the flood, God adds the blessing from 1:22: "Every living creature with you, all flesh—birds, land animals, and every creature that crawls on the earth—bring them out with you. Let them be fruitful and multiply on the earth" (8:17). The exit from the ark onto the dry land recapitulates God's blessing on creatures from the first creation.

God gives his blessing to humans in the flood epilogue, followed by the command to rule the earth and its creatures: "God blessed Noah and his sons and said to them, 'Be fruitful and multiply and fill the earth. Dread and fear of you will come upon every creature on earth, every bird of the sky, everything that moves on the earth, and every fish of the sea. . . . As for you, be fruitful and multiply, teem over the earth, and rule it'" (9:1, 7). These blessings and commands mark the beginning of a new era, which restores the blessings and hierarchy of the first era of creation (1:28), with the addition of the laws of the Noachian covenant to regulate the violence of living creatures, lest they corrupt the earth again. One of the laws, against human bloodshed, is explicitly linked with creation, "for in God's image he made humans" (9:6). This is a new creation with a twist, introducing the concept of laws that creatures must obey. These covenantal laws anticipate the Abrahamic covenant to come, which will be narrowed in scope to a particular people, supplementing the covenant with all living creatures.

Other details of the P flood story also link up with the nexus of creation and covenant. In the P flood chronology, the day when "the water dried off the earth" (8:13) is the first day of the first month. This is the anniversary of the first day of creation, when there was a "first day" (1:5). This is also the day that God commands Moses to set up the tabernacle, whereupon he fills it with his presence: "On the first day of the first month, you shall set up the Tabernacle. . . . And Moses finished the work . . . and the Presence of Yahweh filled the Tabernacle" (Exod 40:2, 33–34; see COMMENTS on Genesis 1). The date of the new year in P (in the spring) commemorates several interrelated beginnings: creation, the postdiluvian era, and the sacred structure of Israelite religion.

The flood, in all these senses, is a connective link between creation and covenant, drawing together threads from both in a movement from chaos to re-creation. It has the seed of new covenants and configurations to come, which will continue to ensure the well-being of the cosmos.

CONTEXTS

The flood plays a key role in the large-scale structure of the P work. It reverses and recapitulates creation in Genesis 1, and anticipates future developments, including the covenant with Abraham (Genesis 17) and its resumption in the Mosaic era. The sign of the Noachian covenant, the rainbow, illuminates the thematic sequence in the covenants. The rainbow is visible to all creatures and to God, and it is the sign that God will never again send a flood to destroy all flesh. The sign of the Abrahamic covenant, circumcision, and the sign of the Mosaic covenant, the Sabbath, are more restricted. Circumcision pertains to the male descendants of Abraham, including Israel and Ishmael. The Sabbath, which commemorates and reactualizes God's rest after creation, is celebrated by Israelites only. The sequence of covenants narrows from universal to particular, even as it maintains a connection with creation.

The composite flood story in Genesis 6–9 provides another literary context for the P story, in which the thematic frameworks of the two stories are merged. As we have seen, the movement from chaos to re-creation is emphasized in the P flood story. God's decisions are consistent and orderly, as is his choice of Noah as new Adam of the second creation. The thematic framework of the J flood story differs. It is not a reversion to chaos and a new creation as much as an episode in Yahweh's relationship to humans, which changes in the movement from Yahweh's recognition of human evil to his reconciliation to flawed humans at the story's end. The emotional and moral tone of Yahweh's encounter with human nature in the J flood is wholly different from the cosmic perspective of God in the P flood. In P, God does not change, but the structure of the cosmos does. In J, human evil does not change, but Yahweh's relationship to it does, with compassion leavening his justice. In the composite story, these features mingle together, yielding a complicated picture of God, humans, the cosmos, and their inner relationships.

God's promise never again to send a flood, expressed in each source, is embedded in these larger issues. In P it is a commitment of the Noachian covenant, which preserves the integrity of the cosmic order. In J it is Yahweh's personal commitment, an expression of his new perception of an imperfect world, in which humans are bound to him by invisible webs of reciprocity. Accordingly, the last scene in the J flood story is Noah's offering of sacrifice to Yahweh, while in P the last scene is God's speech to Noah and his sons. The two versions of the flood story have the same general plot structure—prologue, flood, epilogue—with distinctive conceptual contents and resonances.

The composite text has a multilayered conceptuality: God is decisive and changeable, transcendent and emotional; humanity is prone to violence and evil yet has the capacity to be righteous and law-abiding; the world will not end but has particular rules and limits; and the flood involves fluctuating timelines, numbers of animals, and intensity of waters. The story is clear from a distance, but it becomes mysterious when read closely. The general structure is straightforward, but the details are irregular. Despite R's careful editing and harmonizing additions, the flood narrative has many conceptual gaps, creating the sense of a cryptic text.

The J and P flood stories are independent narrative crystallizations of older traditions, with roots in Mesopotamia. Many features of the older traditions are found in both J and P, such as the righteousness of the flood hero, the preservation of humans and animals on the ark, and the sending of birds to see whether the waters have dried. Some older features are found in only one of the biblical versions, such as the flood hero's sacrifice in the J version and the detailed instructions to build the ark in P. Notice that the priestly laws allow sacrifice only after the priesthood has been instituted and the tabernacle set up, so Noah is not eligible. The P flood story selects only those traditional features that are consistent with its worldview.

The dimensions of the ark and its final landing place are features that illuminate the relationship between the P flood story and its ancient Near Eastern context. The dimensions seem to have symbolic significance as a microcosm of the cosmos, an enclosed world for the duration of the flood. The landing place seems to vary according to the local mental map, attaching itself to the tallest mountains in the vicinity. These features provide a glimpse of how the flood traditions changed over time and space.

The dimensions of the ark vary from a spheroid to a cube to a rectangular box. In Old Babylonian versions, the ark is circular in shape. This is clearest in the so-called Ark Tablet (Finkel 2014: 357–68; Wasserman 2020: 61–76) but also seems readable in the fuller version (*Atra.* III i.28, *kippati*, "circle"; Finkel 2014: 128; Wasserman 2020: 32, 40). In the Ark Tablet, Enki/Ea instructs the flood hero:

The boat which you will build,
    I will draw it out (for you)—a circular plan:
Her length and breadth should be equal,
    Her base should be one *ikû*; her walls should be one *nindanu* (high).

(Wasserman 2020: 66, 69)

This circular boat, whose round base measures 1 *ikû* in area (ca. 0.9 acre = 40,000 square feet) and whose walls are 1 *nindanu* (18 feet) high, is a massive version of the reed coracle boats of Mesopotamia (Finkel 2014: 122–43). Its shape is a flattened spheroid. Enki then commands the flood hero to "roof it over like the Apsû" (*Atra* III i.29), referring to the cosmic subterranean waters. This massive boat, comparable to the Apsû, is latent with cosmic symbolism. As Wasserman (2020: 40–41) observes, "this architectonic detail is not accidental. . . . The Apsû-shaped boat floating on the rising water signals that the Flood dragged the world back to its initial chaotic stage." The boat is a microcosm, a habitable spheroid floating on the waters until the cosmos is reborn.

The later version of the flood in *Gilgamesh* reinterprets the ark's shape. Enki's instructions specify the ark's dimensions but omit its circular shape:

> The boat that you are going to build,
> > her dimensions should correspond:
> Her breadth and length should be equal.

(XI.28–30; George 2003: 704–5)

Utnapishtim builds the ark as a giant cube. It has the same base area as the older circular ark, but with straight walls and edges that are 10 *nindanu* (ca. 180 feet) each:

> On the fifth day I set in place her (outer) surface:
> > one *ikû* was her area, ten *nindanu* each her sides stood high,
> ten *nindanu* each, the edges of her top were equal,
> > I set in place her body, I drew up her design.

(XI.58–59; George 2003: 706–7)

This shape also has cosmic significance. As George (2003: 513) observes, its cubical shape is analogous to a ziggurat: "Marduk's ziqqurrat is a structure with the same overall dimensions (area of base, length, breadth and height) as the ark, and the same sevenfold division in the vertical plane." The vertical division into six decks and a roof "reproduces in miniature the cosmos in its most elaborate structure" (512). The six levels correspond to the levels of the universe: upper, middle, and lower heaven, and upper, middle, and lower Earth (Horowitz 1998: 3–19). The shape differs from the earlier tradition but maintains the symbolic resonance as a microcosm of the world, preserving life in its geometrical structure during the flood.

In the P flood, God instructs Noah to build the ark as a huge rectilinear box: "This is how you shall make it: 300 cubits the ark's length, 50 cubits its width, and 30 cubits its height. Make a roof over the ark and finish it 1 cubit from the top. . . . Make a lower, a second, and a third deck" (6:15–16). The ark is roughly 450 feet long, 75 feet wide, and 45 feet high. It is longer than the Mesopotamian arks, but narrower and shorter. Despite the ark's asymmetry, there is still a resonance of cosmic symbolism. In Genesis 1 God separates three spatial domains as habitats for living creatures: sky, land, and water. The tripartite structure of the ark is analogous to the structure of the world, supporting the seed of all life in a microcosm floating on the primeval waters.

In Berossos's *Babyloniaca,* the ark is "five stades in length and two stades in breadth," roughly 3,000 feet long by 1,200 feet wide. This is a rectilinear ark, like P, but much larger (see Day 2013: 67). The ark is huge in each of its instantiations, but its shape and cosmic symbolism vary, determined by the local imagination and worldview.

The landing place of the ark also changes across the versions (Bailey 1989: 53–82; Finkel 2014: 261–98). The extant Old Babylonian tablets lack this detail. In *Gilgamesh*

XI, the ark lands on Mount Nimush, which is identified with Pir Omar Gudrun, northeast of Kirkuk in Iraqi Kurdistan (George 2003: 516). This is the largest mountain in the Mesopotamian landscape. In the P flood story, "the ark came to rest in the mountains of Ararat" (8:4). This is not a particular mountain, but a mountain range, the tallest in the Near East. The land of Ararat (= Urarṭu) is in eastern Turkey, which became the land of Armenia from the sixth century BCE onward. The landing place of the ark migrates from the tallest mountain in Mesopotamia (Mount Nimush) to the tallest mountain range in the Near East (the mountains of Urarṭu/Ararat). This migration probably reflects a wider horizon of geographical interest from *Gilgamesh* XI to P, the former focused on Mesopotamia and the latter on the wider known world (cf. the mental map in the P Table of Nations in Genesis 10).

The P narrative specifies a whole mountain range rather than a particular mountain. It is possible that this was a strategy to deter people from seeking the ark's remains. If so, the strategy failed. Josephus writes that a particular landing place was commemorated in his time: "The Armenians call this place 'Landing Place,' for there the ark landed safely, and still today they display its remains" (*Ant.* I.92; Feldman 2004: 33). He quotes Berossos's *Babyloniaca* as additional testimony: "It is said that a certain portion of the boat still exists in Armenia on the mountain of the Cordyaeans [Kurdistan] and that some people remove and carry off pieces from the bitumen, and people use what they have carried off for talismans" (*Ant.* I.93; Feldman 2000: 34). For Josephus, Berossos's flood story provided independent testimony for the details of Genesis.

But the location of the ark in Josephus and Berossos seems to have migrated from its earlier landing sites. As Finkel (2014: 292) suggests, Berossos's testimony (quoted above) "sounds like an attempt to harmonize two diverse traditions, Armenia to the north . . . and the Kurdish (Gordyaean) mountains further south, perhaps by then already centred on Mount Cudi." Mount Cudi (Judi in Arabic; Nipur in Akkadian) is near the border of Turkey, Syria, and Iraq. It is the landing place of the ark in Islamic tradition (Qur'an 11:44) and perhaps also in Jewish texts where "the mountains of Ararat" are called "the mountains of Kardu(n)" (targums, Peshitta, *Gen. Rab.* 33.4, etc.). It is possible that the migration of the landing place of the ark to Mount Cudi was motivated by large Assyrian reliefs (eighth–seventh centuries BCE) on the mountain's lower slopes, depicting various dignitaries (Bailey 1989: 66; Anonymous 2014). By the Hellenistic period, local communities may have associated these figures with the flood story.

Another location is provided in the Sibylline Oracles (ca. first century BCE–CE): "There is a certain tall lofty mountain on the dark mainland of Phrygia [in western Turkey]. It is called Ararat. . . . In this place the ark remained on lofty summits when the waters had subsided" (I.261–66; J. J. Collins 1983: 341). In the late second and third centuries CE, Noah's ark is depicted on coins from Apamea, a Phrygian city in the same region as the Sibylline reference. It seems likely that the Jewish community of Apamea identified Noah's flood with a local Phrygian flood tradition, yielding the nearby mountain as the ark's landing place (Trebilco 1991: 86–99).

A late recension of the Samaritan Targum locates the landing place of the ark in "the mountains of Sarandib" (*srndyb*, Gen 8:4; Tal 1980: 25). This is the Arabic name for Sri Lanka. The tenth-century historian al-Ṭabarī affirms the tradition that after being exiled from paradise, "Adam was cast down in Sarandib upon a mountain. . . . [T]he summit of the mountain upon which Adam was cast down is one of those closest to heaven among the mountains of the earth" (Rosenthal 1989: 292). The mountain is now called Sri Padi or Adam's Peak. This exegetical tradition was taken up in the Samaritan Targum, where the ark has migrated again to a higher mountain.

Beginning in the mid-twentieth century, "arkeologists," as they call themselves, have sought evidence of the ark—and the veracity of Genesis—on the tallest mountain in the Ararat range, Mount Ağri in Turkey, which has long been identified as Mount Ararat. Thus far the search, conducted by charlatans and true believers alike, has been fruitless (Bailey 1989: 82–115); but no search has yet been conducted for the ark at Mount Nimush or Adam's Peak. The shape and landing site of the ark are malleable and various, according to the history of mental maps.

The Curse of Canaan (9:18–27; J)

---

9 ¹⁸Noah's sons who left the ark were Shem, Ham, and Japheth. Ham was Canaan's father. ¹⁹These three were Noah's sons, and from them all the earth spread out.

²⁰Noah, a man of the soil, was the first to plant a vineyard. ²¹He drank some wine and became drunk and exposed himself within his tent.ᵃ ²²Ham, Canaan's father, saw his father's nakedness, and he told his two brothers outside. ²³Shem and Japheth took a robe and draped it over both of their shoulders, and they went in backwards and covered their father's nakedness. Since they faced backwards, they did not see their father's nakedness. ²⁴When Noah awoke from his wine, and he knew what his youngest son had done to him, ²⁵he said, "Cursed be Canaan—he shall be the lowest slave to his brothers!" ²⁶He said, "Blessed be Yahweh, the God of Shem—may Canaan be his slave. ²⁷May God enlarge Japheth—may he dwell in Shem's tents, and may Canaan be his slave."

Textual Notes

a. In the MT the *ketiv* ("what is written") is *'hlh,* and the *qere* ("what is read") is *'hlw.* The SP reads *'hlw.* The two variant readings have the same meaning, "his tent," but the reading shared by the *qere* and the SP illustrates the scribal revision of preexilic spelling practices. In preexilic Hebrew (known from inscriptions), a final *he* indicates the vowels *-ō, -ā,* or *-e;* in postexilic Hebrew, a final *he* is restricted to *-ā* and *-e,* and a final *waw* indicates *-ō.* This passage is a good indication of the preexilic composition of the J text (with the spelling *'hlh,* see Baden 2022; see also *l'bdh wlsmrh* in 2:15), and of how postexilic scribes often updated the older spelling style (to *'hlw*), with both forms preserved in the MT (Hendel 1998: 57–58).

Notes

9:18. Noah's sons who left the ark were Shem, Ham, and Japheth. Ham was Canaan's father. This is the first mention of Noah's sons in the J narrative. (P refers to them frequently

346

and lists them in 5:32, 6:10, and 7:13). The change of focus from Noah to his sons provides a transition from the flood story to the postdiluvian events, in which the sons figure prominently.

The aside "Ham was Canaan's father" serves as anticipatory information about Canaan's identity. This addresses the curious problem that, although the story involves the misdeed of Ham, Noah's response is to curse Canaan. This problem is compounded by two further details: according to the order of sons here, Ham is Noah's second son, but in 9:24 the transgression is committed by Noah's "youngest son." And in 9:25, Noah refers to Shem and Japheth as Canaan's "brothers." There is no clear solution to these difficulties (see Skinner 1930: 182; Westermann 1984: 483–84; Vervenne 1995b: 39–41). It is possible, as many commentators have suggested, that two variant stories or traditions are combined here. In one, Noah's sons are Shem, Ham, and Japheth; in another, Canaan is Noah's youngest son, brother to Shem and Japheth. However, as Dillmann (1897: 302) points out, Canaan is asymmetrical to Shem and Japheth, who are fathers of many nations. Although the details are obscure, it is plausible that the J narrative has incompletely harmonized two variant traditions.

It is also possible to read these difficulties in a way that does not require variant traditions. Hoftijzer (1958: 22–23) notes that "his brothers" in 9:25 can simply mean "his kinsmen" and need not imply that Canaan is Noah's son and that Shem and Japheth are his brothers. He also notes that the order of names, "Shem, Ham, and Japheth," does not mean that Ham is necessarily the middle brother. In the Table of Nations, the order is from youngest to oldest brother—Japheth (10:2), Ham (10:6), and Shem (10:21). But the latter verse (from the J source) states that Shem is older than Japheth, perhaps suggesting the order of brothers as Shem, Japheth, and Ham. As for the curse on Canaan rather than Ham, Hoftijzer calls this a "process of actualization," in which the sin of the ancestor is visited on his descendant (24). The story thus argues that the curse of Canaan, which justifies the Israelite displacement of the Canaanites, is a just punishment for the sins of his ancestor.

Whether or not the overlap of the narrative roles of Ham and Canaan derives from the combination of two variant traditions, the logic of the patrilineal inheritance of guilt is at work. This principle is enunciated in the Decalogue, where Yahweh states that he "visits the sins of the fathers on the sons" up to three or four generations (Exod 20:5). It is this rule of the heritability of guilt that allows for the tangled relationship of Ham and Canaan in the current narrative.

9:19. *These three were Noah's sons, and from them all the earth spread out.* The movement from "these three" (*šəlōšâ ʾelleh*) to "from them" (*mēʾelleh*) is the movement from three to many in the repopulation of the earth. This statement is not mere repetition of 9:18 but sets up the thematics of the rest of the primeval narrative.

The verb *nāpəṣâ* ("spread out") is a *qal* of the root *npṣ* (BDB, 659; *HALOT,* 711) or less likely a *niphal* of *pṣṣ* (Dillmann 1897: 304; GKC §67dd). In either case the root is a biform of *pwṣ,* "to spread, disperse, scatter." This sets the stage for the genealogy of the Table of Nations and activates a *Leitwort* of the Tower of Babel story. In the latter, humans build the city and tower "lest we be spread out (*nāpûṣ*) over all the earth," but at the end Yahweh "spread (*hēpîṣām*) them out over all the earth" (11:4, 9). The sequence *npṣ/pwṣ* ("spread out") + *kol-hā ʾāreṣ* ("all the earth") creates a *Leitwort* sequence linking this story and the Babel story. While the several accounts of the spread of humans after the flood are chronologically awkward and somewhat contradictory (note that the Table of Nations and the Tower of Babel story explain cultural and linguistic diversity in different ways), the present clause provides a continuity of theme and diction.

9:20. *Noah, a man of the soil, was the first to plant a vineyard.* The syntax of this verse is unusual. The two verbs—*wayyāḥel* ("began, was first") and *wayyiṭṭaʿ* ("planted")—are converted imperfects, which ordinarily form a temporal or logical sequence. But the definite noun phrase, *'îš hā'ădāmâ* ("the man of the soil, the farmer"), cannot be the object of the verb *wayyāḥel* ("began, was first"). Usually, this verb is continued with an infinitive or participle (as in 4:26 and 10:8, both J). With most commentators (e.g., Dillmann 1897: 304; Skinner 1930: 182), it is easiest to take "the man of the soil" in apposition to Noah, and to take the second verb, *wayyiṭṭaʿ*, as supplementary to *wayyāḥel*, yielding the sentence "Noah, a man of the soil, was the first to plant a vineyard." It is tempting to read "Noah was the first (to be) a farmer," with an ellipsis of "to be," but this is grammatically dubious with the definite article in *'îš hā'ădāmâ* ("the man of the soil"), and is contextually difficult after Adam and Cain, both of whom were farmers, and after Lamech's reference to farming at the birth of Noah (5:29, J).

The verb *wayyāḥel* ("began, was first") suggests a new beginning after the flood and recalls other beginnings in the primeval era—"then was it begun (*hûḥal*) to call on the name of Yahweh" (4:26); Nimrod "was the first (*hēḥēl*) to be a warrior" (10:8); and Yahweh observes of the people of Babel, "this is what they begin (*haḥillām*) to do" (11:6). The verb *hēḥēl* ("to begin, be the first") is a *Leitwort* in the primeval narrative, with positive or negative consequences. This potential ambivalence is in force when Noah first plants a vineyard, since this has positive and negative consequences.

The description of Noah as *'îš hā'ădāmâ* ("the man of the soil") hearkens back to 5:29, where Lamech names his son Noah because he will relieve humans "from our painful manual labor on the soil (*hā'ădāmâ*) that Yahweh has cursed." This in turn hearkens back to the Garden of Eden story and the complex relationship between *hā'ădāmâ* ("the soil") and *hā'ādām* ("the human, man"). For Noah to be "the man of the soil" is to recapitulate the place of the first (hu)man, who was made from the soil and whose destiny it was to work the soil.

The "vineyard" (*kerem, kārem* in pause) is the source of wine, which in the Bible provides nourishment, pleasure, and comfort, although it also holds the danger of drunkenness. The vine is a noble plant; its wine "gladdens God and men" (Judg 9:13) and "gladdens the human heart" (Ps 104:15). It is a balm to those in distress, since it causes them to forget their poverty and troubles (Prov 31:6–7). Wine is used in the sacrificial rites (Exod 29:40) and in various feasts—the word "festival" (*mišteh*) literally means "drinking occasion." The production of wine was a major industry in ancient Israel and an important export. Isaiah's parable of the vineyard depicts Yahweh as a dedicated vintner (Isa 5:1–7). It is possible that wine was "the most commonly consumed beverage in ancient Israel" (King and Stager 2001: 101). From the Israelite point of view, wine was a staple and a blessing. With his naming speech in mind (Gen 5:29, J), Noah's discovery of wine does indeed provide relief to humans from their hard labor on the earth.

Archaeologists and paleobotanists tell us that the wild grape may have been first domesticated in the Early Bronze Age (ca. 3500–2200 BCE) in southern Anatolia and was thereafter transplanted to the Levant, which became famous for its wine. It is possible that Noah was credited as the first to plant a vineyard because he disembarked in Anatolia (Stager 1985b: 173). If so, this would represent an ancient cultural association. But the locale of Noah's vineyard is unclear, since the extant J flood story does not specify the ark's landing place.

9:21. *He drank some wine and became drunk and exposed himself within his tent.* This verse has a quick sequence of three verbs: *wayyēšt* ("he drank"), *wayyiškār* ("he became drunk"), and *wayyitgal* ("he exposed himself"). The narrative is not judgmental about Noah's drunkenness, perhaps since he is the first to drink wine. Elsewhere drunkenness is shameful (e.g., Prov 23:29–34, Hos 4:11, Isa 5:11). It is often used as a metaphor for impending shame and devastation, as in the threat to Edom: "To you also the cup will pass, and you will become drunk and expose yourself" (Lam 4:21).

The scene in which Noah "exposed himself within his tent" may say something about ancient male clothing. In ancient Israel the normal male dress was an outer robe or long shirt that reached below the knees and an undergarment like a skirt or loincloth (King and Stager 2001: 266–71). Pants may have been a Persian innovation, borrowed into Israel during the Persian Empire (Sperling 1999). In the preexilic period, a man was in danger of exposing his genitals when passed out drunk (as here), dancing (as David in 2 Sam 6:16, 20), or ascending steps (at altars in Exod 20:23). To expose one's genitals in public incurred shame and humiliation (see NOTES at 2:25). For this reason, prisoners of war were sometimes transported naked (e.g., Isa 20:4, 2 Chr 28:15, and many Near Eastern reliefs), and the threat of public nakedness is a prominent biblical curse (e.g., Deut 28:48, Isa 47:2–3, Nah 3:5). To have one's sexual parts exposed in public is a sign of loss of control and causes the loss of honor and social status, as when Saul publicly "lay naked all that day and night" (1 Sam 19:24).

Since Noah is "within his tent" (*batôk 'ohŏlōh*), his exposure is private and not a cause of shame. It becomes shameful only when someone sees him who does not belong, breaching the father's domestic space.

9:22. *Ham, Canaan's father, saw his father's nakedness, and he told his two brothers outside.* Ham sees "his father's nakedness" (*'erwat 'ābîw*). The word *'erwâ* refers to genitalia, male or female. To see one's father's genitalia is a shameful act, which generates shame for both parties. To announce this to others exacerbates the transgression, since it makes the father's humiliation public. Both of these acts—the seeing and the telling—are culpable, as Gunkel (1997: 80) observes: "Both are sins. He should not have looked (cf. the counterpart in v. 23) and, at least, should not have spoken of it."

It has often been suggested (beginning with the rabbis and church fathers) that a greater transgression than seeing the father's genitalia is indicated here. Various kinds of sexual transgression—homosexual incest, castration, or even heterosexual incest—have been imputed (see, e.g., Cassuto 1964: 150–53; Bassett 1971; and the critique of Vogels 1987). These interpretations are motivated by three details: (1) the wording of 9:24, where Noah "knew what his youngest son had done to him," suggesting some sort of action that Noah would perceive when he awoke; (2) the biblical references to Canaanite sexual abominations; and (3) the idiom of "seeing" or "exposing" the *'erwat 'ābîkā* ("your father's nakedness") in the laws concerning illicit sexual unions in Leviticus 18 and 20.

The first detail—the wording of 9:24—is suggestive, but not definitive (see below). The second detail—the reputation of the Canaanites—is also suggestive. According to the J Table of Nations, Sodom and Gomorrah are Canaanite cities (10:19), so an implication of sexual violence is possible here. The third of these details—the connection with Leviticus—does not carry weight.

The pertinent passage in Leviticus (from the Holiness source) is as follows: "Your father's nakedness, that is, your mother's nakedness, you shall not expose; she is your mother—you shall not expose her nakedness. The nakedness of your father's wife you shall not expose; it is your father's nakedness" (Lev 18:7–8; similarly, Lev 20:11). This law addresses incest with the mother (or stepmother) as exposing the *'erwat 'ăbîkā* ("your father's nakedness") in the legal sense that the wife's sexuality belongs to her husband. Hence Milgrom (2001: 1537) translates, "The sexual jurisdiction of your father, namely, the sexual organs of your mother you shall not uncover" (Lev 18:7). This use of the idiom "expose the father's nakedness" to refer to having sex with his wife is an innovation in the Holiness source (similarly Ezek 22:10). It is a semantic extension of the literal meaning of seeing or exposing genitalia, as in the law about priestly genitalia (Exod 20:23) and the Noah story (Vogels 1987: 560–61). Hence our story should not be interpreted through the lens of Leviticus 18 and 20 (written after J). The brother's acts of covering their father's sex and averting their eyes indicate that seeing the father's exposed genitalia is the problem.

The last word of the sentence, *baḥûṣ* ("outside"), brings a spatial dimension to Ham's actions and relates to the last word of the previous sentence, *bətôk 'ohŏlōh* ("within his tent"). Ham's movement is from inside to outside, from private space to public space. Ham has transgressed this boundary of the "father's house," which is both a physical layout and a social hierarchy (Stager 1985a: 18–23).

The repetition of the previous aside that Ham is "Canaan's father" (9:18) emphasizes this relationship and anticipates the shift to Canaan in Noah's curse and blessings. The mention of Canaan in the midst of the transgression verbally implicates him in his father's transgression and shame.

9:23. *Shem and Japheth took a robe and draped it over both of their shoulders, and they went in backwards and covered their father's nakedness. Since they faced backwards, they did not see their father's nakedness.* Shem and Japheth are presented as honorable sons, who cover their father's shame. The sequence of verbs shows their deliberate care: "they took . . . they draped . . . they went in . . . they covered . . . they did not see." The final negated verb, "they did not see" (*lō' rā'û*), forms an *inclusio* around Ham's action at the beginning of 9:22, "Ham saw" (*wayyar' ḥām*). There is a strong contrast between these acts of seeing and not-seeing: Ham shames the father, while Shem and Japheth preserve his honor.

The word "robe" (*haśśimlâ*) has the definite article *ha-* but is not grammatically definite (i.e., it is not known to the reader by being previously mentioned or unique), hence the indefinite translation "a robe." This is one of many such instances and may derive from the origin of the definite article as a relative pronoun, "this" (Barr 2014: 473–75). It adds some focus to the word "robe."

The disjunctive clause sequence, "Since they faced backwards, they did not see their father's nakedness" (*ûpənêhem 'ăḥōrannît wə'erwat 'ăbîhem lō' rā'û*), repeats the words "backwards" and "their father's nakedness" from the previous clause to make it absolutely clear that they did not shame their father by seeing his exposed genitals. The brothers are careful and deliberate in their filial behavior, in contrast to Ham's behavior.

As Cassuto (1964: 162) observes, there is a good deal of alliteration in this verse: *śimlâ wayyāśîmû* ("robe and draped"), *šəkem šənêhem* ("shoulders, both of their"), including a lot of sibilants. The suffix "their" (*hem*) occurs four times, emphasizing their filial solidarity and respect for "their father" (*'ăbîhem*).

The obligation of filial piety to a drunken father is nicely illustrated by a Ugaritic passage from the Aqhat epic, where Baal implores El to grant King Danel a son:

> Let him have a son in his house,
>> Offspring within his palace . . .
> To grasp his arm when he is drunk,
>> To support him when sated with wine.

> (*CAT* 1.17.i.25–31; Parker 1997: 53)

9:24. *When Noah awoke from his wine, and he knew what his youngest son had done to him.* The story does not tell how Noah "knew" what Ham "had done to him." This gap in the narrative has given rise to many interpretations (see NOTES at 9:22). Perhaps we are to imagine Noah recognizing the robe covering him as belonging to Shem or Japheth and then interrogating his sons. The words "had done to him" (*'āśâ-lô*) suggest that damage has been done to Noah. In the code of honor and shame, one's honor is a personal possession, and its damage is devastating. The verb *'āśâ* may suggest more, however, perhaps even a hint of Canaanite sexual violence (cf. Sodom and Gomorrah). But if so, it remains only a hint in this direction.

On the curious description of Ham as Noah's "youngest son," see NOTES at 9:18.

9:25–27. The sequence of Noah's curse and blessings consists of two utterances, each introduced by "he said" (*wayyō'mer*). The first utterance is the curse on Canaan, and the second conveys two blessings on Shem and Japheth, including Canaan's servitude to each. The relationships among the brothers are sealed in the father's speech as a consequence of their previous treatment of the father. The curse and blessings are directed toward the descendants of Noah's three sons, following the future orientation introduced in 9:19, "from them all the earth spread out." Interestingly, Noah invokes different divine names in his two blessings—Yahweh (*yhwh*) for Shem, and God (*'ĕlōhîm*) for Japheth, perhaps suggesting a religious difference.

9:25. *he said, "Cursed be Canaan—he shall be the lowest slave to his brothers!"* The curse of Canaan continues the chain of curses from earlier stories, particularly Yahweh's curses on the snake and Cain, "cursed be you" (*'ārûr 'atta;* 3:14, 4:11). The echo of Cain's curse is particularly interesting, since it involves conflict with brothers, and both involve an ethnographic distinction of low status (for Canaan and the Kenites). The idea that Canaan will be the "lowest slave" (*'ebed 'ăbādîm,* lit. "slave of slaves," a superlative construction) to his brothers seems to be a justification and foreshadowing of Yahweh's gift of the land of Canaan to Abraham's descendants (12:7). This promise is preceded by reference to "the land of Canaan" (12:5) and the comment "the Canaanites were then in the land" (12:6), so the identity of the land's inhabitants is not in question. The Canaanites are destined to lose this land, presumably because of the curse on Canaan.

But there are lingering ambiguities. The Canaanites are killed or dispossessed in biblical traditions but do not become slaves (except for the Gibeonites). Moreover, the Canaanites do not become slaves to the Shemites and Japhethites. Of these peoples, only Israel and the Philistines (see Notes at 9:27) dispossess the land of Canaan. Perhaps one Shemite descendant (Israel) and one possible Japhethite descendant (Philistia) are sufficient.

9:26. *He said, "Blessed be Yahweh, the God of Shem—may Canaan be his slave."* The repetition of "he said" (*wayyōʾmer*) in a speech often indicates a dramatic pause, as if the addressee were struck silent (Alter 1996: 39). This may be the effect here, as Noah pauses between the curse and the blessings, and Canaan has no reply.

The blessing of Shem is phrased as a blessing of Shem's god, Yahweh. This seems curious but is perhaps an elliptical way of attaching Shem to the blessings of Yahweh. In this way Shem is blessed, but his lineal descendant Israel maintains the benefits of that blessing.

The archaic prepositional phrase *lāmô* ("his") lends an air of antiquity and authority to Noah's formal utterance. The idea that Canaan will be "his slave" should perhaps be taken as a forecast that Canaan will be conquered or displaced by Shemites (i.e., Israel).

9:27. *May God enlarge Japheth—may he dwell in Shem's tents, and may Canaan be his slave.* The blessing of Japheth has three parts. The first involves a play on the name Japheth—*yapt ʾĕlōhîm ləyepet* ("may God increase Japheth"), using the verb *pth* ("be spacious, enlarge"). The content of the blessing is implicit in Japheth's name. Here Noah invokes *ʾĕlōhîm* ("God") in pointed contrast to the previous invocation of *yhwh ʾĕlōhê šēm* ("Yahweh, the God of Shem"). Noah seems to acknowledge that the Japhethites worship gods other than Yahweh but still refers to their deity as God. This is an ecumenical nomenclature, in which "God" is a cross-cultural designation, and "Yahweh" a particularly Israelite one. In these designations, Noachian religion begins to differentiate into the worship of God and the worship of Yahweh, with both roughly translatable. This ecumenical view may also be found in Yahweh's blessing of Abram, in which "all the families of the earth will be blessed through you" (12:3, J).

The second part of Japheth's blessing, "may he dwell in Shem's tents" (*wəyiškōn bəʾohŏlê-šēm*), suggests future amity between the Japhethites and Shemites, recalling their cooperation in the narrative. But the image of dwelling in someone else's tents can also indicate displacement and conquest, as in Ps 78:55, "He expelled the nations before them . . . he made the tribes of Israel dwell (*wayyaškēn*) in their tents." The obvious candidate for a descendant of Japheth who dwells in Shem's tents (and subjugates Canaan) is the Philistines, who settled the Levantine coast at roughly the same time that Israel emerged in the highlands (see Speiser 1964: 62–63; Seebass 1996: 249–50; Day 2013: 143–47). However, in the Table of Nations, J—or a later glossator—locates the Philistines in the lineage of Ham (10:14), linked with the descendants (and cultural sphere) of Egypt, including Caphtor. (The Japhethite section is lacking in the extant J Table of Nations). Despite this possible incongruity, the Philistines are the best candidates for the actualization of Noah's blessing to Japheth (for other options, see Westermann 1984: 490–91).

The third part of the blessing repeats verbatim the line from Shem's blessing, "and may Canaan be his slave" (*wiyhî kənaʿan ʿebed lāmô*). Japheth and Shem gain equally from Canaan's curse. The brothers who behaved honorably benefit, while the brother who shamed his father loses his status. The command to "honor your father" is acted out in striking and colorful ways in this story and determines the destinies of the three Noachian lineages.

Comments

After the flood, life takes on new complications for Noah and his family. Noah's invention of wine is another step in the ascent of civilization, but it is a dangerous one as Noah's drunkenness exposes him to shame. A father's curse and blessings ensue. The story is both an etiology of wine and a justification for and anticipation of Yahweh's promise of the land of Canaan to Abraham's descendants. The curse of Canaan, in this sense, is a prelude to the rise of Israel.

LITERARY DESIGN

This brief story has a simple literary form, with a brief introduction of the protagonists and a nod toward their genealogical futures (9:18–19), followed by the narrative itself, consisting of an initial situation, complications, recognition, and resolution (9:20–24). The *Leitwort* "father" (*ʾāb*) occurs five times in all, keeping a focus on the authority of the father in matters of family honor and shame.

The introduction of the protagonists adds a crucial piece of anticipatory information, "Ham was Canaan's father" (9:18). This phrase is repeated in the story's complication ("Ham, Canaan's father," 9:22) and resolves with the threefold repetition of "Canaan" as the object of the curse (9:26). The genealogical transfer of shame and curse from Noah's son Ham to Ham's son Canaan is thus prepared by the story's diction already in the introduction.

The initial situation, "Noah, a man of the soil (*ʾîš hā ʾădāmâ*), was the first (or 'began,' *wayyāḥel*) to plant a vineyard," sets the stage for the ensuing complication. It also links the story to two long-range *Leitwort* threads in the J primeval narrative. As a new "beginning" (*ḥll* in the *hiphil*) it resumes this *Leitwort* from 6:1, when humans "began (*hēḥēl*) to multiply on the face of the earth," and 4:26, "then was it begun (*hûḥal*) to call on the name of Yahweh." This thread continues in the following chapter when Nimrod "was the first (*hēḥēl*) to be a warrior on earth" (10:8). This new beginning for Noah is a new step in cultural history and subtly activates these other steps in the primeval narrative.

Noah as "a man of the soil" (*ʾîš hā ʾădāmâ*) resumes the *Leitwort* bond between humans (*hā ʾādām*) and the soil (*hā ʾădāmâ*), which begins in the Garden of Eden (starting with 2:5) and continues to resonate in the subsequent J stories (e.g., 4:2, 11; 5:29; 6:1; 8:21), culminating with Yahweh's promise to bless "all the families of the earth/soil" (12:3) at the transition to the ancestral narratives. As in the earlier stories, this relationship is ambivalent, with good to be gotten from the soil—in this case, grapes and wine—and also negative consequences, including drunkenness and shame.

The resolution of the story, Noah's curse of Canaan, also links up with a previous *Leitwort* thread, another consequence of the relationship between humans and soil. When Noah says, "Cursed be (*ʾārûr*) Canaan" (9:26), he echoes Yahweh's previous utterances, "Cursed be (*ʾārûr*) Cain" (4:11), "Cursed is (*ʾărûrâ*) the soil" (3:17), and "Cursed are (*'ārûr*) you [the snake]" (3:14). In this chain of curses, only this one is uttered by a human, emphasizing Noah's status as father and his authority to curse. As with the relationship between humans and the soil, the fivefold chain of curses will take a turn to fivefold blessings in the transition from the primeval to the ancestral story.

WINE AND SHAME

Noah's invention of viticulture and wine makes him a culture hero, like the Cainites, who are founders of cities, pastoral nomadism, music, and metalworking (4:17–22). Like several of these cultural practices, grape cultivation is an ambivalent gift, both beneficial and dangerous. The benefit is that "wine gladdens life" (Eccl 10:19; cf. Judg 9:13, where it "gladdens gods and humans"). It makes a person forget poverty and toil (Prov 31:7). When Noah is born, his father says, "He will give us relief from our work, from our painful manual labor on the soil that Yahweh has cursed" (Gen 5:29). The invention of wine seems to be part of the "relief" (*nḥm*) that Noah (*nōaḥ*) brings—a wordplay that motivates his name and vocation.

The benefit of wine is highlighted later in Genesis when Isaac gives Esau his blessing, "May God give to you from the dew of heaven and from the fat of the earth, and abundance of grain and new wine" (27:28), and when Jacob foresees that Judah will have an abundance of vineyards and wine:

> He ties his ass to a vine,
> > his ass's foal to a choice vine,
> he washes his clothes in wine,
> > his robe in the blood of grapes. (49:11)

Wine and vineyards are wealth and blessing. But wine is also dangerous, as Lot discovers when his daughters serve him wine on two successive nights, so that "he did not know when she [his daughter] lay down and when she rose" (19:33, 35). The daughters have sex with Lot and become pregnant, with the mistaken intention of preserving humankind. Drinking too much wine exposes the father to transgression, in this case incest. As Hosea warns, "Wine and new wine take away understanding" (Hos 4:11). The blood of the grape is two-faced, a gift and a poison.

This ambivalence plays out in Noah's invention of viticulture and wine. Planting a vineyard is a benefit (cf. the Song of the Vineyard in Isa 5:1–4). Then Noah "drank some wine and became drunk and exposed himself within his tent" (Gen 9:21). This rapid sequence of verbs, "drank . . . became drunk . . . exposed himself," shows the danger of an excess of wine. As the first oenophile, Noah does not know his limits. By becoming drunk and naked, Noah turns from a culture hero to a figure of incipient shame. His shame is actualized when his son sees him naked in his tent.

Noah's drunkenness, exposure, and shame at being seen naked have a relationship to developments in the Garden of Eden. At first "the two of them were naked, the man and his wife, and they felt no shame before each other" (2:25). After they eat the forbidden fruit of the Tree of the Knowledge of Good and Evil, "they knew that they were naked, and they sewed together fig leaves and made loincloths for themselves" (3:7). The transition in Eden is from an initial state of innocence—naked and unashamed—to a state of self-knowledge and moral awareness. At this transition, being seen naked brings shame and triggers the need for clothes to cover their sexed bodies. This relationship of knowledge, nakedness, and shame recurs in Noah's drunkenness, but with variations. He turns from an inventor of civilization to an uncivilized state, a drunken stupor, which leads to exposing his naked body, his experience of shame, and being reclothed by others.

Unlike Adam and Eve, Noah is "in his tent" (9:21), a private domestic space, so his naked body is not in public view. Noah's son breaches this boundary when he "saw his father's nakedness, and he told his two brothers outside" (9:23). The cultural distance between "inside" and "outside" is significant. Being naked inside is protected—the tent is a covering. But the son enters his father's tent without consent. Seeing his father naked exposes not only the father's body but also his vulnerability. Noah is senseless and powerless in his tent. This is the condition of Noah's shame.

As Williams (2008: 220) observes, "The root of shame lies in exposure in a more general sense, in being at a disadvantage . . . a loss of power. The sense of shame is a reaction of the subject to the consciousness of this loss." Noah is unaware of his loss of power in the family structure until he awakens from his stupor: "Noah woke from his wine, and he knew what his youngest son had done to him" (9:24). The emphasis on the family relationship ("his youngest son") makes the locus of lost power clear. Noah's honor as the father has been diminished. Moreover, his youngest son has compounded his shame by telling his brothers outside. He has verbally exposed his father's shame to the other sons.

When Noah becomes aware of what has happened, he responds by reasserting his power with a curse. The son has diminished the father's social capital, and the father restores it by punishing the agent of his loss. In this social exchange, the father restores his honor by casting shame upon the son (or the son's son; see NOTES at 9:18) who shamed him. The social code involves a constant reapportioning of honor and shame, a circulation of capital that regulates relationships, obligations, and power.

The other brothers, in contrast to the shaming son, demonstrate their honor to the father by covering him with a robe while averting their eyes. This is a picture of filial duty. Honorable sons protect the father when he is in a state of powerlessness, such as drunkenness. As the Ugaritic text cited above states, a good son will "grasp his [father's] arm when he is drunk, / To support him when sated with wine" (see NOTES at 9:23). This filial role is fulfilled by Shem and Japheth.

This distribution of honor and shame among Noah's sons yields a hierarchy among them. Ham's son Canaan is cursed to be a slave to his brothers, while Shem and Japheth are blessed. This family relationship turns into an ethnography of power, in which Canaan becomes subservient, and Shem and Japheth will become the masters of Canaan.

Noah's blessings and curses create a genealogical charter for the future hegemony of Israel and Philistia in the land of Canaan, and it sets the stage for Yahweh's promise of the land to Abraham (12:1–4). As Rashi (in Cohen 1997: 2) astutely comments (at Gen 1:1), this is one reason why the Bible begins with Genesis, so that Israel can say to the nations, "He created it [the earth], and he gave it to whoever was upright in his eyes. By his will he gave it to them, and by his will he took it from them and gave it to us." With Noah's curse, the land of Canaan is proleptically taken from Canaan, making it eligible to be the promised land.

Noah's Curse on Canaan shames the future peoples of Canaan, just as the shameful origins of Ammon and Moab (the sons of Lot's incest with his daughters) are borne by their peoples. These stories of shameful family origins populate the genealogy of Genesis to establish an ethnography marked by hierarchies of honor and shame (Hendel 2018). The future focus of this mental map is, of course, Israel. This holds true in the first generation after the flood, when only Noah and his family were on the earth.

CONTEXTS

In the J primeval narrative, this story is the sequel to the flood. As commentators have observed, there is literary parallelism between this story and Cain and Abel: both are sequels to stories of creation or re-creation, and both feature family conflict involving brothers (Sasson 1980: 218; Niditch 1985: 59–60; Carr 1996: 236). Each story features three brothers: Cain, Abel, and Seth (with the latter a substitute for Abel); and Shem, Ham, and Japheth. As noted above, the *Leitwort* sequences also link these stories: Noah's working of the soil (*hā 'ădāmâ*) echoes Adam's, and the curse of Canaan echoes the curse of Cain. The relationships and transgressions differ, since Cain murders his brother, while Ham shames his father. Yet there is a thematic complementarity, in which familial transgressions after new beginnings—after Eden and after the flood—display the evil inclinations of the human heart. Humans are problematic creatures in both eras, violating the ethical norms of family relationships, bringing disorder into the world, and creating ethnographic distinctions and hierarchies.

Another J story that echoes in some respects Noah's drunkenness and the curse of Canaan is the story of Lot and his daughters (19:30–38), which is the epilogue to another destruction, that of Sodom and Gomorrah (Skinner 1930: 312; Zakovitch 1995: 48–49). The destruction by water is echoed by the destruction by fire. Lot's daughters believe that this was a global disaster (like the flood) and that they must bear children to preserve humankind. The older daughter says to the younger, "Come, let us serve our father wine, and let us lay down with him, so that we may bring to life seed from our father" (19:32). As noted above, the drunkenness of the father makes him susceptible to shame. While Noah's son sees him drunk and naked, Lot's daughters make Lot drunk in order to make him naked and have sex with him. In both cases, the children shame the father. (In Lot's case, it is a "measure for measure," since Lot had previously offered the daughters to rape, 19:8.) Both stories end with an ethnographic "othering": Canaan is cursed to be a slave to his brothers, and the children born of incest, Ammon and Moab, bear shameful origins. These stories yield genealogical shame for Canaanites, Ammonites, and Moabites, Israel's predecessors and neighbors.

There is much comparative material for the story's themes and motifs in ancient Near Eastern and Mediterranean texts. The invention and ambivalence of wine (and its counterpart, beer) are prominent topics. Elsewhere, however, wine and beer are invented by gods, who provide its transformative power. Noah's invention of wine seems to be a monotheistic transformation of older traditions.

In the Ugaritic texts, one of Baal's messengers is "Vine" (*gpn*), indicating that the vines depend on Baal's power, probably through his fructifying rain. There is also a god named Trṯ, meaning a kind of wine (cognate with Hebrew *tîrôš*). This wine god is offered sacrifices in Ugaritic ritual texts and must represent, in some sense, the divine power in wine (Healey 1999).

A short Ugaritic text shows the high god El becoming drunk at a banquet and being helped home by his two sons, a distant parallel in the divine domain to Noah's situation:

> [El] drinks wine (*yn*) to satiety,
> > vintage (*trt*) to drunkenness.
> El heads off to his house,
> > arrives at his courts.
> Ṯukamuna and Šunama
> > bear him along.

(CAT 1.114; T. J. Lewis 1997: 195)

Here we see the Father of the Gods becoming drunk at his drinking club and stumbling home safely with the help of two sons. This is a picture of the duties of sons, as Baal tells the childless King Kirta, "To grasp his arm when he's drunk, / To support him when sated with wine" (*CAT* 1.17.i.30–31; Parker 1997: 53). The picture of the drunkenness of El is not shameful as such, since the banquet context may require that he drink wine "to drunkenness" (*škr*). Similarly for Noah, it is not his drunkenness as such that is shameful. His shame is in being seen naked by his son, which the son compounds by exposing the father's nakedness to his brothers outside. Shem and Japheth are good sons, like Ṯukamuna and Šunama, honoring their father by preventing others from seeing him in a state of powerlessness. Good sons—divine or human—act to preserve their father's honor.

In Greece—a wine culture like Israel and Ugarit—Dionysus is the god of wine. In Euripides's *Bacchae*, Dionysus is famed for "inventing liquid wine from grapes as his gift to man. For filled with juice from vines, suffering mankind forgets its grief" (278–80). This characterization of wine is consonant with the Bible's. As in Noah's story, Dionysus's gift is both a benefit and a danger. The god whose power is in the wine brings madness and murder as well as relief. In Greece one drank wine diluted with water to limit the power of Dionysus.

The Table of Nations
(10:1–32; P, J, *R*)

---

10 ¹This is the genealogy of Noah's sons, Shem, Ham, and Japheth. Sons were born^a to them after the flood.

²**Japheth's sons were Gomer and Magog and Maday and Yavan and Tubal and Meshech and Tiras. ³Gomer's sons were Ashkenaz and Diphat^b and Togarmah.** ⁴**Yavan's sons were Elisha and Tarshish, the Kittites and the Rodanites.^c** ⁵From these the maritime nations branched off. These are Japheth's sons^d by their lands, each according to his language, families, and nations.

⁶**Ham's sons were Cush and Egypt and Put and Canaan.** ⁷**Cush's sons were Seba and Havilah and Sabtah and Raamah and Sabteka. Raamah's sons were Sheba and Dedan.** ⁸Cush fathered Nimrod. He was the first to be a warrior on earth. ⁹He became a mighty hunter before Yahweh. Therefore it is said, "Like Nimrod, a mighty hunter before Yahweh." ¹⁰The chief cities of his kingdom were Babel and Erech and Akkad and Calneh, in the land of Sumer. ¹¹From that land he went up to Asshur and built Nineveh and Rehovot-Ir and Calah ¹²and Resen, between Nineveh and Calah, the great city. ¹³Egypt fathered the Ludites and the Anamites and the Lehabites and the Naphtuhites ¹⁴and the Patrusites and the Casluhites, from which came the Philistines, and the Caphtorites. ¹⁵Canaan fathered his firstborn, Sidon, and Heth ¹⁶and the Jebusites and the Amorites and the Girgashites ¹⁷and the Hivites and the Arkites and the Sinites ¹⁸and the Arvadites and the Zemarites and the Hamatites. Afterwards the families of Canaan spread out. ¹⁹Canaan's boundaries extended from Sidon in the direction of Gerar as far as Gaza, and in the direction of Sodom, Gomorrah, Admah, and Zeboiim as far as Lasha. ²⁰**These are Ham's sons according to their families, languages, lands, and nations.**

²¹As for Shem, sons were also born to him. He was the father of *all the sons of* Eber, and he was Japheth's older brother. ²²**Shem's sons were Elam and Asshur and Arpachshad and Lud and Aram.^e** ²³**Aram's sons were Uz and Hul and Gether and Mash.** ²⁴*Arpachshad fathered^f Shelah, and Shelah fathered Eber.* ²⁵As for Eber, two sons

were born. The name of the first was Peleg, for in his time the earth was divided, and the name of his brother was Joktan. ²⁶Joktan fathered Almodad and Shaleph and Hazarmaveth and Yarah ²⁷and Hadoram and Uzal and Diklah ²⁸and Obal and Abimael and Sheba ²⁹and Ophir and Havilah and Jobab—all of these were Joktan's sons. ³⁰Their territory extended from Mesha in the direction of Sepharah, the eastern mountain. **³¹These are Shem's sons according to their families, languages, lands, and nations.**

³²These are the families of Noah's sons according to their genealogy and nations. From these the peoples branched out over the earth after the flood.

Textual Notes

a. Vocalizing the consonants *wywld* as *wayyûlládû* instead of *wayyiwwālədû* (MT); compare 4:18. The *qal* passive is the normal stem for this verb in the J source (Hendel 2000).

b. Reading *dypt* ("Diphat") with 1 Chr 1:6, versus *rypt* ("Riphat") in the MT, SP, and LXX. This is a graphic confusion between *dalet* and *resh* (Hendel 1998: 58).

c. Reading *rdnym* ("Rodanim") with the SP, the LXX, and 1 Chr 1:7, versus *ddnym* ("Dodanim") in the MT. Another graphic confusion between *dalet* and *resh* (Hendel 1998: 6–7, 58).

d. An emendation, *ʾlh bny ypt* ("These are Japheth's sons"), on which most commentators agree. This phrase, or something like it, is required by context (Hendel 1998: 58–59).

e. The LXX adds "and Kenan"; compare 5:9–14. See COMMENTS on 11:10–32 and Hendel 1998: 74.

f. The LXX adds "Kenan, and Kenan begot." See COMMENTS on 11:10–32 and Hendel 1998: 74.

Notes

10:1. This is the genealogy of Noah's sons, Shem, Ham, and Japheth. This is the fourth rubric of the type *ʾēlleh tôlədōt* ("this is the genealogy of . . .") out of five in Genesis 1–11 (2:4, 5:1, 6:9, 10:1, and 11:10). As noted previously, these rubrics provide a structuring principle in the P work and in the final form of Genesis. The idea that the past is structured as a genealogy is deeply rooted in Israel's consciousness.

The clause "This is the genealogy of Noah's sons" has an envelope effect in this chapter, since it is expanded in the final verse: "These are the families of Noah's sons according to their genealogy (*tôlədōtām*)" (10:32). The word "families" (*mišpəhōt*) is drawn from the formula that concludes the lineage of each of Noah's sons (10:5, 20, 31). These repetitions create a tight structure within this chapter: an introduction, three sections of lineages, and a concluding summary.

The three sons of Noah—Shem, Ham, and Japheth—are listed from oldest to youngest here, as previously in P (5:32, 6:10, 7:13) and J (9:18). The genealogy that follows reverses this order, proceeding from youngest to oldest—Japheth (10:2–5), Ham (10:6–20), and Shem (10:21–31). This reversal enables the text to treat the collateral branches (Ham and Japheth) before turning to focus on the line of Shem, the oldest, which will produce Israel. The focus on the Shemites is resumed in the vertical genealogy of 11:10–32. The Hamites and Japhethites have no further genealogical developments. Stylistically, this reversed order creates a chiastic structure, from Shem—Ham—Japheth in 10:1 to Japheth—Ham—Shem in the rest of the chapter.

In the Table of Nations, the genealogical idiom requires that each name signifies a person, but in nearly all cases the person is an ethnonym (cf. "Israel" as an eponymous ancestor and a people). Some names are collective terms, such as *rōdānîm* (Rhodians, 10:4) and the sons of Egypt (Ludim, Anamim, etc., 10:13–14, J), which are in the plural. Among these ancestral names are the names of cities, regions, and ethnic groups. The only name that is solely a person is Nimrod, who is a king and not a nation (10:8–9).

The genealogy in this chapter functions as a social map. The organizing principles are primarily geographical (see Skinner 1930: 193–94): the Japhethites are peoples to the north and west of Israel; the Hamites are peoples to the south (except for Canaan); and the Shemites are peoples to the east (including the lineal ancestor of Israel). The J table differs from the P table in some respects; for instance, it situates the Arabian peoples as Shemites rather than Hamites (see also the differences for Aram [introduced in J in 22:21], Lydia, Asshur, etc.; see NOTES).

R has used the P Table of Nations as the base text, into which portions of the J table have been inserted. These portions are a clause from the introduction to the table (10:1), the introduction of the Shemite genealogy (10:21), and segments of the Hamite and Shemite genealogies (10:8–19, 24–30). Curiously, no portion of the Japhethite genealogy is preserved from J, although J clearly knew the three brothers (9:18–27). The total number of peoples in the table is seventy, a number that seems to represent totality (cf. the seventy sons of Jacob in Genesis 46). R achieved this number by combining thirty-four peoples in P with thirty-six in J (not counting Nimrod, who is not a nation). R combined the two tables to form a coherent whole, while omitting many redundancies.

Sons were born to them after the flood. This verse can be attributed to J because of the similarity of its diction to 10:21 (J): "As for Shem, sons were also born to him." The use of the verb *yld* ("to bear [children]") in the passive is characteristic of J in the primeval narrative, indicating important begettings by Seth (4:26), humankind (6:1), Noah's sons (10:1), Shem (10:21), and Eber (10:25), ancestor of Israel. Here the form *wayyiwwālədû* ("were born" in the *niphal*) should probably be read as a *qal* passive, *wayyulladû*, as in these other verses. The *qal* passive imperfect can be reinterpreted as a *niphal* because the consonantal base *wywldw* can be construed either way. Ginsberg (see Hendel 2000: 42–43) describes such forms as "Masoretically misconstrued." The geographical and ethnic identifications of these sons (and grandsons, etc.) are treated most thoroughly by Lipiński (1990, 1992, 1993, although I occasionally differ); see also Skinner (1930: 196–223) and Day (2022: 163–88).

10:2–5. Japhethites (P). Japheth has seven sons and seven grandsons, a formulaic number. The Japhethites are peoples and places of Anatolia and the islands and coastlands of the northeastern Mediterranean. These peoples are all to the north of Israel. As we will see, the grouping of these names reflects conditions of the seventh to sixth centuries BCE (esp. Gomer, Magog, and Maday).

Japheth (*yepet, yāpet* in pause) is plausibly related to Greek Iapetos, a Titan who is the grandfather of Deucalion, the flood hero (Skinner 1930: 195; Becking 1995). Greek Iapetos has associations with Anatolia (his daughter Ankhialē is the eponymous

Figure 11. Artist's rendition of the world according to the Table of Nations.
(Drawing by William H. C. Propp)

founder of a city in Cilicia), has no Greek etymology, and may be a borrowing from the Near East (West 1966: 202–3).

10:2. *Japheth's sons were Gomer and Magog and Maday and Yavan and Tubal and Meshech and Tiras.* Japheth's sons are generally associated with Anatolia.

Gomer (*gōmer*) corresponds to Akkadian Gimirru/Gimirraya and Greek Kimmerioi, the Cimmerians. These horse-riding pastoralists, originally from southern Russia, entered northern Anatolia in the eighth century BCE. They were a feared military power in Anatolia until ca. 600 BCE, when they were defeated by Lydia and driven out of Anatolia. In Ezek 38:6, Gomer and Togarmah are allies of Gog (see the following NOTE).

Magog (*māgôg*) is not known from ancient Near Eastern sources. It is probably a contraction of Akkadian *māt Gugi,* "the land of Gog/Gyges" (so many commentators). King Gugu (Greek Gyges) founded a powerful royal dynasty in Lydia in western Anatolia and ruled ca. 680–650 BCE. He is mentioned several times in Assyrian annals as *Gugu šar māt Luddi,* "Gog, king of the land of Lydia" (Cogan and Tadmor 1977). Gugu died in battle with the Cimmerians and became the model for the wicked adversary in Ezekiel 38–39, "Gog of the land of Magog, chief prince of Meshech and Tubal" (Ezek 38:2). Perhaps curiously, the P Table of Nations distinguishes between Magog (a Japhethite) and Lud (Lydia, Gen 10:22), a son of Shem. In the J table, the Ludites (Lydians, 10:13) are sons of Egypt and hence are Hamites.

Maday (*māday*) is the land of Media, Akkadian Madaya. The Medes lived in western Iran and had a powerful kingdom in the seventh to sixth centuries BCE. They are mentioned in Assyrian documents beginning in the ninth century BCE. After the Medes and the Babylonians destroyed Nineveh in 612, the Median kingdom extended westward into Anatolia, ruling from central Anatolia to the Persian Gulf. The Median kingdom was conquered by Cyrus of Persia. In Jer 51:28 the "kings of Media" (*malkê māday*) are listed along with other Anatolian adversaries, Ararat and Ashkenaz (see Notes at 10:3).

Yavan (*yāwān*) corresponds to Greek Iaones, the eponymous ancestor of Ionia, originally Iawones (with *digamma*), and Akkadian Yawanu (written Yamanu; see Rollinger 2017: 275–78). Ionia refers to the islands and western coast of Anatolia where Greek colonists settled after ca. 1000 BCE. In Ezek 27:13 Yavan is grouped with other Anatolian peoples, Tubal, Meshech, and Tarshish. In later usage, Yavan comes to mean Greece in general (e.g., Dan 8:21, 10:20, 11:2), rather than Ionia in particular.

Tubal (*tūbal*) corresponds to Akkadian Tabalu, a region and polity in eastern Anatolia. (The shift *Ta* > *Tū* perhaps indicates that the name was mediated to Hebrew via Phoenician; so Lipiński 1990: 46.) Tabal is mentioned in Hittite and Assyrian texts, and in biblical texts it is often listed with Meshech.

Meshech (*mešek*) corresponds to Akkadian Mušku, a people associated with Phrygia in central Anatolia. King Mitâ of Mušku (late eighth century BCE), mentioned numerous times in the Assyrian annals of Sargon II, made Mušku a powerful kingdom. Mitâ is the famous King Midas of Phrygia in Greek sources (Rollinger 2013). In the book of Ezekiel, Meshech is often listed alongside Tubal, its eastern neighbor (Ezek 27:13, 32:26, 38:2, 39:1).

Tiras (*tîrās*) may correspond to the western Anatolian polity called Taruisa/Tarwiza (Troy?) in Hittite records (Bryce 1998: 135–36), although it is not attested in first-millennium texts. Another possibility is the Sea People named Tȑš in Egyptian texts of the late thirteenth century. These may have been mercenaries from western Italy, the Greek Tyrsenoi, Latin Etrusci, to whom Herodotus (perhaps erroneously) attributed Anatolian origins (Drews 1992). A possible link to Thrace, Greek Thrakes, northwest of Anatolia, or its legendary king Teres, has also been proposed (Lipiński 1990: 47). Tiras is not listed elsewhere in the Bible.

10:3. *Gomer's sons were Ashkenaz and Diphat and Togarmah.* The first and third sons have connections or similarities with Gomer (the Cimmerians); the second is obscure.

Ashkenaz ('*aškănaz*) corresponds to Akkadian Iškuza and Greek Skuthai, the Scythians (*HALOT,* 95, plausibly suggests that the Hebrew is a phonetic development from '*aškūz*). The Scythians were horse-riding pastoralists who migrated from Central Asia to southeastern Anatolia and northwestern Iran in the eighth to seventh centuries BCE. During the mid-seventh century the Scythians were a dominant power in the region and allied with Assyria, but their rule collapsed with the decline of the Assyrian Empire in the later seventh century. Ashkenaz is called upon in Jer 51:27, along with

Ararat, Minni, and Media, to go to war against Babylon. Ashkenaz, as fierce horse-riding warrior people, is a "son" of Gomer (the Cimmerians), who possessed similar features. In medieval Hebrew, Ashkenaz refers to Germany, hence its modern meaning.

Diphat (MT *rîpat; dîpat* in 1 Chr 1:6) may correspond to the Persian *dahyu-pati,* meaning "chief of the people/nation" (Lipiński 1990: 49). This title, used by chiefs of Media, may have been misconstrued as a place name. There are no other candidates for the meaning of this name, which is not mentioned elsewhere.

Togarmah (*tōgarmâ*) corresponds to an Anatolian people near the upper Euphrates called Tagarama/Tegarama in Hittite texts, Tagarima in an Akkadian text from Ugarit, and probably Tagari[ma] in an Assyrian text of the ninth century BCE (Astour 1981: 22). The "house/kingdom of Togarmah" (*bêt tôgarmâ*) is an ally of Gomer in Ezek 38:6 and is a trading nation associated with Yavan, Tubal, and Meshech in Ezek 27:14. In medieval Hebrew, Togarmah is the name for Turkey.

10:4. *Yavan's sons were Elisha and Tarshish, the Kittites and Rodanites.* All are island or coastal cultures in the Aegean and Mediterranean regions.

Elisha (*ʾĕlîšâ*) corresponds to Akkadian Alašiya, Ugaritic *ʾalṯy,* the name for Cyprus (or a polity on Cyprus) in second-millennium BCE texts and occasionally later (a fourth-century BCE bilingual Cypriot inscription refers to Apollo Alasiotas, "Apollo of Alashiya"; Day 2013: 155). In the first millennium this island goes by various names—Akkadian Yadnana, from *ʾi danuna,* "island of the Danuna" (*HALOT,* 38), after the Sea People Danuna who settled there; Greek Kupros (Cyprus), from the word "copper," Cyprus's major export; and Hebrew *kittîm/kittîyîm* (Kittim), after the Cypriot city-state called in Greek Kition, Phoenician *kty,* and Latin Citium. The P list of the sons of Yavan contains both the older (Elisha) and the newer (Kittim) names as separate entities. It is possible that the two names refer to different populations on the island (Day 2013: 155).

Tarshish (*taršîš*) corresponds to Assyrian Tarsisi (pronounced *Taršiši*), a polity at the end of the Mediterranean, as indicated in a Neo-Assyrian royal inscription of Esarhaddon: "I wrote to all of the kings who are in the midst of the sea, from Yadnana [Cyprus] and Yaman [Ionia] to Tarsisi, (and) they bowed down at my feet" (Leichty 2011: 135; see Rollinger 2017: 278–79). The association of Tarsisi with Cyprus and Ionia corresponds to the genealogical kinship of Tarshish, Elisha, and Kittim as sons of Yavan in 10:4. Its distant maritime locale also corresponds with its biblical association with "the ends of the earth" (Ps 72:8–10) and Jonah's attempt to flee there (Jonah 1:3). Tarshish in the Bible is famous for its exports of metals, particularly silver, and is linked with the mercantile network of Tyre (Isa 23:1–6; Jer 10:9; Ezek 27:12, 27). Its importance as a trading port is reflected in the famous "Tarshish ships" (1 Kgs 10:22, 22:48; Isa 60:9). Many commentators (see Day 2013: 154–65; Lipiński 1990: 51–52; Elat 1982) identify Tarshish/Tarsisi with Greek Tartessos (perhaps earlier *Tartiš), a Phoenician colony and trading port in southwestern Spain. This is phonetically and geographically more likely than an identification with Akkadian Tarzi, Hittite Tarša, Aramaic *trz,* and Greek Tarsos, a metal-exporting city on the southeastern Anatolian coast. Phoenician Tartessos was a source of metals, famed for its silver, and flourished in the eighth to mid-sixth centuries BCE (Celestino and López-Ruiz 2016). Some silver hoards from the Iron Age Levant have western origins, consistent with Spain, according to isotope tests (Thompson and Skaggs 2013), supporting the identification of Tarshish with Spanish Tartessos.

The Kittites (*kittîm,* sometimes *kittîyîm*), as noted above, correspond to Kition, a city-state in Cyprus. This is the normal name for Cyprus in Classical Hebrew. In Late Biblical Hebrew it was reapplied to the Macedonians (1 Macc 1:1, 8:5) and Romans (see Dan 11:30 and the Dead Sea Scrolls).

The Rodanites (MT *dōdānîm; rōdānîm* in the SP, LXX, and 1 Chr 1:7) correspond to Greek Rodioi, the people of the island of Rhodes. This island, off the coast of Anatolia, was an important commercial center, an entrepôt for Ionia, Greece, Egypt, and the Levant during the Iron Age. Ezekiel 27:15 refers to the "sons of Rodan" (LXX) as traders, together with "many islands" (*'iyyîm rabbîm*).

10:5. *From these the maritime nations branched off.* This remark refers to the descendants of Yavan's sons in 10:4, all of whom are island or coastal peoples. The word *'î* denotes "island," "peninsula," or "coast" (*HALOT,* 38). The phrase *'iyyê haggôyīm,* "island/coastal peoples," is nicely rendered by Speiser (1964: 66) as "maritime nations."

These are Japheth's sons by their lands, each according to his language, families, and nations. This concluding formula ends the Japhethite genealogy. Variations conclude the Hamite and Shemite genealogies: "These are Ham's sons according to their families, languages, lands, and nations" (10:20); and "These are Shem's sons according to their families, languages, lands, and nations" (10:31). These formulaic sentences, together with the opening and closing verses, serve to structure the Table of Nations, following the characteristic P style of variation within repetition. The sequence of categories varies between "land—language—family—nation" (10:5) and "family—language—land—nation" (10:20, 31). There are also slight variations of prepositions (*bəgôyēhem* in 10:5, 20 vs. *ləgôyēhem* in 10:31) and number (*'îš lilšōnô,* "each according to his language," 10:5, vs. *lilšōnōtām,* "their languages," 10:20, 31).

The formulaic phrase "these are Japheth's sons" (*'ēlleh bənê yepet*) is missing in all of the versions of 10:5, and as most commentators have noted, must be supplied (Hendel 1998: 58–59). Without it this verse is only about the "maritime nations" (*'iyyê haggôyîm*), which makes little sense.

10:6–7. Hamites (P). In the P table, Ham has four sons and seven grandsons. The latter number continues the formulaic quality of seven in the Japhethite genealogy. The Hamites are people to the south of Israel, in contrast to the Japhethites to the north. The exception to this spatial opposition is Canaan, who is a son of Ham in J and P. The reason for this placement of Canaan is unclear. It might derive from the proximity of Canaan and Egypt or a memory that Canaan was once part of the Egyptian Empire. In any case it is understandable that Canaan would not be Shemite, since, as Skinner (1930: 202) observes, "it was inevitable that they should find their place as remote from the Hebrews as possible."

Ham (*ḥām*) means "hot," which is an apt designation for these peoples to the south, located primarily in North Africa and the Arabian desert. The name of Ham might be a reformulation or folk etymology of Egyptian *kemet,* "the black (land)," a designation for Egypt (for other possibilities, see Goldenberg 2003: 145–49). In some psalms, Ham is an alternative term for Egypt (Pss 78:51; 105:23, 27; 106:22).

10:6. *Ham's sons were Cush and Egypt and Put and Canaan.* Cush (*kûš*) corresponds to Babylonian Kūšu, Assyrian Kūsu, and Egyptian K'š, the land of Nubia, directly south of Egypt. The Greeks called this region Ethiopia. For the homonym Cush in Mesopotamia, see NOTES at 10:8.

Egypt (*miṣrayim*) corresponds to Ugaritic *mṣrm,* Phoenician *mṣrm* and *mṣrym,* Akkadian Muṣru, and Arabic Miṣr, probably from the common Semitic word for "territory, region" (*miṣru*). The Hebrew form *māṣôr* is used for Egypt occasionally in poetry (2 Kgs 19:24; Isa 19:6, 37:25; Mic 7:12). The ending *-ayim* is probably a pseudo-locative, like *ʾeprayim* (Ephraim), *yərûšālayim* (Jerusalem), and *šāmayim* ("heaven").

Put (*pûṭ*) corresponds to Akkadian Pūṭa and Old Persian Putaya, the land of Libya, west of Egypt. Lipiński (1992: 140) suggests that this name derives from "the name of a Libyan tribe of Cyrenaica which served to designate this region during the 22nd Dynasty (ca. 950–750 BCE)."

Canaan (*kənāʿan*) corresponds to Ugaritic *knʿn,* Phoenician *knʿn,* Akkadian *kina(ḫ)u,* and probably Eblaite Ka-na-na-um. It may derive from the color of the purple dye that the Canaanites extracted from shellfish, the Phoenician purple. The Greek word *Phoinikia* (Phoenicia) probably has the same meaning. In the Bible, Canaan refers to the region of Syria–Palestine, roughly corresponding to the province of Canaan during the Egyptian Empire (Rainey 1996). The people that we call Phoenicians (after Greek usage) called themselves Canaanites.

10:7. *Cush's sons were Seba and Havilah and Sabtah and Raamah and Sabteka. Raamah's sons were Sheba and Dedan.* The sons of Cush (Nubia) are peoples in Africa and Arabia, west and east of the Red Sea.

Seba (*sebāʾ*) is a wealthy kingdom mentioned in Isa 43:3 and 45:14 along with Egypt and Cush, and in Ps 72:10 along with Sheba. It is probably to be located south of Nubia (modern Ethiopia) on the western shore of the Red Sea, which was colonized by Sabaean settlers from South Arabia in the mid-first millennium BCE. By the end of the sixth century BCE local kings ruled there, and in two inscriptions they refer to themselves as rulers of Sbʾ. The Hebrew words *sebāʾ* (Seba) and *šəbāʾ* (Sheba, see below) probably correspond to the different pronunciations of the (originally identical) sibilant in the two Sabaean kingdoms in Africa and Arabia (so W. W. Müller 1992k).

Havilah (*ḥăwîlâ*), a land known for its gold, resins, and precious stones (2:11), is probably the region of Ḥawlan in southern Arabia (modern Yemen), which is known for all of these goods (see W. W. Müller 1992d and NOTES at 2:11). In the J table, Havilah is a son of Joktan (10:29).

Sabtah (*sabtâ*) corresponds to Old South Arabian *šbwt* (Shabwat), the capital of the South Arabian kingdom of Ḥaḍramawt (biblical Hazarmaveth, a son of Joktan in the J table, 10:26). In classical sources this city is called Sabata, Sabatha, Sobota, and other variations (W. W. Müller 1992j). Shabwat was a center of the incense trade.

Raamah (*raʿmâ*), the father of Dedan and Sheba, is listed with Sheba in Ezek 27:22 as a trader in spices, precious stones, and gold. It is in South Arabia and likely corresponds to Old South Arabic *rgmtm,* probably vocalized Ragmatum, an ancient capital of the oasis of Naǵran in southwest Arabia. The earliest reference to Ragmatum is in an inscription from ca. 500 BCE (W. W. Müller 1992i). The LXX Regma indicates that the *ʿayin* of *raʿmâ* was pronounced as a *ǵhayin* (Steiner 2005). The oasis of Naǵran was a branching point on the incense route between Sheba (South Arabia) and Dedan (North Arabia).

Sabteka (*sabtəkāʾ*) probably corresponds to a city in Ḥaḍramawt named *šbkt* (Shabakat). This connection may be supported by the LXX rendering, Sabakatha. It is also possible that this name derives from a Nubian king of Egypt named Shabataka or

Shebitku, who reigned ca. 702–690 BCE. Note that the sequence of *səbā'* . . . *sabtâ* . . . *sabtəkā'* (Seba . . . Sabtah . . . Sabteka) links these names as onomapoetic siblings.

Sheba (*šəbā'*) corresponds to Babylonian Šaba', Old South Arabian Sb', the famed Sabaean kingdom whose queen visits Solomon in 1 Kgs 10:1–10, bringing with her vast amounts of gold, spices, and precious stones (probably reflecting trade relations during the Neo-Assyrian period). Sheba is mentioned several times in Babylonian and Neo-Assyrian texts beginning in the eighth century BCE. It was a wealthy kingdom in South Arabia (modern Yemen) and may have had colonies in North Arabia (Eph'al 1982: 88–89, 227–29) and the western shore of the Red Sea (see above, Seba). The reference here could be to the kingdom or to a colony near Dedan. In the J table, Sheba is a son of Joktan (10:28).

Dedan (*dədān*) corresponds to Akkadian Dadanu, Old South Arabian Ddn, an important city on the incense route in northwest Arabia (the Ḥijaz). Dedan is a prominent trader (Ezek 27:20, 38:13, where it is listed with Sheba) and is located near Edom and Tema (Isa 21:13; Jer 25:23, 49:8; Ezek 25:13).

10:8–19. Hamites (J). The J Table of Nations is only partially preserved, serving to supplement the P version (see NOTES at 10:1). R inserted this J section after the P Hamite genealogy and before the P concluding rubric (10:20). It continues from the P genealogy of the sons of Cush (10:7) and lists the sons of Egypt and Canaan. No sons of Put (10:6) are listed. We may presume that the P table included a fuller Hamite genealogy, including the sons of Put, which has been supplanted by the J section.

The style of the J table differs from that of the P table. J uses the formula "PN$_1$ fathered (*yālad*) PN$_2$, PN$_3$, etc.," varying with the passive (*yullad*), whereas P uses the formula "the sons of (*bəne*) PN$_1$ were PN$_2$, PN$_3$, etc." The J use of *yld* in the *qal* for "fathered" also contrasts with the P use of *yld* in the *hiphil* with the same meaning. The P usage is chronologically later than J (Hendel 2000).

10:8–12. This section is primarily an excursus on Cush's famous son Nimrod, who is the founder-hero of Mesopotamian kingship. The Nimrod account is an epitome of Mesopotamian royal history up to the late eighth century BCE. Several words and phrases in this section—for example, "first to be," "warrior," and "Babel"—create verbal echoes with other parts of the J primeval narrative; compare "the warriors of old" of 6:4 and the builders of Babel in 11:1–9 (note that Nimrod is a builder of cities, including Babel). These linkages are not developed in the text but create a network of associative links. These connections, and the characteristic use of the *qal* of *yld*, indicate that this is a J text.

10:8. *Cush fathered Nimrod. He was the first to be a warrior on earth.* Cush (*kûš*), brother of Egypt and Canaan (10:13–14), has the same genealogical position as Cush (*kûš*) in the P table (10:6–7). In P and elsewhere Cush corresponds to Nubia. But in 10:8 Cush, the father of the legendary Mesopotamian king, arguably corresponds to Akkadian Kaššu/Kuššu and Greek Kossaioi (Kassite) (so many commentators, see Dillmann 1897: 351; Skinner 1930: 208; Speiser 1964: 66). The Kassites ruled in Mesopotamia ca. 1600–1200 BCE, and it is plausible that their name was homologized with Nubian Cush in Hebrew tradition. Another possibility is the Babylonian city Kish (*kiš*), where kingship descended to earth according to the Sumerian King List (Y. Levin 2002). This tradition is attested in first-millennium texts, as in the Late Version of the epic of Adapa (Foster 2005: 545). This problem is difficult to adjudicate, but the Mesopotamian associations of Cush in J are patent.

Nimrod (*nimrōd*) is a Hebrew transformation of the name of the Mesopotamian god Ninurta (see van der Toorn and van der Horst 1990; Machinist 1992; Uehlinger 1999; Day 2022: 196–98). The Hebrew name reflects an original *nimrud*, which is phonetically similar to Ninurt(a). The phonetic changes are minor: nin > nim, and urt > rud (a metathesis from ur to ru, and shift from t to d). Such minor shifts are common in names borrowed across languages. Hence Nimrod is a humanized (or euhemerized) version of the Mesopotamian god Ninurta.

It is possible, as Speiser (1964: 72–73; 1967: 41–52) argues, that the legendary Nimrod is based on the famous Middle Assyrian king Tukulti-Ninurta I, and not directly on the god Ninurta. Later Neo-Assyrian kings claimed to be the "offspring of Tukulti-Ninurta" (Grayson 1996: 202). Since the god Ninurta and the king are correlated in Assyrian royal ideology, this is not a large difference. In our text, the name derives from the god Ninurta, but the deeds are those of a king.

There is also probably a semantic motive in the Hebrew form *nimrōd*, which means "we will rebel" or "let us rebel," a *qal* imperfect or jussive of *mrd*, "to rebel." This sense of the name suggests a political message regarding Mesopotamian kingship, particularly during the era of J, the Neo-Assyrian Empire. The name may be a "hidden transcript," which subtly mocks the Mesopotamian king (Hendel 2005b). As Machinist (1992: 1117) observes, the name is "a Hebrew corruption and denigrative reinterpretation."

In Mic 5:5 "the land of Nimrod" is a synonym for "the land of Assyria." This is an appropriate designation. Ninurta was the son of the god Asshur and the protector of the king in Assyrian royal ideology. Ninurta and the Assyrian king were counterparts. A Neo-Assyrian text states, "the king who stands in the chariot is the warrior king, the lord Ninurta" (Annus 2002: 26). Several names of Assyrian kings incorporate the name Ninurta, including Tukulti-Ninurta I and II, whose name means "my protection is Ninurta." Nimrod as the epitome of the great warrior reflects the tradition of the great warrior god Ninurta and his earthly counterpart, the Assyrian king.

Nimrod's achievement, "he was the first to be a warrior on earth" (*hûʾ hēḥēl lihyôt gibbōr bāʾāreṣ*), verbally echoes other "firsts" with the pattern *hēḥēl* ("begin, be first") + infinitive:

—"Then was it begun (*hûḥal*) to call on the name of Yahweh." (4:26)
—"When humans began (*hēḥēl*) to multiply." (6:1)
—"Noah . . . was the first (*wayyāḥel*) to plant a vineyard." (9:20)
—"this is what they begin (*haḥillām*) to do." (11:6)

This is a *Leitwort* sequence in the J primeval narrative, connecting these disparate stories into a history of civilization, which has both positive and negative valences (see INTRODUCTION IV).

In these respects, it is understandable that Nimrod, the Hebrew reflection of Ninurta, is the hero-founder of Mesopotamian kingship and a mighty warrior and hunter. In this Israelite tradition, the Mesopotamian god is refigured as his earthly counterpart, the Mesopotamian king. The Assyrian coloring of this legendary figure is clearest in 10:11, where Nimrod founds the kingdom of Assyria and its great cities, including Calah and Nineveh. These details reflect the time of the floruit of the Neo-Assyrian Empire, roughly contemporary with the reference in Micah to Assyria as "the land of Nimrod."

10:9. *He became a mighty hunter before Yahweh. Therefore it is said, "Like Nimrod, a mighty hunter before Yahweh."* It is possible, as Dillmann (1897: 352) and others suggest, that 10:9 is an explanatory insertion, clarifying what kind of *gibbōr* ("warrior, hero") Nimrod was—he was a "mighty hunter" (*gibbōr-ṣayid*)—and tying to it a proverbial expression about Nimrod. In any case, the image of the "great hunter" is appropriate for Nimrod, since Ninurta was the patron god of the Assyrian royal hunt and was himself a mighty hunter of mythic monsters.

The phrase *lipnê yhwh* ("before Yahweh," lit. "to the face of Yahweh") has an emphatic function, as if Yahweh is a witness to his past greatness. Compare Jonah 3:3, where Nineveh is described as "a great city before God" (*'îr-gədôlâ lē'lōhîm*). The proverb suggests that Nimrod had become naturalized in Israelite tradition, although Genesis clearly preserves his foreign (Mesopotamian) royal identity.

Nimrod's blend of warrior and hunter also reflects the mythology of Ninurta and the ideology of Assyrian kingship. In war and the hunt, as Annus (2002: 106) comments, "the king acts as Ninurta." Tiglath-Pilesar I punctuates his conquests with accounts of hunting wild animals, as in the following account: "By the command of the god Ninurta, who loves me, with my strong bow, iron arrow-heads, and sharp arrows, I slew four extraordinary strong wild virile bulls in the desert, in the land Mittani. . . . I brought their hides and horns to my city Aššur" (1.vi.58–69; Grayson 1976: 16). Shalmaneser III similarly concludes a military victory with a prodigious hunt: "The gods Ninurta and Nergal, who love my priesthood, gave to me the wild beasts and commanded me to hunt. I killed from my chariot 373 wild bulls (and) 399 lions with my valorous assault. I drove twenty-nine elephants into ambush" (6.iv.40–44; Grayson 1996: 41). As Pongratz-Leisten (2015: 246) comments, "the hunt constituted a perpetual struggle against chaos. . . . When the notion of the hunt entered Assyrian ideological discourse, it was reformulated and reconceptualized within the framework of the king's mythologization as Ninurta."

10:10. *The chief cities of his kingdom were Babel and Erech and Akkad and Calneh, in the land of Sumer.* The word *rē'šît* ("first, chief") means "first" either in temporal order or in terms of importance. Here it means the most important cities of Nimrod's kingdom. But it may also have a temporal nuance, since this is the earlier phase of his kingship, before he moves to Assyria. The temporal movement is from Babylonia (southern Mesopotamia or Sumer) to Assyria (northern Mesopotamia), which correctly sketches, in miniature, the history of Mesopotamian kingship.

Babel (*bābel*) corresponds to Akkadian Babili(m), Babylon (see NOTES at 11:9). Babylon was the preeminent city of southern Mesopotamia from the late second millennium BCE (the reign of Nebuchadnezzar I) to the late fourth century BCE (the reign of Alexander the Great).

Erech (*'erek*) corresponds to Sumerian/Akkadian Uruk, Arabic Warka. Uruk was a prominent city of Sumerian civilization (third millennium BCE) and continued to be a major cultic and urban center throughout Mesopotamian history. The legendary Gilgamesh was its most famous king.

Akkad (*'akkad*) refers to the city Akkade/Agade, capital of the dynasty of Sargon I, ca. 2300–2100 BCE, of the Old Akkadian Empire. The city gave its name to the designation of southern Mesopotamia as "the land of Sumer and Akkad," and to the name of the language Akkadu (Akkadian). It is not clear whether the city Akkade was rebuilt after the Old Akkadian period, but its name and memory were preserved in later Mesopotamian literature.

Calneh (*kalnēh*), Akkadian Kullania/Kinalua, was a prominent city in northern Syria, the capital of the state of Unqi, and (after it was conquered by Assyria in 738 BCE) the name of an Assyrian imperial province. The Assyrian conquest of Calneh is mentioned in Amos 6:2 and Isa 10:9. It is odd for north Syrian Calneh to be included along with other major cities of southern Mesopotamia, prompting Albright (1944) to propose reading consonantal *klnh* as *kullānâ*, "all of them," referring to the previous three cities. This is a plausible reading (cf. this form in Gen 42:36), given the oddity of Calneh in this list. There is also a northern Mesopotamian city named Kullunu, northeast of Nineveh, but it too would seem odd in this list. It is also possible that *kalnēh* is a Hebrew form of a more complex southern Mesopotamian city name, such as Ḥursag-kalama, although this is a minor city.

land of Sumer. The Hebrew word *šinʿār* (Sumer) refers to southern Mesopotamia, the geographical region of Babylonia. It is equivalent in meaning to Akkadian Šumeru (Sumer) but is not etymologically related. Hebrew *šinʿār* corresponds to Akkadian Šanḫar(a) and Egyptian Sangar(a), which indicate an original *Šangar(a). This was a term for Babylonia used during the Late Bronze Age (ca. 1500–1200 BCE). Zadok (1984) proposes that this name derives from a Kassite tribal name Šamḫar, although this is disputed (van der Toorn and van der Horst 1990: 4). The Hebrew use of *šinʿār* (Gen 11:2; 14:2, 9; Josh 7:21; Isa 11:11; Zech 5:11; Dan 1:2) seems to be a survival of an archaic term in the cultural periphery.

10:11. *From that land he went up to Asshur and built Nineveh and Rehovot-Ir and Calah.* The subject of the verb *yāṣāʾ* ("went out") must be Nimrod, although the grammar of the clause suggests that it is Asshur. The grammar would be more natural if Asshur had a directional *he,* meaning "toward Asshur" (*ʾaššurāh*). The directional movement is from southern Mesopotamia (the land of Sumer) to northern Mesopotamia (Assyria). The four great cities of Assyria were Asshur, Calah, Arbela, and Nineveh. In this passage Nimrod is the builder of two of these cities plus two other sites.

Asshur (*ʾaššûr*), Akkadian Aššur, refers to the region of Assyria that includes the city of Asshur. In this passage, in its geographical contrast with Sumer, the region is the main referent. The chief god of Asshur/Assyria is Asshur, a divine personification of the city.

Nineveh (*nînəwēh*), Akkadian Ninuwa, was an important Assyrian city from at least the mid-second millennium BCE. Sennacherib made it the capital of the Neo-Assyrian Empire in ca. 704 BCE, displacing Calah and Dur-Sharrukin. It remained the imperial capital until its destruction in 612 BCE (the fall of Nineveh is the subject of the book of Nahum). The prophet Jonah is sent to "Nineveh, the great city" (Jonah 1:2) to preach repentance to its wicked inhabitants. The ruins of Nineveh came to be called Nabi Yunus ("the prophet Jonah") in Arabic.

Rehovot-Ir (*rəḥōbōt ʿîr*) literally means "city plazas," that is, the public open areas inside the city gates. The corresponding Akkadian phrase is *rēbit āli*, "city plaza." Several Neo-Assyrian texts mention a *rēbit Ninuwa* ("Nineveh Plaza"), a city plaza or district of Nineveh (*AHw,* 964; Sasson 1983: 95). This or a similar Assyrian "city plaza" seems to have been taken up by Israelite tradition as a separate city. Sasson (1983: 96) suggests that it means "broadest among cities," modifying Nineveh, with *rəḥōbōt* ("broad") as a plural superlative and *'îr* ("city") as a collective singular. He admits that the preceding *wə'et* (conjunction + direct object marker) is a problem, since this indicates an object separate from Nineveh. Van der Kooij (2006: 13–14) suggests that Rehovot-Ir may refer to the city of Asshur, which is sometimes referred to in Assyrian texts as *libbu āli*, "the Inner City," after the old city center. Hurowitz (2008: 519 n. 32) suggests that it may refer to Dur-Sharrukin, which was built in or near a Nineveh district.

Calah (*kālaḥ*), Akkadian Kalḥu, was a minor Assyrian city until Ashurnasirpal II made it the capital of the Neo-Assyrian Empire in ca. 883 BCE. It remained the imperial capital until Sennacherib selected Nineveh as his capital, with a brief interruption when Dur-Sharrukin functioned as the capital. Calah was abandoned after the fall of the Neo-Assyrian Empire. In later times its mound came to be known as Nimrud (in Arabic), after Nimrod.

10:12. *and Resen, between Nineveh and Calah, the great city.* Resen (*resen*) may correspond to the Assyrian city of Rēš-Ēni (lit. "head of the spring, source"), some twelve miles north of Nineveh (see Parpola 1970: 293). But this is a minor city, and it seems odd in this sequence. It is possible that it is a cryptic reference to Dur-Sharrukin, Sargon II's short-lived capital (706–704 BCE) near Rēš-Ēni (Hurowitz 2008; van der Kooij 2006: 14–15). But this region is not "between Nineveh and Calah" (*bēn nînəwēh ûbēn kālaḥ*)—Calah is south of Nineveh. It has also been suggested that Resen derives from Akkadian *risnu* ("soaked ground"), perhaps referring to an aqueduct or canal (Lipiński 1966: 85–88). Several major canal systems are known from Assyrian sources, one in the region of Calah and another around Nineveh (Ur 2017: 24–26). Accordingly, Machinist (1992: 1117) suggests, "Resen in Gen 10:12 which is said to be between Nineveh and Calah, could well be an echo, albeit a bit confused, of one or both of these enterprises."

The final aside, "the great city" (*hî' hā'îr haggədōlâ*, lit. "it is the great city"), most naturally applies to the previous word, Calah, but it could also apply to Resen (which was not a great city). Calah was a great city during much of the Neo-Assyrian Empire, particularly the time when it was the imperial capital (ca. 880–706 BCE). Lipiński (1966: 97) suggests that this phrase specifically refers to Calah as "the chief/capital city" (cf. the expression *hakkōhēn haggādōl*, "chief priest"), in which case this passage stems from sometime between ca. 880 and 706 BCE (see also Day 2022: 205–6). The same phrase is used of Nineveh in Jonah 1:2. Some commentators suggest that this is a misplaced gloss intended to describe Nineveh but accidentally appended to the end of the verse (e.g., Skinner 1930: 212).

10:13–14. *Egypt fathered the Ludites and the Anamites and the Lehabites and the Naphtuhites and the Patrusites and the Casluhites, from which came the Philistines, and the Caphtorites.* Egypt has seven sons, a formulaic number (cf. the seven sons and grandsons of Japheth). The identity of these sons as nations or peoples is signaled by the use of the plural for each one, clarifying the ethnographic nature of the genealogy. All of the known peoples are connected to Egypt in some way—by geography or close cultural ties—with the exception of the Ludites.

The Ludites (*lûdîm*) correspond to Akkadian Luddu, Greek Lydia, the land of Lydia in central western Anatolia. Lud/Lydia is a Hamite in J but a Shemite in P (10:22). In the 650s BCE King Gyges/Gog of Lydia was allied with Egypt, which

Lipiński (1992: 150) takes as sufficient reason for Lud to be a son of Egypt in this list. But it is also possible, as many commentators conjecture, that Ludim refer to a North African people (e.g., *HALOT,* 522; Westermann 1984: 519; Wenham 1987: 224), perhaps a scribal mistake for Lubim, the Libyans (Skinner 1930: 212; Seebass 1996: 260). Jeremiah 46:9 mentions Ludim bowmen alongside warriors from Cush and Put (Libya) in the Egyptian army of Pharaoh Necho; similarly, Ezek 30:5 lists together "Nubia, Put, and Lud (*lud*)."

The Anamites (*ʿănāmîm*) are unknown. The Samaritan Pentateuch reads *ʿynmym,* which could be an exegetical rendering, "well of water."

The Lehabites (*ləhābîm*) may correspond to the Libyans, who are usually called *lûbîm* (Nah 3:9; 2 Chr 12:3, 16:8; Dan 11:43). The internal *he* may derive from an Aramaic biform (Lipiński 1992: 151).

The Naphtuhites (*naptūḥîm*) may refer to the people of the Egyptian city of No-Ptaḥ ("city of Ptah" = Memphis; see Lipiński 1992: 151–52), but this city name is not attested. Elsewhere in the Bible this city is called Nōp (e.g., Isa 19:13; Jer 2:16, 44:1). The name is more plausibly derived from *pʾ-tʾ-ḥmw,* the Egyptian term for Lower Egypt, paired with the following term for Upper Egypt (Day 2022: 179).

The Patrusites (*patrūsîm*), Akkadian Paturisi, refer to the people of Upper Egypt (Egyptian *pʾ-tʾ-rsy*). Elsewhere in the Bible this is Patros (in the singular; Isa 11:11; Jer 44:1, 15; Ezek 30:14).

The Casluhites (*kaslūḥîm*) are obscure. It is possible that they are to be identified with the people of Kolḫa, Greek Kolchoi (Colchis), east of the Black Sea, north of Urarṭu (so Lipiński 1992: 152–54), but the association with Egypt makes this difficult.

The brief aside "from which came the Philistines" (*ʾăšer yāṣəʾû miššām pəlištîm*) seems an odd detail about the obscure Casluhites. Elsewhere the Philistines are said to come from Caphtor (Amos 9:7, Jer 47:4). Hence many commentators have plausibly suggested that this explanatory aside was originally added to modify the following name, the Caphtorites. This may have been a marginal or superlinear scribal gloss, which was mislocated in subsequent copying.

The Philistines (*pəlištîm*) were among the Sea Peoples from the Aegean who settled in Cyprus and the Canaanite coast during the twelfth to eleventh centuries BCE (Stager 1995). In Egyptian documents they are the *plšt.* Their material culture was Aegean in origin, and their earliest writing system was an adaptation of Cypro-Minoan. Over time they adapted to local Phoenician and Israelite culture, while preserving some older Aegean features (e.g., the personal name Achish, perhaps meaning "the Achaean").

The Caphtorites (*kaptōrîm*) are the people of Crete, or possibly the Aegean region generally including Crete (Knapp 1995: 1438–39). The word is equivalent to Akkadian Kaptaru, Ugaritic *kptr,* and Egyptian *kftyw.* This term is primarily used in second-millennium texts. Elsewhere in the Bible, the word *kaptōr/kaptōrîm* tends to be used to refer to the distant past, as with the memory of Philistine origins in Caphtor (Amos 9:7, Jer 47:4; cf. Deut 2:23). The term *kərētîm* (Cretans) was also used, sometimes in parallel with Philistines (Ezek 25:16, Zeph 2:5). It is possible that *kərētîm* is the more common first-millennium term. Crete and the Aegean islands had abundant trade relations with Egypt, which accounts for the genealogical affiliation of Caphtor.

10:15–18. *Canaan fathered his firstborn, Sidon, and Heth and the Jebusites and the Amorites and the Girgashites and the Hivites and the Arkites and the Sinites and the*

Arvadites and the Zemarites and the Hamatites. Canaan is a Hamite in P and J. This affiliation may derive from close cultural relations or perhaps from the memory of Canaan as an Egyptian province during the Egyptian Empire (ca. 1500–1200 BCE). Canaan has eleven children—an odd number, which lacks one from the "whole" number twelve. Canaan's children are transparently ethnic groups. The first two are the Phoenicians and the Hittites, and the rest are smaller ethnic groups, marked with the gentilic ending -*î*. The last five are inhabitants of particular cities. It is possible that the entries with the gentilics are expansions to an earlier list with only two sons, Sidon and Heth (Wellhausen 1899: 13; Skinner 1930: 214–15).

Sidon (*ṣîdōn*), Akkadian Ṣidunu, is the name of a prominent Phoenician city. Here and elsewhere it refers to Phoenician people generally (Judg 3:3, 18:7; 1 Kgs 5:20, 16:31). This broader meaning is also found in Akkadian and Phoenician texts.

Heth (*ḥēt*) refers to the Neo-Hittite peoples of the first millennium, who comprised several states in northern Syria and southern Anatolia (Hawkins 1995). These descended from the great Hittite Empire in Anatolia of the second millennium. Some Neo-Hittites also lived farther south, as in "Uriah the Hittite" of David's time (2 Sam 11:3). The Neo-Hittites spoke Luwian and Aramaic. Their geographical location explains their affiliation with Canaan. Note also that Akkadian documents often refer to all of Syria-Palestine as Ḫatti.

The Jebusites (*yəbûsî*) were the ancient inhabitants of Jerusalem and its vicinity according to the biblical texts (e.g., Judg 1:21, 19:10–11; 2 Sam 5:6–8). They are listed along with the Amorites, Girgashites, and Hivites and others in the formulaic list of the dispossessed peoples of Canaan (e.g., Exod 3:8; Deut 7:1, 20:17; Josh 3:10, 9:1; Judg 3:10; similarly, Gen 15:19–21). The Jebusites are not known in extrabiblical texts.

The Amorites (*'ĕmōrî*) are one of the original inhabitants of Canaan according to the lists of dispossessed peoples (e.g., Gen 15:21, Deut 7:1). The term sometimes designated the native Canaanites as a whole. In Neo-Assyrian documents, the term Amurru designated Syria-Palestine generally (like the term Ḫatti, noted above). All these uses descend from the earlier Amorite kingdoms and peoples of the second millennium BCE (Whiting 1995).

The Girgashites (*girgāšî*) are another people of Canaan according to the biblical lists. The personal name Girgišu occurs several times in the Ugaritic Akkadian texts (del Olmo Lete and Sanmartín 2004: 308), and similar names, Grgšy, Grgšt, and Grgšm, occur in Punic texts (Lipiński 1992: 156). These names are plausibly related to the biblical ethnonym.

The Hivites (*ḥiwwî*) are another Canaanite people according to the biblical lists. They seem to be associated with northern Israel—there are Hivites in Shechem (Gen 34:2) and Gibeon (Josh 9:7). In Ugaritic the word *ḥuwwatu* means "country, land" (del Olmo Lete and Sanmartín 2004: 378–79), and therefore *ḥiwwî* may simply mean "those of the land," that is, native people (Lipiński 1992: 157).

The Arkites (*'arqî*) are the inhabitants of the city of Arka (Akkadian Arqā, earlier Irqata), located in northern Phoenicia, modern Tell 'Arqa. The city is mentioned in Akkadian texts of the second and first millennia BCE. It was prominent during Neo-Assyrian times, contributing numerous troops to the battle at Qarqar in 853.

The Sinites (*sînî*) are the inhabitants of the city of Siyan (Ugaritic Syn, Akkadian Siana and variants) in northwest Syria, modern Siano. In light of the toponymic data, the Hebrew consonantal text, *syny*, probably represents *Siyanī, "the Siyanites" (Lipiński 1992: 158). In the biblical reading tradition, the internal consonantal *yod* was taken as a *mater lectionis*.

The Arvadites (*'arwādî*) are the inhabitants of Arwad (Akkadian Arwada and variants), a northern Phoenician city. Arwad is mentioned along Sidon in Ezek 27:8–11 and is mentioned several times in Neo-Assyrian texts.

The Zemarites (*ṣəmārî*) are the inhabitants of the city of Simyra (Akkadian Ṣimirra and variants, earlier Ṣumur; Greek Simyra) in northern Phoenicia. This was also an important city in Neo-Assyrian times.

The Hamatites (*ḥāmātî*) are the inhabitants of Hamath (Akkadian Ḥammatu) in central Syria, on the Orontes River. Hamath was a major city in the first millennium—Amos calls it "Great Hamath" (*ḥāmat rabbâ*, Amos 6:2). Notably, Hamath was allied with Arka, Arwad, Siyan, Israel, and several other "kings from the seacoast" in ninth-century campaigns against Assyria (*ANET*, 278–81).

Afterwards the families of Canaan spread out. This clause anticipates the dispersion of peoples in the Tower of Babel story, but without the negative connotations. The verb *nāpōṣû* ("were spread out") is the same root (in the *niphal*) as the *Leitwort* sequence in the Tower of Babel story: *nāpûṣ* ("[lest] we be spread out," 11:4), *wayyāpeṣ* ("he spread [them] out," 11:8), *hĕpîṣām* ("he spread them out," 11:9). The proximity of this J verse to the Babel story activates this verbal link, but the following verse, listing the boundaries of Canaan, clarifies that this dispersion was within the Canaanite territory. It is an anticipatory gesture, but lacks the drama and conflict to come.

10:19. *Canaan's boundaries extended from Sidon in the direction of Gerar as far as Gaza, and in the direction of Sodom, Gomorrah, Admah, and Zeboiim as far as Lasha.* The description of Canaan's boundary extends from the north (Sidon) to the southwest coast (Gerar, Gaza) and southeast (Dead Sea region). Gaza is a few miles northeast of Gerar, and it is not clear why both are listed. Lasha is unknown but presumably is near the Dead Sea sites of Sodom, Gomorrah, Admah, and Zeboiim. Curiously, the last five children of Canaan are north of the city of Sidon—the Arkites, Sinites, Arvadites, Zemarites, and Hamatites. But since Sidon designates Phoenicia in general (see Notes at 10:15), this disparity may be only apparent.

This boundary formula marks the conclusion of the J Hamite genealogy. This formula recurs in slightly different form at the conclusion of the J Shemite genealogy (10:30). This geographical diction, with the expression *bō'ăkâ* ("in the direction of," lit. "your coming to"), recurs elsewhere in J at 13:10 and 25:18.

10:20. *These are Ham's sons according to their families, languages, lands, and nations.* This formula concludes the P Hamite genealogy (cf. 10:5, 31). The P Hamite genealogy has been truncated after the sons of Cush in 10:7, followed by the J Hamite genealogy for the sons of Cush, Egypt, and Canaan. R inserted the J material into a P framework, while omitting the redundant portion of P. This editorial decision may have been motivated by the abundant detail in the J segment.

10:21. *As for Shem, sons were also born to him. He was the father of all the sons of Eber, and he was Japheth's older brother.* This is the introduction of the J Shemite genealogy, which R has inserted directly before the beginning of the P Shemite genealogy. This "doubling" is sensible, comparable to the end of the Hamite genealogy, where R inserted the P closing formula after the end of the J segment (10:19–20). The other introductory verses in J—for the Japhethites and Hamites—have not been preserved, nor has the J Japhethite section. We may presume that these sections were deemed redundant in conjunction with P, which sheds light on R's editorial sensibilities.

The disjunctive clause "As for Shem, sons were also born to him" (*ûləšēm yullad gam hû'*) signals the beginning of a new sequence, with a focus on Shem. It echoes an earlier genealogical notice, "As for Seth, a son was also born to him" (*ûləšēt gam-hû' yullad bēn*, 4:26). This repetition seems to make Shem (*šēm*) a counterpart of Seth (*šēt*)—their names are similar, and both are the brother from whom the central genealogical branch descends.

It is not clear why Shem is qualified as "Japheth's older brother" (*'ăḥî yepet haggādôl*). He should be "Japheth's and Ham's older brother." In any case, this designation signals that the genealogy is proceeding from youngest to oldest. This fits the tendency whereby the text first addresses the collateral lineages and then turns to the main lineage.

Shem is also qualified as "the father of all the sons of Eber" (*'ăbî kol-bənê-'ēber*), which signals that the main genealogy goes through Eber, who is the eponymous ancestor of the Hebrews. It is likely that R added the phrase "all the sons of" (*kol-bənê*) to accommodate this verse with the harmonizing expansion in 10:24. On this supposition, the J text qualified Shem as "the father of Eber" (*'ăbî 'ēber*) (Skinner 1930: 218–19).

Shem (*šēm*) means "name," which suggests that this is a prestigious lineage, that is, it has a great name. The name Shem may present a positive foil to the desire of the people of Babel to acquire a name (*šēm*, 11:4) and the questionable fame of the *'anšê haššēm* ("men of renown," 6:4). This may also anticipate Yahweh's promise of a great name (*šēm*, 12:2) to Abraham, who is a Shemite.

10:22–23. Shemites (P). The Shemites are peoples to the east of Israel, including the lineal ancestors of Israel. As Skinner (1930: 304) observes, the Shemites in P "are probably arranged in geographical order from SE to NW, till they join hands with the Japhethites." As with the other portions of the P table, this genealogy is shallow, treating only two generations. It is mostly a horizontal genealogy, detailing the collateral branches of the Shemites, with special attention to Aram. The main genealogical line, which issues in Israel, will resume with a vertical genealogy from Shem to Abram in 11:10–26.

Shem's sons were Elam and Asshur and Arpachshad and Lud and Aram. Aram's sons were Uz and Hul and Gether and Mash. Elam (*'êlām*), Akkadian Elamtu, was a people and nation east of Mesopotamia in southwestern Iran. The Neo-Elamite Empire, with its capital in Susa, was a major power from ca. 750 to ca. 640 BCE (Brentjes 1995). Genesis 14 tells of King Chedorlaomer of Elam, a fictional figure whose name has an Elamite flavor.

Asshur (*'aššûr*) is a people and nation in northern Mesopotamia. In J, Asshur is a locale associated with Nimrod, a Hamite (10:11).

Arpachshad (*'arpakšād*) is a mystery. It is often identified with Babylonia, since otherwise Babylonia is not listed in the P Table of Nations. It is possible that the name consists of two element, *'rp + kšd*, with the latter as the name *keśed* (Chesed, Chaldea), designating Babylonia (Skinner 1930: 205; Lipiński 1993: 195–98). The first part could derive from Hurrian *arip-*, a common element in Hurrian personal names (Speiser 1964: 70). A connection with the Assyrian city of Arrapu has been suggested but seems unlikely (note the noncorrespondence of *ḥ* and *k*). Arpachshad is obscure, yet at the same time he is prominent as Israel's lineal ancestor in P's Shemite genealogy (see Notes at 11:10–12).

Lud (*lûd*) is Lydia (Akkadian Luddu, Greek Lydia) in central western Anatolia. In the J table, the Ludim are Hamites (10:13). By their location one would expect Lydia to be a Japhethite people, and Magog arguably represents Lydia in 10:2 (P). Lud is anomalous in the Shemite sequence.

Aram (*'ărām*) refers to the Aramean peoples and nations of Syria. Aram's four sons are Aramean peoples. In J, Aram and various Aramean peoples (including Uz) are descendants of Abraham's brother Nahor (22:20–24).

Uz (*'ûṣ*) is Aram's firstborn son, while in J he is Nahor's firstborn son (22:21). It was presumably an important Aramean town or region. Lipiński (1993: 200) suggests that a certain land of Uz (Akkadian Uṣṣa) in a chronicle of Shalmaneser III refers to a place in northern Syria, which could be the Aramean Uz. Uz is a member of the Edomite genealogy in Gen 36:28, and according to Lam 4:21, Edom "dwells in the land of Uz." Uz is also the homeland of Job (Job 1:1), which suits an Edomite locale. A Safaitic inscription refers to a tribal name *'ḍ* (= Hebrew *'ṣ*) in northwest Arabia near Edom, which may be related to biblical Uz (Knauf 1992b). The location of Aramean Uz remains open.

Hul (*ḥûl*) may refer to the Ḥuleh region of Syria, southeast of the town of Hama (Lipiński 1993: 201).

Gether (*geter*) probably refers to the Aramean region elsewhere called Geshur (*gəšûr*) (2 Sam 15:8, etc.; see Lipiński 1993: 202). This place name, literally "stronghold, fortress," comes from the root *gtr* ("be strong), which was written with a *šin* in Old Aramaic but with a *taw* in Aramaic of the seventh to sixth centuries BCE and later. This graphic and phonological shift (*gšr* > *gtr*) corresponds with the probable date of P (Hendel 2005a: 111).

Mash (*maš*) is obscure. The SP reads *mš'*, probably harmonizing with the place name *mēšā'* in 10:30 (J), while the LXX and 1 Chr 1:17 read *mešek*, a harmonization with the name *mešek* in Gen 10:2 (P) (Hendel 1998: 144).

10:24–30. Shemites (J). The J table resumes with the line of Eber, which splits into the branches of Peleg and Joktan. The text continues with Joktan's line (the collateral lineage), and Peleg's is not resumed. Presumably a J genealogy from Peleg to Abram existed but was not preserved by R because of its redundancy with the P genealogy from Peleg to Abram (11:18–26). The J source is recognizable from the distinctive formula and grammar and the concluding geographical statement (cf. 10:19). The opening verse (10:24) is probably a harmonization, composed by R to accommodate the J section with the P Shemite genealogy in 10:22 and 11:12–15 (Skinner 1930: 219–20).

10:24. *Arpachshad fathered Shelah, and Shelah fathered Eber.* This sequence—arguably a harmonizing bridge between the P and J genealogies—echoes P's vertical genealogy from Arpachshad to Shelah to Eber in 11:12–15, but it uses the *qal* of *yld* ("fathered") in accordance with J's usage. Note that elsewhere R's harmonizations combine the diction of J and P (e.g., 7:3, 8–9, 23).

Shelah (*šelaḥ*, pausal form *šālaḥ*) is from the root *šlḥ*, "to send." It may mean "offshoot, sprout" in personal names (*HALOT*, 1518). There is no evidence for a nation or ethnic group with this name.

Eber ('*ēber*) is the eponymous ancestor of the people called '*ibrî*, "Hebrew." The name is from the root '*br*, "to cross (over)." As the name of a people, it may derive from the geographical designation "other side (of a river)," as in '*ēber hayyardēn* ("the other side of the Jordan," e.g., 50:10). However, the precise nuance is obscure. In any case, the Hebrews are the descendants of Eber in the biblical genealogy and are obliquely signaled by the phrase "sons/children of Eber (*bᵊnê-'ēber*) in 10:21. The ethnic term '*ibrî* ("Hebrew") generally refers to Israelites from a foreign point of view—so Joseph is called an '*îš 'ibrî* ("Hebrew man") by Potiphar's wife (39:14), and he refers to his homeland as '*ereṣ hā'ibrîm* ("land of the Hebrews") when speaking to Egyptians (40:15). In later texts, the term '*ibrî* loses the sense of a foreign appellation, as reflected in the appellation "Abraham the Hebrew" (14:13).

Some scholars derive the term '*ibrî* from the Northwest Semitic word '*apiru* (Ugaritic '*prm*, Akkadian *ḫab/piru*), which in Late Bronze Age usage refers to bands of brigands (Weippert 1971: 63–102; Na'aman 1986). Some early Israelite groups may have been so designated. However, the vocalic pattern of '*ibrî* (a segholate *qitl* + gentilic *î*) is not easily derivable from '*apiru*, which is either a stative adjective (*qatil* pattern) or a passive/stative participle (*qatīl* pattern). The term originally may have meant "dusty one," from '*pr* ("dust"). There is no regular development from *qatil* to *qitl* in Northwest Semitic (although there are some *qatil-*qitl* biforms for body parts in Arabic and Hebrew; see J. Fox 2003: 107–8, 143, 167). Fleming (1998: 74–75) proposes that the tribal term *ḫibrum* (in Akkadian writing) is a better candidate than '*apiru* for the ancestor of '*ibrî*—note that *ḫibrum* is a *qitl* form. The word *ḫibrum* in the Mari texts refers to "a part of the tribal people who live with the flocks, outside the settled villages and towns of the kinsmen they support" (74). Under either of these proposed developments—from '*apiru* or *ḫibrum*— '*ibrî* was reanalyzed as a gentilic noun from the eponymous ancestor, Eber.

Eber, like Abraham, is the ancestor of both Israelites and Arabian peoples (Abraham is the father of Isaac, Ishmael, and the sons of Keturah). In contrast, the Arabian peoples are Hamites in the (relatively later) P table (10:7).

10:25. *As for Eber, two sons were born. The name of the first was Peleg, for in his time the earth was divided, and the name of his brother was Joktan.* Peleg (*peleg*) means "division," which is explained by the aside "in his time the earth was divided (*niplᵊgâ*)." This aside seems to anticipate the Tower of Babel story, in which the people are "spread out" (with the root *pwṣ*). *Peleg* also means "canal" and may refer to a particular site, for example, the place name Palgu (Greek Paliga) at the junction of the Ḫabur and Euphrates Rivers (Skinner 1930: 220; Day 2020: 182). The lineage from Eber and Peleg to Abraham is taken up in 11:16–26 (P).

Joktan (*yoqṭān*) is the father of various Arabian peoples. In later Muslim tradition, the ancestor of the southern Arabs was Qaḥṭān, which may be related to Yoqṭān (Winnett 1970: 181–82). Qaḥṭān was originally a South Arabian tribe. In the genealogy of Abraham and Keturah in 25:1–4 (J), Jokshan (*yoqšān*) is the father of the Arabian peoples Sheba and Dedan (25:2–3). Yoqṭān and Yoqšān are biforms, with the *ṭ/š* alternation perhaps approximating an Old South Arabian emphatic *ḍ* or *ẓ* (Halpern 1988: 312 n. 3). However, there is no such place name or ethnic designation in ancient sources.

10:26–29. *Joktan fathered Almodad and Shaleph and Hazarmaveth and Yarah and Hadoram and Uzal and Diklah and Obal and Abimael and Sheba and Ophir and Havilah and Jobab—all of these were Joktan's sons.* Joktan's thirteen sons—an odd number—are

South Arabian peoples or places, although only a few can be identified with certainty (see Winnett 1970: 183–88; Lipiński 1993: 205–13).

Almodad (ʾalmôdād) may mean "tribe (< ʾahl) of the Beloved (dd)," but there is no known place or people of this name.

Shaleph (šelep) is a South Arabian tribe referred to by Arab geographers as as-Salif and as-Sulaf, and in Minean inscriptions as Slf and Slfn (Lipiński 1993: 207). It is probably located in the region of Ḥaḍramawt.

Hazarmaveth (ḥāṣarmāwet) is the ancient South Arabian kingdom and region of Ḥḍrmwt (Ḥāḍramawt), known from Old South Arabian inscriptions. It was a frankincense-producing region and was an important kingdom from the eighth to seventh centuries BCE to the third century CE (W. W. Müller 1992e).

Yarah (pausal yārah, contextual form yerah), meaning "moon," may correspond to a place name Wrḫn in a Sabaean inscription, or (less likely geographically) a place name Yarki listed in Assurbanipal's campaign against Arab tribes (Lipiński 1993: 209–10; Ephʿal 1982: 162).

Hadoram (hâdôrām) probably corresponds to the South Arabian place name dwrm (Dawram) attested in Sabaean inscriptions. It may have been assimilated to the personal name Hădôrām ("Hadad is exalted"), found twice in the Bible (1 Chr 18:10, cf. 2 Sam 8:10; and 2 Chr 10:18, cf. 1 Kgs 12:18) (W. W. Müller 1992c).

Uzal (ʾûzāl) probably corresponds to the place name ʾAzal, which designates two different sites in South Arabia, one of which has the ruins of an old castle (W. W. Müller 1992l). Uzal refers to a different site from the Uzzal in Ezek 27:19, which is probably an Anatolian city.

Diklah (diqlâ) means "date palm" in Aramaic, and presumably refers to a South Arabian oasis or a region with date palms. W. W. Müller (1992b) observes that this plausibly refers to a place in Old South Arabian inscriptions called nḫl ḫrf, which contains the word "date palm" (naḫl), in the region around Sirwah, an important town in the early Sabaean kingdom. This region was known for its large date palm groves.

Obal (ʾôbāl) corresponds to a South Arabian tribe referred to in Sabaean inscriptions as the bnw ʾblm ("sons of ʿAbil"), whose settlement area was probably in the Yemenite highlands (W. W. Müller 1992g).

Abimael (ʾăbîmāʾēl) consists of ʾăbî ("my father") + enclitic mā + ʾēl ("God"), hence "God is my father." An early Sabaean inscription lists a tribe called ʾbm ʿṯtr, which has a similar construction: ʾab ("father") + enclitic m + the high god ʿAṯtar (W. W. Müller 1992a). It is possible that Abimael refers to this or a similar tribe.

Sheba (šəbāʾ) is listed in the P table as a Hamite (10:7).

Ophir (ʾôpîr) is a wealthy region known for its gold, fine woods, and precious stones. The gold of Ophir is referred to in several biblical texts (e.g., 1 Kgs 9:28, 10:11; 22:49; Ps 45:10; Isa 13:12) and in an eighth-century BCE Hebrew inscription (zhb ʾpr; Tell Qasile). Lipiński (1993: 212–13) plausibly identifies Ophir with the city ẓfr, attested in Sabaean inscriptions, called Ẓafār by Arab authors and identified as the capital of the ancient Himyarite kingdom.

Havilah (ḥăwîlâ) is a South Arabian land famous for its gold and precious stones (2:11–12). It is listed in the P table as a Hamite (10:7).

Jobab (yôbāb) probably corresponds to the prominent Sabaean tribe yhybb (Yuhaybab), in the central highlands of Yemen, mentioned in several Old South Arabian inscriptions (W. W. Müller 1992f). The Hebrew vocalization may be the result of assimilation to the personal name Jobab (*yôbāb*), attested in several biblical texts (Gen 36:33; Josh 11:1; 1 Chr 8:9, 18).

10:30. *Their territory extended from Mesha in the direction of Sepharah, the eastern mountain.* This geographical formula, which ends the J Shemite genealogy, echoes (with variation) the conclusion of the J Hamite genealogy (10:19).

Mesha (*mēšā'*) has the same consonantal spelling as Massa (*maśśā'*), a son of Ishmael (25:14), and may refer to the same tribe and location (Dillmann 1897: 383; and others). The tribe of Massa' is attested several times in Akkadian texts from the eighth century BCE and later and is referred to in the Bible (Prov 30:1, 31:1). It is probably to be located in North Arabia (Eph'al 1982: 218–19). According to the J table, this is the northern terminus of the Joktanite region.

Sephar (*səpār*), which seems to be identified as "the eastern mountain" (*har haqqedem*), is obscure. Lipiński (1993: 214) suggests that Mount Sephar corresponds to Mount Sabir in the highlands of south Yemen. Others identify it with Ẓafār, the capital of the ancient Himyarite kingdom (see above, under "Ophir"), which is modern 'Iṣfār or 'Isfār (Skinner 1930: 222).

10:31. *These are Shem's sons according to their families, languages, lands, and nations.* This verse is the formulaic end of the P Shemite genealogy—compare with 10:5 and 10:20. On the variations among these verses, see NOTES at 10:5. In P it would have followed someplace after 10:23, before the redactional insertion of the J Shemite genealogy.

10:32. *These are the families of Noah's sons according to their genealogy and nations. From these the peoples branched out over the earth after the flood.* This P verse concludes the Table of Nations. It frames the text by echoing and recomposing the opening verse (10:1), supplementing it with diction from the concluding formula for the three genealogies (10:5, 20, 31).

—"This is the genealogy of Noah's sons." (10:1)
—"These are . . . according to his language, families, and nations." (10:5)
—"These are the families of Noah's sons according to their genealogy and nations." (10:32)

In this structured collocation, the Table of Nations comes to a clear conclusion, with the various lines of genealogical exposition tied together.

The final statement, "From these the peoples branched out over the earth after the flood" (10:32), echoes and expands the comment in the Japhethite genealogy, "From these the maritime nations branched off" (10:5). Both have the diction "from these branched out" (*mē'ēlleh niprədû*), but in the final verse it is all nations that branch out over the earth. The term *mē'ēlleh* ("from these") also creates a temporal progression from the beginning of the verse: *'ēlleh . . . mē'ēlleh* ("These are . . . From these"). This last statement moves the end of the text from a static situation ("these are") to a dynamic movement ("from these"), as the peoples fill the earth.

The last two words "after the flood" (*'aḥar hammabbûl*) echo the last two words of 10:1 (J), providing a rhetorical frame for the composite Table of Nations. These words also provide a bridge from the previous flood story and its somber legacy. "After the flood" is the condition of all humanity since everyone descends from Noah's sons and lives on this side of the great destruction.

Comments

DOUBLETS

Like the flood story, the Table of Nations is an example of doublets that have been combined into a single text (Wellhausen 1899: 4–7; Skinner 1930: 187–89; Seebass 1996: 265–67; cf. other models in Carr 1996: 99–101; Witte 1998: 100–114; Hieke 2014: 29–30; Gertz 2018: 299–305). The frameworks of both versions are still visible, although R has shortened the J text (by omitting the Japhethite branch and the beginning of the Hamite branch) and fitted it into the P version. The distinctive styles of J and P are also evident. Some of the divergent details of the two versions are as follows:

- The peoples of South Arabia are descendants of Shem in J but descendants of Ham in P. In J they are the thirteen sons of Joktan (10:26–29), while in P they are the seven sons and grandsons of Cush (10:7). The only names in common are Havilah and Sheba, but all the names are identifiable as South Arabian peoples and locales. This difference probably stems from a different axis of relationship: In J it seems to be primarily economic, reflecting the trade with Arabia in aromatic spices and precious metals (cf. Abraham's wife Keturah, "incense," in 25:1–4, whose sons are peoples and place names in or around northern Arabia). The axis in P seems to be geographical, since Cush (Ethiopia) and South Arabia are neighbors across the Red Sea.
- Eber ('ēber), the eponymous ancestor of the Hebrews ('ibrî), seems to be the son of Shem in J (10:21), while in P he is the son of Shelah in the fourth generation after Shem (11:14–17), according to P's linear genealogy in 11:10–26 (from Shem to Abram). In both versions, Eber is the father of Peleg, but this pair exists at different genealogical depths. This difference reflects the fluidity of genealogies, particularly the "floating gap" in their middle sections (see below).
- Aram is a son of Shem in P (10:22), while in J he is a descendant of Nahor, Abraham's brother (22:21). Nahor's descendants in J (twelve in all) are all Aramean peoples, locales, or individuals. This difference indicates a shift in the perception of ethnic affinity to Aram from J to P, expressed as degrees of genealogical distance. Aram is closer to Abraham in J, probably because of closer cultural ties with Aram in the earlier monarchic era than the later era, when the Aramean polities were absorbed into imperial provinces.
- The affinities of Cush are different in the two versions. Cush is Ethiopia in P (as elsewhere), while in J it also has ties with Mesopotamia. This strange duality of Cush in J is probably due to the homonymity between Cush (Ethiopia) and Cush (Kassite, a Babylonian dynasty, or possibly Kish, where kingship descended from heaven). As noted above, Cush is the father of South Arabian peoples in P, while in J he is the father of Nimrod.
- The Shemite genealogy has a double beginning in 10:21 and 10:22, reflecting two different genealogical styles. The first is in the style of J, "As for Shem, sons were also born to him" (10:21); compare "As for Seth, a son was also born to him" (4:26, J). The

second is in the style of P, "Shem's sons were PN" (10:22); compare the beginnings of the other branches in P, "Japheth's sons were PN" (10:2) "and Ham's sons were PN" (10:6).

When we separate the two versions on the basis of divergent details, internal continuity, and literary style, it becomes clear that R has given priority to the P table for the sons of Japheth. R has carefully edited together the P and J versions of the Hamite and Shemite branches and has presented only the P version of the Japhethite branch.

Let us turn to the details of the two versions, J and P. Each is a segmented genealogy, with vertical and horizontal branching, beginning with Noah and his three sons (10:1, Table 8). This genealogy is purely patrilineal, listing only males. Noah's wife and his sons' wives survive the flood but are not mentioned in the genealogy. (Elsewhere the J genealogies often mention women, e.g., 4:17–18, 11:29, 22:20–24, 25:1–4.) As in the previous genealogies, these four males are individual persons, but their descendants are clearly the names of peoples or locales (with the exception of Nimrod, who is a person). The Table of Nations constructs an ethnographic map of most of the peoples of the world, projected back to the postdiluvian era. Later peoples—Ammon, Moab, Ishmael, Aram (in J), Edom, and Jacob/Israel—belong to later segments of the genealogy.

Table 8. Sons of Noah

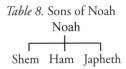

The Table of Nations proceeds in reverse order from the birth order of Noah's sons, starting with the branch most distant from Israel (Japheth) and ending with the branch ancestral to Israel (Shem). This follows the genealogical rule in Genesis that the collateral branches of the genealogy are presented, extending to the present, before returning to the central (Israelite) lineage at the point where the branches diverge (Dillmann 1897: 312). This rule explains the placement of the genealogies of Cain, Lot, Nahor, Ishmael, and Esau, before returning to the lines of Seth, Abraham, Isaac, and Jacob, respectively. So here the Japhethites and Hamites are presented before the central branch of the Shemites.

P's Japhethite genealogy (Table 9) consists of three generations, including Japheth's seven sons and seven grandsons. These are formulaic numbers. The Japhethites are peoples to the north, northeast, and west of Israel, extending from Anatolia to the Mediterranean region as far west as Spain (Tarshish).

Table 9. Japhethite genealogy in P (10:2–5)

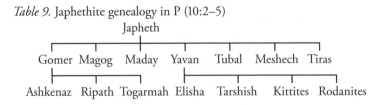

There is no counterpart Japhethite genealogy in J. We may assume that there was one, since Japheth is one of Noah's three sons in J, but R did not include it, perhaps because the P version was fuller. None of these distant peoples (from the viewpoint of Israel) plays a role in the Pentateuch (cf. the sphere of Tyrian trade in Ezek 27:12–25).

The Hamite genealogy is presented in two versions, with some overlap in P (Table 10) and J (Table 11). There are eleven descendants of Ham in P and twenty-three listed in J (including Nimrod, who is a person, not a people or locale). The beginning of this genealogy, the birth of Ham's sons, is lacking in J, perhaps because in it Ham had only three sons. J lists the descendants of Cush, Egypt, and Canaan (not Put).

As noted above, Ham's son Cush has different affinities in the two versions: in P he is the father of South Arabian peoples, and in J he is the father of Nimrod. In both versions the Hamites are in the middle distance from Israel, with the exception of the Ludites (Lydians) in J, who ought to be Japhethites. Both versions include Canaan as a Hamite. This "distancing" of Canaan probably stems from concepts of Israelite ethnicity (see below), not geographical distance.

The Shemite genealogy differs significantly in the two versions (Tables 12 and 13), with little overlap. In P Shem has five sons and four grandsons, while in J he seems to have one son (Eber, see 10:21), two grandsons, and thirteen great-grandsons. R has again fitted the J section into the P section but has preserved both introductions (10:21–22, see above).

As noted above, the Arameans are descended from Shem in P, while in J they are descendants of Nahor (22:20–24). The peoples of South Arabia are descendants of Shem in J, but descendants of Ham in P. This segmented Shemite genealogy, presented last, is a bridge to the linear Shemite genealogy in the next chapter, which branches at Terah's three sons, featuring his firstborn, Abram.

The historical horizons of the two versions of the Table of Nations can be gleaned from some of the details. For P, the sons of Japheth provide some indications. Magog is arguably a contraction from *māt gugi,* "the Land of Gog," referring to Lydia (see NOTES at 10:2). King Gugi/Gyges of Lydia reigned from ca. 680 to 650 BCE, founding a dynasty whose last king, Croesus, was defeated by Cyrus in 546 BCE. The reference to Magog seems to reflect this era, ca. 650–550 BCE (similarly Ezekiel 38). The next son of Japheth, Maday, refers to the Medes, a people of Iran, who with the Babylonians destroyed the Assyrian Empire in 612 BCE, after which the Median kingdom extended westward into Anatolia. The close kinship of Maday and Magog arguably reflects this period of Median expansion. The Median kingdom was conquered by Cyrus in 550 BCE, so the Anatolian connection for Maday seems to reflect the period from 612 to 550 BCE. It is notable that Persia (*pəras*) is lacking in the P table, which suggests that it was composed before the establishment of the Persian Empire under Cyrus (whose title was King of Anshan) and Darius I (whose title was King of Persia). From these Japhethite indications, the P table seems to have been composed sometime between the late seventh and the mid-sixth centuries BCE, the era of the Neo-Babylonian Empire.

For J, the Shemites provide some indications of historical horizons, particularly Nimrod's kingdom and the sons of Joktan. The brief history of Nimrod, whose name derives from Ninurta, the patron god of Neo-Assyrian kings, reflects details of the Neo-Assyrian Empire (see NOTES at 10:8). This corresponds to Micah's use of "the land of Nimrod" to refer to Assyria (Mic 5:5). After Nimrod goes from "the land of Sumer" in southern Mesopotamia to Assyria in the north, he builds several cities: "[he] built Nineveh and Rehovot-Ir and Calah and Resen, between Nineveh and Calah, the great

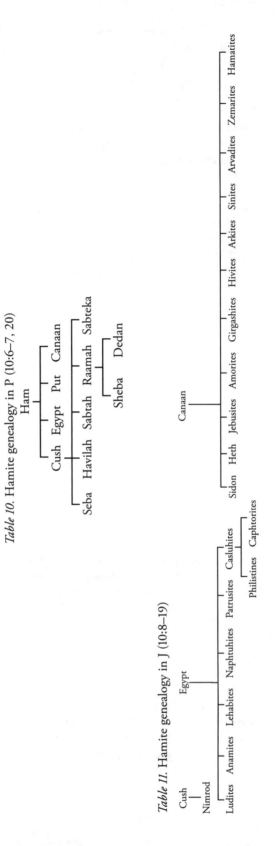

Table 10. Hamite genealogy in P (10:6–7, 20)

Ham
├── Cush ── Egypt ── Put ── Canaan
└── Cush ── Seba, Havilah, Sabtah, Raamah, Sabteka
          └── Raamah ── Sheba, Dedan

Table 11. Hamite genealogy in J (10:8–19)

Cush ── Nimrod
Egypt ── Ludites, Anamites, Lehabites, Naphtuhites, Patrusites, Casluhites ── Philistines, Caphtorites
Canaan ── Sidon, Heth, Jebusites, Amorites, Girgashites, Hivites, Arkites, Sinites, Arvadites, Zemarites, Hamarites

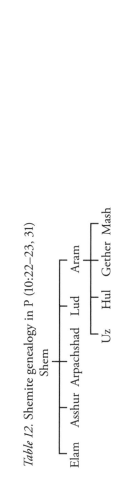

Table 12. Shemite genealogy in P (10:22–23, 31)

Shem

Elam Asshur Arpachshad Lud Aram

Uz Hul Gether Mash

Table 13. Shemite genealogy in J (10:21, 25–30)

Shem

Eber

Peleg Joktan

Almodad Shaleph Hazarmaveth Yarah Hadoram Uzal Diklah Obal Abimael Sheba Ophir Havilah Jobab city" (Gen 10:11). Nineveh and Calah were capital cities of the Neo-Assyrian Empire. According to the grammar, the last phrase, "the great city," refers to Calah, which was the capital city from 883 to 704 BCE, after which Sennacherib moved the capital to Nineveh (which had long been an important Assyrian city). Thereafter Nineveh was "the great city," as it is remembered in Jonah 1:2. Some scholars assume the phrase in Gen 10:11 refers to Nineveh, which requires some grammatical maneuvering. If we read the sentence as it stands, the J table reflects a period sometime in the mid-ninth to eighth centuries BCE (before 704 BCE), at the height of the Neo-Assyrian Empire. If we read this epithet as referring to Nineveh, the Nimrod story may reflect the later Neo-Assyrian period, from 704 to 612 BCE, with no trace of the following Neo-Babylonian period.

The list of Joktan's sons in J shows a detailed knowledge of South Arabian polities and places, probably due to the importance of the incense trade. From the eighth to sixth centuries BCE this lucrative trade was primarily controlled by the South Arabian kingdom of Sheba, with frankincense and other aromatics grown in Hazarmaveth (Ḥaḍramawt) (Breton 1999). The identifiable sons of Joktan are in this zone and reflect a knowledge of this period; hence this section of J is likely no earlier than ca. eighth century BCE, a finding that complements the implications of the Nimrod section. Material evidence of the South Arabian incense trade in the eighth century BCE has been found in the Negev, including a South Arabian inscription at Beersheba (Singer-Avitz 1999: 50–52) and the residue of frankincense on a large limestone altar at Arad (Arie, Rosen, and Namdar 2020).

As we have observed, R generally fitted the J table into the P table, while omitting or abridging several J sections, particularly the opening of the Hamites and the entirety of the Japhethites. R also added two harmonizations to fit together the two Shemite genealogies. The J table seems originally to have the sequence of Shem—Eber (10:21), while the P genealogy has Shem—Arpachshad—Shelah—Eber (10:22 + 11:10–14). To harmonize these variant lineages from Shem to Eber, R added one harmonization to the J table and one to the P. The phrase "all the sons of" (kol-bənê) was inserted into the J text, yielding "He was the father of (all the sons of) Eber" (10:21), which supplies some ambiguity about the sequence from Shem to Eber. To the P text, R added the P genealogy from Shem to Eber drawn from 11:10–14: "Arpachshad fathered Shelah, and Shelah fathered Eber" (10:24). The resulting combination of sources accommodates the J Shemite genealogy to P's longer version, with the differences in genealogical depth harmonized away.

The composite text has seventy nations as the offspring of Shem, Ham, and Japheth, which may have been R's aim. The concept of the seventy nations of the world, derived from this chapter, is somewhat unstable, since it counts Sheba and Havilah twice, once as descendants of Ham (P) and again as descendants of Shem (J). But it is a formulaic number (cf. the seventy sons of Asherah in the Ugaritic Baal myth [CAT 1.4.vi.46], and the seventy members of the house of Jacob in Gen 46:27).

LITERARY DESIGN

The literary styles and organizational structures of the two versions of the Table of Nations are evident in their frameworks. These features create links with other stories in their respective literary strata.

The P table begins with the formulaic introduction, "This is the genealogy (*tôlədôt*) of Noah's sons, Shem, Ham, and Japheth" (10:1). As elsewhere in P, this formula begins a new section of the genealogical narrative, as in 6:9 (Noah) for the P flood story and 11:27 (Terah) for the story of Abram. After this introduction, the three sections of the table use another formulaic introduction, "Japheth/Ham/Shem's sons were PN" (10:2, 6, 22). Each of the three sections ends with another formulaic sentence, which is repeated, with variation, in the final verse:

—"These are Japheth's sons by their lands, each according to his language, families, and nations." (10:5)

—"These are Ham's sons according to their families, languages, lands, and nations." (10:20)

—"These are Shem's sons according to their families, languages, lands, and nations." (10:31)

—"These are the families of Noah's sons according to their genealogy and nations." (10:32)

As is characteristic of P's style, the variations are both large and small. Ham's and Shem's differ only by a preposition (*bə* vs. *lə*). The final summarizing formula (10:32) links the ends of the three sections ("according to their . . . nations") with the opening formula by inserting "their genealogy" (*lətôlədôtām*), creating a framing *inclusio* with "This is the genealogy" (*tôlədôt*, 10:1). The final words of the table, "From these the peoples branched out over the earth after the flood" (10:32), creates a broader frame, picking up the narrative arc of the flood story.

The J table also shows the writer's characteristic style. The preserved sections of the introduction and the Hamite and Shemite genealogies have similar frameworks, including openings, closings, and general diction:

Introduction: "Sons were born to them (*yûl−ədû lāhem bānîm*) after the flood." (10:1b)

Shemite opening: "As for Shem, sons were also born to him (*ûləšēm yullad gam-hû*ʾ)." (10:21)

Eber sublineage opening: "As for Eber, two sons were born (*ûlə ʿēber yullad šənê bānîm*)." (10:25)

Hamite closing: Canaan's boundaries extended from Sidon in the direction of (*miṣṣîdōn bōʾăkâ*) Gerar as far as Gaza, and in the direction of (*bōʾăkâ*) Sodom, Gomorrah, Admah, and Zeboiim as far as Lasha." (10:19)

Shemite closing: "Their territory extended from Mesha in the direction of (*mimmēšāʾ bōʾăkâ*) Sepharah, the eastern mountain." (10:30)

The J opening formula for Shem, repeated for Eber, subtly emphasizes the importance of Eber as ancestor to the Israelites. The closing formula for the Canaanites anticipates a future geographical sequence when Lot sees the valley of Sodom and Gomorrah (13:10, J, with the rare *bōʾăkâ*). This closing formula also repeats at the end of Ishmael's genealogy, where his descendants dwell "from Havilah as far as Shur . . . in the direction of (*bōʾăkâ*)" (25:18, J).

Another *Leitwort* sequence links the J table with narratives that come before and after. The story of the curse of Canaan begins with an anticipatory aside: "These three were Noah's sons, and from them all the earth spread out (*nāpəṣâ*)" (9:18). This *Leitwort* is taken up in the genealogy of the Canaanites: "Afterwards the families of Canaan spread out (*nāpōṣû*)" (10:18). These are different roots (*nps* and *pwṣ*), but with the same sound and meaning. The positive sense of people "spreading out" after the flood and in the table changes into an anxious fear in the Tower of Babel story, when the people plan to build a great city and tower "lest we be spread out (*nāpûṣ*) over all the earth" (11:4). In consequence, Yahweh "spread them out (*wayyāpeṣ*) from there over all the earth, and they ceased building the city" (11:8). In this *Leitwort* sequence, "spreading out" (*nps/pwṣ*) takes on a doubled sense. The outcome—people spreading over the whole earth— is the same, but in the Babel story it is a consequence of human hubris rather than the natural genealogical growth of humankind. The *Leitwort* sequence binds these stories together, but it has resonances that are complicated and ambivalent, as is characteristic of the J source.

MENTAL MAPS

The Table of Nations is a mental map, merging ethnography and genealogy. This means that the descendants of Shem, Ham, and Japheth are, for the most part, the eponymous ancestors of peoples, nations, or cultural regions, such as Egypt and Canaan. Some of these descendants are not individual ancestors but are explicitly groups. In P, two of the offspring of Yavan are written in the plural, the Kittites (*kittîm*) and the Rodanites (*rōdānîm*, 10:4). In J, the offspring of Egypt are all written in the plural, for example, the Ludites (*lûdîm*, 10:13), and most of the offspring of Canaan are written with a gentilic ending, for instance, the Amorites (*hā'ĕmōrî*, 10:15). An exception to these rules in J is Nimrod, who is a person (a "humanized" version of Ninurta) and does not have children but rather founds kingdoms and cities. But Nimrod represents Mesopotamia and as such fits into the general picture. The text is an ethnographic table of peoples and nations, mapped onto the genealogy of the sons of Noah.

Some of the principles of this mental map are familiar from other traditional tribal cultures that use genealogies to organize their social relationships. Evans-Pritchard (1940: 108) elucidated some of these principles, emphasizing that the genealogies are "a projection into the past of actual relations between groups of persons. . . . [They are a means of] coordinating relationships." The genealogies encode these relationships by using concepts that he calls "structural time" and "structural distance." Structural time refers to the genealogical branching point of the common ancestor: "Any kinship relationship must have a point of reference on a line of ascent, namely a common ancestor, so that such a relationship has a time connotation" (106). The depth of time in the genealogies varies according to structural distance, which refers to "the distance between groups of persons . . . expressed in terms of values" (110). This means that groups that are at the same geographical distance may have different "structural distances" from the genealogical subject (Israel in our case) and so are nested in the genealogy at different time depths.

We can see these principles at work in the Table of Nations. Those peoples with the least structural distance from Israel have the closest common ancestor, and vice versa. Structural distance includes differing measures of geographical, linguistic, religious, and cultural distance.

The Japhethites are the most structurally distant from Israel. These are peoples of Anatolia, Iran, and the northern Mediterranean islands and coast, a geographical crescent from the northeast to the far west (Tarshish in Spain). These peoples are distant geographically and culturally from Israel and speak mostly unintelligible languages (to a Hebrew speaker). These are peoples at the extremes of the known world.

In the middle structural distance are the Hamites. These are mostly peoples of North Africa and the eastern Mediterranean, geographically to the west of Israel, with exceptions. This branch includes Ham's youngest son, Canaan. Although Canaan is geographically proximate to Israel, it is structurally distant, on the basis of perceived differences in religion, culture, and values. The proximity of Canaan to Egypt also suits its Hamite affiliation. As noted above, P places the South Arabian peoples in the middle distance (as sons of Ham), whereas J places them in closer structural distance (as sons of Shem). In J, Mesopotamia is in the middle distance (Nimrod is a Hamite), while P places Mesopotamia in closer proximity to Israel (Asshur and Arpachshad are sons of Shem). These different genealogical relationships may reflect changing perceptions of structural distance (including economic and political relationships) from the Neo-Assyrian to the Neo-Babylonian eras.

Shem, as the ancestor of Israel, is the ancestor of peoples structurally closer to Israel, geographically to the east, with some exceptions. In P, Mesopotamia and Aram are Shemites, which makes sense culturally, geographically, and linguistically. Elam is east of Mesopotamia, and so also a Shemite. Shem's other son in P, Lud (Lydia), is the odd man out, since as a people of western Anatolia he should be a Japhethite. For J, the South Arabian peoples, to the east, are sons and grandsons of Shem. This connects with the even closer structural distance of the peoples of northern Arabia (the sons of Abraham and Keturah) and the Arab tribes of the Syro-Palestinian deserts (the sons of Ishmael). As noted above, the J table expresses a closer kinship to the Arab peoples than the P table. The Arameans are also closer kin in J. The P table makes them sons and grandsons of Shem, while in J they are sons of Nahor, Abraham's brother (22:20–24). The closer common ancestor in J means in genealogical terms a closer structural distance and stronger sense of kinship.

These principles explain why the closest peoples to Israel in genealogical terms—Ammon, Moab, Ishmael, and Edom—are not listed in the Table of Nations. They branch off from the main genealogy during the era of Abraham, Isaac, and Jacob/Israel. (J includes the Arameans and the north Arabian peoples in this genealogical era.) The peoples in the table are most of the people in the world, but the latecomers—including the eponymous ancestors of Israel and its tribes—will have their day.

A degree of historical memory is mingled with the genealogy's structural time. The history of Mesopotamian kingship embedded in the Nimrod story is accurate in its general scope. Mesopotamian kingship did begin in Sumer and Babylonia and then moved north to Assyria. The large-scale sweep of Mesopotamian history (up to the Neo-Assyrian period) is accurately represented. There are old cultural memories here, in this case laced with implicit critique.

In the time scale of this genealogical map, Israel clearly remembered that it was a historical latecomer, and accordingly comes later in the genealogy than Mesopotamia, Egypt, Canaan, and other peoples and nations in the table. Most of these other peoples regarded themselves as autochthonous, as the original inhabitants of their land. Israel was aware of its belatedness in the Near East, and hence it is not a near offspring of Noah or his sons. Its origin is differently configured. As expressed in the motif of the ascent of the younger son, Israel achieves status in the world despite its belatedness. In Israel's genealogical self-fashioning, the prestige of antiquity is not available. This is an accurate historical memory. Israel's lateness in the genealogical map is compensated by divine favor, that is, by its origins as a chosen people.

CONTEXTS

The Table of Nations is recast by the Chronicler in his epitome of the Genesis genealogies in 1 Chronicles 1. The Chronicler reduces the genealogies to their essence, turning the genealogies of Genesis 5 and 11 into two sequences of names, and enclosing within them a condensed version of the Table of Nations:

—Adam, Seth, Enosh, Kenan, Mahalalel, Jared, Enoch, Methuselah, Lamech, Noah, Shem, Ham, and Japheth (1 Chr 1:1–4, cf. Gen 5:1–32)
—The sons of Japheth . . . The sons of Ham . . . The sons of Shem . . . (1 Chr 1:4–23, cf. Gen 10:2–29)
—Shem, Arpachshad, Shelah, Eber, Peleg, Reu, Serug, Nahor, Terah, Abram, that is, Abraham (1 Chr 1:24–27, cf. Gen 11:10–27 + Gen 17:5)

As Japhet (1993: 54) observes, this genealogical reduction of Genesis 1–11 is formally "an *inclusio:* a framework enclosing a central passage." The portions of the Table of Nations that are included are presented whole, with no deviations from Genesis 10. This section, Japhet comments, "provide[s] an ethnic backdrop of the 'seventy nations' of the world against which the history of Israel is about to be described" (56).

The reduction of the Table of Nations and the genealogies of Genesis 5 and 11 allows the Chronicler to move quickly to the genealogy of Israel, leading to the history of David in 1 Chronicles 10–29. The long beginning of Chronicles presents a new kind of genealogical narrative, stripped down to its pure structure.

Genealogies served as mental maps for other tribal polities and kingships in the ancient Near East. In our sources they serve to adjudicate disputes, create alliances, and establish political authority. Amorite culture of the early second millennium BCE provides many examples. For instance, genealogical ties (by marriage) are invoked by a son of an Amorite chieftain in a letter to King Bilalama of Eshnunna: "I am your brother, your flesh and blood am I. A stranger might be hostile, but I remain at your beck and call. You must therefore listen to me and thus honor me in the eyes of the Amorites" (Whiting 1995: 1235). Genealogical relationships are an index to loyalties and political favor.

A genealogy of Amorite tribal ancestors, in varying versions, is found in the opening section of the second-millennium Assyrian Royal Chronicle and the Genealogy of the Hammurapi Dynasty (Table 14) (Glassner 2004: 71–74, 136–37; Finkelstein 1966; see R. R. Wilson 1977: 86–114). The first twelve names in the Assyrian list are mostly eponymous ancestors of Amorite tribes or locales, with an admixture of other names. The correspondences between these two versions (some are double names) are indicated in the second column (Finkelstein 1966: 98–99).

Table 14. Versions of Amorite royal genealogy

Assyrian (A) Royal Chronicle	Genealogy of the Hammurapi Dynasty
1. Ṭudiya	1. Aram-madara (A5 + 6)
2. Adamu	2. Ṭûbti-yamūta (A1 + 2)
3. Yangi	3. Yamquzzu-ḫalama (A3 + 4)
4. Suḫlāmu	4. Ḥeana (A10)
5. Ḥarḫaru	5. Namzu (A7)
6. Mandaru	6. Didānu (A9)
7. Imṣu	7. Zummabu (A11)
8. Ḥarṣu	8. Namḫû (A12)
9. Didānu	
10. Ḥanû	
11. Zuabu	
12. Nuabu	

Although presented as a linear genealogy of "kings who dwelled in tents" (*šarrū ašibutū kultāri*) (Glassner 2004: 136–37), this list is probably a reworking of a segmented Amorite genealogy, whose branches cannot now be untangled. The apical ancestor, Ṭudiya, is a synonym for Amorite, while Adamu is a place name. Didānu/Ditānu is a royal ancestor at Ugarit. Ḥanû is a major tribal grouping or term for pastoralists in the region of Mari, and Namḫû is probably the Numḫa tribe known from Mari. Several sequences are rhyming pairs—Ḥarḫaru and Mandaru, Imṣu and Ḥarṣu, Zuabu and Nuabu—probably indicating an oral background. These names and their tribal/geographical referents are comparable to the names in the Table of Nations but arranged as a linear royal dynasty instead of a segmented ethnographic map.

The Tower of Babel (11:1–9; J)

---

11 ¹All the earth had one language and one set of words.ᵃ ²As they journeyed in the east they came upon a valley in the land of Sumer, and they settled there. ³Each one said to his neighbor, "Come, let us mold bricks and bake them in fire"—for bricks served as stone for them, and pitch served as mortar for them. ⁴They said, "Come, let us build for ourselves a city and a tower with its top in heaven, and let us make a name for ourselves, lest we be spread out over all the earth."

⁵Yahweh came down to see the city and the tower that the children of humans had built. ⁶Yahweh said, "Behold, they are one people with one language for all of them, and this is what they begin to do. Now there will be no restraining them from whatever they plan to do. ⁷Come, let us go down and confuse their language there, so that no one will understand his neighbor's language." ⁸Yahweh spread them out from there over all the earth, and they ceased building the city.ᵇ ⁹Therefore they call its name Babel, for there Yahweh confused all the earth's language, and from there Yahweh spread them out over all the earth.

Textual Notes

a. The LXX adds *lkl,* "for all," harmonizing with *lklm,* "(one language) for all of them" (11:6).

b. The SP and LXX add *w't hmgdl,* "and the tower," harmonizing with *w't hmgdl,* "(the city) and the tower" (11:5, cf. 11:4).

Notes

11:1–4. The Tower of Babel story has two sections, 11:1–4 and 5–9, the first section focused on the humans' words and deeds and the second on Yahweh's response. Each verse of the first section has echoes and inversions in the second, where the humans' initial linguistic and cultural unity, which leads to their ambitious plans, is reversed into linguistic confusion and global dispersion. As commentators have long noted, the narrative has a conceptual structure of "measure for measure" (*middâ kəneged middâ*, so Rashi on 11:4 and 7). The dense *Leitwort* sequences and inversions highlight the primacy of language in this story—the complexity of language is both a subject of the story and a feature of its verbal texture.

11:1. *All the earth had one language and one set of words.* This initial situation is described without judgment or comment. The verse is echoed twice in the second section as its implications unfold. The first echo occurs in Yahweh's speech in 11:6, "Behold, they are one people with one language for all of them," when he perceives the danger of their unified actions. The second echo occurs at the end of the story, when Yahweh reverses the initial unity into a permanent diversity, "Yahweh confused all the earth's language" (11:9).

The phrases "all the earth" (*kol-hā ʾāreṣ*) and "one language" (*śāpâ ʾeḥāt*) begin *Leitwort* sequences, each occurring (with variation) four times (and 11:1, 4, 8, 9; and 11:1, 6, 7, 9). The first phrase has shifts of meaning between people and geography. Initially "all the earth" signifies all people, to which Yahweh responds by spreading them "over all the earth" (*ʿal-pənê kol-ha ʾāreṣ*, 11:4, 8, 9) in a geographical sense. There is irony in these two senses of "all the earth," as the humans' desire to be forever unified is reversed by Yahweh into its other meaning, which the humans fear ("lest we be spread out over all the earth," 11:4). With these *Leitwort* nuances, the story reverses the initial situation of "all the earth," and dispersal and confusion ensue.

Similar changes are sounded in the *Leitwort* chain of "one language," as it becomes destabilized into its opposite—a diversity of mutually unintelligible languages. In 11:1 we are told that everyone speaks "one language," which is exemplified in 11:3, where people speak to each other, with particular attention to the features of the words. In 11:4 the people formulate an ambitious plan through their mutually intelligible speech. In the second section Yahweh perceives the problem stemming from "one people with one language" (11:6) and determines to confuse "their language" (11:7), which is confirmed in the conclusion, "for there Yahweh confused all the earth's language" (11:9), fusing together these two *Leitwort* sequences.

The phrase "one language" is qualified in 11:1 by an odd phrase, "one set of words" (*dəbārîm ʾăḥādîm*, lit. "one words") (see Skinner 1930: 225; Uehlinger 1990: 350–60). As Gunkel (1997: 95) observes, this phrase adds emphasis to the topic of language. In this phrase the word "one" (*ʾăḥādîm*) is in the plural to agree with "words" (*dəbārîm*) (cf. Ezek 37:17, where *ʾăḥādîm* also means "one"). There is an implicit paradox here—how can many be one? This semantic incongruity is highlighted by the repetition of the word "one" in the singular and plural—*ʾeḥāt . . . ʾăḥādîm* ("one [singular] . . . "one [plural]"). Importantly, this intimation of plurality occurs in language speaking about language. As Uehlinger (1990: 360) observes, this conveys an "aspect of relative differentiation." This tension of unity and plurality anticipates the thematics of the story, in which "one people with one language" become many.

The identity of the "one language and one set of words" has long posed a puzzle for interpreters. Since the represented speech is Hebrew, early interpreters identified this language as Hebrew (Kugel 1998: 235–37). According to Jub. 12:25–26, God instructed an angel to teach Hebrew to Abraham, thereby restoring the "language of creation." Some modern scholars have proposed that the story refers to Sumerian or

Babylonian, since the story is set in Sumer (Hamilton 1990: 350–51). Other candidates proposed include Syriac, Gaelic, Gothic, Swedish, Scythian, Cimbric, and esoteric or spiritual speech (Olender 1992: 1–11; Eco 1995: 7–33).

According to the story, Yahweh confused the original language, hence it is lost forever. It may be a primeval ideal, like the Garden of Eden, not amenable to recovery. The story represents this language through Hebrew narration, laced with Hebrew word-plays, so it is reasonable for early interpreters to infer that the lost language is Hebrew. But this is an effect of the narration—like foreigners speaking accented English in an American film. In any case, this pertains to the paradox of a story told in an intelligible language about a lost original language.

11:2. *As they journeyed in the east they came upon a valley in the land of Sumer, and they settled there.* This clause begins with *wayhî*, as does 11:1. It is unusual for two successive clauses to have this structure, since it often serves to introduce a new episode or story. Some commentators take this as a clue that two different texts have been combined (e.g., Skinner 1930: 224; Seybold 1976: 458–59; cf. Gunkel 1997: 94–95). However, as Uehlinger (1990: 312) observes, this is not a cogent argument, since the grammatical function differs in the two verses. In 11:1 *wayhî* introduces a new narrative discourse ("and it was that . . ."), and in 11:2 *wayhî* + *bə* + infinitive introduces a temporal clause, ("when, as . . ."), which provides the background for the punctual action that follows. The two *wayhî* clauses provide background for the narrative in complementary ways.

The word *miqqedem* ("in the east") means "off in the east," with a partitive nuance for the preposition *min,* as in several other passages with the same form (2:8, 12:8, and 13:11, all J; see BDB, 578). As in 2:8, there is also a resonance of "in antiquity," since *miqqedem* can have both meanings, and this is the temporal setting of the story. The use of this word recalls its earlier uses—the location of Eden "in the east" (2:8), the monsters who stand guard "east of the Garden of Eden" (3:24), and Cain's wanderings "east of Eden" (4:16). The east is the location of human beginnings.

The people "came upon a valley in the land of Sumer." This is the Tigris–Euphrates Valley, which the Greeks called Mesopotamia ("Between the Rivers"). The word "Sumer" (*šinʿār*) corresponds in meaning to the Akkadian Šumeru, "Sumer," although the two words are not cognate (see NOTES at 10:10). Sumer is the southern region of Mesopotamia. The story acknowledges the great antiquity of Mesopotamian civilization, although it inverts the Mesopotamian pride in its heritage by making its most famous city a symbol of shame rather than pride. This locale sets the stage for the naming of the city of Babel in 11:9.

The settling of humans in one place—"they settled there (*šām*)"—is undone in the second section. In 11:7 Yahweh says, "let us . . . confuse their language there (*šām*)," and in 11:8 "Yahweh spread them out from there (*miššām*)." These repetitions combine, with variations, in the concluding summary: "there (*šām*) Yahweh confused all the earth's language" and "from there (*miššām*) Yahweh spread them out" (11:9). As Cassuto (1964: 233) observes, there is an alliteration of *šin*'s in the sequence *šinʿār wayyēšəbû šām* ("Sumer, and they settled there") and in the later repetitions of *šām* ("there") and *šēm* ("name," 11:4, 9).

11:3. *Each one said to his neighbor, "Come, let us mold bricks and bake them in fire"—for bricks served as stone for them, and pitch served as mortar for them.* The opening frame for the speech—*wayyō᾽mərû ᾽iš ᾽el-rē᾽ēhû* ("each one said to his neighbor")—emphasizes the proximity of the humans, the ease with which they speak, and even the sense of an identical speech spoken by each one. Their one language and one set of words yield one repeated discourse. The word *rē᾽ēhû* means "his friend, companion, neighbor," and all these senses seem to be conveyed. The easy ability of humans to speak to each other is reversed in the second part, with Yahweh's decision to confuse their language so that "no one will understand his neighbor's language" (*lō᾽ yišmə᾽û ᾽iš śəpat rē᾽ēhû,* 11:7).

The brief speech and the narrator's explanatory aside are filled with alliteration and verbal play, foregrounding the workings of language. The request "Come, let us mold bricks and bake them in fire" (*hābâ nilbənâ ləbēnîm wəniśrəpâ liśrēpâ*) has assonance and rhyme, with four of the five words ending with the same vocalic shape (*bâ, nâ, pâ, pâ*). The clauses *nilbənâ ləbēnîm* (lit. "let us brick bricks") and *niśrəpâ liśrēpâ* (lit. "let us fire with fire") both use the same root for the verb and noun and the same verbal pattern, creating a dense circularity of sound and meaning. The hailing word, *hābâ* ("Come"), introduces the sentence and rhymes with the other verbs. It is as if this were a perfect language, in which sound and meaning correspond naturally.

The narrator's explanatory aside—"for bricks served as stone for them, and pitch served as mortar for them"—introduces the issue of translation; that is, it annotates the speech for the comprehension of its audience. The details concern the materials used for architecture in Mesopotamia versus Israel. Bricks baked in fire (i.e., kiln-fired mud-bricks) were the durable building material used in southern Mesopotamia, since stone deposits were rare and forests nonexistent (Moorey 1994: 302–32). In Israel, stone was plentiful and was the preferred building material; so the narrator translates the Mesopotamian custom into Israelite terms—*they* use baked bricks joined together with pitch, whereas *we* use stone joined together with clay-based mortar.

With this explanatory aside, the story adds authentic detail to the Mesopotamian setting, and at the same time it foregrounds the linguistic dimension. The words in the speech correspond to *their* culture, which must be translated to be comprehensible in *our* culture. The difference of cultures and lexicons is intimated in this aside, bringing our attention momentarily to the differentiated world that is the outcome of the story.

The people's call, *hābâ nilbənâ* ("Come, let us mold"), echoes in the second section in Yahweh's call, *hābâ . . . wənābəlâ* ("Come . . . let us confuse," 11:7). The first verbs are the same and the second are near anagrams, with the letters *lb* reversed and two *n*'s reduced to one. Hence making bricks (*nilbənâ*) turns to making confusion (*nābəlâ*). In this way Yahweh transposes the human speech to yield his precisely appropriate response.

11:4. They said, "Come, let us build for ourselves a city and a tower with its top in heaven." The continuation of the speech brings the seemingly benign intention expressed in 11:3 to a new level, as the plan becomes more ambitious. This intensification is expressed in a vertically ascending sequence: "city" to "tower" to "top" to "heaven." The movement is from human geography upward to the divine world.

In the context of stories where becoming "like gods" is prohibited (2:4–3:24) and sex and marriage with the Sons of God lead to dire consequences (6:1–4), the human ascent to heaven is potentially alarming, as Yahweh makes clear in his response. The human desire is not motivated solely by the quest for honor ("make a name"), but also by a sense of vulnerability ("lest we be spread out"). The story seems to suggest that human ambition is a complicated mixture of pride and anxiety.

The two segments of speech in 11:3–4 each begin with *wayyōʾmərû . . . hābâ* ("They said . . . 'Come'"), followed by cohortative verbs. Some commentators take this repetition as an indication that the two speeches stem from different stories or different phases of composition (e.g., Westermann 1984: 546; Uehlinger 1990: 310, 329–30). In view of the thematic connections of the two speeches, I think this explanation is unnecessary. It is preferable to take the beginning of 11:4 as a resumptive repetition, returning the narrative to the humans' speech after the narrator's aside in 11:3b. The deliberate repetition of a sequence to resume a previous narrative thread is a common technique in biblical narrative.

The call *hābâ nibneh* ("Come, let us build") adds to and echoes the previous call, *hābâ nilbənâ* ("Come, let us mold"), and differs by a single *lamed* in the cohortative verb. The idea of building something occurs naturally after making bricks, and the sounds of the words flow naturally. This call to "build" echoes in the second section with Yahweh's perception of what the humans had "built" (*bānû*, 11:5) and in the consequence that they ceased "building" (*libnōt*, 11:8).

The plan to build "a city and a tower" (*ʿîr ûmigdāl*) evokes the landscape of Mesopotamia, where the city walls and temple towers seem to rise from the plain. As Edzard (1987: 14) observes, "Anyone travelling through flat and level Babylonia and approaching a city would already see from a great distance something high, gigantic, mountain-like rising up." The word *migdāl* ("tower, citadel") refers to the Mesopotamian temple tower or ziggurat (Akkadian *ziqqurratu;* Kellermann 1997; cf. Uehlinger 1990: 376–77). Speiser (1967: 59) has suggested that the phrase *ʿîr ûmigdāl* should be seen as a hendiadys, "city crowned by a tower," which is possible but not necessary. The phrase "city and tower" recurs in Yahweh's perception of the situation in 11:5, but when the humans cease their work, only "the city" is mentioned (see NOTES at 11:8).

The phrase *rōʾšô baššāmayim* ("its top in heaven") has some ambiguity since it can be a literal description or hyperbolic (see Uehlinger 1990: 378–80). The literal sense is found in Jacob's dream, where he sees a stairway with "its top reaching to heaven" (*rōʾšô maggîaʿ haššāmáymâ*, 28:12) on which angels travel between heaven and earth. The figurative or hyperbolic meaning is found in the description of Canaanite cities in Deut 1:28 and 9:1, where the spies see "great cities with fortifications up to heaven (*baššāmayim*)." Jeremiah uses a similar hyperbole in his threat to Babylon: "Even if Babylon should ascend to heaven, / if she fortify her strong heights" (Jer 51:53). These are figurative uses of the expression "reaching to heaven," like our word "skyscraper."

For the temples and temple towers of the ancient Near East, the trope of reaching to heaven mingles the literal and the hyperbolic. They are cosmic bonds between heaven and earth, even if they do not physically reach heaven. For instance, the ziggurat of Eridu is named "Eunir ["House-ziggurat"], which has grown high, (uniting) heaven and earth" (Sjöberg and Bergmann 1969: 17). As Edzard (1987: 15) observes, "the reference to the heavens has a deeper meaning. They describe the cosmic function of the shrine. . . . [T]he temple is a link between heaven and earth: thus *dur-an-ki,* 'link of heaven and earth' is the name of the holy quarter in Nippur."

Figure 12. Tower of Babel stele (George 2011). King Nebuchadnezzar II stands before a plan and profile of the restored ziggurat. The inscription to the left reads, "Etemenanki, the ziqqurrat of Babylon." From relief (detail restored) on basalt stele (sixth century BCE), Schøyen collection, Oslo. (Drawing by William H. C. Propp)

The ziggurat of Babylon was named Etemenanki, "House, Foundation of Heaven and Earth." It was a seven-storied temple tower with Marduk's shrine at the top. In a foundation cylinder (sixth century BCE), Nebuchadnezzar II described his plan to restore this ziggurat: "Etemenanki, to raise its top to heaven" (*Étemenanki ana ullîm rēšiša šamāmī;* Uehlinger 1990: 224; George 2011: 166). This inscription drew on old language. Already in the late third millennium BCE King Gudea of Lagash described the temple Ebabbar in these terms: "the house has raised its top to heaven" (Edzard 1987: 15). A recently published stele has a relief of Nebuchadnezzar facing the newly restored ziggurat of Babylon (see fig. 12).

"let us make a name for ourselves, lest we be spread out over all the earth." This cohortative clause is in sequence with the previous one, "Let us build. . . ." It may convey a sense of purpose or result, *"so that* we may make a name for ourselves" (*IBHS* §34.6). While the grammar suggests a causal link, the logical connection between the two clauses is clear—great deeds establish a great name. For example, because of Yahweh's great deeds at the exodus, "You made yourself a name" (Jer 32:20; similarly, Isa 63:12, Neh 9:10). Making a name implies fame, glory, and remembrance by future generations.

In our verse, the alliteration of šāmayim ("heaven") and šēm ("name") confirms this sense—a tower with its top in šāmayim will secure their šēm.

In Israel and the ancient Near East, kings established a lasting name by their great building projects (Uehlinger 1990: 380–96). The fame of Solomon rests in part on his construction of the Jerusalem temple (1 Kings 6–8), as does that of Gilgamesh on his construction of the great walls of Uruk (*Gilg.* I.11–21). As Ben Sira writes, "Children and the building of a city establish one's name" (Ben Sira 40:19). These are human forms of immortality. The building project in Babel is a way to establish a name that transcends the lifespans of its builders, establishing a kind of immortality.

The humans are motivated not only by a desire for fame, but also by a fear of disunity and dispersion. Desire and fear are mingled in their plan. In the second part, Yahweh reverses their plan and instantiates their fears—dispersal, anonymity, disunity. The people's words, "lest we be spread out over all the earth," recur in the narrator's voice when "Yahweh spread them out from there over all the earth" (11:8), and echo again in the concluding summary (11:9). The people's fear becomes the seed of its realization. In the narrative grammar, the people's motive clause ("lest we be spread out") becomes Yahweh's result clause ("Yahweh spread them out"), without the negation ("lest").

11:5–9. The second section effects a shift of perspective from the words and deeds of the human builders to those of Yahweh. The humans are objects of Yahweh's perception and plan, which decisively counters the humans' plan. Yahweh creates new conditions to limit the scope of human power, yielding the multiplicity of languages and civilizations that exist in the present world.

11:5. *Yahweh came down to see the city and the tower that the children of humans had built.* The background image is of Yahweh dwelling in heaven. The moment when "Yahweh came down" (*wayyēred yhwh*) from heaven toward earth neatly reverses the verticality from earth to heaven in the humans' plan and shifts the perspective to Yahweh's "sight." As Cassuto (1964: 244–45) observes, "they imagined that the top of their tower would reach the heavens, but in God's sight their gigantic structure was . . . a terrestrial not a celestial enterprise." The statement of Yahweh's descent "to see" (*lirʾōt*, i.e., to investigate) human misdeeds recurs in the Sodom and Gomorrah story, "I will go down so that I may see" (*ʾērădâ-nnāʾ wəʾerʾeh*, 18:21, J).

The phrase "the city and the tower" echoes the human words in 11:4, but now they are known and definite ("*the* city and *the* tower") and can be seen. This is the first of many verbal echoes that bind the first and second sections, reframing the human speech from Yahweh's perspective.

The comment "that the children of humans had built" (*ʾăšer bānû bᵊnê hāʾādām*) is alliterative, bringing attention to the linguistic interpenetration of sound and meaning. This sequence echoes the human words "let us build for ourselves" (*nibneh-llānû*, 11:4) but adds an ominous note as it shifts to Yahweh's perspective. The term for humans is *bᵊnê hāʾādām* ("sons/children of humans/Adam"), which subtly evokes their first ancestor. The transgression of the human/divine boundary by the first humans is now, in a sense, recapitulated by their descendants. What once was an individual breach of boundaries is now a collective breach, as humans attempt to ascend to heaven.

11:6. *Yahweh said, "Behold, they are one people with one language for all of them, and this is what they begin to do. Now there will be no restraining them from whatever they plan to do."* Yahweh now perceives the scope of the human plan. The formal structure of this verse—*wayyōʾmer yhwh hēn . . . wə ʿattâ . . .* ("Yahweh said, 'Behold . . . Now . . . '")—is the same as in the Eden story, *wayyōʾmer yhwh . . . hēn . . . wə ʿattâ . . .* ("Yahweh . . . said, 'Behold . . . Now . . . ,'" 3:22). In both places Yahweh perceives the danger of the human situation, which in Eden could lead to humans becoming immortal by eating from the Tree of Life. Here Yahweh sees the danger of similarly catastrophic results, and so he resolves to confuse their speech and scatter them. Yahweh's perception of the implications of human deeds in Babel echoes the comparable moment in Eden, aligning the first and last stories in the J primeval narrative.

The sequence "they are one people with one language for all of them" echoes the opening, "all the earth had one language" (11:1), but with a small change. Now Yahweh sees them as "one people (*ʿam ʾeḥād*) with one language (*śāpâ ʾaḥat*)." This perception, from Yahweh's perspective, of "one people" motivates his reversal of their situation into a multiplicity of peoples and languages.

In his diagnosis of the problem—"Now there will be no restraining them from whatever they plan to do"—Yahweh does not elucidate precisely what the transgression is. This ambiguity allows for many interpretations. The only clearly objectionable part of the humans' plan is that the tower will have "its top in heaven" (11:4; cf. Hiebert 2007: 37–38). The implication is that only divine beings—Yahweh and other divinities, such as the Sons of God—may cross between heaven and earth. By attempting to do so, the humans are attempting to transgress the proper boundary between the divine world and the human world. (Note also the implicit criticism of the ideology of Babylonian temple towers; see Comments.) Yahweh determines to safeguard this separation, as he does in the Garden of Eden story.

The clause *kōl ʾăšer yāzəmû la ʿăśôt* ("whatever they plan to do") echoes Yahweh's earlier words in the verse, *zeh haḥillām la ʿăśôt* ("this is what they begin to do"), but shifts them into the future tense, anticipating an endless expansion of the humans' ambitious and disruptive plans.

11:7. *Come, let us go down and confuse their language there, so that no one will understand his neighbor's language.* Yahweh's decision to confuse the people's language echoes the form of the people's previous speech in 11:3–4. In each case the imperative sequence consists of *hābâ* ("come") followed by two cohortative verbs, "Let us X . . . and Y." Yahweh's speech also has an elegant rhythm. The first three words, *hābâ nērədâ wenābəlâ* ("Come, let us go down and confuse"), each end with the same sound—*bâ, dâ, lâ.* The next two words, *šām śəpātām* ("their language there"), begin with sibilants and end with *ām,* creating a two-part rhyme. Here we see Yahweh as the master of language, who reverses the people's previous words. The word *ñabəlâ* ("let us confuse") is a near-anagram of *nilbənâ* ("let us mold [bricks]," 11:3), showing Yahweh's ability already to confuse their speech. Again, the story foregrounds the topic of language through rhyme, alliteration, and other linguistic devices.

Although this divine speech echoes the prior human speech, where "each one said to his neighbor, 'Come, let us . . . '" (11:3), it is not entirely clear whom Yahweh is addressing. In the context of Yahweh's plural address in Eden, "Behold, the human has become like one of us" (3:22), and the plural address in the P creation story, "Let us make humans in our image, according to our likeness" (1:26), it is most plausible to understand Yahweh's plural address here as directed to his divine assembly. This is the heavenly host, consisting of Sons of God, angels, and assorted other lesser deities (cf. 1 Kgs 22:19; Isaiah 6; Ps 82:1; etc.). As in the previous plural addresses, the speech is followed by Yahweh's solo actions. Having announced his intention to his heavenly court, God acts on his own authority.

There is some friction between Yahweh's injunction, *nērədâ* ("Let us go down"), and the previous statement, *wayyēred yhwh* ("Yahweh came down," 11:5). Both are forms of the verb *yrd*, "to go down." Some scholars take this repetition as a clue that two different versions or layers of tradition have been combined here (so Gunkel 1997: 94; Skinner 1930: 227; Westermann 1984: 540). It is perhaps easier to see this as another repetition with dramatic effect, resuming Yahweh's act of "going down" from heaven to earth, which counters the humans' problematic plan to ascend from earth to heaven.

The motive, "so that no one will understand [lit. 'hear'] his neighbor's language" (*'ăšer lōʾ yišmə'û 'îš śəpat rē'ēhu*), echoes and reverses the speech situation in which "each one said to his neighbor" (*wayyōʾmərû 'îš 'el-rē'ēhû*, 11:3). The previous ease of speech will be countered by the institution of linguistic and geographical difference.

11:8. *Yahweh spread them out from there over all the earth.* Following Yahweh's speech about confusing their language, he moves to scatter the people across the earth. This logical swerve may be a seam between two narratives or traditions (so many commentators) or may be an associative link between confusing their language and scattering them. That is to say, the problem of "one people with one language" (11:6) is resolved by scattering the people and confusing their language. Yahweh's two actions are complementary but unfold serially. One of these is spoken of in 11:7, the other is accomplished in 11:8, and both are linked in the concluding summary in 11:9. This is arguably a literary effect, using ellipsis and association. The fulfillment of Yahweh's plan also has linguistic complexity, which is resolved in the concluding verse.

The report of Yahweh's action in 11:8 echoes the people's speech in 11:4, "lest we be spread out over all the earth." In this story words have consequences. The people's words are fulfilled in a manner precisely opposite their intention. The people's speech is, in this respect, the seed of their undoing.

they ceased building the city. This clause echoes and reverses the humans' speech, "Let us build for ourselves a city and a tower" (11:4). Interestingly, the tower is not mentioned here; however, their association is established in the repetition of "city and tower" in 11:4–5. The focus now turns to the city, whose name is the subject of the following clause. The tower, which was previously prominent because of "top in heaven," is now in the background as a feature of the infamous city. This technique of shifting focalization between associated objects is a frequent feature of biblical narrative (e.g., the two trees in Eden).

11:9. *Therefore they call its name Babel, for there Yahweh confused all the earth's language, and from there Yahweh spread them out over all the earth.* The etiology of Babylon is the final gesture of the story. This summarizing conclusion brings together the topics of 11:7–8, the confusion of languages and the scattering of the people, situating them in relation to the infamous city. Only here is the identity of the city revealed.

Babel (Akkadian Bābilim; Greek Babylon) was the most famous Mesopotamian city of first millennium BCE, rising to prominence around 1100 BCE under Nebuchadnezzar I. He may have built Etemenanki, the ziggurat of the temple of Marduk in Babylon (von Soden 1985). The city and its ziggurat were destroyed and restored multiple times during the first millennium BCE, until their final demise after Alexander the Great. The name of Babylon was understood to mean "the gate of god" (*bāb-ilim*) in Akkadian, although this was probably a folk etymology of a pre-Akkadian toponym (Gelb 1994: 268).

The biblical explanation of the name of the city is a satirical wordplay. The name is *bābel* (Babel) because there Yahweh *bālal* ("confused") the world's original language. In biblical narrative, the name of a thing highlights the essence of that thing, so the great city is portrayed as a place of confusion. This politically charged etiology merges the distant past with the present, as Babylon existed in Israelite times as a famous city. In this temporal shift, the myth becomes a subtle geopolitical critique. Babel, signifying confusion, is an ironic name for the great Mesopotamian city. The founders of the city of Babylon, who desired fame—a lasting name—achieved instead a name of infamy.

The assonance of *šemāh* ("its name"), *šām* ("there"), and *miššām* ("from there") in 11:9 emphasizes the name and locale of Babylon, the geographical site of primal transgression and punishment. The confusion and dispersal occurred "there," pointing to Babylon and "its name." According to the temporal frame of the story, the city and its tower lay in ruins, as it had many times since. But it was Yahweh who first ruined Babylon—perhaps a vicarious triumph for a people under Mesopotamian rule.

The last phrase in this story, "all the earth" (*kol-hā ʾāreṣ*), occurs twice in 11:9, bringing together both meanings of geography and population. In the last clause it refers to the geography of "all the earth," and in the previous clause it refers to its people, "all the earth's language." These phrases echo previous repetitions and create an envelope structure with the opening, "all the earth" (11:1). This is a story about how "all the earth" changed from a primal unity—of culture, geography, language, and plans—to the present diversity and divisions. The messiness of the human world—our cultural rivalries, our inability to communicate with our neighbors, and even the infamy of Babylon—is the unintended result of our ancestors' desires. "All the earth" now means something different from what it meant at the beginning of the story, even as it repeats the same words.

Comments

The Tower of Babel story is about the origins of the multiplicity of languages and peoples across the earth. It explains how these features of the world came into their present form. But the story is not simply an explanation of causes (etiology). It is also a profile of human anxiety and hubris, a warning about the dangers of civilization, and a linguistic echo chamber that focalizes language. It also has a partially submerged political message, criticizing by verbal mimicry the empire whose most fabled city was Babylon. The collective transgression at Babel echoes the transgression of the first couple in Eden with the attempt to broach the boundary of divine and human and the resulting expulsion and exile into the present world. The transgression at Babel continues to resonate in the present, as communication is marked by babbling confusion among scattered peoples.

LITERARY DESIGN

The Tower of Babel story, only nine verses long, is a literary gem (see Fokkelman 1991: 11–46; Weinfeld 1982: 82–83; Baden 2009b). As a narrative about language, it utilizes language in a sophisticated and deliberate way, using all the effects of the J author, including *Leitwort* repetitions, a balanced literary structure, and speeches laced with irony and moral complexity. It is a brilliantly imagined short work, drawing on traditional themes and motifs, and with a subtle political edge.

The story's structure has two matching sections and a conclusion. The first section (11:1–4) focuses on the human world and human speech, and the second section (11:5–8) shifts the focus to Yahweh's perspective and his speech and punishment. After this zigzagging between earth and heaven and their respective agents, the final verse (11:9) ties the threads together in a concluding summary. The verbal correspondences and variations that echo in these sections include the following, some in combination. Each varying construction is listed separately.

Language (śāpâ)
"one language" (śāpâ 'aḥat, 'eḥāt in pause, 11:1, 6), sections 1 and 2
"their language" (śəpātām, 11:7), section 2
"his neighbor's language" (śəpat rēʿēhû, 11:7), section 2
"all the earth's language" (śəpat kol-hāʾāreṣ, 11:9), conclusion

Earth, land (ʿereṣ)
"all the earth" (kol-hāʾāreṣ, 11:1, 9), section 1 and conclusion
"over all the earth" (ʿal-pənê kol-hāʾāreṣ, 11:4, 8, 9), sections 1, 2, and conclusion
"land of Sumer" (ʾereṣ šinʿār, 11:2), section 1

One (ʾeḥād/ʾaḥat)
"one language" (śāpâ 'aḥat/'eḥāt, see above), sections 1 and 2
"one set of words" (dəbārîm 'ăḥādîm, 11:1), section 1
"one people" (ʿam ʾeḥād, 11:6), section 2

One person (ʾîš) + his neighbor (rēʿēhû)
"each one . . . to his neighbor" (wayyōʾmərû ʾîš ʾel-rēʿēhû, 11:3), section 1
"no one . . . his neighbor's language" (lōʾ yišməʿû ʾîš śəpat rēʿēhû, 11:7), section 2

Come, let us (hābâ + cohortative)
"Come, let us mold bricks" (hābâ nilbənâ, 11:4), section 1
"Come, let us build" (hābâ nibneh, 11:5), section 2
"Come, let us go down" (hābâ nērədâ, 11:7), section 2

City and tower (ʿîr + migdāl)
"a city and a tower" (ʿîr ûmigdāl, 11:4), section 1
"the city and the tower" (ʾet-hāʿîr wə ʾet-hammigdāl, 11:5), section 2

To build (bnh)
"let us build for ourselves" (nibneh-llānû, 11:4), section 1
"the children of humans had built" (bānû bənê hāʾādām, 11:5), section 2
"they ceased building" (wayyaḥdəlû libnōt, 11:8), section 2

Name (šēm)
"Let us make a name" (naʿăśe-llānû šēm, 11:4), section 1
"they call its name" (qārāʾ šəmāh, 11:9), conclusion

There (šām)
"they settled there" (wayyēšəbû šām, 11:2), section 1

"confuse their language there" (*wənābəlâ šām*, 11:7), section 2

"spread them out from there" (*wayyāpeṣ . . . ʾōtām miššām*, 11:8), section 2

"there confused" (*šām bālal*, 11:9), conclusion

"from there spread them out" (*ûmiššām hĕpîṣām*, 11:9), conclusion

To spread out (*pwṣ*)

"lest we be spread out" (*pen-nāpûṣ*, 11:4), section 1

"Yahweh spread them out" (*wayyāpeṣ yhwh*, 11:8), section 2

"Yahweh spread them out" (*hĕpîṣām yhwh*, 11:9), conclusion

To confuse (*bālal*)

"let us confuse" (*nābəlâ*, 11:7), section 2

"Yahweh confused" (*bālal yhwh*, 11:9), conclusion

In addition to these multiple echoes, the first and last verses (11:1, 9) form a frame around the whole. The first verse has "all the earth" (*kol-hāʾāreṣ*) and "one language" (*śāpâ ʾeḥāt*), and the last verse has "all the earth's language" (*śəpat kol-hāʾāreṣ*) and "over all the earth (*ʿal-pənê kol-hāʾāreṣ*), creating a movement from one people in one place with one language to many peoples and languages spread out over all the earth. The phrase "all the earth" (*kol-hāʾāreṣ*) has a mobile meaning in this framework, shifting from people in 11:1 and 9a to a spatial focus, "over all the earth" (echoing 11:4 and 8). This semantic mobility subtly displays the mobility of language itself, as language and people become spread across the earth at the story's end.

Intermingled with the echoing diction are many untranslatable sound-plays, as in the following instances of alliteration:

—*nilbənâ ləbēnâ wəniśrəpâ liśrēpâ* ("let us mold bricks and bake them in fire," 11:3)

—*hallabēnâ lə ʾeben wəhaḥēmar . . . laḥōmer* ("bricks as stone, and pitch . . . as mortar," 11:3)

—*bānû bənê hā ʾādām* ("the children of humans had built," 11:5)

—*šām śəpātām* ("their language there," 11:7)

—*bābel . . . bālal* ("Babel . . . confused," 11:9)

These verbal and sonic repetitions, in varying forms and constructions, compose much of the text. They are indicated below by italics. The whole narrative is, in a sense, constructed as an echo chamber of language:

Section 1

All the earth had *one language* and *one* set of words. As they journeyed in the east they came upon a valley in *the land* of Sumer, and they settled *there. Each one* said *to his neighbor, "Come, let us mold bricks and bake them in fire"*—for *bricks* served *as stone* for them, *and pitch* served *as mortar* for them. They said, *"Come, let us build* for ourselves *a city and a tower* with its top in heaven, and let us make a *name* for ourselves, lest we be *spread out over all the earth."*

Section 2

Yahweh came down to see *the city and the tower* that *the children of humans had built.* Yahweh said, "Behold, they are *one* people with *one language* for all of them, and this is what they begin do. Now there will be no restraining them from whatever they plan to do. *Come, let us* go down and *confuse their language there*, so that *no one* will understand *his neighbor's language."* Yahweh *spread them out from there over all the earth*, and they ceased *building the city.*

Conclusion

Therefore they call its *name Babel*, for *there* Yahweh *confused all the earth's language*, and *from there* Yahweh *spread them out over all the earth*.

Notice that many of the repetitions create echoes between section 1 and section 2, focalizing the clash between the human perspective and the divine perspective. This perspectival shift brings in its wake a series of recognitions and reversals. First, "Yahweh came down to see the city and the tower"—a vertical descent, which reverses the upward movement of building a tower "with its top in heaven." Yahweh recognizes the implications of the building activities, and he reverses the people's aspirations by confusing their language and spreading them over all the earth. Their anxiety about being "spread out over all the earth" comes to pass precisely because of their attempt to prevent it. The people not only fail to "make a name" for themselves, but their legacy is the name of Babel, explained as "confusion," the ruins of their aspirations.

In this nexus of verbal and sonic echoes, language itself is artfully focalized as a site of human transgression and its consequence. The solution to unified and excessive human aspirations, Yahweh explains, is a permanently altered—and mutually unintelligible—array of languages and peoples. The effectiveness of language is radically limited in the present world.

Some of these *Leitwort* repetitions have links with other texts in the J primeval narrative. The building activity by the *bǝnê hāʾādām* ("sons/children of humans," 11:5) subtly indicates their genealogical origins as the "children of Adam." This creates a link with the transgression in Eden, which also violated the boundaries of human and divine and led to expulsion and exile. The foiled desire for a "name" (*šēm*, 11:4, 9) echoes the obscure description of the Nephilim as "men of great name" (*ʾanšê haššēm*, 6:4). These children of the Sons of God and daughters of humans are, like the builders of Babel, (in)famous yet anonymous. The desire for a great name is a negative foil for the next story, where Yahweh says to Abram, "I will make your name great" (12:2). In contrast to the builders of Babel, Abram's obedience and virtue—he teaches "the way of Yahweh" to his descendants (18:19)—are the right ways to gain a great name. The name of Abram endures, in contrast to the names of the builders of Babel.

Another *Leitwort* with links to other J stories is "spread out" (*pwṣ*, 11:4, 8, 9). This activates an association with the two previous J texts, the Table of Nations and the curse of Canaan. The latter begins with a genealogical comment: "These three were Noah's sons, and from them all the earth spread out" (*nāpǝṣâ kol-hāʾāreṣ*, 9:19). Then in the J Table of Nations, "the families of Canaan spread out" (*nāpōṣû mišpǝḥôt hakkǝnaʿănî*, 10:18). The "spreading out" of the Canaanites is one instance of the global "spreading out" from Noah's sons. These verbs are *nāpaṣ*, a biform of *pûṣ*. In the Babel story, the prior genealogical "spreading out" is changed into an anxiety and fear that motivates the builders of Babel, "lest we be spread out over all the earth" (*pen-nāpûṣ ʿal-pǝnê kol-hāʾāreṣ*, 11:4). Although this verb is a biform of the previous ones, the prefixed *nun* makes it fit sonically with this *Leitwort* sequence: *nāpǝṣâ—nāpōṣû—nāpûṣ*.

In this *Leitwort* sequence, the Babel narrative transforms the genealogical spread of branching humanity into a psychological portrait of human anxiety and hubris. When Yahweh "spread them out (*wayyāpeṣ* and *hēpîṣām*) over all the earth" (11:8, 9), he actualizes their fear and negates their aspiration. This reversal creates the differentiation of peoples along with their mutually unintelligible languages as a punishment. This "spreading out" contrasts with its previous representation as a natural result of the descent of humankind. The Babel story overlays the durative spread of humans across the earth in the previous texts with a punctual story of the multiplicity of peoples as a sign of collective human failure and its corresponding punishment.

CULTURE AND CRITIQUE

The Tower of Babel story is the capstone of a narrative sequence, beginning with the expulsion from Eden, that traces the steps of human civilization. This is an ambivalent process, consisting of benefits and deficits. The founding of cities is similarly ambiguous. Cain builds the first city (4:17), which seems to color urban life as tainted with violence. The next city mentioned is Babel (Babylon), which is the first of Nimrod's chief (*rē'šît*) cities "in the land of Sumer" (10:10). The concept that Babylon was the first city is widespread in Mesopotamian tradition after around 1100 BCE (see below). This cultural memory is accurately reflected in the history of Nimrod's kingdom. But the connection of Babylon and the other cities with the archetypal Mesopotamian king gives them an ambiguous coloring coming from a people subjected to Mesopotamian hegemony.

The story of humankind attempting to build with its top in heaven" (11:4) while dwelling "in the land of Sumer" (11:2) is a thematic doublet of the first city of Nimrod's kingdom. It is also, less precisely, a doublet of Cain's founding of the first city, which is similarly "in the east" (4:16). In our story, Babylon is the first city. The Mesopotamian coloring as well as the people's plan to build the tower "up to heaven" make this first city an object of transgression, guilt, and shame. The first city is remembered as an infamy, not as a moral or cultural ascent. Its ruins are reflected in the divided condition of humankind, who are spread across the world and cannot communicate because of their mutually unintelligible speech. Civilization is associated with hubris and the desire to transgress the proper limits of humankind, to ascend via their humanmade tower up to heaven.

Yahweh's speech in the story articulates the problem at the heart of human civilization: "Behold, they are one people with one language for all of them, and this is what they begin to do. Now there will be no restraining them from whatever they plan to do" (11:6). As a unified community with a single language, the people have the power to implement their aspirations, "whatever they plan to do" (*kōl 'ăšer yāzəmû la 'ăśôt*). Yahweh's recognition of the people's capacity "to plan, consider, devise" (*zmm*) echoes his recognition of the evil of "every design of their heart's imaginings" (*kol-yēṣer maḥšəbōt libbô*, 6:5) in the J flood story, which motivates Yahweh to send the flood to destroy them. In the Babel story, Yahweh does not destroy them—he has promised not to do so (8:21–22)—but he negates their cultural capacity to implement their dangerous aspirations. He does so by dividing and scattering them, geographically and linguistically, so that they are no longer "one people with one language" and no longer able to implement "whatever they plan." The ruins of Babylon are a monument to the limits of civilization—and its insatiable hubris—in a world where humankind is divided and weak.

Wellhausen (1885: 303) aptly describes the ambivalence of civilization in the Babel story, situating it within the growth of civilization in the J primeval narrative: "With his [man's] growing civilization grows also his alienation from the highest good; and—this is evidently the idea, though it is not stated—the restless advance never reaches its goal after all; it is a Sisyphus-labor; the tower of Babel, which is incomplete to all eternity, is the proper symbol for it." The ambivalent steps of civilization in Genesis 1–11 are like Sisyphus pushing his boulder up the mountain, only to watch it roll back down. It is an incessant and potentially dangerous labor, with a limited reward.

In the double temporality of myth, in which the past illuminates the present and contemporary concerns shape the past, the builders of Babel have a double reference. In the story's genealogical context, they are collectively "the children of humans" (bənê hā'ādām, 11:5), which evokes their descent from Adam ('ādām or hā'ādām). As "one people" (11:6) who are scattered across "the whole earth" (11:8, 9), they are the ancestors of all the different peoples of the earth. Their hubris, guilt, and shame are features of the collective past of every people. Civilization carries reminders of their transgression, particularly when one encounters other nations and their languages, with their divide of incomprehension. The Babel story explains and illuminates this problematic complexity of cultural and linguistic difference in the present world.

But the myth also conveys what Scott (1990) calls a "hidden transcript," in which a subject people criticize their rulers through indirection, mimicry, and mockery. The hidden transcript takes place "in public view but is designed to have a double meaning" (19). If we read the Babel story against the grain in this sense, it is obvious that Babylon signifies not simply Babylon in the past, but the most famous city of Mesopotamia in the present. If the J writer composed this text in the Neo-Assyrian era, then the hubris, guilt, and shame of the people of Babel are imputed, to some degree, to the rulers of the current Mesopotamian empire, whose ideal was "one people" with one imperial order (see below). Even if the city and tower of Babylon were intact at this time, in the mind's eye of the story, Babel is perpetually destroyed and "confused" (bālal). The mythic ruins of Babel are projected onto the actual city, which was the "cosmic center" of Mesopotamian civilization. This is the hidden transcript of the story, which is only slightly hidden. The infamy of Babel pertains to the current imperial aspirations of the "people of Babel," who still seek to climb to heaven, make a great name, and violate the limits of Yahweh's cosmic order. By the story's end, so this hidden transcript may suggest, they will not prevail. Babylon will be utterly confused. This is not an explicit sense of the story, but may be a hidden sense, a bit of anti-imperial mimicry, intimated between the lines of the myth.

CONTEXTS

In the prophetic visions of the new era, the limits and divisions of the present world will be overcome in a cosmic repetition of the first era. In a supplement to the prophecies of Zephaniah, the new era will include a purified language, with which all the peoples of the world will call on Yahweh:

Therefore, wait for me—declares Yahweh—
> for the day when I arise in the future. . . .
For then I will change the peoples to a pure language,
> so that all of them will call on the name of Yahweh,
> to serve him in unison. (Zeph 3:8, 9)

There is no allusion to the Tower of Babel story in this text, but it repeats the motif of the division of peoples and languages (cf. the Table of Nations, Gen 10:5, 20, 31). The condition of the new era will recapitulate the original era, when all people were one and had the same speech. In the prophetic vision, Yahweh will "change the peoples to a pure language," healing the division of the peoples and the confusion of languages. As with the seraphic purification of Isaiah's "unclean lips" (*śəpātayim*) (Isa 6:5–7), Yahweh will purify the peoples' language (*śāpâ*) so that they may speak a pure speech and worship Yahweh in unison.

The idea of a future universal language, which reverses the primeval confusion of tongues, is a recurring desire of humankind (cf. the Sumerian "Spell of Nudimmud," where "on that day . . . the language of all mankind is one" [Alster 1973: 104; similarly, Vanstiphout 2003: 65]). The return to paradise in the ideal future entails a return to one people and a unified language, whether it be Hebrew, Sumerian, or Esperanto. In this ideal era there will be no more transgressions, no aspirations to fame, power, and self-transcendence. The first time will become the end-time, canceling the discontents of civilization.

In Mesopotamian traditions of the late second and first millennia BCE, Babylon was the "cosmic capital" and first city, founded by the gods in primeval times. This concept originally belonged to the Sumerian cities of Nippur and Eridu and was appropriated by Babylon during the Old and Middle Babylonian periods (George 1997; Lambert 2013: 200–201). Babylon became a political center in the eighteenth century BCE, and it was elevated to the status of cosmic center by the twelfth century BCE, which was probably the time of the composition of *Enuma Elish* and its exaltation of the god Marduk and his city, Babylon (Lambert 2013: 248–77). Babylon continued to be the most fabled city of Mesopotamia until its decline during the Hellenistic period. This tradition of Babylon as the first city and cosmic center is a key context for the Babel story. This was true even in the Neo-Assyrian period, as is clear in a letter from a Babylonian official to his Assyrian counterpart: "When he has entered Babylon, he will have trodden on the center of the lands" (Lambert 2013: 201).

In a list of Babylon's names and attributes, Babylon is called "the city whose brickwork is most ancient" (*ālu ša libittašu maḫrat*) and "the bond of heaven and earth" (*markas šamê u erṣeti*) (George 1997: 126–27, 139–40). Babylon as the first city is also attested in the myth "The Founding of Eridu," in which Babylon inherits the older status of Eridu. The first work of creation is the founding of Babylon: "Babylon was made, Esagil was completed" (*Bābilu epuš, Esagil šuklul,* line 14; Lambert 2013: 372–73).

The temple of Marduk in Babylon was Esagil, which means "House Whose Top Is High." Its temple tower (*ziqquratu*) was Etemenanki, "House, Foundation of Heaven and Earth" (George 1993: 149). The tower's name describes it as a cosmic axis linking heaven and earth. These are cosmic qualities that are the context of the Tower of Babel story.

The earliest mention of the tower (*ziqquratu*) of Babylon is in *Enuma Elish* (George 2005: 87). The mythic attributes of the city, its temple, and its ziggurat are expressed in Marduk's address to the gods after his creation of the world:

> Above the Apsû, the emerald (?) abode . . .
> Beneath the celestial parts, whose floor I made firm,
> > I will build a house to be my luxurious abode.
> Within it I will establish its shrine,
> > I will found my chamber and establish my kingship. . . .
> I shall call its name "Babylon," "The Homes of the Great Gods."
>
> > > (V.117–29; Lambert 2013: 104–5)

After Marduk creates humans, he commands the gods to build Babylon and its temple complex:

> "Build Babylon, the task you have sought.
> > Let bricks for it be molded, and raise the shrine!"
> The Anunnaki wielded the pick.
> > For one whole year they made the needed bricks.
> When the second year arrived,
> > they raised the peak of Esagil, a replica of the Apsû.
> They built the lofty temple tower (*ziqqurat*) of the Apsû.
>
> > > (VI.59–63; Lambert 2013: 112–13)

The raising of the temple's peak is a wordplay on the name of Esagil, "House Whose Top Is High." This passage, including its wordplay, is similar to the Babel story, whose people desired to build "a city and a tower with its top in heaven" (Gen 11:4) and molded and baked the needed bricks (11:3). The cosmic ideology and architectural technology of Babylon and its temple complex are echoed in the Tower of Babel story. We need not assume a direct textual connection with *Enuma Elish,* but a knowledge of the prestige of Babylon.

The status of Babylon persisted through the Neo-Assyrian period, the probable era of the J author. As Speiser (1967: 57–58) observes, when the seventh-century Neo-Assyrian king Esarhaddon restored Ešarra, the temple of the god Aššur, his annals use the language of the building of Babylon in *Enuma Elish*:

> For one whole year they molded bricks. . . .
> When the second year arrived
> I raised high the top of Ešarra, the dwelling of Aššur, my lord,
> up to heaven.
>
> > > (Esarhaddon 57.v.1, 29–34; Leichty 2011: 126)

For the Neo-Assyrian king, Babylon and its temple were the cosmic center, whose prestige he sought to transfer to Aššur's temple by this textual echo. Similarly, in a tablet of the Aššur recension of *Enuma Elish,* an Assyrian scribe changed the city's name from Bābili (Babylon) to Baltil (Aššur) (V.129, 137; Lambert 2013: 105, ms E). These allusions and revisions attempt to appropriate the cosmic status of Babylon for Aššur and show that the prestige of Babylon persisted through the Neo-Assyrian period. This is the conceptuality of Babylon that the Tower of Babel story evokes and contests.

Uehlinger (1990) has proposed that the Babel story has a specific Mesopotamian political-historical context in the fate of the new capital city (Dur-Sharrukin, "Fortress of Sargon") that Sargon II dedicated in 706 BCE, but which was abandoned at his death six months later. Since this interpretation requires omitting Babylon from the original story, it seems unnecessarily complicated. But Uehlinger's general point that the story presents an implicit critique of Mesopotamian imperial ideology is valid. As he observes, the Babel story is "a political-theological reflection . . . on the theme of Yhwh's opposition to claims to world domination" (536). I have described this as a hidden transcript of the story, an implicit critique of imperial aspirations.

As Uehlinger (1990: 453–502) observes, a recurring theme of Neo-Assyrian imperial ideology is that it unifies all the peoples of the world, including foreign people with mutually unintelligible languages. This is expressed in an inscription of Sargon II, describing the foreign peoples that he settled in Dur-Sharrukin: "Subjects from the four corners of the world, of different tongues, of untranslatable speech, inhabitants of mountains and plains, but all subjects of the light of the gods, the lord of totality, whom I had deported by order of my lord Aššur and by the power of my scepter, I imposed one command over them and I settled them" (Liverani 2017: 160). The empire aspired to transform the chaos of many subjects of "different tongues, untranslatable speech" into a single unified command (*pâ išten,* lit. "one mouth"). This ideology of "one people, one rule" is subverted in the Babel story, as the unified city of Babel—and its lofty aspirations—is destroyed when Yahweh confuses the people's speech and scatters them across the earth. The myth seems to mimic and subvert the dominant Assyrian imperial ideology.

As with the context offered by *Enuma Elish* and other Mesopotamian texts, it is not necessary to posit direct textual knowledge of Assyrian royal texts for the Babel story to critique the pretensions of the ruling empire. It is enough to be a subject people of the Neo-Assyrian Empire to know its pretensions of world domination. The Babel story's hidden transcript (which is only slightly hidden) undermines the claim to power of the contemporary empire, subjecting it to Yahweh's judgment and punishment. It simultaneously exposes the problem of the origins of civilization in primeval times. The first city, the Babel of confusion, is an emblem of infamy. Its hubris and fate are consistent with the Mesopotamian omen, "If a city rises to the sky like a mountain, that city will be reduced to a heap of ruins" (*Šumma ālu,* I 16).

Generations from Shem to Abram (11:10–32; **P**, J, *R*)

---

11   [10]This is the genealogy of Shem. Shem was 100 years old and fathered Arpachshad, two years after the flood. [11]After he fathered Arpachshad, Shem lived 500 years. He fathered sons and daughters. [12]Arpachshad lived 35 years and fathered Shelah. [13]After he fathered Shelah, Arpachshad lived 403 years. He fathered sons and daughters. [14]Shelah lived 30 years and fathered Eber. [15]After he fathered Eber, Shelah lived 403 years. He fathered sons and daughters. [16]Eber lived 34 years and fathered Peleg. [17]After he fathered Peleg, Eber lived 370[a] years. He fathered sons and daughters. [18]Peleg lived 30 years and fathered Reu. [19]After he fathered Reu, Peleg lived 209 years. He fathered sons and daughters. [20]Reu lived 32 years and fathered Serug. [21]After he fathered Serug, Reu lived 207 years. He fathered sons and daughters. [22]Serug lived 30 years and fathered Nahor. [23]After he fathered Nahor, Serug lived 200 years. He fathered sons and daughters. [24]Nahor lived 29 years and fathered Terah. [25]After he fathered Terah, Nahor lived 119 years. He fathered sons and daughters. [26]Terah lived 70 years and fathered Abram, Nahor, and Haran.

[27]This is the genealogy of Terah. Terah fathered Abram, Nahor, and Haran, and Haran fathered Lot. [28]Haran died before his father Terah in the land of his kin, *in Ur of the Chaldeans.* [29]Abram and Nahor took for themselves wives. Abram's wife's name was Sarai, and Nahor's wife's name was Milcah, the daughter of Haran, who was the father of Milcah and Iscah. [30]Sarai was barren; she had no son.[b] [31]**Terah took his son Abram, and Haran's son Lot, his grandson, and his daughter-in-law Sarai, his son Abram's wife, and he sent them[c] from Ur of the Chaldeans to go to the land of Canaan. They came to Haran and settled there.** [32]The days of Terah's life were 205 years, and Terah died in Haran.

Textual Notes

a. Reading 370 with the LXX. Usually in this chronology this date (Eber's remainder) would correspond to the formula MT = LXX = (SP + 100). Here the LXX (370) and

408

SP (270) indicate that the archetypal reading is 370. MT's 430 is probably the result of a scribal confusion with the previous number 34, where *šlšym šnh w'rb'* ("thirty years and four," v. 17) is a reminiscence and transposition of *'rb' wšlšym šnh* ("four and thirty years," v. 16) (Hendel 1998: 71–73).

b. Reading *yld* ("son, child") with the SP. The MT reads *wld*, which is most likely the result of a graphic confusion of *yod* and *waw*, two graphically similar letters (see Textual Note 2:12b). Although **wld* is the original spelling for "child, son" in Semitic (and remains the spelling in Arabic), the shift of the word initial *waw* to *yod* is a characteristic feature of the Northwest Semitic language group, to which Hebrew belongs. Interestingly, because of this scribal error, the word *wld* became a specialized term for "embryo" in postbiblical Hebrew (Hendel 1998: 59).

c. Reading *wywṣ' 'tm* ("and he sent them") with the SP and LXX. The MT reads *wyṣ'w 'tm* ("they went with them"), which makes no sense and differs only in the placement of *waw* (a vowel marker) in the first word. A scribe in the proto-MT tradition presumably made a slight error (Hendel 1998: 59–60).

Notes

11:10–26. *The genealogy of Shem.* This section gives the genealogy of the postdiluvian ancestors. The rubric "this is the genealogy of Shem" (*'ēlleh tôlədōt šēm*, 11:10) introduces a new section of Genesis (see Notes at 2:4, 5:1, 6:9). It also resumes the linear genealogy from the "book of Adam's genealogy" (*sēper tôlədōt 'ādām*, 5:1), complementing the segmented Sethite genealogy in the Table of Nations (10:21–31). A second section of this chapter begins with the rubric "this is the genealogy of Terah" (11:27). These genealogical sections (the latter supplemented with J text) serve as a temporal bridge from the primeval era to the era of Abraham's family. The generally decreasing lifespans—from Shem's 600 down to Nahor's 148—also serve to indicate a transition from the primeval era to the ancestral era.

11:10–11. *This is the genealogy of Shem. Shem was 100 years old and fathered Arpachshad, two years after the flood. After he fathered Arpachshad, Shem lived 500 years. He fathered sons and daughters.* The genealogical entries from Shem to Terah have the following form, with variations: "PN₁ lived X years and fathered PN₂. After he fathered PN₂, PN₁ lived Y years. He fathered sons and daughters." This repeats the pattern in Genesis 5 but lacks its concluding formula: "All the days of PN₁'s life were Z years, and he died." The entry for Terah, however, has this concluding formula in slightly altered form (11:32). The lack of this formula in the sequence from 11:10 to 11:26 may be due to P's propensity for stylistic variation or may point to the secondary origin of this section, which may have been incompletely modeled after Genesis 5 (so Carr 1996: 72). I incline to the former explanation, since a textual and genealogical continuity between the two sections is indicated by the connecting verses of 5:32 + 7:6 + 9:28–29.

The entries for Shem and Terah have other variations to this pattern. Shem's entry begins *šēm ben-X šānâ* ("Shem was X years old") rather than *šēm ḥay X šānâ* ("Shem lived X years"). This stylistic variation also occurs in Noah's entry, *nōaḥ ben-X šānâ* (5:32), providing a measure of continuity between father and son. The other variation is the additional phrase "two years after the flood" (see below). Terah's entry varies with several expansions, including the redactional insertion of J material in 11:28–30 and the listing of his three sons, Abram, Nahor, and Haran (11:26). This feature mirrors the listing of Noah's three sons at the end of Genesis 5.

The phrase "two years after the flood" addresses a chronological difficulty. According to this verse Shem was 100 years old when he fathered Arpachshad, but according to the chronological data in 5:31 and 7:6, Shem was 100 years old at the onset of the flood. But the text seems to exclude Arpachshad from the ark, since it states, "Noah went out [of the ark] with his sons, his wife, and his sons' wives with him" (8:18). There is no mention of a grandson. Someone, possibly the P writer, added this chronological note to remove this potential difficulty (Hendel 1998: 75–76). However, the glossator failed to adjust Shem's age—he should be 102 years old when he "fathered Arpachshad two years after the flood." This chronological problem probably derives from the combination of the "book of Adam's genealogy" with the P flood story, which produced several other chronological conundrums (see COMMENTS).

Arpachshad is listed as Shem's son in the P Table of Nations (10:22). There he is Shem's third son, after Elam and Asshur. The genealogy here resumes the Shem–Arpachshad line as a vertical genealogy, after the branching Shemite genealogy in Genesis 10. This follows the typical biblical pattern of first treating the collateral lineages and then turning back to the main genealogical branch.

11:12–19. The first four generations of Shemites—Arpachshad, Shelah, Eber, and Peleg—are listed in the Table of Nations (see 10:22–25). Arpachshad is listed in the P table, and all four are listed in the J table. Presumably, the J source contained a continuation of this genealogy until Abraham, but this section was not preserved.

11:20–26. The next four generations of Shemites—Reu, Serug, Nahor, and Terah— seem to derive their names from places in Upper Mesopotamia in or near the region of Haran, with the possible exception of Reu (see COMMENTS).

Reu (rə'û) is rendered in the LXX as Ragau, which may reflect original *Raḡaw (Zadok 1980: 110; Layton 1990: 97). Zadok (1980: 109–10) suggests a correspondence with the place name Til Raḫawa, attested in a Neo-Assyrian text. The association of "bowmen from Til Raḫawa" with an Aramean leader, Ayababa, may indicate a location in Upper Mesopotamia. Frayne (2001: 233) suggests that Reu-Ragaw may correspond to the city of Raqqim (modern ar-Raqqa), attested in Old Babylonian texts, located south of Haran in the Baliḫ Valley. Another possibility is that rə'û corresponds with the name of an Aramean tribe, Ru'ua, that dwelled in or near Babylonia in the eighth to seventh centuries (Skinner 1930: 232; Zadok 1980: 110). A less likely possibility is that rə'û is a short form of a name like rə'û'ēl (Reuel), meaning "God is a friend" (so most commentators; but see Layton 1990: 97). The MT vocalization of Reu may be a harmonization with the name Reuel.

Serug (śərûḡ) has long been identified with the place name Sarūgi, attested in Neo-Assyrian texts of the ninth to seventh centuries BCE (Hess 1992b). It corresponds with the modern Turkish city Suruç, called Saruḡ by Syrian and Arab writers, located west of Haran in the Baliḫ Valley. This city has some association with Batna, a city known from Old Assyrian texts—it is possible that Batna and Sarūgi are alternative or overlapping names for the same city (Frayne 2001: 219–20). The place name may have a connection with the Aramean subtribe Sarūgu, known from Neo-Assyrian texts, which may descend from the Old Babyloniania subtribe Ašarugāyum, known from the Mari letters (Durand 2004: 194–95; Younger 2016: 658–59).

Nahor (*nāḥôr*) corresponds to the place name Naḥur, a city frequently attested in second-millennium texts (Hess 1992a). Naḥur is located in the Ḥabur River Valley, about one hundred miles east of Haran, in the Old Babylonian district of Idamaraṣ (Beitzel 1992: 44, 52; Astour 1995: 1409; Heimpel 2003: 618). It was linked to Haran by an important trade route. During much of the second millennium it was the seat of a district governor (*šāpiṭum*), and in the Mari letters it is a place where the kings of Idamaraṣ assemble (Heimpel 2003: 311). In the Middle Assyrian era it was conquered by Adad-Narari I (Grayson 1987: 159–60) and probably in the Neo-Assyrian era by Adad-Narari II (restored reading, Naḥ[ur]; Grayson 1991: 148–49).

Although the biblical name Nāḥôr is best identified with Naḥur (**naḥur > nāḥōr* by normal phonological development), other Mesopotamian sites have similar names. Til Naḥiri is a settlement listed in the Neo-Assyrian "Harran Census" located in the outskirts of Haran (Frayne 2001: 225). An older site, Niḥriya, is located in the Baliḥ Valley north of Haran (Beitzel 1992: 53–54). The Akkadian verb *naḥāru,* "to be shriveled, withered," may be connected to these geographical names.

Terah (*teraḥ*) corresponds to Til Turaḥi (variant Til ša Turaḥi), a city in the Baliḥ Valley, west of the Baliḥ River. It had a palace of a local king in the mid-ninth century BCE, when it was conquered by Shalmaneser III (*COS* 2.263–69; Kraeling 1922). Its precise location is uncertain—it may correspond to modern Tell Tcheraf (Frayne 2001: 229). The Akkadian word *turaḥu* means "wild goat, gazelle," hence Til Turaḥi is "Gazelle Hill."

11:26. *Terah lived 70 years and fathered Abram, Nahor, and Haran.* Seventy is a good age—seven connoting completion or wholeness—to bear three sons. The branching of Terah's line into three sons corresponds to the branching of Noah's line into three sons in the antediluvian genealogy in Genesis 5. Abram, Nahor, and Haran are the tenth generation in the postdiluvian genealogy, which also makes a symmetry with the ten generations of the antediluvian genealogy (Adam to Noah).

Abram ('*abrām*) means "the Father is exalted." It is a sentence name, with the divine element '*ab* ("father") as subject and *rām* ("be exalted, high") as predicate. For Abram this name is doubly significant, since it exalts God at the same time as it anticipates Abram's destiny as an exalted father, as when God changes the name to Abraham, "for I hereby make you a father of a multitude of nations" (17:5, P). The name Abraham, a variant of Abram, is here explained as if it were a melding of '*abrā(m)* ("father") + *hām(ôn)* ("multitude"). This is an exegetical wordplay or midrash on the name.

Names related to '*abrām* are common in the second and first millennia BCE (see Thompson 1974: 33 and references). Examples include three names from Late Bronze Age Ugarit: *a-bi-ra-mu* (in cuneiform script) and two foreigners (from Cyprus and Egypt) named '*abrm* (in alphabetic script). A Late Bronze Age name from Egypt is written '*ibrm*. A Neo-Assyrian name is *abi-ra-mi*. All of these names correspond to '*abrām* or '*ăbîrām*.

A Neo-Babylonian site called Bīt Abīram, "House of Abiram," in the Nippur countryside southeast of Babylon was in or near the region of exiled Judeans in the sixth century and later (Joannès and Lemaire 1996). The site was named after the household and lineage of a person named Abiram. It is possible that the site was named for biblical Abram; compare the nearby city of Judean exiles named āl-Yāhūdu, "Judah-town"

(Pearce and Wunsch 2014). However, the connection between Bīt Abīrâm and the community of the "house of Abram" may be coincidental, a historical irony.

A tenth-century place name in the Negev may incorporate the name Abram, but this is unclear. A place name in the victory stele of the Egyptian king Shishak/Sheshonq I is, in Egyptian syllabic writing, *p3 ḥqr' 'brm* (Ritner 2009: 208, #71; K. A. Wilson 2005: 120–21). It consists of three elements: the Egyptian definite article *p3;* the word *ḥqr',* which probably represents Semitic *ḥql,* "field, territory" (Akkadian *eqlu,* Aramaic *ḥaqlā',* and perhaps Hebrew *ḥelqâ;* see K. A. Wilson 2005: 118–20; Atwood 2018); and *'brm,* which may represent the name *'abrām* (so Ritner 2009: 208, 212 n. 43; Hoch 1994: 18, 205, 235–37). There are, however, other possibilities for the writing *'brm,* including *'abilīm,* "streams," which in the singular is common in Palestinian toponyms (Y. Levin 2010: 205). It is possible—but no more—that the Negev place is "the Field of Abram," perhaps commemorating biblical Abram in the region where tradition placed his home.

Nahor (*nāḥôr*) is named after his grandfather. This was a common custom (papponymy) in the biblical world. The "city of Nahor" (*'îr nāḥôr*) is Haran (*ḥārān*) in 24:10. This locale coheres with Nahor's role as the father of the Arameans, who dwell in Upper Mesopotamia during the Israelite era. In 22:20–24 (J), Nahor is the father of twelve sons, who are eponyms of Aramean tribes or places. In 28:2 (P), Nahor's descendants live in Paddan-Aram ("the Field of Aram").

Haran (*ḥārān*), the youngest son, echoes the city name Haran (*ḥārān*) and may derive from the place name with a weakening of the initial *ḥet* to *he* (Wellhausen 1885: 313). In Num 32:36, the tribe of Gad builds (or restores) a town called *bêt ḥārān* ("House of Haran"). This Transjordanian locale coheres with Haran's genealogical position as the ancestor (through Lot) of the peoples of Moab and Ammon (Gen 19:37–38).

11:27–32. The genealogy of Terah. The *tôlǝdōt* ("genealogy, descendants") formula occurs in 11:27 for the fifth time (see 2:4, 5:1, 6:9, 11:10), introducing the next section of Genesis. This section (11:27–25:19) focuses on Abram, the firstborn of Terah, but also relates the genealogical histories of Nahor (22:20–24) and Haran's son Lot (Genesis 12–14, 19). This section is a new beginning but continues in these verses the genealogical style of the previous section (11:10–26). R has incorporated text from J in 11:28–30. The birth and migration of Abram is a hinge between the primeval narrative and the ancestral narrative, and a turning point in Genesis.

11:27. *This is the genealogy of Terah. Terah fathered Abram, Nahor, and Haran, and Haran fathered Lot.* After the *tôlǝdōt* rubric, the text returns to the genealogy with a resumptive repetition of the last half of 11:26, "(he) fathered Abram, Nahor, and Haran." This sequence also constitutes a circular *inclusio* (see INTRODUCTION I). The following comment "and Haran fathered Lot" provides anticipatory information for the subsequent narrative. After Haran's death, Lot becomes the head of Haran's lineage and makes the journey to Haran and Canaan.

The name Lot (*lôṭ*) is obscure. It is probably related to the name Lotan (*lôṭān*), the firstborn son of Seir and a Horite chief (36:20–22), who is connected with the region of Edom, south of Ammon and Moab (Lot's grandchildren). The word *lôṭ* means a kind of "covering" (Isa 25:7) and may refer to the garments of the tribal people of Lot/Lotan (Knauf 1992a).

11:28. *Haran died before his father Terah in the land of his kin, in Ur of the Chaldeans.* R has supplemented the P text of the descendants of Terah with 11:28–30 from the J source (Emerton 1992). R (or a later scribe) added the gloss "in Ur of the Chaldeans" to harmonize the J and P texts (see below). Signs of J include the phrase *bə'ereṣ môladtô* ("in the land of his kin"), which is expanded in Abram's call to go *mē'arṣəkā ûmimmôladtəkā* ("from your land and from your kin," 12:1), and the *Leitwort* and motif of the barren wife (11:30). These are connective features in the J narrative.

The death of Haran "before" (*'al-pənê*, "in the face/presence of") his father, that is, during Terah's lifetime, strikes a tragic note. The disrupted chain of generations anticipates the generational problems of Abram. Haran's death makes Lot fatherless—the opposite of Abram's problem—and Abram takes on Lot as a presumptive heir in the narrative that follows.

The repetition of the place of Haran's death—"in the land of his kin, in Ur of the Chaldeans" (*bə'ereṣ môladtô bə'ûr kaśdîm*)—poses a puzzle. Many commentators regard the explanatory phrase "in Ur of the Chaldeans" as a redactional gloss, which serves to harmonize the J locale "in the land of his kin" with the P location "Ur of the Chaldeans" (11:31) (e.g., Westermann 1985: 139; Emerton 1992: 39–40). There appear to be two traditions of the patriarchal homeland, one in the region of Haran, which coheres with the geographical connections of the several ancestral names (see NOTES above on Reu, Serug, Nahor, Terah, and Haran), and another in Ur of the Chaldeans. Elsewhere the J source attests only the Haran tradition, where Nahor's descendants live (see 29:5, "Laban, son of Nahor"). Note that in P neither Nahor nor Haran (who is phonetically associated with Haran) leaves Ur of the Chaldeans (11:31). The implication is that the "land of his kin" (*'ereṣ môladtô*) in J has been secondarily identified with "Ur of the Chaldeans." This clarifies why Yahweh calls Abram to go "from your land and from your kin" (12:1) at the time when Abram is in Haran. The collocation of *'ereṣ* ("land") and *môledet* ("kin") refers to Haran in both J texts. This is the ancestral homeland in J (see COMMENTS).

Ur of the Chaldeans (*'ûr kaśdîm*) is the ancient city of Ur in southern Mesopotamia (Millard 2001; Day 2022: 207–16). The specification that this is Ur "of the Chaldeans" makes it clear that this is southern Mesopotamia. The Chaldeans were a tribal people of uncertain origin who became prominent in southern Mesopotamia in the eighth to sixth centuries BCE (Frame 1997). Their ethnym (Akkadian *kaldu*, Greek Chaldaioi) is represented in Hebrew as *kaśdîm*, with the letter *śin*. The variation between *śin* and *l* indicates that the original consonant was a lateral fricative [ɬ], perhaps of East Arabian origin (Steiner 1977: 137–43). It is possible that the Chaldeans were originally an Arabian people (Frame 1997: 483).

The phrase "land of the Chaldeans" (*'ereṣ kaśdîm*) occurs in biblical writings of the seventh to sixth centuries BCE referring to southern Mesopotamia (Babylonia) (Jer 24:5, 25:12, 50:1–51:54; Ezek 1:3, 12:13; on this gloss in Isa 23:13, see Clements 1980: 194). This chronological horizon corresponds with P's usage of "Ur of the Chaldeans."

In Gen 15:7 (a later text), God proclaims that "I brought you out of Ur of the Chaldeans." This text exegetically blends the P and J versions of Abram's migration. Note that the P migration from Ur is due to Terah's agency, not God's (11:31). In postbiblical tradition, the name Ur (*'ûr*) is linked with its Hebrew homonym, "fire" (*'ûr*), generating the legend of Abram burning down the house of idols in Ur and Haran perishing in the fire (Jub. 12:12–14; Kugel 1998: 267–70; Day 2022: 216–25).

11:29. *Abram and Nahor took for themselves wives. Abram's wife's name was Sarai, and Nahor's wife's name was Milcah, the daughter of Haran, who was the father of Milcah and Iscah.* The details of Abram's and Nahor's marriages fill out the picture of Abram's kin, preparing for Yahweh's call to Abram to go "from your land and your kin" (12:1). They also provide anticipatory information for Sarai's barrenness (11:30) and the later progeny of Nahor and Milcah (22:20–23), all J.

Sarai (*śārāy*) is an archaic form of *śārâ*, "princess" (Layton 1990: 241–49). The *-ay feminine ending is found in Northwest Semitic languages of the second millennium BCE (Amorite and Ugaritic) and is primarily restricted to women's names and feminine proper nouns. An equivalent personal name is attested in Ugaritic, *śry,* and three similar names are found in Amorite (*šar-ra-a-ia, šar-ra-ia,* and *šar-ri-ia;* Layton 1990: 246).

Milcah (*milkâ*) means "queen." The Akkadian cognate of Sarai/Sarah is *šarratu,* "queen," which could suggest a closer affinity between the two women, perhaps even a play on their two names. There is no reason to suspect that the two were goddesses in origin, as is sometimes conjectured. Unlike Sarai, Milcah's ancestry is noted since she is already part of the "house of Terah." She is Haran's daughter, Nahor's and Abram's niece. According to biblical custom and law, marriage with a niece was permitted (Lev 18:6–16).

The note that Haran was father of Milcah and Iscah (*yiskâ*) adds additional genealogical information about Abram's extended family (the "house of the father"), but Iscah is not again mentioned. In postbiblical traditions, she is sometimes identified with Sarai, giving Sarai an ancestry and making her Abram's niece (Targum Jonathan).

11:30. *Sarai was barren; she had no son.* This brief aside provides important anticipatory information for the subsequent narrative, beginning with the call of Abram, when Yahweh promises to make him "a great people" (12:2). Since Sarai is barren, the promise immediately becomes problematic. This is the problem around which the Abraham narrative revolves, whether directly or indirectly, involving Sarai, Hagar, presumptive heirs (Lot, Eliezer, Ishmael), and Isaac.

The form of this comment is doubled, comparable to poetic parallelism—first we are told "Sarai was barren (*'āqārâ*)," followed by a concrete detail, "she had no son" (*'ên lāh yeled*), which genealogically specifies and intensifies the problem. The word *yeled* (see TEXTUAL NOTE b) can mean either "son" or "child," and both are implied in Sarai's barrenness. In the long view of the narrative, the focus is on Sarai's inability to bear a son, which will be remedied in Genesis 18 and 21. Yahweh's promise to Abram, which in J follows immediately upon this verse, expands the implications of Sarai's situation. Notably, this anticipatory information is given to the reader, but there is no suggestion that Abram or Sarai is yet aware of this condition (see 16:1 in J, and 15:2). This narratorial aside introduces a distance in knowledge between the characters and the audience, which gives the promise a touch of suspense, a fraught background.

The *Leitwort* and motif of the barren wife will recur, with variations, in the next two generations. Rebekah and Rachel are, like Sarai, *'āqārâ* ("barren," 25:21 and 29:31, both J). This motif creates dramatic tension and has the theological effect of requiring divine intervention. It also marks the future heir as special, a consequence of divine favor.

11:31. *Terah took his son Abram, and Haran's son Lot, his grandson, and his daughter-in-law Sarai, his son Abram's wife, and he sent them from Ur of the Chaldeans to go to the land of Canaan. They came to Haran and settled there.* The P genealogical narrative continues (from 11:27) with the migration of Terah, Abram, Lot, and Sarai to Haran. This P narrative will resume in 12:4b–5 with the migration of Abram, Sarai, and Lot from Haran to Canaan. As addressed above (NOTES to 11:28), two migration traditions have been combined here, one from Haran and the other from Ur. The Haran migration appears to be the older one and is the only tradition in J. The P source combines the Haran tradition with the Ur tradition, yielding a two-part migration.

The reason for P's location of the patriarchal homeland in Ur is unclear. The most plausible explanation was proposed by Wellhausen (1885: 342): "If we . . . consider that Abraham is said to have migrated into Palestine from Ur, from Chaldea, it is hardly possible to reject the idea that the circumstances of the exile had some influence in molding the priestly form of the patriarchal legend." The exiled communities of Judah were settled in Lower Mesopotamia in 597 BCE and afterwards, which may be contemporary with P. The royal household lived in Babylon, while the majority were settled in the environs of Nippur, including a new site called āl-Yahūdu, "Judah-town" (Pearce and Wunsch 2014). Abram's journey from Ur (an ancient city south of this region) to Haran would have passed near these settlements. On some level, the P displacement of the ancestral homeland southward may suggest a desire that the exiles will resume Abram's journey to the promised land, following the route from Ur to Canaan.

Disputes involving Abraham and the promised land seem to have troubled the exiles (see Ezek 11:15, 33:23–24). As Greenberg (1997: 690) comments, "Abraham appears to have exercised a fascination upon the battered remnants of the national collapse in the homeland and in Babylonia." P's revision of the ancestral homeland may offer a different approach to this Abrahamic dilemma, recasting the exiles as legitimate heirs of the ancestral homeland, now revised to Ur of the Chaldeans.

The statement that Terah "sent them from Ur of the Chaldeans to go to the land of Canaan" is P's alternative to the J tradition of Yahweh's call to Abram (12:1–3). In P there is no explicit motive for this journey, and it has no theological content. Terah is the mover, not God. The P story of Abram has its climax in the Abrahamic covenant (Genesis 17), which is the only P text in which God speaks to Abram. As Zakovitch (1999: 438) observes, "the Priestly document prefers to begin the presentation of the relationship between God and Abraham in the land of Canaan, in a covenant between them." In P Abram journeys from Ur to Haran to Canaan at the behest of his father, but receives God's promises and the covenant only later, twenty-four years after leaving Haran at the mature age of ninety-nine (17:1; Hendel 2019: 586–90).

The city of Haran (*ḥārān*), first mentioned here, is Akkadian Ḥarrānu (the *reš* in the Hebrew is virtually doubled; cf. LXX Charran), meaning "way, road." Haran was a prominent city in the Baliḥ River Valley, located at the crossroads of important trade routes (Esse 1984; and COMMENTS).

Nahor and Milcah do not accompany Terah, Abram, Sarai, and Lot to Haran. Yet in both J and P, Nahor's descendants dwell in Haran (see 25:19, P; 29:5, J). Haran is "the city of Nahor" (*'îr nāḥôr*) in 24:10—a relatively late text (Hendel and Joosten 2018: 81–82) that follows the tradition associating Nahor with Upper Mesopotamia (see NOTES at 11:22 for the correlation with the place name Naḥur).

11:32. *The days of Terah's life were 205 years, and Terah died in Haran.* This verse resumes the genealogical entry for Terah that was probably derived from the "book of

Adam's genealogy" (see NOTES at 5:1). It follows from 11:26: "Terah lived 70 years and fathered Abram, Nahor, and Haran." Instead of the formula in 11:10–26, "After he fathered PN_2, PN_1 lived Y years. He fathered sons and daughters," it repeats, with variations, the formula in Genesis 5, "All the days of PN_1 were Y years, and he died." The entry for Terah, including the birth of Abram, is the last in the style of the "book of Adam's genealogy."

The notice "in Haran" was probably added by the P source (so most commentators). It emphasizes the movement from Ur to Haran (11:31). The death of Terah is a turning point for Abram, since he now becomes the head of the household, the "house of the father" (*bêt-'āb*) in Haran. In the next stage of the journey to Canaan, Abram will be the father figure, as he transitions toward his destiny as the ancestor of Israel (Hendel 2019a).

Comments
EDITIONS

There are three editions of the postdiluvian chronology in Genesis 11 (Hendel 1998: 71–80). This is similar to the case of multiple editions of the antediluvian chronology in Genesis 5 but has a different local cause. The clues in this chapter are as follows: In the MT, all the postdiluvian ancestors, including Noah and Shem, are alive at Abraham's birth, and three (Shem, Shelah, and Eber) survive him; in the SP, only Abraham's father, Terah, is alive at his birth; and in the LXX, only the previous three ancestors, Terah, Nahor, and Serug, are alive at Abraham's birth, and none survives him. The situations in the SP and LXX conform to normal genealogical time, whereas the MT has a remarkable situation of the contemporaneity of the postdiluvian generations. This is a noteworthy disparity between the MT on one side and the SP and LXX on the other.

In this case, it is relatively easy to show that the chronologies in the SP and LXX have a partially shared strategy of revising a chronology that is nearly identical to that of the MT. The formula is as follows:

Proto-SP
> *Arpachshad to Serug:* Add one hundred to the age at begetting, and subtract one hundred from the remainder, leaving the age at death unchanged.
> *Nahor:* Add fifty to the age at begetting, and subtract fifty from the remainder, leaving the age at death unchanged.
> Result: All the ancestors before Terah die before Abraham's birth.

Proto-LXX
> *Arpachshad to Serug:* Add one hundred to the age at begetting.
> *Nahor:* Add fifty to the age at begetting.
> Result: All the ancestors before Serug die before Abraham's birth.

The motive for these systematic revisions is to remove the perceived problem of the contemporaneity of Abraham's postdiluvian ancestors. This chronological issue was not rectified—and perhaps not seen as a problem—in the proto-MT textual tradition. It became an object of exegetical ingenuity in midrashic interpretation, as when Abraham sent Isaac to study in the academy of Shem (*Gen. Rab.* 56.11).

As shown in Table 15, the archetype, which approximates the original P chronology, is equal to the MT in all numbers except for Eber's remainder, 430 years. This is

Table 15. Editions of postdiluvian chronology

	Archetype	MT	SP	LXX
Shem *b*	100	″	″	″
r	500	″	″	″
d	—	—	600	—
	(1842 AM)	(2156 AM)	(1807 AM)	(2742 AM)
Adjustment	+2	″	″	″
Arpachshad *b*	35	″	135	135
r	403	″	303	430
d	—	—	438	—
	(1747 AM)	(2061 AM)	(1612 AM)	(2674 AM)
Kenan II *b*	—	—	—	130
r	—	—	—	330
				(2839 AM)
Shelah *b*	30	″	130	130
r	403	″	303	330
d	—	—	433	—
	(1812 AM)	(2126 AM)	(1877 AM)	(2969 AM)
Eber *b*	34	″	134	134
r	370	430	270	″
d	—	—	404	—
	(1813 AM)	(2187 AM)	(1978 AM)	(3143 AM)
Peleg *b*	30	″	130	130
r	209	″	109	″
d	—	—	239	—
	(1682 AM)	(1996 AM)	(1947 AM)	(3112 AM)
Reu *b*	32	″	132	132
r	207	″	107	″
d	—	—	239	—
	(1712 AM)	(2026 AM)	(2077 AM)	(3242 AM)
Serug *b*	30	″	130	130
r	200	″	100	″
d	—	—	230	—
	(1735 AM)	(2049 AM)	(2200 AM)	(3365 AM)
Nahor *b*	29	″	79	79
r	119	″	69	129
d	—	—	148	—
	(1683 AM)	(1997 AM)	(2248 AM)	(3373 AM)
Terah *b*	70	″	″	″
r	—	—	—	—
d	205	″	145	″
	(1769 AM)	(2083 AM)	(2324 AM)	(3449 AM)
Abraham	(1634–1809 AM)	(1948–2123 AM)	(2249–2424 AM)	(3314–3489 AM)

Note: b, age at begetting; *r,* remainder of lifespan; *d,* age at death (= *b* + *r*); AM, *anno mundi*; ″, unchanged from archetype; —, a lack in the text.

probably a scribal reminiscence and transposition of the previous number, 34 years (see TEXTUAL NOTE a). The year of death after creation (*anno mundi*, AM), which is not in the text but easily added up, is supplied in parentheses. The other values given are *b*, age at begetting; *r*, remainder of lifespan; and *d*, age of death (= *b* + *r*). Note that only the SP regularly supplies the number for *d*, and the LXX has an extra ancestor, Kenan, who shares the name of Kenan (*qênān*) in 5:9–14.

The formula in which *b* (archetype) = M = (SP/LXX – 100) is consistent from Arpachshad through Serug, as is the formula *b* (archetype) = M = (SP/LXX – 50) for Nahor. There are some variants in the formula for *r*, in which *r* (archetype) = M/LXX = (SP + 100) for Arpachshad through Serug. These variants may be due to scribal errors, as with Eber's *r* in the MT (see above) or Arpachshad's and Shelah's *r* values in the LXX. Nahor's *r* in the LXX is arguably a minor textual change from '*śrh* ("ten") to '*śrym* ("twenty") (Hendel 1998: 73).

The addition of Kenan II in the proto-LXX seems to be a harmonization with the ten-generation structure of the chronology in Genesis 5. Although this makes the antediluvian and postdiluvian chronologies formally equivalent, it overlooks the implicit point of the original chronology that Abraham is the tenth generation from Noah. The values for Kenan II reproduce those of his son, Shelah.

The addition in proto-SP of the death formula, "All the days of PN were *X* years, and he died," is a parallel case of harmonization with the formal structure of the antediluvian chronology. It would appear that the postdiluvian chronology lacked this feature, which was easily supplied by a proto-SP scribe.

The two-year adjustment to the birth of Arpachshad "two years after the flood" (11:10, all versions) seems to be an adjustment, perhaps by P or R, of the combination of the "book of Adam's genealogy" with the P flood narrative. Shem's age at begetting of one hundred years indicates that Arpachshad was born in the year of the flood. (Note that Noah was five hundred years old when he begat Shem and was six hundred when the flood began; 5:32, 7:6). But no infant enters or exits the ark (7:7, 13; 8:18; all P). The two-year gap reconciles the birth of Arpachshad with the flood narrative.

LITERARY DESIGN

This section consists of two parts: the postdiluvian genealogy (11:10–26) and the opening of the Abram narrative (11:27–32). The first part is entirely P, and the second part is a combination of P (11:27, 31–32) and J (11:28–30) (Emerton 1992; Hendel 2011: 186–90). R added a brief harmonization ("in Ur of the Chaldeans," 11:28) to bridge the different locations of Abram's homeland (see below).

The postdiluvian genealogy resumes the form of the antediluvian genealogy in Genesis 5, the "book of Adam's genealogy" (*sēper tôlədōt 'ādām*, 5:1), with some modifications. The supplements include the introductory rubric "This is the genealogy of Shem" ('*elleh tôlədōt šēm*, 11:10), marking this as a new section of Genesis, and the rubric that follows the genealogy, "This is the genealogy of Terah" ('*ēlleh tôlədōt teraḥ*, 11:27), marking the beginning of the next section. Another supplement is the temporal detail "two years after the flood," which reconciles the genealogy with the flood chronology, noting that Arpachshad was born after the year-long duration of the flood (see NOTES at 11:10). The main structural change is the absence of the death formula in the postdiluvian genealogy. Compare the formulaic diction (which varies at some points) in the antediluvian and postdiluvian genealogies:

PN$_1$ lived X years, and he fathered PN$_2$. After he fathered PN$_2$, PN$_1$ lived Y years, and he fathered sons and daughters. All the days of PN$_1$ were Z years, and he died. (5:3–32)

PN$_1$ lived X years, and he fathered PN$_2$. After he fathered PN$_2$, PN$_1$ lived Y years, and he fathered sons and daughters. (11:10–26)

We do not know whether the death formula was lacking in the postdiluvian section of the "book of Adam's genealogy" or whether it was omitted by a later writer (P or R). But the death formula is provided for Terah in the last verse of the chapter (11:32), which serves to enclose the beginning of the Abram story within the genealogical structure.

The antediluvian and postdiluvian genealogies have another layer of symmetry, with some variation, in the overall shape of two segments. The antediluvian section has the form of a linear genealogy of ten generations from Adam to Noah, plus a segmented generation of three sons: "Noah fathered Shem, Ham, and Japheth" (5:31). The postdiluvian section has essentially the same form, but with a difference. The linear genealogy has nine generations from Shem to Terah and ends with a tenth segmented generation of three sons: "[Terah] fathered Abram, Nahor, and Haran" (11:26). Both segments have nine or ten generations plus a final threefold generation, but they differ in the location of the branching. This is so that Shem can occur twice, once (with his brothers) at the end of the antediluvian genealogy, and again as the apex of the postdiluvian genealogy. This yields a variation within a formal symmetry (Table 16).

Table 16. Antediluvian and postdiluvian genealogies

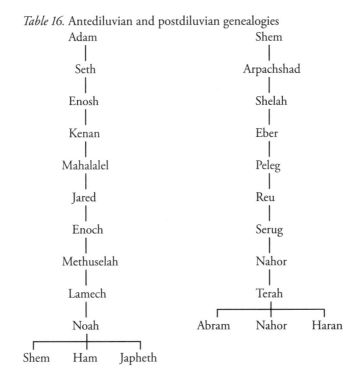

Notably, the edition of the postdiluvian genealogy in proto-LXX adds a generation to the postdiluvians, that of Kenan, son of Arpachshad, which serves to harmonize the structure of the two genealogies (Hendel 1998: 74–75). But in so doing, this edition adds a confusion—there is already a Kenan, son of Enosh—and loses the emphasis on Abram as the tenth generation.

The story of Abram begins, as noted above, with the P rubric, "This is the genealogy of Terah" (11:27). The P text continues with a resumptive repetition of Terah's sons, yielding a circular *inclusio*: "[he] fathered (*wayyôled*) Abram, Nahor, and Haran. This is the genealogy (*tôlədōt*) of Terah. Terah fathered (*hôlîd*) Abram, Nahor, and Haran" (11:26–27). The threefold repetition of *yld* (in varying *hiphil* and denominative forms) creates a dense emphasis on fathering children in this patriline. These will be a key concern in the narrative of Abram that follows.

The J account of Abram's family in 11:28–30 is presumably a fragment of a fuller J introduction to the Abram story, which R has truncated and folded into the P text. Since it is an excerpted text, it is difficult to comment on its literary form, except that the preserved portion sets the backdrop for several *Leitwort* repetitions and thematic transformations that follow in the J narrative. The most ominous is the terse but emphatic anticipatory detail, "Sarai was barren; she had no son" (11:30). The *Leitwort* "barren" (*ʿăqārâ*) and the theme of the desire for a male heir will resound in the following narrative for three generations. (The *Leitwort* *ʿăqārâ* recurs in each generation: for Rebekah in 25:21 and Rachel in 29:31.) The phrase "in the land of his kin" (*bə'ereṣ môladtô*, 11:28) and the description of kinship relations in the patrimonial house of Terah (11:29–30) echo in Yahweh's call to Abram, "Go from your land (*'arṣəkā*) and your kin (*môladtəkā*) and your father's house (*bêt 'ābîkā*)" (12:1). As Alter (1996: 50) observes, the "two terms [in 'land of his kin'] are broken out from each other to yield the focusing sequence" of land—kin—father's house. The descriptive sequence in 11:28–30 is taken up and given dramatic intensity in Yahweh's address to Abram. The J sequence prepares the way for Abram's initiation into his new identity as the chosen patriarch (Hendel 2019a: 572–76).

HOMELANDS

According to Genesis 1–11, history begins in and around Mesopotamia. Yahweh plants a garden "in Eden, in the east," where he places "the human he had formed" (2:8). From Eden branch the Tigris and Euphrates, the great rivers of Mesopotamia (2:14–15). Cain is condemned to wander "east of Eden" (4:16). Noah's ark comes to rest in "the mountains of Ararat" (8:4), north of Mesopotamia. The first people "journeyed in the east" and "came upon a valley in the land of Sumer, and they settled there" (11:2) and built the city and tower of Babylon (11:9). In our section, Terah took Abram, Sarai, and Lot and "sent them from Ur of the Chaldeans to go to the land of Canaan. They came to Haran and settled there" (11:31). Ur is in Lower Mesopotamia, and Haran is in Upper Mesopotamia. After this initial stage in the journey to Canaan, Abram and his family are still dwelling in Mesopotamia. Humankind in general comes from "the east," and Abram's homeland is in Mesopotamia.

Aside from these explicit statements, Abram's genealogy has implicit links to Mesopotamian locales. In the last four generations of the postdiluvian genealogy, all the names other than Abram are cognate with place names in Upper Mesopotamia (Table 17 and Notes to 11:20–26). Here are the equivalences in Hebrew and Akkadian:

Śərûg = *Sarūgi*, village in the region of Haran in the Baliḫ River Valley
Nāḥôr = *Naḫur*, city east of Haran in the upper Ḫabur River Valley
Teraḥ ~ *(Til) Turaḫi*, village in the region of Haran in the Baliḫ River Valley, with slightly different vocalic pattern
Ḥārān ~ *Ḥarrān*, city of Haran, with weakening of initial guttural (*ḥ > h*)

Table 17. Ancestral names and toponyms

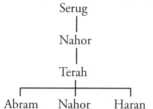

These names of Abram's ancestors and kin correspond to the region of Abram's homeland in Upper Mesopotamia (Delitzsch 1888: 362; Dillmann 1897: 403–4; Albright 1957: 236–37). This is curious, because these correspondences in the P genealogy conflict with P's narrative, in which Abram's homeland was in Ur of the Chaldeans in Lower Mesopotamia, and the family later journeyed to Haran in Upper Mesopotamia (11:31). This internal contradiction in P may suggest that the implicit association with Haran is primary, as it is in J, and the explicit association with Ur is secondary, perhaps a reinterpretation or updating of older tradition in P (see Notes at 11:31).

The brief J account of Abram's family in 11:28–30, truncated and interpolated into the surrounding P text, subtly foregrounds some key themes that will be developed in the following J narrative. As noted above, R harmonized this section with the P text by supplying "in Ur of the Chaldeans" after "in the land of his kin" (11:28), thus identifying this homeland with the locale in the following P text (11:31). But there is only one journey in J, from Haran to Canaan, and it occurs at Yahweh's request in the call to Abram in 12:1–4a. The preserved beginning of the Abram story in J is as follows: "Haran died before his father Terah in the land of his kin (*bə'ereṣ môladtô*) . . . Abram and Nahor took for themselves wives. Abram's wife's name was Sarai, and Nahor's wife's name was Milcah, the daughter of Haran, who was the father of Milcah and Iscah. Sarai was barren; she had no son" (11:28–30). As noted above, the description of Terah's household—the social unit called the "house of the father"—sets the backdrop for Yahweh's resonant command to Abram, "Go from your land and your kin and your father's house" (12:1). This request moves from the place ("your land") to the local genealogical relationships ("your kin") to the family unit ("your father's house"). To leave one's homeland, which encompasses place, genealogy, and family, is a difficult request. Yet the consequence is direct: "Abram went out, as Yahweh had told him" (12:4), showing Abram's response to Yahweh's extraordinary request.

The description in J of Abram's "father's house" (*bêt 'āb*) yields a rich network of family relationships, with Terah as paterfamilias and Abram as the firstborn son

(Table 18). This represents the "house of the father" (*bêt-'āb*), a kinship unit that designates an extended or joint family, who ideally lived in a single dwelling, a multiroom house (Stager 1985a). As Schloen (2001: 108) observes, "Such a household typically consisted of a conjugal couple and their unmarried children, together with their married sons and their wives and children, as well as other unmarried or dependent paternal kinsfolk and servants." Terah's wife is not named, but the genealogy then branches to include male and female members of the patrimonial household.

Table 18. Genealogy of Terah's household

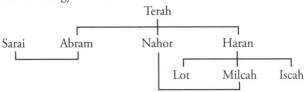

But this is not a static picture; there are indications of trouble in the household. Haran dies before his father. Iscah seems to be an unmarried daughter. The marriage of Nahor with his niece Milcah preserves the continuity of Haran's lineage. (Nahor and Milcah's sons—mostly the names of Aramean tribes and locales—are presented in 22:20–23.) Abram and Sarai's problem is tersely stated, but its consequence is clear: "And Sarai was barren; she had no son" (11:30). The lineage of Abram is in crisis.

This picture of Abram's household is the backdrop for the turning point of the divine call to Abram. Yahweh's promise, "I will make you a great people" (12:2), is in tension with the trouble in Abram's lineage. This crisis between the family reality and the divine promise provides the motive force for much of the subsequent Abram narrative.

Although the J narrative is truncated and folded into P, it is relatively clear that the ancestral homeland is in the region of Haran. This is shown in several sources in the ancestral narrative. In J, Rebekah instructs Jacob, "Rise and flee to Laban, my brother, in Haran" (27:43), and he later arrives in Haran, home of Laban, descendant of Nahor (29:5). In the doublet in P, she instructs him, "Rise and go to Paddan-Aram, the house of Bethuel, your mother's father, and take from there a wife from the daughters of Laban, your mother's brother" (28:2). In a supplemental story (Genesis 24), Abraham's servant goes to the ancestral homeland, called Aram Naharaim ("Aram of the Two Rivers") and "the city of Nahor" (24:10), to bring back a bride for Isaac from Nahor's lineage.

The region of Haran is the region where Abraham and Nahor were born and where Nahor's line persists. Jacob marries patrilateral and matrilateral cousins (Leah and Rachel), and Isaac marries a patrilateral cousin (Rebekah), both of which conform to the endogamous (inner lineage) ideal. The journeys back and forth between the homeland and the promised land are essential features in the ancestral narrative. Let us turn to the historical and cultural contexts of these memories of ancestral homelands.

CONTEXTS

Outside of Genesis, the cultural memory of the homeland in Mesopotamia, whether in Haran or Ur, is evoked several times, usually in passages that are dependent on Genesis.

For instance, Joshua recounts at the covenant ceremony in Shechem: "In olden times, your fathers dwelled in the land across the river—Terah, father of Abraham and father of Nahor—and they served other gods. I took your father, Abraham, from the land across the river, and I led him through all the land of Canaan" (Josh 24:2–3). This summary draws on passages in Genesis (harmonizing the Abram story with Jacob's burial of foreign gods), but using Deuteronomic language, with the formulaic ʾĕlōhîm ʾăḥērîm ("other gods") rather than ʾĕlōhê hannēkār ("foreign gods," Gen 35:2–4). Another text dependent on Genesis is Neh 9:7, which draws on the diction of Gen 15:7 and 17:5: "You brought him out of Ur of the Chaldeans, and you changed his name to Abraham." These citations show the textual authority of Genesis and the connective way that the stories were understood.

The only mention of the ancestral homeland that is likely independent of Genesis is Hos 12:13–14. In this text the prophet recounts Jacob's flight to the ancestral homeland for a wife:

> Jacob fled to the field of Aram,
>> Israel served for a wife,
>> and for a wife he guarded. (Hos 12:13)

The prophet then juxtaposes this episode with Moses and the exodus:

> By a prophet Yahweh brought up Israel from Egypt,
>> and by a prophet he was guarded. (Hos 12:14)

In this contrast, Hosea prefers the exemplary prophet, Moses, by whom Israel was guarded (nišmar) during Israel's exodus from Egypt, to the relative weakness of Jacob, who fled to Aram, served (ʿbd) for a wife, and "guarded" (šāmar) sheep. The heroic prophet is contrasted with the frightened and subservient patriarch.

In the context of other mentions of Aram in Hosea, this text arguably expresses a criticism of Israel's recent history with Aram. As Blum (2009: 310) observes, in light of the text's focus on "the name of the place to which Jacob fled . . . [and] Israel's dependency (ʿbd) there, the contemporary reader cannot but think of the recent history of catastrophic events." Israel had been the junior ally with Damascus in campaigns against Assyria, which ended with disaster in 734–732 BCE. The story of Jacob's journey to Haran is used by the prophet as a critique of Israel's servitude to Aram-Damascus—and an assertion of the superiority of prophets (like Hosea).

This allusion to Jacob's flight to the ancestral homeland, which activates the audience's knowledge of the story, indicates that this cultural memory was current in the eighth century BCE. Hosea describes this homeland as the "field of Aram" (śadēh ʾărām). This geographical designation is consonant with Genesis, where in P the region is called Paddan-Aram, "the Way (or Field) of Aram" (25:20, 28:2, etc.) In 24:10 the region is called Aram-Naharaim, "Aram of the Two Rivers," referring to the region of Upper Mesopotamia whose general boundaries are the Euphrates and the Ḥabur (or possibly the Tigris) Rivers. This term is frequent elsewhere (e.g., Deut 23:5, Judg 3:8).

In most biblical texts, the ancestral homeland is described as Aram, and the kinfolk who live there are Aramean. In P, Rebekah is "the daughter of Bethuel the Aramean from Paddan-Aram, and sister of Laban the Aramean" (Gen 25:20, similarly 28:5). In the episode where Jacob flees from him, Laban is called "Laban the Aramean" (31:20–24, J), and the two make a pact at the boundary between Israel and Aram in Gilead.

In Nahor's genealogy in 22:20–24 (J), Nahor fathers twelve sons who bear the names of Aramean peoples, cities, and tribes, including his son Chesed (*keśed*, Chaldea) and grandson Aram (*'ărām*). The Aramean identity of the ancestral homeland is a persistent feature, which is recalled in the ritual declaration on the festival of the first fruits, "my father was a perishing (or wandering) Aramean" (*'ărammî 'ōbēd 'ābî*, Deut 26:5). Like many ritual texts, this is an alliterative and rhyming sequence, with repetition of word-initial sounds (*'aleph* + *ā, ō, ā*), twice a medial *bet*, twice a rhyming final vowel (*-î*), and the final focusing synthesis, *'ābî* ("my father").

But there are problems with the Aramaic ethnicity and locale of the ancestors across the Euphrates. Despite their occasional military alliances, there was a cultural clash between Aram and Israel during this period. This tension is highlighted when Laban and Jacob separate in Gilead and make a pact of truce (Genesis 31). Laban names the ritual memorial stones in Aramaic, *yəgar śāhădûtā'* ("mound of witness"), while Jacob gives them a Hebrew name, *gal'ēd*, playing on the name Gilead (31:47). Laban's use of Aramaic is a code-switching device that emphasizes his foreign identity. At this geographical boundary between Aram and Israel, the separateness of Laban "the Aramean" from Jacob/Israel is crucial. The bond of kinship, activated in the ancestral homeland, now turns into an opposition, a cultural rupture between Aram and Israel. The Aramean ethnicity and language of the ancestral kin is a boundary condition in this story. The Aramean ancestors are kin but are also hostile foreigners. This is a paradox in the biblical memory of the ethnic homeland. To explore this issue more deeply, we turn to the ancient historical context.

The region of Upper Mesopotamia around Haran—the Baliḥ and upper Ḥabur Valleys, in Arabic the Jazira—was populated by Aramean and other tribal peoples since at least the twelfth century BCE, when this area was called "the land of the Arameans" (*KUR armāya;* Younger 2016: 36–37). This area was intermittently invaded by Assyrian kings until the ninth century BCE, when the region was incorporated into the Assyrian Empire. The ninth-century conquest of Haran and other Aramean locales and tribes is mentioned in 2 Kgs 19:12 (= Isa 37:12), where Sennacherib boasts in a letter, "My fathers destroyed Gozan, Haran, Reṣeph, and the Bet-Adenites." Haran was a prominent city in the Neo-Assyrian era, serving as an administrative center of the western empire (Liverani 2014: 505). It is mentioned in Ezek 27:23 as a trading partner of Tyre, reflecting its location on a major trade route between Assyria and the west.

Some of the Samarian exiles in 722 BCE were resettled in Gozan in the upper Ḥabur Valley (2 Kgs 17:6). But the deportation of the "lost tribes" to various regions of Assyria, designed to eliminate the formerly rebellious vassal state, is unlikely to have yielded a memory of the region of Haran as the ancestral homeland. As the allusion in Hosea indicates, this memory was alive before the end of the Northern Kingdom.

From an Israelite perspective, the Arameans of Upper Mesopotamia were a world away. The Arameans familiar in biblical sources are closer to home, consisting of western polities such as Rehob, Zobah, and Geshur, and above all, Aram-Damascus (e.g., 2 Sam 8:3–8; 2 Kings 5–6; Amos 1:3–5; Isa 7:1–9). Fleming (1998: 57) aptly describes this complication for Genesis: "The Genesis tradition of a north Syrian origin for Abraham and his family is both central to the narrative and difficult to explain in terms of peoples and regional political relations during the lives of the Israelite states. . . . [This is] a region different from the familiar Aram centered at Damascus. These are not the

Arameans known to the writers' direct experience." The Arameans of Haran and its environs were outside the usual horizons of Israelite experience.

As the story of Jacob and Laban at Gilead shows, another problem with this Aramean connection is language. Aramaic and Hebrew are both Northwest Semitic languages but have many contrasting features and are relatively distant within this group (Garr 1985: 216–35). According to the Bible, Hebrew and Old Aramaic were not mutually intelligible. When an Assyrian official speaks to Hezekiah's officials in Hebrew, they implore him, "Please speak to your servants in Aramaic, for we understand it, but do not speak to us in Judean in the hearing of the people on the wall" (2 Kgs 18:26 = Isa 36:11). Palace officials learned Aramaic as the language of international diplomacy, but to ordinary Hebrew speakers it was unintelligible (Garr 1985: 231). This linguistic disjunction poses a complication to the memory that the ancestors were Arameans of Upper Mesopotamia. Yet this is the claim of the genealogy and narrative of Genesis.

Let us explore the wandering routes of these cultural memories, what we may call the "mnemohistory" of the ancestral homeland in Upper Mesopotamia. A clue is the floating temporality of the place names in Abram's genealogy: Haran, Nahor, Serug, and Terah. As we have seen, these are places in Upper Mesopotamia. While Ḥarrān was a prominent city in the second and first millennia, Naḫur disappeared after the Middle Assyrian period (ca. twelfth century BCE), and its role as a regional center was replaced by other cities. Sarūgi and Turaḫi, towns in the region of Ḥarrān, are first mentioned in Neo-Assyrian royal inscriptions of the mid-ninth century BCE. Sarūgi is also mentioned in the "Harran Census" of the eighth century BCE. These two towns are not known in our sources before the Neo-Assyrian period. As these details indicate, there is a floating time range when these places flourished, but perhaps no single time when they were all in existence. This floating temporality poses a complication and a possible solution.

This temporal context of the ancestral homeland in Upper Mesopotamia arguably requires a longer time span, what Braudel (1980: 27–49) calls the *longue durée* (see Burke 2021: 1–13). This term designates the slow movement of social, economic, and demographic change in a given zone, including cyclical and durative cultural practices. In our case this ecological zone consists of the semiarid steppes and highlands of the Levant, extending in a crescent from Israel and Transjordan to Upper Mesopotamia. These areas were primarily pastoralist zones inhabited by tribal peoples in the eighteenth to twelfth centuries BCE and beyond. This zone began to be intensively settled during the Iron Age, yielding new territorial tribal polities, including the Aramean states, Israel, Ammon, Moab, and Edom. As Liverani (2014: 435) comments: "In terms of demography and settlements, the areas that were not particularly suitable for irrigation (such as semi-arid plateaus, hills and mountains) that declined in the Late Bronze Age suddenly became the preferred areas for Iron Age settlements. Sedentarisation, then, led to a significant change in the areas formerly used as pastureland in the Late Bronze Age." This ecological zone has a long continuity of tribal culture, which interacted in various ways with territorial states and empires whose networks of trade and conquest impacted the region during the second millennium BCE. In the wake of the rising and falling political powers, the ethnic identities of the tribes and tribal confederations also oscillated, collapsing and recrystallizing under various names and configurations, including Amorite, Sutû, Aḫlamu, Aramean, and Israelite.

In older scholarship, each of these peoples was seen as a different population, who displaced each other by migration or invasion. More recently, the waves of new ethnic and tribal identities have been more plausibly analyzed as adaptations by local groups to social and ecological changes. As Pitard (1994: 209–10) states:

> The early sources give no clear hint that the Arameans were newcomers into Upper Mesopotamia. They are portrayed as large, tribally oriented groups with substantial pastoral components and also large numbers of members living in towns and villages. This description is quite similar to that of the large tribes that inhabited this area during the eighteenth century, as known from the Mari archives. It seems quite unlikely that the Arameans were immigrants into Syria and Upper Mesopotamia at all, but rather that they were the West Semitic–speaking peoples who had lived in that area throughout the second millennium, some as pastoralists and some in villages, towns, and cities.

Similarly, G. M. Schwartz (1989: 255) writes, "The sequence of designations from Amorite to Aramean probably reflects changing ethnic or tribal affiliations." The change of names reflects perceptions of ethnicity and kinship—which can change over time and circumstances—not a wholly new population.

The Mari letters (mid-eighteenth century BCE) that address tribal affairs in the regions of Ḫarrān (in the territorial coalition of Zalmaqum) and Naḫur (in the Idamaraṣ coalition) illustrate the kinds of political relationships between tribes, cities, and kings that characterize this geographical zone for many centuries. For instance, kings must deal diplomatically with the tribal chiefs and elders. As a diplomat advises Zimri-Lim, king of Mari:

> Write to the Idamaraṣ elders and to Aduna-Addu [king of Ḫanzat in Zalmaqum] for them to come to you, then come to a peace agreement [lit. "kill a donkey"] and talk frankly with them. Keep these people under your control. Your flocks are now pasturing in their district, (so) your messengers should be in constant contact with Aduna-Addu. Previously, Yaḫdun-Lim, when he would go to that land, would give gifts to the Idamaraṣ elders, and his flocks were secure; there was neither deception nor transgression. Now then, act in the same way as your father. (A.2730; Sasson 2015: 137–38)

Gifts, ceremonies, and peace treaties are key instruments of diplomacy when dealing with tribes in this region, then as now.

An example of tribal diplomacy in action is a letter from a tribal chief to Zimri-Lim telling how he resolved a crisis over grain reserves by giving gifts and making a treaty establishing "peace" (*salimum*) between the pastoralist tribes and kings of Idamaraṣ (A.4341; Guichard 2013). This chief averted conflict "for the Ḫana pastoralists and my lord's flocks" (lines 20–21).

In a Middle Assyrian letter from Tell Ṣābi Abyad (thirteenth to twelfth centuries BCE), a fortified farmstead in the Baliḫ Valley south of Haran, a regional Assyrian official upbraids his chief steward for failure to arrange properly a dinner with local Sutû tribal leaders (the Sutû tribal confederation is attested in the Mari letters, and the term persists, sometimes generalized as "nomad," to the first millennium; see Heltzer 1981; Younger 2016: 88–94): "What is this, that you do not execute my orders as I tell you?

Why did you not give orders to your brewer to send a potter to Dunni-Aššur? Let a written assignment go out from you to your brewer in Saḫalu that he should make available beer and *tariḫu*-vessels when the Sutû come to have dinner with me. Who else would I ask, who else would give it to me?" (Fales 2014: 233). Diplomacy with tribal leaders, it seems, goes well with Assyrian beer and fine crockery.

A generation later, an official of the regional Assyrian polity, who held the title "grand vizier, king of Hanigalbat," made a treaty with Sutû chiefs of the Niḫsānu tribe. A provision stipulates that leaders of other Sutû tribes serve as witnesses in disputed legal cases: "[I]f there are legal problems regarding compensation for unlawfully taken property, (to which) attention has been given, then the [. . .] of the Ešrayû and the [chief]s of the Qaʾirānu sit as witnesses" (Wiggermann 2010: 56). During the Middle Assyrian period, Sutû tribes are attested from the Baliḫ and Ḫabur Valleys to "the foot of Mt. Lebanon" (Grayson 1991: 98, 107; Younger 2016: 92).

Tiglath-Pilesar I (1114–1076 BCE) records a similar geographical range in his campaigns against tribal peoples he calls "Aḫlamû-Arameans," perhaps meaning "pastoral nomads in the land of the Arameans" (*aḫlamī KUR armāya;* Fales 2017: 142–50). These tribes lived in the region from Upper Mesopotamia to Mount Lebanon. Most of his campaigns were to the west of the Euphrates: "I crossed the Euphrates twenty-eight times, twice in one year, in pursuit of the Aḫlamû-Aramaeans. I defeated them from the foot of Mt. Lebanon, the city of Tadmor of the land of Amurru as far as Rāpiqu of Karduniaš (Babylonia)" (Pakute Inscription; Grayson 1976: 37–38). The geographical spread of the Aḫlamû-Arameans is equivalent to the range of the Sutû, and before them the Yaminites of the Mari letters (Fleming 1998: 61–62; Sasson 2015: 146), extending westward from Upper Mesopotamia to the Beqaʿ Valley of Lebanon.

Throughout this long period of tribal formation and reformation, with changing adaptations to regional economies and polities, a tribal way of life persisted, which is portrayed in the narrative and genealogy of Abraham. This portrait of the ancestors and their tribal homeland suggests a continuity with Levantine tribal culture in the *longue durée*. As Fleming (1998: 65) comments, "The Bible's location for Abraham's origin does not present Israel as an isolated phenomenon but makes Israel kin to a whole range of peoples." These peoples lived to the north (Aram), east (Ammon, Moab, Edom), and south (Ishmaelites and other Arab peoples). The biblical memory of the Upper Mesopotamian homeland is an origin story and ethnic map for all these tribal peoples and polities contemporary with Israel.

These peoples shared a cultural pattern as tribal, segmentary societies, linked by genealogical ties, with a mixture of pastoralist, agricultural, and village lifeways. Their ecological zones were also largely shared, primarily in the semiarid steppe and highland regions, between the sown (i.e., the irrigated or riverine lowlands) and the desert.

The biblical memories of Haran and the land of Nahor—of an ancestral homeland in Upper Mesopotamia—seem strikingly specific. We do not know whether this memory was shared with other peoples. It seems to be a feature of the *longue durée* of tribal memories in the Levant. It belongs to the deep past and the present, a conjuncture of history and tribal memory. It may illustrate the mixture of past and present in biblical memory. As Zumthor (1990: 87) observes, "No epic is totally devoid of historical ingredients regardless of the mythic opacity of its discourse. . . . The universal feature of epic . . . is this interpenetration of elements."

In sum, the ancestors' journeys from Upper Mesopotamia to the southern Levant and back again retrace the path of ancient pasturelands, in the footsteps of Amorites, Sutû, Aḥlamû, and Arameans. There are old tracks in this cultural memory, mingled with present concerns. It has a particular relevance in our passage because it brings the ancestors from the ancient east—the place of creation and dispersion—to the promised land.

Index of Subjects

Note: Page numbers in *italics* refer to figures; numbers in **bold** refer to tables.

Babylon, 39, 40, 58, 169, 363, 394, 395, 398–99, 403–4, 405; destruction of, 19–20; hanging gardens of, 163; ziggurat of, 395, 405–6

Babylonian exile, 43, 303

baptism, 46

"Be Fruitful and Multiply," 13, 40–41, 126–27, 136, 326–27, 329–30

Bethuel, 423

Biblical Hebrew. *See* Hebrew

Boaz, 229

Cain, 9, 32, 40, 96–97; birth of, 213, 215; curse of, 9, 222–25, 240; descendants of, 226–35, 238, 250; as farmer, 216; and the Kenites, 214–15; killing Abel, 220–21; mark of, 226; meaning of name, 213–14; sacrifice of, 216–17; wife of, 227

Cain and Abel, 38, 204–5, 220–21; Genesis text, 96–97; literary design, 236–39; notes and commentary, 211–42

Cainites, 10

Calah, 370

Calneh, 369

Canaan (land of), 24, 277, 373

Canaan (son of Ham), 9, 32, 301, 347, 364–65, 387; descendants of, 371–73. *See also* Curse of Canaan

Canaanites, 351–52

Caphtorites, 370–71

Casluhites, 370–71

Cave of the Patriarchs, 35

chaos and re-creation, 339–41

cherub/cherubim, 25, 194–97, 205, 206, 207

Chesed, 424

Christ, 35, 46, 49, 204

Church of the Holy Sepulcher, 35

circumcision, 321, 330, 332, 341

City of Four, 35

civilization, 39–40, 404

contexts: of Abraham/Abram's story, 422–28; of Adam to Noah genealogy, 259–62; of Cain and Abel, 240–42; of the Curse of Canaan, 356–57; of the Eden narrative, 204–10; of the flood narrative (J), 300–306; of the flood nar-

rative (P), 341–45; of Sons of God and Daughters of Humans, 275–82; of the Table of Nations, 388–89; of the Tower of Babel, 404–7

corruption and destruction, 12

Creation narrative: creation out of nothing, 109; days (day 1), 107–16, 142–43 (day 2), 116–20, 142–43 (day 3), 120–22, 142–43 (day 4), 122–25, 142–43 (day 5), 125–27, 142–43 (day 6), 127–38, 142–43 (day 7), 138–41; diptych design of, 142–44; double representations of, 45–46; Egyptian, 149–50, 162; and the flood narrative, 146; Genesis text, 93–94, 105–6; and the Gospel of John, 46; in Isaiah, 148; *Leitwort* style, 13; Mesopotamian, 118–19, 123, 124, 148–52, 158, 161; notes and commentary, 107–52; plot structure of, 31–32; textual notes, 106–7. *See also* Garden of Eden

culture and critique, 403–4

cuneiform texts, 53, 303, 411

Curse of Canaan, 9, 32, 241, 351; Genesis text, 100–101; notes and commentary, 346–57. *See also* Canaan (son of Ham)

Cush, 364–65, 379

Cyrus, 381

Daniel, 129, 263, 288, 301

Darius I, 381

David (King), 134, 166, 229, 241

Dedan, 365, 366

deities (Babylonian): Anat, 281; Anu, 56, 209; Apsu, 58, 111, 118, 144, 149–50, 159, 164, 343, 406; Aruru, 57, 210; Astarte/Ishtar, 57, 292; Athtar, 206; Atum, 150; Baau, 110; Bau, 110; Ea, 58, 161, 208, 209, 287, 299, 342, 384; Enki, 56–57, 170, 268, 287, 288, 289, 294, 299, 300, 302, 303, 314, 342–43; Enlil, 54, 56–57, 58, 129, 132, 149, 150–51, 170, 249, 265, 270, 287, 288, 294, 299, 300, 302–3, 305–6; Id, 159; Mami, 161, 170, 299, 300, 302, 305, 306, 333; Marduk (Bēl), 58, 113, 118, 132, 140, 148, 149, 151, 170, 229, 332, 343, 395, 398, 405–6; Mummu, 112, 144; Nabu (Nebo), 148; Namma, 111; Namtar, 56;

Nikkal-Ib, 124; Ninsun, 57; Nintu, 56–57; Ninurta, 19, *127,* 210, 367–68, 381, 386; Šamaš, *124,* 132; Šapšu, 124; Siduri, 209; Tiamat, 58, 111, 118, 140, 149, 150, 151, 332; Yariḫu, 124

deities (Canaanite): Baal, 112, 197, 356, 384; "Earth-and-Heaven," 109; El, 129, 168, 266, 281, 357; Sea, 197

deities (Egyptian): Atum, 150; Geb, *119,* 150; Maat (Ma'at), 207, 261; Nun, 150; Nut, 119, *119,* 150; Osiris, *119;* Ptah, 113, 371; Re, *119;* Shu, *119,* 150; Thoth, 261

deities (Greek/Roman): Aphrodite, 292; Ares, 279; Dionysus, 357; Eros, 151; Hephaestus, 279; Hermes, 279; Poseidon, 279; Zeus, 279–80

demons, 57, 179, 219, 278, 303

destruction and restoration, 299–300

Diklah, 376–77

Diphat, 362–63

double representations, 5–8, **6**

doublets: in the Flood narrative, 334–35; in the Garden of Eden, 197, 205–6; in the Table of Nations, 379–84

dove, 18, 291–93, 324

earth, creation of, 121, 157–58. *See also* Creation narrative

Eber, 373–76, 379, 384, 385, 388, 410, 416, 418

Egypt (son of Ham), 364–65, 370

Egyptian cosmos, *119*

Elam, 374

Eliezer, 414

Elisha, 363

Elkanah, 229

'ĕlōhîm, 157, 201, 202, 262. *See also* angels; Sons of God; Yahweh/God

Enkidu, 39, 57–58, 137, 183, 210, 327

Enmeduranki, 261

Enoch, 44–45, 227–28, 247–51, 254, 262, 388

Enosh, 234–35, 238, 247, 254, 388

Erech, 368

Esagil, 405, 406

Esau, 229, 241

Etemenanki, 395, 398

Eunir, 394

Euphrates River, 94, 153, 168, 169–70, 302, 363, 376, 392, 420, 423, 424, 427

Eve: creation of, 51, 95–96, 172, 174–77, 201–3; eating the forbidden fruit, 37–38, 181–82; as mother of all life, 191–92; and the snake, 95, 177–81; sons of, 23; tomb of, 35. *See also* nakedness

flood hero, 57, 161, 209, 249–51, 252, 261, 281, 291–92, 294, 299, 300, 303–6, 314–15, 319, 324, 342–43, 360

Flood narrative, 11, 13, 41; according to J, 283–306; according to P, 307–45; and baptism, 46; chronology of, 319–20; and the creation narrative, 146; disharmonies in, 9; double representations of, 6–7; Genesis text, 98–100; location of, 323, 342–45; Mesopotamian, 25, 54–55, 291, 292, 294, 299–300, 302–5, 314–15, 320, 323, 324–25, 342–44; Noah's perceptions, 18; question of the Nephilim, 9, 271–72, 275, 278. *See also* ark; Noah

food laws, 27, 29

fratricide, 32, 221, 222, 223, 238, 239–40, 285

Garden of Eden, 10, 11, 30; creation of, 163–64; eating the forbidden fruit, 181–82; expulsion from the garden, 194, 201, 203–4; in Ezekiel, 206–7; Genesis text, 94–96; guardians of, 195–97, 205, 206, 207; as historical record, 48–51; interrogation and punishment, 38, 184–92; notes and commentary, 153–210; as purely symbolic, 48; repetitions of, 34; return to, 34–35; river in, 167–70. *See also* Creation narrative; innocence, loss of

genealogies, 5–8, 418–20; of Abram/Abraham, 420–21, **421**; of Adam, 7, 8, 97, 235, 243–62; Amorite, 388–89, **389**; antediluvian and postdiluvian, 256–59, **256, 257, 417, 419, 421**; Cainite, 226–35, 238, 250; of Enoch, 247–51; as ethnic genre, 22–24; in Genesis 5, 256–59; Hamite, **382**; of heaven and earth, 156; of Israel, 23; Japhethite, **380**; and memory, 35–36; as mental maps,

genealogies (*continued*)
388; of morals, 41–42; of Noah's sons,
359–89; of Shem, 7, **383**; from Shem
to Abram, 102, 408–28; Sumerian King
List, 259–61, **260**; of Terah, 422, **422**.
See also Table of Nations

Genesis: age of, 14–21; allegorical interpretation of, 45–46, 50; apocalyptic
interpretations of, 34, 44–46, 47, 48,
50, 204, 208, 262; author(s) of, 5;
Dead Sea Scrolls texts, 3, 364; figural
interpretations of, 44–53; as genealogy
and mythology, 21–36; historical context
of, 53–55; interpretations of, 42–44,
55–56; and Isaiah, 148; in Jeremiah, 147;
midrashic interpretations, 46–50; moral
world of, 36–42; in Nehemiah, 147;
origin of name, 4; plain sense of, 51–53;
in the Psalms, 147; scribal revisions
and new editions, 14; settings of the
sources, 18–20; sources and style, 4–5;
supplements, 13–14; textual families and
sources, 3–4

Genesis J: Abraham narrative, 205; dating
of, 14–15, 20–21; discontinuities, 7,
9–10; distinctive function words, 15–16;
diversity and continuity, 8–10; double
representation and redaction, 5–8, **6**;
Leitwort style and literary design, 10–12;
linguistic distinctions, 16–17; setting
and literary tradition, 18–20; stylistic
continuity, 10

Genesis P: dating of, 20–21; disharmonies,
7; diversity and continuity, 8–10; double
representation and redaction, 5–8, **6**;
Leitwort style and literary design, 12–13;
setting and literary tradition, 20; *tôlǝdôt*
genre, 22–24; unity and sequence, 8–9

Genesis R: double representation and
redaction, 5–8, **6**; transitional glosses,
7–8, 13–14, 290

genres: analytical, 21–22, 25–26; ethnic vs.
analytical, 21–24

Gether, 374–75

giants, 9, 252, 271, 272, 275–79, 281–82

Gihon, 169

Gilgamesh, 39, 40, 209–10, 278–79, 396

Girgashites, 371–72

"God Saw That It Was Good," 12–13, 114,
137–38, 339–40

Gomer, 361–62

Gudea (king of Lagash), 395

Hadoram, 376–77

Hagar, 414

Ham, 9, 252, 311, 346–47, 350, 359, 379,
380, 385

Hamatites, 372, 373

Hamites, 364–66, 373, 381, **382**, 385–88

Hammurapi Dynasty, 388–89, **389**

Haran, 410, 412–13, 414, 416, 421, 424, 427

Havilah, 168, 365, 376–77, 379

Hazarmaveth, 376–77

heaven: creation of, 157–58; naming of,
120; vault of, 116–19, 125

Hebrew, 21, 50, 108–9, 110, 120, 126,
128, 129, 136, 147, 156, 157, 163, 166,
168–70, 176, 191, 192, 214, 215, 219,
228, 229, 230, 231, 247, 258, 270, 271,
280, 304, 315, 321, 323, 356, 362, 363,
365, 367, 369, 373, 375, 376, 378, 379,
391–92, 409, 412, 413, 415, 421, 424,
425; Archaic Biblical (ABH), 15, 229,
269; Biblical, 15–16, 21, 158, 194, 229,
232, 314, 315, 317; Classical Biblical
(CBH), 15, 18–19, 43, 108, 109, 192,
213, 220, 269, 364; inscriptional, 252,
377; Late Biblical (LBH), 15, 108, 269,
364; medieval, 363; northern dialect,
269; paleo-, 3–4, 226; postbiblical, 108,
263, 409; postexilic, 346; preexilic,
346; Qumran, 15; Transitional Biblical
(TBH), 15, 148

Heth, 371–72

Hivites, 371–72

homelands, 420–22

hubris, 19, 29, 40, 386, 399, 403, 404, 407

Hul, 374–75

humans: creation of, 11, 128–36, 159–64;
as evil, 284–85, 299, 300; woman, 135,
160, 172, 174–77

hybrid creatures, *196*, 274–75, 279. *See also*
cherub/cherubim; Nephilim

imagery: "Adam and Eve" seal, *179*;
Babylonian snake-dragon, *187*; Egyptian

cosmos, *119;* Mesopotamian warrior god and dragon, *127;* Noah's ark, *316;* palm tree and winged hybrid creatures, *196;* Temple of the Babylonian sun god, *124;* Tower of Babel stele, *395*

immortality, 25, 34, 57, 164–65, 178, 193–94, 207–10, 249, 270, 272, 303, 396

innocence, loss of, 37, 39, 167, 177, 181, 183, 191, 198, 202, 203, 210, 354

Irad, 228

Isaac, 241, 414, 422

Iscah, 414

Ishmael, 241, 414

Jabal, 9, 230–31

Jacob, 51, 229, 241, 422–23, 424, 425

Japheth, 9, 252, 311, 346–47, 350, 352, 359, 360–61, 364, **380**, 385

Japhethites, 360–64, 380–81, **380**, 386–88

Jared, 247, 253, 254, 388

Jebusites, 371–72

Job, 111, 162, 191, 215, 218, 222, 239, 301, 375

Jobab, 101, 359, 376–78

Joktan, 376–77, 379, 381, 384

Joseph, 51, 220, 221

Joshua, 277, 422–23

Jubal, 9, 231

Kenan, 247, 254, 388

Kenan II, 418

Kenites, 214–15, 227, 240, 242

Keturah, 227, 376, 379, 387

Khnumhotep II, *230*

Kittites, 363–64

Laban, 422, 423, 424, 425

Lamech (descendant of Cain), 9, 38–39, 40, 226–30, 232–33, 238, 240, 388

Lamech (father of Noah), 251, 253, 254

languages: Akkadian, 53, 111, 114, 116, 117, 139, 161, 163, 168–70, 174, 186, 191, 192, 207, 229, 234, 269, 279, 303–4, 314, 315, 316, 319, 323, 324, 344, 361–63, 365, 366, 368–76, 378, 392, 394, 398–99, 411–15, 421; Amorite, 228, 229, 414; Arabic, 108, 213, 228, 229,

231, 315, 344, 365, 368, 369, 370, 376, 409, 424; Aramaic, 3, 16, 43, 110, 129, 163, 191, 192, 215, 252, 262, 263, 266, 278, 302, 303, 363, 371, 372, 375, 377, 412, 424, 425; Egyptian, 53, 234, 287, 364, 369, 371, 412; Greek, 4, 45, 108, 113, 157, 169, 244, 260, 278, 280, 313, 360–66, 371, 373, 375, 376, 398, 413; Luwian, 372; Old Persian, 53, 169, 363, 365; and the Tower of Babel, 390–93, 397–404, 405; Ugaritic, 109, 110, 111, 116, 126, 159, 206–7, 229, 230, 269, 279, 280, 281, 296, 315, 321, 351, 355, 356–57, 363, 365, 371, 372, 376, 384, 414; universal, 405. *See also* Hebrew

Leah, 241, 422

Lehabites, 370–71

Leitwort style, 198, 204–5, 222, 236, 264, 295, 337–39, 391, 402–3; in Classical Hebrew, 18; in J, 10–12, 236, 237, 272–73; in P, 12–13, 136, 145–46

lifespans, 246–55, **254**, 259–61, 302–3, 319, 416, **417**; limited, 268–70, 275

light: creation of, 46, 47–48, 49, 110–11, 113–15, 119, 122, 141, 142–43, 148; vs. darkness, 115–16, 117, 122, 143; as divine attribute, 113, 151–52; of heavenly bodies, 47–48, 50, 122–25, 138, 142, 143, 145, 147; spiritual, 49

literary design: Adam to Noah genealogy, 255–56; Cain and Abel, 236–39; the Curse of Canaan, 353–54; of the flood narrative (J), 297–98; of the flood narrative (P), 335–39; Garden of Eden, 197–200; Table of Nations, 384–86; Tower of Babel, 399–403

literary devices: hendiadys, 110, 188, 217, 223, 394; *inclusio,* 13, 41, 107, 156, 290, 310, 312, 313, 318, 330, 336–37, 350, 385, 388, 412, 420; merisms, 109, 110, 138, 157, 165, 187; parallelisms, 12, 13, 16, 110, 112–13, 115, 134–35, 139, 140, 141, 143, 156, 158, 175–76, 184, 187, 188, 191, 213, 218, 226, 228–29, 231–35, 237, 248, 255, 289, 291, 296, 310, 311, 320, 328–29, 331, 356, 414; rhyming, 110, 135, 175, 188, 223, 233–34, 298, 313, 314, 320, 389, 393,

literary devices (*continued*)
397, 424; sevenfold repetition, 38, 48,
96–97, 106–7, 114, 120, 137, 211–12,
225, 233–34, 238, 288, 343; wordplay,
107, 110, 120, 121, 127, 130, 157, 158,
174, 176, 177, 187, 188, 213, 215, 226,
228, 230, 231, 235, 238, 248, 251, 252,
286, 293, 295, 321, 322, 354, 392, 399,
406, 411. See also *Leitwort* style

living creatures: on the ark, 288–91,
317–18; on the earth, 127–28, 172–74;
in the sea, 125–26; in the sky, 125–26,
309; taxonomy of, 200–202. *See also*
humans; hybrid creatures

Lot, 205, 238, 322, 354, 356, 380, 385,
412–15, 420

Lud, 374–75, 387

Ludites, 370–71

Maday, 361–62, 381

Magog, 361–62, 381

Mahalalel, 247, 254, 388

marriage: with deities, 57, 124, 267;
institution of, 23, 29, 176–77, 197, 229,
264–65, 414, 422; between Sons of God
and the Daughters of Humans, 265,
267, 268, 270, 273, 275, 393

Mash, 374–75

Mehiyael, 228–29

memory, cultural, 35–36, 425

mental maps, 386–88

Mesha, 378

Meshech, 361–62

Mesopotamian flood hero, 249

metalworkers, 213–14, 231–32, 240, 242

Methuselah, 247, 251, 253–55, 388

Methushael, 228–29

midrash, 46–50

Milcah (wife of Nahor), 414, 415

monotheism, 25, 54–55, 148–49, 266, 275,
299, 300, 317, 356

moral codes/themes, 36–37; civilization
and its discontents, 39–40; genealogy of
morals, 41–42; and the image of God,
40–41; sex, shame, and guilt, 37–39

Mosaic covenant, 316

Moses, 5, 11, 12, 13, 23, 45, 50, 51, 52, 115,
146, 156, 167, 179, 224, 235, 239, 247,

271, 276, 286, 287, 289, 314, 318–19,
330, 341, 423; death of, 4, 141, 321; Law
of, 43; lifespan of, 247, 270

mythology: as analytical genre, 25–36;
double temporality of, 404; as explanation, 26–28, 151; function of, 26; as
legitimation and orientation, 28–30;
and memory, 35–36; as sacred narrative,
30–33; use of repetition in, 33–35

Naamah (sister of Tubal-Cain), 232

Nahor, 379, 388, 410, 411–12, 415, 416,
421, 422, 424, 427

nakedness: of Adam and Eve, 32, 37–38,
95, 154, 166, 177, 179, 182–85, 193, 198,
199, 201, 202, 203; of Noah, 9, 32 40,
346, 349–50, 354–57

Naphtuhites, 370–71

Nebuchadnezzar I, 398

Nebuchadnezzar II, 395, *395*

Nephilim, 9, 270–74, 276–80

Nimrod, 9, 19, 40, 366–70, 381, 384, 387

Nineveh, 53, 101, 163, 358, 362, 368,
369–70, 381, 384

Noachian covenant, 295–97, 311–12, 316,
330–34

Noah, 11, 32, 41, 46, 98–100, 248–52;
birth of, 251; building an altar, 294;
descendants of, 388; drunkenness of,
9, 301, 349–51, 354–56; finding divine
favor, 286–87, 310–11; lifespan of, 319;
nakedness of, 9, 32 40, 346, 349–50,
354–57; naming of, 251–52; perceptions
of, 18; planting a vineyard, 348–49, 353;
righteousness of, 39, 288, 310–11; sending out of birds, 18, 291–93, 324–25;
sons of, 9, 23, 100–101, **380**, 385, 416;
variations of, 11. *See also* Flood narrative

Obal, 376–77

ocean (sea): and the creation, 109–12, 117,
121, 150, 340; and the flood, 290, 319,
320, 322, 335, 336, 340

Ophir, 376–77

original sin, 48, 56, 204

Panzuzu, 179

Patrusites, 370–71

Peleg, 10, 375–76, 379, 388, 410

Philistines, 370–71

Pishon, 168–69

plants, 136–37, 158

Platonic allegory, 46–47, 50

polytheism, 25, 54–55, 148, 267

Put, 364–65

Raamah, 365

Rachel, 241, 414, 422

rainbow, 27, 117, 322, 330, 332–33, 339, 341

Rebekah, 414, 422, 423

Rehovot-Ir, 369–70

Rephaim, 277, 279, 281–82

Resen, 370

Reu, 388, 410

river, 159; division of 167–70. *See also* Euphrates River; Tigris River

Rodanites, 363–64

Rosetta Stone, 53

Sabbath law, 28–29, 33–34, 138–41, 146, 330

Sabtah, 365

Sabteka, 365–66

sacrifices, 29; of Cain and Abel, 216–18, 239; of the flood hero, 305–6; by the Israelites, 147; of Noah, 289, 294–95, 306

Šalappāya tribe, 242

Sarai/Sarah (wife of Abram), 102, 173, 408, 414–15, 420–22

Sargon II, 407

Sarug, 421

Satan, 56, 187, 204

scrolls, 19

sea monsters/dragons, 25, 107, 111, 126, 147, 152

Seba, 365

Sennacherib, 424

Sephar, 378

Serug, 388, 410, 416, 418

Seth, 234, 238, 246, 247, 264, 379–80, 388; lifespan of, 254

sexuality, 37–38, 39; consequence of, 265; and sexual awareness, 166–67; and sexual hierarchy, 202–3

Shaleph, 376–77

Sheba, 365, 366, 376–77, 379

Shelah, 375, 379, 384, 388, 410, 416, 418

Shem, 9, 252, 311, 346–47, 350, 359, 360, 379–80, **380**, 384, 385, 416, 418

Shemites, 373–80, 381, **383**, 385–88, 409–16

Sidon, 371–72

Sinites, 371–73

snake: as animal of the field, 173, 178, 179; association with magic, 178–79; curse on, 186–87, 208, 351; in the Garden of Eden, 30–31, 51, 95, 154, 157, 166, 171, 177–83, 185–87, 197–200, 208; in *Gilgamesh,* 57, 209–10; as Satan, 56, 179, 204; as trickster, 178, 209–10; and West Semitic goddesses, 179

Sodom and Gomorrah, 205, 221, 222, 274, 290, 350, 351, 356, 358, 373, 385, 396

Solomon, 134, 229, 396

Solubba (Sleyb) tribe, 242

Song of Deborah, 242

Song of Lamech, 232–34

Song of Moses, 23

Sons of God, 25, 97–98, 397; biblical mentions of, 265–66; and the Daughters of Humans, 263–82; Genesis text, 97–98; as hybrids, 274–75. *See also* angels; *ĕlōhîm*

Sumer, land of, 369, 392

Sumerian King List, 259–61, **260**

Sutû tribes (Suteans), 234, 425–28

tabernacle, 12, 145, 146–47, 314, 319, 325, 341, 342

Table of Nations, 30, 101; contexts, 388–89; double representations of, 6–8; genealogy of Shem, 7; Genesis text, 101; as mental map, 386–88; notes and commentary, 358–89

Tarshish, 363–64

Terah, 381, 388, 409, 411, 412, 414–16, 421

Tetragrammaton, 157. *See also* Yahweh/God

Tiglath-Pilesar I, 427

Tigris River, 94, 153, 168, 169–70, 302, 392, 420, 423

Tiras, 361–62

Togarmah, 362–63

Torah, 4, 20, 43, 47

Index of Modern Authors

Aharoni, Y., 214
Aḥituv, S., 108
Albertz, R., 40
Albright, W. F., 369, 421
Allen, J. P., 113, 119, 150, 163
Al-Rawi, F. N. H., 224
Alster, B., 111, 405
Alter, R., 10, 11, 12, 134, 173, 174, 175, 177, 199, 232, 319, 320, 352, 420
Amit, Y., 10
Anderson, G. A., 108, 131, 217
Annus, A., 367, 368
Anonymous (2014), 344
Arie, E., 384
Arlow, J., 26
Armstrong, J. F., 315
Arneth, M., 14
Arnold, B. T., 20, 123
Assmann, J., 35
Astour, M. C., 363, 411
Attridge, H. W., 46, 110, 112, 151
Atwood, P., 412
Auerbach, E., 10, 33, 43, 184
Augustine, 48–49

Baden, J. S., 5, 8, 346, 399
Bailey, L. R., 343, 344, 345
Baker, L. S., 5

Bakhtin, M., 30, 33
Bal, M., 160
Barr, J., 108, 130, 131, 155, 158, 171, 178, 191, 193, 205, 325, 350
Barré, M. L., 219
Barth, F., 242
Barton, J., 5, 36, 224
Bascom, W., 25
Bassett, F. W., 349
Batto, B. F., 140
Bauks, M., 22, 37, 109, 149, 152, 162, 165, 166, 256
Beal, R. H., 151
Becking, B., 219, 360
Beckman, G., 229
Beitzel, B., 411
Ben-Amos, D., 21
Ben-Dov, J., 248, 309, 320, 325, 326
Benjamin, W., 33, 35, 42, 55
Bergmann, E., 394
Berman, J. A., 5
Bernstein, M. J., 263
Berry, G. R., 269
Bird, P., 130, 131, 132, 188, 203
Blenkinsopp, J., 14, 15, 318, 325
Bloch, M., 21
Blum, E., 5, 22, 165, 166, 172, 244, 246, 423

Index of Ancient Sources

Note: Page numbers in **bold** refer to tables.

10:20	362
11:2	362
11:30	364
11:43	371

HOSEA

1:2	108
4:11	349, 354
11:11	292
12:13	216, 423
12:13–14	423
12:14	423
13:3	321

JOEL

2:3	163

AMOS

	276
1:3–5	424
2:9	271, 277
3:15	296
5:19	325
6:2	369, 373
6:4	206
7:3	286
7:4	320
9:7	371

JONAH

1:2	369, 370, 384
1:3	363
3:3	368
4:6	157

MICAH

4:9	188
5:5	367, 381
6:2	109
7:12	365
7:17	186

NAHUM

2:8	292
3:5	349
3:9	371

HABAKKUK

1:2	311
3:9	332
3:11	332

ZEPHANIAH

1:5	138
2:5	371
3:8	405
3:9	405

HAGGAI

2:12	16

ZECHARIAH

5:11	369
7:10	329
14:8	296
14:20	230

MALACHI

1:7	294
1:12	294
3:10	321

New Testament

MATTHEW

24:37	46

LUKE

17:26	46

JOHN

1:1	46
1:9	46
1:14	46

ROMANS

5:14	46, 204
5:18	204
15:4	44

I CORINTHIANS

15:45	34, 46

Greek and Latin Literature

Ancient Hebrew and Related Inscriptions

Ancient Near Eastern Texts